CORPOR...

SHOWCASE 10

PHOTOGRAPHY ILLUSTRATION & GRAPHIC DESIGN

FOREWORD

For 10 years, Corporate Showcase has presented the best and most innovative photographers, illustrators and graphic designers specializing in corporate assignments. This year is no different. More than 200 artists in these pages will show you the most current and distinctive visual trends in corporate communications, including executive portraiture, product shots, industrial land-scapes, collages, computer enhancements, and logo and design work.

With this 10th anniversary edition, we begin moving through the decade of the 1990's. We expect the business climate to be more cost-conscious, and executives to be more environmentally conscious. Yet the need for companies to spend time and money communicating their unique corporate identity will continue to grow, and with it the need for finding new ways of expressing that identity.

The business of business communications, which includes TV commercials, print ads, annual reports, brochures, and now, newer forms of media, changes with each new year. It requires a fresh look, a new idea, an innovative concept. That is the role of Corporate Showcase 10.

President and Publisher	**Ira Shapiro**
Senior Vice President	**Wendl Kornfeld**
Vice President Sales and Marketing	**Marie-Christine Matter**
Marketing Director	**Ann Middlebrook**
Production Director	**Karen M. Bochow**
Data Systems Manager/Distribution/Grey Pages	**Scott Holden**

Published by
American Showcase, Inc.
915 Broadway, 14th Floor
New York, New York 10010
(212) 673-6600
FAX: (212) 673-9795

Corporate Showcase 10
Hardback 0931144-68-X
Softback 0931144-69-8
ISSN 0742-9975

Cover Credits:
Front Cover Photograph:
Charles Callaghan
Title Page Illustration:
Steve Dininno

Inside you'll find:

More than 1,200 full-color photographs and illustrations, reproduced at award-winning standards of color and clarity;

Articles by designers, ad agency creatives, corporate marketing people and others in the field who offer their experiences and their insights;

A national directory section with thousands of updated phone listings and addresses for photographers, illustrators, graphic designers, reps, stock photo agencies and other production support services; and

A listing of the associations, guilds, and clubs within the advertising and graphic arts community.

Corporate Showcase 10 is an essential sourcebook for established professionals—graphic designers, corporate communications directors, and others involved in corporate advertising and promotion—as well as for students and those starting out in these fields.

We're confident that you'll find the range of talent presented here stimulating, accessible, and of value to your own creative work.

Ira Shapiro
Publisher

Advertising Sales

Advertising Coordinator
Shana Ovitz

Sales Representatives
New York
John Bergstrom
Barbara Preminger
Joe Safferson
Dave Tabler

Rocky Mountain
Kate Hoffman
(303) 493-1492

West Coast
Ellen Kasemeier
(805) 298-3104

Administration

Controller
Joel Kopel

Accounts Manager
Connie Malloy

Office Manager
Elaine Morrell

Accounting Assistants
Mila Livshits
Myron Yang

Administrative Assistant
Paula Cohen

Marketing

Promotion/New Projects Manager
Mitchell Hinz

Marketing Coordinator
Lisa Wilker

Book Sales Coordinator
Cynthia Breneman

Production

Production Manager
Chuck Rosenow

Project Manager
Tracy Russek

Production Administrator
Diane Cerafici

Traffic Coordinator
Sandra Sierra

Special Thanks to: Ron Canagata, Ken Crouch, Julia Curry, Jeffrey Gorney, Anne Newhall, Tony Oppenheim, George Phillips, Adam Seifer, Ian Thomson

Mechanical Production
American Showcase, Inc.

Grey Pages Production
Goodman/Orlick Design

Typesetting
The Ace Group, Inc.

Color Separation
Universal Colour Scanning Ltd.

Printing and Binding
Everbest Printing Co., Ltd.

U.S. Book Trade Distribution
Watson-Guptill Publications
1515 Broadway New York,
New York 10036 (212) 764-7300
Watson-Guptill ISBN: 8230-6193-0

For Sales outside the U.S.
Rotovision S.A.
9 Route Suisse
1295 Mies, Switzerland
Telephone: 022-755-3055
Telex: 419246 ROVI FAX: 022-755-4072

Contents

Viewpoints

Graphic Arts Organizations

Grey Pages

Indexes

Alphabetical Listing

*Advertising
Photographers
of America Inc.*

Advertising Photographers
Any Street
Anywhere, USA

Dear Advertising Photographer:

In May, 1981, a group of advertising photographers met to address some of the problems dealing with our specialty. Before long, we formed the Advertising Photographers of America. And today, we have more than 2,000 members in eight chapters—and we're growing.

Here's the point. If you're an advertising photographer, by God, you should be a member of APA!

Why? Because we know it's a tough world out there. And we're dealing every day with the problems, joys, legalities, tax ramifications, technologies, trends, negotiating skills, personalities and opportunities of our professional niche called advertising photography.

And we've got the muscle and knowledge to make a difference in your business.

So, if you're an ad photographer and you're not an APA member, you're missing the boat. We talk your language. We understand. And we help.

Call the regional office nearest you...and get the scoop.

Happy Decade,

Mickey McGuire
President, APA National

APA/Atlanta
1157 West Peachtree Street
Atlanta, GA 30309
404-892-6263

APA/Chicago
1725 West North Avenue
Chicago, IL 60616
312-342-1717

APA/Detroit
32588 Dequindre
Warren, MI 48092
313-978-7373

APA/Los Angeles
7201 Melrose Avenue
Los Angeles, CA 90046
213-935-7283

APA/Miami
2545 Tiger Tail Avenue
Coconut Grove, FL 33033
305-856-8338

APA/New York
27 West 20th Street
New York, NY 10011
212-807-0399

APA/Portland
135 Somerset Street
Portland, ME 04101
207-773-3771

APA/San Francisco
375 7th Street
San Francisco, CA 94103
415-621-3915

Illustrators & Graphic Designers

◆ Kolea Baker • Artist Representative • 2819 First Avenue Suite 240 • Seattle , Washington 98121 • 206 . 443 . 0326 • Fax 206 . 448 . 4219

11

THE ILWU AND THE PORT OF SEATTLE: PARTNERS IN BUILDING A STRONG COMMUNITY

◆ Kolea Baker • Artist Representative • 2819 First Avenue Suite 240 • Seattle , Washington 98121 • 206 . 443 . 0326 • Fax 206 . 448 . 4219

◆ ◆ ◆ ◆

◆ Kolea Baker • Artist Representative • 2819 First Avenue Suite 240 • Seattle , Washington 98121 • 206 . 443 . 0326 • Fax 206 . 448 . 4219

We don't use design just to change the way things look. We use it to change the way people think. About you, your products, your company.

Con Edison

It's forward-focus design that gets noticed. That solves problems. That builds awareness and boosts sales. In ads/brochures and catalogs/

Madison Square Garden Network

logos and symbols/posters/direct response/corporate identity programs.   For clients like Citibank.   Con Edison.   Letraset.   McGraw-Hill.

Letraset

Madison Square Garden Network. Sony.   We're Glazer & Kalayjian, Inc., a communications design group. And we're proud to be a part

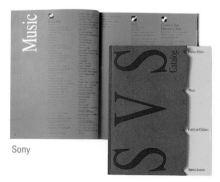

Sony

McGraw-Hill

of the 37th Annual Cannes International Advertising Film Festival as Official Design Consultant.   Our congratulations to the winners.

Glazer and Kalayjian, Inc. Communications Design Group   301 East 45th Street, New York, NY 10017   212-687-3099

Glazer and Kalayjian, Inc.

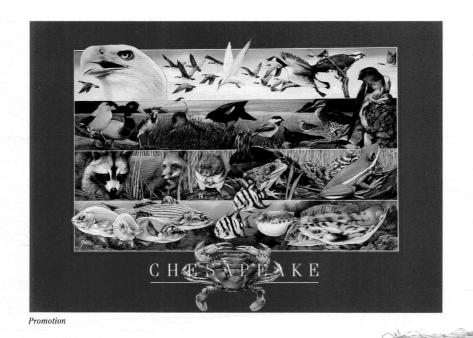

Promotion

Random House Pub.

Jack Graber
Represented by Walter Supley, the Creative Advantage, inc.
620 Union Street, Schenectady, New York 12305 (518) 370-0312
FAX (518) 370-1636

Southland Mall

Purina

Atlanta Zoo

McDonald's

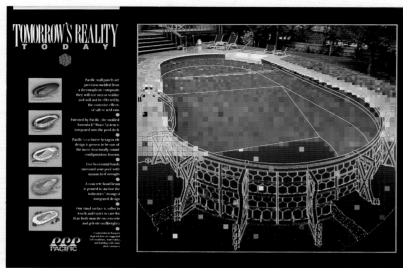

We do it.
Award winning images and imagers.
Experience.
Logo design to holograms.
Laser show in the Arizona desert?
Oh yes.
Artistry.
Technical Expertise.
You and us.
Exciting Possibilities.
Motivated, Aware, Ready.

Every rule abo ut WHaT is appropriate narrows»whAt is possible.

the Creative Advantage, inc.
620 Union Street
Schenectady, New York 12305
(518) 370-0312   FAX (518) 370-1636

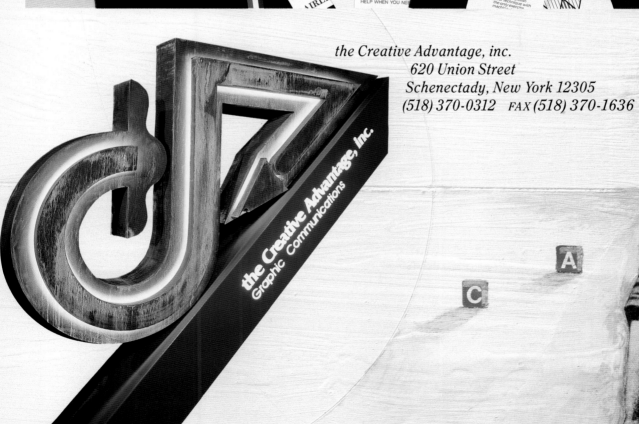

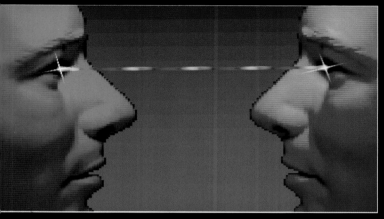

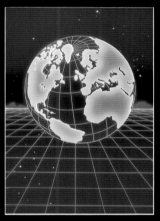

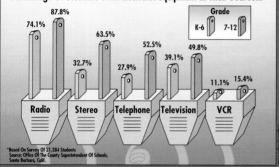

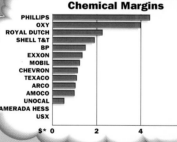

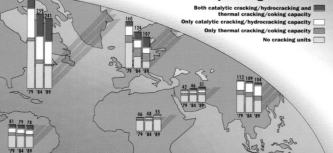

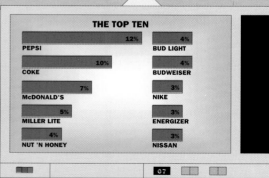

2H Studio
Roger Huyssen and Gerard Huerta
45 Corbin Drive
Darien, Connecticut 06820
(203) 656-0200 • (203) 656-0505

For additional work see back flaps
of American Showcase Illustration
Volume 14.

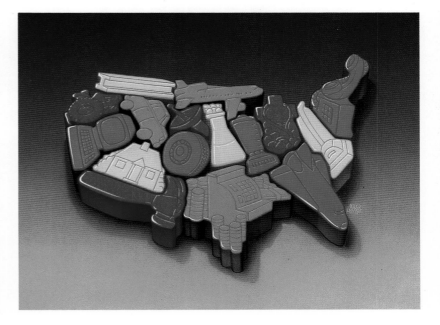

Gerard Huerta

ROGER HUYSSEN

21

Eliot Bergman, Inc.
362 West 20th Street
New York, New York 10011
(212) 645-0414 • FAX: (212) 633-6654
(212) 645-0414 Modem

Represented by:
Asciutto Art Representatives, Inc.
19 East 48th Street
New York, New York 10017
(212) 838-0050 • FAX: (212) 838-0506

Eliot Bergman designs
illustrated charts, diagrams and maps.

Additional work:
American Showcase 12, 13
Corporate Showcase 8, 9

Clients Include: ADT, AT&T, Inc.
Magazine, The Insurance Information
Institute, Ogilvy & Mather, McGraw-Hill,
Medical Tribune, Met Life, Scott
Foresman, Security Pacific, Times Mirror.

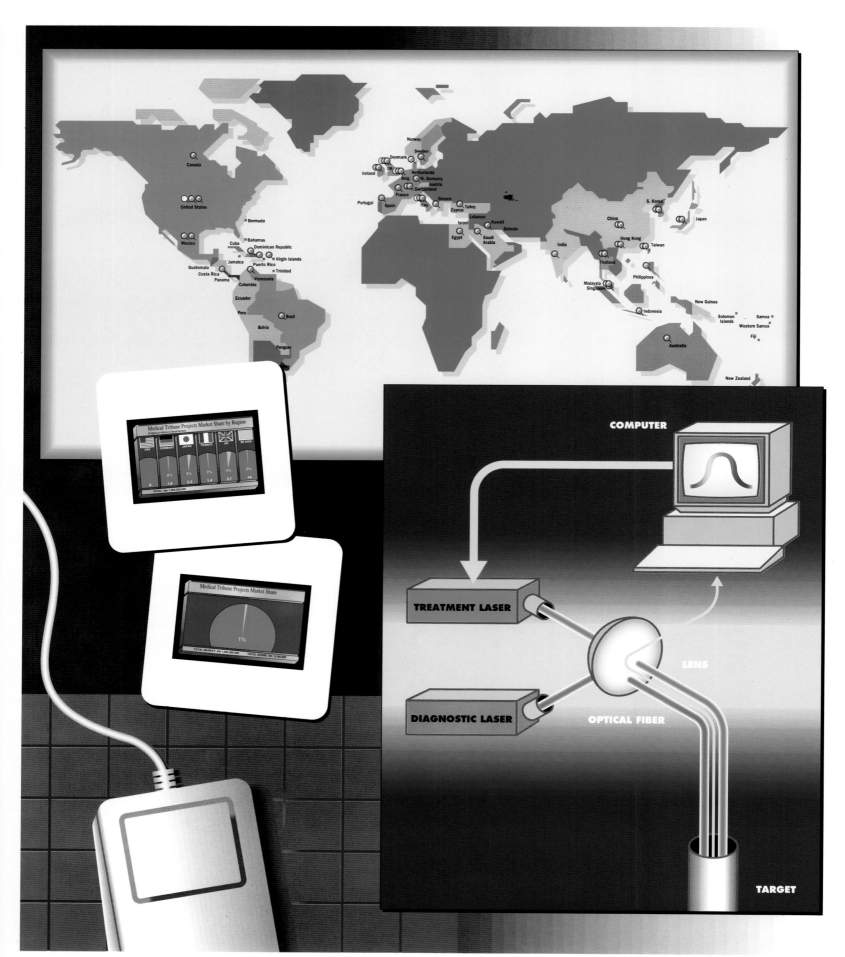

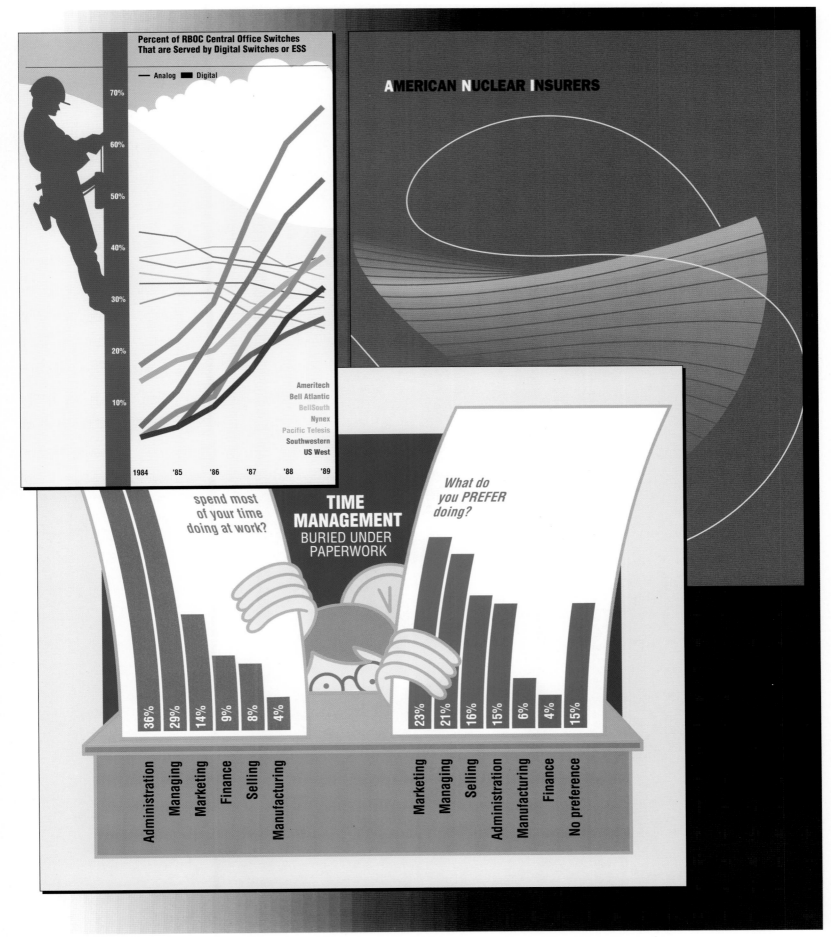

Percent of RBOC Central Office Switches That are Served by Digital Switches or ESS

— Analog ■ Digital

70%
60%
50%
40%
30%
20%
10%

Ameritech
Bell Atlantic
BellSouth
Nynex
Pacific Telesis
Southwestern
US West

1984　'85　'86　'87　'88　'89

AMERICAN NUCLEAR INSURERS

spend most of your time doing at work?

TIME MANAGEMENT
BURIED UNDER PAPERWORK

What do you PREFER doing?

36% Administration
29% Managing
14% Marketing
9% Finance
8% Selling
4% Manufacturing

23% Marketing
21% Managing
16% Selling
15% Administration
6% Manufacturing
4% Finance
15% No preference

Guy Billout
225 Lafayette Street
Suite 1008
New York, New York 10012
(212) 431-6350
FAX: (212) 941-0787

Series for an advertising campaign for
National Westminster Bank (U.K.)

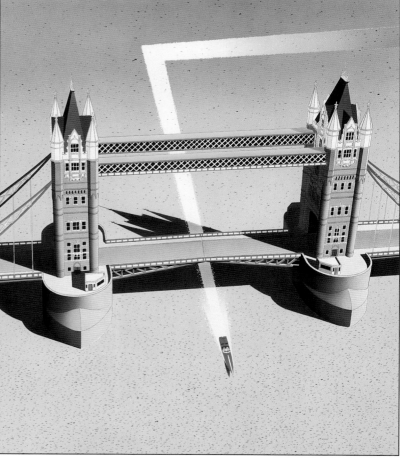

Guy Billout
225 Lafayette Street
Suite 1008
New York, New York 10012
(212) 431-6350
FAX: (212) 941-0787

Ted E. Borgert III

Technical Illustrations
Box 1622
Cincinnati, Ohio 45201
For Voice, Message or FAX dial:
(513) 721-8322

• Specializing in the creation of artistic technical images from blueprints, photos and sketches.

• Supplying industry and government with color renderings and line drawings of architectural and mechanical subjects.

Clients and Projects include: Anheuser-Busch, Apple Computer, Boeing, Chrysler, Compaq, Cummins Engine Co., Ford, General Electric, General Motors, John Deere, Kellogg, Litton, NYNEX, Monarch Marking, Proctor & Gamble, Reynolds & Reynolds, and Stanley Tools.

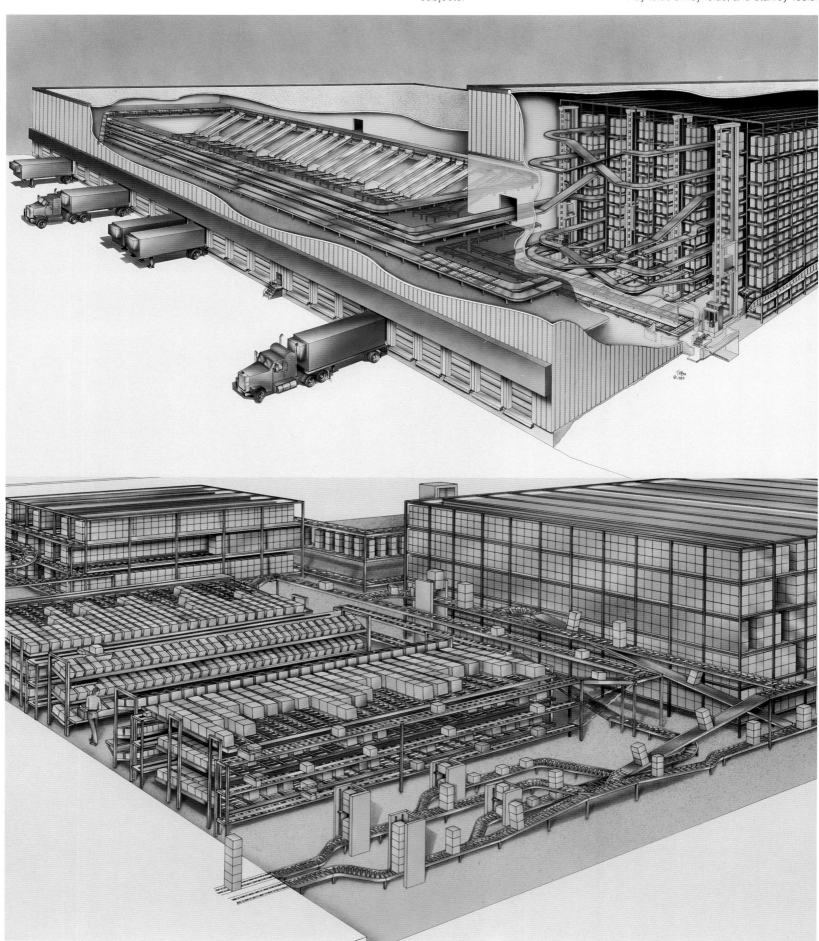

Bracchi Beresford Draplin
152 East 33rd Street
New York, New York 10016
(212) 532-3298
FAX: (212) 689-7652

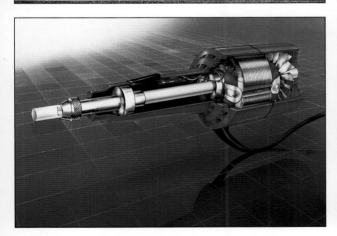

Jennifer Collins
320 East 42nd Street
Apartment 112
New York, New York 10017
(212) 297-0474
(212) 949-6081
FAX Available

Steve Dininno
553 East Fulton Street
Long Beach, New York 11561
(516) 431-1495
FAX: (516) 889-6510

Partial Client List:
DuPont Pharmaceuticals, N.B.C., Boston Globe, Washington Post, Playboy, Maryland Casualty, BusinessWeek, N.C.R. Computers, M.C.I., Capital Bancorp, Liant Software, MassMutual, Penthouse Magazine, Coopers & Lybrand.

Work Featured in:
Creative Illustration 1, 2; Art Directors Club Annual 1987; American Showcase 12, 13, 14; Print Regional Design 1990; New York Gold 3; Conceptual Illustration 1.

Articles About My Work:
Artist's Magazine, Art Direction Magazine, New York Newsday Magazine

Cathy Hull
165 East 66th Street
New York, New York 10021
(212) 772-7743
FAX: (212) 535-1877

See The Light. Visual Commentary
for The Design Scene, Print Magazine.

Franck Levy
305 East 40th Street
New York, New York 10016
(212) 557-8256

Abbott, ADP, AT&T, Bloomingdale's, Berkley Publishing, CBS Records, Citibank, Canon, Chesebrough Ponds, Children's Television Network, Coca Cola, DuPont, Eli Lilly, Hanes, IBM, Johnson & Johnson, The Journal of Commerce, Lotus, Morgan Stanley, McGraw Hill, New York Daily News, New York Times Magazines, Northwest Airlines, NYNEX, Parke Davis, Procter & Gamble, Sears, Simon and Schuster, U.S. Navy, Xerox, Ziff-Davis, etc....

Member of the Society of Illustrators

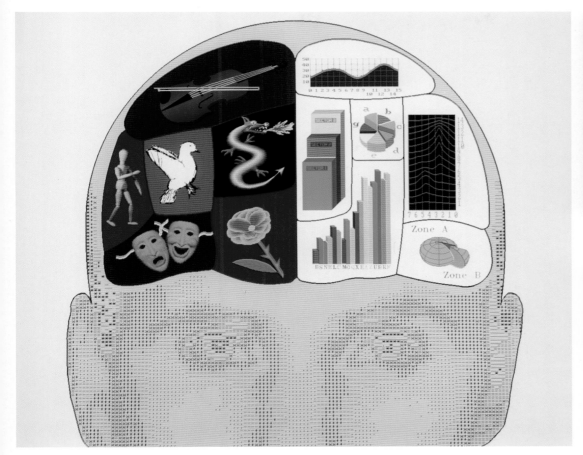

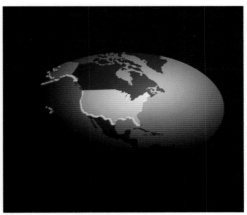

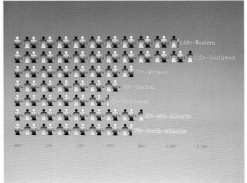

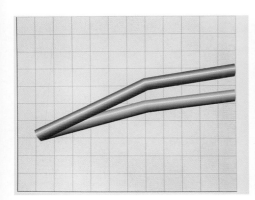

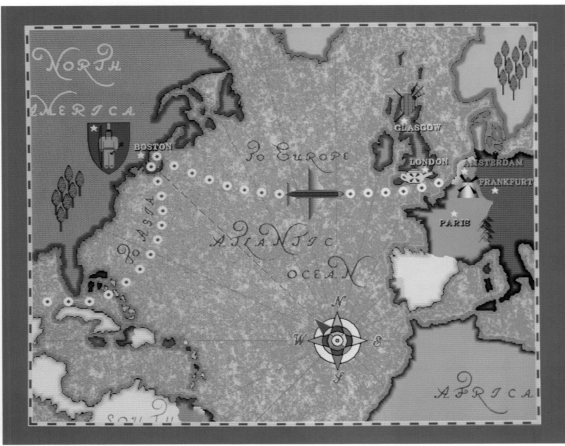

Hal Lōse
533 West Hortter Street
Toad Hall
Philadelphia, Pennsylvania 19119
(215) 849-7635
FAX: (215) 849-7635

Member:
Society of Illustrators
Graphic Artists Guild
© Hal Lōse 1991

Comps overnite! With Fax & FedEx,
we can do business wherever you are
(even in Philadelphia).
Design, Layouts or Comps can be
as rough or finished as you want.
I comp to please.

PENNSYLVANIA HOUSE

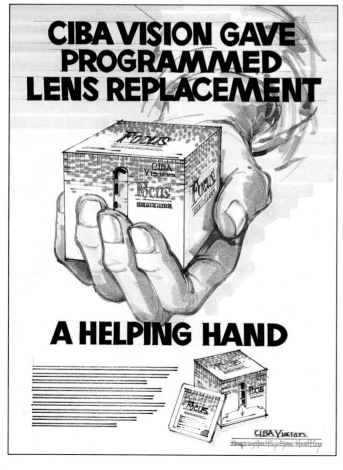

CIBA VISION GAVE
PROGRAMMED
LENS REPLACEMENT

A HELPING HAND

Tinted soft contact lenses?
Know your options.

CIBASOFT & STD

Frances Middendorf
337 East 22nd Street, #2
New York, New York 10010
(212) 473-3586
FAX: (212) 473-3586

Alden Burleigh
7 North Main Street
Fall River, Massachusetts 02720
(508) 677-1688
FAX: (508) 677-1688

The New York Times
Flying Magazine
American Lawyer Media
East-West Journal
North Star Records
Rhode Island Monthly
Gralla Publications

Creativity Award 1990 from Art
Direction Magazine

Member of the Graphic Artists Guild
and The National Arts Club

The Miller Group, Ltd.
250 Bell Street, Suite 260
Reno, Nevada 89503
(702) 333-9009
FAX: (702) 329-6568
(702) 324-3500 Modem

When Sending the Very Best Isn't Good Enough.

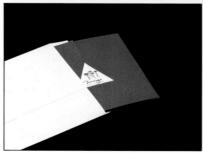  

Special event invitations that really pull.

John Schreck
101 Spring Hill Road
Fairfield, Connecticut 06430
(203) 259-6824

"Nothing astonishes men so much as common sense and plain dealing."
—Ralph Waldo Emerson

Professional photographers and their clients share at least one common trait: they own businesses which have to be run like businesses, if they are to succeed.

Every business has needs and the right to fulfill them. Consequently, many business owners appreciate that a mutual concern for each other's needs is simply common sense. And, plain dealing, through negotiations aimed at meeting each other's needs, is the way to a fair deal.

There has been a storm brewing for years in the communication arts industry, and at the center of that storm is: copyright ownership. It has taken on greater proportions than almost any other issue in the industry's history, as copyright ownership and "work for hire" seem to be catalysts in the never ending battle of demands and claims between the photographer and client. This storm must blow itself out. The alternative, to carry out the analogy, is unending storm damage. With so much at stake for both sides, this conflict must be resolved.

People fight out of need more than greed, and the key to resolving any conflict is to meet the needs of both parties. Hence the first step requires an acknowledgment of these needs by the parties involved.

Let's look at the needs of the typical client being serviced by the typical photographer. Clients need to:

• Exploit every dollar they expend to the maximum.
• Maximize their income to assure their future profits.

• Protect their image and name from harm.
• Avoid disadvantaging themselves in future dealings.
• Avoid liability and damage from unforeseen circumstances.

Now, when a client makes a demand that a photographer sign over his or her copyright, it is usually for one of these underlying, abstract, but understandable reasons.

However, what the photographer hears from the client is something quite different: clients say that a copyright must be transferred to protect a proprietary process, or corporate identity; they say that they do not want to have to renegotiate additional use; they say that they must have it because their legal departments have told them that this is the way to do it.

All of these arguments are understandable, but unconvincing to the majority of photographers who put their hearts and souls into their work. Photographers, like their clients, are businesses, and in fact, share many of the same needs. And, when working together, clients and photographers also have similar interests: both desire a quality job, which they can exploit, and from which they can obtain future value, and for which they will exchange fair value. This makes perfect sense. Now let's get to plain dealing.

Photographers have to recognize that their clients have the right to fulfill their needs. Supporting that right and fulfilling those needs is good business. Clients must also recognize that photographers have the right to fulfill their own needs and recognize and support that right.

However, many businesses fail to see the needs of their photographers. They take a short-sighted view of the business relationship, and try to "win it all" in their negotiations, under the assumption that the supply of talented photographers will never shrink. In other words, they put copyright control as their "bottom line", and tell photographers to "take it or leave it."

No one can see far enough into the future to determine if the ranks of qualified photographers will totally dry up as a result of battles over copyright. However, copyright transfer demands can be a death blow to a photographer's business, and the pool of photographic talent working right now is being affected, and will continue to be affected.

"Take it or leave it" copyright demands bring to mind the story of the short-sighted businessman who made such a good deal with a critical supplier that it put the supplier out of business, which in turn crippled the buyer's business when other suppliers could not meet his demands.

So let's examine the other side of the story: why should a photographer need to retain the copyright to his or her work? The answers are simple. His or her business needs are:

• To establish a body of work, which serves as asset and identity.
• To have the right to promote themselves by showing the fruits of their labors.
• To increase future income and profitability to assure future stability and growth.
• To guard against improper exploitation of creative efforts.

Continued on page 60

Susan Swan
83 Saugatuck Avenue
Westport, Connecticut 06880
(203) 226-9104
FAX: (203) 454-7956

Clients:

Chemical Bank; CMP Publications; Harcourt Brace Jovanovich; Scholastic; Houghton Mifflin Company; Holt Rinehart

Winston; Bantam Doubleday Dell; Silver Burdett and Ginn; Putnam; Macmillan; Walker and Company; Scott Foresman and Company; Harper and Row; Children's Television Workshop.

Member Graphic Artist's Guild

© Susan Swan 1991

Will Nelson

**Sweet
Represents**
(415) 433-1222
716 Montgomery Street, San Francisco, California 94111

Elizabeth Uyehara
1020 Westchester Place
Los Angeles, California 90019
(213) 731-4168
FAX: (213) 731-0033

Clients:
American Film Magazine
California Magazine
Entrepreneur Magazine
LA Weekly
Los Angeles Reader
Los Angeles Times Calendar

Los Angeles Times Book Review
MPI Home Entertainment
Muscle & Fitness Magazine
New Perspectives Quarterly
Plaza Communications
Reason Magazine
Writer's Guild of America, West

ELIZABETH UYEHARA

Rosemary Webber
644 Noank Road
Mystic, Connecticut 06355
(203) 536-3091

Selected Client List: The New Yorker; The Wall Street Journal; Success Magazine; IBM; Westinghouse; Heinz; Security Pacific; Manufacturers Hanover; Mobil; Foote, Cone & Belding; MGM Grand; Schroders.

Artwork has been the subject of articles written in American Artist, May 1989; Communication Arts, February 1987; Washington Journalism Review, March 1987; Advertising Age, August 1985; Manhattan Inc., September 1984; Inc. Magazine, October 1982; Society of Newspaper Design Illustration Awards 2 years.

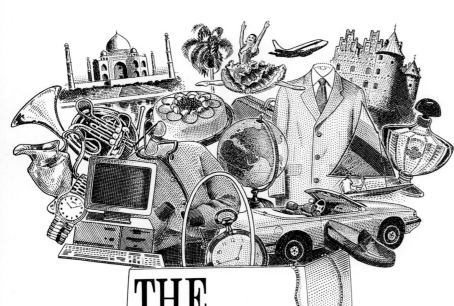

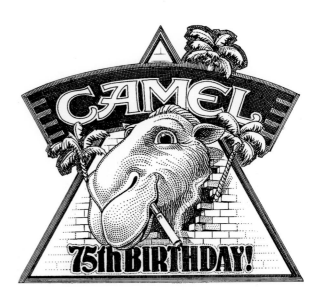

IndexIllustrators & Graphic Designers

Photography

NYC/Northeast

Connecticut
Delaware
Maine
Maryland
Massachusetts
New Hampshire
New Jersey
New York
North Carolina
Pennsylvania
Rhode Island
Vermont
Virginia
Washington, DC
West Virginia

JON ORTNER

NEW YORK CITY • 212/873-1950

JON ORTNER

NEW YORK CITY • 212/873-1950

BILL GALLERY

Photo essays...fly on the wall photography with a sense of composition and emotion. Real life, available light, I don't hide the wastebasket. See *Mead Annual Report Show* 87, 88 & 90 for the Lotus annual reports, and *Annual Report Trends* 88 for Apple Computer. Member ASMP.

86 South Street
Boston, MA 02111
617.542.0499

TED HOROWITZ

CORPORATE PHOTOGRAPHY

203·454·8766

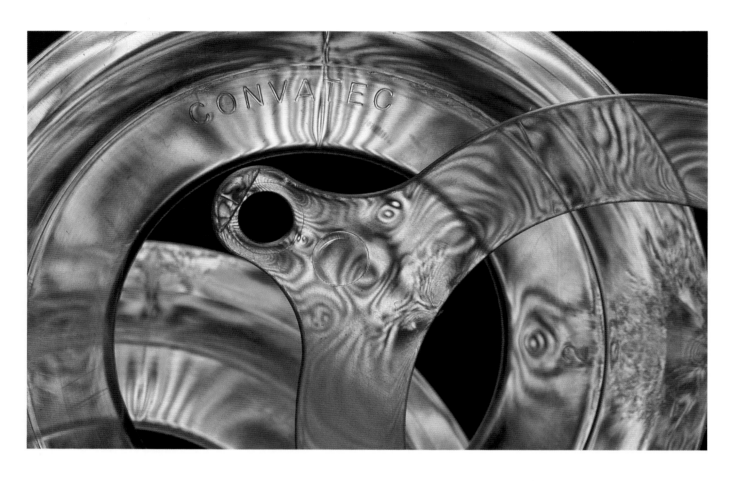

TED HOROWITZ

CORPORATE PHOTOGRAPHY

203·454·8766

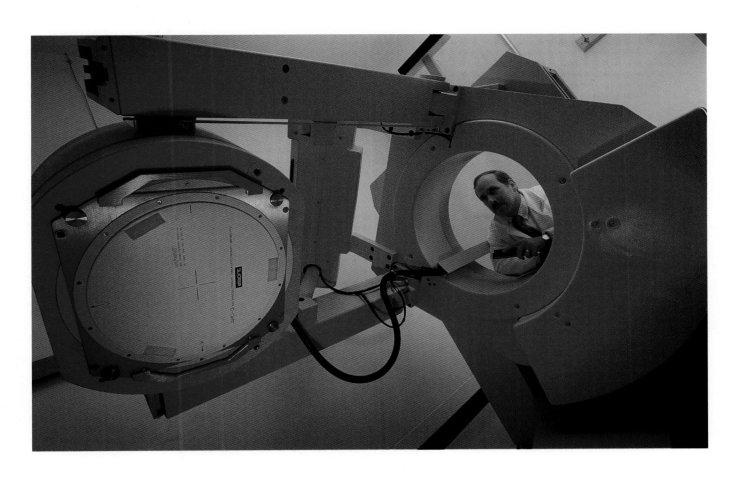

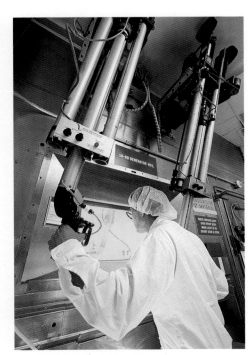

paras

Michael Paras

668 Avenue of the Americas

N.Y., N.Y. 10010

212 243-8546

Fax 212 243-8547

Pobereskin

ADVERTISING

CORPORATE

EDITORIAL

**Joseph Pobereskin
New York**

(212) 619-3711

ASSIGNMENTS

AND

STOCK

SIMMONS

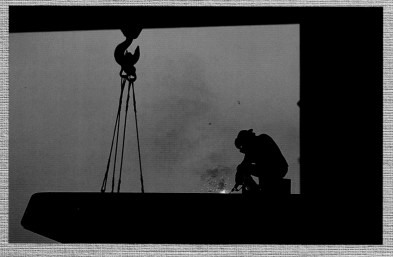

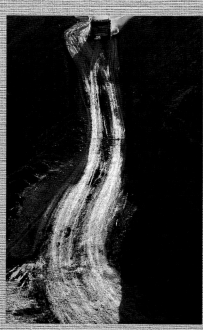

Specializing in location photography for Advertising, Annual Reports, Corporations & Industry. Clients include: Acushnet, Amtrak, Analog Devices, Apollo Computer, Bank of Boston, Bank of New England, Bose Corp., The Boston Company, BJK&E, Citibank, Codex, Commercial Union Assurance, Data General, Deere & Company, Delta Airlines, Hysol, Digital Equipment Corp., EG&G, Ensign Bickford Aerospace, Fairchild, Fidelity, Foote Cone & Belding, General Electric, Gillette, Goodyear, W. R. Grace, Graylock Industries, Grumman Aerospace, Gunn Associates, HBM Creamer, HHCC, Heublein, Hewlett Packard, IBM, John Hancock, Keiler Advertising, Kimberly-Clark, Leonard Monihan Lubars & Partners, LTX, Measurex, Mobay, Moore Business Forms, Nashua Corp., New England Electric, Pfizer Inc., Pitney-Bowes, Polaroid, Prime Computer, Putnam Funds, Rockwell International, Schorr & Howard Co., Scott Paper, Scudder Fund Distributors, Sheraton Corp., State Street Bank & Trust, Sun Co., Teradyne, TWA, 3M, J. Walter Thompson, Time Magazine, Time-Life Books, Touche-Ross, Unionmutual, Warner Communications, S. D. Warren, Young & Rubicam.

ERIK LEIGH SIMMONS
60 K Street
Boston, Massachusetts 02127
(617) 268-4650

A mini portfolio is available upon request.

Stock photography available through The Image Bank.

k a t h e r i n e
LAMBERT

WASHINGTON DC
2 0 2 - 8 8 2 - 8 3 8 3

WILMINGTON TRUST

ROY F. WESTON, INC

DUPONT

ralph

mercer

photography

617 951 4604
617 951 2696 fax

451 D street
9th floor
boston/ma
02210

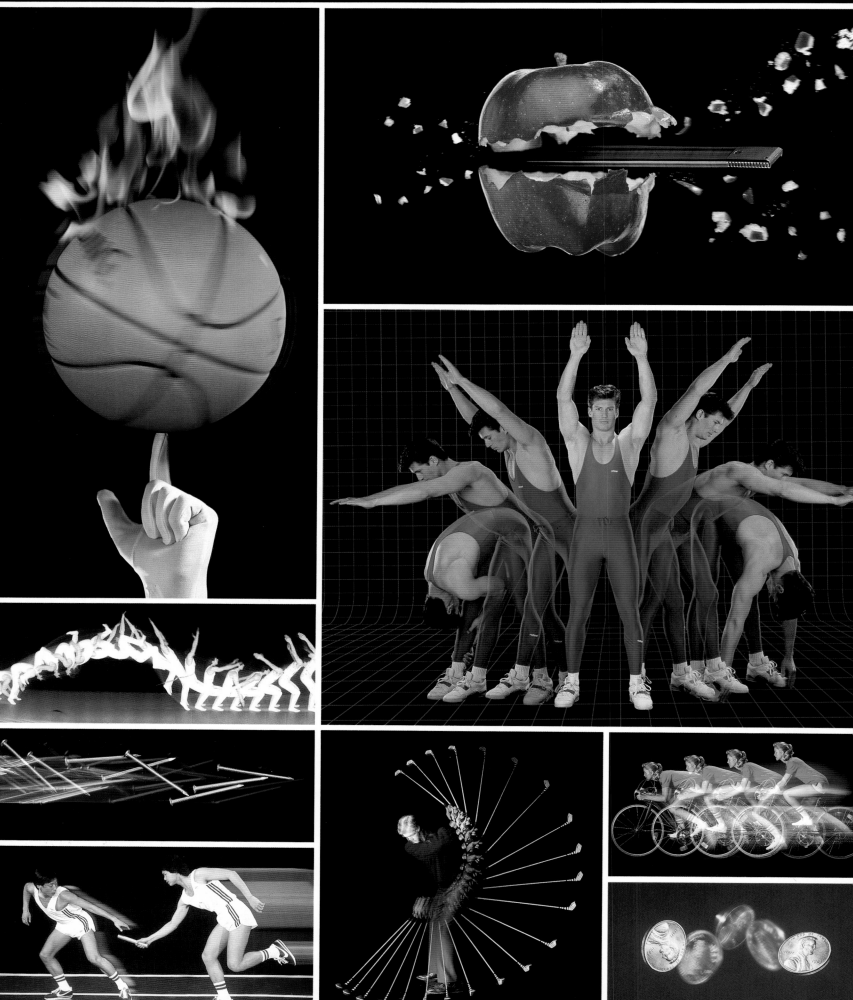

The Globus Brothers Photography Tel: 243-1008
Fax: 645-0332

Timkin Co.

Partial client list:

Alling & Cory

Bausch & Lomb

Castle/MDT

Chase

Corning Glass Works

Eastman Dental Center

Eastman Kodak Co.

General Motors

Leica Incorporated

Nalge Co.

Rochester City School District

Synon Incorporated

Timkin Co.

Xerox Corporation

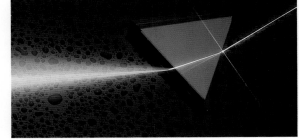

GENE MYERS

Stock Available

250 N. Goodman St.

Rochester, New York 14607-1128

Eastman Kodak Co.

716 - 244 - 4420

716 - 244 - 9146 FAX

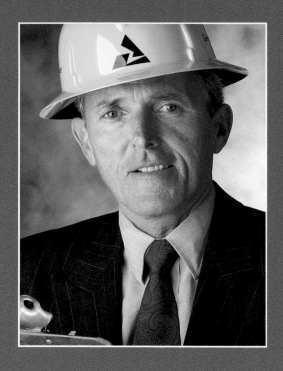

Martin De Leon

Martin De Leon Photography
286 Fifth Avenue
New York, NY 10001
212 714-9777

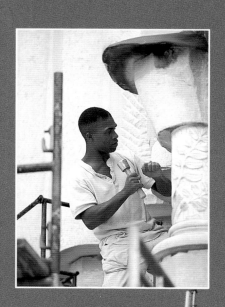

**Stephen Barth
Photography**
37 South Clinton Street
Doylestown, Pennsylvania 18901
(215) 340-0900
RD 7 Hickory Hill Road
Bethlehem, Pennsylvania 18015
(215) 866-4377

Member ASMP
© 1991 Stephen Barth Photography
Extensive Stock Photo file
In-House Modeling Agency

Specializing in corporate, advertising, industrial and editorial photography for the financial, healthcare, pharmaceutical, and education industries.

Stephen Barth
PHOTOGRAPHY

TWO STUDIO LOCATIONS:

■ **BUCKS
COUNTY**

■ **ALLENTOWN,
BETHLEHEM,
EASTON**

Continued from page 36

Like the business's needs, these are logical. But now let's look at a list of specific needs of the client with regards to a photography assignment. From each job, the client needs:

• The right to increase usage, and expand to other media.
• To control and maximize the benefit from expense.
• To maintain necessary confidentiality and exclusivity of use.
• To have predictable costs, and avoid uncertain future pricing.
• To profit from commissioned creative works.

Interestingly enough, this set of needs is not irreconcilable with those of a photographer. In fact it is competitive and complimentary at the same time.

The competitive aspect rests solely in the price to be negotiated. Each party wants the most they can get from their time and for their money. This kind of competitive interest is good for the relationship and usually easily negotiated. The interests of each party are complimentary in that neither side is in conflict with the other. The needs of each can be met with simple understanding based on common sense and plain dealing. Here's how:

First, it should be stated that copyright can be bought or sold when deemed appropriate by both the client and the photographer (anyone can sell an asset if he or she chooses.) However, it isn't usually necessary.

Realistically, there is no client need or interest regarding copyrightable work which can not be licensed or contractually provided for by the photographer/copyright owner. For example, pricing of future uses, expanded circulation, re-uses, etc. can all be agreed to in the early stages of a negotiation. Whether by fixed fee, percentage of original fee or by no increase in fee at all, both the financial interest of the client, as well as the right to exercise such future uses at will, absolutely can and should be protected.

Clients often have a need to protect certain assets, their image, processes, executives and employees from undesired exposure. This proprietary interest can and must be protected. Again, this can be done by guarantee of the photographer, who as copyright owner, should agree to not license such images for any other use by anyone, except the original client. When clients protect their needs and secure their interests in such a manner, it allows the photographer to exploit the value of the non-proprietary images for his or her future gain, whether it is from the promotional value of the work, or from the residual value in the rights not granted to the original client.

From the photographers side, the majority of photographers make some share of their revenues from the sale of such residual rights. These revenues contribute to the profitability of the business, which in turn keeps the general cost of assignment photography lower. It is simple mathematics. If a photographer cannot use a commissioned work to obtain residual income, it will simply drive the price of commissioned work up and up. If you take away that right, you must pay the price to cover the loss of that right.

Hence, a simple understanding of the needs of client and photographer can lead to a dramatically improved working relationship: one in which the photographer and the client work together to produce the finest possible result and the best possible price; one in which the photographer and the client get all the value to which they are entitled by their needs, not their wants; one in which the mutual dependency of both is recognized and provided for.

The simple fact is that all of this conflict over copyright ownership could be put to rest with common sense and plain dealing.

Creative photography is not a commodity. The "I paid for it; I own it" attitude simply isn't in the best interests of the business relationship. Unlike a commodity, a photograph can be used over and over again. It can be everlasting. No stationer would sell a box of envelopes if the box never ran out. That stationer would soon learn that the only way to stay in business would be to lease the use of the endless supply of envelopes.

The interests of photographers and clients are not irreconcilable. These interests can easily be accommodated by simple negotiations aimed at meeting the needs of both the client and the photographer.

Let's hope that common sense and plain dealing soon eliminate the current trend of "take it or leave it."

Richard Weisgrau
Executive Director
ASMP - American Society of
Magazine Photographers, Inc.
© 1991, ASMP

Steve Burns
30 Westwood Avenue
PO Box 175
Westwood, New Jersey 07675
(201) 358-1890

For additional work see:
Corporate Showcase 9
Corporate Showcase 8
New Jersey Source 2

Member ASMP.
Stock available.

STEVE BURNS

201 358-1890

Walter P. Calahan
(703) 998-8380 Office & FAX

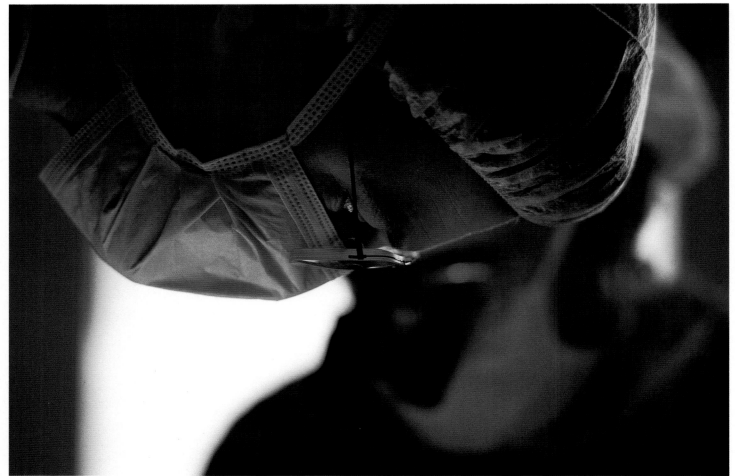

Dr. Timothy Colton, surgeon

*Olympic Training Center,
Lake Placid, N.Y.*

Spirit of Massachusetts, dawn

4656 34th Street, South, Suite B-2, Arlington, Virginia 22206-1740

Walter P. Calahan

(703) 998-8380 Office & FAX

Clients:
Ameritech
Equifax
McGraw-Hill
Philip Morris
Time-Warner
Whittle Communications

Also See:
Corporate Showcase, Volume 8,
page 204
Corporate Showcase, Volume 9,
pages 160-161
Creative Sourcebook of Washington,
D.C., 5th Edition, page 278

Desiree C. Vass, 90, with Easter flowers

4656 34th Street, South, Suite B-2, Arlington, Virginia 22206-1740

Charles Callaghan
(215) 822-8258

I work in the real world.

A world where corporations and agencies demand more than just technical expertise.

It's a world demanding creativity, visual excellence and total responsibility.

The decisions come easily and I'm proud of my work.

Given the opportunity, I'll express your visual direction.

CALLAGHAN

Arlene Collins
64 North Moore Street
Studio 3E
New York, New York 10013
(212) 431-9117
FAX: (212) 226-8466

In Canada represented by:
Diane Jameson
(416) 369-9442
FAX: (416) 366-5525

ASMP Member
Clients include: NCR Corporation,
Canada Wire, Noranda Mines, Kodak
(Canada), Maclean Hunter Annual
Report, Hill & Knowlton (Canada).

Jeff Comella
12 Pecan Drive
Pittsburgh, Pennsylvania 15235
(412) 795-2706

Location assignments for
annual report, corporate
communications, advertising,
and editorial clients.

Call for portfolio.

See additional photographs:
Corporate Showcase Volume 9,
page 123.

Member ASMP
© 1991 Jeff Comella

C O M E L L A

Steve Dunwell
20 Winchester Street
Boston, Massachusetts 02116
(617) 423-4916 • FAX: (617) 695-0059

Fine photography for business
and industry.
Annual reports, brochures and
special books.

Member ASMP

DUNWELL

Claudio Edinger
456 Broome Street
New York, New York 10013
(212) 219-8619
FAX: (212) 219-8669
(212) 699-1417 Mobile Phone

Salvatore Silipigni – *Pittsburgh Symphony Orchestra*

Martha Everson
219 Fisher Avenue
Brookline, Massachusetts 02146
(617) 232-0187

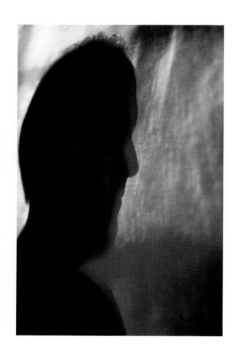

MARTHA

Robert I. Faulkner
14 Elizabeth Avenue
East Brunswick, New Jersey 08816
(201) 390-6650

Photography of architecture and interior design.

Clients include: Stubbins Assoc., Haines Lundberg Waehler, The Grad Partnership, CUH2A, Hillier Group, Martin Organization, Kling Lundquist, Short & Ford, Lutron Electronics, Johnson & Johnson, Steelcase, Gunlocke, Prudential, Hilton Hotels, Merck, General Electric, Schering Plough, Walden Books, ADP Corp., Phillips Lighting, Torcon Construction, Henderson Corp., Trammell Crow, Lincoln Properties, Cushman Wakefield, Hartz Mountain, DKM Properties, Tower Center Assoc., Beta West, Trafalgar House, Toll Bros. Hills Dev., Pace Advertising, CN Communications, ANR Advertising.

Richard Frasier
2857 Nutley Street
Fairfax, Virginia 22031
(703) 385-3761

So he does it all? They've all done it all! To stay afloat while working towards a specialty. But Rich thinks that "doing it all" is a specialty. That studio, corporate, location, fashion, stock and architecture are all part of the same picture. That experience gained in one area enhances performance in all the others. Remarkable photos make true believers. So, he does it all.

—Andy Attiliis, Attiliis & Assoc.

Say a booking has stock value too? Rich will discuss the possibilities and afford my client an appropriate consideration. —Linda Sherman, Linda Sherman Design, Inc.

Designer eye. Listens well, *then thinks* (important). Little bulb starts blinking (blinking hell, sometimes his whole head lights up). Incredible range!—J. Michael Welton, The Welton Agency

That case of Leicas convinced me — even in the field he goes for studio quality. —Larry Johnston, VP, Spectrum Publishing

And his book (no quick peek, identify style, file neatly away person here)! I was compelled to go on. —Kathryn Rebeiz, Publisher, Washington Entertainment Magazine

Kenneth Gabrielsen
Photography
11 Tuttle Street
Stamford, Connecticut 06902
(203) 964-8254

Client list available upon request.

Call for Stock list.

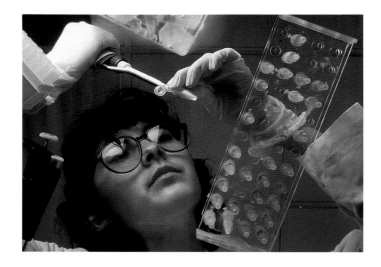

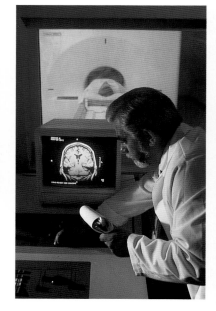

Garry Geer
Geer Photography
183 Saint Paul Street
Rochester, New York 14604
(716) 232-2393

Specializing in corporate, editorial,
and advertising photography.

Jon Goell
535 Albany Street
Boston, Massachusetts 02118
(617) 423-2057 • FAX: (617) 542-8206

Corporate Annual Reports /
Editorial / Advertising / Stock

Partial Client List: Addison Wesley,
BTA, BBN, Boston Magazine,
Business Week, CFO, Continental
CableVision, Converse, DEC, Egerton,
Inc Magazine, HBMC Direct, Polaroid,
Prime Computervision, Thrift Fund.

Jon Goell
535 Albany Street
Boston, Massachusetts 02118
(617) 423-2057 • FAX (617) 542-8206

Photographs © Jon Goell 1991

Executives for an English annual report

JON GOELL
617·423·2057

surgeon for editorial spread
set and shot @ left for cover

Tom Graves
136 East 36 Street
New York, New York 10016
(212) 683-0241
FAX: (212) 779-3126

Thoughtful photography
for discerning clients.

Call us for printed samples.

David M. Grossman
211 East 7th Street
Brooklyn, New York 11218
(718) 438-5021

Corporate Annual Reports, Posters, Ads:

Memorial Sloan Kettering, New York Public Library, United Way, Gannett Foundation.

Manning Gurney
25 West 38th Street, 3rd floor
New York, New York 10018
(212) 391-0965

Studio Portraits
Executive Makeovers

Time Inc.
AT & T
Loving & Weintraub
N.C.C.I

HEAD DESIGNER CIAO SPORT

C.E.O. THEATRICAL ORGANIZATION

REPORTER WABC T.V.

ATTORNEY

C.E.O. KENAR ENTERPRISE

BEFORE

MUSEUM DIRECTOR

Ron Hagerman
389 Charles Street
Providence, Rhode Island 02904
(401) 272-1117

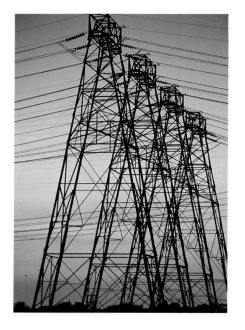

Don Hamerman
(212) 627-5474 New York City
(203) 325-1977 Connecticut
FAX: (203) 353-0606

Portraits. Reportage.

Kent Hanson
147 Bleecker Street, #3R
New York, New York 10012
(212) 777-2399

Editorial, Advertising, and
Corporate Photography.

Portfolio and Stock Photography
available upon request.

Glen Hitchcox
7 Blauvelt Street
Nanuet, New York 10954
(914) 623-5859
FAX: (914) 623-7259

Corporate
Industrial
Architectural
Editorial

Stock Available

As editor of *Photo District News*, I like to believe we're completely plugged into the business of commercial photography and are reporting on news and trends in a timely and accurate manner. Alas, our efforts have not always been appreciated.

Such has been the case, in recent years, with our coverage of corporate photography. Annual reports, we've noted, have been looking better and better. Editorial and advertising photographers, we also noted, seemed to be finding new opportunities (and happiness) in corporate and annual report photography. The field was positively blossoming.

That's what we saw, and that's what we wrote about.

And that's when we noticed that not everyone was happy with us. Some felt that we were making too much of this trend. In fact, one big name corporate photographer took me aside at a party to complain about all the coverage of his specialty in *PDN*. "It used to be no one wanted to be a corporate photographer," he said morosely. "Now everyone wants to be one....Could you please tone it down?"

So when asked to say a few words here about the state of corporate photography, I decided to take his advice. Let me say, once and for all, that corporate photography is not all it's cracked up to be.

It's true, the money is better (far better, I'm afraid) than in editorial photography. It's also true that the advertising photography market seems to be in a slump. Finally, it's true that annual report photographers have enjoyed an unprecedented amount of creative freedom in recent years. But then, have you considered what they have to work with?

In other words, have you considered how tough a job it is to make corporate America look good?

Consider, for a moment, your average CEO. He (and it is usually a he) is not what most of us would term unduly photogenic. He's also no fool: He knows he's not photogenic. More importantly, he also knows that a photo session is going to take him away from his daily business of improving profitability. Therefore, the idea of getting his picture taken does not fill him with great joy. In fact, it makes him cranky—which makes him even less photogenic than usual.

But duty calls, so he agrees to pose.

Would you want to photograph this man? Before answering, consider this well-known photographer's take on photographing executives (which is one of his specialities): "They don't want you to show them in any inherently revelatory manner. What they do want is to be shown exactly the way they looked when they were practicing in front of the bathroom mirror earlier that morning, which is the way their wives helped them to look."

Now, be honest, would you want to photograph this cranky, unphotogenic man?

Let's assume you feel confident of your ability to take on the corporate executive. Then you are ready to consider the next major challenge of corporate photography: your average corporate location. This is the lab/office/factory where the day-to-day work of the corporation is performed.

Continued on page 90

Tom Iannuzzi
141 Wooster Street, #6A
New York, New York 10012
(212) 505-9108 • (212) 563-1987
FAX Available

Corporate
and Editorial
Photography

Tom Iannuzzi

George Kamper Productions Ltd.
15 West 24th Street
New York, New York 10010
(212) 627-7171

Rep: Ursula Kreis (212) 562-8931
FAX: (212) 562-7959

Michigan Rep: Stage III (313) 978-7373
FAX: (313) 978-9085

With his in-camera photo montages, George Kamper photographically interprets abstract ideas and tells a story visually by combining diverse elements not commonly seen together in one photograph. All effects are done in front of the camera—on the set or on location. The process can first be polaroided, so there are no surprises. Since the resulting chrome is the final image, there is no additional production cost.

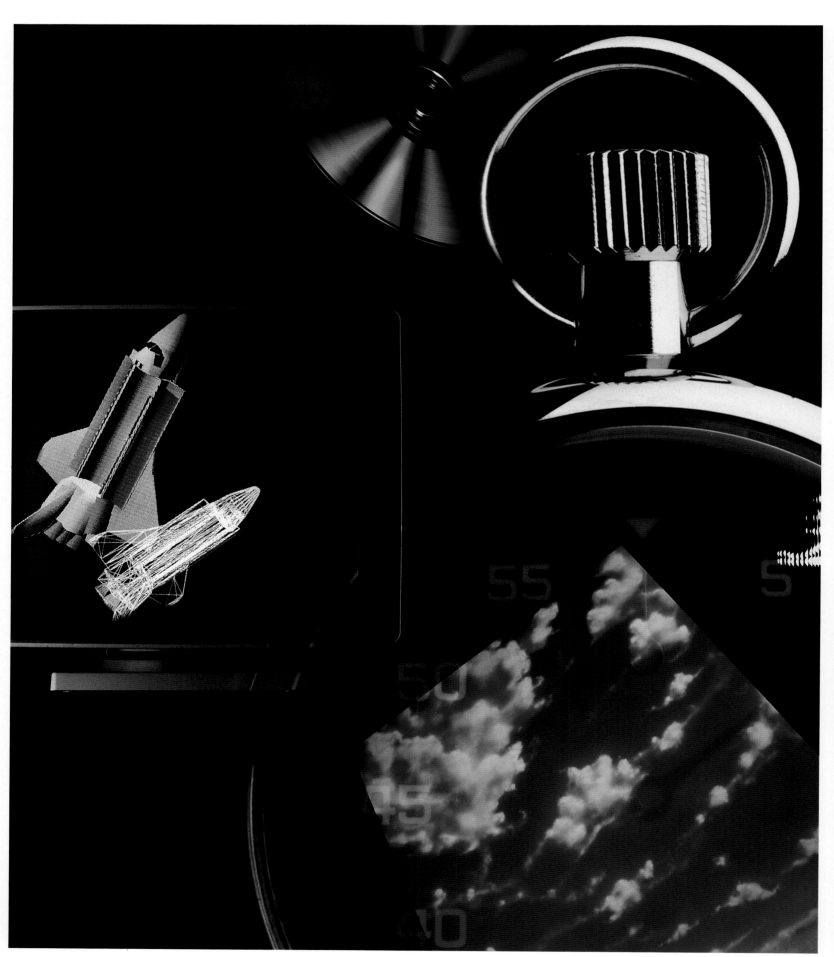

**George Kamper
Productions Ltd.**
15 West 24th Street
New York, New York 10010
(212) 627-7171

Rep: Ursula Kreis (212) 562-8931
FAX: (212) 562-7959

Michigan Rep: Stage III (313) 978-7373
FAX: (313) 978-9085

With his in-camera photo montages, George Kamper photographically interprets abstract ideas and tells a story visually by combining diverse elements not commonly seen together in one photograph. All effects are done in front of the camera—on the set or on location. The process can first be polaroided, so there are no surprises. Since the resulting chrome is the final image, there is no additional production cost.

Kevin Lein Photography
83 Leonard Street, 3rd floor
New York, New York 10013
(212) 966-2764
FAX: (212) 966-2784

Principal Clients:
Avenue, Capital (Italy), Class (Italy),
Family Media, Finalco, Parade,
Parents, R.H. Macy Corporate Buying,
The America First Companies,
Town & Country.

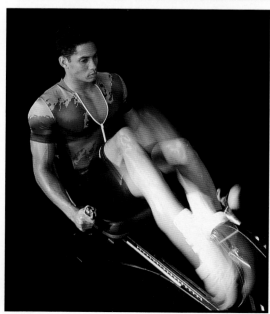

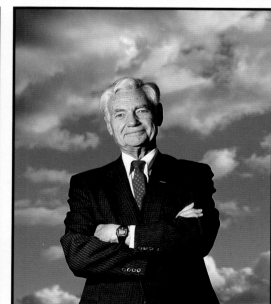

Jook Leung
photography
35 South Van Brunt Street
Englewood, New Jersey 07631
(201) 894-5881
FAX: (201) 894-5882

Jook is a photo-illustrator combining his expertise in photography with digital and optical imaging techniques...

Stock photography is also available.

Additional work can be seen in:
American Showcase:
Volume 14, Page 122
Volume 13, Page 113
Volume 12, Page 105
Volume 11, Page 118
and Corporate Showcase:
Volume 9, Page 94

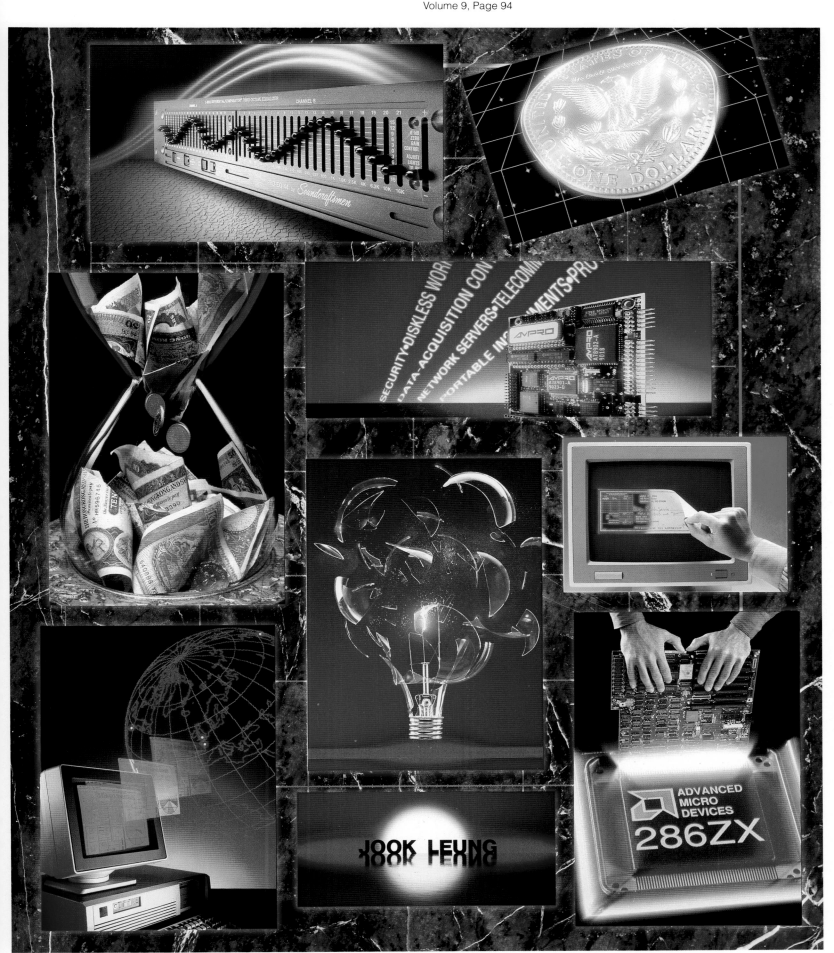

Continued from page 84

Labs, in my experience anyway, tend to feature lots of bright white formica and/or tile and chrome (both highly reflective), and fluorescent lights (which impart such a pleasant green tone to everything.) Offices also tend to favor this lighting—and the green is usually augmented by the glow emanating from the nearly ubiquitous computer terminals on everyone's desk. Factories are either over-lit or dismally dark and dreary. And both factories and offices tend to be messy and disorganized.

To add to your location woes, consider this: the curmudgeonly CEO you've just photographed—to say nothing of the designer who's hired you—wants to present a totally different picture of this lab/office/factory than the one you see before you when you arrive. Not only is he likely to reject a cinema verité approach, he's apt to be highly indignant if you attempt it.

Creating the fantasy location the CEO—and the designer—have in mind takes considerable ingenuity and skill. It also often requires a considerable amount of lighting equipment that you and your hapless assistant will have to schlep to said location.

Which brings us to a whole other issue: Have you considered exactly where these labs/offices/factories are located? Usually, in locations neither glamorous (far from it!) nor accessible.

So you have to ask yourself: Would you like to photograph this location?

Having covered who and what corporate photographers are likely to be called upon to shoot, let's consider the client itself, the corporation.

Given the proprietary nature of most corporations, the corporate photographer may well be dealing with a client who's even tougher on rights and usage than his editorial or advertising colleagues. Not only may the corporate client suffer from the I-paid-for-it-so-I-own-it syndrome so pervasive in the industry, he or she may feel the need to own these precious images outright, lest they be published in a context less than flattering to the corporation. To put it another way, corporations tend to be a tad white-knuckle about control.

Would you want to deal with this client?

So there it is, the other side of corporate photography: it's a very tough business. So let's not hear any more complaints at parties, okay?

Elizabeth Forst
Editor-in-Chief
Photo District News

John Loy

Photography

1611 Shipley Road
Wilmington, DE 19803

Ph 302 762 3812
Fx 302 762 8424

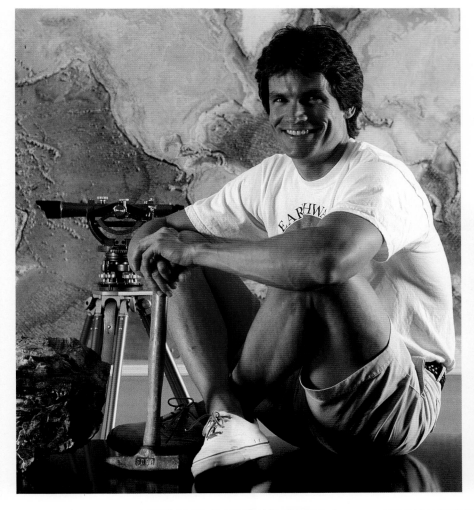

Partial List of Clients: Mercedes Benz Dealers, Litton/
Clifton Precision, W. L. Gore & Associates, Brown
Shoe Company, Bell Atlantic, The Linpro Company,
Drexel University, Kent General Hospital, West Chester
University, Daroff Designs, Inc., Barclay's Bank.

Larry Maglott
249 A Street
Boston, Massachusetts 02210
(617) 482-9347

Larry Maglott
249 A Street
Boston, Massachusetts 02210
(617) 482-9347

Kevin R. McDonald Studio
319 Newtown Turnpike
Redding, Connecticut
(203) 938-9276
FAX available

Specializing in:
Corporate Annuals
Medical, Health & Fitness
Editorial Fashion
Portraits
Advertising

To view more work:
See Corporate Showcase Vol. #7
Traveling Portfolio
available upon request.

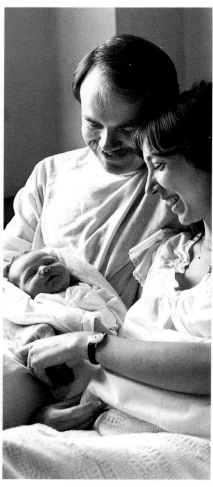

Abraham Menashe
Humanistic Photography
306 East 5th Street
New York, New York 10003
(212) 254-2754
FAX: (212) 505-6857

Life affirming photography. Highlighting the human factor by focusing on people and their vital spirit.

On Location Worldwide for Advertising, Editorial, Corporate clients.

Stock: From birth to old age. Medical / Health Care / Social Service / Religions / Handicapped & much more.

Donald L. Miller
295 Central Park West
New York, New York 10024
(212) 496-2830

Specializing in C.E.O.'s, Chairmen, Presidents, Directors, and top management.

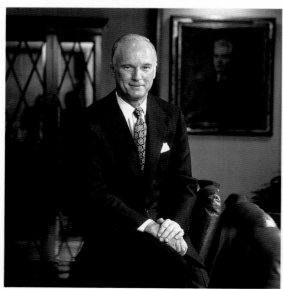

Donald L. Miller
295 Central Park West
New York, New York 10024
(212) 496-2830

Specializing in C.E.O.'s, Chairmen,
Presidents, Directors, and top
management.

**Gary Mirando
Photography**
27 Cleveland Street
Valhalla, New York 10595
(914) 997-6588
FAX: (914) 428-2953

Corporate
Industrial
Editorial
Travel and Stock

Greg Pease
Greg Pease & Associates, Inc.
23 East 22nd Street
Baltimore, Maryland 21218
(410) 332-0583
FAX: (410) 332-1797

Stock photography available
Studio Manager: Kelly Baumgartner

Specializing in corporate/industrial
photography
Also see:
American Showcase 4 through 14
Corporate Showcase 1, 4 through 9

A selection from:
Westmoreland Coal Company
1990 Annual Report

Alex Pietersen
67 N The Village Green
Budd Lake, New Jersey 07828
(201) 347-7504

Representatives:
Warner & Associates (201) 755-7236
1425 Belleview Avenue
Plainfield, New Jersey 07060
Black Star (212) 679-3288
116 East 27th Street
New York, New York 10016
Orion Press Tokyo Japan

No computer, copystand, animation
stand or lasers are used to create these
images.
Additional work can be seen in
Corporate Showcase 4 and 6

Clients:
Deltakos (Div. of J. Walter Thompson)

Saatchi & Saatchi • Nelson
Communications • Eli Lilly • Upjohn Co.
Squibb • Merck International • Allied
Chemical • A T & T • Tobor Pictures Ltd.
Robocop 1 & 2 • W. H. Freeman and
Company Publishers • Silver Burdett &
Ginn • The Mennen Company • I.B.M.
Ryder Trucks Inc. • U.S. Comstruct

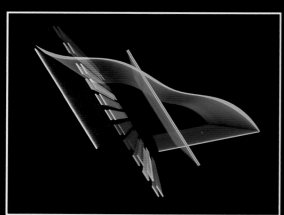

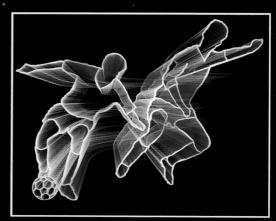

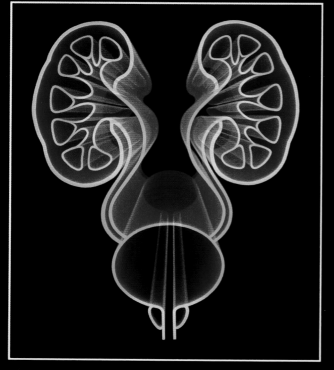

alex pietersen

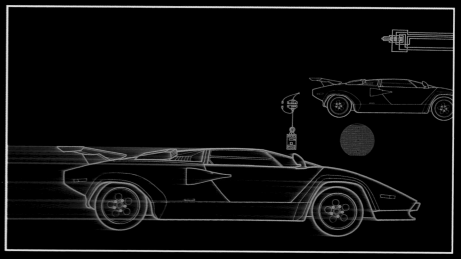

Bill Ray

350 Central Park West
New York, New York 10025
(212) 222-7680

Represented by:
Marlys Ray

Black & white samples and portfolio
on request.

Clockwise from upper left:
Lord Richardson, Morgan Stanley,
London.
David M. Kelly, President, CEO; Bernard
L. Madoff, Chairman, National Securities
Clearing Corp.
S. Parker Gilbert, Chairman (right);
Richard B. Fisher, President (seated);

Robert F. Greenhill, Vice Chairman
(standing), Morgan Stanley.
Walter Max, President of steam turbine
division, Turbodyne Corp.
J. Carter Bacot, Chairman, CEO; Peter
Herrick, President, and members of the
Steering Committee, The Bank of New
York.

Seth Resnick
28 Seaverns Avenue, Suite 8
Boston, Massachusetts 02130
(617) 983-0291
FAX: (617) 522-7291

Location photography for:
Annual Reports, Corporate,
Advertising, Editorial, Stock

Recent clients: AARP Ameritech,
Bitstream, Business Week, Cimflex
Teknowledge, Computerland,
Continental, Dallas First, Dial, DuPont,
Forbes, Inc., Lotus, Magnavox, Money,
National Geographic, Ryder, The New
York Times, Tufts, USCI.

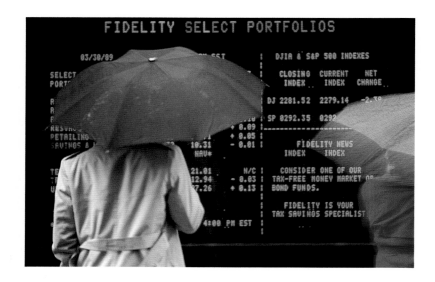

Seth Resnick
28 Seaverns Avenue, Suite 8
Boston, Massachusetts 02130
(617) 983-0291
FAX: (617) 522-7291

Location photography for:
Annual Reports, Corporate,
Advertising, Editorial, Stock

Recent clients: AARP Ameritech,
Bitstream, Business Week, Cimflex
Teknowledge, Computerland,
Continental, Dallas First, Dial, DuPont,
Forbes, Inc., Lotus, Magnavox, Money,
National Geographic, Ryder, The New
York Times, Tufts, USCI.

Spirits and Submarines: How to Satisfy Corporate Clients and Pacify Angry Gods

We were in paradise.

It was a spectacular setting for a photo shoot: lush vegetation, waterfalls, the ocean waves crashing, the mountains looming in the distance. We were in Hawaii at the site of a new hotel and condominium complex. And overnight, somehow, huge boulders that had been removed from the site had mysteriously returned to their ancient locations.

The geologists for the project could not give us any logical explanation of how giant rocks could move of their own accord <u>at all</u>, much less the distance that some of them did move. <u>This</u> was a problem. Not only were the photo session and marketing brochure at stake, but an investment of millions of dollars in the land—none of it could be sold if it was "unstable."

We soon learned that the development was taking place on ancient Hawaiian burial ground, and the locals insisted that the boulders were being moved by the spirits of long-dead nobles, disturbed by the sudden activity in the area. Faced with a problem that was obviously not going to be solved by conventional scientific wisdom, the developer agreed to have the land blessed by a native priest.

The boulders stayed in place. We got the photos, and did the brochure.

Admittedly, design firms do not often encounter situations where the local gods are offended, but we were prepared to respond to any type of circumstance. Like the forces that caused the rocks to move, what distinguishes one design firm from another is the ability to go beyond the obvious, to create a unique (and sometimes intangible) statement.

Large and small corporations alike require visual communication tools to express their messages: to report the annual financial position of the company, introduce products and services, or present a new corporate identity, program, or logo.

That's where design firms come in. We create those tools, in a style appropriate to the client and product. We use computer technology, photography, illustration and creative printing techniques to make new and exciting images. Most competent designers are able to produce attractive work. What makes the difference between competent and good is the designer's ability to identify with the client, and develop a working relationship with the company itself. And fundamental to this relationship is the concept of <u>partnership</u>, and trust in each other's judgement. The design firm and the client, we have found, have to "co-produce" each project. But, as in any relationship, this requires work.

One of the most important abilities a design firm can have for a corporate client is similar to what makes a good reporter: to be able to take a mass of information, sometimes in a very complex technical environment, and <u>identify the story</u>. You could generalize this by saying "understand the client's business," but it's a little more complicated.

For example, one of our current clients produces computer software for manufacturing companies. It is used in three different types of manufacturing processes: "discrete" (which is the assembly of parts into a final product, like a TV set or furniture); "process" (which involves raw materials); and "mixed-mode" (where products are created and then transferred to high-volume packaging lines, like ice cream and pharmaceuticals.) Whew!

No one at my firm, including myself, is a manufacturing specialist, chemist or computer scientist. Our initial interviews and preparation—completed over several weeks—didn't leave us really sure about the distinctions within this complex subject, let alone about the science of the software itself. It wasn't until we stepped back from this milieu of technical wizardry that we arrived at the design answer: it was the software's <u>function</u> that mattered, and, fundamentally, that function was managing inventory and resources.

In giving us two weeks of intensive briefings, the client had been trying to give us the best possible background, making sure we had all the information we needed. But, as had the client, we lost the forest in the (technological) trees, until we stepped out of the park.

This is an important point: a design firm, as a third-party resource, sees things from an outside perspective. What this means is that we tend to view a company from a point of view more like that of the audience with whom it needs to communicate. And this can create tension if it is not done in a setting of partnership, and of trust, in the design firm-client relationship. Because to be effective, designers must provide what the <u>client really needs</u>, not just what the client <u>wants</u>.

Continued on page 110

Mark Richards
58 Falcon Street
Needham, Massachusetts 02192
(617) 449-7135
(800) 829-7135

Simon & Schuster
Buyer Advertising
Optical Corp. of America
New England Card and Index

Awards/Memberships
Photographic Resource Center
Cambridge Art Association
One person show Polaroid Corporate
Headquarters
Horesman-Calumet Large Format
Photography Honorable Mention
Creative Club of Boston, Merit Award

Team Work

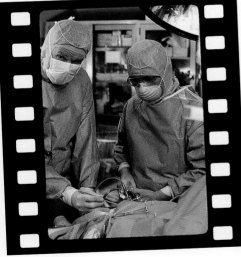

Precision

The Dean

Service

Taste

**Richardson/Wright
Photography**
Tim Wright
PO Box 8296
Richmond, Virginia 23226
(804) 272-1439
FAX: (804) 330-7390

Specializing in location photography
for advertising, corporate and editorial
markets.

Partial client list: E.R. Carpenter, James
River Corporation, Business Week, Time
and U.S. News & World Report
Magazine.

•Portfolio and stock list available upon
request.

TIM WRIGHT

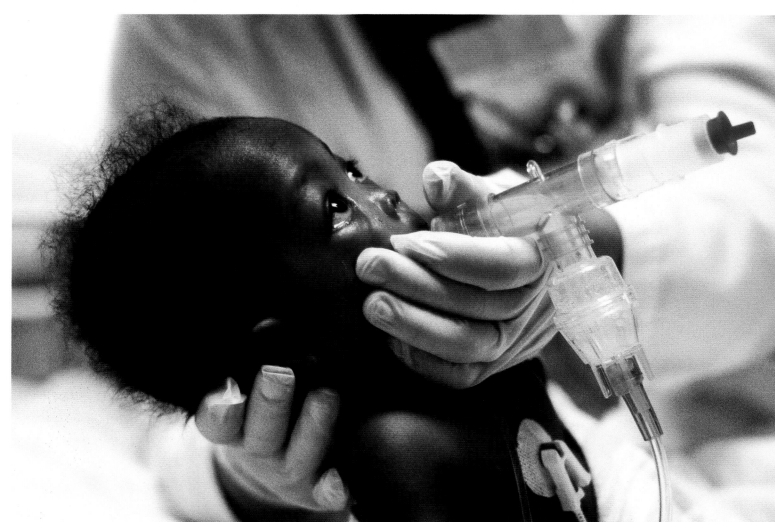

Richardson/Wright Photography
Lynda Richardson
PO Box 8296
Richmond, Virginia 23226
(804) 272-0965
FAX: (804) 330-7390

Ray Pfortner
Peter Arnold, Inc.
1181 Broadway
New York, New York 10001
(212) 481-1190
(800) 289-7468

Specializing in studio and location photography of the world's wildlife for advertising, corporate and editorial markets.

Partial client list: Browning-Ferris Industries, South African Tourism Board, Vulcan Materials Company, National Geographic Society and the National Wildlife Federation.

•Portfolio and stock list available upon request.

John Rörström
13 Summit Street
East Hampton, Connecticut 06424
(203) 267-7255

Location and studio portraiture,
international travel, stock available.

Stanley Rowin
791 Tremont Street
Boston, Massachusetts 02118
(617) 437-0641

SIMPLE. POWERFUL. PASSIONATE.

Continued from page 104

For instance, the audience of a particular company, and its essential message, may change as the company evolves. In the process of designing and producing communication tools, the design firm must recognize those changes and provide advice and perspective.

We've had one client for the entire 16 years of our existence. It started out as a small housing corporation, and has grown into the largest housing developer in California and in France and a major financial services provider. But there is more to the story than just corporate growth.

As the company has expanded, the market it serves has itself grown and changed. This has meant keeping the image of the company up-to-date and relevant to its new consumer needs. The company is now also publicly traded, and must comply with many legal requirements. Our design firm has evidently been successful at unifying the corporate message of this company, while still communicating with the quite different audiences that are important to each subsidiary. We have won some important design awards, and still have the client.

This is not to boast. This is to say that, with the development of a good working partnership with a corporate client, design firms can continue to serve their needs effectively over a period of many years, despite changes in business, markets and audience.

And sometimes, a commitment to a firm has unforeseen benefits. Let me leave you with an anecdote:

We had a client who specialized in defense electronics, but was expanding into civilian markets. One of its successful military products was a "rotator servo" control unit for submarines. These are fairly arcane devices to begin with, and it was neither possible (from a security standpoint) nor desirable (who but an expert could identify it?) to use a product shot.

So we looked for a submarine photo. And I mean we looked. The U.S. Navy offered to stage the shot we wanted, but we didn't want to spend tax dollars for private purposes. Finally, we gathered several shots we thought would do the job, had them enlarged, and put them on the walls of the room for our client presentation.

A visiting intelligence expert and one of the company's staff happened by, and glanced in. They were incredulous. "Where did you get that picture?!!" one asked. We told him we'd have to track back through the records, but that we could find out. "But, why?" we asked. "That's a Russian submarine," he responded, "and to my knowledge, nobody has a photo like that of that vessel!"

Ah, well. They do now.

By the way, the annual report turned out beautifully, even without the Soviet sub. Sometimes, by going the extra mile for a client, you get results you never expected.

Joan Libera
Founder/Principal
Libera & Associates
Los Angeles, CA

James Rudnick

(212) 466-6337

Location photography for corporate, advertising, and editorial clients.

Corporate and advertising clients include: American Express, American Maize, Champion Paper, Citibank, Danaher, Liberty Mutual, RJR Nabisco, Pepsico, and Sony.

Publications include: Time, Esquire, National Geographic, and Travel & Leisure.

Stock photography available upon request.

Robert Severi
Washington, DC
(301) 585-1010

Represented in New York City by:
Gamma-Liaison - assignments
(212) 447-2515
Woodfin Camp - stock
(212) 481-6900

Additional work can be seen in:
American Showcase 8, page 233
American Showcase 10, page 223
A.R. 5, pages 204-205
A.R. 6

Call studio to receive our regular
mailings, client list or portfolio.

Robert Severi
Washington, DC
(301) 585-1010

Represented in New York City by:
Gamma-Liaison - assignments
(212) 447-2515
Woodfin Camp - stock
(212) 481-6900

Additional work can be seen in:
American Showcase 8, page 233
American Showcase 10, page 223
A.R. 5, pages 204-205
A.R. 6

Big Fish, Powerful Ideas and Generic Communications

'm standing knee deep in the Missouri River in Montana with fly rod in hand. The sun is hot, the water is cold and some thirty feet away a large wild rainbow trout rises to devour some aquatic morsel. I watch intently; this is some fish. My total being becomes obsessed with outwitting a fish with a brain the size of a pea. To make it more preposterous, if I catch it I'll just let it go anyway.

I continue to observe closely and ask myself, "What fly do I use? How large? What color? Fish it on the surface? Just below the surface?" I'll figure it out. I'll solve the problem. The trout will be caught, but when?

Suddenly, slam, bam. The line goes tight...fish on. I pull up. The fish runs, jumps, runs again. The reel sings, the rod bends. It's exciting. It's thrilling. It's fun. It is totally satisfying and I love it.

We're sitting at the conference table in our office in New York. It's hot out, but the air conditioning is cool. We are all intense, wound a little tight. This is some project. It's a big product launch and we're all obsessed with making it absolutely great.

We talk. We joke. We doodle. We look at Corporate Showcase. We ask each other, "What's good about this product? What's different? Why buy it? What if? What type? What color? How big?" We'll figure it out. The problem will be solved. It will be great, but when?

Suddenly, slam, bam. Flash...the idea hits. That's it. Our imaginations run wild, they jump and run again. The idea sings, it bends. It's exciting. It's thrilling. It's fun. It is totally satisfying and we love it.

A trout is a very selective creature... you can't fool him with a *generic* fly... it just won't work.

So here's the point. The best communications...the ones that are exciting and memorable and work... contain designs, images and words that deliver *real ideas,* not generic ones.

Unfortunately, too much of today's communication is filled with generic imagery. A "Your Company Name Goes Here" way of thinking is fast becoming the norm in our business culture. How many annual reports have you seen with a photograph of "The Corporate Huddle": a group of three people; one person with a red article of clothing; the other pointing at something; and the third staring into space. Or the busy investment banker with a phone in each ear and a grimace on his face.

It's hard work to come up with the big idea, the great image, the unique design. But what gets me up in the morning is the challenge of solving a problem and creating something new and yes, different.

Helpful hints to eliminate generic communications:

1. Never use the words *excellence, commitment* or *teamwork.*

2. Don't use tabletop shots of foreign currency to illustrate *global capability.*

3. Never do a shot from the steps of the Federal Reserve in NYC with the New York Stock Exchange in the background.

4. Try very hard not to print faux textures like marble and granite for backgrounds.

5. Never use a photograph of a woman with a bow tie. Always use photographs of men with bow ties.

The creative community has a professional obligation to its clients to go beyond the generic. To provide fresh solutions instead of the same old stuff. We can't let boring become the norm.

Remember: you can't catch the attention of great clients with generic ideas.

Arnold Wechsler
President
Wechsler & Partners Inc.
Marketing and Design
New York City

Stephen Sherman
49 Melcher Street
Fifth Floor
Boston, Massachusetts 02210
(617) 542-1496 Voice/FAX

Stock Photography Available

Clients Include:
Bell Atlantic, Bomzer Design,
Computerworld, Curran & Connors,
Coopers & Lybrand, Ernst & Young,
Equafax, GTE Labs, Hologic, Inc.,
IDS/American Express, Information
Week, New England Telephone,
NYNEX, Polaroid, Sun Microsystems

To view additional work, please see:

Corporate Showcase 8, Page 193
Corporate Showcase 9, Page 147

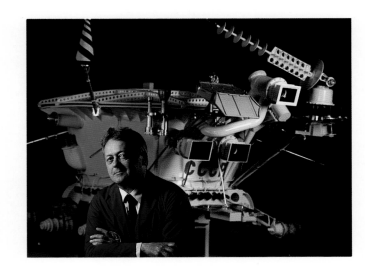

Dana Sigall Photography
348 Congress Street
Boston, Massachusetts 02210
(617) 357-5140
FAX: (617) 426-5125

P L A N

C O M M I T

S U P P O R T

E M P O W E R

A selection from Organizational Dynamics, Inc. marketing brochure: **Implementing Total Quality**. Design and art direction: Mary Kiene.

Peter Steiner
183 Saint Paul Street
Rochester, New York 14604
(716) 454-1012
FAX: (716) 454-1916

A m e r i c a n   A i r l i n e s   *A p p l e*   *B B D & O*   *K o d a k*

S a a t c h i & S a a t c h i   O g i l v y & M a t h e r   X e r o x

Tom Stewart
205 Johnson Point Road
Penobscot, Maine 04476
(207) 326-9370

Tom Stewart
205 Johnson Point Road
Penobscot, Maine 04476
(207) 326-9370

To see more work:
Corporate Showcase 9, pages 150 & 151
Corporate Showcase 8, pages 194 & 195

If you came across a bottle labeled with a skull and crossbones, you would not be tempted to taste its contents. A red traffic light automatically makes your foot push the brake pedal. Symbols are graphic devices prompting you to action: sometimes warning of impending danger, other times informing or classifying. They are shorthand for complex ideas. Symbols overcome language barriers and provide instant recognition. The yellow box says Kodak, even if you are illiterate. The curly script says Coca-Cola, even before you read the words. Flags are symbols: the Union Jack means England, the red disc, Japan, the Stars and Stripes, America, reaffirming not just the fact but a lot of the legends around the fact. The symbol is a powerful conjurer of a thousand images, all at once.

The danger in using symbols is the danger of cliché: an effective symbol has always been seen a thousand times before. Milton Glaser's ingenious I ♥ New York has now been copied in hundreds of versions, varying from imitation to insanity.

Because of its ability to compel people to action, the symbol has become a selling tool. Companies are protecting their logotypes with copyrights and restricting their use via complicated manuals. Books governing the applications of the IBM or AT&T logos are the size of a small telephone directory. Updating or changing a trademark like Mobil's, replacing the prancing Pegasus with the updated red "O," cost close to a hundred million dollars.

For a designer or photographer, the use of the symbol depends on the ingenuity with which you apply it in a way different from its original intent. The surrealists picked on the Mona Lisa as "The Painting," not because it was the greatest painting ever made, but because of its fame, its history of having been stolen and returned. It was a perfect target. They defaced it, collaged it, paraphrased it, copied it, and each time it became even more "valuable." The Greek Pygmalion legend of the sculptor who shaped the perfect woman and made her come to life became G.B. Shaw's Pygmalion and later, in its third reincarnation, Lerner & Loewe's My Fair Lady. The symbol thrives on revival and is strengthened through each adaptation. It reduces misunderstandings created by language and other differences. Symbols are a reaffirmation of our basic sameness.

Henry Wolf
From: Visual Thinking: Methods for Making Images Memorable
© 1988 Henry Wolf
Published by American Showcase

Steven Stone
20 Rugg Road
Allston, Massachusetts 02134-1627
(617) 782-1247
FAX: (617) 787-2332

Stock Agent:
The Picture Cube
89 Broad Street
Boston, Massachusetts 02110
(617) 367-1532
FAX: (617) 482-9266

Clients Include: Boston Magazine,
Business Week, Alsys, Cognition, CMP
Publications, EG&G, Data General,
Emery Air Freight, Kiddie Products,
Milton Bradley, Museum of Fine Arts-
Boston, New Balance, Polaroid, Whittle
Communications.

For Additional Work See:
Corporate Showcase #9, Page 153
Corporate Showcase #8, Page 199
Worksource 1989, Pages 226 & 227
Worksource 1988, Pages 258 & 259

Randall Tagg
18 Broxbourne Drive
Fairport, New York 14450
(716) 425-3139

Randall Tagg
18 Broxbourne Drive
Fairport, New York 14450
(716) 425-3139

Michel Tcherevkoff
873 Broadway
New York, New York 10003
(212) 228-0540
FAX: (212) 353-2054

Represented in New York by
Madeleine Robinson (212) 243-3138

1. AT&T, AD: J. Stacy Rogers
2. AT&T, AD: J. Stacy Rogers
3. National Geographic, AD: Dave
   Seager

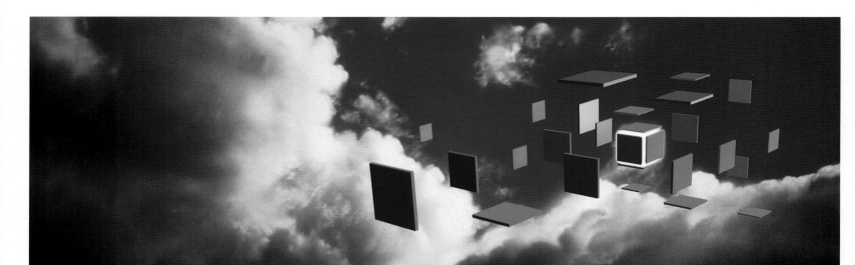

1.

2.

3.

Michel Tcherevkoff
873 Broadway
New York, New York 10003
(212) 228-0540
FAX: (212) 353-2054

4. Stock: Michel Tcherevkoff
5. Dean Witter, AD: Creighton Phillips
6. Mobil, AD: Bob DeGaetano
7. Computer Imagery: Michel Tcherevkoff

© 1990 Michel Tcherevkoff

If you want the "big picture" and buy photography, write to us on your company letterhead and we'll send you a complimentary full color copy of "Tcherevkoff, The Image Maker".

4.

5.

6.

7.

Nicholas E. Waring
Washington, DC
(301) 864-8115
FAX: (301) 864-8229

Represented By:
Catherine Bopp
(703) 680-3703 Phone

The Art Directors Club of
Metropolitan Washington
1988, 1989
1990 Best of Show Annual Report
ADDY 89
Also see: The Washington Creative
Sourcebook 1989

John Wee
J. W. Photography
115 Pius Street
Pittsburgh, Pennsylvania 15203
(412) 381-6826

Advertising • Annual Report
Architectural • Stock

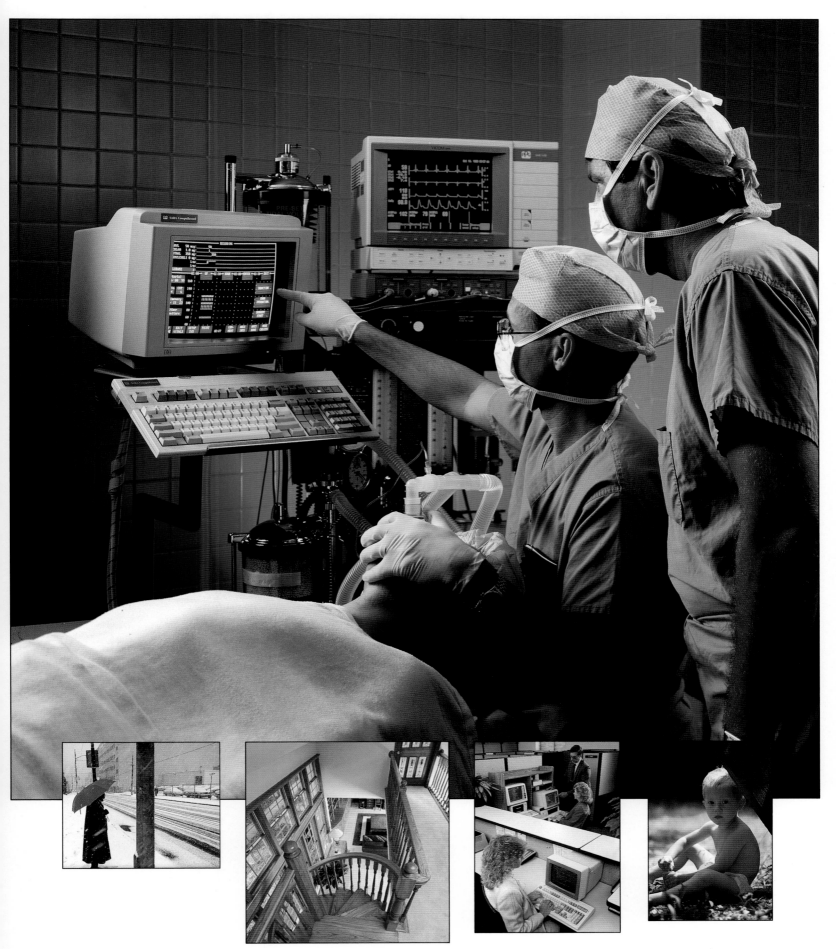

David Witbeck
77 Ives Street
Providence, Rhode Island 02906
(401) 274-9118

Believable pictures of real people
in real situations.

See also Corporate Showcase 9.

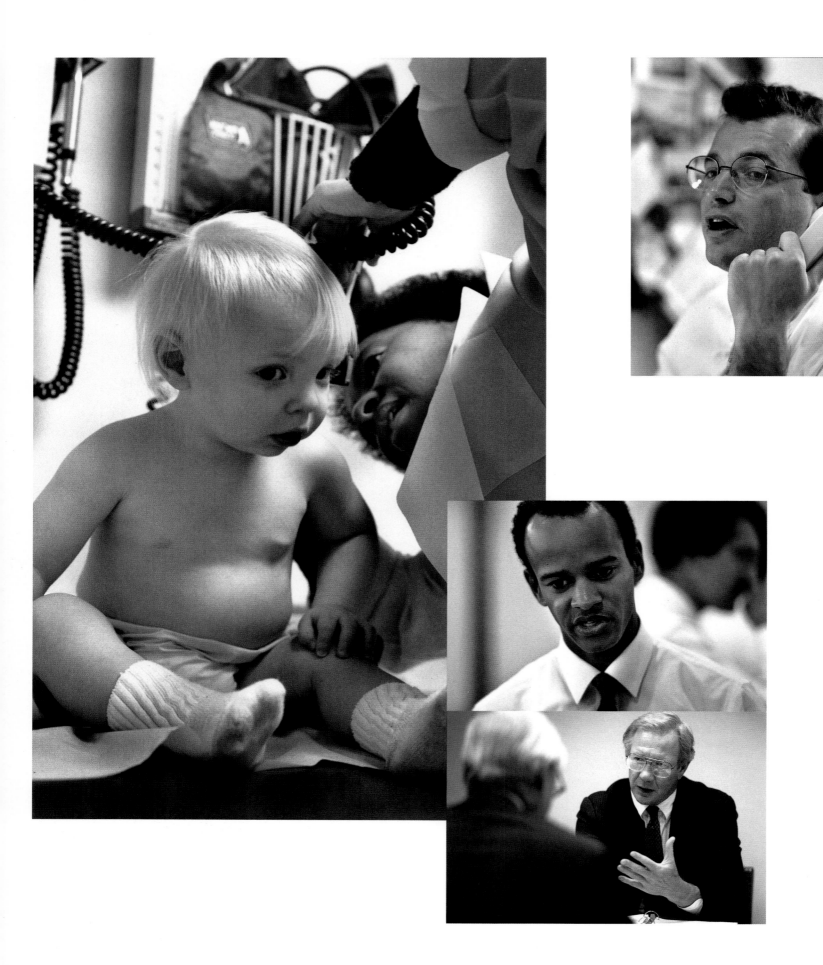

DAVID WITBECK
PHOTOGRAPHER

southeast

Alabama
Florida
Georgia
Kentucky
Louisiana
Mississippi
South Carolina
Tennessee

Positive IMAGE CORP.

COMMERCIAL PHOTOGRAPHY

MarkEscher

428 Armour Circle, N.E./Atlanta, Georgia 30324/404-874-3272

JERRY BURNS

331 Elizabeth Street, NE   Atlanta, Georgia 30307   404.522.9377

Call or write for a copy of the award-winning Jerry Burns CD Sampler.

Ian Barr
2640 SW 19th Street
Fort Lauderdale, Florida 33312
(305) 584-6247

Werner J. Bertsch
Fotoconcept Inc.
Fort Lauderdale, Florida, USA
(305) 463-1912
FAX: (305) 463-8864

Worldwide Corporate, Editorial,
and Travel Photographer.

A large variety of work has been
published in International and
National Consumer Magazines, Trade
Publications, and in Advertising.
Stock Photography available.

**Billy Brown
Photography, Inc.**
2700 Seventh Avenue South
Birmingham, Alabama 35233
(205) 251-8327
FAX: (205) 326-3018

People and Location Photography for
Annual Reports, Advertising, Corporate
and Travel.

Stock Available Through: Comstock
Member ASMP, AIGA

All Photos © Billy Brown 1991

Katie Deits

Camera Graphics, Inc.
2001 Bomar Drive, Suite 4
North Palm Beach, Florida 33408
(407) 775-3399 or 622-7330
(407) 346-2969 Mobile
FAX: (407) 622-2727

Creative interpretation of your ideas
into powerful photographs.

Extensive experience in aerial,
corporate, editorial, health care,
and industrial photography.

Outstanding photography...every time.

Call for portfolio
Member ASMP, PPA

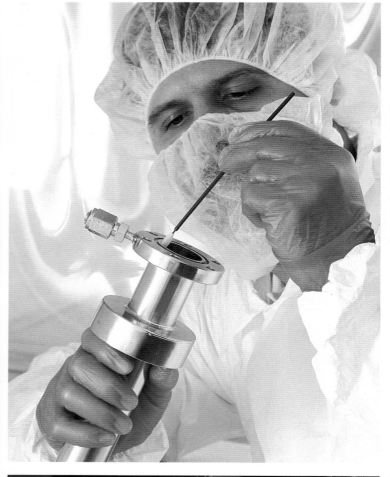

Fred S. Gerlich Photography
1220 Spring Street
Atlanta, Georgia 30309
(404) 872-3487
FAX: (404) 872-8346

G E R L I C H

Specializing in Location & Studio Photography For Annual Reports, Corporate-Industrial Communications & Advertising. ■

Clients Include:

American Hospitex
Amoco
Apple Computer
Atlanta Magazine
Anaconda Ericsson
Blue Cross & Blue Shield
Budweiser
Burger King
Childress Klein Properties
CNN
Coats & Clark
Coca-Cola USA
Curtis 1000
Georgia Federal Bank
Graphic Industries
Harris-Lanier
HBO & Company
Hitachi
Hyatt Regency Hotels
IBM
Kentucky Fried Chicken
Kimberly Clark Corporation
Marriott Hotels
Milliken Textiles
Mobile
Monsanto
Nissan
Northern Telecom
Panasonic
Piccadilly Cafeterias, Inc.
R. J. Reynolds
Royal Insurance Co.
Samna Corporation
Scripto
Sears
Southern Bell
The United Way
Touche Ross
Union Carbide
United Technologies
U.S. Forestry Dept.
WSB-TV
Yamaha

Additional Photography
Can Be Seen In Corporate
Showcase #7 , Page 158.

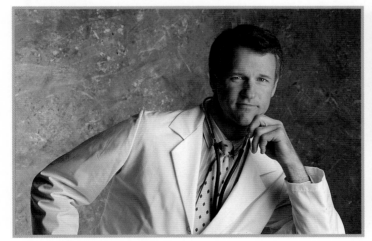

Bob Greenberg
15505 Bull Run Road
Miami Lakes, Florida 33014
(305) 433-8888

Studio and location photography
for advertising and corporate
communications.

Product illustration, exterior
architecture, aerial photography.

Stock available

Member A.S.M.P.

Chipp Jamison
2131 Liddell Drive, NE
Atlanta, Georgia 30324
(404) 873-3636
FAX: (404) 873-4034

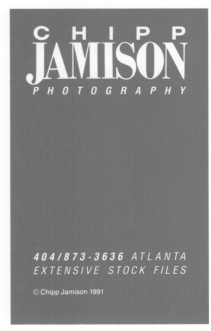

CHIPP
JAMISON
PHOTOGRAPHY

404/873-3636 ATLANTA
EXTENSIVE STOCK FILES

© Chipp Jamison 1991

142

KPC Photography

Box 32188
Charlotte, North Carolina 28232
(704) 358-5855
FAX: (704) 358-5865

Art Gentile
Dustin Peck
John Daughtry

- Corporate Communications
- Public Relations
- Industrial
- Executive Portraiture
- Architectural & Interiors
- ASMP • NPPA

KPC PHOTOGRAPHY

David Luttrell
5117 Kesterwood Drive
Knoxville, Tennessee 37918
(615) 688-1430

Deborah Gray Mitchell

7000 Northeast 4th Court
Miami, Florida 33138
(305) 757-4233
FAX: (305) 751-7574

Covering South Florida and beyond, award-winning photographer Deborah Gray Mitchell will deliver the shots you need in or out of the studio for corporate, advertising and editorial assignments.

A fully bilingual staff provides access to the Latin American market.

Member ASMP

© 1990 Deborah Gray Mitchell

Rhea Rippey
Corporate Photographic Services
Post Office Box 50093
Nashville, Tennessee 37205-0093
(615) 646-1291 Office
(615) 351-4976 Mobile
FAX: (615) 386-9503

Centrally based in the Eastern US, Rhea (pronounced "Ray") delivers color location photography in 35mm, 70mm, and 4x5 formats to his corporate, industrial, and editorial clients utilizing Nashville's American hub for assignment logistics into the Southeast and beyond.
Member ASMP   © 1990 Rhea Rippey

Bob Schatz
112 Second Avenue North
Nashville, Tennessee 37201
(615) 254-7197 Studio
(615) 943-4222 Mobile

Stock Available.

A partial list of clients:
Nissan, Northern Telecom, Trane Corp.,
BG Automotive Motors, PICA, Emery
Worldwide, Intergraph, Time, Success,
Financial World.

For additional work see:
Corporate Showcase 8
American Showcase 13
ASMP Silver Book 6 & 7

Carmen Schettino
5638 Country Lakes Drive
Sarasota, Florida 34243
(813) 351-4465

• Creative • Capable • Versatile • Efficient

With over 25 years experience photographing executives of corporate America, Carmen Schettino has the ability to capture the essence of the person while being respectful of time and pressure. His superior knowledge of lighting and his feeling for people are reflected in his photographic works of art.

Partial Client List: J.C. Penney, Pulsar Time Inc., Avon, Centrico, Eastman Kodak, Ingersol Rand, Minolta Corp., Rolls Royce, Seiko, Fortunoff, IBM, Abex Corp., American Express, Independence Bank, Medical Economics, Sanyo, Western Union, Prudential Insurance.

schettino

Ron Sherman
PO Box 28656
Atlanta, Georgia 30328-0656
(404) 993-7197
FAX: (404) 993-6106

Location photography for annual reports, advertising, corporate, industrial, editorial, travel and sports assignments.

Stock Photography Available. 50,000 color and 100,000 black & white images.

Samples published in Corporate Showcase 9, 7, 6, 5, 4, 3, American Showcase 10 and 8 and ASMP Book 1981, 2, 3, 4.

Member ASMP
© 1991 Ron Sherman
Design: Patt Farrell

C A P

COMPUTER AIDED PHOTOGRAPHY

Making the impossible possible by using a combination of photography and computer technology. Tonal ranges are controllable and the scope of the image is unlimited. We can now go beyond photography and into the future to make your ideas into an image with impact.

FROM THIS

TO THIS

DIFFERENCES IN LIGHTING QUALITY AND QUANTITY CAN BE CONTROLLED WHETHER IN A LARGE

INDUSTRIAL INTERIOR OR OUTSIDE FACILITY WITH DEEP SHADOWS AND BRIGHT HIGHLIGHTS.

Midwest

Illinois
Indiana
Iowa
Kansas
Michigan
Minnesota
Missouri
Nebraska
North Dakota
Ohio
South Dakota
Wisconsin

BEN WEDDLE

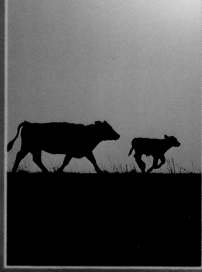

When you need someone
who knows agriculture
from "A" to "E-I-E-I-O,"
do what the following inter-
national clientele have done:
Ralston-Purina, Dow-Elanco,
Mobay, American Cyanamid,
Boehringer-Ingelheim, IH Case,
DeKalb-Pfizer, Terra International,
American Angus.

Call Ben Weddle
Photographer/ Producer
218 Delaware Street, Suite 108
Kansas City, Missouri 64105
(816) 421-2902 • Stock photos available

© copyright Ben Weddle 1991

ANDREW**SACKS**

ANDREW**SACKS**

20727 SCIO CHURCH ROAD • CHELSEA (DETROIT), MICHIGAN 48118 • STUDIO AND LOCATION PHOTOGRAPHY
EDITORIAL AND CORPORATE ASSIGNMENTS • CALL FOR SAMPLE PORTFOLIO • 313 475-2310 • FAX 313 475-3010
ADDITIONAL STOCK FROM TONY STONE WORLDWIDE • 800-234-7880

LARRY HAMILL

Assignment • Stock

77 Deshler • Columbus • Ohio • 43206

614-444-2798

D . R . GOFF

QUICKSILVER PHOTOGRAPHY ▪ 66 WEST WHITTIER STREET ▪ COLUMBUS, OHIO 43206 ▪ 614-443-6530

1611 NORTH SHEFFIELD CHICAGO IL 60614
312.642.6650 FAX 312.337.3204

Alex Atevich
325 North Hoyne Avenue
Chicago, Illinois 60612
(312) 942-1453
FAX: (312) 942-1455

Gregory D. Baker
4630 Charles
Rockford, Illinois 61108
(815) 398-1114

Warren Denning

231 Ohio Street
Wichita, Kansas 67214
(316) 262-4163

Location and studio photography for advertising, corporate and editorial clients.

Clients Include:
Beech Aircraft Corporation; Cessna Aircraft Company; The Coleman Company, Inc.; Dewar's Blended Scotch Whiskey; Federal Land Bank; George Dickel Tennessee Sour Mash Whiskey; Hallmark; Learjet Corporation; Mastercraft Skis; NCR Corporation; Pepsico; Pioneer Balloon Company; Pizza Hut; Pratt and Lambert, Inc.; The Traveler's Insurance Companies.

Rick Dieringer
19 West Court Street
Cincinnati, Ohio 45202
(513) 621-2544

Advertising, fashion and
corporate/industrial photography

See also Corporate Showcase 4, 6, 7,
8, 9; American Showcase 13 and 14.

© 1990 Rick Dieringer

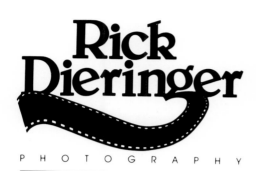

Rick Dieringer

P H O T O G R A P H Y

19 West Court Street
Cincinnati, Ohio 45202
513/621-2544

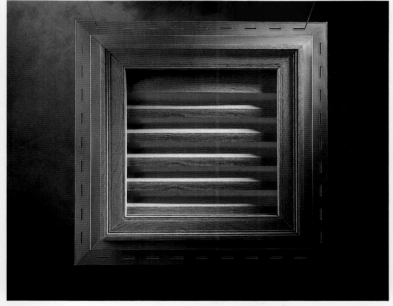

**Jeff Frey
Photography, Inc.**
405 East Superior Street
Duluth, Minnesota 55802
(218) 722-6630

Photographers:
Jeffrey Frey
Steven M. Tiggemann
J. Scott Lawrence

Custom Lab connected.
Member: ASMP, PPA, NPPA.

Studio & location: advertising,
architectural, corporate, editorial,
education, health care, industrial,
people, and product.
For more samples see page 196
Corporate Showcase 9.
Clients include: Blandin Paper Co.,
Chromaline Corp., C.G. Bretting, DM

& IR Railroad, Edgell Communications,
First Bank System, Grand Trunk Railroad,
Lakehead Pipe Line, Lake Superior
Paper Industries, M E International,
Minnesota Power, Mueller Brass;
Norwest Bank, Pentair, Pettibone,
Potlatch, Reach All, The Moline Co.,
U S West Communications.

DULUTH ENTERTAINMENT CONVENTION CENTER

ST. LUKE'S HOSPITAL REGIONAL TRAUMA CENTER

LAKE SUPERIOR PAPER INDUSTRIES

MUELLER BRASS

Eric H. Futran
3454 North Bell
Chicago, Illinois 60618
(312) 525-5020

Over fifteen years experience in a vast array of commercial venues. An eye toward strong graphics mixed with an easy going manner and common sense on location.

Recent work for Allied Van Lines, Allstate, ARA Services, Cahners Publishing, Follett, IIT, Kelloggs, Kraft General Foods, Molex, Northwestern Steel, Nabisco Brands, Welbilt.

John Gilroy Photography
2407 West Main Street
Kalamazoo, Michigan 49007
(616) 349-6805
(616) 381-8764

John is chosen for assignments where the search for visual potential and the creative use of lighting for graphic emphasis are the challenge.

Images shown (L-R): feature article, CI0 Magazine; calendar, Mossberg Printing Company; public interest report, The Dow Chemical Company; annual report, The Upjohn Company; magazine cover, Consumers Power Company.

For more samples of work see Corporate Showcase 4-9.

166

Tom Jelen
PO Box 115
Arlington Heights, Illinois 60006
(708) 506-9479

Panoramic Stock Images
230 North Michigan Avenue
Chicago, Illinois 60601
(312) 236-8545

APA, ASMP

Copyright Tom Jelen

David Joel Photography Inc.
1515 Washington Avenue
Wilmette, Illinois 60091
(Chicago area)
(708) 256-8792

Specializing in Multiple Strobe-Light Applications on Location.

Partial client list: Quaker Oats, CNA Financial, Whirlpool, U.S. Gypsum, American National Can, Philip Morris Cos., Sara Lee Corporation, Del Monte, Illinois Bell, MIT, Baxter Travenol, Underwriters Laboratories, Kraft Inc.

For more samples see:
p. 211 Corporate Showcase 5;
p. 169 Corporate Showcase 6;
p. 183 Corporate Showcase 7;
p. 244 Corporate Showcase 8;
p. 203 Corporate Showcase 9.

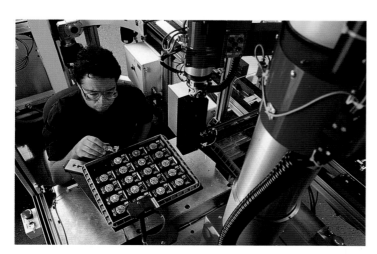

Dawson Jones, Inc.
23 North Walnut Street
Dayton, Ohio 45449
(513) 859-7799

TRAVERSIE
JONES
PHOTOGRAPHERS

CLIENTS INCLUDE

A.H. Robins
Accu-Ray
Airborne Express
Amcast
Bordens
Cahners Publishing Co.
Codex Corp.
Consolidated Freightways
Copeland Corporation
Dayco
Digital Equipment
Entrepreneur Magazine
Family Circle Magazine
Hooper & Nezi
INC Magazine
J. Walter Thompson
Krug International
Kuhn & Wittenborn
Legate-Stashower
Lord Sullivan Yoder
M. A. Hanna Co.
Marketing Services, Inc.
McGraw-Hill
The Mead Corporation
Mead Data Central
Mitchel & Comer
Mosinee Paper
Nations Business
NCR
PennCorp Financial
Polessi Clancy
ProClinica
R.G. Smith Enterprises
Reynolds+Reynolds
Robbins & Myers
Scott Foresman
Society Bank
Sonoco Products
Standard Register
Success Magazine
Sulzer Escher Wyss
Venture Magazine
Wolf Blumberg Krody
Zylke & Associates

STOCK AVAILABLE

Dayton
Stills, Atlanta
Stock, Boston
The Stockhouse, Houston
Tony Stone Worldwide
Uniphoto, Washington, DC

DAWSON JONES, INC.

23 North Walnut Street
Dayton, Ohio 45449
Telephone: 513-859-7799

© Dawson Jones, Inc. 1991

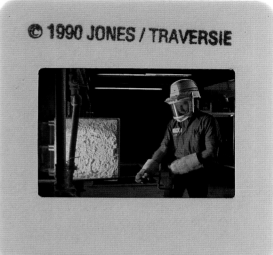

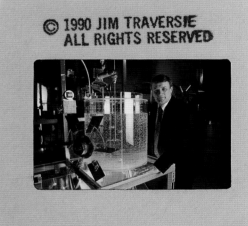

David Kogan
1242 West Washington Boulevard
Chicago, Illinois 60607
(312) 243-1929
FAX: (312) 243-3299

Location and Studio Photography for annual reports, corporate communications and advertising.

Additional Language: French

Recent clients include: Reliance Comm/Tec; Viskase Corp.; AT&T; Architex International; Baltimore Sun; Readers Digest; Control Data; Pillsbury.

Also see Corporate Showcase 2, 3, 4, 5, 6, 7, 8, and 9.

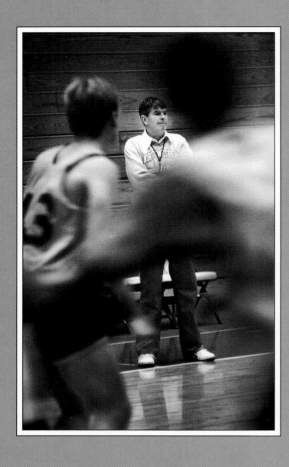

Avis Mandel Photography
1550 North Lake Shore Drive
Suite Ten/G
Chicago, Illinois 60610
(312) 642-4776 • FAX: (312) 642-6887

Avis Mandel Photography

o

1550 North Lake Shore Drive

Suite Ten / G

Chicago, Illinois 60610

312 / 642.4776

Fax 312 / 642.6887

Funny you should inquire right now about how we use architectural photographers. I was going over the numbers last night, preparing myself for the annual Catch-22 budget negotiations with my management. I can't ask for a figure until I know which projects we want to shoot and who will shoot them. But I can't decide who to hire until I know how much money I've got.

(Of the 200-plus photographers in this book, fewer than 25 specialize in architecture. I wonder why...)

Some things depend on other things, and for us, the choice of photographer depends partly on the project. The process begins when our five studio directors send their favorite architectural projects to our managing principal, who evaluates them in light of their ability to represent the firm's work. Since we never advertise (well, hardly ever), he looks for a distinctive design, size, or client type that will best tell our story in visual terms.

Our various publishing venues are design and trade magazines or local, regional, or national papers; design competitions; and in-house publications such as fact sheets and "Genslereports." We package high quality prints in our photobrochures, and we use slides when making presentations to potential clients.

Once we make our decision about what projects to shoot, and have some specific goals in mind, we're ready to turn to the choice of a photographer. One very smart marketing coordinator we know divides them into three groups: photographers that deliver top-flight, fail-safe photography, for commeasurate fees; those who are rising stars, priced in the mid-range; and the newcomers, breaking in and breaking even, with a small profit margin.

Looking at potential "shooters" this way makes a lot of sense. By matching the level of photographers and projects, for our modest jobs we get good pictures and a young photographer builds a portfolio of excellent work, and our budget stretches; for our mid-range jobs we get excellent quality at a fair price; and for our showcase work we hire the best that money can buy.

Regardless of the level, we prefer to work with people whose professional standards match our own. What this means for us is being available when we want to shoot and going back cheerfully (like the druids to Stonehenge) to get that perfect shot as the first light strikes the facade at sunrise. We review everyone's portfolio carefully, with an eye for particular qualities. When the subject is architecture, an absolute requisite is the ability to select point of view and control the light. The photo, after all, has to compensate for the viewer's inability to walk through the building and see it three-dimensionally.

Specific questions we ask ourselves are these:

• How does this photographer handle the technical aspects of light? An interior space may mix halogen, tungsten, fluorescent, and natural light in a single area. Each registers a different color on film and often, especially in huge spaces like airport terminals, can't be completely controlled.

Continued on page 182

Michael K. McCann
15416 Village Woods Drive
Eden Prairie, Minnesota 55347
(612) 949-2407

Mike McCann photographs people and product on location or in his studio. Portfolio upon request.

In the 12 years he has been in business, Mike has worked for clients including: ADC Telecommunicatons, Avis, Bankers Systems, Coldwell Banker, Dayton Hudson, Fluoroware, 3M, Toro and Radisson Hotels.

MINNEAPOLIS

Parallel Productions, Inc.
Tom Berthiaume
1008 Nicollet Mall
Minneapolis, Minnesota 55403
(612) 338-1999

■

Greg LeMond / Three-time winner of the Tour de France

B E R T H I A U M E

People

Parallel Productions, Inc.
Mark Lafavor
1008 Nicollet Mall
Minneapolis, Minnesota 55403
(612) 338-1999

LA FAVOR

Still Life

T. Shaun Proctor
409 North Racine
Chicago, Illinois 60622
(312) 829-5511
FAX: (312) 829-6261

Partial list of clients includes:
Cahners Publishing / Holsum Bakers
Diners Club / Ace Hardware / Borg
Warner Automotive / Miller Breweries

Dove International / Owens Corning
MacDonalds Corporation / Quaker
Oats / General Electric / Chicago
Bears / Amoco Oil

Proctor
Proctor

**Tom Rogowski
Photography, Inc.**
214 East 8th Street
Cincinnati, Ohio 45202
(513) 621-3826
FAX: (513) 621-3837

Location and Studio Photography
for Advertising and Corporate
Communications.

A client list and a Free Minifolio of
work are available upon request.

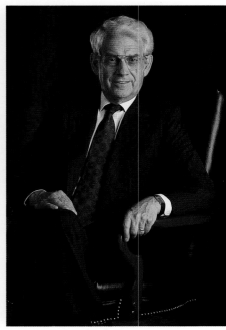

Tony Schanuel
10901 Oasis Drive
St. Louis, Missouri 63123
(314) 849-3495
(314) 231-9200 Studio

Advertising, Corporate and
Editorial Location Photography

Member: ASMP
International travel

Partial client list includes: AT&T,
Anheuser-Busch, John Deere, Forbes,
Ford Motors, First Data Resource,
Graybar Corporation, Kraft Foods,
Monsanto, Moog Automotive, Medicine
Shoppe International, Purina Mills,
Southwestern Bell, Sigma Chemical,

Union Pacific Railroad, Union Pacific
Technologies, Whittle Communications.

See Corporate Showcase #9

© Tony Schanuel, 1991

SCHANUEL

Paul Schlismann
Photography
PO Box 412
Deerfield (Chicago), Illinois 60015
(708) 945-0768

Corporate
Industrial
Architectural & Interiors
Aerial
Studio & Location

PAUL   SCHLISMANN

(708) 945-0768

Continued from page 174

• Does the portfolio reveal experience in shooting subtly varied material surfaces? Does it catch the quiet emphasis of light wood grains against pale fabrics and glass surfaces?

• Does this photographer have a track record in the industry? How often have major industry publications used his or her work? (Ever on the cover?) Have other top design firms hired this photographer? Has the work brought any awards to the design firm? And now that our firm has projects in Europe and the far side of the Pacific Rim, do we find international representation in the portfolio?

• And the toughest question of all: Does the portfolio show an ability to capture in two dimensions those elements of a three-dimensional project that advance the practice of design? We work hard to realize our creative vision of architectural spaces that serve people well and that they love to be in. That is part of what has made us the number one interior design firm in the nation. We feel a responsibility to our clients, ourselves, and the profession to reach for equal excellence in the way that vision is pictured. Maybe it doesn't always seem fair to the photographer, but we expect to recognize our vision in the final photo.

(Actually, as I write all this, I'm realizing that architectural photography is darned hard work.)

After asking all these impossible questions, and finding photographers who fit the bill (in the end, we always do), I'm ready to make Catch-22 make sense. I carve out estimates for each shoot. Each total reflects the number of shots we expect, the photographer's fees, expenses, and assistant's fees; and the cost of processing film. Sometimes a truly dark-horse project enters the running after the annual budget is out of the gate. In this case, the project designer may, with the approval of the managing principal, create a special budget. The designer takes preliminary photographs and uses these to secure commitments from the client, vendors, and consultants who have an interest in the finished projects. They are usually glad to share the total cost in exchange for professionally shot transparencies of their part of the project.

After that, it's easy. All we have to do is complete the shoot, print the piece, make the brochure, and get it all out!

(You know, I'm starting to think the real reason there are so few architectural photographers is that buildings don't cooperate in the photo shoot. They just sit there. No winks, no smiles, no tilting the chin or crossing the legs. Sigh. But, then, there are some of us who think a great photograph of a great building is a pretty sexy accomplishment...)

Mary McKinley
Marketing Coordinator
Gensler and Associates/Architects
Los Angeles, CA

John Sykaluk Photography
2500 North Main Street
Rockford, Illinois 61103
(815) 968-3819 Office
(815) 963-3102 Studio

Studio and Location Photography

"Creating the right mood is what makes the image come alive. Capturing your audience through photography is what we're about."

Also see Corporate Showcase 9, page 184.

All photos © John Sykaluk 1990.

DESIGN: LESLIE MANGAS

John Sykaluk Photography

→ 815/968-3819

Van Inwegen Photography
(312) 477-8344
FAX: (312) 404-9647

Represented By:
Linda Frank
(312) 528-1890

Van Inwegen Photography
(312) 477-8344
FAX: (312) 404-9647

Represented By:
Linda Frank
(312) 528-1890

Robert VanMarter
1209 Alstott Drive South
Howell, Michigan 48843 (Detroit)
(517) 546-1923

Advertising and corporate
photography on location and
in the studio.

Member ASMP

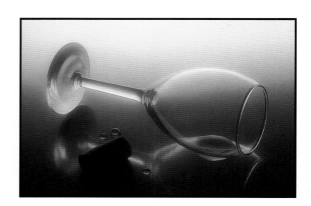

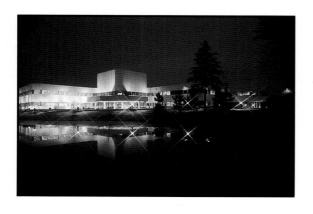

**James Visser
Photography**
4274 Shenandoah Avenue
Saint Louis, Missouri 63110
(314) 771-6857

Corporate, editorial and advertising
location photography.

Specializing in people, the places where
they work and the things they make.

See additional samples in ASMP
6 & 7 and Corporate Showcase 8 & 9.

Peter Yates
1208 Bydding Road
Ann Arbor, Michigan 48103
(313) 995-0839
FAX: (313) 668-2659

Clients include:
Ameritech
Business Week
Chrysler
Forbes

Fortune
General Motors
IBM
Mazda

Monsanto
Newsweek
Sports Illustrated
Time

Bruce Zake
633 Huron Road
Cleveland, Ohio 44115
(216) 694-3686 Studio
(216) 765-3191 Digital Pager

Photography of people and places on location for annual reports as well as advertising, corporate communications, and editorial publications.

Please Refer to:
Corporate Showcase 7 Page 204
Corporate Showcase 8 Page 268
Corporate Showcase 9 Page 217

Why do some creative people never seem to run out of ideas?

Because they read ARCHIVE.

ARCHIVE, the magazine that presents the top advertising campaigns from around the world, is just the source of creativity you need. Send $43.97 for a full year (six issues), and more than 120 pages of the most innovative TV, print and poster ads will begin arriving at your door. Or call 1-800-825-0061 for even faster service.

ARCHIVE Magazine
915 Broadway
New York, NY
10010

southwest

**Arizona
Arkansas
New Mexico
Oklahoma
Texas**

Keith Wood Photography, Inc
1308 Conant
Dallas Texas 75207
214 634 7344
Fax 214 637 2756

To me, the biggest drilling platform in the North Sea or the deepest mine in the Far East is nothing without people. Massiveness is meaningless and cold. My problem comes when I have to capture the integrity of the project while maintaining the human side of that project. It's much like studying the atmosphere of a beehive and realizing that any exposure of its interior destroys continuity ... the bees don't act naturally. It's really no different when a photographer enters an environment where he doesn't belong. It's an unnatural situation.

Over the years I have entered many unusual and exciting atmospheres around the world. I've worked in places where western photographers have rarely been. I have to quickly learn local customs, mannerisms and taboos (never touch a Cambodian kid's head). I try to learn at least a working bit of the language so I can put my subject at ease ... Hell, I'm the major representative of my client when I'm in the field.

Good photography is really just an exchange. I take a bit of the subject's time and soul and I try to leave him with a pleasant experience and a little ego boost. It's funny, but corporate executives are often harder to relax than a Java native. The only way I can capture a good image is to let them know I'm on their side and dedicated to making them look as good as possible in their space. I love it ... it's a lot more than pushing buttons.

Arco Chemical
Arco Oil and Gas
C.I.O. Magazine
Diamond Shamrock/
    Oil & Gas
Dresser Industries
Fina
First Mississippi Gold/
    First Mississippi Corporation
Humana Hospitals
Inc. Magazine
Kimberly-Clark
Maxus Energy
Motorola Corporation
Old El Paso
Oryx Energy Company
Petrolite Oil Field Svcs.
Schlumberger Inc.
Swearingen/
    Commercial Real Estate
Texas Industries

Self Promotion Indonesia 1990

Self Promotion Indonesia 1989

Self Promotion Indonesia 1990

Keith Wood Photography, Inc
1308 Conant
Dallas Texas 75207
214 634 7344
Fax 214 637 2756

Fina Annual Report 1990

Self Promotion

Oryx Energy 1990

Browning Ferris Ind. Annual Report 1990

Old El Paso 1990

Oryx Energy Annual Report 1990

Arco North Sea

Phil Hollenbeck
2833 Duval Drive
Dallas, Texas 75211
214 331 8328

The Storyteller's Eye. The ability to see and capture that moment when composition, light and subject come together to perfectly tell the story. Whether I'm on assignment or in the car, I'm always watching for those moments. If I have to make a quick U-turn on a busy highway to get a shot I just noticed, I will. It's that important to me to capture the moment and record it.

the Storyteller's eye

ASMP

194

MICHAEL   NORTON

3427   EAST   HIGHLAND

PHOENIX,   ARIZONA   85018

602•840•9463

Jess Alford
1800 Lear Street
Number Three
Dallas, Texas 75215
(214) 421-3107

Advertising, Corporate, Industrial,
Editorial and Travel Photography
on Location.

Clients include: Anheuser Busch, Frito
Lay, IBM, NEC, Texas Instruments,
Trammell Crow, et al.

Nash Baker
2208 Colquitt
Houston, Texas 77098
(713) 529-5698

Clients include:
Chevron, Hardees, 3M Corporation,
University of Texas Medical Branch.
© 1990 Nash Baker

Graphic Arts Organizations

ALASKA

Alaska Artists Guild
PO Box 101888
Anchorage, AK 99510
(907) 248-4818

ARIZONA

Arizona Artist Guild
8912 North Fourth Street
Phoenix, AZ 85020
(602) 944-9713

CALIFORNIA

Advertising Club of Los Angeles
3600 Wilshire Boulevard, Suite 432
Los Angeles, CA 90010
(213) 382-1228

APA Los Angeles, Inc.
7201 Melrose Avenue
Los Angeles, CA 90046
(213) 935-7283

APA San Francisco
22 Cleveland Street
San Francisco, CA 94103
(415) 621-3915

Art Directors and Artists Club
2791 24th Street
Sacramento, CA 95818
(916) 731-8802

Book Club of California
312 Sutter Street, Suite 510
San Francisco, CA 94108
(415) 781-7532

Los Angeles Advertising Women
3900 West Alameida
The Tower Building, 17th Floor
Burbank, CA 91505
(818) 972-1771

San Francisco Art Directors Club
Box 410387
San Francisco, CA 94141-0387
(415) 387-4040

San Francisco Creative Alliance
Box 410387
San Francisco, CA 94141-0387
(415) 387-4040

Society of Illustrators of Los Angeles
5000 Van Nuys Boulevard, Suite 300
Sherman Oaks, CA 91403
(818) 784-0588

**Society of Motion Pictures &
TV Art Directors**
11365 Ventura Boulevard, #315
Studio City, CA 91604
(818) 762-9995

Visual Artists Association
2550 Beverly Boulevard
Los Angeles, CA 90057
(213) 388-0477

Western Art Directors Club
PO Box 996
Palo Alto, CA 94302
(408) 379-2114

Women's Graphic Commission
1126 Highpoint Street
Los Angeles, CA 90035
(213) 935-1568

COLORADO

Art Directors Club of Denver
1900 Grant Street
Denver, CO 80203
(303) 830-7888

**International Design Conference
in Aspen**
Box 664
Aspen, CO 81612
(303) 925-2257

CONNECTICUT

Connecticut Art Directors Club
PO Box 639
Avon, CT 06001
(203) 651-0886

DISTRICT OF COLUMBIA

American Advertising Federation
1400 K Street NW, Suite 1000
Washington, DC 20005
(202) 898-0089

American Institute of Architects
1735 New York Avenue, NW
Washington, DC 20006
(202) 626-7300

American Society of Interior Designers
National Headquarters
608 Massachusetts Avenue, NE
Washington, DC 20002
(202) 546-3480

**Art Directors Club of Metropolitan
Washington**
1420 K Street NW, Suite 500
Washington, DC 20005
(202) 842-4177

NEA: Design Arts Program
1100 Pennsylvania Avenue, NW
Washington, DC 20506
(202) 682-5437

FLORIDA

APA Miami
2545 Tiger Tail Avenue
Coconut Grove, FL 33033
(305) 856-8336

GEORGIA

APA Atlanta
POB 20471
Atlanta, GA 30325-1471
(404) 881-1616

Art Directors Club of Atlanta
125 Bennett Street, NW
Atlanta, GA 30309
(404) 352-8726

Atlanta Art Papers, Inc.
PO Box 77348
Atlanta, GA 30357
(404) 588-1837

Creative Arts Guild
PO Box 1485
Dalton, GA 30722-1485
(404) 278-0168

HAWAII

APA Hawaii
733 Auahl Street
Honalulu, HI 96813
(805) 524-8269

ILLINOIS

APA Chicago
1725 West North Avenue, #2D2
Chicago, IL 60622
(312) 342-1717

Institute of Business Designers
341 Merchandise Mart
Chicago, IL 60654
(312) 467-1950

American Center For Design
233 East Ontario Street, Suite 500
Chicago, IL 60611
(312) 787-2018

Women in Design
2 North Riverside Plaza, Suite 2400
Chicago, IL 60606
(312) 648-1874

INDIANA

Advertising Club of Indianapolis
3833 North Meridian
Suite 305 B
Indianapolis, IN 46208
(317) 924-5577

Continued on page 206

Jay Brousseau
2608 Irving Boulevard
Dallas, Texas 75207
(214) 638-1248
FAX: (214) 638-1249

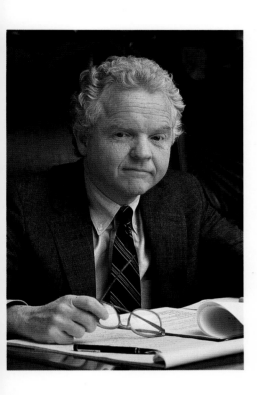

<u>*Clients include:*</u>

Boeing

Burlington Northern

Chevron

Continental Airlines

Fortune

Singer Corporation

Steve Chenn Photography
6301 Ashcroft
Houston, Texas 77081
(713) 271-0631 • FAX: (713) 271-5918

If you'd like to see more work for stock and assignment, please call or write on your company letterhead for our mini-portfolio.

Steve Chenn Photography
6301 Ashcroft
Houston, Texas 77081
(713) 271-0631 • FAX: (713) 271-5918

For additional work refer to Corporate
Showcase Volumes 1, 2, 3, 8 & 9.

Ralph Cole, Inc.
Photographer
PO Box 2803
Tulsa, Oklahoma 74101
(918) 585-9119

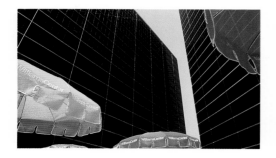

George Craig
314 East Thirteenth Street
Houston, Texas 77008
(713) 862-6008 • FAX: (713) 863-1422

Shooting stars or guitars, hi-tech to high-fi. High flying images that tell your story.
Creative excellence combined with technical abilities and a down to earth attitude has enabled me to satisfy these recent clients:
Bali Blinds, Briggs Weaver, Businessland, Compaq Computers, Cushman & Wakefield, Ensco, Gulf Printing Company, Life-Tech, Louana Foods, Poole Company, Rhom & Haas, Texas Marine, U.S. Postal Service and Warner Brothers.

Crossley & Pogue
1412 West Alabama
Houston, Texas 77006
(713) 523-5757
FAX: (713) 523-6712

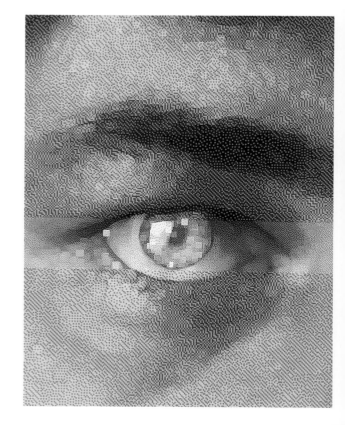

**Greg Dawson
Photography**
211 Beall Street
Houston, Texas 77008
(713) 862-8301
FAX: (713) 862-5461

Major Clients Include:
Coca-Cola Foods, Continental Airlines,
Coors, Exxon, GeoQuest, HCA, Hoechst
Celanese, Masoneilan/Dresser, MCI,
Purina, Seagull Energy, Shell, Stewart
& Stevenson, Sysco, Texaco, Texas
Childrens Hospital, Uncle Bens, WNS

Continued from page 198

IOWA

Art Guild of Burlington
Arts for Living Center
PO Box 5
Burlington, IA 52601
(319) 754-8069

MAINE

APA Portland
135 Somerset Street
Portland, ME 04101
(207) 773-3771

MASSACHUSETTS

Boston Visual Artists Union
33 Harrison Avenue
Boston, MA 02111
(617) 695-1266

Creative Club of Boston
155 Massachusetts Avenue
Boston, MA 02115
(617) 338-6452

Center for Design of Industrial Schedules
221 Longwood Avenue
Boston, MA 02115
(617) 734-2163

Graphic Artists Guild
425 Watertown Street
Newton, MA 02158
(617) 244-2110

Guild of Boston Artists
162 Newbury Street
Boston, MA 02116
(617) 536-7660

Society of Environmental Graphic Designers
47 Third Street
Cambridge, MA 02141
(617) 577-8225

MICHIGAN

APA Detroit
32588 Dequindre
Warren, MI 48092
(313) 795-3540

Michigan Guild of Artists and Artisans
118 North Fourth Avenue
Ann Arbor, MI 48104
(313) 662-3382

MINNESOTA

Advertising Federation of Minnesota
4248 Park Glen Road
Minneapolis, MN 55416
(612) 929-1445

MISSOURI

Advertising Club of Greater St. Louis
10 Broadway, #150-A
St. Louis, MO 63102
(314) 231-4185

Advertising Club of Kansas City
9229 Ward Parkway, Suite 260
Kansas City, MO 64114
(816) 822-0300

American Institute of Graphic Arts
112 West Ninth
Kansas City, MO 64105
(816) 474-1983

NEW JERSEY

Federated Art Associations of New Jersey, Inc.
PO Box 2195
Westfield, NJ 07091
(201) 232-7623

Point-of-Purchase Advertising Institute
66 North Van Brunt Street
Englewood, NJ 07631
(201) 894-8899

NEW YORK

The Advertising Club of New York
155 East 55th Street
New York, NY 10022
(212) 935-8080

The Advertising Council, Inc.
261 Madison Avenue, 11th Floor
New York, NY 10016
(212) 922-1500

APA
Advertising Photographers of America, Inc.
27 West 20th Street, Room 601
New York, NY 10011
(212) 807-0399

Advertising Production Club of N.Y.
60 East 42nd Street, Suite 1416
New York, NY 10165
(212) 983-6042

TANY Inc.
408 8th Avenue, #10A
New York, NY 10001
(212) 629-3232

Advertising Women of New York Foundation, Inc.
153 East 57th Street
New York, NY 10022
(212) 593-1950

A.A.A.A.
American Association of Advertising Agencies
666 Third Avenue, 13th Floor
New York, NY 10017
(212) 682-2500

American Booksellers Association, Inc.
137 West 25th Street
New York, NY 10001
(212) 463-8450

American Council for the Arts
1285 Avenue of the Americas, 3rd Floor
New York, NY 10019
(212) 245-4510

The American Institute of Graphic Arts
1059 Third Avenue, 3rd Floor
New York, NY 10021
(212) 752-0813

American Society of Interior Designers
New York Metro Chapter
200 Lexington Avenue
New York, NY 10016
(212) 685-3480

American Society of Magazine Photographers, Inc.
419 Park Avenue South, #1407
New York, NY 10016
(212) 889-9144

Art Directors Club of New York
250 Park Avenue South
New York, NY 10003
(212) 674-0500

Association of American Publishers
220 East 23rd Street
New York, NY 10010
(212) 689-8920

Association of the Graphic Arts
5 Penn Plaza, 20th Floor
New York, NY 10001
(212) 279-2100

The Children's Book Council, Inc.
568 Broadway
New York, NY 10012
(212) 966-1990

CLIO
336 East 59th Street
New York, NY 10022
(212) 593-1900

Continued on page 246

**Steve Foxall
Photography, Inc.**
Dallas, Texas USA
(214) 824-1977
FAX number upon request

Additional images in Corporate
Showcase Vol. 9, Pg. 233.

Studio and location photography for
Corporate Advertising and Editorial
clients.

Mark Green
2406 Taft Street
Houston, Texas 77006
(713) 523-6146
FAX: (713) 523-6145

Mark Green
2406 Taft Street
Houston, Texas 77006
(713) 523-6146
FAX: (713) 523-6145

Ray Hand
10921 Shady Trail
Suite 100
Dallas, Texas 75220
(214) 351-2488
FAX: (214) 351-2499

Ray Hand
10921 Shady Trail
Suite 100
Dallas, Texas 75220
(214) 351-2488
FAX: (214) 351-2499

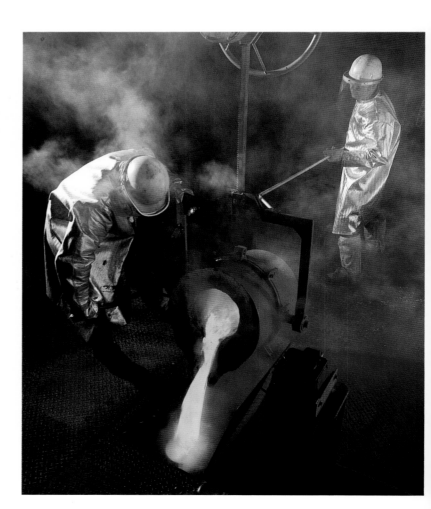

American Airlines
American Express
B.F. Goodrich/Aerospace
CLR/Fast Tax
Datapoint
Dun & Bradstreet
Frito Lay
Harris Corp.

Kodak
Mayflower Group
Northern Telecom
Pepsi
Texas Instruments
UniRoyal
United Way
Westvaco

Michael Hart
7320 Ashcroft, Suite 105
Houston, Texas 77081-6113
(713) 271-8250
FAX: (713) 271-6008

Last year, we worked on Annual Reports for Borden, Browning-Ferris, Chemical Bank, Compaq, Cooper Industries, Equus Capital, First City BankCorp, GNI, Kent Electronics, Pride Petroleum, Shell, Tenneco, Vallen, and YMCA of Greater Dallas.

We photographed in fifteen states and five foreign countries, and our subjects ranged from CEO's to sugar cane harvesters.

MEXICO

TENNESSEE

ENGLAND

MONTANA

GERMANY

BELGIUM

Michael Hart
7320 Ashcroft, Suite 105
Houston, Texas 77081-6113
(713) 271-8250
FAX: (713) 271-6008

Our Black-and-White portfolio is available upon request. You are also invited to write or fax on your letterhead to be added to our mailing list.

Member/ASMP

COLORADO

TEXAS

VIRGINIA

WISCONSIN

Doug Hoke
805 Northwest 49th
Oklahoma City, Oklahoma 73118
(405) 840-1256 (With FAX)

DOUG HOKE
PHOTOGRAPHY

George Mayer
1356 Chemical
Dallas, Texas 75207
(214) 424-4409
FAX: (214) 630-9765

Clients Include:
Apple Computer
The Beard Agency Inc.
Frito-Lay
Hill & Knowlton
Southland Corp.

Photographing people and
the places where they work
for advertising, corporate
communications, and editorial
assignments

Dennis Meyler
1903 Portsmouth, Suite 25
Houston, Texas 77098-4235
(713) 520-1800 Office
FAX: (713) 523-4839

Advertising/Corporate/Editorial/Industrial

For additional work see American
Showcase Volumes 7, 8, 9 & 10 and
Corporate Showcase Volumes 7, 8, & 9.

Partial Client List: 3M, Artesia Waters,
Planned Parenthood, Prudential
Insurance, Reed Tool, Schlumberger,
Anadrill, Shell Oil, Sterling Electronics,
Coldwell Banker, Dr. Pepper, The
Coastal Corporation, Hughes Tool, IBM,

Anderson Clayton Foods, Exxon,
Curtin Matheson Scientific, Texaco,
Lyondell Petrochemical, Granada
Corporation, ARCO, Conoco,
Entertainment Marketing, Zapata
Corporation.

Dale O'Dell
2040 Bissonnet
Houston, Texas 77005
(713) 521-2611

Studio and location photography.
Special-effects utilizing computer
graphics, optical effects and computer-
photographic composites. Dale is a
specialist in illustrating difficult to
visualize concepts.

See also: American Showcase Vol.
13 & 14; CA Photo Annuals 1985, 1987,
1988, 1989.
Clients include: ATT, Chevron, Compaq,
GTE, Meridian Oil, Panasonic, Citgard
Oil, Southwestern Bell, Texaco, Aramco.

Frank Simon
4030 North 27th Avenue, Suite B
Phoenix, Arizona 85017
(602) 279-4635

Bob Werre Photography

2437 Bartlett Street
Houston, Texas 77098
(713) 529-4841
FAX: (713) 529-4130

Bob is an accomplished and versatile photographer handling corporate, editorial and advertising assignments—formats up to 8x10—studio or location.

For additional images see Showcase 6, 7, 8, and Showcase 13.

The business of commercial art and photography.

The more than 300 SPAR members nationwide represent the best talent in the business.

For over 20 years, while we've been bringing talent and client together, SPAR members also have been working to promote high professional standards and to foster cooperation and understanding.

Our members today are not just salespeople but marketing specialists with a wide range of capabilities.

We are truly professionals doing business with professionals.

SOCIETY OF PHOTOGRAPHER AND ARTIST REPRESENTATIVES, INC.
1123 Broadway, Room 914 New York, New York 10010 212-924-6023

west

Alaska
California
Colorado
Hawaii
Idaho
Montana
Nevada
Oregon
Utah
Washington
Wyoming

PETE SALOUTOS

SEATTLE 206 842 0832   LOS ANGELES 213 397 5509   REPRESENTED BY KOLEA BAKER 206 443 0326

6750 55th Avenue South
Seattle, WA 98118
(206) 721-5151

6750 55th Avenue South
Seattle, WA 98118
(206) 721-5151

CHOICES

CORPORATE

TRAVEL

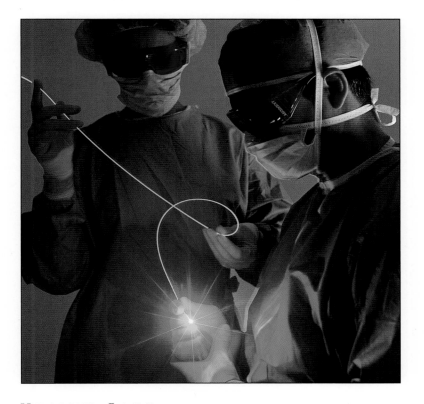

HEALTH CARE

EDITORIAL

4

P
O
R
T
F
O
L
I
O
S

Electronic Imaging by Andrew Rodney with the use of the Apple Macintosh.

501
NORTH DETROIT ST.
LOS ANGELES
CA 90036
213 939 7427

D E R E K
S M I T H

P H O T O G R A P H E R

568 South 400 West

Salt Lake City, Utah 84101

801 • 363 • 1061

SOONER OR LATER YOU'LL GET TO SHOOT IN UTAH!

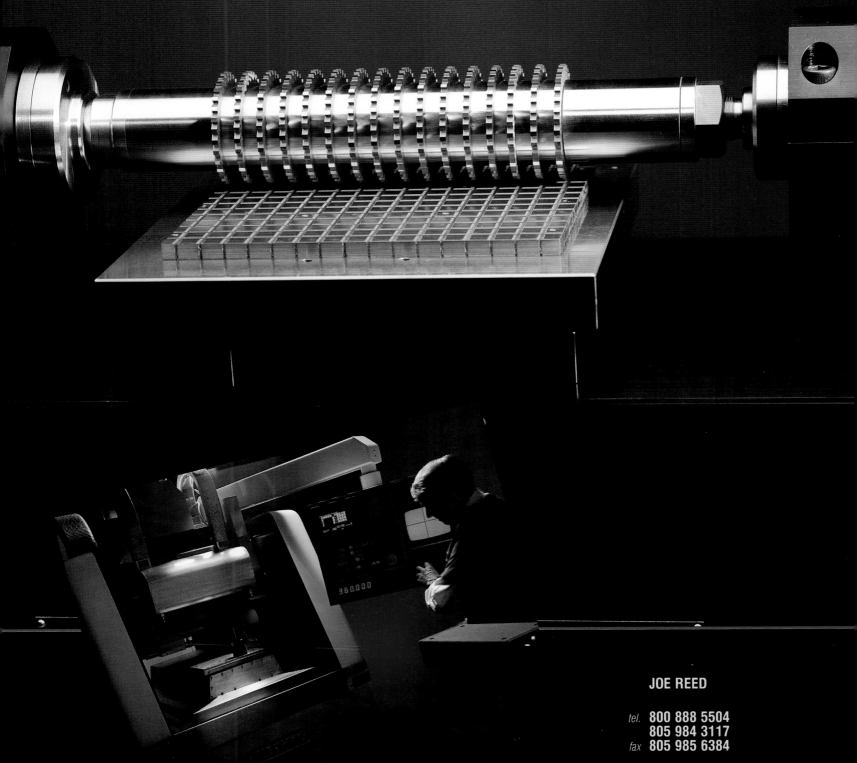

VIEWFINDERS
visual communications

JOE REED

tel. **800 888 5504**
805 984 3117
fax **805 985 6384**

suite **120**
3401 WEST FIFTH
OXNARD CALIFORNIA
zip **93030**

G.E. HADEL

"Two roads diverged...and I—
I took the one less travelled by,
and that has made all the difference."

Robert Frost-The Road Not Taken

Clients Include:
Kingston Technology
Intercommunications Inc.
John Creel Advertising
Centennial Corporation
TRAVCOA
Le Meridien Hotel
(Newport Beach, CA)

Gregg E. Hadel Photographer • 15431 Redhill • Suite "E" • Tustin, CA 92680 • (714) 259-9224 • FAX (714) 259-1566

Gary L. Benson
11110 34th Place SW
Seattle, Washington 98146
(206) 242-3232

Images discovered on location.
Photography for corporate, annual
report, editorial and advertising
assignments.

Clients include: Forbes, GTE, Safeco
Insurance Co., Puget Sound Freight/
Truck Lines, Chevron USA, US West.
Additional work: Corporate Showcase
8 & 9.

GARY BENSON
PHOTOGRAPHY

Steven Bloch
Portland, Oregon
(503) 224-8018

Call

AND

EVERYTHING

IN

BETWEEN

BIKE MESSENGER

PRESIDENT CONMETCO

STEVEN BLOCH   **PHOTOGRAPHER**   431 NW FLANDERS   PORTLAND, OREGON 97209

TELEPHONE   (503) 224•8018   FACSIMILE (503) 223•8685   CELLULAR (503) 780•350.1

CLIENTS: BLACKSTAR, INTEL, LAMB WESTON, BURGERVILLE, AT&T, TIME LIFE, WEYERHAEUSER, FAIRCHILD PUBLICATIONS, FREIGHTLINER, PACIFIC POWER, ESCO, PGE.

L·I·F·E I·M·A·G·E·S

**Mert Carpenter
Photography**
202 Granada Way
Los Gatos, California 95030
(408) 370-1663
FAX: (408) 370-1668

Corporate Location and Architecture

More than a decade of shooting
assignments nationwide.

Greg Cava
2912 South Highland
Suite J
Las Vegas, Nevada 89109
(702) 735-2282
FAX: (702) 735-6703

Location and studio photography for advertising, editorial and corporate assignments.

Client list includes:
American Airlines
HBO
CBS Fox Video
L.A. Raiders
Caesars World, Inc.
The Mirage

FIB Nevada
UNLV Athletics
The Boyd Group
Numont Mining Corp.

© 1990 Greg Cava

237

**Michael Christmas
Photography**
9863 Pacific Heights Boulevard
Suite A
San Diego, California 92121
(619) 554-0226
(213) 302-8437 Los Angeles
(415) 677-7965 San Francisco

Client list:
Citicorp, Hewlett-Packard, Nissan, Pro-Kennex Tennis & Golf, Kunnan Sports, Hang Ten, Avis, Cobra Golf, Uni-Vite, United Way/Chad, Just Say No Drug Program, Diatek, Ahlstrom/Pyropower, Deloitte Haskins & Sells, Bank of Commerce San Diego, First Commercial Bank Sacramento, Firestone, San Diego Convention Center and Soup Exchange Restaurants.

CHRISTMAS
PHOTOGRAPHY

David/Gayle Photography

Dave Robinson Photographer
3223 1st Avenue South, Suite "B"
Seattle, Washington 98134-1819
(206) 624-5207
FAX: (206) 343-0491

Photo Illustration, studio set construction, special effects when appropriate, a product photographer who works well with people. Specializing in problem solving and communicating through photography.

Award winning photography for Boeing Aerospace, Microsoft, Accel/The Exchange, Fluorocarbon, Associated Grocers, Apple Computer Dealers Association, General Automotive, John Fluke Manufacturing, Lunstead Furniture, Rane Corporation, Hotel Captain Cook (Alaska), Holiday Inn,

Westin Hotels, photo illustrations for numerous book covers and CD/tape jackets, product catalogs for Kenworth Trucks, Paccar Parts, Kidder Skis, Weisfields and Boma Jewelry, package illustration for Teltone, Microsoft, Microrim and more.

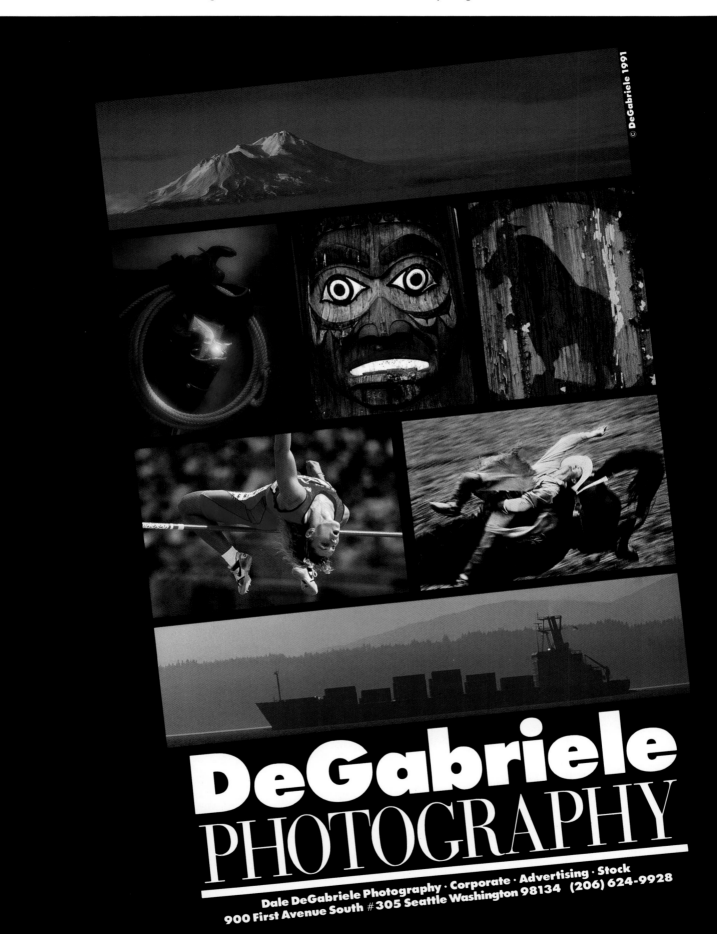

Fritz Dent
219 First Avenue North #395
Seattle, Washington 98109
(206) 233-0685

David Franzen
Franzen Photography
746 Ilaniwai Street, Suite 200
Honolulu, Hawaii 96813
(808) 537-9921
FAX: (808) 528-2250

Notes:
All photos: © David Franzen
Member ASMP

Awards of Excellence: PRSA and IABC

Latest book: "The Art of Mauna Kea"

Clients:
Alexander & Baldwin
Chevron, USA
Ellerbe Becket
Forbes Magazine
Four Seasons Hotels
Hill & Knowlton

Specializing in:
Aerial
Annual Report
Architectural/Interior
Corporate/Industrial
Travel/Resort

HAWAII

Jerome Hart
4612 Northeast Alameda
Portland, Oregon 97213
(503) 224-3003
FAX: (503) 222-2677

New York Representative:
M.J. Koreiva
(212) 246-3316

Clients include: Nike, First Interstate
Bank, Louisiana Pacific, Georgia Pacific,
Tektronix, Pacificorp, Doernbecher
Children's Hospital, Freightliner, Mentor
Graphics, PGE, Rouse Company,
University of Oregon.

JEROME HART
PHOTOGRAPHY

Adobe   AT&T   Bayer USA   Citicorp   Clorox   Pacific Bell   Westinghouse

HILDRETH
photographer

4 1 5 . 8 2 1 . 7 3 9 8

Robert Holmgren
319 Central Avenue
Menlo Park, California 94025
(415) 325-6837

Location photography of people at
work for corporate and editorial clients.

SAN FRANCISCO PRODUCTION GROUP

NEW UNITED MOTOR COMPANY (NUMMI)

RONALD BALDWIN (CEO) GEOTHERMAL RESOURCES

UNIVERSITY OF CALIFORNIA

PACIFIC LUMBER COMPANY

Continued from page 206

Graphic Artists Guild
11 West 20th Street
New York, NY 10011
(212) 463-7730

Guild of Book Workers
521 Fifth Avenue, 17th Floor
New York, NY 10175
(212) 757-6454

Institute of Outdoor Advertising
342 Madison Avenue
New York, NY 10173
(212) 986-5920

International Advertising Association, Inc.
342 Madison Avenue, Suite 2000
New York, NY 10017
(212) 557-1133

The One Club
3 West 18th Street
New York, NY 10011
(212) 255-7070

The Public Relations Society of America, Inc.
33 Irving Place
New York, NY 10003
(212) 995-2230

Society of American Graphic Artists
32 Union Square, Room 1214
New York, NY 10003
(212) 260-5706

Society of Illustrators
128 East 63rd Street
New York, NY 10021
(212) 838-2560

Society of Photographers and Artists Representatives
1123 Broadway, Room 914
New York, NY 10010
(212) 924-6023

Society of Publication Designers
60 East 42nd Street, Suite 1416
New York, NY 10165
(212) 983-8585

Television Bureau of Advertising
477 Madison Avenue
New York, NY 10022
(212) 486-1111

Type Directors Club of New York
60 East 42nd Street, Suite 1416
New York, NY 10165
(212) 983-6042

U.S. Trademark Association
6 East 45th Street
New York, NY 10017
(212) 986-5880

Volunteer Lawyers for the Arts
1285 Avenue of the Americas, 3rd Floor
New York, NY 10019
(212) 977-9270

Women in the Arts
c/o Roberta Crown
1175 York Avenue, #2G
New York, NY 10021
(212) 751-1915

NORTH CAROLINA

Davidson County Art Guild
224 South Main Street
Lexington, NC 27292
(704) 249-2742

OHIO

Advertising Club of Cincinnati
PO Box 43252
Cincinnati, OH 45243
(513) 575-9331

Design Collective
D.F. Cooke
130 East Chestnut Street
Columbus, OH 43215
(614) 464-2883

PENNSYLVANIA

Art Directors Club of Philadelphia
2017 Walnut Street
Philadelphia, PA 19103
(215) 569-3650

TEXAS

Advertising Club of Fort Worth
1801 Oak Knoll
Colleyville, TX 76034
(817) 283-3615

Art Directors Club of Houston
PO Box 271137
Houston, TX 77277
(713) 961-3434

Dallas Society of Visual Communications
3530 High Mesa Drive
Dallas, TX 75234
(214) 241-2017

VIRGINIA

Industrial Designers Society of America
1142 East Walker Road
Great Falls, VA 22066
(703) 759-0100

National Association of Schools of Art and Design
11250 Roger Bacon Drive, #21
Reston, VA 22090
(703) 437-0700

WASHINGTON

Allied Arts of Seattle, Inc.
107 South Main Street
Seattle, WA 98104
(206) 624-0432

Seattle Ad Federation
2033 6th Avenue, #804
Seattle, WA 98121
(206) 448-4481

WISCONSIN

Coalition of Women's Art Organizations
123 East Beutel Road
Port Washington, WI 53074
(414) 284-4458

Milwaukee Advertising Club
231 West Wisconsin Avenue
Milwaukee, WI 53203
(414) 271-7351

Diane Huntress

3337 West 23rd Avenue
Denver, Colorado 80211-4501
(303) 480-0219

ASMP • NPPA

Among our Capabilities:
Location Portraiture
Reportage
Studio and Hand-Tinting
Sports and Travel
Architecture
Movement

Among our Clients:
American Express
Continental Airlines
Dun & Bradstreet
DuPont
Phillips Petroleum
Time, Inc.

Jim Karageorge
610 22nd Street, #309
San Francisco, California 94107
(415) 648-3444
FAX: (415) 255-9707

Transforming locations
Large photo this page was shot on
location

Mead Annual Report Show 1987-89
AR 100 and AIGA Shows

See previous pages in Corporate
Showase Vols. 1-5 & 7-9

Stock is available through the studio
and through H. Armstrong Roberts
(215) 386-6300

Call the studio for a complete portfolio

© 1991 Jim Karageorge

Jim Karageorge
610 22nd Street, #309
San Francisco, California 94107
(415) 648-3444
FAX: (415) 255-9707

Transforming locations

Mead Annual Report Show 1987,
'88, '89
Multiple awards in the AR 100 and
AIGA shows.

See previous pages in Corporate
Showcase Vols. 1-5 & 7-9

Stock is available through the studio
and through H. Armstrong Roberts
(215) 386-6300

Call the studio for a complete portfolio

© 1991 Jim Karageorge

David Lissy
14472 Applewood Ridge Road
Golden, Colorado 80401
(303) 277-0232

Recent Clients Include:
Breckenridge Resort
Colorado Tourism Board
Front Range Airport-Denver
Hart Bornhoft Group
Head Sportswear
Hostmark

Merkley Ski Hats
Quintessence-Aspen Cologne for
Women
Radisson Hotel-Denver
Texaco/Havoline Grand Prix of Denver
Tyrolia

Awards:
Eastman Kodak Professional
Photographers Showcase at Epcot
Center

Marc D. Longwood
Sacramento, California USA
(916) 635-0652
FAX... Please ask

I'm a well educated and expressive sort of guy who quickly builds rapport with people. Not only subjects, but everyone else who helps setup a successful shot...from roughnecks to Ph.D.s.

And, you can trust me to understand your communication objectives and run with it.

I'm only a phone call away.
There's the number...Let's talk.

Ernst & Young

Apple Computer

Intel

AT&T

Genesis Electronics

Pacific Bell Telephone

Pacific Telesis

Pitney Bowes

Price Waterhouse

Wells Fargo Bank

Duewag Corporation

Dow Chemical

Pacific Southwest
Airlines

Wickland Oil

Sutter Health

Foundation Health
Corporation

Advanced Counter
Measure Systems

Beneficial Equities

Alcatel Transcom
Electronics

California Chamber
of Commerce

Business Week

Fortune

PC World

Macintosh Today

Infoworld

LA Times

LONGWOOD
PHOTOGRAPHY
PEOPLE & LOCATION

Annual Reports
Corporate
Industrial
Advertising
Editorial

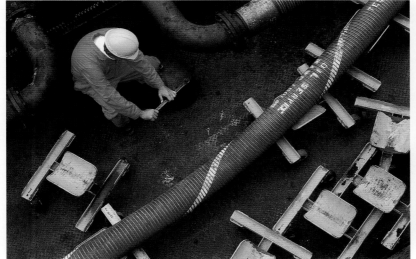

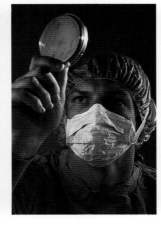

251

Kent Miles Photography

Represented by:
Pix Producers, Inc.
500 Greenwich Street, Suite 501
New York, New York 10013
(212) 226-0012
FAX: (212) 226-2329

Evocative photographs in Black and White and in Color.

Assignment and Stock photography on location, emphasizing people and portraiture, travel, pictorial and documentary subjects for Advertising, Corporate and Editorial clients.

Portfolios and client list available on request.
Also see our pages in American Showcase 12-14 and Corporate Showcase 6-9.

Member ASMP

"EEKA THE SWAMP-THING" WITH AMBER, HER PET ANACONDA AT THE BANGOR, MAINE, STATE FAIR, 1988.

Milroy/McAleer Photography
711 West 17th Street, G-7
Costa Mesa, California 92627
(714) 722-6402
FAX: (714) 722-6371

Milroy/McAleer are a team of photographers specializing in location photography working with and without people.

To see more examples of our work see Corporate Showcase #7 & #8. In addition see The Black Book 1989, 1990 and 1991; or call to see a portfolio.

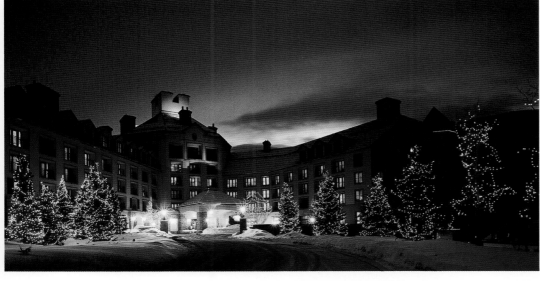

**David Muench
Photography, Inc.**
David Muench, Marc Muench
PO Box 30500
Santa Barbara, California 93130
(805) 967-4488
FAX: (805) 967-4268

Seasons, elements, familiar sites and places not yet discovered. Unique way of viewing the American landscape, North, South, East, West. Light, timing and angles create new dimensions to constantly updated large stock collection. Landscapes throughout America with & without people in unusual surroundings. Assignments are welcomed with stock available in 4 x 5, 6 x 7 & 35mm formats.

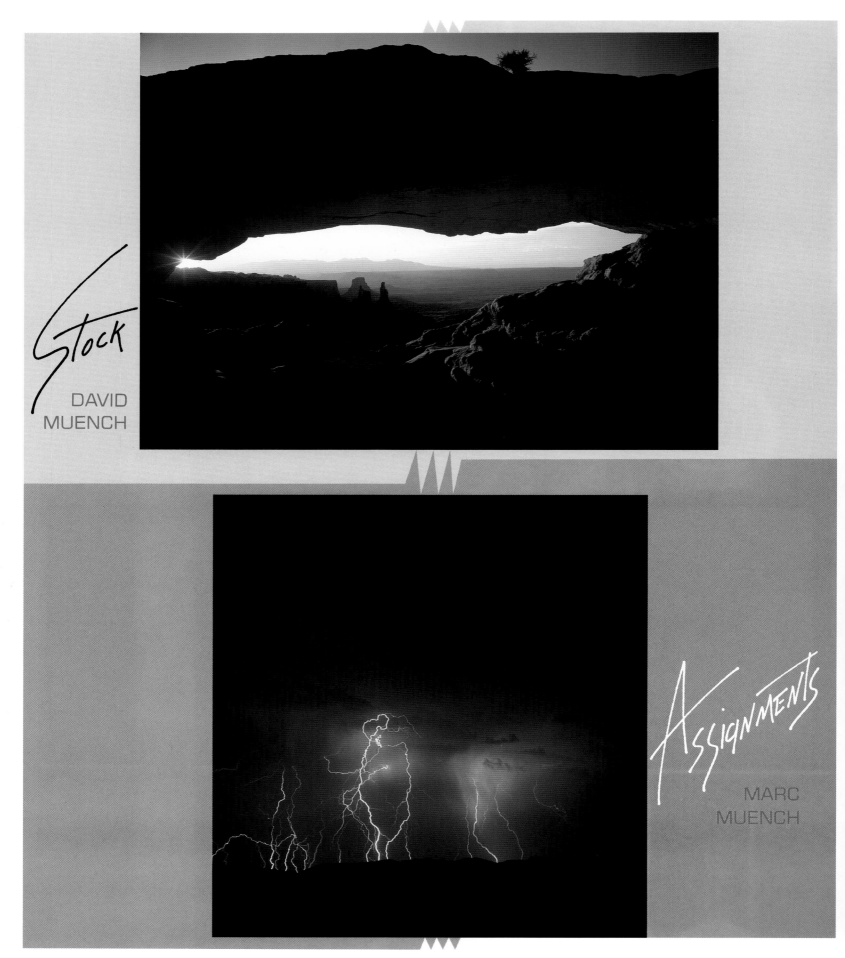

Stock

DAVID
MUENCH

Assignments

MARC
MUENCH

Ray Ng
1855 Blake Street
Denver, Colorado 80202
(303) 292-0112

RAY NG

CLIENTS INCLUDE:

BUSINESS WEEK

CHANGING TIMES

DISCOVER

FORBES

FORTUNE

GERRY BABY PRODUCTS

MEDICAL DYNAMICS

QUARK INC.

TIME/LIFE BOOKS INC.

U S NEWS & WORLD REPORT

U S WEST

WHITTLE COMMUNICATIONS

David E. Perry
PO Box 4165 Pioneer Square Station
Seattle, Washington 98104
(206) 932-6614 Phone
FAX: (206) 935-8958

One of the first questions I ask is how you want your images to feel. Button-down-honest? Playfully-candid? Daydream-innocent...? They must effect an emotional response from the viewer that somehow clothes the facts being presented.

Additional work in American Showcase, Volumes 7 & 9-12 and Corporate Showcase, Volumes 8 & 9.

Doug Plummer
501 North 36th Street, Suite 409
Seattle, Washington 98103
(206) 789-8174
FAX: (206) 632-1259

People and locations worldwide.

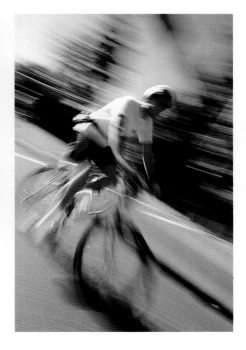

DOUG PLUMMER
p h o t o g r a p h e r
2 0 6 . 7 8 9 . 8 1 7 4

John Ripley
290 Green Street
San Francisco, California 94133

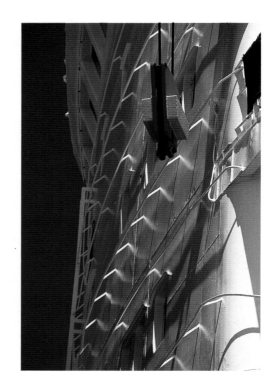

RIPLEY

San Francisco
415.781.4940

David Scott Smith
Photographer
1437 Avenue E
Billings, Montana 59102
(406) 259-5656

Additional work can be seen in
Corporate Showcase volumes 6,
8 and 9.

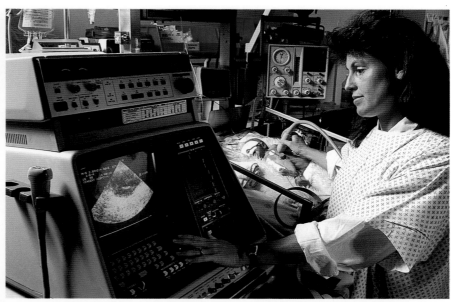

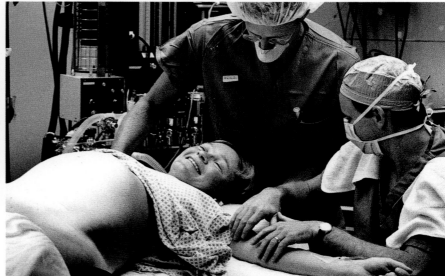

David X. Tejada
1553 Platte Street
Suite 205
Denver, Colorado 80202
(303) 458-1220

TEJADA

PHOTOGRAPHY

1553 Platte Street   Suite 205
Denver, Colorado 80202   303 458 1220

T E J A D A

P H O T O G R A P H Y

1553 Platte Street   Suite 205
Denver, Colorado 80202   303 458 1220

**Thomas Upton
Photographer**
1879 Woodland Avenue
Palo Alto, California 94303
(415) 325-8120

Photography for Medicine, Health
and Business

Clients include:
Ask Computer Systems, Baxter
Gurian & Mazzei, Children's Hospital
at Stanford, Hewlett Packard, Oracle,
Stanford University Hospital, Syntex.

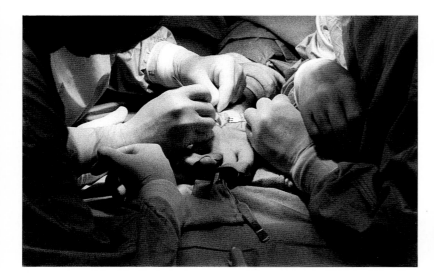

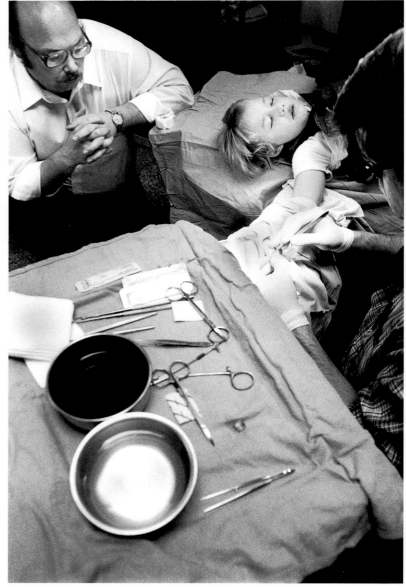

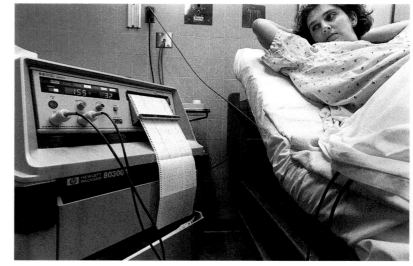

Richard Wheeler
1116 4th Street
San Rafael, California 94901
(415) 457-6914

corporate/industrial photography
b&w and color
from california to new york,
apalachicola to coeur d'alene

Do it by the book.

How do you decide on an appropriate fee for artwork you sell or buy? How do you write a contract that's fair to both artist and buyer? What are the implications of new technologies in the art marketplace? If you're an artist, what business practices should you expect from your clients? And if you're a buyer, what should you expect from a professional artist?

Artists and buyers alike will find good answers to questions like these in *Pricing and Ethical Guidelines,* 7th Edition. Published by The Graphic Artists Guild, the *Guidelines* contains the result of the Guild's extensive survey of pricing levels in every branch of the graphic arts, as well as a wealth of information on estimates, proposals, contracts, copyrights, and many other aspects of the business relationship between artist and buyer.

To order your copy of this indispensable reference, send $22.95 plus $3.50 shipping and handling, along with your name and address, to the **Graphic Artists Guild, 11 West 20th St., New York, NY 10011.** New York residents please add 8¼% sales tax (total $28.63).

International

David Robert Austen
David Austen Associates
GPO Box 2480
Sydney 2001 Australia
61 (2) 957-2511
FAX: 61 (2) 957-2511
Couriers: 297 Miller Street
North Sydney 2062 Australia

Assignment representation:
Linda D. Duncan, in our office.
Picture Group, Providence, R.I., USA
Gamma Press Images, Paris, France
Pacific Press Service, Tokyo, Japan

Member: American Society of Magazine
Photographers

Partial list of assignments:
American Express • Ampol Petroleum
Bank of America • Bechtel Power
Corporation • BHP • Esso • IBM
Lend Lease • Mobil • Johnson Wax
National Geographic Magazine
New York Times • Smithsonian Institution
Time-Life Incorporated

Stock representation:
Pacific Press Service
Stock, Boston
Tony Stone Worldwide
Photo Library of Australia
Picture Group
West Stock
ZEFA

Nancy Cohen
95 Atchison Street
Crows Nest, New South Wales 2065
Australia
(61) 2 439-1805 Phone/FAX

An American based in Australia. Specializing in people, places, and events for Corporate, Editorial, and Industrial clients. A strong sense of reality, action, warmth, and design. On location in Australia, the Pacific, Asia, and beyond.

Clients: Exxon, Esso, OTC, Caltex, Telecom, NCR.

Stock: Black Star

When ideas don't come to you out of the blue, look here.

There's no question that American Showcase produces the #1 sourcebooks for locating freelance photographers and illustrators.

But for creatives everywhere, Showcase is the best source for something even more important: INSPIRATION.

Page after page of images, styles, and techniques will provide you with an inexhaustible source of creative ideas.

Illustration Showcase 14, divided into two easy-to-use volumes, gives you 1226 pages of the highest quality full-color reproductions -- more than 6,000 images, from the very best in the illustration field, for only $65.00.

And Photography Showcase 14 offers 360 pages of the highest quality full-color images by today's top and up-and-coming photographers, for only $39.95.

To purchase either of these books, simply send a check or money order for the correct amount to American Showcase, 915 Broadway, New York, NY 10010, with a return address, or call us at (212) 673-6600 to place your credit card order by phone (we accept all major cards.) We'll even pick up the postage and handling (New York residents, please add sales tax.)

Now <u>that's</u> an idea.

AMERICAN SHOWCASE

Stock & Services

Philip Derenzis
421 North 23rd Street
Allentown, Pennsylvania 18104
(215) 776-6465

Natures Moods & Seasons—
Landscapes & Abstracts. Travel,
Industry, Rural Scenics, Clouds,
Backgrounds, Fireworks, Animals.

Bette S. Garber
3160 Walnut Street
Thorndale, Pennsylvania 19372
(215) 380-0342
FAX: (215) 380-8881

Specializing in the Trucking Industry

Stock Photos/Assignments
Member: American Society of
Magazine Photographers
All photos © Bette S. Garber

WANTED

Problem-solvers. Sages. Wits. Philosophers. Boat-rockers.

We hope you've enjoyed reading the **VIEWPOINTS** in Corporate Showcase 10. This popular feature is designed to enlighten and entertain our readers by providing unique insights on the current state of photography, graphic design, illustration, advertising, and corporate marketing.

We'd like to take this opportunity to invite you to share your own thoughts, opinions and methods with thousands of your colleagues worldwide.

The average **VIEWPOINT** is 1,000 words but we'll consider longer (or shorter) pieces. Have the article titled, typed double-space, and be sure to include your own name, job title, company and address. If we publish your submission in our next Showcase, you will receive a copy of the book, 500 reprints of your article and our eternal gratitude. (Of course, we can't guarantee that yours will be published, but we do promise to acknowledge and read every submission.)

Go ahead, write down all those things you've always wanted to get off your chest. Speak out to those photographers, illustrators and designers you hire…share confidences with your colleagues …tell off your boss. Do it while you're feeling outraged/satisfied/ frustrated about the work you create. Do it today and mail it to:

Mitchell Hinz
New Projects Manager
American Showcase, Inc.
915 Broadway
New York, New York 10010

Thanks a lot. We're looking forward to hearing from you and hope to see you in **CORPORATE SHOWCASE VOLUME 11!**

Tom & Pat Leeson
"American Gone Wild" Collection
PO Box 2498
Vancouver, Washington 98668
(206) 256-0436

50,000 transparencies capturing North America's wildside- elk bugling, deer running, wolves howling, many endangered species.

Dynamic bald eagles- flying, fishing, fighting, nesting, perching & portraits. See our award-winning photo book The American Eagle.

We specialize also in travel photography of the Canadian Rockies, Alaska and the Pacific Northwest; old growth forests and western national parks.

Tom & Pat Leeson
"American Gone Wild" Collection
PO Box 2498
Vancouver, Washington 98668

IndexPhotographers

Creation by design, not accident.

Outstanding visual images rarely just happen. They are the result of careful premeditation, planning and design.

This new book by Henry Wolf, one of today's foremost photographers and art directors, examines the many creative methods he employs – from use of strange perspective to settings in improbable places to unexpected combinations.

Here are 17 chapters of techniques for translating words into photographic images that will be more com-

pelling, more unique and therefore more memorable.

Any visual communicator will find inspiration in these pages.

Clothbound with hundreds of full-color photographs, as well as reproductions of many classic works of art that have been an influence on them.

184 pages. $45.00. All major credit cards accepted. Order now! American Showcase, 915 Broadway, New York, New York 10010, (212) 673-6600.

P H O N E   L I S T I N G S
&   A D D R E S S E S   O F
R E P R E S E N T A T I V E S ,
V I S U A L   A R T I S T S
&   S U P P L I E R S

C O N T E N T S

R E G I O N S

New York City

Northeast
Connecticut
Delaware
Maine
Maryland
Massachusetts
New Hampshire
New Jersey
New York State
Pennsylvania
Rhode Island
Vermont
Washington, D.C.
West Virginia

Southeast
Alabama
Florida
Georgia
Kentucky
Louisiana
Mississippi
North Carolina
South Carolina
Tennessee
Virginia

Midwest
Illinios
Indiana
Iowa
Kansas

Miichigan
Minnesota
Missouri
Nebraska
North Dakota
Ohio
South Dakota
Wisconsin

Southwest
Arizona
Arkansas
New Mexico
Oklahoma
Texas

Rocky Mountain
Colorado
Idaho
Montana
Utah
Wyoming

West Coast
Alaska
British Columbia
California
Hawaii
Nevada
Oregon
Washington

International

R E P S

N Y C

A

Abel Partners/210 E 67th St #35 212-628-6209
Mike Dietz, (I), Peter Johansky, (P), Robert S Levy, (I), Harry
Pincus, (I), Bob Stuhmer, (I)

Altamore, Bob/237 W 54th St 4th Fl...............................212-977-4300
Cailor/Resnick , (P)

American Artists/353 W 53rd St #1W..............................212-682-2462
Keith Batcheller, (I), Bart Bemus, (I), Roger Bergendorff, (I), Dan
Bridy, (I), Robert Burger, (I), Chris Butler, (I), Gary Ciccarelli, (I),
Jim Deigan, (I), Jacques Devaud, (I), Bob Dorsey, (I), Lane
DuPont, (I), Michael Elins, (I), Malcolm Farley, (I), Russell Farrell,
(I), George Gaadt, (I), Rob Gage, (P), Bill Garland, (I), Jackie
Geyer, (I), Dave Gilo, (I), John Hamagami, (I), Pam Hamilton, (I),
Steve Hendricks, (I), Doug Henry, (I), John Holm, (I), Chris
Hopkins, (I), Mitch Hyatt, (I), Richard Kriegler, (I), Alan Leiner, (I),
Ned Levine, (I), Maurice Lewis, (I), Ed Lindlof, (I), Jerry LoFaro,
(I), Ron Mahoney, (I), Mick McGinty, (I), Jean-Claude Michel, (I),
James Needham, (I), David Noyes, (I), Erik Olson, (I), Jim
Owens, (I), Charles Passarelli, (I), Tony Randazzo, (I), Jan
Sawka, (I), Todd Schorr, (I), Michael Schumacher, (I), Joe
Scrofani, (I), Jim Starr, (I), Mike Steirnagle, (I), Peter Van Ryzin,
(I), Tony Ward, (P), Stan Watts, (I), Will Weston, (I), Ron Wolin, (I),
Jonathan Wright, (I), Gary Yealdhall, (I), Andy Zito, (I)

Anton, Jerry/107 E 38th St #5A......................................212-633-9880
Bobbye Cochran, (I), Abe Echevarria, (I), Norman Green, (I),
Aaron Rezny, (P), Chris Vincent, (I), Oliver Williams, (I)

Aparo, Vincent/65 W 68th St..212-877-5439
Barry Seidman, (P)

Arnold, Peter Inc/1181 Broadway 4th Fl.........................212-481-1190
Yann Arthus-Bertrand, (P), Fred Bavendam, (P), Dieter Blum,
(P), Herb Comess, (P), Martha Cooper, (P), Dennis diCicco,
(P), Bob Evans, (P), Helmut Gritscaher, (P), Jacques Jangoux,
(P), Manfred Kage, (P), Steve Kaufman, (P), Stephen
Krasemann, (P), Werner Muller, (P), Jim Olive, (P), Hans
Pfletschinger, (P), Jeffrey L Rotman, (P), Galen Rowell, (P),
David Scharf, (P), Erika Stone, (P), Bruno Zehnder, (P)

Art & Commerce/108 W 18th St 212-206-0737
William Claxton, (P)

The Art Farm/420 Lexington Ave 212-688-4555
Bruce Aruffenbart, (I), Dick Carroll, (I), Computer Paint Group,
(I), Sururi Gumen, (I), Bob Lubbers, (I), Dick Naugler, (I), Scott
Pike, (I), Bob Walker, (I), Kong Wu, (I), Bill Zdinak, (I)

Artco/232 Madison Ave #402..212-889-8777
Ed Acuna, (I), Alexander & Turner , (I), George Angelini, (I),
Frank Bolle, (I), Gene Boyer, (I), Dan Brown, (I), Alain Chang,
(I), Anne Cook, (I), Jeff Cornell, (I), Bob Dacey, (I), Beau &
Alan Daniels, (I), Mort Drucker, (I), Lisa Falkenstern, (I), Ed
Gazsi, (I), Gary Glover, (I), Lisa Henderling, (I), Kathy Jeffers,
(I), David Loew, (I), Rick McCollum, (I), John Jude Palencar,
(I), Barry Phillips, (I), Al Pisano, (I), Jean Restivo, (I), Marcel
Rozenberg, (I), Mark Smollin, (), Leslie Szabo, (I), Brian Twede,
(I), Sally Vitsky, (I), Rob Zuckerman, (I)

Artists Associates/211 E 51st St #5F..............................212-755-1365
Norman Adams, (I), Don Brautigam, (I), Michael Deas, (I), C
Michael Dudash, (I), Mark English, (I), Robert Heindel, (I),
Steve Karchin, (I), Dick Krepel, (I), Skip Liepke, (I), Fred Otnes,
(I), Norman Walker, (I)

Arton Associates/216 E 45th St 212-661-0850
Ned Butterfield, (I), Paul Giovanopoulis, (I), Laurent Hubert, (I),
Jacob Knight, (I), Carveth Kramer, (I), Michelle Laporte, (I),
Karen Laurence, (I), Katrina Taylor, (I)

Artworks/270 Park Ave S #10B.......................................212-260-4153
Michelle Amatrula, (I), Tudor Banus, (I), Ken Dewey, (I), Donna
Diamond, (I), Richard Dickens, (I), Sandra Filippucci, (I), Peter
Fiore, (I), Dennis Lyall, (I), Marcia Pyner, (I), Romas , (I), Mort
Rosenfeld, (I), Larry Schwinger, (I), Evan T Steadman, (I)

Asciutto Art Reps/19 E 48th St 212-838-0050
Anthony Accardo, (I), Eliot Bergman, (I), Alex Bloch, (I), Olivia
Cole, (I), Daniel Delvalle, (I), Suzanne DeMarco, (I), Len

Epstein, (I), Simon Galkin, (I), Meryl Henderson, (I), Nurit
Karlin, (I), Morissa Lipstein, (I), Loreta Lustig, (I), Sal
Murdocca, (I), James Needham, (I), Charles Peale, (I), Jan
Pyk, (I), Fred Winkowski, (I)

B

Badd, Linda/568 Broadway #601 212-431-3377
Tom Clayton, (P)

Bahm, Darwin/6 Jane St...212-989-7074
Harry DeZitter, (P), Gordon Kibbe, (I), Joan Landis, (I), Rick
Meyerowitz, (I), Don Ivan Punchatz, (I), Arno Sternglass, (I),
John Thompson, (I), Robert Weaver, (I)

Baker, Valerie/152 W 25th St 12th Fl..............................212-807-7113
Michel Legrand, (P)

Barboza, Ken Assoc/853 Broadway #1603.....................212-505-8635
Anthony Barboza, (P), Leonard Jenkins, (I), Peter Morehand,
(P), Marcus Tullis, (P)

Barich, Liz/245 E 58th St 212-752-8174
Nathaniel Kramer, (P), Roger Neve, (P), Yoichrio Sato, (P)

Barefoot, Elenor/105 Hudson St #208.............................212-226-3430

Barnes, Fran/25 Fifth Ave #9B..212-505-2720

Barracca, Sal/381 Park Ave S #919................................212-889-2400
Jeanette Adams, (I), Alan Ayers, (I), Mark Buehner, (I), Tom
Galasinski, (I), Robert Grace, (I), Rich Grote, (I), Alan
Gutierrez, (I), Mitchell Heinze, (I), Ken Hodges, (I), Daniel
Horne, (I), John Huxtable, (I), Tim Jacobus, (I), Paul Jennis, (I),
Ken Laager, (I), Richard Lauter, (I), Robert Lawson, (I), Lina
Levy, (I), Peg Magovern, (I), David Mann, (I), Bruce Minney, (I),
Yan Nascimbene, (I), Larry Noble, (I), John Pahlsson, (I), Keith
Parkinson, (I), Brad Purse, (I), Larry Selman, (I), Peter Siu, (I),
Gary Smith, (I), Jim Thiesen, (I), Josie Yee, (I), John Zielinski,
(I), Ivan Zorad, (I)

Becker, Erika/150 W 55th St..212-757-8987
Esther Larson, (I)

Becker, Noel/150 W 55th St...212-757-8987
Sy Vinopoll, (P)

Beidler, Barbara/648 Broadway #506..............................212-979-6996
Luca Babani, (P), Richard Dunkley, (P), Teresa Ginori, (P), Bob
Hiemstra, (P), Robert Levin, (P), Nana Watanabe, (P)

Beilin, Frank/405 E 56th St...212-751-3074

Bernstein & Andriulli/60 E 42nd St #505........................212-682-1490
Tony Antonios, (I), Per Arnoldi, (I), Pat Bailey, (I), Garin Baker, (I),
Garie Blackwell, (I), Melinda Bordelon, (I), Rick Brown, (I), Daniel
Craig, (I), Creative Capers , (I), Everett Davidson, (I), Nina Duram,
(I), Jon Ellis, (I), Ron Fleming, (I), Victor Gadino, (I), Joe Genova,
(I), Marika Hahn, (I), Veronika Hart, (I), John Harwood, (I), Bryan
Haynes, (I), Catherine Huerta, (I), Kevin Hulsey, (I), Tim Jessell, (I),
Mary Ann Lasher, (I), Bette Levine, (I), Todd Lockwood, (I), Lee
MacLeod, (I), Greg J Martin, (I), David B McMacken, (I), Michael
Molkenthin, (I), Chris Moore, (I), Bill Morse, (I), Frank Moscati, (I),
Pete Mueller, (I), Craig Nelson, (I), Jeff Nishinaka, (I), Greg J
Petan, (), Laura Phillips, (I), Jake Rajs, (P), Mike Rider, (I), Peggi
Roberts, (I), Ray Roberts, (I), Joe Salina, (I), Goro Sasaki, (I),
Marla Shega, (I), Chuck Slack, (I), Peter Stallard, (I), J C Suares,
(I), Thomas Szumowski, (I), Murray Tinkelman, (I), Clay Turner, (I),
Pam Wall, (I), Brent Watkinson, (I), Chuck Wilkinson, (I), Paul
Wollman, (I), James Wood, (P), Matthew Zumbo, (I)

Big City Prodctns/5 E 19th St #303 212-473-3366
Howard Berman, (P), Steve Bronstein, (P), Earl Culberson, (P),
David Massey, (P), Dan Weaks, (P)

Black Star/116 E 27th St 212-679-3288
John W. Alexanders, (P), Nancy Rica Schiff, (P), Arnold
Zann, (P)

Black, Fran/116 E 27th St 212-725-3806
Frank Founier, (I), Diane Padys, (P), Garth Vaughan, (I), Harris
Welles, (P), Tom Zimberoff, (P)

Black, Pamela/73 W Broadway 212-385-0667
Larry Bercow, (P), David Hedrich, (P), William Heuberger, (P),
William Hueberger, (P), Irida Icaza, (P), Al Payne, (P),Photo
Group , (P), Rick Young, (P)

Bloncourt, Nelson/666 Greenwich St.............................212-924-2255
Chris Dawes, (P)

Boghosian, Marty/201 E 21st St #10M...........................212-353-1313
James Salzano, (P)

Booth, Tom Inc/425 W 23rd St #17A..............................212-243-2750
William Garrett, (P), Tom Gilbert, (P), Joshua Greene, (P),
Gordon Munro, (P), Robert Reed, (P), Lara Rossignol, (P),

David Seidner, (P), Geoff Spear, (P)
Boyer, Susan/7 E 20th St 212-533-3113
Brett Froomer, (P)
Brackman, Henrietta/415 E 52nd St 212-753-6483
Brennan, Dan/568 Broadway #1005 212-925-8333
Knut Bry, (P), Mark Bugzester, (P), Alejandro Cabrera, (P),
Anthony Horth, (P), Stevie Hughes, (P), Kenji Toma, (P), Claus
Wickrath, (P)
Brindle, Carolyn/203 E 89th St #3D 212-534-4177
Brody, Sam/12 E 46th St #402 212-758-0640
Fred Hilliard, (I), Carroll Seghers II, (P), Allen Lieberman, (I),
Steve Peringer, (I), Elsa Warnick, (I), Paul Wright, (I)
Brown, Deborah & Assoc/7 W 22nd St 10th Fl 212-463-7732
Brown, Doug/17 E 45th St #1008 212-953-0088
Dennis Blachut, (P), Abe Seltzer, (P)
Bruck, Nancy & Eileen Moss/100 Bleecker St #6D 212-982-6533
Gary Feinstein, (P), Warren Gerbert, (I), Ken Goldammer, (I),
Joel Peter Johnson, (I), Lionsgate , (I), Adam Niklewicz, (I),
Pamela Patrick, (I), Ben Perini, (I), Scott Pollack, (I)
Bruml, Kathy/201 W 77th St 212-874-5659
Grant Peterson, (P)
Buck, Sid & Kane, Barney/566 Seventh Ave #603 212-221-8090
Jacques Alschech, (I), Mario Avila, (I), Ken Call, (I), Claudia
Callander, (I), Helen Chung, (I), Jack Degraffenried, (I),
Joseph Denaro, (I), Michael Farina, (I), Ann Fox, (I), Nate
Giorgio, (I), Laura Hesse, (I), John Hickey, (I), David Jarvis,
(I), Mark Kaufman, (I), Steven Keyes, (I), Harvey Kurtzman,
(I), Bob Labsley, (I), Saul Lambert, (I), Dan Lavigne, (I), Peter
Lloyd, (I), Ted Lodigensky, (I), Rich Mahon, (I), Robert
Melendez, (I), Jess Nicholas, (I), Gary Nichols, (I), Wally
Niebart, (I), Paul Palnik, (I), Ric Powell, (I), Joseph Sellers, (I),
Tad Skozynski, (I), Lynn Stephens, (I), Bill Thomson, (I),
Vahid, (I), Larry Winborg, (I)
Burris, Jim/350 W 39th St 212-239-6767
Bush, Nan/135 Watts St 212-226-0814
Barry Lategan, (P), Bruce Weber, (P)
Byrnes, Charles/435 W 19th St 212-627-3400
Steve Steigman, (P)

C

Cahill, Joe/636 Ave of Americas #2C 212-751-0529
Shig Ikeda, (P), Brad Miller, (P)
Camp, Woodfin & Assoc/116 E 27th St 212-481-6900
Robert Azzi, (P), Kip Brundage, (P), Jason Laure, (P)
Canter, Theresa/80 Charles St #3W 212-924-5887
Caputo, Elise & Assoc/240 E 27th St 212-725-0503
Becker/Bishop , (P), Steve Brady, (P), Didier Dorot, (I), James
Kozyra, (P), Peter Papadopolous, (P), Bill Robbins, (P)
Carp, Stan/2166 Broadway 212-362-4000
Dennis Gray, (P), Dennis Kitchen, (P), Allen Vogel, (P)
Casey, Judy/96 Fifth Ave 212-255-3252
Richard Bailey, (P), Martin Brading, (P), Calliope , (P), Torkil
Gudnason, (P), Christopher Micaud, (P), Jim Reiher, (P)
Casey, Marge/245 E 63rd St #201 212-486-9575
Albaino Ballerini, (P), Geoffrey Clifford, (P), Michael Luppino,
(P), Louis Wallach, (P), David Weiss, (P)
Chislovsky, Carol/853 Broadway #1201 212-677-9100
Karen Bell, (I), Taylor Bruce, (I), Russell Cobane, (I), Jim
Cohen, (I), Jon Conrad, (I), Bob Cooper, (I), Jan Evans, (I),
Chris Gall, (I), Jeff George, (I), Bob Gleason, (I), Ignacio
Gomez, (I), Ken Graning, (I), Steve Gray, (I), Mark Herman, (I),
Mike Kowalski, (I), Joe Lapinski, (I), Julie Pace, (I), Vincent
Petragnani, (I), Ed Scarisbrick, (I), Chuck Schmidt, (I), Rick
Schnieder, (I), Sandra Shap, (I), Randy South, (I), Nighthawk
Studios, (I), C A Trachok, (I)
Collignon, Daniele/200 W 15th St 212-243-4209
Dan Cosgrove, (I), Bill Frampton, (I), David Gambale, (I),
Steve Lyons, (I), Dennis Mukai, (I), Mitch O'Connell, (I),
Cindy Pardy, (I), Irena Roman, (I), Hisashi Sekine, (I),
Doug Suma, (I), Alex Tiani, (I), Varlet-Martinelli , (I),
Don Weller, (I)
Conlon, Jean/461 Broome St 212-966-9897
Elizabeth Brady, (I), Roberto Brosan, (P), Kenro Izu, (P), Ivano
Piza, (P), Evan Polenghi, (P)
Cornelia/56-58 Warren St #5E 212-732-6240
Tom Fogliani, (P), Denis Malerbi, (P), Richard Pierce, (P), Jim
Varriale, (P)

Creative Freelancers/62 W 45th St 212-398-9540
Peter Angelo, (I), Dani Antman, (I), Harold Brooks, (I), R S
Brown, (I), Bill Brummard, (I), Tom Burasiewicz, (I), Ernest
Burden, (I), Wende Caporale, (I), Robert Chronister, (I), Judy
Clifford, (I), Dan Cooper, (I), Donna Corvi, (I), Rudy Cristiano,
(I), Tom Daly, (I), Howard Darden, (I), Steve Dinnino, (I), Glen
Dodds, (I), Arthur Donovan, (I), Peggy Dressel, (I), John
Duncan, (I), Steven Duquette, (I), John Edens, (I), Anne Feiza,
(I), Karl Fischer, (I), Gregg Fitzhugh, (I), Lynn Foster, (I),
Claudia Fouse, (I), Stephen Fritsch, (I), Peter Gallagher, (I),
Greta Gallivan, (I), Ted Glazer, (I), Julie Grau, (I), David Grove,
(I), Marika Hahn, (I), Blake Hampton, (I), Gary Hanna, (I),
Paula Havey, (I), R Mark Heath, (I), Amy Huelsman, (I), Peter
Hunt, (I), Peter Ivanoff, (I), Chet Jezierski, (I), Dennis Kendrick,
(I), Jeff Kronen, (I), George Ladas, (I), Alice Landry, (I), Buddy
Leahy, (I), Anita Lovitt, (I), Sam Mclean, (I), A J Miller, (I),
Jacqui Morgan, (I), Merideth Nemirov, (I), Michael Ng, (I), Jan
North, (I), Russ North, (I), Vilma Ortiz, (I), Richard Parisi, (I),
Masood Parvez, (I), Robert Pasternak, (I), Elle Peek, (I),
George Poladian, (I), Mike Rodericks, (I), Meryl Rosner, (I),
Barry Ross, (I), Joanna Roy, (I), Glen Schofield, (I), Clare
Sieffert, (I), Tom Starrace, (I), John Suchy, (I), Steve Sullivan,
(I), Steve Sweny, (I), Glen Tarnowski, (I), Bill Teodecki, (I), Dana
Ventura, (I), Kurt Wallace, (I), Joanne Wanamaker, (I), Laura
Westlake, (I), Roger White, (I), Mary O'Keefe Young, (I)
Creative Workforce/568 Broadway 212-645-4885
Ashkan Sahihi, (P)
Cuevas, Robert/118 E 28th St #306 212-679-0622
James Joern, (P), Barnett Plotkin, (I)
Cullom, Ellen/55 E 9th St 212-777-1749
Robert Grant, (P)

D

Dagrosa, Terry/12 E 22nd St 212-254-4254
Davies, Nora/370 E 76th St #C103 212-628-6657
Halley Ganges, (P), Michael Pateman, (P)
Dedell, Jacqueline Inc/58 W 15th St 6th Fl 212-741-2539
Cathie Bleck, (I), Ivan Chermayeff, (I), Teresa Fasolino, (I),
David Frampton, (I), Griesbach/Martucci , (I), Hiroko, (I), Paula
Munck, (I), Edward Parker, (I), Ivan Powell, (I), Keith Richens,
(I), Barry Root, (I), Kimberly B Root, (I), Isadore Seltzer, (I),
Mick Wiggins, (I), Richard Williams, (I)
Des Verges, Diana/73 Fifth Ave 212-691-8674
Paccione Photography, (P)
DeVito, Kitty/43 E 30th St 14th Fl 212-889-9670
DiBartolo/Lemkowitz/310 Madison Ave 212-297-0041
Chris Collins, (P), George Hausman, (P), Steve Krongard, (P),
Gary Kufner, (P), Robert Mizono, (P), Michael O'Neill, (P),
James Porto, (P)
DiParisi, Peter/250 W 99th St #3A 212-663-8330
Gary Buss, (P), Ellen Denuto, (P), Lucille Khornack, (P), Cyndy
Warwick, (P)
Donner & Co, Tracey/444 E 82nd St #6L 212-737-5549
Dorman, Paul/430 E 57th St 212-826-6737
Studio DGM, (P)
Dorr, Chuck/45 W 21st St #6A 212-627-9871
Robert Carroll, (P)
Drexler, Sharon/451 Westminster Rd, Brooklyn 718-284-4779
Les Katz, (I)
DuCane, Alex/111 E 64th St 212-772-2840
Tony Kent, (P), Niel Kirk, (P), Cheryl Koralik, (P), Christopher
Micaud, (P), Maria Robledo, (P)

E

Edwards, Libby/1650 Third Ave #4A 212-534-6688
Elliott Banfield, (I), Mario Belcastro, (I), Patricia Cullen Clark,
(I), Michael Donato, (I), Vilma Ortiz, (I)
Enright, Catherine/106 E 81st St 212-288-0249
Erlacher, Bill/Artists Assoc/211 E 51st St #5F 212-755-1365
Michael Deas, (I), Mark English, (I), Alex Gnidziejko, (I), Dick
Krepel, (I), Fred Otnes, (I), Daniel Schwartz, (I), Norman Walker, (I)
Eyre, Susan/292 Marlboro Rd, Brooklyn 718-282-5034

F

Feinstein, Ron/312 E 9th St 212-353-8100

Feldman, Robert/133 W 17th St #5A 212-243-7319
Brian Hagiwara, (P), Alen MacWeeney, (P), Elizabeth Naples, (P), Terry Niefield, (P)
Fischer, Bob/135 E 54th St...212-755-2131
Alex Chatelain, (P), James Moore, (P)
Fishback, Lee/350 W 21st St...212-929-2951
AEL , (I)
Folio Reps/450 Seventh Ave #902...212-268-1788
Syd Brak, (I), Nick Cudworth, (I), Stanislaw Fernandez, (I), David Juniper, (I), Jean-Christian Knaff, (I), Gary Long, (I), John Mac, (I), James Marsh, (I), Ean Taylor, (I), Mike Terry, (I), George Underwood, (I), Povl Webb, (I), Ray Winder, (I)
Ford, Walter/86-21 60th Rd #4, Rego Park 718-397-9087
Ron Elstadt, (I), Wilfred Spoon, (I), Bill Vann, (I)
Foster, Pat/6 E 36th St #1R..212-685-4580
Keith Birdsong, (I), Dru Blair, (I), Ken Otsuka, (I)
Foster, Peter/870 UN Plaza..212-593-0793
Donald Penny, (P), Charles Tracey, (P)
Friess, Susan/36 W 20th St..212-675-3033
Richard Goldman, (P)
Friscia, Salmon/20 W 10th St..212-228-4134
Daniel Sussman, (P)

G

Gaynin, Gail/241 Central Park West 212-580-3141
Terry Clough, (P)
Gebbia, Doreen/312 W 88th St #2R..212-496-1279
Bruce Plotkin, (P)
Ginsberg/Kirk/407 Park Ave S #25F...212-679-8881
Godfrey, Dennis/231 W 25th St #6E..212-807-0840
Jeffrey Adams, (I), Daryl Cagle, (I), Joel Nakamura, (I), Wendy Popp, (I), David Stimson, (I)
Goldman, David Agency/41 Union Sq W #918..................................212-807-6627
Michele Barnes, (I), Norm Bendell, (I), Keith Bendis, (I), Jay Brenner, (P), John Paul Endress, (P), Mitchell Rigie, (I), David Rosso, (I), James Yang, (I), Kang Yi, (I)
Gomberg, Susan/41 Union Sq W #636 212-206-0066
Neil Brennan, (I), Colin Brown, (I), Steve Carver, (I), Robert Dale, (I), G Allen Garns, (I), Ralph Giguere, (I), Franklin Hammond, (I), Fran Hardy, (I), Jacobson/Fernandez , (I), Jeff Leedy, (I), Daniel McGowan, (I), Messi & Schmidt, (I), Marti Shohet, (I), James Tughan, (I), Mark Weakley, (I)
Goodwin, Phyllis A/10 E 81st St 212-570-6021
Whistl'n Dixie, (I), Carl Furuta, (P), Howard Menken, (P), Carl Zapp, (P)
Gordon, Barbara Assoc/165 E 32nd St..212-686-3514
Craig Bakley, (I), Ron Barry, (I), Bob Clarke, (I), James Dietz, (I), Jim Dietz, (I), Wendy Grossman, (I), Glenn Harrington, (I), Robert Hunt, (I), Nenad Jakesevic, (I), Jackie Jasper, (I), Elizabeth Kenyon, (I), Sonja Lamut, (I), William Maughn, (I), Roy McKie, (I), Jackie Vaux, (I)
Gotham Art Agency/1123 Broadway #600..212-989-2737
Manuel Boix, (I), Petra Mathers, (I), JJ Sempe, (I), Peter Sis, (I), Tomi Ungerer, (I), F K Waechter, (P)
Grande, Carla/444 W 52nd St 212-977-9214
John Dugdale, (P), Helen Norman, (I)
Grant, Lucchi/800 West End Ave #15C...212-663-1460
Green, Anita/718 Broadway 212-674-4788
Rita Maas, (P), Michael Molkenthin, (P)
Grien, Anita/155 E 38th St 212-697-6170
Dolores Bego, (I), Fanny Mellet Berry, (I), Julie Johnson, (I), Hal Just, (I), Jerry McDaniel, (I), Don Morrison, (I), Alan Reingold, (I), Alex "Mangal" Zwarenstein, (I)

H

Hajjar, Rene/240 E 27th St...212-685-0679
Chris Jones, (P)
Handelman, H Lee/77 Fifth Ave 212 645-7946
Moshe Brakha, (P)
Hankins + Tegenborg Ltd/60 E 42nd St #1940...................................212-867-8092
Peter Attard, (I), Bob Berran, (I), Ralph Brillhart, (I), Joe Burleson, (I), George Bush, (I), Michael Cassidy, (I), Frederico Castelluccio, (I), Jamie Cavaliere, (I), Jim Cherry, (I), Mac Conner, (I), John Dawson, (I), Guy Deel, (I), Chris Dellorco, (I), Ron DiScensa, (I), John Taylor Dismukes, (I), Bill Dodge, (I), Danilo Ducak, (I), Marc Ericksen, (I), Robert Evans, (I),

George Fernandez, (I), David Gaadt, (I), Steve Gardner, (I), James Griffin, (I), Ray Harvey, (I), Edwin Herder, (I), Michael Herring, (I), Kevin Hulsey, (I), Aleta Jenks, (I), Rick Johnson, (I), Mia Joung, (I), Tom Kasperski, (I), Dave Kilmer, (I), Uldis Klavins, (I), Richard Lauter, (I), Bob Maguire, (I), John Mazzini, (I), Neal McPheeters, (I), Cliff Miller, (I), Wendell Minor, (I), Miro, (I), Mitzura, (I), Sam Montesano, (I), Jeffery Oh, (I), Greg Olanoff, (I), Matt Peak, (I), Walter Rane, (I), Kirk Reinert, (I), Frank Riley, (I), Don Rodell, (I), Sergio Roffo, (I), Kenneth Rosenberg, (I), Ron Runda, (I), Peter Van Ryzin, (I), Harry Schaare, (I), Bill Schmidt, (I), Diane Slavec, (I), Dan Sneberger, (I), Frank Steiner, (I), Robert Travers, (I), Bob Trondsen, (I), Victor R Valla, (I), Jeff Walker, (I), Romeo Washington, (I), John Youssi, (I)
Hansen, Wendy/126 Madison Ave...212-684-7139
Metin Enderi, (P), Minh , (P), Masaaki Takenaka, (P)
Head, Olive/155 Riverside Dr #10C...212-580-3323
Lauren Hammer, (P), Nesti Mendoza, (P)
Henderson, Akemi/44 W 54th St...212-581-3630
Phil Cantor, (P), Hitoshi Fugo, (P), Sonia Katchian, (P), Rei Ohara, (P), Atsuko Ohtsuka, (P), Bob Osborn, (P), Liu Chung Ren, (P), Toshiro Yoshida, (P)
Henry & Co/272 Park Ave 47th Fl 212-586-8762
Henry, John/237 E 31st St...212-686-6883
Lane (Ms) Berkwit, (P), Lois Greenfield, (P), Irutchka, (P)
Herron, Pat/80 Madison Ave 212-753-0462
Larry Dale Gordon, (P), Hiro, (P), Malcolm Kirk, (P)
Heyl, Fran/230 Park Ave #2525 212-581-6470
Hill, Lilian/107 W 25th St #3A...212-627-5460
Holmberg, Irmeli/280 Madison Ave #1402 212-545-9155
Toyce Anderson, (I), Lee Lee Brazeal, (I), Dan Bridy, (I), Robert Byrd, (I), Lindy Chambers, (I), Hank Haselaar, (I), Deborah Healy, (I), Stephen Johnson, (I), Sue Llewellyn, (I), John Martinez, (I), Lu Matthews, (I), Marilyn Montgomery, (I), Cyd Moore, (I), John Nelson, (I), Ann Neuman, (I), Jacqueline Osborn, (I), Deborah Pinkney, (I), Nikolai Punin, (I), Bob Radigan, (I), Donald Ranaldi, (I), Bill Rieser, (I), Lilla Rogers, (I), Joel Spector, (I), Randie Wasserman, (I)
Holtzberg, Diana/166 Second Ave #11K...212-829-9838
Ori Hofmekler, (I)
Hovde, Nob/1438 Third Ave 212-753-0462
Larry Dale Gordon, (P),Hiro , (P), Malcolm Kirk, (P)
Hurewitz, Gary/38 Greene St..212-925-2999
Howard Berman, (P), Steve Bronstein, (P)
Husak, John/236 W 26th St #805...212-463-7025
Frank Marchese, (G), William Sloan, (I)

IJ

Iglesias, Jose/1123 Broadway #1113 212-929-7962
Stan Fellerman, (P), John Uher, (P)
In Focus Assoc/21 E 40th St #903..212-779-3600
Andrew Eccles, (P), Carol Ford, (P), Robert Jefferds, (P), Jeff McNamara, (P)
Italia, Mark/648 Broadway #401 212-353-8975
New Media Design, (I), Arden von Hager, (I), Van Howell, (I), Izumi Inoue, (I), David Lovatt Smith, (I), Ted Wright, (I)
Ivy League of Artists/156 Fifth Ave #617...212-243-1333
Ernest Albanese, (I), Cheryl Chalmers, (I), William Colrus, (I), Joseph Dawes, (I), Richard DelRossi, (I), John Dyess, (I), Paula Goodman, (I), Mark Hannon, (I), Tad Krumeich, (I), Chris Murphy, (I), Justin Novack, (I), Frederick Porter, (I), Tom Powers, (I), Tanya Rebelo, (I), Herb Reed, (I), John Rice, (I), Allison Staffin, (I), B K Taylor, (I), Kyuzo Tsugami, (I), Allen Welkis, (I), Debora Whitehouse, (I)
Jedell, Joan/370 E 76th St...212-861-7861
George Agalias, (P), David Hecker, (P)
Johnson, Arlene/5 E 19th St 212-725-4520
Johnson, Bud & Evelyne/201 E 28th St..212-532-0928
Wayne Alfano, (I), Kathy Allert, (I), Betty de Araujo, (I), Irene Astrahan, (I), Cathy Beylon, (I), Lisa Bonforte, (I), Carolyn Bracken, (I), Roberta Collier, (I), Frank Daniel, (I), Larry Daste, (I), Betty DeAraujo, (I), Jill Dubin, (I), Carolyn Ewing, (I), Bill Finewood, (I), George Ford, (I), Robert Gunn, (I), Erasmo Hernandez, (I), Tien Ho, (I), Mei-ku Huang, (I), Yukio Kondo, (I), Tom LaPadula, (I), Leonard Lubin, (I), Turi MacCombie, (I), Darcy May, (I), Eileen McKeating, (I), John O'Brien, (I), Heidi

Petach, (I), Steven Petruccio, (I), Frank Remkiewicz, (I), Christopher Santoro, (I), Stan Skardinski, (I), Barbara Steadman, (I), Tom Tierney, (I)
Joyce, Tricia/342 W 84th St 212-724-4590
Reuven Afanador, (P), Michael Biondo, (P)

K

Kahn, Harvey Assoc Inc/14 E 52nd St 212-752-8490
Bernie Fuchs, (I), Nick Gaetano, (I), Gerald Gersten, (I), Robert Peak, (I), Bill Sienkiewicz, (I)
Kane, Odette/236 W 27th St 10th Fl 212-807-8730
Richard Atlan, (I), Maria Perez, (I), Charles Seesselberg, (P)
Kaplan, Holly/43 Crosby St 212-925-2929
Bruno , (P)
Kauss, Jean-Gabriel/235 E 40th St 212-370-4300
Gianpaolo Barbieri, (P), Rodger Duncan, (I), Jesse Gerstein, (P), Francois Halard, (P), Mark Hispard, (P), Dominique Isserman, (P), Thibault Jeanson, (P), Elizabeth Novick, (P), Isabel Snyder, (P), Lance Staedler, (P)
Kenney, John Assoc/145 E 49th St 212-758-4545
Gary Hanlon, (P), Elizabeth Heyert, (P)
Ketcham, Laurie/210 E 36th St #6C 212-481-9592
Lee Friedman, (P), David Hamsley, (P), Dick Nystrom, (P), Rudolph Vandommele, (P)
Ketchum, Laurie/210 E 36th St #6C 212-481-9592
Scott Clarke, (P), Rudolph Van Dommele, (P)
Kim/137 E 25th St 11 Fl 212-679-5628
Carl Shiraishi, (P)
Kimche, Tania/425 W 23rd St #10F 212-242-6367
Paul Blakey, (I), Kirk Caldwell, (I), Richard Goldberg, (I), Hom & Hom , (I), Rafal Olbinski, (I), Miriam Schottland, (I), E T Steadman, (I), Christopher Zacharow, (I)
Kirchoff-Wohlberg Inc/866 UN Plaza #525 212-644-2020
Angela Adams, (I), Bob Barner, (I), Esther Baron, (I), Maryjane Begin, (I), Liz Callen, (I), Steve Cieslawski, (I), Brian Cody, (I), Gwen Connelly, (I), Donald Cook, (I), Floyd Cooper, (I), Betsy Day, (I), Rae Ecklund, (I), Lois Ehlert, (I), Al Fiorentino, (I), Frank Fretz, (I), Jon Friedman, (I), Dara Goldman, (I), Jeremy Guitar, (I), Konrad Hack, (I), Ron Himler, (I), Rosekrans Hoffman, (I), Kathleen Howell, (I), Chris Kalle, (I), Mark Kelley, (I), Christa Kieffer, (I), Dora Leder, (I), Tom Leonard, (I), Susan Lexa, (I), Don Madden, (I), Susan Magurn, (I), Jane McCreary, (I), Lyle Miller, (I), Carol Nicklaus, (I), Sharon O'Neil, (I), Robin Oz, (I), Diane Paterson, (I), Jim Pearson, (I), J Brian Pinkney, (I), Charles Robinson, (I), Bronwen Ross, (I), Mary Beth Schwark, (I), Robert Gantt Steele, (I), Arvis Stewart, (I), Pat Traub, (I), Lou Vaccaro, (I), Joe Veno, (I), Alexandra Wallner, (I), John Wallner, (I), Arieh Zeldich, (I)
Klein, Leslie D/255 Sherman St, Brooklyn 718-438-7553
Klimt, Bill & Maurine/15 W 72nd St 212-799-2231
Randy Berrett, (I), Wil Cormier, (I), Jamie DeJesus, (I), Doug Gray, (I), Mark Heath, (I), Paul Henry, (I), Roger Leyonmark, (I), Jeffrey Lindberg, (I), Frank Morris, (I), Shusei Nagaoka, (I), Alan Neider, (I), Gary Penca, (I), Leonid Pinchevsky, (I), Bill Purdom, (I), Rob Sauber, (I), Mark Skolsky, (I), Carla Sormanti, (I), Susan Tang, (I), Greg Winters, (I)
Knight, Harrison/1043 Lexington Ave #4 212-288-9777
Barbara Campbell, (P)
Korman, Alison/95 Horatio St 212-633-8407
David Bishop, (P), Susan Kravis, (I)
Korn, Elaine Assoc/234 Fifth Ave 212-679-6739
Garry Gross, (P), Josh Haskins, (P), Klaus Laubmayer, (P), Francis Murphy, (P), Jim Wood, (P)
Korn, Pamela & Assoc/32 W 40th St #9B 212-819-9084
Brian Ajhar, (I), Wendy Braun, (I), Jeff Moores, (I), Kurt Vargo, (I)
Kramer, Ina/104 E 40th St #111 212-599-0435
Lewis Calver, (I), Sharon Ellis, (I), Ken & Carl Fischer, (P), Jeffrey Holewski, (I), Ellen G Jacobs, (I), Lauren Keswick, (I), Robert Margulies, (I), William Westwood, (I)
Kramer, Joan & Assoc/720 Fifth Ave 212-567-5545
Richard Apple, (P), Bill Bachmann, (P), Roberto Brosan, (P), David Cornwell, (P), Micheal DeVecka, (P), Clark Dunbar, (P), Stan Flint, (P), Stephen Frink, (P), Peter Kane, (P), John Lawlor, (P), Roger Marschutz, (P), James McLoughlin, (P), Ralph Merlino, (P), Frank Moscati, (P), Bill Nalton, (P), John Russell, (P), Ed Simpson, (P), Roger Smith, (P), Glen Steiner, (P), Janice Travia, (P), Ken Whitmore, (P), Gary Wunderwald, (P),

Edward Young, (P), Eric Zucker, (P)
Kreis, Ursula G/63 Adrian Ave, Bronx 212-562-8931
Bill Farrell, (P), George Kamper, (P)
Krongard, Paula/210 Fifth Ave #301 212-683-1020
Douglas Foulke, (P), Bill White, (P)

L

Lada, Joe/330 E 19th St 212-254-0253
Lalleman, Sylvan/340 E 51st St #10H 212-838-7180
Lamont, Mary/200 W 20th St 212-242-1087
Jim Marchese, (P)
Lander, Jane/333 E 30th St 212-679-1358
Mel Furukawa, (I), Helen Guetary, (I), Cathy Heck, (I), Frank Riley, (I)
Lane, Judy/444 E 82nd St 212-861-7225
Larkin, Mary/308 E 59th St 212-308-7744
Lynn St John, (P), Charles Masters, (P)
Lavaty, Frank & Jeff/509 Madison Ave 10th Fl 212-355-0910
John Berkey, (I), Jim Butcher, (I), Royd Crosthwaite, (I), Bernard D'Andrea, (I), Domenick D'Andrea, (I), Don Daily, (I), Michael Davis, (I), Donald Demers, (I), Roland DesCombes, (I), Chris Duke, (I), Bruce Emmett, (I), Gervasio Gallardo, (I), Tim Hildebrandt, (I), Martin Hoffman, (I), Stan Hunter, (I), Chet Jezierski, (I), David McCall Johnston, (I), Mort Kunstler, (I), Paul Lehr, (I), Lemuel Line, (I), Robert LoGrippo, (I), Darrel Millsap, (I), Carlos Ochagavia, (I), Ben Verkaaik, (I)
Lee, Alan/33 E 22nd St #5D 212-673-2484
Jim Barber, (P)
Leff, Jerry Assoc Inc/420 Lexington Ave #2760 212-697-8525
Franco Accornero, (I), Lisa Adams, (I), Ken Barr, (I), Tom & Greg Beecham, (I), Semyon Bilmes, (I), Alex Boies, (I), Ron Broda, (I), Bradford Brown, (I), Mike Bryan, (I), Michael Bull, (I), Brian Callanan, (I), Gwen Connelly, (I), Denise Chapman Crawford, (I), Joe DiCesare, (I), Ron DiCianni, (I), Bill Donovan, (I), Norm Eastman, (I), Lisa French, (I), Charles Gehm, (I), Penelope Gottlieb, (I), Kate Brennan Hall, (I), Richard High, (I), Terry Hoff, (I), Lars Justinen, (I), Lingta Kung, (I), Ron Lesser, (I), Francis Livingston, (I), Steven Mach, (I), Dennis Magdich, (I), Michele Manning, (I), Frank Marciuliano, (I), Alan Mazzetti, (I), Gary McLaughlin, (I), Celia Mitchell, (I), Rick Ormond, (I), John Parsons, (I), Kenn Richards, (I), Sue Rother, (I), Rob Ruppel, (I), John Sayles, (I), Jackie Snider, (I), Mary Thelen, (I), James Woodend, (I), Judy York, (I)
Legrand, Jean Yves/41 W 84th St #4 212-724-5981
Lehman, Patty/8 Gramercy Park S #6E 212-260-1768
John Fortunato, (P), David Harry Stewart, (P), Peter Zeray, (P)
Leone, Mindy/381 Park Ave S #710 212-696-5674
Bill Kouirinis, (P)
Leonian, Edith/220 E 23rd St 212-989-7670
Philip Leonian, (P)
Lerman, Gary/113 E 31st St #4D 212-683-5777
John Bechtold, (P), Jan Cobb, (P)
Levin, Bruce/231 E 58th St #22B 212-832-4053
Levy, Leila/4523 Broadway #7G 212-942-8185
David Bishop, (P), Yoav Levy, (P)
Lewin, Betsy/152 Willoughby Ave, Brooklyn 718-622-3882
Ted Lewin, (I)
LGI/241 W 36th St 7th Fl 212-736-4602
John Bellissimo, (P), Bruce Birmelin, (P), Jim Bridges, (P), Peter Dokus, (P), Douglas Dubler, (P), Lynn Goldsmith, (P), Todd Grey, (P), Stephen Harvey, (P), Marc Hauser, (P), Christopher Kehoe, (P), Richard Pasley, (P), Don Weinstein, (P)
Lindgren & Smith/41 Union Sq W #1228 212-929-5590
Julian Allen, (I), Barbara Banthien, (I), Bradley Clark, (I), David Dees, (I), Regan Dunnick, (I), Cameron Eagle, (I), Douglas Fraser, (I), Joe & Kathy Heiner, (I), Lori Lohstoeter, (I), Richard Mantel, (I), John Mattos, (I), Margo Nahas, (I), Kathy O'Brien, (I), Michael Paraskevas, (I), Judy Pedersen, (I), Charles S Pyle, (I), Tim Raglin, (I), Ed Sorel, (I), Robert Gantt Steele, (I), Cathleen Toelke, (I), Cynthia Torp, (I), Jean Wisenbaugh, (I), Darryl Zudeck, (I)
Liz-Li/260 Fifth Ave 212-889-7067
Bruce Davidson, (P), Martin Mistretta, (P), Roy Volkmann, (P)
Locke, John Studios Inc/15 E 76th St 212-288-8010
Tudor Banus, (I), John Cayea, (I), Andre Dahan, (I), Oscar DeMejo, (I), Jean-Pierre Desclozeaux, (I), James Endicott, (I), Jean Michel Folon, (I), Michael Foreman, (I), Andre Francois,

(I), George Giusti, (I), Edward Gorey, (I), Dale Gottlieb, (I), Catherine Kanner, (I), Peter Lippman, (I), Richard Oden, (I), William Bryan Park, (I), Robert Pryor, (I), Hans-Georg Raugh, (I), Fernando Puig Rosado, (I), Ronald Searle, (I), Peter Sis, (I), Roland Topor, (I), Carol Wald, (I)

Lott, Peter & George/60 E 42nd St #1146 212-953-7088
Juan C Barberis, (I), Ted Chambers, (I), Tony Cove, (I), David Halpern, (I), Keith Hoover, (P), Ed Kurtzman, (I), Eric J W Lee, (I), Wendell McClintock, (I), Mark Nagata, (I), Tim O'Brien, (I), Marie Peppard, (I), John Suh, (I), Barbara Tyler, (I)

Lynch, Alan & Colm/155 Ave of Americas 10th Fl 212-255-6530
Michael Armson, (I), John Clementson, (I), Stephen Hall, (I), John Harris, (I), Jane Human, (I), Daniel Torres, (I), Jenny Tylden-Wright, (I), Jim Warren, (I), Jane Woolley, (I), Janet Woolley, (I)

M

Manasse, Michele/16 W 75th St 2nd Fl 212-873-3797
Sheldon Greenberg, (I), Narda Lebo, (I), Wallop Manyum, (I), Roger Roth, (I), John Segal, (I), Terry Widener, (I)

Mandell, Ilene/61 E 86th St 212-860-3148

Mann & Dictenberg Reps/20 W 46th St 212-944-2853
Brian Lanker, (P), Al Satterwhite, (P), Ulf Skogsbergh, (P)

Marek & Assoc Inc/160 Fifth Ave #914 212-924-6760
Walter Chin, (P), Han Feurer, (P), Marco Glaviano, (P), Eddy Kohli, (P), Marie Josee Lafontaine, (MU), Just Loomis, (P), Deborah Turbeville, (P)

Marlon Inc/115 5th Ave #8C 212-777-5757
Piero Gemelli, (P), Christophe Jouany, (P)

Marshall, Mel & Edith/40 W 77th St 212-877-3921

Martin, Bruce Rough Riders/55 Mercer St 2nd Fl 212-219-1543

Mason, Kathy/111 W 19th St #2E 212-675-3809
Don Mason, (P)

Mason, Pauline/267 Wycoff St, Brooklyn 718-624-1906
Clifford Harper, (I), Peter Knock, (I), Peter Till, (I)

Mattelson Assoc/37 Cary Rd, Great Neck, NY 212-684-2974
Karen Kluglein, (I), Marvin Mattelson, (I)

McKay, Colleen/229 E 5th St #2 212-598-0469
Marili Forastieri, (P), Lilo Raymond, (P), Robert Tardio, (P)

Mendola Ltd/420 Lexington Ave #PH4,5 212-986-5680
Gus Alavezos, (I), Paul R Alexander, (I), Steve Brennan, (I), David Bull, (I), Jim Campbell, (I), Ellis Chappell, (I), Garry Colby, (I), Jim Deneen, (I), Vincent DiFate, (I), John Eggert, (I), Dominick Finelle, (I), Phil Franke, (I), Hector Garrido, (I), Elaine Gignilliat, (I), Chuck Gillies, (I), Dale Gustafson, (I), Chuck Hamrick, (I), Attila Hejja, (I), Dave Henderson, (I), Mitchell Hooks, (I), James Ibusuki, (I), Bill James, (I), Bob Jones, (I), Dean Kennedy, (I), Alfons Kiefer, (I), Joyce Kitchell, (I), Michael Koester, (I), Ashley Lonsdale, (I), Dennis Luzak, (I), Jeffrey Lynch, (I), Jeffrey Mangiat, (I), Edward Martinez, (I), Bill Maughan, (I), Geoffrey McCormack, (I), Mark McMahon, (I), Ann Meisel, (I), Roger Metcalf, (I), Ted Michener, (I), Mike Mikos, (I), William Miller, (I), Tom Newsome, (I), Chris Notarile, (I), Peter Pioppo, (P), RadenStudio, (I), Delro Rosco, (I), Robert Sauber, (I), Brian Sauriol, (I), David Schleinkofer, (I), Bill Silvers, (I), Mike Smollin, (I), Kipp Soldwedel, (I), John Solie, (I), Cliff Spohn, (I), Robert Tanenbaum, (I), Jeffrey Terreson, (I), Thierry Thompson, (I), Stan Wan, (P), Mark Watts, (I), Mike Wimmer, (I), Ben Wohlberg, (I), David Womersley, (I)

Mennemeyer, Ralph/286 Fifth Ave 4th Fl 212-279-2838
Beth Baptiste, (P), Paul Christensen, (P), Katrina , (P), Ted Morrison, (P), Steve Robb, (P)

Miller, Jessica/24 W 30th St 9th Fl 212-213-1195
Valerie Curry, (P), Steve Landis, (P)

Miller, Susan/1641 Third Ave #29A 212-427-9604
Desmond Burdon, (I), Ainslie MacLeod, (I), Bill Robbins, (I), Richard Hamilton Smith, (I), David Zimmerman, (P)

Mintz, Les/111 Wooster St #PH C 212-925-0491
Istvan Banyai, (I), Robert Bergin, (I), Bernard Bonhomme, (I), Grace DeVito, (I), Curt Doty, (I), Mark Fisher, (I), Mark S Fisher, (I), Amy Hill, (I), Shirley Kaneda, (I), Bobbie Moline Kramer, (I), Elizabeth Lennard, (I), Roberta Ludlow, (I), David Lui, (I), Julia McLain, (I), Burton Morris, (I), Rodica Prato, (I), Karen Socolow, (I), Tommy Soloski, (I), Barton Stabler, (I), Maria Stroster, (I), Sarah Waldron, (I), Dennis Ziemienski, (I)

Monaco Reps/280 Park Ave S 212-979-5533
Jeff Berlin, (P), Hans Gissinger, (P), Frank Hom, (P), Roger Neve, (P), John Peden, (P), Danny Sit, (P), Otto Stupakoff, (P)

Morgan, Vicki Assoc/194 Third Ave 212-475-0440
Nanette Biers, (I), Ray Cruz, (I), Patty Dryden, (I), Vivienne Flesher, (I), Bob Hickson, (I), Joyce Patti, (I), Ward Schumacher, (I), Joanie Schwarz, (I), Kirsten Soderlind, (I), Nancy Stahl, (I), Steam/Dave Willardson , (I), Dahl Taylor, (I), Willardson + Assoc, (I), Bruce Wolfe, (I), Wendy Wray, (I), Brian Zick, (I)

Moscato, Lynn/118-14 83rd Ave #5B, Kew Gardens.....................718-805-0069

Mosel, Sue/310 E 46th St 212-599-1806

Moses, Janice/155 E 31st St #20H...............................212-7929
Chris Sanders, (P)

Moskowitz, Marion/342 Madison Ave #469 212-719-9879
Dianne Bennett, (I), Diane Teske Harris, (I), Arnie Levin, (I), Geoffrey Moss, (I)

Moss & Meixler/36 W 37th St 212-868-0078
Suzanne Buckler, (P), Leon Lecash, (P), Louis Mervar, (P)

Moss, Eileen & Nancy Bruck/333 E 49th St #3J 212-980-8061
Tom Curry, (I), Warren Gebert, (I), Joel Peter Johnson, (I), Lionsgate , (I), Adam Niklewicz, (I), Pamela Patrick, (I), Ben Perini, (I), Robert Pizzo, (I), Scott Pollack, (I)

Muth, John/37 W 26th St 212-532-3479
Pat Hill, (P)

N

Neail, Pamela R Assoc/27 Bleecker St 212-673-1600
Steven Alexander, (I), Margaret Brown, (I), Sean Daly, (I), Gregory Dearth, (I), David Guinn, (I), Celeste Henriquez, (I), Thea Kliros, (I), Michele Laporte, (I), Marina Levikova, (I), Tony Mascio, (I), Peter McCaffrey, (I), Cary McKiver, (I), CB Mordan, (I), Manuel Nunez, (I), Brenda Pepper, (I), Janet Recchia, (I), Linda Richards, (I), Kenneth Spengler, (I), Glenn Tunstull, (I), Jenny Vainisi, (I), Vicki Yiannias, (I), Pat Zadnik, (I)

Network Representatives/206 W 15th St 4th Fl 212-727-0044
Marc Anthony, (P), Ross Whitaker, (P)

Newborn, Milton/135 E 54th St 212-421-0050
John Alcorn, (I), Stephen Alcorn, (I), Braldt Bralds, (I), Robert Giusti, (I), Dick Hess, (I), Mark Hess, (I), Victor Juhasz, (I), Simms Taback, (I), David Wilcox, (I)

OP

O'Rourke-Page Assoc/219 E 69th St #11G 212-772-0346
Honolulu Crtv Grp, (P), Sam Haskins, (P), Lincoln Potter, (P), Jim Raycroft, (P), Eric Schweikardt, (P), Smith/Garner, (P), William Sumner, (P), John Thornton, (P), Gert Wagner, (P), John Zimmerman, (P)

Onyx/110 Greene St #804 212-925-5440
Max Aguilera, (P), Eika Aoshima, (P), Fredrich Cantor, (P), Nancy Ellison, (P), Darryl Estrine, (P), Michael Garland, (P), D Gorton, (P), Mark Hanauer, (P), Bonnie Lewis, (P), Aaron Rapoport, (P), Joyce Ravid, (P), Tim Redel, (P), Philip Saltonstall, (P), Bonnie Schiffman, (P), Mark Sennet, (P), Brian Smale, (P), Davies & Starr, (P), David Strick, (P), Bob Wagoner, (P), Barbara Walz, (P), Timothy White, (P), Tom Wolff, (P), Firooz Zahedi, (P), Elizabeth Zeschin, (P)

The Organisation/267 Wyckoff St, Brooklyn 718-624-1906
Grahame Baker, (I), Enikoe Bakti, (I), Zafer Baran, (I), Roy Castle, (I), Yvonne Chambers, (I), Emma Chichester Clark, (I), Maxwell Dorsey, (I), David Eaton, (I), Mark Entwisle, (I), Michael Frith, (I), Peter Goodfellow, (I), Glyn Goodwin, (I), Neil Gower, (I), Susan Hellard, (I), Leslie Howell, (I), Nicholas Hutchinson, (I), Natacha Ledwidge, (I), Michael McCabe, (I), Alan Morrison, (I), Katherine Mynott, (I), Lawrence Mynott, (I), Michael O'Shaughnessy, (I), Guy Passey, (I), Janet Pontin, (I), Fred Preston, (I), Ruth Rivers, (I), Max Schindler, (I), Jayne Simkins, (I), Linda Smith, (I), Amanda Ward, (I), Nadine Wickenden, (I)

Palmer-Smith, Glenn Assoc/104 W 70th St 212-769-3940
Jim Brill, (P), Charles Nesbitt, (P)

Parallax Artist's Reps/350 Fifth Ave 212-695-0445
Hilmar Meyer-Bosse, (P), Pauline St Denis, (P)

Penny & Stermer Group/31 W 21st St 7th Fl Rear.......................212-243-4412
Manos Angelakis, (F), Doug Archer, (I), Ron Becker, (I), Scott Gordley, (I), Mike Hodges, (I), Michael Hostovich, (I), Don Kahn, (I), Julia Noonan, (I), Thomas Payne, (I), Deborah Bazzel Pogue, (I), Terri Starrett, (I), James Turgeon, (I), Judy Unger, (I)

Petrie, Jack/28 Vesey St #2213 212-301-5196
Stan Ellerman, (P), Gary Hanlon, (P)

Photography Bureau/400 Lafayette St #4G....................212-255-3333
Pierce, Jennifer/1376 York Ave 212-744-3810
Pinkstaff, Marsha/25 W 81st St 15th Fl.................212-246-2300
Neal Barr, (P), Mark Weiss, (P), Peter Zander, (P)
Polizzi, Antonia/125 Watts St 212-925-1571
Pritchett, Tom/130 Barrow St #316....................212-688-1080
George Kanelous, (I), George Parrish, (I), Terry Ryan, (I)
Pushpin Assoc/215 Park Ave S #1300..................212-674-8080
Sergio Baradat, (I), Gary Baseman, (I), Lou Beach, (I), Eve
Chwast, (I), Seymour Chwast, (I), Robert Crawford, (I), Alicia
Czechowski, (I), Dave Jonason, (I), Hiro Kimura, (I), Frank Miller,
(I), R Kenton Nelson, (I), Roy Pendleton, (I), George Stavrinos, (I)

R

Rapp, Gerald & Cullen Inc/108 E 35th St #1C 212-889-3337
Ray Ameijide, (I), Emmanuel Amit, (I), Michael David Brown, (I),
Lon Busch, (I), Ken Dallison, (I), Jack Davis, (I), Bob
Deschamps, (I), Bill Devlin, (I), Ray Domingo, (I), Lee Duggan,
(I), Dynamic Duo Studio, (I), Randy Glass, (I), Lionel Kalish, (I),
Tak Kojima, (P), Laszlo Kubinyi, (I), Sharmen Liao, (I), Lee
Lorenz, (I), Allan Mardon, (I), Hal Mayforth, (I), Elwyn Mehlman,
(I), Alex Murawski, (I), Lou Myers, (I), Bob Peters, (I), Jerry
Pinkney, (I), Camille Przewodek, (I), Charles Santore, (I), Steve
Spelman, (P), Drew Struzan, (I), Michael Witte, (I)
Ravis, Sara/33 Bleecker St 2nd Fl 212-777-0847
Ray, Marlys/350 Central Pk W............................212-222-7680
Bill Ray, (P)
Reactor Worldwide Inc/227 W 29th St #9R..............212-967-7699
Jamie Bennett, (I), Federico Botana, (I), Henrik Drescher, (I),
Gail Geltner, (I), Steven Guarnaccia, (I), Jeff Jackson, (I), Jerzy
Kolacz, (I), Ross MacDonald, (I), James Marsh, (I), Simon Ng,
(I), Tomio Nitto, (I), Bill Russell, (I), Joe Salina, (I), Jean Tuttle,
(I), Maurice Vellekoop, (I), Rene Zamic, (I)
Reese, Kay Assoc/225 Central Park West...............212-799-1133
Gerry Cranham, (P), Ashvin Gatha, (P), Arno Hammacher, (P),
Simpson Kalisher, (P), Jay Leviton, (P), George Long, (P), Jon
Love, (P), Lynn Pelham, (P), Milkie Studio, (P), T Tanuma, (P)
Reid, Pamela/66 Crosby St.............................212-925-5909
Thierry des Fontaines, (P), Bettina Rheims, (P), Bert Stern, (P)
Renard Represents/501 Fifth Ave #1407................212-490-2450
Steve Bjorkman, (I), Joseph Cellini, (I), Rob Day, (I), Glenn
Dean, (I), Carol Donner, (I), Bart Forbes, (I), Dan Garrow, (I), Tim
Girvin, (I), Jud Guitteau, (I), William Harrison, (I), Jane Hurd, (I),
Hideaki Kodama, (I), John Martin, (I), Wayne McLoughlin, (I),
Richard Newton, (I), Robert Rodriguez, (I), Theo Rudnak, (I),
Maso Saito, (I), Kazuhiko Sano, (I), Michael Schwab, (I), Doug
Struthers, (I), Jozef Sumichrast, (I), Kim Whitesides, (I)
Rep Rep/211 Thompson St #1E..........................212-475-5911
Rob Fraser, (P), Marcus Tullis, (P)
Ridgeway, Karen/330 W 42nd St #3200NE..............212-714-0130
Ron Ridgeway, (I)
Riley Illustration/81 Greene St.........................212-925-3053
Bill Benoit, (I), Quentin Blake, (I), William Bramhall, (I), CESC,
(I), Paul Degen, (I), Chris DeMarest, (I), Jeffrey Fisher, (I), Paul
Hogarth, (I), Benoit Van Innis, (I), Pierre Le-Tan, (I), Paul
Meisel, (I), Jim Parkinson, (I), Cheryl Peterson, (I), J J Sempe,
(I), David Small, (I)
Riley, Catherine/12 E 37th St...........................212-532-8326
Jon Riley, (P)
Robinson, Madeline/31 W 21st St.......................212-243-3138
Russell Kirk, (P), Chuck Kuhn, (P), Michel Tcherevkoff, (P)
Roman, Helen Assoc/140 West End Ave #9H.............212-874-7074
Lou Carbone, (I), Roger T De Muth, (I), Mena Dolobowsky, (I),
Naiad Einsel, (I), Walter Einsel, (I), Myron Grossman, (I), Jeff
Lloyd, (I), Sandra Marziali, (I), Andrea Mistretta, (I)
Rudoff, Stan/271 Madison Ave.........................212-679-8780
David Hamilton, (P), Gideon Lewin, (P)

S

S I International/43 East 19th St........................212-254-4996
Jack Brusca, (I), Oscar Chichoni, (I), Daniela Codarcea, (I),
Richard Corben, (I), Richard Courtney, (I), Bob Cowan, (I), Robin
Cuddy, (I), Dennis Davidson, (I), Allen Davis, (I), Andre Debarros,
(I), Ted Enik, (I), Fernando Fernandez, (I), Blas Gallego, (I),
Vicente Gonzalez, (I), Mel Grant, (I), Devis Grebu, (I), Oscar Guell,
(I), Steve Haefele, (I), Sherri Hoover, (I), Susi Kilgore, (I), Richard

Leonard, (I), Sergio Martinez, (I), Fred Marvin, (I), Francesc
Mateu, (I), Jose Miralles, (I), Isidre Mones, (I), Steve Parton, (I),
Joan Pelaez, (I), Jordi Penalva, (I), Vince Perez, (I), Martin Rigo,
(I), Melodye Rosales, (I), Eve Rose, (I), Doug Rosenthal, (I),
Vicente Roso, (I), Artie Ruiz, (I), Paul Tatore, (I), Paul Wenzel, (I)
Sacramone, Dario/302 W 12th St........................212-929-0487
Tohru Nakamura, (P), Marty Umans, (P)
Samuels, Rosemary/14 Prince St #5E....................212-477-3567
Beth Galton, (P), Chris Sanders, (P)
Sander, Vicki/155 E 29th St #28G.......................212-683-7835
John Manno, (P)
Santa-Donato, Paul/25 W 39th St #1001.................212-921-1550
Satterwhite, Joy/80 Varick St #7B.......................212-219-0808
Al Satterwhite, (P)
Saunders, Gayle/145 E 36th St #2......................212-481-3860
Steven Klein, (P), Tiziano Magni, (P), Michael O'Brien, (P)
Saunders, Michele/84 Riverside Dr #5..................212-496-0268
Ricardo Bertancourt, (P), David Hamilton, (P), Uwe Ommer, (P)
Schecter Group, Ron Long/212 E 49th St...............212-752-4400
Scher, Dotty/235 E 22nd St............................212-689-7273
Harry Benson, (P), Marty Jacobs, (P), David Katzenstein, (P),
Denis Waugh, (P)
Schneider, Jonathan/175 Fifth Ave #2291................212-459-4325
Dennis Dittrich, (I), Mike Kreffel, (I), Adam Max, (I), Harley
Schwadron, (I), Steve Smallwood, (I), Jay Taylor, (I)
Schochat, Kevin R/150 E 18th St #14N...................212-475-7068
Thom DeSanto, (P), Mark Ferri, (P)
Schub, Peter & Robert Bear/136 E 57th #1702 212-246-0679
Robert Freson, (P), Irving Penn, (P), Rico Puhlmann, (P)
Seigel, Fran/515 Madison Ave 22nd Fl..................212-486-9644
Kinuko Craft, (I), John Dawson, (I), Catherine Deeter, (I), Lars
Hokanson, (I), Mirko Ili'c, (I), Earl Keleny, (I), Larry McEntire, (I),
Michael Vernaglia, (I)
Shamilzadeh, Sol/214 E 24th St #3D....................212-532-1977
Rick Muller, (P), The Strobe Studio, (P)
Sharlowe Assoc/275 Madison Ave.......................212-288-8910
Claus Eggers, (P), Nesti Mendoza, (P)
Sheer, Doug/59 Grand St..............................212-274-8446
Siegel, Tema/234 Fifth Ave 4th Fl.......................212-696-4680
Loretta Krupinski, (I)
Sigman, Joan/336 E 54th St............................212-832-7980
Robert Goldstrom, (I), John H Howard, (I)
Smith, Emily/30 E 21st St..............................212-674-8383
Jeff Smith, (P)
Solomon, Richard/121 Madison Ave.....................212-683-1362
Kent Barton, (I), Thomas Blackshear, (), Steve Brodner, (I),
John Collier, (I), Paul Cox, (I), Jack E Davis, (F), David A
Johnson, (I), Gary Kelley, (I), Bill Nelson, (I), C. F. Payne, (I),
Douglas Smith, (I), Mark Summers, (I)
Stein, Jonathan & Assoc/353 E 77th St..................212-517-3648
Mitch Epstein, (P), Burt Glinn, (P), Ernst Haas, (P), Nathaniel
Lieberman, (P), Alex McLean, (P), Gregory Murphey, (P), Joel
Sternfeld, (P), Roy Wright, (P), Jeffrey Zaruba, (P)
Stevens, Norma/1075 Park Ave.........................212-427-7235
Richard Avedon, (P)
Stockland-Martel Inc/5 Union Sq W 6th Fl...............212-727-1400
Joel Baldwin, (P), Hank Benson, (P), Richard Corman, (P),
Anthony Gordon, (P), Tim Greenfield-Sanders, (P), Hashi, (P),
Walter Iooss, (P), Nadav Kander, (P), Eric Meola, (P), Sheila
Metzner, (P), Tim Mitchell, (P), Claude Mougin, (P), Michael
Pruzan, (P), Bruce Wolf, (P)
Stockwell, Jehremy/307 W 82nd St/Box C................212-595-5757
Michael Conway, (I)
Stogo, Donald/310 E 46th St...........................212-490-1034
Tom Grill, (P), John Lawlor, (P), Tom McCarthy, (P), Manuel
Morales, (I), David Stoecklein, (P), Peter Vaeth, (P)

TUV

Thomas, Pamela/254 Park Ave S #5D....................212-529-4033
Tise, Katherine/200 E 78th St..........................212-570-9069
Raphael Boguslav, (I), John Burgoyne, (I), Bunny Carter, (I),
Judy Pelikan, (I)
Tralongo, Katrin/144 W 27th St.........................212-255-1976
Mickey Kaufman, (P)
Turk, Melissa/370 Lexington Ave #1002 212-953-2177
Juan Barberis, (I), Barbara Bash, (I), Susan Johnston Carlson,
(I), Paul Casale, (I), Robert Frank, (I), Wendy Smith-Griswold, (I)

Umlas, Barbara/131 E 93rd St..212-534-4008
Hunter Freeman, (P), Nora Scarlett, (P)
Vallon, Arlene/47-37 45th St #4K, Long Island Clty.........................718-706-8112
Van Arnam, Lewis/881 7th Ave #405.....................................212-541-4787
Paul Amato, (P), Mike Reinhardt, (P)
Van Orden, Yvonne/119 W 57th St..212-265-1223
Visages /560 Broadway #407..212-541-7550
Trel Brock, (P), Gwendolyn Cates, (P), Chris Cuffaro, (P),
Nicola Dill, (P), Ruedi Hofmann, (P), Paul Jasmin, (P), Laura
Levine, (P), Blake Little, (P), Jim McHugh, (P), Thierry Mugler,
(P), Albane Navizet, (P), Dewey Nicks, (P), Albert Sanchez,
(P), Thomas Schenk, (P), Michael Tighe, (P)
Von Schreiber, Barbara/315 Central Park West #4N.....................212-580-7044
Josef Astor, (P), Oberto Gili, (P), Erica Lennard, (P), Dennis
Manarchy, (P), Sarah Moon, (P), Jean Pagliuso, (P), Neal Slavin, (P)

WYZ

Ward, Wendy/200 Madison Ave #2402 212-684-0590
Mel Odom, (I)
Wasserman, Ted/51 E 42nd St...212-867-5360
Michael Englert, (P), Steven Green-Armytage, (P)
Wayne, Philip/66 Madison Ave #9C.......................................212-696-5215
Denes Petoe, (P), Douglas Whyte, (P)
Weber, Tricia Group/125 W 77th St.......................................212-799-6532
Raul Colon, (I), Abe Gurvin, (I), Rick Lovell, (I), Bill Mayer, (I),
David McKelzey, (I), Pat Mollica, (I), John Robinette, (I), Jim
Salvati, (I), Danny Smythe, (I)
Weissberg, Elyse/299 Pearl St #5E..212-406-2566
Jack Reznicki, (P)
Wilson, Scott/160 Fifth Ave #818..212-633-0105
John Falocco, (P)
Yellen, Bert & Assoc/420 E 54th St #21E 212-838-3170
Bill Connors, (P), Jody Dale, (P), Harvey Edwards, (P), Robert
Farber, (P), Joe Francki, (P), Tim Geaney, (P), James
Robinson, (P), Olaf Wahlund, (P)
Young, Georgiana/200 E 94th St #904 212-410-1770
Deborah Attoinese, (P), David Lawrence, (P)

NORTHEAST

A

Ackermann, Marjorie/2112 Goodwin Lane, North Wales, PA.........215-646-1745
H Mark Weidman, (P)
Alfieux, Barbara/72 Williamson Ave, Hillside, NJ 201-923-0011
William Bennett, (P)
Anderson, Laurel/5-A Pirates Lane, Gloucester, MA.......................508-281-6880
John Curtis, (P)
Artco/227 Godfrey Rd, Weston, CT..203-222-8777
Ed Acuna, (I), Alexander & Turner , (I), George Angelini, (I),
Frank Bolle, (I), Gene Boyer, (I), Dan Brown, (I), Alain Chang,
(I), Anne Cook, (I), Jeff Cornell, (I), Bob Dacey, (I), Beau &
Alan Daniels, (I), Mort Drucker, (I), Lisa Falkenstern, (I), Ed
Gazsi, (I), Gary Glover, (I), Lisa Henderling, (I), Kathy Jeffers,
(I), David Loew, (I), Rick McCollum, (I), John Jude Palencar,
(I), Barry Phillips, (I), Al Pisano, (I), Jean Restivo, (I), Marcel
Rozenberg, (I), Mark Smollin, (), Leslie Szabo, (I), Brian Twede,
(I), Sally Vitsky, (I), Rob Zuckerman, (I)
The Art Source/444 Bedford Rd, Pleasantville, NY.........................914-747-2220
James Barkley, (I), Karen Baumann, (I), Larry Bernette, (I),
Paul Birling, (I), Vince Caputo, (I), Robert Cassila, (I), Betsy
Feeney, (I), Scott Gladden, (I), Robert Lee, (I), Robert Marinelli,
(I), Michael McGovern, (I), John Ramon, (I), Mary Rankin, (I),
Richard Rockwell, (I)
Artists International/7 Dublin Hill Dr, Greenwich, CT.....................203-869-8010
Tony Chen, (I), David Chestnut, (I), Bill Cleaver, (I), Eric
D'Zenis, (I), ino , (I), Michael Hampshire, (I), John Nez, (I), Earl
Parker, (I), Paul Vaccarello, (I)

B

Bancroft, Carol & Friends/7 Ivy Hill Rd/Box 959, Ridgefield, CT ..203-438-8386
Lori Anderson, (I), Mary Bausman, (I), Kristine Bollinger, (I),
Stephanie Britt, (I), Chi Chung, (I), Jim Cummins, (I), Susan
Dodge, (I), Andrea Eberbach, (I), Barbara Garrison, (I), Toni

Goffe, (I), Ethel Gold, (I), Mark Graham, (I), Linda Graves, (I),
John Gurney, (I), Fred Harsh, (I), Ann Iosa, (I), Laurie Jordan,
(I), Ketti Kupper, (I), Karen Loccisano, (I), Laura Lydecker, (I),
Stephen Marchesi, (I), Judy Mastrangelo, (I), Kathleen
McCarthy, (I), Elizabeth Miles, (I), Yoshi Miyake, (I), Steven
Moore, (I), Nancy Munger, (I), Rodney Pate, (I), Cathy Pavia,
(I), Ondre Pettingill, (I), Larry Raymond, (I), Beverly Rich, (I),
Gail Roth, (I), Sandra Shields, (I), Cindy Spencer, (I), Linda
Boehm Weller, (I), Ann Wilson, (I)
Benezra, Adam/20 W Emerson St, Melrose, MA 617-662-8660
Tracy Flickinger, (I)
Beranbaum, Sheryl/115 Newbury St, Boston, MA.......................617-437-9459
David Barber, (I), Ronald Dellicolli, (I), James Edwards, (I),
Bob Eggleton, (I), Mike Gardner, (I), Michael Joyce, (I), Manuel
King, (I), Greg Mackey, (I), Michael McLaughlin, (I), Stephen
Moscowitz, (I), Matthew Pippin, (I)
Birenbaum, Molly/7 Williamsburg Dr, Cheshire, CT 203-272-9253
Peter Beach, (I), Alice Coxe, (I), W E Duke, (I), Sean Kernan,
(P), Joanne Schmaltz, (P), Paul Selwyn, (I), Bill Thomson, (I)
Bogner, Fred/911 State St, Lancaster, PA.................................717-393-0918
brt Photo Illustration, (P)
Bookmakers Ltd/25-Q Sylvan Rd S, Westport, CT........................203-226-4293
David Bolinsky, (I), Steve Botts, (I), Dawn DeRosa, (I), George
Guzzi, (I), Lydia Halverson, (I), Keith LoBue, (I), Judith
Lombardi, (I), Kathy McCord, (I), David Neuhaus, (I), Karen
Pellaton, (I), Marsha Serafin, (I), Dick Smolinski, (I), Sharon
Steuer, (I), Harriet Sullivan, (I)
Brewster, John Creative Svc/597 Riverside Ave, Westport, CT ..203-226-4724
Don Almquist, (I), Mike Brent, (I), Wende L Caporale, (I), Lane
Dupont, (I), Tom Garcia, (I), Steve Harrington, (I), Jim Herity,
(P), Seth Larson, (I), Dolph LeMoult, (I), Howard Munce, (I),
Alan Neider, (I), Nan Parsons, (I), Rick Schneider, (I), Steven
Stroud, (I), Al Weston, (I)
Breza-Collier, Susan/105 Prospect Ave, Langhorne, PA................215-752-7216
Browne, Pema Ltd/Pine Rd HCR Box 104B, Neversink, NY...........914-985-2936
Robert Barrett, (I), Todd Doney, (I), Richard Hull, (I), Ron
Jones, (I), Kathy Krantz, (I), John Rush, (I), John Sandford, (I)
Bruck, J S/PO Box 474, Woodbury, CT....................................203-263-0093

C

Cadenbach, Marilyn/149 Oakley Rd, Belmont, MA 617-484-7437
Jack Richmond, (P)
Campbell, Rita/129 Valerie Ct, Cranston, RI...............................401-826-0606
Campbell, Suzi/365 Beacon St, Boston, MA 617-266-7365
Carothers, Stuart/72 Manor Lane, Morrisville, PA.......................215-736-9452
Michael Berry, (I)
Caton, Chip/15 Warrenton Ave, Hartford, CT..............................203-523-4562
Bob Durham, (I), Phillip Dvorak, (I), Mike Eagle, (I), Andy
Giarnella, (I), Simpson Kalisher, (P), Kathleen Keifer, (I), Diana
Minisci, (I), Mark Panioto, (P), Bob Rich, (I), Alna Roman, (I),
Linda Schiwall-Gallo, (I), Frederick Schneider, (I), Shaffer-Smith
Photo , (P), Marc Sitkin, (P), Janet Street, (I), Andy Yelenak, (I)
City Limits/80 Wheeler Ave, Pleasantville, NY 914-747-1422
Colucci, Lou/POB 2069/86 Lachawanna Ave, W Patterson, NJ........201-890-5770
Conn, Adina/3130 Wisconsin Ave NW #413, Washington, DC..........202-296-3671
Rosemary Henry-May, (I), Carl Schoanberger, (I), Peter
Steiner, (I)
Cornell/McCarthy/2-D Cross Hwy, Westport, CT...........................212-454-4210
Creative Advantage Inc/620 Union St,
Schenectady, NY (P 16,17)..**518-370-0312**
Jack Graber, (I), Richard Siciliano, (P)
Creative Arts International/1024 Adams St, Hoboken, NJ..........201-659-7711
Stephanie Causey, (I), David Chen, (I), Gene Garbowski, (I),
Wayne Parmeter, (I), Jerry Pavey, (I), Michael Powell, (I), Mark
Seidler, (I)

DE

D'Angelo, Victoria/620 Centre Ave, Reading, PA 215-376-1100
Andy D'Angelo, (P)
Ella/229 Berkeley #52, Boston, MA..617-266-3858
Lizi Boyd, (I), Krista Brauckman, (I), Wilbur Bullock, (I), Rob
Cline, (I), Richard Cowdrey, (I), Jack Crompton, (I), Sharon
Drinkwine, (I), Anatoly Dverin, (I), Scott Gordley, (I), Robert
Gunn, (I), Kevin Hawkes, (I), Doug Henry, (I), Roger Leyonmark,
(I), Masato Nishimura, (I), Carol O'Malia, (I), Kathy Petrauskas,
(I), Phil Porcella, (P), Phillip Porcella, (P), Molly Quinn, (I), Jim

Raycroft, (P), Cheryl Roberts, (I), Bruce Sanders, (I), Ron Toelke, (I), Rhonda Voo, (I), Bryan Wiggins, (I), Francine Zaslow, (P)

Ennis Inc/78 Florence Ave, Arlington, MA................................617-643-2656

Erwin, Robin/54 Applecross Cir, Chalfont, PA................................215-822-8258
Callaghan Photography, (P)

Esto Photographics/222 Valley Pl, Mamaroneck, NY 914-698-4060
Peter Aaron, (P), Dan Cornish, (P), Scott Frances, (P), Jeff Goldberg, (P), John Margolies, (P), Peter Mauss, (P), Jock Pottle, (P), Ezra Stoller, (P)

FG

Fort, Faris/1850 Ingelside Terrace, Washington, DC 202-667-2004
Scott Bryant, (P), Robert A Rathe, (P)

Geng, Maud/25 Gray St, Boston, MA 617-236-1920
Caroline Alterio, (I), Peter Barger, (I), Suzanne Barnes, (I), Jean-Christian Knaff, (I), Jon McIntosh, (I), Glenn Robert Reid, (I), Mike Ryan, (P), Vicki Smith, (I)

Giandomenico, Terry (Ms)/13 Fern Ave, Collingswood, NJ 609-854-2222
Bob Giandomenico, (P)

Giannini & Talent/201 Tulip Ave, Takoma Park, MD................202-328-9076

Giraldi, Tina/42 Harmon Pl, N Haledon, NJ 201-423-5115
Frank Giraldi, (P)

Goldstein, Gwen/8 Cranberry Lane, Dover, MA................................508-785-1513
Michael Blaser, (I), Cathy Diefendorf, (I), Lane Gregory, (I), Barbara Morse, (I), Terry Presnall, (I), Susan Spellman, (I), Gary Torrisi, (I)

Goodman, Tom/1424 South Broad St, Philadelphia, PA................215-468-5842
Jerome Lukowicz, (P), Matt Wargo, (P), Lee Wojnar, (P)

H

Heine, Karl Promotions/193 Seymour Ave, Derby, CT 203-854-9393

Heisey, Betsy/109 Somerstown Rd, Ossining, NY 914-762-5335
Whitney Lane, (P)

HK Portfolio/458 Newtown Trnpk, Weston, CT 203-454-4687
Bert Badson, (I), Anthony Carnabuci, (I), Abby Carter, (I), Randy Chewning, (I), Carolyn Croll, (I), Eldon Doty, (I), JAK Graphics, (I), Anne Kennedy, (I), Benton Mahan, (I), Susan Miller, (I), Stephanie O'Shaughnessy, (I), Jan Palmer, (I), Sandra Speidel, (I), Peggy Tagel, (I), Jean & Mou-sein Tseng, (I), George Ulrich, (I), Randy Verougstraete, (I), Scott Webber, (I), David Wenzel, (I)

Holt, Rita/920 Main St, Fords, NJ 212-683-2002
David Burnett, (P), David Burnette, (P), Chuck Ealovega, (P), Derek Gardner, (P), Donna & Rodney Rascona, (P)

Hone, Claire/859 N 28th St, Philadelphia, PA................................215-765-6900
Stephen Hone, (P)

Hopkins, Nanette/751 Conestoga Rd, Rosemont, PA 215-649-8589

Hubbell, Marian/99 East Elm St, Greenwich, CT................................203-629-9629

Hummer, Dave/88 St Frances St, Newark, NJ 201-344-4214

JKL

Jagow, Linda/PO Box 425, Rochester, NY................................716-546-7606
John Berg, (I), Ron Brancato, (I), Dave Calver, (I), Bob Clarke, (I), Alan Cober, (I), Leslie Cober, (I), Bob Conge, (I), Susan Covert, (I), Roger T DeMuth, (I), Bob Dorsey, (I), Maliki Malik, (I), Jean K Stephens, (I)

Kerr, Ralph/239 Chestnut St, Philadelphia, PA 215-592-1359

Knecht, Cliff/309 Walnut Rd, Pittsburgh, PA 412-761-5666
David Bowers, (I), Janet Darby, (I), Jim Deigan, (I), Jackie Geyer, (I), Lou Pasqua, (I), Deborah Pinkney, (I), George Schill, (I), Lee Steadman, (I), Jim Trusilo, (I), Phil Wilson, (I)

Kurlansky, Sharon/192 Southville Rd, Southborough, MA...........508-872-4549
Colleen, (I), John Gamache, (I), Peter Harris, (I), Geoffrey Hodgkinson, (I), Bruce Hutchison, (I), Stacey Lewis, (I), Dorthea Sierra, (I), Julia Talcott, (I)

Leyburn, Judy/235 Haynes Rd, Sudbury, MA 508-443-8871
Mark Steele, (I)

Lipman, Deborah/506 Windsor Dr, Framingham, MA 508-877-8830
Mark Fisher, (I), Richard A. Goldberg, (I), Katherine Mahoney, (I), Elivia Savadier, (I), Susan Smith, (I), Karen Watson, (I)

M

McNamara, Paula B/182 Broad St, Wethersfield, CT 203-563-6159
Jack McConnell, (P)

Metzger, Rick/5 Tsienneto Rd, Derry, NH................................603-432-3356
Jon Chomitz, (P), Dave Deacon, (R), Hotshots , (P), Kevin Prieur, (P)

Monahan, Terry/16 Kinsman Pl, Natick, MA................................508-651-0671

Morgan, Wendy/5 Logan Hill Rd, Northport, NY................................516-757-5609
Karl Edwards, (I), Scott Gordley, (I), Fred Labitzke, (I), Preston Lyon, (P), Al Margolis, (I), ParaShoot, (P), David Rankin, (I), Mark Sparacio, (I)

Moser, Trixie/PA................................215-236-3156
Stan Fellerman, (P), John Uher, (P)

Murphy, Brenda/72 High St #2, Topsfield, MA 508-887-3528
Jeanne Abboud, (I), Diane Bigda, (I), Joe Goebel, (I), Howie Green, (I), Diane Kunic, (I), William Kurt Lumpkins, (I), Valentine Sahleanu, (I), David Schuster, (I), Mark Seppala, (I), Paul Wasserboehr, (I), Richard Watzulik, (I)

OP

O'Connor, Leighton/15 Ives St, Beverly, MA................................617-426-2099
Linc Cornell, (P), Joe Veno, (I)

O'Leary, Gin/1260 Boylston St, Boston, MA 617-267-9299

Oreman, Linda/22 Nelson St, Rochester, NY................................716-244-6956
Nick Agnello, (I), Jim Bliss, (I), Laura Cowles, (I), Paul Facklam, (I), Bill Finewood, (I), Peter Lautenslager, (I), Bob Radigan, (I), Pete Smith, (I), Vicki Wehrman, (I)

Palulian, Joanne Reps/18 McKinley St, Rowayton, CT................203-866-3734
M John English, (I), Bonnie Hofkin, (I), Gayle Kabaker, (I), David Lesh, (I), Kirk Moldoff, (I), Dickran Palulian, (I), Bonnie Timmons, (I)

Pickles, Carolyn/PO Box 80370, Springfield, MA................................413-732-3522
Eric Poggenpohl, (P)

Publishers Graphics/251 Greenwood Ave, Bethel, CT 203-797-8188
Robert Alley, (I), Deborah Borgo, (I), Patti Boyd, (I), Robin Brickman, (I), Ray Burns, (I), Eulala Conner, (I), Helen Davie, (I), Marie DeJohn, (I), Leslie Dunlap, (I), Julie Durrell, (I), Allan Eitzen, (I), Marlene Ekman, (I), Gioia Fiammenghi, (I), Walter Gaffney-Kessell, (I), T.R. Garcia, (I), Joan Goodman, (I), Dana Gustafson, (I), Susan Hall, (I), Paul Harvey, (I), Jean Helmer, (I), Pamela Johnson, (I), John Jones, (I), G Brian Karas, (I), Kathie Kelleher, (I), Jane Kendall, (I), Kees de Kiefte, (I), Robin Kramer , (I), Gary Lippincott, (I), Bob Marshall, (I), Vikki Marshall, (I), Lisa McCue, (I), Nancy Munger, (I), Robert A Parker, (I), Anna Pomaska, (I), Sandy Rabinowitz, (I), David Rickman, (I), S.D. Schindler, (I), Joel Snyder, (I), Lynn Sweat, (I), Barbara Todd, (I), James Watling, (I), Ulises Wensell, (I)

Putscher, Tony/1214 Locust St, Philadelphia, PA................................215-569-8890

R

Redmond, Sharon/8634 Chelsea Bridge Way, Lutherville, MD 301-823-7422
Don Carstens, (P), Jim Owens, (I), Carol Wells, (I)

Reese-Gibson, Jean/4 Puritan Rd, N Beverly, MA 508-927-5006
Dennis Helmar, (P), Dan Morrill, (P), Steve Rubican, (P)

Reitmeyer, Roxanne/2016 Walnut St, Philadelphia, PA................215-972-1543
Terrence McBride, (P)

Resources/511 Broadway, Saratoga Springs, NY 518-583-3676
Russell Ley, (P), Larry Van Valkenburg, (P)

Robbins, David Group/237 Hopmeadow St, Simsbury, CT.............203-658-2583
Rob Brooks, (I), Mike Eagle, (I), Kim Perkins, (I), Dan Snyder, (I), Andy Yelenak, (I)

Roderick, Jennifer/60 Oak St, Harrison, NY................................914-835-4175
Brian Goble, (P)

Roland, Rochel/20150 Locust Dale Terrace, Germantown, MD 301-353-9431
Michael Pohuski, (P), Jim Sloane, (P), Ann Whiting, (I)

Rotella, Robert/6 Partridge Ct, Newtown, PA................................215-968-3696
Ralph Giguere, (I), Abbott, Jim, (P), Michael LaRiche, (P)

ST

Satterthwaite, Victoria/115 Arch St, Philadelphia, PA 215-925-4233
Michael Furman, (P)

Schnitzel, Gary/PO Box 297, Pineville, PA................................215-598-0214

Sequis Ltd/9 W 29th St, Baltimore, MD................................301-467-7300

Sheehan, Betsy/7928 Ruxway Rd, Baltimore, MD................................301-828-4020

Snitzel, Gary/1060 Durham Rd, Pineville, PA................................215-598-0214

Sonneville, Dane/PO Box 155, Passaic, NJ................................212-603-9530
Leland Bobbe, (P), Jim Kinstrey, (I), John Pemberton, (P), Jamie Phillips, (P), Bob Shein, (I)

Soodak, Arlene/11135 Korman Dr, Potomac, MD................................301-983-2343

The Source/2276 Mount Carmel Ave, Glenside, PA................................215-885-8227
Dimitrios Bastas, (I), Dan Fione, (I), Thomas Hamilton, (I), Tom

Quirk, (I), Drew Strawbridge, (I)
Star, Lorraine/1 Canterbury Circle, Kennebunk, ME........................207-967-5319
Stemrich, J David/213 N 12th St, Allentown, PA 215-776-0825
Mark Bray, (I), Bob Hahn, (P)
Stoller, Erica/222 Valley Pl, Mamaroneck, NY 914-698-4060
Ternay, Louise/119 Birch Ave, Bala Cynwyd, PA 215-667-8626
Vince Cuccinotta, (I), Don Everhart, (I), Greg Purdon, (I), Peter
Sasten, (G), Bill Ternay, (I), Victor R Valla, (I)
TVI Creative Specialists/1146 19th St NW, Washington, DC........202-331-7722
Don Carstens, (P), Mark Freeman, (I), Doug Hansen, (P), Gary
Iglarshi, (I), Isaac Jones, (P), Eucalyptus Tree Studio, (I)

UVW

Unicorn/120 American Rd, Morris Plains, NJ 201-292-6852
Greg Hildebrandt, (I)
Veloric, Philip M/128 Beechtree Dr, Broomall, PA 215-356-0362
Michael W Adams, (I), Deb Troyer Bunnell, (I), Suzanne K
Clee, (I), Rick L Cooley, (I), Don Dyen, (I), Len Ebert, (I), Kathy
Hendrickson, (I), Patricia Gural Hinton, (I), John Holder, (I),
Robert R Jackson, (I), Polly Krumbhaar Lewis, (I), Nancy Il, (I),
Richard Loehle, (I), Laurie Marks, (I), Denise Prowell, (I), Eileen
Rosen, (I), Ed Sauk, (I), Dennis Schofield, (I), Samantha Carol
Smith, (I), Wayne Anthony Still, (I), Brad Strode, (I), Gary
Undercuffer, (I), Lane Yerkes, (I)
Warner, Bob/1425 Belleview Ave, Plainfield, NJ................................908-755-7236
Hank Morgan, (P), Lou Odor, (P)
Wolfe, Deborah Ltd/731 North 24th St, Philadelphia, PA.................215-232-6666
Skip Baker, (I), Robert Burger, (I), Rick Buterbaugh, (I), Jenny
Campbell, (I), Ray Dallastra, (I), Deborah Danilla, (I), Pat
Duffy, (I), Jeff FitzMaurice, (I), John Paul Genzo, (I), Patrick
Gnan, (I), Jim Himsworth, (I), Michael Hostovich, (I), Robin
Hotchkiss, (I), Marianne Hughes, (I), Neal Hughes, (I), Scott
Johnston, (I), Eric Joyner, (I), Russell Kirk, (P), Andy Meyer,
(I), Tom Miller, (I), Verlin Miller, (I), Bill Morse, (I), Steven Nau,
(I), Lisa Pomerantz, (I), Bob Roper, (I), Michel Tcherevkoff,
(P), Richard Waldrep, (I)
Wolff, Timmy/1509 Park Ave, Baltimore, MD 301-383-7059

S O U T H E A S T

A

Aldridge, Donna/755 Virginia Ave NE, Atlanta, GA 404-872-7980
Ted Boonthanakit, (I), Thomas Gonzalez, (I), Chris Lewis, (I),
Carol H Norby, (I), Marcia Wetzel, (I)
Anders, Phil/704 Churchill Dr, Chapel Hill, NC...................................919-929-0011
Jan Lukens, (I), Chuck Primeau, (I)

B

Beck, Susanne/2721 Cherokee Rd, Birmingham, AL 205-871-6632
Charles Beck, (P)
Bowlus, Peter/8453 NW 70th St, Miami, FL.......................................305-594-5902
Brenner, Harriet/2625 SW Westlake Cir, Palm City, FL...................407-286-9781
Dick Krueger, (P), Erich Schremp, (P), Tony Soluri, (P)
Burnett, Yolanda/571 Dutch Vall Rd, Atlanta, GA 404-881-6627
Al Clayton, (P), Michael Harrell, (I), Martin Pate, (I), Steve
Spetseris, (I), Pamela Trowe, (I), Michael West, (P)

C

Cary & Co/666 Bantry Lane, Stone Mountain, GA 404-296-9666
Robert August, (I), Mike Hodges, (I), Johnna Hogenkamp-
Bandle, (I), Kevin Hulsey, (I), David Marks, (I), Charlie
Mitchell, (I), Greg Olsen, (I), Kathi Roberts, (I), John
Sommerfeld, (P)
Comport, Allan/241 Central Ave, St Petersburg, FL.........................813-821-9050
Sally Wern Comport, (I)
Couch, Tom/1164 Briarcliff Rd NE #2, Atlanta, GA 404-872-5774
Granberry/Anderson Studio, (P)
Cuneo, Jim...813-848-8931

FGH

Flesher, Robert/102 Waterford Ct, Peachtree City, GA....................404-487-2472

Forbes, Pat/11459 Waterview Cluster, Reston, VA 703-478-0434
Kay Chernush, (P), Lautman Photography, (P), Claude
Vasquez, (P), Claudio Vazquez, (P), Taren Z, (P)
Gaffney, Steve/4701 Kenmore Ave, Alexandria, VA.......................703-751-1991
ightscapes Photo , (P), Lisa Masson, (P)
Green, Cindy/280 Elizabeth St #A-105, Atlanta, GA 404-525-1333
Hathcox, Julia/5730 Arlington Blvd, Arlington, VA.............................703-845-5831
David Hathcox, (P)

J

Jernigan, Jack/4209 Canal St, New Orleans, LA...............................504-486-9011
Robert Anderson, (I), Kenneth Harrison, (I), Kathleen Joffrion,
(I), Wendi Schneider, (I)
Jett & Assoc Inc/21 Theatre Square #200, Louisville, KY 502-561-0737
Gary Bennett, (I), Dan H Brawner, (I), Annette Cable, (I), Mark
Cable, (I), John Mattos, (I), Mario Noche, (I), Cynthia Torp, (I),
Jeff Tull, (I), David Wariner, (I), Roy Wiemann, (I), Wayne
Williams, (I), Paul Wolf, (I)

KLM

Kohler, Chris/1105 Peachtree St, Atlanta, GA...................................404-292-4727
Lee, Wanda/3647 Cedar Ridge Dr, Atlanta, GA 404-432-6309
Paul Larkin, (P), Rodger Macuch, (P)
Linden, Tamara/3565 Piedmnt/2 Piedmnt Ctr#300, Atlanta, GA 404-262-1209
Gail Chirko, (I), Tom Fleck, (I), Joe Ovies, (I), Charles
Passarelli, (I), Larry Tople, (I)
McGee, Linda/1816 Briarwood Ind Ct, Atlanta, GA 404-633-1286
McLean Represents/571 Dutch Valley Rd, Atlanta, GA 404-881-6627
Michael Harrel, (I), Mitch Hyatt, (I), Martin Pate, (I), Steve
Spetseris, (I), Pamela Trowe, (I)
Moore, Carolyn/PO Box 37108, Charlotte, NC 704-335-1733
Morrah, Linda/301 Calvin St, Greenville, SC....................................803-242-9108

P

Perry, Sarah/968 Homewood Ct, Decatur, GA..................................404-634-2349
Tom Cain, (I), John Findly, (I), David Kacmarynski, (I), Kelly
Maddox, (I), Joe Peery, (I), Phil Perry, (I)
Peters, Barbara/2217 Cypress Isl Dr #205, Pompano Bch, FL 305-978-0675
Jacques Dirand, (P), Lizzie Himmel, (P)
Pollard, Kiki/848 Greenwood Ave NE, Atlanta, GA...........................404-875-1363
Betsy Alexander, (G), Lindy Burnett, (I), Cheryl Cooper, (I),
David Guggenheim, (P), Dennis Guthrie, (I), Kathy Lengyel, (I),
Pat Magers, (I), Julie Muller-Brown, (I), Frank Saso, (I), James
Soukup, (I), Elizabeth Traynor, (I)
Prentice, Nancy/919 Collier Rd NW, Atlanta, GA..............................404-266-0088
Arliss Day, (I), Rene Faure, (I), Doris Galloway, (I), Pat
Harrington, (I), Kenny Higdon, (P), Ed Hurlbeck, (I), George
Parrish, (I), Robbie Short, (I), Morris Ward, (I), Derek Yanicer,
(I), Bruce Young, (I)

RST

Ross, Adora Adam/1507 Tace Dr NW, Palm Bay, FL........................407-728-3099
Silva, Naomi/2161 Peachtree St NE #502, Atlanta, GA....................404-355-6674
Daryl Cagle, (C), Kevin Hamilton, (I), Rob Horn, (L), Cyd
Moore, (I), Mike Moore, (I), Rick Paller, (I), Alan Patton, (I),
Gary Penca, (I), Geo Sipp, (I), Don Sparks, (P)
Sullivan, Tom/3805 Maple Court, Marietta, GA 404-971-6782
Sumpter, Will/1728 N Rock Springs Rd, Atlanta, GA........................404-874-2014
Charles Cashwell, (I), Flip Chalfant, (P), Brit Taylor Collins, (I),
Bob Cooper, (I), David Gaadt, (I), Brenda Losey, (I), David
Moses, (I), Jackie Pitman, (I), Drew Rose, (I), Garcia Studios,
(P), Clark Tate, (I), Phil Wende, (I)
Trlica/Reilly: Reps/PO Box 1325, Charlotte, NC 704-372-6007
Gerin Choiniere, (P), Sally Wern Comport, (I), Gary Crane, (I),
Laura Gardner, (I), Marcus Hamilton, (I), Steve Knight, (P),
Mike McMahon, (I), Gary Palmer, (I), Harry Roolaart, (I), Greg
Rudd, (I), Walter Stanford, (I), David Taylor, (I), Jack Vaughan,
(I), John White, (I), David Wilgus, (I)

WY

Wells, Susan/5134 Timber Trail, Atlanta, GA.....................................404-255-1430
Paul Blakey, (I), Ted Burn, (I), David Clegg, (I), Cam DeLeon,
(I), Elaine Dillard, (I), Laura Hesse, (I), Bob Hogan, (I), Don

Loehle, (I), Richard Loehle, (I), Randall McKissick, (I), Christine Mull, (I), John Nelson, (I), Bob Radigan, (I), Tommy Stubbs, (I), Monte Varah, (I), Beth White, (I)

Wetherington, Kathleen/PO Box 8702, Atlanta, GA 404-248-9773
Williams, Phillip/1270 W Peachtree St #8C, Atlanta, GA 404-873-2287
oris/Pittman , (G), Abe Gurvin, (I), Jack Jones, (I), Rick Lovell, (I), Bill Mayer, (I), David McKelvey, (I), Pat Mollica, (I), Tom Nikosey, (I), John Robinette, (I), Danny Smythe, (I), Dale Verzaal, (I)
Yeaswich & Welch/1177 Louisiana Ave, Winter Park, FL 407-647-3001

MIDWEST

A

Allan, Nancy/2479 W 11th St #2479, Cleveland, OH 216-621-3838
Altman, Elizabeth/1420 W Dickens, Chicago, IL 312-404-0133
Ben Altman, (P), Ron Coppock, (P), Don DuBroff, (P), Jack Perno, (P), Abby Sadin, (P), Russell Thurston, (I)
Art Staff Inc/1000 John R Rd #110, Troy, MI 313-583-6070
John Arvan, (I), Joy Brosious, (I), Ralph Brunke, (I), Ricardo Capraro, (I), Larry Cory, (I), Caryl Cunningham, (I), Sheryl DeMorris, (I), Brian Foley, (I), Dennis Goldsworthy, (I), Jim Gutheil, (I), Vicki Hayes, (I), Jim Hodge, (I), Ben Jaroslaw, (I), Dan Kistler, (I), Baron Lesperance, (I), John Martin, (I), Dick Meissner, (I), Heidi Meissner, (I), Dick Miller, (I), Jerry Monteleon, (I), Linda Nagle, (I), Colin Payne, (I), Jeff Ridky, (I), Al Schrank, (I), Jim Slater, (I), Chris Szetela, (I), Ken Taylor, (I), Alan Wilson, (I)
Atols, Mary/405 N Wabash #1305, Chicago, IL...............................312-222-0504

B

Ball, John/203 N Wabash, Chicago, IL...312-332-6041
Wilson-Griak Inc, (P)
Bartels, Ceci Assoc/1913 Park Ave, St Louis, MO 314-241-4014
Jim Arndt, (P), Bill Bruning, (I), Justin Carroll, (I), Gary Ciccarelli, (I), David Davis, (I), Paul Elledge, (P), Mark Fredrickson, (I), Lisa French, (I), Stephen Grohe, (P), Michael Halbert, (I), Bill Jenkins, (I), Keith Kasnot, (I), Leland Klanderman, (I), Shannon Kriegshauser, (I), Greg MacNair, (I), Pete Mueller, (I), John Nelson, (I), Adam Niklenicz, (I), Jim Olivera, (I), Kevin Pope, (C), Guy Porfirio, (I), Jean Probert, (I), Mike Randal, (I), B B Sams, (C), Todd Schorr, (I), Jay Silverman, (I), Terry Sirrell, (I), Terry Speer, (I), Judy Unger, (I), Wayne Watford, (I), Morgan Weistling, (I), Linden Wilson, (I), Ted Wright, (I)
Bauer, Frank/207 E Buffalo St #543, Milwaukee, WI.........................414-291-0300
Bryan Peterson, (I)
Bernstein, Joanie/PO Box 3635, Minneapolis, MN...........................612-374-3169
Mark Chickinelli, (I), Lee Christiansen, (I), Eric Hanson, (I), Jack A Molloy, (I), Stan Olson, (I), Dan Picasso, (I)
Blockey, Gloria/3313 Croft Dr, Minneapolis, MN 612-781-7385
Bonnen, Ed/444 Lentz Ct, Lansing, MI.......................................517-371-3086
Darwin Dale, (P), Barbara Hranilouish, (I), Kim Kauffman, (P)
Bracken, Laura/215 W Illinois, Chicago, IL 312-644-7108
William Sladcik, (P), James Wheeler, (P)
Brenna, Allen Associates/9376 Amsden Way, Minneapolis, MN..612-349-3805
Dezso Csanady, (I), Don Ellwood, (I), Lou Flores, (I), Richard Kriegler, (I), Kelly Provo, (I), Mike Sobey, (I)
Brooks & Assoc/855 W Blackhawk St, Chicago, IL.........................312-642-3208
Nancy Brown, (P), David Kogan, (P), VanKirk Photo, (P)
Burchill, Linda/260 E Chestnut, Chicago, IL 312-664-4703
Bussler, Tom/642 N Clark, Chicago, IL..312-642-6499
Sid Evans, (P), Phoenix Group, (I)

C

Coleman, Woody/490 Rockside Rd, Cleveland, OH........................216-661-4222
Eric Apel, (I), Sandy Appleoff, (I), Jeffrey Bedrick, (I), Alex Bostic, (I), Larry Elmore, (I), Jack Jones, (I), Michael Koester, (I), Vladimir Kordic, (I), John Letostak, (I), Jeff Lloyd, (I), Charles Manus, (I), Al Margolis, (I), Manuel Morales, (I), Bill Morse, (I), David Moses, (I), Ernest Norcia, (I), Vincent Perez, (I), Bob Radigan, (I), James Seward, (I), Marla Shegal, (I), Tom Shephard, (I), David Taylor, (I), Ezra Tucker, (I), Tom Utley, (I), Monte Varah, (I)

Cowan, Pat/604 Division Rd, Valparaiso, IN.....................................219-462-0199
Ralph Cowan, (P)
Creative Source Inc/360 North Michigan Ave, Chicago, IL 312-649-9777

D

Demunnik, Jack/Twin Springs Farms, Durango, IA.........................319-588-3019
DeWalt & Assoc/210 E Michigan St #403, Milwaukee, WI 414-276-7990
Mel Drake, (G), Tom Fritz, (P), Rick Karpinski, (I), Dennis Matz, (I), Mark Mille, (I)
Dodge, Tim/301 N Waters St 5th Fl, Milwaukee, WI.........................414-271-3388
Ken Hanson, (G), Dave Vander Veen, (P), Peter Wells, (I), Matthew Zumbo, (I)
Dolby, Karen/333 N Michigan #2711, Chicago, IL 312-855-9336
Diane Davis, (I), Richard Dionisio, (P), Jan Jones, (I), Peg McGovern, (I), Julie Pace, (I), Fran Vuksanovich, (I), Eddie Yip, (I)

E

Edsey, Steve/520 N Michigan Ave #706, Chicago, IL......................312-527-0351
Stuart Block, (P), Chuck Bracke, (I), Michael Carroll, (I), Rick Clubb, (I), Wil Cormier, (P), Deszo Csanady, (I), Mike Dammer, (I), Tom Durfee, (I), Mike Hagel, (I), Lou Heiser, (I), Keith Jay, (I), Al Lipson, (I), Betty Maxey, (I), Joe McDermott, (I), Tom McKee, (I), Bob Perzel, (P), Mike Phillips, (I), John Rau, (I), Joe Sapulich, (I), Harlan Scheffler, (I), Sussan Shipley, (I), Mike Sobey, (I), Sam Thiewe, (I), Bobbi Tull, (I), Terry Wickart, (I)
Eldridge Corp/916 Olive St #300, St Louis, MO............................314-231-6800
Jana Brunner, (I), Bob Commander, (I), David FeBland, (I), Ted Fuka, (I), Kuni Hagio, (I), John Van Hamersveld, (I), Charles White III, (I), Bud Kemper, (I), Tom Killeen, (I), Doug Klauba, (I), Nora Koerber, (I), Greg Litwicki, (I), Tom Lungstrom, (I), Jane Meredith, (I), Bill Miller, (I), Marilyn Montgomery, (I), Garry Nichols, (I), Virginia Peck, (I), Carol Robbins, (I), Jay Vigon, (I), Mark Wickart, (I)
Erdos, Kitty/210 W Chicago, Chicago, IL 312-787-4976
Finished Art, (I), Jim Durish, (I), Tom Zamiar, (P)

FG

Falvey, Lee/169 E Wisconsin Ave, Oconomowoc, WI 414-567-8867
Feldman, Kenneth/1821 N Dayton, Chicago, IL.............................312-337-0447
Fiat, Randi & Assoc/211 E Ohio #621, Chicago, IL 312-784-2343
David Csicsko, (I), Marc Hauser, (P), John Kleber, (I)
Frazier, Bob/617 W Fulton St, Chicago, IL....................................312-845-9650
Freeman, Lisa/2507 Brewster Rd, Indianapolis, IN.........................317-872-7856
Joe LaMantia, (I), Joseph Mahler, (I), Dianne McElwain, (I), Mark Schroeder, (I), Juana Silcox, (I)
Goodman, Munro/405 N Wabash #1912, Chicago, IL......................312-321-1336
Tom Bookwalter, (I), Chris Butler, (I), Bill Cigliano, (I), Pat Dypold, (), Malcolm Farley, (I), Clint Hansen, (I), Quang Ho, (I), Ben Luce, (I), Randy Nelsen, (I), David Schweitzer, (I), Michael Steirnagle, (I)
Graphic Access/444 N Wells St, Chicago, IL................................312-222-0087

H

Handelan-Pedersen/1165 North Clark, Chicago, IL 312-664-1200
Hanson, Jim/777 North Michigan Ave #706, Chicago, IL 312-337-7770
Richard Fegley, (P), John Fry, (P), Glen Gyssler, (P), Maria Krajcirovic, (P), Rob Porazinski, (I), Hannes Schmid, (P), Craig Smallish, (I), Christian Vogt, (P), Richard Wahlstrom, (P), Harry Whitver, (I)
Harlib, Joel Assoc/405 N Wabash #3203, Chicago, IL....................312-329-1370
Richard Anderson, (I), Nick Backes, (I), Michael Backus, (I), Bart Bemus, (I), Tim Bieber, (P), Al Brandtner, (I), Russell Cobane, (I), Esky Cook, (I), Mike Dean, (I), Lawrence Duke, (I), Chuck Eckart, (I), Paul Elledge, (P), Robert Farber, (P), Randy Glass, (I), Abe Gurvin, (I), Scott Harris, (I), Karel Havlicek, (I), Barbara Higgins-Bond, (I), Roger Hill, (I), David McCall Johnston, (I), Tim Langenderfer, (I), Richard Leech, (I), Peter Lloyd, (I), Albert Lorenz, (I), Kenvin Lyman, (I), Don Margolis, (I), Bill Morse, (I), Dennis Mukai, (I), Steve Nozicka, (P), Fred Pepera, (I), Kevin Pope, (I), Ray Roberts, (I), Buc Rogers, (I), Delro Rosco, (I), Delro Rosco, (I), Boris Vallejo, (I), Bill Vann, (I), Kim Whitesides, (I), Donald Wilson, (I), Michael Witte, (I), Bruce Wolfe, (I), Jonathan Wright, (I), Bob Ziering, (I)

Harmon, Ellen/950 W Lake St, Chicago, IL 312-829-8201
Harry Przekop, (P)
Harris, Gretchen & Assoc/5230 13th Ave S, Minneapolis, MN.....612-822-0650
Ken Jacobsen, (I), Nathan Jarvis, (I), Jim Rownd, (I), Mary
Worcester, (I)
Hartig, Michael/3602 Pacific St, Omaha, NE 402-345-2164
Hellman Assoc Inc/1225 W 4th St, Waterloo, IA 319-234-7055
Kim Behm, (I), Deb Bovy, (I), Greg Hargreaves, (I), Dan
Hatala, (I), Steve Hunter, (I), Doug Knutson, (I), Paul Lackner,
(I), Pat Muchmore, (I), John Thompson, (I), Todd Treadway, (I)
Higa, Tracy/1605 N Mohawk St, Chicago, IL..................................312-440-1692
Hogan, Myrna & Assoc/333 N Michigan, Chicago, IL....................312-372-1616
Horton, Nancy/939 Sanborn, Palatine, IL 708-934-8966
Hull, Scott Assoc/68 E Franklin St, Dayton, OH 513-433-8383
Mark Braught, (I), Tracy Britt, (I), Andy Buttram, (I), John Buxton,
(I), John Ceballos, (I), Greg Dearth, (F), Andrea Eberbach, (I),
David Groff, (I), Peter Harritos, (I), Julie Hodde, (I), Bill James, (I),
Greg LaFever, (I), John Maggard, (I), Gregory Manchess, (I),
Larry Martin, (I), Ted Pitts, (I), Mark Riedy, (I), Don Vanderbeek, (I)

IK

Image Source/801 Front St, Toledo, OH 419-697-1111
Jay Langlois, (P), Joe Sharp, (P)
Kamin, Vince & Assoc/111 E Chestnut, Chicago, IL 312-787-8834
Sara Anderson, (I), Tom Berthiaume, (P), Steve Bjorkman, (I),
Dave Jordano, (P), Mary Anne Shea, (I), Dale Windham, (P)
Kapes, Jack/233 E Wacker Dr #1412, Chicago, IL 312-565-0566
Stuart Block, (P), John Cahoon, (P), Carl Faruta, (P), Dan
Romano, (I), Nicolas Sidjakov, (G)
Kastaris, Harriet & Assoc/3301 S Jefferson, St Louis, MO 314-773-2600
Eric Dinyer, (I), Rip Kastaris, (I), Tony Schanuel, (P), Jeff Tull,
(I), Arden Von Haeger, (I), April Goodman Willy, (I)
Keltsch, Ann/9257 Castlegate Dr, Indianapolis, IN 317-849-7723
Kleber, Gordon/1723 N Honore, Chicago, IL..................................312-276-4419
Knutsen, Jan/10740 Toledo Ct, Bloomington, MN...........................612-884-8083
Kogen, Judi/315 W Walton, Chicago, IL 312-266-8029
Richard Izui, (P)
Koralik, Connie/900 West Jackson Blvd #7W, Chicago, IL..............312-944-5680
Ron Criswell, (I), Ted Gadecki, (I), Myron Grossman, (I), Robert
Keeling, (I), Chuck Ludecke, (I), Bob Scott, (I), Bill Weston, (I),
Andy Zito, (I)
Kuehnel, Peter/19 E Pearson St #125, Chicago, IL 312-642-6499
Ted Carr, (I), Ray Perkins, (P), Phoenix Studio, (I)

LM

Lux & Assocciates, Frank/20 W Hubbard #3E, Chicago, IL.......312-222-1361
Maloney, Tom & Assoc/307 N Michigan Ave #1008, Chicago, IL....312-704-0500
Nicolette Anastas, (I), Dan Clyne, (I), Colleen Quinn, (I)
McGrath, Judy/612 N Michigan Ave 4th Fl, Chicago, IL...................312-944-5116
Sandi Appleoff, (I), Bob Bullivant, (P), Joanne Carney, (P), Bret
Lopez, (P)
McNamara Associates/1250 Stephenson Hwy, Troy, MI 313-583-9200
Max Alterruse, (I), Perry Cooper, (I), Garth Glazier, (I), Hank
Kolodziej, (I), Kurt Krebs, (I), Jack Pennington, (I), Tony
Randazzo, (I), Gary Richardson, (I), Don Wieland, (I)
McNaughton, Toni/233 E Wacker #2904, Chicago, IL.....................312-938-2148
Pam Haller, (P), Rodica Prato, (I), James B. Wood, (P)
Miller, Richard/405 N Wabash #1204, Chicago, IL..........................312-527-0444
Montagano, David/405 N Wabash #1606, Chicago, IL 312-527-3283
Murphy, Sally/307 North Michigan Ave #1008, Chicago, IL 312-346-0720

NO

Neis, The Group/11440 Oak Drive, Shelbyville, MI 616-672-5756
Bender + Bender , (P), Tom Bookwalter, (I), Gary Eldridge, (I),
Bill Ross, (I)
Nicholson, Richard B/2310 Denison Ave, Cleveland, OH 216-398-1494
Jon DeVaul, (P), Mark Molesky, (P), Mike Steinberg, (P)
Nicolini, Sandra/230 N Michigan #523, Chicago, IL........................312-871-5819
Elizabeth Ernst, (P), Tom Petroff, (P)
O'Brien, Dan/444 N Michigan Ave, Chicago, IL..............................312-580-0880
O'Farrel, Eileen/311 Good Ave, Des Plaines, IL 708-297-5447
Robert Lightfoot, (P)
O'Grady Adv/111 E Wacker Dr #3000, Chicago, IL 312-726-9833
Jerry Dunn, (P)
Ores, Kathy/411 S Sagamon #2B, Chicago, IL 312-410-7139

Osler, Spike/2616 Industrial Row, Troy, MI.....................................313-280-0640
Madison Ford, (P), Rob Gage, (P), Eric W Perry, (P), Dennis
Wiand, (P)

P

Paisley, Shari/402 Newberry Ave, La Grange Park, IL.....................708-482-9060
Peterson, Vicki/211 E Ohio, Chicago, IL...312-467-0780
John Cascarano, (P), Whistln Dixie, (I), Elyse Lewin, (P),
Howard Menken, (P), Heimo Schmidt, (P)
Phase II/35 W Wacker Dr #3700, Chicago, IL...................................312-855-9500
Steve Snodgrass, (I)
Pohn, Carol/2259 N Wayne, Chicago, IL..312-348-0751
Ron Amis, (I), Diane O'Quinn Burke, (I), Hedwig , (I), Carl
Heinz, (I), Carl Leick, (I), Roger Marchultz, (P)
Pool, Linda/7216 E 99th St, Kansas City, MO.................................816-761-7314
Michael Radencich, (P)
Potts, Carolyn & Assoc/4 E Ohio #11, Chicago, IL 312-944-1130
Kevin Anderson, (P), Mark Battrell, (P), Karen Bell, (I), John
Craig, (I), Alan Dolgins, (P), Byron Gin, (I), Bob Gleason, (I),
Jewell Howard, (I), Alan Kaplan, (P), Don Loehle, (I), John
McCallum, (P), Susan Nees, (I), Joe Ovies, (I), Donna Ruff, (I),
Jack Slattery, (I), Rhonda Voo, (I), Leslie Wolf, (I)
Potts, Vicki/PO Box 31279, Chicago, IL 312-631-0301
Preston, Lori/449 W Belden Ave #1F, Chicago, IL 312-528-5483

R

Rabin, Bill & Assoc/680 N Lake Shore Dr #1020, Chicago, IL 312-944-6655
John Alcorn, (I), Steve Alcorn, (I), Joel Baldwin, (P), Joe
Baraban, (P), Roger Beerworth, (I), Michael Bennallack-Hart,
(I), Hank Benson, (P), Guy Billout, (I), Howard Bjornson, (P),
Thomas Blackshear, (I), R O Blechman, (I), Charles William
Bush, (P), Richard Corman, (P), Etienne Delessert, (I), Anthony
Gordon, (P), Tim Greenfield-Sanders, (P), Robert Guisti, (I),
Lamb & Hall, (P), Min Jae Hong, (I), Walter looss, (P), Victor
Juhasz, (I), Nadav Kander, (P), Art Kane, (P), Steve Mayse, (I),
Eric Meola, (P), Sheila Metzner, (P), Jonathan Milne, (I), Claude
Mougin, (P), Robert Rodriguez, (I), Michael Schwab, (I), Ink
Tank, (I), Ezra Tucker, (I), David Wilcox, (I), Bruce Wolf, (P)
Ray, Rodney/405 N Wabash #2709, Chicago, IL.............................312-222-0337
David M Beck, (I), Mort Drucker, (I), Jim Endicott, (I), Rick Farrell,
(I), Marla Frazee, (I), Mark Frueh, (I), Ken Goldammer, (I), Rick
Gonnella, (I), Robert Gunn, (I), Tom Nikosey, (I), Tony Petrucelli,
(P), Robert Pryor, (I), Paul Rogers, (I), Gary Ruddell, (I), Dick
Sakahara, (I), Tim Schultz, (P), Danny Smythe, (I), Greg Wray, (I)
Ritchey, Deborah/920 N Franklin #202, Chicago, IL.......................312-642-5763
Roche, Diann/301 E Armour Blvd #315, Kansas City, MO 816-561-4473

S

Sell, Dan/233 E Wacker, Chicago, IL..312-565-2701
Alvin Blick, (I), Paul Bond, (I), Bob Boyd, (I), Lee Lee Brazeal, (I),
Daryll Cagle, (I), Kirk Caldwell, (I), Wayne Carey, (I), Justin Carroll,
(I), Mike Elins, (I), Bill Ersland, (I), Eucalyptus Tree Studio , (I), Rick
Farrell, (I), Dick Flood, (I), Bill Harrison, (I), Barry Jackson, (I), Dave
Kilmer, (I), Dave LaFleur, (I), Tom Lochray, (I), Gregory Manchess,
(I), Bill Mayer, (I), Frank Morris, (I), Stanley Olson, (I), WB Park, (I),
Hank Parker, (I), Ian Ross, (I), Mark Schuler, (I), R J Shay, (I), Dale
Verzaal, (I), Phil Wendy, (I), Paul Wolf, (I), John Zielinski, (I)
Shulman, Salo/215 W Ohio, Chicago, IL 312-337-3245
Stan Stansfield, (P)
Skillicorn, Roy/233 E Wacker #1209, Chicago, IL..........................312-856-1626
Tom Curry, (I), David Scanlon, (I)
Spectrum Reps/206 N 1st St, Minneapolis, MN...............................612-332-2361
Steiber, Doug/405 N Wabash #1503, Chicago, IL...........................312-222-9595

TVWZ

Trott, David/1237 Chicago Rd, Troy, MI...312-583-2828
Tuke, Joni/325 W Huron #310, Chicago, IL.....................................312-787-6826
Dan Blanchette, (I), Mary Grandpre, (I), Chris Hopkins, (I), Susan
Kinast, (P), Cyd Moore, (I), Sherry Neidigh, (I), Michel Tcherevkoff,
(P), Bill Thomson, (I), Pam Wall, (I), John Welzenbach, (P)
Virnig, Janet/2216 E 32nd St, Minneapolis, MN.............................612-721-8832
Rick Allen, (I), Mary Grandpre, (I), Robin Moline, (I), Brian Otto,
(I), Kate Thomssen, (I), Kevin Whaley, (I)
Wainman, Rick & Assoc/166 E Superior #212, Chicago, IL..........312-337-3960

Zann, **Sheila**/502 N Grove, Oak Park, IL 708-386-2864

SOUTHWEST

AB

Art Rep Inc/3525 Mockingbird Lane, Dallas, TX 214-521-5156
Lee Lee Brazeal, (I), Kirk Caldwell, (I), Lindy Chambers, (I),
Ellis Chappell, (I), Tom Curry, (I), Tom Dolphens, (I), M John
English, (I), Kent Kirkley, (P), Matthew Savins, (I), Stephen
Turk, (I), Andrew Vracin, (P), Terry Widener, (I)
Boster, Barbara/3910 Buena Vista #10, Dallas, TX 214-559-3640
Witlandson & Assoc, (I), Karen Blessen, (I), Lamb & Hall, (P),
John Katz, (P), Gary McCoy, (P), Jim Myers, (P), R J Shay, (I)

C

Campbell, Pamela/314 Rock Island, Angleton, TX........................713-523-5328
Charles Brown, (I), George Campbell, (I), Frankie Flores, (I),
Alexander Molinello, (I), Tom Nikosey, (I), Larry Noble, (I),
Jack Slattery, (I)
Cedeno, Lucy/PO Box 254, Cerrillos, NM 505-473-2745
David Michael Kennedy, (P)
Cobb, Friend & Johnson/2811 McKinney Ave #206, Dallas, TX ...214-855-0055
Kent Barker, (P), Connie Connally, (I), Ray-Mel Cornelius, (I),
Michael Johnson, (P), Donald Keene, (I), Geof Kern, (P),
Mercedes McDonald, (I), Michael McGar, (I), Hilary Mosberg,
(I), Richard Myers, (P), R Kenton Nelson, (I), Bryan Peterson,
(I), Steve Pietzsch, (I), Theo Rudnak, (I), Tom Ryan, (P), Jim
Sims, (P), James N Smith, (I), Joel Spector, (I), Kelly Stribling,
(I), Malcolm Tarlossky, (I), James Tennison, (I), Michele Warner,
(I), Neill Whitlock, (P)
Cuomo, Celeste/2919 Welborn #101, Dallas, TX........................214-559-0805

DF

Davis, Brooke/2515 McKinney #900, Dallas, TX 214-969-0034
DiOrio, Diana/2829 Timmons Ln, Houston, TX............................713-960-0393
Whistling Dixie, (I), Tommy Ewasko, (P), The Straight Line
Group, (I), Larry Keith, (I), Bahid Marinfar, (I), Thom Ricks, (I)
Freeman, Sandra/3333 Elm St #105, Dallas, TX 214-871-1956
Jennifer Harris, (I), Mary Haverfield, (I), Rusty Jones, (I), Lynn
Rowe Reed, (I), Gretchen Shields, (I)

HK

Hawkins, Berry/8602 Santa Clara, Dallas, TX....................214-327-7889
Matt Bowman, (P)
KJ Reps/2919 Welborn #101, Dallas, TX 214-559-0805
Kline, Sandy/637 Hawthorne, Houston, TX..........................713-522-1862
Tom Bookwalter, (I), Lee Lee Brazeal, (I), Mark Chickinelli, (I),
Keith Graves, (I), Mary Charles Kubricht, (I), Rolf Laub, (I),
Dave Maloney, (I), Jimmy Margulies, (I), Mike Robins, (I), Chris
Summers, (P), Denise Watt, (I)

LP

Lynch, Andrea/5521 Greenville #104-338, Dallas, TX.......................214-369-6990
Lynch, Larry/5521 Greenville #104-338, Dallas, TX 214-369-6990
Joel Armstrong, (I), Morton Beebe, (P), Amy Bryant, (I),
David Bullock, (P), Denise Chapman-Crawford, (I), Bob
Depew, (I), Glenn Gustafson, (I), Kate Brennan Hall, (I), Dan
Ham, (P), Aaron Jones, (P), Jeff Kosta, (P), Gary Nolton,
(P), Ambrose Rivera, (I), John Saxon, (P), Mike Wimmer, (I)
Photocom Inc/2412 Converse, Dallas, TX.........................214-428-8781
Robb Depenport, (P), Bart Forbes, (I), Claude Mougin, (P),
Tom Nikosey, (I), Andy Post, (P), Michael Steirnagle, (I),
Richard Wahlstrom, (P), Gordon Willis, (P)
Production Services/1711 Hazard, Houston, TX..........................713-529-7916

RST

Ryan, Linda/7028 Wabash Circle, Dallas, TX 214-826-8118
Dean St Clair, (I), Alan Cook, (P), Becky Cutler, (I), Faith
DeLong, (I), Andrzej Dudzinski, (I), William Harrison, (I), Chris
Hoover, (I), Mark Mroz, (I), John Nelson, (I), Bob Radigan, (I),

Kevin Short, (I), Pete Smith, (I)
Sands, Trudy/233 Yorktown, Dallas, TX............................214-748-8663
Simpson, Elizabeth/1415 Slocum St #105, Dallas, TX 214-761-0001
Kathleen Kinkopf, (I)
Those Three Reps/2909 Cole #118, Dallas, TX 214-871-1316
Bill Debold, (P)

W

Washington, Dick/717 W Ashby, San Antonio, TX..........................512-733-6128
Patti Bonham, (I), Stephen Durke, (I), Rick Kroninger, (P), Mark
Mroz, (I), Reuben Njaa, (P), Dan Soder, (I), Mark Weakley, (I)
Whalen, Judy/2336 Farrington St, Dallas, TX..........................214-630-8977
Ken Coffelt, (I), Robert LaTorre, (P)
Willard, Paul Assoc/4160 N Craftsman Ct #202, Scottsdale, AZ....602-423-1500
Mary Flock, (I), Jack Graham, (I), Gary Krejca, (I), Kevin
MacPherson, (I), Frank Medeola, (I), Curtis Parker, (I), Nancy
Pendleton, (I), Guy Porfirio, (I), Charles Thomas, (I), Wayne
Watford, (I), Jean Wong, (I)

ROCKY MTN

BCF

Brogren-Kelly/3113 E 3rd St #220, Denver, CO 303-399-3851
Ron Sauter, (I), Elsa Warnick, (I)
Cleary, T Brian/205 N Trade Center Tr, Mustang, OK 405-376-0909
Comedia/1664 Lafayette St, Denver, CO..............................303-832-2299
Foremark Studios/PO Box 10346, Reno, NV 702-786-3150

GN

Gibson, Susan/1063 Fillmore St, Denver, CO 303-333-8949
Vicki Gullickson, (I), Jeff Lauwers, (I), Matthew McFarren, (I),
Lee Milne, (P), Randy Nelson, (I)
Goodman, Christine/1869 S Pearl St #201, Denver, CO 303-733-8722
Carol Guenzi Agents Inc/130 Pearl St #1602, Denver, CO..........303-733-0128
No Coast Graphics/2629 18th St, Denver, CO..........................303-458-7086
Robert August, (I), John Cuneo, (I), Bill Kastan, (I), Patrick
Merewether, (I), Tom Nikosey, (I), Jim Salvati, (I)
Norman, Mary Lou/1664 Lafayette St, Denver, CO 303-832-2299

WEST COAST

AB

Amour, Nona/PO Box 2340, San Anselmo, CA 415-459-0319
Rick Brown, (I), Jay Daniel, (P), Mike Kowalski, (I), Jeff Leedy,
(I), Bill Reitzel, (P), Don Winston, (P), James Wolnick, (I), Diane
Woods, (P)
Arnold, Wendy/4620 Coldwater Cnyn, Studio City, CA 818-762-8850
Ayerst, Deborah/2546 Sutter St, San Francisco, CA 415-567-3570
**Baker, Kolea /2819 First Ave #240, Seattle, WA
(P 10-13)** **206-443-0326**
George Abe, (I), Don Baker, (I), Jeff Brice, (I), Elaine Cohen,
(I), Tom Collicott, (P), Philip Howe, (I), Studio MD, (I), Pete
Saloutos, (P), Bruce Sharp, (I), Al Skaar, (I), Jere Smith, (I), Kris
Wiltse, (I), Glenn Yoshiyama, (I)
Braun, Kathy/75 Water St, San Francisco, CA..........................415-775-3366
Pat Allen, (PS), Laurence Bartone, (P), Steve Bonini, (P),
Sandra Bruce, (L), Michael Bull, (I), Eldon Doty, (I), Jim Fulp,
(I), Lamb & Hall, (P), John Holder, (I), John Huxtable, (I), Bob
Johnson, (I), Jackie Osborn, (I), Stephen Osborn, (I), Gary
Pierazzi, (AB), Ray Smeraldo, (I), Koji Takei, (I)
Brenneman, Cindy/1856 Elba Cir, Costa Mesa, CA 714-641-9700
Dean Armstrong, (P), Steve Ellis, (I), Pierre Kopp, (P), Gregory
Miller, (I), Brian Murray, (I), Jim Stefl, (I)
Brock, Melissa Reps/43 Buena Vista Trail, San Francisco, CA 415-255-7393
John Cuneo, (I)
Brown, Dianne/402 N Windsor Blvd, Los Angeles, CA....................213-462-5598
David LeBon, (P), Bill Werts, (P)
Burlingham, Tricia/9538 Brighton Way #318, Beverly Hills, CA......213-271-3982
Greg Gorman, (P), Robert Grigg, (P), Kam Hinatsu, (P), Karen
Krasner, (P), Dennis Manarchy, (P), Peggy Sirota, (P)

Busacca, Mary/1335 Union St, San Francisco, CA............................415-776-4247
Richard Anderson, (I), Olden Budwine, (I), Mark Busacca, (I),
George Campbell, (I), Ignacio Gomez, (I), Paul Hoffman, (P),
John Lund, (P), Tom Nikosey, (I), Michael Pearce, (I), Jack
Slattery, (I), Willardson & Assoc, (I)
Bybee, Gerald/1811 Folsom St, San Francisco, CA.........................415-863-6346

C

Campbell, Marianne/240 Stewart St 2nd Fl, San Francisco, CA.....415-227-0939
Will Mosgrove, (P)
Carriere, Lydia/PO Box 8382, Santa Cruz, CA.................................408-425-1090
Willis Preston Campbell, (P), Don Faia, (GD), Danilo Gonzalez,
(I), Jeff Hicks, (P), Steve Kurtz, (P), John Sutton, (P)
Collier, Jan/166 South Park, San Francisco, CA 415-552-4252
Barbara Banthien, (I), Gary Baseman, (I), Bunny Carter, (I),
Chuck Eckart, (I), Rae Ecklund, (I), Douglas Fraser, (I), Robert
Hunt, (I), Yan Nascimbene, (I), Kathy O'Brien, (I), David
Rawcliffe, (P), Steve Scott, (I), Robert Gantt Steele, (I), Cynthia
Torp, (I), ahid , (I), Don Weller, (I)
Conrad, James/2149 Lyon #5, San Francisco, CA 415-921-7140
Cook, Warren/PO Box 2159, Laguna Hills, CA 714-770-4619
Kathleen Norris Cook, (P)
Cordove-Molmud, Laura/500 South Barrington #6, LA, CA 213-472-3078
Cormany, Paul/11607 Clover Ave, Los Angeles, CA.......................213-828-9653
Cormany, Tom Reps/7825 Manchester Ave, Playa Del Rey, CA 213-578-2191
Mark Busacca, (I), Greg Call, (I), Dave Clemons, (I), Jim
Heimann, (I), Rich Mahon, (I), Penina Meisels, (P), Ted Swanson,
(I), Stan Watts, (I), Will Weston, (I), Dick Wilson, (I), Andy Zito, (I)
Cornell, Kathleen/741 Millwood Ave, Venice, CA 213-301-8059
Jay Ahren, (P), John Cuneo, (I), Nancy Duell, (I), Seith Erlich,
(P), William Thompson, (P), Glen Wexler, (P)
Courtney & Natale/8800 Venice, Los Angeles, CA 213-202-0344
Dianne Bennett, (I), Jan Evans, (I), Stan Gorman, (I), Diane Teske
Harris, (I), Ling Ta Kung, (I), Jeff Leedy, (I), Sen Maruyama, (I),
Nancy Ohanian, (P), Julie Perron, (I), Chuck Schmidt, (I)
Creative Resource/2956 Nicadia Dr, Los Angeles, CA 213-470-2644

D

DeMoreta, Linda/1839 9th St, Alameda, CA....................................415-769-1421
Sam Allen, (I), Piet Halberstadt, (I), Ron Miller, (P), Steven
Nicodemus, (I), Vida Pavesich, (I), Michael Pierazzi, (P), Zhee
Singer, (I), Steven Underwood, (P)
Dicker, Debbie/765 Clementina St, San Francisco, CA.....................415-621-0687
Keith Ovregaard, (P)
Dodge, Sharon/3033 Thirteenth Ave W, Seattle, WA 206-284-4701
Robin Bartholick, (P), Art Bemus, (I), Rick Farrell, (I), John &
Lani Fortune, (I), Jud Guitteau, (I), Steven Hunt, (P), Aaron
Jones, (P), Brian Karas, (I), Jerry Nelson, (I), Frank Renlei, (I),
Patricia Ridenour, (P), John Schilling, (I), Paul Schmid, (I),
Keith Wither, (I), Jeff Zaruba, (P)
Dubow, Chuck/10966 Strathmore Dr #8, Los Angeles, CA..............213-208-8042
Terry Anderson, (I), Dick Ellescas, (I), David Galchutt, (I),
Richard Ikkanda, (I), Paul Kratter, (I), Bob Maile, (L)

EF

Epstein, Rhoni/Photo Rep/3814 Franklin Ave, Los Angeles, CA.......213-663-2388
Ericson, William/1024 Mission St, South Pasadena, CA 213-461-4969
Feliciano, Terrianne/16812 Red Hill #B, Irvine, CA 714-250-3377
Fleming, Laird Tyler/5820 Valley Oak Dr, Los Angeles, CA 213-469-3007
Haskell Wexler, (F), Vilmos Zsigmond, (F)
Fox & Spencer/8350 Melrose Ave #201, Los Angeles, CA..............213-653-6484
France Aline Inc/1076 S Ogden Dr, Los Angeles, CA 213-933-2500
Dan Arsenault, (P), Guy Billout, (I), Thomas Blackshear, (I), Elisa
Cohen, (I), Elliot Crowley, (P), Peter Greco, (L), Steve Huston, (I),
Steve Johnson, (I), Rick Kroninger, (P), John Mattos, (I), Steve
Mayse, (I), Jacqui Morgan, (I), Joel Nakamura, (I), Manuel
Nunez, (I), Robin Ruppel, (I), Teri Sandison, (P), Ezra Tucker, (I),
Kim Whitesides, (I), Bruce Wolfe, (I)

G

Gardner, Jean/348 N Norton Ave, Los Angeles, CA 213-464-2492
Richard Hume, (P), Brian Leatart, (P), Brett Lopez, (P), Rick
Rusing, (P), Steve Smith, (P), Tim Street-Porter, (P)
George, Nancy/302 N LaBrea Ave #116, Los Angeles, CA 213-655-0998

Robert Cooper, (I), Daniels & Daniels, (I), Diane Davis, (I),
Bruce Dean, (I), Dean Foster, (I), Bob Gleason, (I), Penelope
Gottlieb, (I), Steve Hendricks, (I), Hank Hinton, (I), Gary
Hoover, (I), Richard Kriegler, (I), Gary Lund, (I), Julie Pace, (I),
Jeannie Winston, (I), Corey Wolfe, (I)
Glick, Ivy/350 Townsend St #426, San Francisco, CA 415-543-6056
Jerry Dadds, (I), Jane Dill, (I), Don Dudley, (I), Malcolm Farley,
(I), Martin French, (I), Derek Grinnell, (I), Matthew Holmes, (I),
Rhonda Voo, (I)
Goldman, Caren/4504 36th St, San Diego, CA................................619-284-8339
Pete Evaristo, (I), Smith, Mark GW, (I), Sparky LeBold, (I),
Susie McKig, (I), Gary Norman, (I), Gary Norman, (I), Randy
Verougstaete, (I)
Graham, Corey/Pier 33 North, San Francisco, CA 415-956-4750
Frank Ansley, (I), Byron Coons, (I), Gordon Edwards, (P), Trick
Films, (F), Bob Gleason, (I), Chuck Kuhn, (P), Rudi Legme, (P),
Peg Magovern, (I), Patricia Mahoney, (I), Peg McGovern, (I),
Joel Nakamura, (I), Sarn, (I), Gretchen Schields, (I), Mark
Schroeder, (I), Doug Suma, (I)
Group West Inc/5455 Wilshire Blvd #1212, Los Angeles, CA 213-937-4472
Mike Cressy, (I), Larry Salk, (I), Ren Wicks, (I)

H

Hackett, Pat/101 Yesler #502, Seattle, WA 206-447-1600
Bill Cannon, (P), Jonathan Combs, (I), Steve Coppin, (I), Eldon
Doty, (I), Larry Duke, (I), Bill Evans, (I), Martin French, (I),
David Harto, (I), Chris Hopkins, (I), Gary Jacobsen, (I), Larry
Lubeck, (R), Dan McGowan, (I), Bill Meyer, (I), Leo Monahan,
(I), Bruce Morser, (I), Dennis Ochsner, (I), Chuck Pyle, (I), Jill
Sabella, (P), Yutaka Sasaki, (I), John C Smith, (I), Kelly Smith,
(I), Chuck Solway, (I), Dean Williams, (I)
Hall, Marni & Assoc/PO Box 481251, Los Angeles, CA 213-934-9420
Kevin Aguilar, (I), Dave Arkle, (I), Dave Erramouste, (I), Stan
Grant, (I), Dennis Gray, (P), Pam Hamilton, (I), Miles Hardiman,
(I), Elyse Lewin, (P), Jill Sabella, (P), Nancy Santullo, (P), Perry
Van Shelt, (I), John Turner, (P)
Hardy, Allen/1680 N Vine #1000, Los Angeles, CA 213-466-7751
Hart, Vikki/780 Bryant St, San Francisco, CA..................................415-495-4278
Jan Evans, (I), G K Hart, (P), Kevin Hulsey, (I), Aleta Jenks, (I),
Tom Kamifuji, (I), Julie Tsuchiya, (I), Jonathan Wright, (I)
Hedge, Joanne/1838 El Cerrito Pl #3, Los Angeles, CA..................213-874-1661
Cathy Detter, (I), Future Fonts, (L), Ignacio Gomez, (I), Rick
McCollum, (I), David McMacken, (I), Vida Pavesich, (I), Ken
Perkins, (I), Laura Phillips, (I), Jim Salvati, (I), Dave Schweitzer,
(I), Steven Scott, (I), Dayal Studio, (I), Julie Tsuchiya, (I), Brent
Watkinson, (I)
Henderson, Judi/245 S Van Ness 3rd Fl, San Francisco, CA...........415-864-0516
Hillman, Betsy/Pier 33 North, San Francisco, CA 415-391-1181
Istvan Banyai, (I), John Hyatt, (I), John Marriott, (P), Angel City
Prod, (TV), Randy South, (I), Greg Spalenka, (I), Kevin Spaulding,
(I), Joe Spencer, (I), Jeremy Thornton, (I), Jackson Vereen, (P)
Hjul, Diana/8696 Crescent Dr, Los Angeles, CA..............................213-654-9513
Neal Brisker, (P), John Reed Forsman, (P), Jim Greenberg, (P)
Hodges, Jeanette/12401 Bellwood, Los Alamitos, CA 213-431-4343
Ken Hodges, (I)
Hughes, April & Assoc/300 Ridgewood Ave, Mill Valley, CA 415-398-6542
Dennis Dittrich, (I), Ernie Friedlander, (P), Mitch Heinze, (I),
Kim Mak, (I), Paul Matsuda, (P), Sandra Speidel, (I)
Hunter, Nadine/80 Wellington Ave/Box 307, Ross, CA 415-456-7711
Rebecca Archey, (I), Charles Bush, (P), Jim Endicott, (I), Jud
Guitteau, (I), Bret Lopez, (P), Mercedes McDonald, (I),
Cristine Mortensen, (I), Alan Ross, (P), Jan Schockner, (L), Liz
Wheaton, (I)

JK

Jorgensen, Donna/PO Box 19412, Seattle, WA 206-284-5080
Mel Curtis, (P), Fred Hilliard, (I), Mits Katayama, (I), Richard
Kehl, (I), Doug Keith, (I), David Lund, (I), Cheri Ryan, (I),
Nancy Stentz, (I)
Karpe, Michele/6671 Sunset Blvd #1592, Los Angeles, CA............213-465-0140
Stephen Danelian, (P), Claude Morigin, (P), Victoria Pearson,
(P), Mike Reinhardt, (P), Lara Rossignol, (P), Greg Spalenka,
(I), George Stavrinos, (I)
Kirsch Represents/7316 Pyramid Dr, Los Angeles, CA 213-651-3706
David Kimble, (I), Joyce Kitchell, (I), Royce McClure, (I), Todd
Smith, (P), Jeff Wack, (I)

Knable, Ellen/1233 S La Cienega Blvd, Los Angeles, CA 213-855-8855
Henry Bjorn, (P), Roger Chouinard, (I), Bob Commander, (I),
John Dearstyne, (I), Coppos Films, (F), Randy Glass, (I), Joe
Heiner, (I), Kathy Heiner, (I), Jeff Nadler, (P), Margo Nahas, (I),
Paul Sanders, (P), Jonathan Wright, (I), Brian Zick, (I)
Koeffler, Ann/1425 N Alta Vista Blvd #402, Los Angeles, CA..........213-850-8222
Istvan Banyai, (I), Karen Bell, (I), Gerald Bybee, (P), Dick Cole,
(I), Byron Coons, (I), Jan Evans, (I), Jonathon Gelber, (P),
Chuck Kuhn, (P), Rik Olson, (I), Frank Ordaz, (I), Dan Picasso,
(I), Katherine Salentine, (I), Sandra Speidel, (I), James Stagg,
(I), Pam Wall, (I)
Kovac & Sweeney/4617 Ocean Front Walk, Marina Del Ray, CA ...213-964-2429
Hank Benson, (P), Mark Scott, (P), Nancy Stahl, (P)

L

Lawrence, Lydia/190 Cervantes Blvd #7, San Francisco, CA..........415-267-3087
Byron Gin, (I), Lon Goddard, (I), Nancy A Haig, (I), Pamela
Hamilton, (I), Johhny Karwan, (I), Andy Zito, (I)
Laycock, Louise/1351 Ocean Frt Walk #106, Santa Monica, CA....213-204-6401
Lesli-Art Inc/PO Box 6693, Woodland Hills, CA 818-999-9228
Lilie, Jim/251 Kearny St #511, San Francisco, CA........................415-441-4384
Ron Chan, (I), Craig Marshall, (I), Bruno Mezzapelle, (I),
Robert Rodriguez, (I), Dugald Stermer, (I), Ezra Tucker, (I),
Stan Watts, (I), Dennis Ziemienski, (I)
London, Valerie/9756 Charleville Blvd, Beverly Hills, CA 213-277-8090
Ludlow, Catherine/1632 S Sherburne Dr, Los Angeles, CA 213-859-9222
Dewy Nicks, (P)
Luna, Tony/45 E Walnut St, Pasadena, CA 818-584-4000

M

Marie, Rita & Friends/183 N Martell Ave #240, Los Angeles, CA..213-934-3395
David M Beck, (I), Mort Drucker, (I), Jim Endicott, (I), Rick
Farrell, (I), Marla Frazee, (I), Mark Frueh, (I), Ken Goldammer,
(I), Rick Gonnella, (I), Robert Gunn, (I), Tony Petrucelli, (P),
Robert Pryor, (I), Renwick , (I), Paul Rogers, (I), Gary Ruddell,
(I), Dick Sakahara, (I), Tim Schultz, (P), Danny Smythe, (I),
Greg Wray, (I)
Martha Productions/4445 Overland Ave, Culver City, CA...............213-204-1771
Bob Brugger, (I), Kirk Caldwell, (I), Brian Cronin, (I), Stan
Evenson Dsgn, (GD), Mike Elins, (I), Allen Garns, (I), Jeff
George, (I), Bryon Gin, (I), Mark Jasin, (I), John Kleber, (I),
Catherine Leary, (I), R Kenton Nelson, (I), Cathy Pavia, (I),
Delro Rosco, (I), Laurie Rosenwald, (I), Kevin Short, (I), Steve
Vance, (I), Rhonda Voo, (I), Wayne Watford, (I)
McGuiness, Charlotte/2120 N 60th St, Seattle, WA........................206-524-8308
Paul Ackerman, (P), Jim Mears, (P), Dave Niedopytalski, (P)
Mix, Eva/2129 Grahn Dr, Santa Rosa, CA 707-579-1535
Morgan, Michele/4621 Teller #108, Newport Beach, CA................714-474-6002
Bill Brown, (I), Rob Court, (I), Elaine DaVault, (I), Kevin
Davidson, (I), Diane Davis, (I), Dave Hudson, (I), Darlene
McElroy, (I), Morgan Pickard, (I)
Mulhauser & Young/945 Front St #206, San Francisco, CA 415-392-0542
Judy Clifford, (I), Celeste Ericsson, (I), Martin Schweitzer, (P),
Ed Taber, (I), Carlotta Tormey, (I)

NOP

Newman & Franks/2956 Nicada Dr, Los Angeles, CA 213-470-0140
Gene Allison, (I), Darryl Cagle, (I), Jim Desing, (L), Carol Etow, (I),
Nick Galloway, (I), Joan Hoch, (I), Tim Huhn, (I), Michael
Humphries, (I), Steven Klipenstein, (I), Starky LeBold, (I), John
Metowan, (I), Peter Palombi, (I), Jeff Petersen, (I), David Sarman,
(P), Theona Stokes, (I), Glenn Tarnowski, (I), Chuck Untersee, (P)
Newman, Carol/1119 Colorado Ave #23, Santa Monica, CA...........213-394-5031
Onyx/7515 Beverly Blvd, Los Angeles, CA..213-965-0899
Ostan/Prentice/Ostan/1245 McClellan Dr, Los Angeles, CA.........213-305-7143
Parrish, Dave/Photopia/PO Box 2309, San Francisco, CA 415-441-5611
Curtis Degler, (P), Steve Gill, (C), Curtis Martin, (P), Jeff Richey,
(P), Pete Saloutos, (P), Vince Valdes, (P)
Partners & Artists Assoc /13480 Contour, Sherman Oaks, CA....818-995-6883
Pate, Randy/3408 W Burbank Blvd, Burbank, CA
(P 18) **818-985-8181**
Chris Dellorco, (I), John Taylor Dismukes, (I), Robert Florczak,
(I), Bryan Haynes, (I), Chris Hopkins, (I), Robert Hunt, (I),
Marvin Mattelson, (I), Mick McGinty, (I), Kazuhiko Sano, (I),
Soapstone Studios, (I), Hugh Syme, (I)

Peek, Pamela/10834 Blix #116, Toluca Lake, CA 818-760-0746
Pelkin, Christine/1962 San Pablo Ave #3, Berkeley, CA 415-841-2238
Rob Barber, (I), John Chui, (I), Penina Meisels, (P), Frank
Remkiewicz, (I), Tom Skrivan, (P), Nita Winter, (P), Tom Wyatt, (P)
Peterson, Linda/310 1st Ave S #333, Seattle, WA..........................206-624-7344
Piscopo, Maria/2038 Calvert Ave, Costa Mesa, CA.........................714-556-8332
Jack Boyd, (P), J W Burkey, (P), John Connell, (P), Yuri Dojc,
(P), Stan Sholik, (P)
Platte, Franz/3537 17th St, San Francisco, CA..................................415-431-0657
Pohl, Jacqueline/66 Broadway, San Francisco, CA.........................415-421-4220
Jon Conrad, (I), Steven Hunt, (P), Aaron Jones, (P), John
Mattos, (I), Margo Nahas, (I), Sarah Waldron, (I)
Pribble, Laurie/911 Victoria Dr, Arcadia, CA 818-574-0288
Steve Bjorkman, (I), Greg Hally, (I), John Hull, (I), John
Huxtable, (I), Catherine Kanner, (I), Mercedes McDonald, (I),
Ken Rosenberg, (I), Andrea Tachiera, (I), Brent Watts, (I)

R

Rappaport, Jodi/5410 Wilshire Blvd #1008, Los Angeles, CA 213-934-8633
Repertory Reps/6010 Wilshire Blvd #505, Los Angeles, CA...........213-931-7449
Kaz Aizawa, (I), Richard Arruda, (I), Rhonda Burns, (I), Craig
Calsbeek, (I), Jon Conrad, (I), Laurie Gerns, (I), Scott Hensey,
(MM), Hom & Hom , (I), Haruo Ishioka, (I), Robert Jacobs, (R),
Russell Kirk, (P), Bob Maile, (L), Karl Parry, (P), Deb Polston,
(I), Teresa Powers, (I), Robert Schaefer, (I), Maryann Thomas,
(I), Larry Vigon, (G), Steve Walters, (I)
Rosenthal, Elise/3443 Wade St, Los Angeles, CA 213-390-9595
Dave Allen, (I), Joel Barbee, (I), Jody Eastman, (I), Marc
Erickson, (I), Robert Evans, (I), Bill Hall, (I), Mark Heath, (I), Jim
Henry, (I), Reggie Holladay, (I), Mia Joung, (I), Dennis Kendrick,
(I), Rick Kinetader, (I), Kyounja Lee, (I), Roger Leyonmark, (I),
Roger Loveless, (I), David Mann, (I), Roger Marchutz, (P),
Kathleen McCarthy, (I), Erik Olsen, (I), Erik Van der Palen, (I),
Tom Pansini, (I), Kim Passey, (I), Stephen Peringer, (I), Bob
Radigan, (I), Ed Renfro, (I), Ching Reyes, (I), Scott Ross, (I),
Larry Salk, (I), Chris Tuveson, (I), Bill Vann, (I), Ren Wicks, (I),
Larry Winborg, (I), Kenny Yamada, (I), Allen Yamashiro, (I)

S

Salisbury, Sharon/116 W Blithedale, Mill Valley, CA........................415-383-5943
Antar Dayal, (I), Cathy Deeter, (I), Jim Endicott, (I), Phil Frank,
(I), Joel Glenn, (P), Hank Hinton, (I), Tom Landecker, (P),
Michelle Manning, (I), Jock McDonald, (P), Doug Suma, (I)
Salzman, Richard W/716 Sanchez St, San Francisco, CA 415-285-8267
Doug Bowles, (I), Ruben DeAnda, (I), Kristen Funkhouser, (I),
Manuel Garcia, (I), Marty Gunsaullus, (I), Denise Hilton-Putnam,
(I), Jewell Homad, (I), Dan Jones, (I), Chris McAllister, (I), Dave
Mollering, (I), Everett Peck, (I), Greg Shed, (I), Walter Stuart, (I)
Santee Lehmen Dabney Inc/900 1st Ave S #404, Seattle, WA 206-467-1616
Scott, Freda/244 Ninth St, San Francisco, CA..................................415-621-2992
Sherry Bringham, (I), Ed Carey, (P), Terry Hoff, (I), Scott
Johnson, (I), Gayle Kabaker, (I), Francis Livingston, (I), Alan
Mazzetti, (I), R J Muna, (P), Sue Rother, (I), Susan Schelling,
(P), William Thompson, (P), Carolyn Vibbert, (I), Pam Wall, (I)
Scroggy, David/2124 Froude St, San Diego, CA...............................619-222-2476
Ed Abrams, (I), Jodell D Abrams, (I), Rick Geary, (I), Jean
"Moevius" Giraud, (I), Jack Molloy, (I), Hal Scroggy, (I), Lionel
Tallaro, (I)
Shaffer, Barry/PO Box 48665, Los Angeles, CA................................213-939-2527
Sharp & Assoc/3952 W 59th St, Los Angeles, CA 213-290-1430
Alan Dockery, (P), Lois Frank, (P), John LeCoq, (P), Paul
Maxon, (P), Bob McMahon, (I), Greg Morales, (I), C David
Pina, (L), Lionel Tallaro, (P)
Slobodian, Barbara/745 N Alta Vista Blvd, Hollywood, CA 213-935-6668
Pearl Beach, (I), Bob Greisen, (I), Scott Slobodian, (P)
Sobol, Lynne/4302 Melrose Ave, Los Angeles, CA...........................213-665-5141
Laura Manriquez, (I), Arthur Montes de Oca, (I)
Stefanski, Janice Reps/2022 Jones St, San Francisco, CA 415-928-0457
Jeffrey Bedrick, (I), Adrian Day, (I), Karl Edwards, (I), Emily
Gordon, (I), Gary Hanna, (I), Gary Hanna, (I), Barbara Kelley,
(I), Laurie La France, (I), Beth Whybrow Leeds, (I), Katherine
Salentine, (I)
Stelling, Terry/588 Wisconsin St, San Francisco, CA......................415-826-2132
Studio Artists Inc/638 S Van Ness Ave, Los Angeles, CA 213-385-4585
Chuck Coppock, (I), George Francuch, (I), Bill Franks, (I)
Susan & Company/2717 Western Ave, Seattle, WA........................206-728-1300

Bry Barnard, (I), David M Davis, (I), Gary Eldridge, (I), Iskra Johnson, (I), Larry Jost, (I), Kristin Knutson, (I), Don Mason, (P), Karen Moskowitz, (P), Stephen Peringer, (I), Joe Saputo, (I), John Schmelzer, (I)

Sweet, Ron/716 Montgomery St,
San Francisco, CA (P 38,39)..........................**415-433-1222**
Randy Barrett, (I), Batista/Moon , (P), Charles Brown, (I), Randy Glass, (I), Richard Leech, (I), Tom Lochray, (I), Steve Mayse, (I), Will Nelson, (I), Will Nelson, (I), Darrell Tank, (I), Jeffrey Terreson, (I), Jack Unruh, (I), Bruce Wolfe, (I), James B Wood, (P)

TV

Thornby, Kirk/611 S Burlington, Los Angeles, CA.............................213-933-9883
Tos, Debbie/111 Tamarind Ave, Hollywood, CA 213-466-0033
Carl Furuta, (P), Michael Going, (P), David Kramer, (P), Michael Salas, (P)
Townsend, Kris/58 Polhemus Way, Larkspur, CA 415-243-2484
David W Hamilton, (P)
Valen Assocs/950 Klish Way, Del Mar, CA..619-259-5774
George Booth, (C), Richard Cline, (C), Whitney Darrow, (C), Eldon Dedini, (I), Joe Farris, (C), Bob Handelsman, (C), Stan Hunt, (C), Henry Martin, (C), Warren Miller, (I), Frank Modell, (C), Mischa Richter, (C), Victoria Roberts, (C), Henry Syverson, (C), Robert Weber, (I), Gahan Wilson, (I), Bill Woodman, (I), Jack Ziegler, (C)
Vandamme, Vicki/35 Stillman #206, San Francisco, CA 415-543-6881
Lee Lee Brazeal, (I), Kirk Caldwell, (I), John Collier, (I), Kathy & Joe Heiner, (I), Alan Krosnick, (P), Steve Lyons, (I), Dennis Mukai, (I), Jennie Oppenheimer, (I), Will Rieser, (I), Kim Whitesides, (I), Nic Wilton, (I)

W

Wagoner, Jae/654 Pier Ave #C, Santa Monica, CA...........................213-392-4877
Stephen Durke, (I), Ken Durkin, (I), William Harrison, (I), Steve Jones, (I), Nobee Kanayama, (I), Leo Monahan, (I), Jeff Nishinaka, (I), Doug Suma, (I), Don Weller, (I)
Wiley, David/1535 Green St #207, San Francisco, CA 415-441-1623
Steve Bjorkman, (I), Chris Consani, (I), Ben Garvie, (I), Ben Garvie, (I), Ben Garvie, (I), Brent Lindstrom, (P), Scott Sawyer, (I), Keith Witmer, (I), Paul Wolf, (I)
Winston, Bonnie/195 S Beverly Dr #400, Beverly Hills, CA 213-275-2858
Eshel Ezer, (P), Marco Franchina, (P), Joe Hill, (P), Mark Kayne, (P), Francesco Scavullo, (P), Veronique Vial, (P)

I N T E R N A T I O N A L

Kane, Dennis/135 Rose Ave, Toronto , ON 416-323-3677
Miller + Comstock Inc/180 Bloor St W #1102, Toronto , ON..........416-925-4323
Organisation, The/69 Caledonian Rd, London, England, ...071-281-5176
Grahame Baker, (I), Emma Chichester Clark, (I), Neil Gower, (I), Katherine Mynott, (I), Michael O'Shaughnessy, (I), Max Schindler, (I)
Sharp Shooter/524 Queen St E, Toronto , ON 416-860-0300
Vernell, Maureen/128 Fieldgate Dr, Nepean , ON............................613-825-4740

ILLUSTRATORS

NYC

A

Aagaard, Gary/312 5th St #3, Brooklyn	718-499-4687
Abraham, Daniel E/Box 2528/Rockefeller Sta	718-499-4006
Abrams, Kathie/548 Ninth St, Brooklyn	718-499-4408
Accardo, Anthony/19 E 48th St 3rd Fl	212-838-0050
Accornero, Franco/620 Broadway	212-674-0068
Acuna, Ed/232 Madison Ave #402	212-889-8777
Adams, Angela/866 UN Plaza #525	212-644-2020
Adams, Jeanette/261 Broadway	212-732-3878
Adams, Jeffrey/231 W 25th St #6E	212-807-0840
Adams, Lisa/100 W 12th St #4H	212-691-3238
Adams, Norman/211 E 51st St #5F	212-755-1365
Adelman, Morton/144-69 28th Ave	718-961-5072
Aiese, Bob/60 Pineapple St, Brooklyn	718-596-2240
Ajhar, Brian/32 W 40th St #9B	212-819-9084
Albahae, Andrea/2364 Brigham St 1st Fl, Brooklyn	718-934-7004
Alcorn, John/135 E 54th St	212-421-0050
Alcorn, Stephen/135 E 54th St	212-421-0050
Alexander & Turner/232 Madison Ave #402	212-889-8777
Alexander, Pat/19 E 83rd St #4B	212-288-3345
Allaux, Jean Francois/21 W 86th St	212-496-8593
Allen, Julian/31 Walker St	212-925-6550
Allen, Michael Illus/89 Fifth Ave	212-924-3432
Allen, Terry/164 Daniel Low Terr, Staten Island	718-727-0723
Allert, Kathy/201 E 28th St	212-532-0928
Aloisio, Richard/145 E 16th St	212-473-5635
Alpert, Alan/405 E 54th St	212-741-1631
Alpert, Olive/9511 Shore Rd, Brooklyn	718-833-3092
Alter, Judy/539 Naughton Ave, Staten Island	718-667-5643
Ameijide, Ray/108 E 35th St #1C	212-889-3337
Amicosante, Vincent/280 Madison Ave #1402	212-545-9155
Amit, Emmanuel/108 E 35th St #1C	212-889-3337
Amrine, Cynthia/240 E 27th St	212-679-0129
Anderson, Rolf/45 W 84th St	212-787-3305
Anderson, Toyce/280 Madison Ave #1402	212-545-9155
Angelakis, Manos/31 W 21st St 7th Fl Rear	212-243-4412
Angelini, George/232 Madison Ave #402	212-889-8777
Angelo, Peter/500 W 43rd St #7G	212-947-7454
Angerame, Diane/57-30 254th St, Little Neck	718-428-7794
Antonios, Tony/60 E 42nd St #505	212-682-1490
Arcelle, Joan/430 W 24th St	212-924-1865
Arisman, Marshall/314 W 100th St	212-662-2289
Aristovulos, Nick/16 E 30th St	212-725-2454
Arnold, Robert/149 W 14th St	212-989-7049
Arnoldi, Per/60 E 42nd St #505	212-682-1490
Asbaghi, Zita/104-40 Queens Blvd, Forest Hills	718-275-1995
Assel, Steven/472 Myrtle Ave, Brooklyn	718-789-1725
Astrahan, Irene/201 E 28th St	212-532-0928

B

Bacall, Aaron/204 Arlene St, Staten Island	718-494-0711
Bailer, Brent/104 E 40th St	212-661-0257
Bailey, Pat/60 E 42nd St #505	212-682-1490
Baker, Garin/60 E 42nd St #505	212-682-1490
Baker, Grahame/267 Wyckoff St, Brooklyn	718-624-1906
Banfield, Elliott/110 Horatio St	212-255-3950
Banner, Shawn/170 Broadway #201	212-312-6447
Baradat, Sergio/210 W 70th St	212-721-2588
Baran, Zafer/267 Wycoff St, Brooklyn	718-624-1906
Barancik, Cathy/18 E 78th St	212-472-3838
Barberis, Juan C/60 E 42nd St #1146	212-953-7088
Barbour, Karen/51 Warren St 5th Fl	212-619-6790
Barner, Bob/866 UN Plaza #525	212-644-2020
Barnes, Michele/111 Sullivan St #3B	212-219-9269
Baron, Esther/866 UN Plaza #525	212-644-2020
Barr, Ken/420 Lexington Ave #2760	212-697-8525
Barrall, Tim/372 Bleecker St #2	212-243-9003
Barrera, Alberto/463 West St #1017D	212-645-2544

Barrett, Ron/2112 Broadway #402A	212-874-1370
Barritt, Randi/240 W 15th St	212-255-5333
Barry, Ron/165 E 32nd St	212-686-3514
Bartholomew, Caty/217 Dean St, Brooklyn	718-596-8863
Barton, Kent/121 Madison Ave	212-683-1362
Baseman, Gary/443 12th St #2D, Brooklyn	718-499-9358
Bates, Harry	718-693-6304
Bauer, Carla Studio/156 Fifth Ave #1100	212-807-8305
Bauman, Jill/PO Box 152, Jamaica	718-631-3160
Baumann, Karen/43 E 19th St	212-688-1080
Baxter, Daniel/88 First Pl Parlr Fl, Brooklyn	718-522-1549
Becker, Ron/265 E 78th St	212-535-8052
Beecham, Tom/420 Lexington Ave #2738	212-697-8525
Begin, Maryjane/866 UN Plaza #525	212-644-2020
Bego, Dolores/155 E 38th St	212-697-6170
Belair & Inoue Visual Comm/323 Park Ave S	212-473-8330
Belcastro, Mario/1650 Third Ave #4A	212-534-6688
Bemus, Bart/353 W 53rd St #1W	212-682-2462
Bendell, Norm/41 Union Sq W #918	212-807-6627
Benney , Robert/50 W 96th St	212-222-6605
Benson, Linda M./558 7th St #3A, Brooklyn	718-499-9492
Berger, Stephen/43 E 19th St	212-254-4996
Bergin, Robert/111 Wooster St #PH C	212-925-0491
Bergman, Eliot, Inc./362 W 20th St #201 (P 22,23)	**212-645-0414**
Berkey, John/509 Madison Ave 10th Fl	212-355-0910
Berran, Bob/60 E 42nd St #1940	212-867-8092
Berrett, Randy/15 W 72nd St	212-799-2231
Berry, Fanny Mellet/155 E 38th St	212-697-6170
Beylon, Cathy/201 E 28th St	212-532-0928
Bianco, Gerard/1040 82nd St, Brooklyn	718-836-8637
Biers, Nanette/194 Third Ave	212-475-0440
Billout, Guy/225 Lafayette St #1008 (P 24,25)	**212-431-6350**
Bilmes, Semyon/420 Lexington Ave #2760	212-697-8525
Biniasz, Paul/132 W 21st St 12th Fl	212-979-0025
Bjorkman, Steve/501 Fifth Ave #1407	212-490-2450
Black & White Dog Studio/3240 Henry Hudson Pkwy #6H, Bronx	212-601-8820
Blackshear, Lisa/11 W 17th St	212-675-1083
Blackshear, Thomas/121 Madison Ave	212-683-1362
Blackwell, Garie/60 E 42nd St #505	212-682-1490
Blair, Dru/6 E 36th St #1R	212-685-4580
Blake, Bob/251 W 97th St #6B	212-316-4656
Blake, Quentin/81 Greene St	212-925-3053
Blas, Bob/43 E 19th St	212-254-4996
Bleck, Cathie/58 W 15th St 6th Fl	212-741-2539
Bliok, Leo/990 Ave of Americas	212-629-8559
Bloch, Alex/19 E 48th St 3rd Fl	212-838-0050
Bloom, Tom/235 E 84th St #17	212-628-6861
Blubaugh, Susan M/330 E 11th St #3	212-533-1646
Blum, Zevi/81 Greene St	212-925-3053
Bogan, Paulette/287 W 4th St #1	212-243-1694
Boguslav, Raphael/200 E 78th St	212-570-9069
Boies, Alex/420 Lexington Ave #2760	212-697-8525
Bolognese, Don/19 E 48th St	212-838-0050
Bonforte, Lisa/201 E 28th St	212-532-0928
Bonhomme, Bernard/111 Wooster St #PH C	212-925-0491
Bono, Mary M/288 Graham Ave, Brooklyn	718-387-3774
Bordelon, Melinda/60 E 42nd St #505	212-682-1490
Bornstein, Peter/474 Fifth Street #4, Brooklyn	718-768-0443
Bostic, Alex/330 Haven Ave #4N	212-568-2848
Botana, Federico/227 W 29th St #9R	212-967-7699
Botas, Juan/110 Suffolk St #6A	212-420-5984
Bowie, Effie/152 E 94th St #12A	212-289-5469
Boyd, Harvey/24 Fifth Ave	212-475-5235
Boyer, Gene/232 Madison Ave #402	212-889-8777
Bozzo, Frank/400 E 85th St #5J	212-535-9182
Bracchi Beresford Draplin/152 E 33rd St 4th Fl (P 27)	**212-532-3298**
Brachman, Richard/30-44 34th St #5F, Astoria	718-204-6879
Bracken, Carolyn/201 E 28th St	212-532-0928
Brady, Elizabeth/461 Broome St	212-966-9897
Brak, Syd/450 Seventh Ave #902	212-268-1788
Bralds, Braldt/135 E 54th St	212-421-0050
Bramhall, William/81 Greene St	212-925-3053
Brandt, Joan/15 Gramercy Park S	212-473-7874
Braun, Wendy/32 W 40th St #9B	212-819-9084
Brautigam, Don/211 E 51st St #5F	212-755-1365
Breakey, John/611 Broadway #811	212-982-0188
Breinberg, Aaron/66-15 Thorton Pl, Forest Hills	718-261-2544

Brennan, Neil/41 Union Sq W #636 212-206-0066
Brennan, Steve/420 Lexington Ave #PH4,5 212-986-5680
Bricher, Scott/330 W 42nd St #3200NE 212-714-0147
Brillhart, Ralph/60 E 42nd St #1940 212-867-8092
Brindak, Hermine/29 W 15th St #B 212-620-0604
Broda, Ron/420 Lexington Ave #2760 212-697-8525
Brodner, Steve/121 Madison Ave 212-683-1362
Brofsky, Miriam/186 Riverside Dr 212-595-8094
Brooks, Andrea/99 Bank St 212-924-3085
Brooks, Clare Vanacore/415 W 55th St 212-245-3632
Brooks, Ed/20 W 87th St #6A 212-595-5980
Brooks, Hal/20 W 87th St #6A 212-595-5980
Brooks, Leo/3039 Wallace Ave #6E, Bronx 212-882-0148
Brooks, Lou/415 W 55th St 212-245-3632
Brooks, Lou Productions/415 W 55th St 212-245-3632
Brothers, Barry/1922 E 18th St, Brooklyn 718-336-7540
Brown, Bradford/4103 Lowerre Pl, Bronx 212-231-8223
Brown, Colin/41 Union Sq W #636 212-206-0066
Brown, Dan/232 Madison Ave #402 212-889-8777
Brown, Donald/20 Bay St Landing #2D, Staten Island 212-532-1705
Brown, Judith Gwyn/522 E 85th St 212-288-1599
Brown, Michael David/108 E 35th St #1C 212-889-3337
Brown, Peter D/235 E 22nd St #16R 212-684-7080
Brown, Rick/60 E 42nd St #505 212-682-1490
Brown, RS/62 W 45th St 212-398-9540
Bruce, Taylor/853 Broadway #1201 212-677-9100
Bruinsma, Martin/377 Broome St #10 212-226-5460
Brusca, Jack/43 E 19th St 212-254-4996
Bryan, Diana/200 E 16th St #1D 212-475-7927
Bryan, Mike/420 Lexington Ave #2760 212-697-8525
Bryant, Rick J/18 W 37th St #301 212-594-6718
Buchanan, Yvonne/18 Lincoln Pl #2L, Brooklyn 718-783-6682
Buehler, Mark/418 Atlantic Ave, Brooklyn 718-797-3689
Bull, Michael/420 Lexington Ave #2760 212-697-8525
Burgoyne, John/200 E 78th St 212-570-9069
Busch, Lon/108 E 35th St #1C 212-889-3337
Buschman, Lynne/186 Franklin St 212-925-4701
Bush, George/60 E 42nd St #1940 212-867-8092
Byrd, Bob/280 Madison Ave #1402 212-545-9155

C

Caggiano, Tom/83-25 Dongan Ave, Elmhurst 718-651-8993
Cagle, Daryl/95 Horatio St 212-807-0840
Cain, David/200 W 20th St #607 212-633-0258
Callen, Liz/866 UN Plaza #525 212-644-2020
Campbell, Jim/420 Lexington Ave #PH4,5 212-986-5680
Cantarella, Virginia Hoyt/107 Sterling Pl, Brooklyn 718-622-2061
Carbone, Kye/241 Union St, Brooklyn 718-802-9143
Carpenter, Joe/72 Spring St #1003 212-431-6666
Carpenter, Polly/72 Spring St 212-431-6666
Carr, Noell/30 E 14th St 212-675-1015
Carter, Bunny/200 E 78th St 212-570-9069
Carter, Penny/12 Stuyvesant Oval #4A 212-473-7965
Carver, Steve/41 Union Sq W #636 212-206-0066
Casale, Paul/5304 11th Ave, Brooklyn 718-871-6848
Cascio, Peter/810 Seventh Ave 41st Fl 212-408-2177
Cassidy, Michael/60 E 42nd St #1940 212-867-8092
Cassler, Carl/420 Lexington Ave #PH4,5 212-986-5680
Castelluccio, Frederico/60 E 42nd St #1940 212-867-8092
Catrow, David/ 212-627-7058
Cavaliere, Jamie/60 E 42nd St #1940 212-867-8092
Celsi, David/43 W 27th St #9R 212-889-6196
Ceribello, Jim/11 W Cedar View Ave, Staten Island 718-317-5972
Cesc/81 Greene St 212-925-3053
Chabrian, Deborah/420 Lexington Ave #PH 4,5 212-986-5680
Chalmers, Cheryl/156 Fifth Ave #617 212-243-1333
Chambless-Rigie, Jane/64-66 Seventh Ave #3D 212-627-9821
Chang, Alain/232 Madison Ave #402 212-889-8777
Chappell, Ellis/420 Lexington Ave #PH4,5 212-986-5680
Charmatz, Bill/25 W 68th St 212-595-3907
Chermayeff, Ivan/58 W 15th St 6th Fl 212-741-2539
Chester, Harry/501 Madison Ave 212-752-0570
Chironna, Ronald/122 Slosson Ave 2nd Fl, Staten Island 718-720-6142
Chow, Tad/50-44 68th St, Woodside 718-899-9813
Christiansen, Kent/320 E 50th St #2C 212-754-3017
Christiensen, kent/320 E 50th St #2C 212-754-3017
Chronister, Robert/3140 Rt 209, KIngston 914-687-4911
Chwast, Eve/215 Park Ave S #1300 212-674-8080
Chwast, Jacqueline/23-83 37th St, Astoria 718-626-0840
Chwast, Seymour/215 Park Ave S #1300 212-674-8080
Ciardiello, Joe/2182 Clove Rd, Staten Island 718-727-4757
Ciccarelli, Gary/353 W 53rd St #1W 212-682-2462
Ciesiel, Christine G/101 MacDougal St 212-353-8678
Cieslawski, Steve/866 UN Plaza #525 212-644-2020
Clark, Emma Chichester/267 Wyckoff St, Brooklyn 718-624-1906
Clarke, Robert/200 W 54th St #9C 212-581-4045
Clementson, John/155 Ave of Americas 10th Fl 212-255-6530
Clifford, Judy/62 W 45th St 212-398-9540
Cober, Leslie/431 E 83rd St 212-515-4536
Cody, Brian/866 UN Plaza #525 212-644-2020
Coffey, Deborah C/339 E 33rd St #1R 212-532-5205
Cohen, Adam/74 Charles St #2B 212-691-4074
Cohen, Hayes/36-35 193rd St #3, Flushing (P 20) 718-321-7307
Cohen, Stacey L/252 W 76th St #3A 212-724-2774
Colby, Garry/420 Lexington Ave #PH4,5 212-986-5680
Cole, Olivia/19 E 48th St 3rd Fl 212-838-0050
Collier, John/121 Madison Ave 212-683-1362
Collier, Roberta/201 E 28th St 212-532-0928
Collins, Jennifer/320 E 42nd St #112 (P 28) 212-297-0474
Colon, Ernie/43 E 19th St 212-254-4996
Colrus, William/156 Fifth Ave #617 212-243-1333
Comitini, Peter/30 Waterside Plaza 212-683-5120
Cone, William/575 Park Ave 212-751-4812
Confer, Mitchell/505 Court St #3A, Brooklyn 718-858-2159
Connelly, Gwen/420 Lexington Ave #2760 212-697-8525
Conner, Mona/1 Montgomery Pl #8, Brooklyn 718-636-1527
Continuity Graphics Assoc'd Inc/62 W 45th St 212-869-4170
Conway, Michael/316 E 93rd St #23 212-722-3300
Cook, Anne/232 Madison Ave #402 212-889-8777
Cook, David/60 E 42nd St #1940 212-867-8092
Cook, Donald/866 UN Plaza #525 212-644-2020
Cooper, Dan/62 W 45th St 212-398-9540
Cooper, Dana/35 E 85th St #4D 212-794-3969
Cooper, Floyd/866 UN Plaza #525 212-644-2020
Cooperstein, Sam/677 West End Ave 212-864-4064
Corben, Richard/43 E 19th St 212-254-4996
Corio, Paul/208 E 7th St #10 212-228-4630
Cormier, Wil/15 W 72nd St 212-799-2231
Cornell, Jeff/232 Madison Ave #402 212-889-8777
Cornell, Laura/118 E 93rd St #1A 212-534-0596
Corvi, Donna/568 Broadway #604 212-925-9622
Couch, Greg/51 Seventh Ave, Brooklyn 718-789-9276
Courtney, Richard/43 E 19th St 212-254-4996
Cove, Tony/60 E 42nd St #1146 212-953-7088
Cox, Paul/121 Madison Ave 212-683-1362
Craig, Daniel/60 E 42nd St #505 212-682-1490
Creative Capers/60 E 42nd St #505 212-682-1490
Crews, Donald/653 Carroll St, Brooklyn 718-636-5773
Cristiano, Rudy/62 W 45th St 212-398-9540
Crosthwaite, Royd/509 Madison Ave 10th Fl 212-355-0910
Cruse, Howard/88-11 34th Ave #5D, Jackson Heights 718-639-4951
Cruz, Ray/194 Third Ave 212-475-0440
Csatari, Joe/420 Lexington Ave #2911 212-986-5680
Cudworth, Nick/450 Seventh Ave #902 212-268-1788
Cuevas Stillerman Plotkin/118 E 28th St #306 212-679-0622
Cummings, Pat/28 Tiffany Pl, Brooklyn 718-834-8584
Cummings, Terrence/210 W 64th St #5B 212-586-4193
Cusack, Margaret/124 Hoyt St, Brooklyn 718-237-0145
Cushwa, Tom/303 Park Ave S #511 212-228-2615
Czechowski, Alicia/215 Park Ave S #1300 212-674-8080

D

D'Andrea, Bernard/509 Madison Ave 10th Fl 212-355-0910
D'Andrea, Domenick/509 Madison Ave 10th Fl 212-355-0910
D'Onofrio, Alice/866 UN Plaza #4014 212-644-2020
Dacey, Bob/232 Madison Ave #402 212-889-8777
Dale, Robert/1573 York Ave #3N 212-535-2505
Dallison, Ken/108 E 35th St #1C 212-889-3337
Daly, Sean/85 South St 212-668-0031
Damore, Georgan/280 Madison Ave #1402 212-545-9155
Daner, Carole/200 W 20th St #101 212-243-8152
Daniel, Frank/201 E 28th St 212-532-0928
Daniels, Beau & Alan/232 Madison Ave #402 212-889-8777
Daniels, Sid/12 E 22nd St #11B 212-673-6520

Darden, Howard/62 W 45th St 212-398-9540
Daste, Larry/201 E 28th St 212-532-0928
Davidson, Dennis/43 E 19th St 212-254-4996
Davidson, Everett/60 E 42nd St #505 212-682-1490
Davis, Allen/141-10 25th Rd #3A, Flushing 718-463-0966
Davis, Harry R/189 E 3rd St #15 212-674-5832
Davis, Jack/108 E 35th St #1C 212-889-3337
Davis, Jack E/121 Madison Ave 212-683-1362
Davis, Nelle/20 E 17th St 4th Fl 212-807-7737
Davis, Paul/14 E 4th St 212-420-8789
Dawson, John/515 Madison Ave 22nd Fl 212-486-9644
Day, Betsy/866 UN Plaza #525 212-644-2020
De Seve, Peter/25 Park Pl, Brooklyn 718-398-8099
DeAraujo, Betty/201 E 28th St 212-532-0928
Deas, Michael/39 Sidney Pl, Brooklyn 718-852-5630
Deel, Guy/60 E 42nd St #1940 212-867-8092
Dees, David/41 Union Sq W #1228 212-929-5590
Deeter, Catherine/515 Madison Ave 22nd Fl 212-486-9644
Degen, Paul/81 Greene St 212-925-3053
DeGraffenried, Jack/566 Seventh Ave #603 212-221-8090
DeJesus, Jamie/15 W 72nd St 212-799-2231
Delmirenburg, Barry/301 E 38th St 212-573-9200
DelRossi, Richard/156 Fifth Ave #617 212-243-1333
Delvalle, Daniel/19 E 48th St 212-838-0050
Demarest, Chris/81 Greene St 212-925-3053
DeMichiell, Robert/226 W 78th St #26 212-769-9192
Denaro, Joseph/566 Seventh Ave #603 212-221-8090
Deneen, Jim/420 Lexington Ave #2911 212-986-5680
DeRijk, Walt/43 E 19th St 212-254-4996
Dervaux, Isabelle/204 Ave B 212-505-0511
Deschamps, Bob/108 E 35th St #1C 212-889-3337
DesCombes, Roland/509 Madison Ave 10th Fl 212-355-0910
Design Loiminchay/503 Broadway 5th Fl 212-941-7488
Design Plus/156 Fifth Ave #1232 212-645-2686
Desimini, Lisa/532 E 82nd St #19 212-737-1535
DeSpain, Pamela Mannino/344 E 63rd St #2C 212-486-2315
Dettrich, Susan/253 Baltic St, Brooklyn 718-237-9174
Devaud, Jacques/353 W 53rd St #1W 212-682-2462
Devlin, Bill/108 E 35th St #1C 212-889-3337
Diamantis, Kitty/19 E 48th St 3rd Fl 212-838-0050
Diamond Art Studio/11 E 36th St 212-685-6622
Diamond, Donna/420 Lexington Ave PH 212-986-5680
Diamond, Ruth/95 Horatio St #521 212-243-3188
DiCianni, Ron/420 Lexington Ave #2760 212-697-8525
DiComo Comp Art/120 E 34th St #12K-L 212-689-8670
Diehl, David/222 W 20th St #16 212-242-8897
Dietz, Jim/165 E 32nd St 212-686-3514
DiFabio, Jessica/56 Jane St #1B 212-645-3620
Dilakian, Hovik/111 Wooster St #PH C 212-925-0491
Dinnerstein, Harvey/933 President St, Brooklyn 718-783-6879
Dininno, Steve/62 W 45th St 212-398-9540
Dittrich, Dennis/42 W 72nd St #12B 212-864-5971
Dodds, Glenn/238 E 36th St 212-679-3630
Dodge, Bill/60 E 42nd St #1940 212-867-8092
Doktor, Patricia/95 Horatio St #9A 212-645-4452
Dolobowsky, Mena/140 West End Ave #9H 212-874-7074
Domingo, Ray/108 E 35th St #1C 212-889-3337
Doniger, Nancy/402A 19th St, Brooklyn 718-965-0284
Donner, Carol/501 Fifth Ave #1407 212-490-2450
Donze, Lisa/33-48 28th St, Astoria 718-956-9082
Doquette, Steve/62 W 45th St 212-398-9540
Doret, Michael/12 E 14th St #4D 212-929-1688
Doret/Smith Studios/12 E 14th St #4D 212-929-1688
Doty, Curt/4 S Portland Ave #2, Brooklyn 718-797-5115
Dowdy, Michael/3240 Henry Hudson Pkwy #6H, Bronx 212-601-8820
Downes, Nicholas/PO Box 107, Brooklyn 718-875-0086
Draper, Linda/95 Horatio St #205 212-581-4609
Drescher, Henrik/151 First Ave #55 212-777-6077
Drovetto, Richard/355 E 72nd St 212-861-0927
Dryden, Patty/194 Third Ave 212-475-0440
Duarte, Mary Young/350 First Ave #9E 212-674-4513
Dubanevich, Arlene/866 UN Plaza #4014 212-644-2020
Duburke, Randy/272 Wyckoff St, Brooklyn 718-522-6793
Ducak, Danilo/60 E 42nd St #1940 212-867-8092
Dudash, C Michael/211 E 51st St #5F 212-755-1365
Dudzinski, Andrzej/52 E 81st St 212-772-3098
Duggan, Lee/108 E 35th St #1C 212-889-3337
Duke, Chris/509 Madison Ave 10th Fl 212-355-0910
Dunnick, Regan/41 Union Sq W #1228 212-929-5590
Duquette, Steven/62 W 45th St 212-398-9540
Duram, Nina/60 E 42nd St #505 212-682-1490
Dyess, John/156 Fifth Ave #617 212-243-1333
Dynamic Duo Studio/382 Lafayette St 212-254-8242

E

Eagle, Cameron/41 Union Sq W #1228 212-929-5590
Eastman, Norm & Bryant/420 Lexington Ave #2738 212-697-8525
Ecklund, Rae/41 Union Sq W #1228 212-929-5590
Eckstein, Linda/534 Laguardia Pl #5S 212-522-2552
Edmunds, Douglas/126 W 22nd St 212-627-4040
Eggert, John/420 Lexington Ave #PH4,5 212-986-5680
Ehlert, Lois/866 UN Plaza #525 212-644-2020
Eisner, Gil/310 W 86th St #11A 212-595-2023
Elins, Michael/353 W 53rd St #1W 212-682-2462
Ellis, Dean/30 E 20th St 212-475-1483
Elmer, Richard/504 E 11th St #FE1A 212-522-1051
Ely, Richard/207 W 86th St 212-757-8987
Emerson, Carmela/217-11 54th Ave, Bayside 718-224-4251
Emerson/Wajdowicz/1123 Broadway 212-807-8144
Endewelt, Jack/50 Riverside Dr 212-877-0575
Enik, Ted/82 Jane St #4A 212-620-5972
Enric/43 E 19th St 212-688-1080
Entwisle, Mark/267 Wycoff St, Brooklyn 718-624-1906
Erickson, Mary Anne/25 Fifth Ave #14H 212-979-8246
Evans, Jan/853 Broadway #1201 212-677-9100
Evcimen, Al/305 Lexington Ave #6D 212-889-2995
Eversz, Kim Wilson/268 Union St #3, Brooklyn 718-237-8546
Ewing, Carolyn/201 E 28th St 212-532-0928

F

Fabricatore, Carol/1123 Broadway #612 212-463-8950
Falkenstern, Lisa/232 Madison Ave #402 212-889-8777
Fanelli, Carolyn/19 Stuyvesant Oval 212-533-9829
Farina, Michael/566 Seventh Ave #603 212-221-8090
Farrell, Russell/353 W 53rd St 212-682-2462
Farrell, Sean/320 E 42nd St #112 212-949-6081
Fascione, Sabina/194 Third Ave 212-475-0440
Fasolino, Teresa/58 W 15th St 6th Fl 212-741-2539
Faulkner, Matt/35 Pineapple St #1A, Brooklyn 718-858-1724
Faust, Clifford/322 W 57th St #42P 212-581-9461
FeBland, David/670 West End Ave #11B 212-580-9299
Feingold, Deborah/430 Broome St 212-911-0018
Fennimore, Linda/808 West End Ave #801 212-866-0279
Fernandez, Fernando/43 E 19th St 212-254-4996
Fernandez, George/60 E 42nd St #1940 212-867-8092
Fernandez, Stanislaw/115 Fourth Ave #2A 212-533-2648
Fertig, Howard/7-15 162nd St #6C, Beechhurst 718-746-6265
Fichera, Maryanne/120 E 34th St #12K-L 212-689-8670
Field, Lori Nelson/860 W 181st St #41A 212-795-4281
Fine, Robert/43 E 19th St 212-254-4996
Finelle, Dominick/420 Lexington Ave #PH4,5 212-986-5680
Fiorentino, Al/866 UN Plaza #525 212-644-2020
Fischer, Rick/156 Fifth Ave #1222 212-645-6772
Fisher, Jeffrey/81 Greene St 212-925-3053
Fisher, Mark/111 Wooster St #PH C 212-925-0491
Fitzhugh, Gregg/62 W 45th St 212-398-9540
Flaherty, David/449 W 47th St #3 212-262-6536
Flanagan, Dan/427 15th St #1C, Brooklyn 718-499-5253
Fleming, Ron/60 E 42nd St #505 212-682-1490
Flesher, Vivienne/194 Third Ave 212-475-0440
Forbes, Bart/501 Fifth Ave #1407 212-490-2450
Forrest, Sandra/332 W 88th St #C1 212-769-4375
Foster, B Lynne/540 Ft Washington Ave #3D 212-740-7011
Fox, Barbara/301 W 53rd St 212-245-7564
Frampton, David/58 W 15th St 6th Fl 212-741-2539
Francis, Judy E/110 W 96th St #2C 212-866-7204
Frank, Scott J/518 E 80th St #2A 212-861-0635
Fraser, Douglas Illust/41 Union Sq W #1228 212-929-5590
Freas, John/353 W 53rd St #1W 212-682-2462
Freda, Tony/36-34 30th St, Long Island City 718-482-7455
Freelance Solutions/369 Lexington Ave 18th Fl 212-490-3334
French, Lisa/420 Lexington Ave #2760 212-697-8525
Fretz, Frank/866 UN Plaza #525 212-644-2020
Fricke, Warren/15 W 72nd St 212-799-2231

Fried, Janice/459 Ninth St, Brooklyn.................................718-832-0881
Friedman, Barbara A/29 Bank St 212-242-4951
Friedman, Jon/866 UN Plaza #525.................................212-644-2020
Frisari, Frank/9508 112th St, Richmond Hill..................718-441-0919
Frith, Michael/267 Wycoff St, Brooklyn 718-624-1906
Furukawa, Mel/116 Duane St...................................212-349-3225

G

Gabriel, Don/43 E 19th St...................................212-254-4996
Gadino, Victor/1601 Third Ave.................................212-534-7206
Gaetano, Nick/14 E 52nd St...................................212-752-8490
Gala, Tom/420 Lexington Ave #2911.............................212-986-5680
Galindo, Felipe/96 Ave B 2nd Fl...............................212-477-2485
Galkin, Simon/19 E 48th St 3rd Fl.............................212-838-0050
Gall, Chris/853 Broadway #1201................................212-677-9100
Gallardo, Gervasio/509 Madison Ave 10th Fl....................212-355-0910
Gambale, David/200 W 15th St..................................212-243-4209
Gampert, John/PO Box 219, Kew Gardens.........................718-441-2321
Gardner, Steve/60 E 42nd St #1940.............................212-867-8092
Garguila, Joanna/107 St Mark's Pl #1H.........................212-777-0392
Garland, Bill/353 W 53rd St #1W...............................212-682-2462
Garns, G Allen/41 Union Sq W #636.............................212-206-0066
Garrick, Jacqueline/333 E 75th St.............................212-628-1018
Garrido, Hector/420 Lexington Ave #PH4,5......................212-986-5680
Garrison, Barbara/12 E 87th St................................212-348-6382
Garrow, Dan/501 Fifth Ave #1407...............................212-490-2450
Gartel, Laurence/270-16 B Grand Central Pkwy, Floral Park.....718-229-8540
Gates, Donald/19 E 48th St 3rd Fl.............................212-838-0050
Gayler, Anne/320 E 86th St #4F................................212-734-7060
Gazzo, Peppi/220 Cabrini Blvd #4H.............................212-568-2337
Geary, Rick/1 Irving Pl #G24A.................................212-677-9045
Gebert, Warren/333 E 49th St #3J..............................212-980-8061
Gehm, Charles/420 Lexington Ave #2760.........................212-697-8525
Geiser, Janie/340 E 9th St....................................212-353-5015
Geller, Amy/11-15 45th Ave, Long Island City..................718-786-5277
Gem Studio/420 Lexington Ave #220.............................212-687-3460
Genova, Joe/60 E 42nd St #505.................................212-682-1490
Gentile, John & Anthony/244 W 54th St 9th Fl..................212-757-1966
George, Jeff/853 Broadway #1201...............................212-677-9100
Geras, Audra/501 Fifth Ave #1407..............................212-490-2450
Gerberg, Darcy/149 W 24th St..................................212-243-3346
Gersten, Gerry/1380 Riverside Dr..............................212-928-7957
Gerwitz, Rick/93 Perry St #11.................................212-989-9342
Giavis, Ted/420 Lexington Ave #PH 4,5.........................212-986-5680
Giglio, Mark/235 Elizabeth St #21.............................212-431-8926
Giglio, Richard/2231 Broadway #17.............................212-724-8118
Gignilliat, Elaine/420 Lexington Ave #PH4,5...................212-986-5680
Giguere, Ralph/41 Union Sq W #636.............................212-206-0066
Gillies, Chuck/420 Lexington Ave #PH4,5.......................212-986-5680
Gillot, Carol/67 E 11th St #708...............................212-353-1174
Giorgio, Nate/566 Seventh Ave #603............................212-221-8090
Giovanopoulos, Paul/119 Prince St.............................212-677-5919
Girvin, Tim/501 Fifth Ave #1407...............................212-490-2450
Giuliani, Bob/19 E 48th St....................................212-838-0050
Gladstone, Dale/128 N 1st St, Brooklyn........................718-782-2250
Glass, Randy/108 E 35th St #1C................................212-889-3337
Glazer & Kalayjian/301 E 45th St (P 14,15)..................212-687-3099
Glick, Judith/301 E 79th St...................................212-734-5268
Glover, Gary/232 Madison Ave #402.............................212-889-8777
Goldman, Dara/866 UN Plaza #525...............................212-644-2020
Goldstrom, Robert/471 Fifth St, Brooklyn......................718-768-7367
Goodell, Jon/866 UN Plaza #4014...............................212-644-2020
Goodfellow, Peter/267 Wycoff St, Brooklyn 718-624-1906
Goodman, Paula/156 Fifth Ave..................................212-243-1333
Gordley, Scott/31 W 21st St 7th Fl Rear.......................212-243-4412
Gore, Elissa/583 W 215th St #A3...............................212-567-2161
Gorton, Julia/85 South St #6N.................................212-825-0190
Gorton/Kirk Studio/85 South St #6N............................212-825-0190
Gottfried, Max/82-60 116th St #CC3, Kew Gardens...............718-441-9868
Gourley, Robin/244 Fifth Ave 11th Fl..........................212-679-4420
Gowdy, Carolyn/81 Greene St...................................212-925-3053
Gower, Neil/267 Wyckoff St, Brooklyn..........................718-624-1906
Grace, Alexa/70 University Pl.................................212-254-4424
Graham, Mariah/670 West End Ave...............................212-580-8061
Graham, Thomas/408 77th St #D4, Brooklyn......................718-680-2975
Grajek, Tim/184 E 2nd St #4F..................................212-995-2129
Gran, Julia/3240 Henry Hudson Pkwy #6H, Bronx.................212-601-8820

Grant, Bill/119 Amherst St, Brooklyn..........................718-891-4936
Graphic Chart & Map Co/236 W 26th St #8SE.....................212-463-0190
Grashow, David/81 Greene St...................................212-925-3053
Gray, Doug/15 W 72nd St.......................................212-799-2231
Gray, Susan/42 W 12th St #5...................................212-675-2243
Grebu, Devis/43 E 19th St.....................................212-254-4996
Greenstein, Susan/4915 Surf Ave, Brooklyn.....................718-373-4475
Gregoretti, Robert/41-07 56th St, Woodside....................718-779-7913
Greif, Gene/270 Lafayette St #1505............................212-966-0470
Greiner, Larry/236 W 26th St 8th Fl...........................212-982-2428
Griesbach/Martucci/58 W 15th St 6th Fl........................212-741-2539
Griffel, Barbara/23-45 Bell Blvd, Bayside.....................718-631-1753
Griffin, James/60 E 42nd St #1940.............................212-867-8092
Grimmett, Douglas/467 Ave of Americas.........................212-627-8216
Grossman, Robert/19 Crosby St.................................212-925-1965
Grossman, Wendy/355 W 51st St #43.............................212-262-4497
Guarnaccia, Steven/430 W 14th St #508.........................212-645-9610
Guip, Amy/430 Lafayette St Loft 3.............................212-674-8166
Guitar, Jeremy/866 UN Plaza #525..............................212-644-2020
Guitteau, Jud/501 Fifth Ave #1407.............................212-490-2450
Gumen, Murad/33-25 90th St #6K, Jackson Heights...............718-478-7267
Gurbo, Walter/208 E 13th St #6N...............................718-634-0072
Gurney, John Steven/261 Marlborough Rd, Brooklyn..............718-462-5073
Gustafson, Dale/420 Lexington Ave #PH4,5......................212-986-5680
Gutierrez, Rudy/330 Haven Ave #4N.............................212-568-2848

H

Haas, Arie/62 W 45th St.......................................212-398-9540
Hack, Konrad/866 UN Plaza #525................................212-644-2020
Hahn, Marika/Oak Tree Rd/Box 670, Palisades...................914-365-3317
Haimowitz, Steve/67-40 Yellowstone Blvd, Forest Hills.........718-520-1461
Hall, Deborah Ann/105-28 65th Ave #6B, Forest Hills...........718-896-3152
Hall, Joan/155 Bank St #H954..................................212-243-6059
Hall, Stephen/155 Ave of Americas 10th Fl.....................212-255-6530
Hamann, Brad/330 Westminster Rd, Brooklyn.....................718-287-6086
Hampton, Blake/62 W 45th St...................................212-398-9540
Hamrick, Chuck/420 Lexington Ave #PH 4,5......................212-986-5680
Hanna, Gary/62 W 45th St 212-398-9540
Hannon, Mark/156 Fifth Ave #617...............................212-243-1333
Hardy, Fran/41 Union Sq W #636................................212-206-0066
Harris, Diane Teske/342 Madison Ave #469......................212-719-9879
Harris, John/155 Ave of Americas 10th Fl......................212-255-6530
Hart, John/494 State St, Brooklyn.............................718-852-6708
Hart, Thomas/82-67 Austin St #506, Kew Gardens................212-984-3108
Hart, Veronika/60 E 42nd St #505..............................212-682-1490
Harte, Cheryl/124 E 85th St #1F...............................212-879-3886
Harvey, Ray/60 E 42nd St #1940................................212-867-8092
Harwood, John/60 E 42nd St #505...............................212-682-1490
Haselaar, Henk/280 Madison Ave #1402..........................212-545-9462
Havilland, Brian/34 E 30th St.................................212-481-4132
Haynes, Bryan/60 E 42nd St #505...............................212-682-1490
Heath, R Mark/62 W 45th St....................................212-398-9540
Heck, Cathy/333 E 30th St.....................................212-679-1358
Heindel, Robert/211 E 51st St #5F.............................212-755-1365
Hejja, Attila/420 Lexington Ave #PH4,5........................212-986-5680
Hellard, Susan/267 Wycoff St, Brooklyn........................718-624-1906
Heller, Debbie/601 West End Ave #11B..........................212-580-0917
Heller, Karen/300 W 108th St..................................212-866-5879
Henderling, Lisa/232 Madison Ave #402.........................212-889-8777
Henderson, Alan/31 Jane St #10B...............................212-243-0693
Henderson, Meryl/19 E 48th St 3rd Fl..........................212-838-0050
Henrie, Cary/310 E 46th St #5H................................212-986-0299
Henriquez, Celeste/27 Bleecker St.............................212-673-1600
Henry, Paul/15 W 72nd St......................................212-799-2231
Herbert, Jonathan/324 Pearl St #2G............................212-571-6256
Herder, Edwin/60 E 42nd St #1940..............................212-867-8092
Hering, Al/277 Washington Ave #3E, Brooklyn...................914-471-7326
Herman, Mark/853 Boradway #1201...............................212-677-9100
Herman, Tim/853 Broadway......................................212-677-9100
Hesse, Laura/566 Seventh Ave #603.............................212-221-8090
Hewitt, Margaret/31 Ocean Pkwy #2C, Brooklyn..................718-436-2039
Hewitt/Low Studios/31 Ocean Parkway #2C, Brooklyn.............718-436-2039
Hickes, Andy/315 W 23rd St #3A................................212-989-9023
Hickson, Bob/194 Third Ave....................................212-475-0440
High, Richard/420 Lexington Ave #2760.........................212-697-8525
Hill, Amy/111 Wooster St #PH C................................212-925-0491
Himler, Ron/866 UN Plaza #525.................................212-644-2020

Hirashima, Jean/161 E 61st St #5C 212-593-9778
Hiroko/67-12 Yellowstone Blvd #E2, Forest Hills 718-896-2712
Hoff, Terry/420 Lexington Ave #2760 212-697-8525
Hoffman, Ginnie/108 E 35th St #1 212-889-3337
Hoffman, Martin/509 Madison Ave 10th Fl 212-355-0910
Hoffman, Rosekrans/866 UN Plaza #525 212-644-2020
Hofhiemer, Steven/102-25 67th Rd #5E, Forest Hills 718-997-0399
Hofmekler, Ori/166 Second Ave #11K 212-829-9838
Hogarth, Paul/81 Greene St 212-925-3053
Holland, Brad/96 Greene St 212-226-3675
Holm, John/353 W 53rd St #1W 212-682-2462
Holst, Joani/1814 Bay Ridge Pkwy, Brooklyn 718-236-6214
Holter, Susan/Goodman, Al/422 E 81st St 212-744-7870
Hom & Hom/425 W 23rd St #10F 212-242-6367
Hong, Min Jae/310 E 23rd St #10J 212-674-4320
Honkanen, William/19 Stanton St #31 212-995-0751
Hooks, Mitchell/321 E 83rd St 212-737-1853
Hosner, William/853 Broadway 212-677-9100
Hostovich, Michael/127 W 82nd St #9A 212-580-2175
Howard, John/336 E 54th St 212-832-7980
Howell, Kathleen/866 UN Plaza #525 212-644-2020
Huang, Mei-ku/201 E 28th St 212-532-0928
The Hub/16 E 16th St 4th Fl 212-675-8500
Hubert, Laurent/216 E 45th St 212-661-0850
Huerta, Catherine/337 W 20th St #4M 212-682-1490
Huffman, Tom/130 W 47th St #6A 212-755-3185
Hughes, Mary Ellen/403 E 70th St 212-288-8375
Hull, Cathy/165 E 66th St (P 30) 212-772-7743
Human, Jane/155 Ave of Americas 10th Fl 212-255-6530
Hunt, Jim/853 Broadway 212-677-9100
Hunt, Robert/165 E 32nd St 212-686-3514
Hunter, Stan/509 Madison Ave 10th Fl 212-355-0910

I

Ilbusuki, James/420 Lexington Ave #PH4,5 212-986-5680
Ice, Monica/19 E 48th St 212-838-0050
Ilic, Mirko/95 Horatio St #526 212-645-8180
Illumination Studio/330 Haven Ave #4N 212-568-2848
Incandescent Ink Inc/111 Wooster St #PH C 212-925-0491
Incisa, Monica/300 E 40th St #7D 212-986-5344
The Ink Tank/2 W 47th St 14th Fl 212-869-1630
Inoue, Izumi/325 W 37th St 4F 212-643-9147
Iskowitz, Joel/420 Lexington Ave #2911 212-986-5680
Ivens, Rosalind/156 Prospect Park W #3L, Brooklyn 718-499-8285

J

Jaben, Seth Design/47 E 3rd St #3 212-673-5631
Jacobson/Fernandez/41 Union Sq W #636 212-206-0066
Jaffee, Al/140 E 56th St #12H 212-371-5232
Jakesevic, Nenad/165 E 32nd St 212-686-3514
James, Bill/420 Lexington Ave #PH4,5 212-986-5680
Jamieson, Doug/42-20 69th St, Woodside 718-565-6034
Janoff, Dean/514 W 24th St 3rd Fl 212-807-0816
Jasper, Jackie/165 E 32nd St 212-686-3514
Jeffers, Kathy/151 W 19th St 212-255-5196
Jeffries, Shannon/494 State St, Brooklyn 718-643-1755
Jennis, Paul/420 Lexington Ave #2911 212-986-5680
Jessell, Tim/60 E 42nd St #505 212-682-1490
Jetter, Frances/390 West End Ave 212-580-3720
Jezierski, Chet/62 W 45th St 212-398-9540
Jinks, John/690 Greenwich St #BD 212-675-2961
Jirecke, Danusia/114 E 7th St #15 212-691-1313
Jobe, Jody/875 W 181st St 212-795-4941
Johnson, David A/121 Madison Ave 212-683-1362
Johnson, Doug/45 E 19th St 212-260-1880
Johnson, Iskra/353 W 53rd St #1W 212-682-2462
Johnson, Joel Peter/333 E 49th St #3J 212-980-8061
Johnson, Julie/155 E 38th St 212-697-6170
Johnson, Lonni Sue/11 Riverside Dr #3JW 212-873-7749
Johnson, Stephen/280 Madison Ave #1402 212-545-9155
Johnston, David McCall/509 Madison Ave 10th Fl 212-355-0910
Jonason, Dave/215 Park Ave S #1300 212-674-8080
Jones, Bob/420 Lexington Ave #PH 4,5 212-986-5680
Jones, Randy/323 E 10th St 212-677-5387
Jones, Russell/199 Eighth Ave #C4, Brooklyn 718-965-3224
Jones, Taylor/19 E 48th St 3rd Fl 212-838-0050
Joung, Mia/60 E 42nd St #1940 212-867-8092
Julian, Claudia/301 W 45th St #7A 718-891-7957
Juniper, David/450 Seventh Ave #902 212-268-1788
Just, Hal/155 E 38th St 212-697-6170
Justinen, Lars/420 Lexington Ave #2760 212-697-8525

K

Kagansky, Eugene/515 Ave I #2H, Brooklyn 718-253-0454
Kalish, Lionel/30 E 10th St 212-228-6587
Kalle, Chris/866 UN Plaza #525 212-644-2020
Kaloustian, Rosanne/208-19 53rd Ave, Bayside 718-428-4670
Kanarek, Michael/54 W 21st St 212-989-8377
Kaneda, Shirley/34 W 56th St #4F 212-246-6335
Kanelous, George/130 Barrow St #316 212-688-1080
Kaniliotis, Thanos/245 E 40th St #20C 212-682-2554
Kantra, Michelle/26 W 97th St #4A 212-316-3176
Kaplan, Mark/156 Fifth Ave #617 212-243-1333
Kappes, Werner/134 W 26th St #903 212-242-6777
Karchin, Steve/211 E 51st St #5F 212-755-1365
Karlin, Bernie/41 E 42nd St #PH 212-687-7636
Karlin, Eugene/3973 48th St, Sunnyside 714-472-4625
Karlin, Nurit/19 E 48th St 212-838-0050
Karn, Murray/120 E 86th St 212-289-9124
Katz, Les/451 Westminster Rd, Brooklyn 718-284-4779
Kaufman, Mark/5123 Reeder St, Elmhurst 718-672-3257
Kaufmann, Berl/65-65 Booth St #605, Rego Park 718-275-7974
Kaufthial, Henry/220 W 19th St #1200 212-633-0222
Keleny, Earl/515 Madison Ave 22nd Fl 212-486-9644
Kelley, Barbara/555 10th St, Brooklyn 718-788-2465
Kelley, Gary/121 Madison Ave 212-683-1362
Kelley, Mark/866 UN Plaza #525 212-644-2020
Kelly, Kevin/601 E 11th St #3B 212-505-2711
Kendrick, Dennis/99 Bank St #3G 212-924-3085
Kernan, Patrick/413 W 48th St 212-924-7800
Keyes, Steven/566 Seventh Ave #603 212-221-8090
Kibbee, Gordon/6 Jane St 212-989-7074
Kiefer, Alfons/420 Lexington Ave #PH4,5 212-986-5680
Kieffer, Christa/866 UN Plaza #525 212-644-2020
Kimura, Hiro/298 Clinton Ave, Brooklyn 718-638-0372
Kirk, Daniel/85 South St #6N 212-825-0190
Klavins, Uldis/60 E 42nd St #1940 212-867-8092
Klein, David G/408 Seventh St, Brooklyn 718-788-1818
Klein, Hedy/111-56 76th Dr #B3, Forest Hills 718-793-0246
Klein, Renee/164 Daniel Low Terr, Staten Island 718-727-0723
Klein/Allen Studio/164 Daniel Low Terr, Staten Island 718-727-0723
Kletsky, Olga/63-89 Saunders St #5G, Rego Park 718-897-1771
Knaff, Jean-Christian/450 Seventh Ave #902 212-268-1788
Knafo, Hai/370 Union St, Brooklyn 212-416-2469
Knettell, Sharon/108 E 35th St #1 212-889-3337
Knight, Jacob/216 E 45th St 212-661-0850
Kodama, Hideaki/501 Fifth Ave #1407 212-490-2450
Kojoyian, Armen/52 Clark St #5K, Brooklyn 718-797-5179
Kondo, Vala/230 W 79th St #52 212-517-4052
Kondo, Yukio/201 E 28th St 212-532-0928
Koren, Edward/81 Greene St 212-925-3053
Kovalcik, Terry/124 W 18th St 5th Fl 212-620-7772
Kramer, Carveth/216 E 45th St 212-661-0850
Krauter, George/89 Fifth Ave 212-924-3432
Kretschmann, Karin/323 W 75th St #1A 212-724-5001
Kronen, Jeff/231 Thompson St #22 212-475-3166
Krumeich, Tad/156 Fifth Ave #617 212-243-1333
Kubinyi, Laszlo/108 E 35th St #1C 212-889-3337
Kuchera, KAthleen/25 Prince St #5 212-966-6605
Kuester, Bob/353 W 53rd St #1W 212-682-2462
Kuhn, Grant/233 Bergen St, Brooklyn 718-596-7808
Kukalis, Romas/420 Lexington Ave #2911 212-986-5680
Kung, Lingta/420 Lexington Ave #2760 212-697-8525
Kunstler, Mort/509 Madison Ave 10th Fl 212-355-0910
Kuper, Peter/250 W 99th St #9C 212-864-5729
Kurman, Miriam/422 Amsterdam #2A 212-580-1649
Kursar, Ray/1 Lincoln Plaza #43R 212-873-5605
Kurtzman, Edward/60 E 42nd St #411 212-953-7088
Kurtzman, Harvey/566 Seventh Ave #603 212-221-8090

L

Lablak, Teresa A/206-02 50th Ave, Bayside 718-224-8597

Lacey, Lucille/87-25 86th St, Woodhaven 718-805-2215
Lackner, Paul/19 E 48th St 212-838-0050
Ladas, George/157 Prince St...........212-673-2208
Laird, Campbell/162 E 23rd St #3B...........212-505-5552
Lakeman, Steven/115 W 85th St...........212-877-8888
Lamut, Sonja /165 E 32nd St...........212-686-3514
Landis, Joan/6 Jane St...........212-989-7074
Landry, Alice/62 W 45th St...........212-398-9540
Lang, Gary/420 Lexington Ave #2738...........212-697-8525
Langenstein, Michael/56 Thomas St 2nd Fl...........212-964-9637
LaPadula, Tom/201 E 28th St...........212-532-0928
Lapinski, Joe/853 Broadway #1201...........212-677-9100
Laporte, Michele/579 Tenth St, Brooklyn 718-499-2178
Larrain, Sally Marshall/19 E 48th St 3rd Fl...........212-838-0050
Larson, Miriam/410 Riverside Dr #92...........212-713-5765
Lasher, Mary Ann/60 E 42nd St #505...........212-682-1490
Laslo, Larry/179 E 71st St 212-737-2340
Lau, Rikki/60 E 12th St #6D...........212-674-5971
Laurence, Karen/216 E 45th St...........212-661-0850
Lauter, Richard/381 Park Ave S #919...........212-889-2400
Lavigne, Dan/566 Seventh Ave #603...........212-221-8090
Law, Polly/305-A President St, Brooklyn 718-875-4425
Lazure, Catherine/593 Riverside Dr #6D...........212-690-1867
Le-Tan, Pierre/81 Greene St 212-925-3053
Leder, Dora/866 UN Plaza #525...........212-644-2020
Ledwidge, Natacha/267 Wycoff St, Brooklyn 718-624-1906
Lee, Bill/792 Columbus Ave #1-O 212-866-5664
Lee, Eric J W/60 E 42nd St #1146 212-953-7088
Lee, Jody A/175 Ninth Ave...........212-741-5192
Leedy, Jeff/41 Union Sq W #636 212-206-0066
Leer, Rebecca J/560 W 43rd St #11K...........212-563-4980
Lehr, Paul/509 Madison Ave 10th Fl...........212-355-0910
Leiner, Alan/353 W 53rd St #1W...........212-682-2462
Lennard, Elizabeth/111 Wooster St #PH C...........212-925-0491
Leon, Karen/154-01 Barclay Ave, Flushing 718-461-2050
Leonard, Richard/212 W 17th St #2B 212-243-6613
Leonard, Tom/866 UN Plaza #525...........212-644-2020
Lesser, Ron/420 Lexington Ave #2760...........212-697-8525
Levin, Arnie/342 Madison Ave #469...........212-719-9879
Levine, Andy/30-85 36th St #2, Astoria 718-956-8539
Levine, Bette/60 E 42nd St #505...........212-682-1490
Levine, Marsha E/140-55 34th Ave #4P, Flushing...........718-445-9410
Levy, Franck/305 E 40th St #5Y (P 31) **212-557-8256**
Lewin, Ted/152 Willoughby Ave, Brooklyn 718-622-3882
Lewis, Tim/184 St Johns Pl, Brooklyn 718-857-3406
Lexa, Susan/866 UN Plaza #525...........212-644-2020
Liao, Sharmen/108 E 35th St #1C...........212-889-3337
Liberatore, Gaetano/43 E 19th St...........212-254-4996
Lieberman, Ron/109 W 28th St...........212-947-0653
Liepke, Skip/211 E 51st St #5F...........212-755-1365
Lilly, Charles/24-01 89th St, E Elmhurst 718-803-3442
Lindberg, Jeffrey/449 50th St, Brooklyn 718-492-1114
Lindeman, Nicky/548 Hudson St...........212-645-8180
Lindgren, Goran/19 E 48th St 3rd Fl...........212-838-0050
Lindlof, Ed/353 W 53rd St #1W...........212-682-2462
Lindquist, Mark/1762 First Ave 212-534-3899
Line, Lemuel/509 Madison Ave 10th Fl...........212-355-0910
Lionsgate/333 E 49th St #3J...........212-980-8061
Lippman, Peter/410 Riverside Dr #134 212-865-1823
Lipstein, Morissa/19 E 48th St...........212-838-0050
Little Apple Art/409 Sixth Ave, Brooklyn 718-499-7045
Littrell, Kandy/2 W 47th St...........212-869-1630
Livingston, Francis/420 Lexington Ave #2760 212-697-8525
Lloyd, Peter/566 Seventh Ave #603...........212-221-8090
Lockwood, Todd/60 E 42nd St #505...........212-682-1490
Lodigensky, Ted/566 Seventh Ave #603...........212-221-8090
Lofaro, Gerald/270 Lafayette St #308...........516-752-7519
LoGrippo, Robert/509 Madison Ave 10th Fl...........212-355-0910
Lohsteoter, Lori/41 Union Sq W #1228...........212-929-5590
Long, Gary/450 Seventh Ave #902...........212-268-1788
Lonsdale, Ashley/420 Lexington Ave #PH4,5...........212-986-5680
Lorenz, Lee/108 E 35th St #1C...........212-889-3337
Lovitt, Anita/308 E 78th St...........212-628-8171
Low, William/31 Ocean Pkwy #2C, Brooklyn...........718-436-2039
Luce, Ben/5 E 17th St 6th Fl...........212-255-8193
Ludlow, Roberta/111 Wooster St #PH C...........212-925-0491
Lui, David/111 Wooster St #PH C...........212-925-0491
Lulevitch, Tom/101 W 69th St #4D...........212-362-3318

Lustig, Loretta/19 E 48th St 3rd Fl...........212-838-0050
Lyall, Dennis/420 Lexington Ave #PH 4,5 212-986-5680
Lynch, Jeffrey/420 Lexington Ave #PH4,5 212-986-5680

M

Mac, John/450 Seventh Ave #902...........212-268-1788
MacCombie, Turi/201 E 28th St 212-532-0928
MacDonald, Ross/27 1/2 Morton St #20 212-727-8067
MacLeod, Lee/60 E 42nd St #505...........212-682-1490
Madden, Don/866 UN Plaza #525...........212-644-2020
Magdich, Dennis/420 Lexington Ave #2760 212-697-8525
Magnuson, Diana/461 Park Ave S 212-696-4680
Maguire, Bob/60 E 42nd St #1940 212-867-8092
Magurn, Susan/866 UN Plaza #525...........212-644-2020
Mahon, Rich/566 Seventh Ave #603...........212-221-8090
Mahoney, Ron/353 W 53rd St #1W...........212-682-2462
Maisner, Bernard/184 Second Ave #2A...........212-475-5911
Malonis, Tina/32-11 31st Ave #1, Astoria...........718-956-7924
Mangal/155 E 38th St...........212-697-6170
Mangiat, Jeffrey/420 Lexington Ave #PH4,5...........212-986-5680
Mannes, Don/325 E 77th St #5D...........212-288-1661
Manning, Michele/420 Lexington Ave #2760...........212-697-8525
Mantel, Richard/114 E 32nd St #1103...........212-929-5590
Manyum, Wallop/37-40 60th St, Woodside...........718-476-1478
Marchetti, Lou/420 Lexington Ave #PH 4,5...........212-986-5680
Marciuliano, Frank/420 Lexington Ave #2760...........212-697-8525
Marden, Phil/329 Third Ave #10 212-689-6033
Mardon, Allan/108 E 35th St #1C...........212-889-3337
Margulies, Robert/561 Broadway #10B...........212-219-9621
Marich, Felix/853 Broadway...........212-677-9100
Marinelli, Robert/165 Bryant Ave, Staten Island 718-979-4018
Marridejos, Fernando/130 W 67th St #1B...........212-724-7339
Marsh, James/450 Seventh Ave #902...........212-268-1788
Martin, Greg J/60 E 42nd St #505 212-682-1490
Martin, John/501 Fifth Ave #1407 212-490-2400
Martinez, Edward/420 Lexington Ave #PH4,5 212-986-5680
Martinez, John/280 Madison Ave #1402...........212-545-9155
Martinez, Sergio/43 E 19th St...........212-254-4996
Martinot, Claude/145 Second Ave #20 212-473-3137
Marvin, Fred/43 E 19th St...........212-254-4996
Maryles, Helen/43 W 16th St #1B...........212-727-1092
Marziali, Sandra/140 West End Ave #9H...........212-874-7074
Masi, George/111 Wooster St #PH C...........212-925-0491
Mason, Brick/349 E 14th St #3R...........212-777-4297
Mason, Tod/19 E 48th St 3rd Fl...........212-838-0050
Masuda, Coco/1 Union Sq #803 212-255-7381
Mathieu, Joseph/81 Greene St...........212-925-3053
Mattos, John/41 Union Sq W #1228...........212-929-5590
Maughan, Bill/420 Lexington Ave #PH4,5...........212-986-5680
Maxwell, Brookie/53 Irving Pl...........212-475-6909
May, Darcy/201 E 28th St...........212-532-0928
Mayforth, Hal/108 E 35th St #1C...........212-889-3337
Mazarin, C S/157 E 99th St #16...........212-410-9628
Mazzella, Mary Jo/541 Edison Ave, Bronx...........212-862-3560
Mazzetti, Alan/420 Lexington Ave #2760...........212-697-8525
McArthur, Dennis/170-44 130th Ave #8D, Jamaica...........718-987-3946
McCaffery, Peter/27 Bleecker St 212-673-1600
McClintock, Wendell/60 E 42nd St #1146...........212-953-7088
McCollum, Rick/232 Madison Ave #402...........212-889-8777
McConnell, Gerald/10 E 23rd St 212-505-0950
McCormack, Geoffrey/420 Lexington Ave #PH4,5...........212-986-5680
McCreanor, Mike/156 Fifth Ave...........212-243-1333
McCreary, Jane/866 UN Plaza #525...........212-644-2020
McCutheon, Kathleen/261 W 19th St...........212-989-3954
McDaniel, Jerry/155 E 38th St...........212-697-6170
McEntire, Larry/515 Madison Ave 22nd Fl...........212-486-9644
McGurl, Michael/83 Eighth Ave #2B, Brooklyn 718-857-1866
McKeating, Eileen/340 W 11th St #2ER...........212-627-7715
McKenzie, Crystal/30 E 20th St #502...........212-598-4567
McLain, Julia/111 Wooster St #PH C...........212-925-0491
McLaughlin, Gary/420 Lexington Ave #2760...........212-697-8525
McLean, Wilson/902 Broadway #1603...........212-752-8490
McMacken, David B/60 E 42nd St #505 212-682-1490
McMullan, James/222 Park Ave S #10B...........212-473-5083
McPheeters, Neal/16 W 71st St 212-799-7021
Mead, Kimble Pendleton/125 Prospect Park West, Brooklyn 718-768-3632
Mehlman, Elwyn/108 E 35th St #1C 212-889-3337

Meisel, Ann/420 Lexington Ave #PH4,5 212-986-5680
Meisler, Meryl/553 8th St, Brooklyn 718-768-3991
Melendez, Robert/566 Seventh Ave #603 212-221-8090
Merrell, Patrick/124 W 18th St 5th Fl 212-620-7777
Messi, Enzo & Schmidt, Urs/41 Union Sq W #636 212-206-0066
Meyerowitz, Rick/68 Jane St 212-989-2446
Michaels, Bob/267 Fifth Ave #402 212-532-0916
Michal, Marie/108 E 35th St #1 212-889-3337
Michel, Jean-Claude/353 W 53rd St #1W 212-682-2462
Midda, Sara/81 Greene St 212-925-3053
Middendorf, Frances/337 E 22nd St #2 (P 33) 212-473-3586
Mikos, Mike/420 Lexington Ave #PH 4,5 212-986-5680
Milbourn, Patrick/327 W 22nd St #3 212-989-4594
Milgrim, David/8 Grammercy Park S #2G 212-673-1432
Miliano, Ed/248 West 88th #23-B 212-873-4721
Miller, A J/62 W 45th St 212-398-9540
Miller, Cliff/60 E 42nd St #1940 212-867-8092
Miller, Douglas/36-34 30th St, Long Island City 718-482-7455
Mills, Elise/150 E 79th St #3 212-794-2042
Minor, Wendell/277 W 4th St 212-691-6925
Miro/60 E 42nd St #1940 212-867-8092
Mitchell, Celia/2229 19th St, Long Island City 718-626-4095
Mitchell, Judith/270 Riverside Dr #1D 212-666-5143
Mitsuhashi, Yoko/27 E 20th St Grnd Fl 212-979-1266
Mitzura/60 E 42nd St #1940 212-867-8092
Miyamoto, Linda/PO Box 2310, Brooklyn 718-596-4787
Mones-Mateu/43 E 19th St 212-254-4996
Montesano, Sam/60 E 42nd St #1940 212-867-8092
Montgomery, Marilyn/280 Madison Ave #1402 212-545-9155
Montiel, David/115 W 16th St #211 212-929-3659
Moonlight Press Studio/362 Cromwell Ave, Ocean Breeze ..718-979-9695
Moore, Christian/400 E 77th St #7A 212-288-3718
Moore, Cyd/280 Madison Ave #1402 212-545-9155
Moores, Jeff/32 W 40th St #9B 212-819-9084
Moore, Marlene/400 E 77th St #7A 212-288-3718
Moorhead, Meg/205 E 77th St 212-628-4285
Moraes, Greg/60 E 42nd St #428 212-867-8092
Morgan, Jacqui/692 Greenwich St 212-463-8488
Moritsugu, Alison/504 W 111th St #62 212-316-5315
Morris, Frank/23 Bethune St #2 212-989-2598
Morrison, Don/155 E 38th St 212-697-6170
Morse, Bill/60 E 42nd St #505 212-682-1490
Moscarillo, Mark/90 W Broadway #2B 516-563-8114
Moss, Geoffrey/315 E 68th St 212-472-9474
Mossey, Belinda/526 2nd St, Brooklyn 718-499-2588
MS Design/27 W 20th St #1005 212-242-6525
Mueller, Pete/60 E 42nd St #505 212-682-1490
Mulligan, Donald/418 Central Pk W #81 212-666-6079
Munck, Paula/58 W 15th St 6th Fl 212-741-2539
Munson, Don/235 W 76th St #9E 212-572-2251
Murawski, Alex/108 E 35th St #1C 212-889-3337
Murdocca, Sal/19 E 48th St 3rd Fl 212-838-0050
Murphy, Chris/156 Fifth Ave #617 212-243-1333
Myers, David/228 Bleecker St #8 212-989-5260
Myers, Lou/108 E 35th St #1C 212-889-3337
Mynott, Katherine/267 Wyckoff St, Brooklyn 718-624-1906
Mynott, Lawrence/267 Wyckoff St, Brooklyn 718-624-1906

N

Nagaoka, Shusei/15 W 72nd St 212-799-2231
Nagata, Mark/60 E 42nd St #1146 212-953-7088
Nahas, Margo Z/41 Union Sq W #1228 212-929-5590
Nahigian, Alan/33-08 31st Ave #2R, Long Island City 718-274-4042
Najaka, Marlies Merk/241 Central Pk W #7A 212-580-0058
Nakai, Michael/218 Madison Ave #5R 212-213-5333
Narashima, Tomo/1160 Third Ave #9K 212-988-3828
Nascimbene, Yan/381 Park Ave S #919 212-889-2400
Nazz, James/42 Stuyvesant St 212-228-9713
Needham, James/19 E 48th St 212-838-0050
Neff, Leland/506 Amsterdam Ave #61 212-724-1884
Nelson, Bill/121 Madison Ave 212-683-1362
Nelson, Craig/60 E 42nd St #505 212-682-1490
Nelson, John/280 Madison Ave #1402 212-545-9155
Nelson, John Illus/101 N 3rd St, Brooklyn 718-387-5168
Nelson, Lori/860 W 181st St #41A 212-795-4281
Nessim, Barbara/63 Greene St 212-219-1111

Neubecker, Robert/395 Broadway #14C 212-219-8435
Neumann, Ann/280 Madison Ave #1402 212-545-9155
Neuworth, Pauline/230 Fifth Ave #2000 212-686-3383
Newman, Nurit/241-20 Northern Blvd #3C, Douglaston ...718-229-5026
Newton, Richard/501 Fifth Ave #1407 212-490-2450
Neyman-Levikova, Marina/155 E 38th St 212-697-6170
Ng, Michael/58-35 155th St, Flushing 718-461-8264
Nicastre, Michael/420 Lexington Ave #2738 212-697-8525
Nicholas, Jess/566 Seventh Ave #603 212-221-8090
Nicklaus, Carol/866 UN Plaza #525 212-644-2020
Nicotra, Rosanne/420 Lexington Ave #2738 212-697-8525
Niklewicz, Adam/333 E 49th St #3J 212-980-8061
Nishinaka, Jeff/60 E 42nd St #505 212-682-1490
Noftsinger, Pamela/600 W 111th St #6A 212-316-4241
Noome, Michael/420 Lexington Ave/Penthouse 212-986-5680
Noonan, Julia/873 President St, Brooklyn 718-622-9268
North, Jan Coffman/62 W 45th St 212-398-9540
North, Russ/5 Grammercy Park W 212-228-8639
Notarile, Chris/420 Lexington Ave #PH4,5 212-986-5680
Novak, Justin/156 Fifth Ave #617 212-243-1333

O

O'Brien, Tim/60 E 42nd St #1146 212-953-7088
O'Leary, Danny/342 E 65th St #5RW 212-628-5322
O'Shaughnessy, Michael/267 Wyckoff St, Brooklyn 718-624-1906
Oberheide, Heide/295 Washington Ave #5B, Brooklyn 718-622-7056
Ochagavia, Carlos/509 Madison Ave 10th Fl 212-355-0910
Ockenfels III, Frank/245 E 30th St 212-683-1304
Odom, Mel/252 W 76th St #B1 212-724-9320
Oelbaum, Fran/196 W 10th St #2A 212-691-3422
Okuyan, Selime/69-01 Northern Blvd #2L, Woodside 718-476-1457
Olanoff, Greg/60 E 42nd St #1940 212-867-8092
Olbinski, Rafal/425 W 23rd St #10F 212-242-6367
Olitsky, Eve/235 W 102nd St #12K 212-678-1045
Olson, Erik/516 9th St, Brooklyn 718-965-0914
Olson, Richard A/85 Grand St 212-925-1820
Orit Design/27 W 24th St 10th Fl 212-727-1140
Orita, Vilma/201 Ocean Pkwy #3A, Brooklyn 718-851-5758
Ortiz, Jose Luis/66 W 77th St 212-877-3081
Osaka, Rick/14-22 30th Dr, Long Island City 718-956-0015
Oz, Robin/866 UN Plaza #525 212-644-2020

P

Palencar, John Jude/232 Madison Ave #402 212-889-8777
Palma, Eric/113 N 8th St, Brooklyn 718-388-6091
Pantuso, Mike/350 E 89th St 212-534-3511
Paragraphics/427 3rd St, Brooklyn 718-965-2231
Paraskevas, Michael/41 Union Sq W #1228 212-929-5590
Pardy, Cindy/200 W 15th St 212-243-4209
Parisi, Richard/62 W 45th St 212-398-9540
Parker, Edward/58 W 15th St 6th Fl 212-741-2539
Parker, Robert Andrew/81 Greene St 212-925-3053
Parry, Ivor/280 Madison Ave, New York 212-779-1554
Parsons, John/420 Lexington Ave #2760 212-697-8525
Parton, Steve/368 Broadway #302 212-766-2285
Passarelli, Charles/353 W 53rd St #1W 212-682-2462
Pasternak, Robert/114 W 27th St #55 212-675-0002
Paterson, Diane/866 UN Plaza #525 212-644-2020
Patrick, Pamela/333 E 49th St #3J 212-980-8061
Patti, Joyce/194 Third Ave 212-475-0440
Pavlov, Elana/377 W 11th #1F 212-243-0939
Payne, C F/121 Madison Ave 212-683-1362
Peak, Matt/60 E 42nd St #1940 212-867-8092
Peak, Robert/14 E 52nd St 212-752-8490
Peale, Charles/19 E 48th St 212-838-0050
Pearson, Jim/866 UN Plaza #525 212-644-2020
Pechanec, Vladimir/34-43 Crescent St #4C, Long Island City ..718-729-3973
Pedersen, Judy/305 Second Ave #710 212-777-8077
Peele, Lynwood/344 W 88th St 212-799-3305
Pelaez, Joan/43 E 19th St 212-254-4996
Pelavin, Daniel/80 Varrick St 212-941-7418
Pelikan, Judy/200 E 78th St 212-570-9069
Pelosi, Mary Jane/PO Box 677/Throgs Neck Sta, Bronx ...212-792-4263
Penalva, Jordi/43 E 19th St 212-254-4996
Pendleton, Roy/215 Park Ave S #1300 212-674-8080
Penelope/420 Lexington Ave #2738 212-679-8525

Peralta, Gina/39-33 57th St #2D, Woodside 718-565-0919
Percivalle, Rosanne/430 W 14th St #413 212-633-2480
Perez, Maria/236 W 27th St 10th Fl 212-807-8730
Perez, Vince/43 E 19th St 212-254-4996
Perini, Ben/333 E 49th St #3J 212-980-8061
Perlow, Paul/123 E 54th St #6E 212-758-4358
Personality Inc/501 Fifth Ave #1407 212-490-2450
Petan, Greg J/60 E 42nd St #505 212-682-1490
Peters, Bob/108 E 35th St #1C 212-889-3337
Peterson, Cheryl/81 Greene St 212-925-3053
Peterson, Robin/411 West End Ave 212-724-3479
Petragnani, Vincent/853 Broadway #1201 212-677-9100
Petruccio, Steven/201 E 28th St 212-532-0928
Pettingill, Ondre/2 Ellwood St #3U 212-942-1993
Phillips, Barry/232 Madison Ave #402 212-889-8777
Phillips, Laura/60 E 42nd St #505 212-682-1490
Piglia, Paola/28 Cliff St #3 212-393-9207
Pincus, Harry/160 Sixth Ave @ 210 Spring St 212-925-8071
Pinkney, J Brian/866 UN Plaza #525 212-644-2020
Pinkney, Jerry/108 E 35th St #1C 212-889-3337
Pirman, John/57 W 28th St 212-679-2866
Pisano, Al/22 W 38th St 212-213-3204
Pizzo, Valerie/425 W 57th St #3K 212-333-5402
Platinum Design/14 W 23rd St 2nd Fl 212-366-4000
Podwill, Jerry/108 W 14th St 212-255-9464
Pogue, Deborah Bazzel/31 W 21st St 7th Fl 212-243-4412
Poladian, Elena & Girair/42 E 23rd St #6N 212-213-3460
Polengi, Evan/159 25th St, Brooklyn 718-499-3214
Polishook, Emily/34-50 28th St #5B, Astoria 212-705-3473
Popp, Wendy/231 W 25th St #6E 212-807-0840
Porter, Frederick/156 Fifth Ave #617 212-243-1333
Powell, Ivan/58 W 15th St 6th Fl 212-741-2539
Powers, Tom/156 Fifth Ave #617 212-243-1333
Prato, Rodica/111 Wooster St #PH C 212-925-0491
Pratt, Russell E/150 E 35th St #440 212-685-7955
Przewodek, Camille/108 E 35th St #1C 212-889-3337
Puente, Lyle/324 E 5th St, Brooklyn 718-436-4447
Punin, Nikolai/280 Madison Ave #1402 212-545-9155
Purdom, Bill/780 Madison Ave/Box 6 212-988-4566
Pyk, Jan/19 E 48th St 3rd Fl 212-838-0050

QR

Quartuccio, Dom/410 W 24th St #9M 212-727-7329
Quon, Mike Design Office/568 Broadway #703 212-226-6024
RadenStudio/420 Lexington Ave #PH4,5 212-986-5680
Radigan, Bob/280 Madison Ave #1402 212-545-9155
Raglin, Tim/138 W 74th St 212-873-0538
Ranaldi, Donald/280 Madison Ave #1402 212-545-9155
Randazzo, Tony/353 W 53rd St #1W 212-682-2462
Rane, Walter/60 E 42nd St #1940 212-867-8092
Reay, Richard/515 W 236th St, Bronx 212-884-2317
Rebelo, Tanya/156 Fifth Ave #617 212-243-1333
Reed, Herb/156 Fifth Ave #617 212-243-1333
Reim, Melanie/214 Riverside Dr #601 212-749-0177
Reingold, Alan/155 E 38th St 212-697-6170
Renfro, Ed/250 E 83rd St #4E 212-879-3823
Reynolds, Gene/71 Thompson St 212-431-3072
Reynolds, Scott/308 W 30th St #9B 212-629-5610
Rice, John/156 Fifth Ave #617 212-243-1333
Rich, Norman/2557 Marion Ave #3G, Bronx 212-733-5140
Richards, Linda/27 Bleecker St 212-673-1600
Richardson, Ruth/5 Ludlow St 212-219-2056
Rickerd, Dave/50 W 23rd St 5th fl 212-627-4111
Rider, Mike/60 E 42nd St #505 212-682-1490
Ridgeway, Ronald/330 W 42nd St #3200 NE 212-714-0130
Rigo, Martin/43 E 19th St 212-254-4996
Risko, Robert/201 W 11th St #2C 212-989-6987
Rivers, Ruth/267 Wycoff St, Brooklyn 718-624-1906
Rixford, Ellen/308 W 97th St 212-865-5686
Roberts, Peggi/60 E 42nd St #505 212-682-1490
Roberts, Phil/420 Lexington Ave #2911 212-986-5680
Roberts, Ray/60 E 42nd St #505 212-682-1490
Robinson, Charles/866 UN Plaza #525 212-644-2020
Robinson, Lenor/201 E 69th St #6E 212-734-0944
Rochon, Joanne/21 Prince St #2 212-334-9120
Rodell, Don/60 E 42nd St #1940 212-867-8092
Rodriguez, Robert/501 Fifth Ave #1407 212-490-2450
Rogers, Lilla/483 Henry St, Brooklyn 718-624-6862
Rohr, Dixon/430 W 34th St #5E 212-268-6907
Roman, Barbara/345 W 88th St #5B 212-362-1374
Romer, Dan/125 Prospect Park W, Brooklyn 718-768-3632
Romero, Javier/9 W 19th St 5th Fl 212-727-9445
Root, Barry/58 W 15th St 212-741-2589
Rosato, John/420 Lexington Ave PH 212-986-5680
Rose, Bob/873 Broadway 212-982-9535
Rosebush Visions Corp/154 W 57th St #826 212-398-6600
Rosen, Terry/101 W 81st St #508 212-580-4784
Rosenfeld, Mort/420 Lexington Ave #2911 212-986-5680
Rosenwald, Laurie/45 Lispenard St 212-675-6707
Rosenzweiz, Myra/310 W 90th St 212-362-9871
Rosner, Meryl/21 Grammercy Park #3A 212-219-3463
Ross Culbert Lavery Russman/15 W 20th St 9th Fl 212-206-0044
Ross, Bronwen/866 UN Plaza #525 212-644-2020
Ross, Ian/203 W 84th St #2A 212-721-5268
Ross, Richard/80 Eighth Ave #303 212-242-3900
Rother, Sue/420 Lexington Ave #2760 212-697-8525
Rothman, Mike/21 W 74th St 212-438-4954
Roy, Joanna/62 W 45th St 212-398-9540
Rozenberg, Marcel/232 Madison Ave #402 212-889-8777
Ruffins, Reynold/15 W 20th St 9th Fl 212-627-5220
Ruiz, Artie/43 E 19th St 212-254-4996
Rundo, Ron/60 E 42nd St #1940 212-867-8092
Russell, Bill/227 W 29th St 9th Fl 212-967-6443
Ryan, Terry/130 Barrow St #316 212-688-1080

S

Sabanosh, Michael/433 W 34th St #18B 212-947-8161
Sabin, Robert/60 E 42nd St #1940 212-867-8092
Saksa Art & Design/41 Union Sq W #1001 212-255-5539
Salerno, Steve/541 Hudson St #2 212-727-1599
Salina, Joe/60 E 42nd St #505 212-682-1490
Samuels, Mark/25 Minetta Ln #4A 212-777-8580
Sanders, Jane/47-51 40th St #6D, Sunnyside 718-786-3505
Sanjulian/43 E 19th St 212-688-1080
Santore, Charles/108 E 35th St #1C 212-889-3337
Santoro, Christopher/201 E 28th St 212-532-0928
Sargent, Claudia K/15-38 126th St, Queens 718-461-8280
Sasaki, Goro/60 E 42nd St #505 212-682-1490
Sauber, Rob/10 Plaza St #12C, Brooklyn 718-636-9050
Saurda, Tomas/875 Third Ave 4th Fl 212-303-8326
Sauriol, Brian/420 Lexington Ave #2911 212-986-5680
Sawka, Jan/353 W 53rd St #1W 212-682-2462
Sayles, Elizabeth/10 E 23rd St 7th Fl 212-420-0292
Sayles, John/420 Lexington Ave #2760 212-697-8525
Scarisbrick, Ed/853 Broadway #1201 212-677-9100
Schaare, Harry/60 E 42nd St #1940 212-867-8092
Schacht, Michael/925 Park Ave 212-734-5318
Schaer, Miriam/522 E 5th St 212-673-4926
Schaller, Tom/2112 Broadway #407 212-362-5524
Schanzer, Roz/461 Park Ave S 212-696-4680
Scheckman/Ferguson/145 E 22nd St 212-473-8747
Scheuer, Phil/126 Fifth Ave #13B 212-620-0728
Schindler, Max/267 Wyckoff St, Brooklyn 718-624-1906
Schleinkofer, David/420 Lexington Ave #PH4,5 212-986-5680
Schmidt, Bill/60 E 42nd St #1940 212-867-8092
Schmidt, Chuck/853 Broadway #1201 212-677-9100
Schneegass, Martinu/241 Eldridge St #2R 212-529-7445
Schreier, Joshua/466 Washington St 212-925-0472
Schumacher, Michael/353 W 53rd St #1W 212-682-2462
Schumaker, Ward/194 Third Ave 212-475-0440
Schumer, Arlen/382 Lafayette St 212-254-8242
Schwab, Michael/501 Fifth Ave #1407 212-490-2450
Schwark, Mary Beth/866 UN Plaza #525 212-644-2020
Schwartz, Daniel/48 E 13th St 212-533-0237
Schwartz, Judith/231 E 5th St 212-777-7533
Schwarz, Jill Karla/80 N Moore St 212-227-2444
Schwarz, Joanie/194 Third Ave 212-475-0440
Scott, Bob/106 Lexington Ave #3 212-684-2409
Scrofani, Joseph/353 W 53rd St #1W 212-682-2462
Searle, Ronald/15 E 76th St 212-288-8010
Seaver, Jeffrey/130 W 24th St #4B 212-741-2279
Segal, John/165 W 91st St #5A 212-662-3278
Seiffer, Alison/77 Hudson St 212-227-0087
Sekine, Hisashi/200 W 15th St 212-243-4209

Seltzer, Isadore/285 Riverside Dr #2B 212-666-1561
Sempe, J J/81 Greene St 212-925-3053
Sery, Guy A/117 E 57th St 212-371-9771
Sessler, Carol/305 W 84th St #5A 212-580-1233
Shafer, Ginger/113 Washington Pl 212-989-7697
Shahidi, Behrooz/160 Fifth Ave #812A 212-989-2967
Shahinian, Brenda/81 Greene St 212-925-3053
Shannon, David/306 E 50th St #2 212-688-8475
Shap, Sandra/853 Broadway #1201 212-677-9100
Shega, Marla/60 E 42nd St #505 212-682-1490
Shenefield, Barbara/85 Barrow St #6K 212-633-8755
Shepherd, Cameron/520 Broadway #7Rear 212-334-0962
Sherman, Maurice/209 E 23rd St 212-679-7350
Shohet, Marti/41 Union Sq W #1001 212-627-1299
Sieffert, Clare/62 W 45th St 212-398-9540
Sienkiewicz, Bill/14 E 52nd St 212-752-8490
Silva, Jorge/111 Wooster St PHC 212-925-0491
Silverman, Burt/324 W 71st St 212-799-3399
Silvers, Bill/420 Lexington Ave #PH4,5 212-986-5680
Singer, Paul Design/494 14th St, Brooklyn 718-499-8172
Sis, Peter/10 Bleecker St #7B 212-260-0151
Skardinski, Stan/201 E 28th St 212-532-0928
The Sketch Pad Studio/6 Jane St 212-989-7074
Skolsky, Mark/257 12th St, Brooklyn 718-499-1148
Skopp, Jennifer/1625 Emmons Ave #6H, Brooklyn 718-646-2344
Skorodumov, Alexander/285 Ft Washington Ave 718-575-1678
Slack, Chuck/60 E 42nd St #505 212-682-1490
Slackman, Charles B/320 E 57th St 212-758-8233
Sloan, William/236 W 26th St #805 212-463-7025
Slvavec, Diane/60 E 42nd St #1940 212-867-8092
Small, David/81 Greene St 212-925-3053
Smalley, Guy/40 E 34th St #203 212-683-0544
Smith, Brett/353 W 53rd St #1W 212-682-2462
Smith, Douglas/121 Madison Ave 212-683-1362
Smith, Gary/31 W 21St E 7th Fl 212-243-4412
Smith, Laura/12 E 14th St #4D 212-206-9162
Smith, Linda/267 Wyckoff St, Brooklyn 718-624-1906
Smith, Mary Anne/45 Perry St #19 212-691-3570
Smith, Trudi/866 UN Plaza #4014 212-644-2020
Smith, Vicki/504 E 5th St #6C 212-475-1671
Smollin, Michael/420 Lexington Ave #PH4,5 212-986-5680
Smythe, Danny/38 W 39th St 212-768-0481
Sneberger, Dan/60 E 42nd St #1940 212-867-8092
Snelson, Kenneth/140 Sullivan St, 212-580-1233 212-777-0356
Sobel, Phillip Eric/80-15 41st Ave #128, Elmhurst 718-476-3841
Socolow, Karen/111 Wooster St #PH C 212-925-0491
Soderlind, Kirsten/194 Third Ave 212-475-0440
Soldwedel, Kipp/420 Lexington Ave #PH 4,5 212-986-5680
Solie, John/420 Lexington Ave #PH4,5 212-986-5680
Solomon, Debra/536 W 111th St #55 212-662-5619
Soloski, Tommy/111 Wooster St #PH C 212-925-0491
Sorenson, Marco/325 W 37th St #5F 212-473-1052
Sormanti, Carla/15 W 72nd St 212-799-2231
Sorvino Ligasan Design Assoc/1616 York Ave #5 212-879-8197
Sottung, George/420 Lexington Ave #2911 212-986-5680
Spacek, Peter/611 Broadway #610 212-505-6802
Spangler, Ken/43-17 55th St, Woodside 718-898-8591
Spengler, Kenneth/21-58 Hughes Ave, Bronx 212-295-0346
Spiak, Al/146 Reade St 212-941-4680
Spiak, Sharon/146 Reade St #4 212-941-4680
Spohn, Cliff/420 Lexington Ave #PH4,5 212-986-5680
Spohn, Sachi/420 Lexington Ave PH 212-986-5680
Spollen, Chris/362 Cromwell Ave, Ocean Breeze 718-979-9695
Sposato, John/43 E 22nd St #2A 212-477-3909
Stabin, Victor/100 W 15th St #4I 212-243-7688
Staffin, Allison/156 Fifth Ave #617 212-243-1333
Stahl, Nancy/194 Third Ave 212-475-0440
Stallard, Peter/60 E 42nd St #505 212-682-1490
Staples, Matthew/141 W 36th St 14th Fl 212-279-7935
Starrace, Tom/54 W 21st St #308 212-633-1079
Starrett, Terri/31 W 21st St 7th Fl Rear 212-243-4412
Steadman, Barbara/330 E 33rd St #10A 212-684-6326
Steadman, E T/425 W 23rd St #10F 212-242-6367
Steiner, Frank/60 E 42nd St #1940 212-867-8092
Stephens, Lynn/777 West End Ave #9A 212-864-1487
Stern, Kalika/308 E 79th St #6H 212-734-4503
Sternglass, Arno/622 Greenwich St 212-675-5667
Sterrett, Jane/160 Fifth Ave #700 212-929-2566

Stewart, Arvis/866 UN Plaza #525 212-644-2020
Stillman, Susan/126 W 71st St #5A 212-724-5634
Stimson, David/231 W 25th St #6E 212-807-0840
Stolper, Karen/255 W 14th St #4H 212-675-5150
Strachan, Bruce/999 Lorimer St, Brooklyn 718-383-1264
Streeter, Sabina/141 Wooster St 212-254-7436
Struthers, Doug/501 Fifth Ave #1407 212-490-2450
Struzan, Drew/108 E 35th St #1C 212-889-3337
Studio M/60 E 42nd St #505 212-682-1490
Stuhmer, Bob/36 E 23rd St 212-995-5223
Suares, J C/60 E 42nd St #505 212-682-1490
Suh, John/60 E 42nd St #1146 212-953-7088
Sullivan, Suzanne Hughes/77 W 55th St #3B 212-581-6112
Summers, Mark/121 Madison Ave 212-683-1362
Sutton, Judith/239 Dean St, Brooklyn 718-834-8851
Sweny, Stephen/217 E 29th St #52 212-532-4072
Szpura, Beata/48-02 69th St, Woodside 718-424-8440
Szumowski, Thomas/60 E 42nd St #505 212-682-1490

T

Taba, Eugene/1185 Sixth Ave 8th Fl 212-730-0101
Taback, Simms/15 W 20th St 9th Fl 212-627-5220
Taleporos, Plato/333 E 23rd St #2EE 212-689-3138
Tanenbaum, Robert/420 Lexington Ave #PH4,5 212-986-5680
Tankersley, Paul/29 Bethune St 212-924-0015
Tarnowski, Glen/62 W 45th St 212-398-9540
Tauss, Marc/484 W 43rd St #40H 212-410-2827
Taylor, B K/156 Fifth Ave #617 212-243-1333
Taylor, Bridget Starr/675 Hudson St #2S 212-924-9468
Taylor, Dahl/194 Third Ave 212-475-0440
Taylor, Doug/106 Lexington Ave 212-674-6346
Taylor, Ean/450 Seventh Ave #902 212-268-1788
Taylor, Katrina/216 E 45th St 212-661-0850
Taylor, Toni L/1560 Leland Ave, Bronx 212-824-9252
Tedesco, Michael/120 Boerum Pl #1E, Brooklyn 718-596-4179
1091/45 W 18th St 7th Fl Tower 212-645-5325
Tenga, Kathlyn/31-42 32nd St, Astoria 718-626-4344
Tenorio, Juan/830 Amsterdam Ave 212-663-2626
Terreson, Jeffrey/420 Lexington Ave #PH4,5 212-986-5680
Terry, Mike/450 Seventh Ave #902 212-268-1788
Teters, Jerry/302 W 109th St #8 212-222-2858
Thompson, Thierry/420 Lexington Ave #PH4,5 212-986-5680
Thomson, Bill/566 Seventh Ave #603 212-221-8090
Thonnessen, Sabina/141 Wooster St #3B 212-254-7436
Thorpe, Peter/254 Park Ave S #6D 212-477-0131
Thorspecken, Thomas/615 E 14th St #7A 212-995-5647
Tierney, Tom/201 E 28th St 212-532-0928
Tod-Kat Studios/353 W 53rd St #1W 212-682-2462
Tokyo, Max/236 W 26th St #805 212-463-7025
Tom, Jack/80 Varick St #3B 212-941-1860
Tomkin, Tom/317 W 95th St #4F 212-932-2490
Toriello, Steven/846 Carroll St, Brooklyn 718-230-4867
Torp, Cynthia/41 Union Sq W #1228 212-929-5590
Torres, Daniel/155 Ave of Americas 10th Fl 212-255-6530
Trachok, C A/853 Broadway #1201 212-677-9100
Travers, Robert/60 E 42nd St #1940 212-867-8092
Trondsen, Bob/60 E 42nd St #1940 212-867-8092
Trull, John/1573 York Ave 212-535-5383
Tsugami, Kyuzo/156 Fifth Ave #617 212-243-1333
Tunstull, Glenn/201 Clinton Ave #14G, Brooklyn 718-834-8529
Turner, Clay/60 E 42nd St #505 212-682-1490
Tylden-Wright, Jenny/155 Ave of Americas 10th Fl 212-255-6530

UV

Uhler, Kimanne/205 DeKalb Ave, Brooklyn 718-855-1488
Ulrich, Mark/59 W 19th St #2B2 212-989-9325
Underwood, George/450 Seventh Ave #902 212-268-1788
Uram, Lauren/251 Washington Ave #4R, Brooklyn 718-789-7717
Vaccaro, Lou/866 UN Plaza #525 212-644-2020
Vahid/566 Seventh Ave #603 212-221-8090
Vainisi, Jenny/58 Middagh St #16, Brooklyn 718-858-4914
Vantine, Laura/499 Sinclair Ave, Staten Island 718-356-9311
Vargo, Kurt/32 W 40th St #9B 212-819-9084
Varlet-Martinelli/200 W 15th St 212-243-4209
Vaux, Jacquie Marie/165 E 32nd St 212-686-3514
Vecchio, Carmine/10-40 Jackson Ave, LOng Island City 718-786-2020

Velasquez, Eric/226 W 113th St..212-866-2209
Vellekoop, Maurice/227 W 29th St #9R.................................212-967-7699
Veltfort, Anna/16-B W 86th St..212-877-0430
Verkaaik, Ben/509 Madison Ave 10th Fl.................................212-355-0910
Victor, Joan B/863 Park Ave #11E...212-988-2773
Villa, Roxanne/105 Montague St #403, Brooklyn...................718-797-0348
Vitale, Stefano/478 Bergen St, Brooklyn...............................718-789-8688
Vitsky, Sally/232 Madison Ave #402......................................212-889-8777
Viviano, Sam J/25 W 13th St..212-242-1471
Vollath, Guenther/156 Fifth Ave #617.....................................212-243-1333
Vosk, Alex/521 E 82nd St #1A..212-737-2314
Voth, Gregory/67 Eighth Ave...212-807-9766

W

Wacholder, Lisa Roma/2613 Ave J, Brooklyn........................718-951-7218
Walker & Assoc/18 E 64th St #4B...212-759-5590
Walker, Jeff/60 E 42nd St #1940...212-867-8092
Walker, John S/47 Jane St..212-242-3435
Wall, Pam/60 E 42nd St #505..212-682-1490
Wallace, Kurt/62 W 45th St...212-398-9540
Waller, Charles/35 Bethune St PH C.......................................212-989-5843
Wallner, Alexandra & John/866 UN Plaza #4014....................212-644-2020
Walsh, Terry/31 W 21st St 7th Fl...212-243-4412
Ward, Donna/19 E 48th St 3rd Fl...212-838-0050
Ward, John/43-36 Robinson St #5H, Flushing 718-358-6423
Warren, Jim/155 Ave of Americas 10th Fl...............................212-255-6530
Warren, Valerie/14 E 4th St #1103..212-505-5366
Wasserman, Randie/28 W 11th St #2B.....................................212-645-7226
Wasson, Cameron/4 S Portland Ave #3, Brooklyn..................718-875-8277
Watkinson, Brent/60 E 42nd St #505.......................................212-682-1490
Watts, Mark/420 Lexington Ave #PH4,5...................................212-986-5680
Watts, Sharon/201 Eastern Parkway, Brooklyn 718-398-0451
Weakley, Mark/41 Union Sq W #636.......................................212-206-0066
Weaver, Robert/42 E 12th St..212-254-4289
Webb, Povl/450 Seventh Ave #902..212-268-1788
Weber, Rosemary/229 W 78th St...212-724-6529
Weiman, Jon/2255 Broadway #306...212-787-3184
Weiner, Jeffrey/214 E 90th St #4RE...212-876-2335
Weinman, Jon/2255 Broadway #306...212-787-3184
Weisbecker, Philippe/476 Broadway #4M.................................212-966-6051
Weisser, Carl/38 Livingston St #33, Brooklyn.........................718-834-0952
Weissman, Sam/2510 Fenton Ave, Bronx.................................212-654-5381
Westerberg, Rob/34-64 Hillside Ave #4V..................................212-567-1884
Whistl'n Dixie/10 E 81st St..212-570-6021
White, Debra/4 South Portland Ave #4, Brooklyn.....................718-797-5115
White, Roger/160 West End Ave #3K..212-362-1848
Whitehead, Samuel B/304 Seventh Ave #1, Brooklyn..............718-768-0803
Whitehouse, Debora/156 Fifth Ave #617..................................212-682-1490
Whitesides, Kim/501 Fifth Ave #1407.......................................212-490-2450
Wickenden, Nadine/267 Wycoff St, Brooklyn...........................718-624-1906
Wiemann, Roy/PO Box 271/Prince St Sta.................................212-431-3793
Wiggins, Mick/58 W 15th St 6th Fl...212-741-2539
Wilkinson, Bill/155 E 38th St..212-697-6170
Wilkinson, Chuck/60 E 42nd St #505.......................................212-682-1490
Willardson + Assoc/194 Third Ave...212-475-0440
Williams, Elizabeth/349 E 82nd St #8.......................................212-517-4593
Williams, Oliver/66 Madison Ave #11J......................................212-674-1903
Williams, Richard/58 W 15th St 6th Fl......................................212-741-2539
Wilson, Amanda/346 E 20th St...212-260-7567
Wilson, Harvey/316 Clinton Ave, Brooklyn...............................718-857-8525
Wimmer, Mike/420 Lexington Ave #PH4,5.................................212-986-5680
Wind, Bodhi/43 E 19th St...212-254-4996
Winder, Ray/450 Seventh Ave #902..212-268-1788
Winkowski, Fred/48 W 71st St..212-724-3136
Winterhale, John/329 E 13th St..212-254-6665
Winterrowd, Turk/755 1st St #2, Brooklyn................................718-768-2181
Winterson, Finn/401 Eighth Ave #43, Brooklyn 212-219-2711
Witte, Michael/108 E 35th St #1C...212-889-3337
Wohlberg, Ben/43 Great Jones St..212-254-9663
Wolfe, Bruce/194 Third Ave...212-475-0440
Wolfgang, Sherri/382 Lafayette St...212-254-8242
Wollman, Paul/60 E 42nd St #505..212-682-1490
Womersley, David/420 Lexington Ave #PH4,5..........................212-986-5680
Wood, Clare/54 Berkeley Pl, Brooklyn.....................................718-783-3734
Woodend, James/420 Lexington Ave #2760..............................212-697-8525
Woolley, Jane/155 Ave of Americas 10th Fl.............................212-255-6530
Wray, Wendy/194 Third Ave...212-475-0440

Wyatt, Kathy/43 E 19th St..212-254-4996
Wynne, Patricia/446 Central Pk West 212-865-1059

Y

Yalowitz, Paul/598 Freeman Ave, Brentwood 212-532-0859
Yang, James/41 Union Sq W #918..212-807-6627
Yankus, Marc/570 Hudson St #3..212-242-6334
Yealdhall, Gary/353 W 53rd St #1W...212-682-2462
Yee, Josie/211 W 20th St #6E...212-206-1260
Yeldham, Ray/420 Lexington Ave #2911....................................212-986-5680
Yemi/7 E 14th St #812..212-627-1269
Yiannias, Vicki/27 Bleecker St..212-673-1600
Yip, Jennie/625 E 82nd St, Brooklyn...718-444-6750
York, Judy/420 Lexington Ave #2760...212-697-8525
Yourke, Oliver/525-A Sixth Ave, Brooklyn 718-965-0609
Yule, Susan Hunt/176 Elizabeth St...212-226-0439

Z

Zacharow, Christopher/109 Waverly Pl #4R...............................212-460-5739
Zagorski, Stanislaw/142 E 35th St..212-532-2348
Zaid, Barry/219 W 81st..212-580-1993
Zamchick, Gary/155 E 23rd St #308...212-529-0544
Zann, Nicky/155 W 68th St #1114...212-724-5027
Zeldich, Arieh/866 UN Plaza #525..212-644-2020
Zick, Brian/194 Third Ave...212-475-0440
Ziegler, Gavin/PO Box 21076..212-957-8007
Ziemienski, Dennis/111 Wooster St #PH C...............................212-925-0491
Ziering, Bob/151 W 74th St #2B..212-873-0034
Zimmerman, Jerry/124 W 18th St 5th Fl....................................212-620-7774
Zimmerman, Robert/530 1st St, Brooklyn..................................718-768-2664
Zudeck, Darryl/41 Union Sq W #1228.......................................212-929-5590
Zumbo, Matthew/60 E 42nd St #505..212-682-1490
Zwarenstein, Alex "Mangal"/155 E 38th St 212-697-6170

N O R T H E A S T

A

Abe, Yoshiko/165 Jacoby St, Maplewood, NJ............................201-378-9188
Abel, Ray/18 Vassar Pl, Scarsdale, NY.....................................914-725-1899
Abell, Patrick/601 Himes Ave #107, Frederick, MD 301-696-8545
Ackerman, Angela/11 Colonial Dr, Framingham, MA.................508-788-0879
Adam Filippo & Moran/1206 Fifth Ave, Pittsburgh, PA..............412-261-3720
Adams, Michael W/3002 Fifth St, Trooper, PA 215-539-5679
Addams, Charles/PO Box 8, Westport, CT.................................203-227-7806
Ahle, Dorothy/8 Grimshaw St, Malden, MA 617-321-8302
Ahmed, Ghulan Hassan/1258 Walker Ave, Baltimore, MD.........301-433-0478
Albanese, Ernest/136 Park Ave #2, Hoboken, NJ.....................201-659-9335
Alcorn, Bob/434 South Main St, Heightstown, NJ......................609-448-4448
Alde, David/1801 Clydesdale Pl NW, Washington, DC 202-234-1196
Aldrich, Susan/31 Clearbrook Dr, Smithtown, NY.....................516-261-6220
Alexander, Christian/566 Commonwealth Ave #404, Boston, MA........617-247-7443
Alexander, Paul R/37 Pine Mountain Rd, Redding, CT 203-544-9293
Alexander, Steven/113 77th St, N Bergen, NJ...........................201-861-6314
Alsop, Mark/RR 5 Milltown Rd, Brewster, NY............................914-287-7352
Alterio, Caroline/25 Gray St, Boston, MA..................................617-236-1920
Ames, Sharon/1017 Bellmore Rd, North Bellmore, NY 415-665-5144
Amorosi, Tom/6 Compton St, E Rockaway, NY.........................516-596-0160
Ancas, Karen/84 Keystone St, W Roxbury, MA.........................617-323-8466
Anderson, John/501 N Calvert St, Baltimore, MD......................301-332-6508
Anderson, Philip/245 Broadway, Arlington, MA..........................617-641-3823
Anderson, Richard/490 Bleeker Ave, Mamaroneck, NY 914-381-2682
Andri, Richard/46 Cherrywood Dr, Manhasset Hill, NY..............516-358-7986
Angrisani, Chris/2825 Terrace Dr #202, Chevy Chase, MD 301-587-0378
Ansall, Joseph/70233 Cipriano Ct, Lanham, MD........................301-552-4935
Anthony, Jay B/806 N Calvert St, Baltimore, MD.......................301-727-6764
Antkowiak, Jeff/8193 Mountain Estate Ct, Pasadena, MD..........301-360-2535
Anzalone, Lori/35-02 Berdan Ave, Fairlawn, NJ.........................201-796-5588
Apple, Margot/March Rd, Ashfield, MA......................................413-625-9514
Ardissone, Mary/PO Box 6539, Silver Spring, MD.....................301-209-0054
Armstrong, Stuart/1503 Dublin Dr, Silver Spring, MD................301-681-6178
Aronson, Ruth/124 Hornbeam Lane, Kinnelon, NJ.....................201-838-2207
Aruta, Mark/5115 41st St NW, Washington, DC..........................202-364-0384
Arvis, Tom/11228 Troy Rd, Rockville, MD 301-468-0828

Asmussen, Don/18 Norumbega Terrace #6, Waltham, MA....617-647-0299
Asprino, Donna/49 Warren Ave #4, Boston, MA....617-426-5067
Astrachan, Michael/204 Carmalt Rd, Hamden, CT....203-498-0455
Atkinson-Mavilia, Peg/45 Captain Pierce Rd, Scituate, MA....617-545-7654
Avishai, Susan/28 Marlboro St, Newton, MA....617-969-7246

B

B&G Associates/520 Adams St, Hoboken, NJ....201-653-5542
Bach, Josh/326 S 19th St #11A, Philadelphia, PA....215-732-1359
Bacon, Paul/106 Vineyard Ave, Highland, NY....914-691-9233
Bailey, Brian/461 9th St, Palisades Park, NJ....201-585-2937
Bailey, Jean/174 Farm Rd, Sherborn, MA....508-655-7770
Baird, Jack/47 Middle St, Portland, ME....207-772-3992
Baiungo, Charles/61 Congress St, Bangor, ME....207-947-2966
Baker, Lori/RR 1/PO Box 880, Randolph Ctr, VT....802-426-3800
Baker, Skip/731 N 24th St, Philadelphia, PA....215-232-6666
Baker, Susan Harriet/315 West Side Dr #303, Gaithersburg, MD....301-258-0126
Bakley, Craig/68 Madison Ave, Cherry Hill, NJ....609-428-6310
Baldwin, James/1467 Jordan Ave, Crofton, MD....301-721-1896
Ball, Harvey/340 Main St, Wooster, MA....617-752-9154
Bang, Molly Garrett/43 Drumlin Rd, Falmouth, MA....508-540-5174
Bangham, Richard/2006 Cascade Rd, Silver Spring, MD....301-649-4919
Banta, Susan/17 Magazine St, Cambridge, MA....617-876-8568
Baquero, George/145 Clinton Pl #2B, Hackensack, NJ....201-342-9362
Barancik, Bob/135 S 18th St #403A, Philadelphia, PA....215-977-9540
Barber, David/21 Taft St, Marblehead, MA....617-631-6130
Barbier, Suzette/7 Devotion St #3, Brookline, MA....617-739-2822
Barger, Peter/25 Gray St, Boston, MA....617-236-1920
Barkley, James/444 Bedford Rd, Pleasantville, NY....914-747-2220
Barnard, Bryn/PO Box 285, Woodbury, NJ....609-853-4252
Barner, Bob/65 Mt Vernon St, Boston, MA....617-523-0953
Barnes, Ken/52 Mercator Lane, Willingboro, NJ....609-871-6051
Barnes, Kim/17 Pinewood St, Annapolis, MD....301-261-8662
Barnes, Suzanne/188 Central St #5, Somerville, MA....617-628-0837
Barr, Ken/770 Boylston St #17F, Boston, MA....617-267-5275
Barr, Loel (Ms)/22301 Flintridge Dr, Brookville, MD....301-774-4634
Barrett, Andrea/164 Elm Street, Kingston, MA....617-585-5791
Barrett, Debby/49 Hamilton St, Everett, MA....617-387-2031
Barrett, Jennifer/5510 Glenwood Rd, Bethesda, MD....301-654-4603
Barrett, Tom/7118 Wayne Ave, Upper Darby, PA....215-352-9530
Barrett, Victor/65 Ashburton St, Providence, RI....401-273-9898
Barrette, Steve/38 Quail Run, Massapequa, NY....516-797-2146
Barruso, Joe/30 Mildred Ave, Poughkeepsie, NY....813-530-4236
Bartlett, Christopher/2211B Woodbox Lane, Baltimore, MD....301-484-1906
Bartlett, David/8 E Hawthorne Dr, LaPlata, MD....301-932-0039
Baruffi, Andrea/341 Hudson Terrace, Piermont, NY....914-359-9542
Bastas, Dimitrios/2276 Mt Carmel Ave, Glenside, PA....215-885-8227
Bauer, Stephen/3000 Chestnut Ave #34, Baltimore, MD....301-243-0643
Becker, N Neesa/241 Monroe St, Philadelphia, PA....215-925-5363
Becker, Polly/591 Tremont St, Boston, MA....617-247-0469
Beim, Judy/359 3rd St, Clifton, NJ....201-478-4309
Beisel, Dan/4713 Ribble Ct, Ellicott City, MD....301-461-6377
Belove, Janice/46 Carolin Rd, Montclair, NJ....201-744-3760
Belser, Burkey/1818 N St NW #110, Washington, DC....202-775-0333
Ben-Ami, Doron/14 Fox Run Ln, Newtown, CT....203-270-1849
Bendis, Keith/275 Tanglewylde Rd, Lake Peekskill, NY....914-528-7378
Bennett, James/165 Seventh St #1, Hoboken, NJ....201-963-1457
Benshoshan, Orna (Ms)/34 Bernard St, Lexington, MA....617-863-1689
Benson, John D/2111-A Townhill Rd, Baltimore, MD....301-665-3395
Bensusen, Sally/2853 Ontario Rd NW #615, Washington, DC....202-462-0601
Berg, John/377 Hudson St, Buffalo, NY....716-884-8003
Berg, Linda/34 Westwood Dr, E Rochester, NY....716-385-8513
Berger, Charles/53 Maplewood Dr, Plainview, NY....516-931-5085
Bergin, Kiernan/41 Stevenson Pl, Kearny, NJ....201-998-1901
Berlin Productions/200 William St, Port Chester, NY....914-937-5594
Berman, Craig/16 Taylor St, Dover, NJ....201-366-4407
Berman, Michael/49 S Cedar Brook Rd, Cedar Brook, NJ....609-561-4188
Berman, Simi/Box 58, Chesterfield, NH....606-256-8477
Bernette, Larry/444 Bedford Rd, Pleasantville, NY....914-747-2220
Berney, Katherine/24 Cameron Ave #2, Somerville, MA....617-776-4242
Berry, Rick/93 Warren St, Arlington, MA....617-648-6375
Bersani, Shennen/14 Rockwell Ave, Brockton, MA....508-583-1648
Bianco, Peter/40 Henry St #11, Framingham, MA....508-875-9007
Biedrzycki, David/8 Pilgrim Lane, Medfield, MA....617-648-6139
Biegel, Michael David/14 W Maple Ave, Allendale, NJ....201-825-0084
Bigda, Diane/72 High St #2, Topsfield, MA....508-887-3528
Billin-Frye, Paige/216 Walnut St NW, Washington, DC....202-291-3105
Bingham, Edith/ PO Box 255, Washington, NH....603-495-3961
Birling, Paul/444 Bedford Rd, Pleasantville, NY....914-747-2220
Birmingham, Lloyd P/500 Peekskill Hollow Rd, Putnam Valley, NY....914-528-3207
Birnbaum, Meg/331 Harvard St #14, Cambridge, MA....617-491-7826
Blackwell, Deborah/3 River St, Sandwich, MA....508-888-4019
Blackwell, Patrick/PO Box 324, North Truro, MA....508-487-3336
Blahd, William/3717 Alton Pl NW, Washington, DC....202-686-0179
Blake, Marty/PO Box 266, Jamesville, NY....315-492-1332
Blaser, Michael/8 Cranberry Lane, Dover, MA....508-785-1513
Blasutta, Mary Lynn/Rider Hollow Rd, Arkville, NY....914-586-4899
Blauers, Nancy/50 Walnut St, Stratford, CT....203-377-6109
Bliss, Harry/1703 South 10th St, Philadelphia, PA....215-551-0888
Bliss, Philip/22 Briggs Ave, Fairport, NY....716-377-1609
Blum, Marianne/400 Executive Blvd, Elmsford, NY....914-592-2031
Bochner, Nurit/5 Bayley Ave, Yonkers, NY....914-965-4827
Boger, Diane/3426 16th St NW #205, Washington, DC....202-328-2156
Bolinsky, David/25-Q Sylvan Rd S, Westport, CT....203-226-4293
Bolle, Frank/5 Church Hill Rd, Redding Ridge, CT....203-938-9399
Bollinger, Kristine/7 Ivy Hill Rd/Box 959, Ridgefield, CT....203-438-8386
Bolster, Robert/7 Hope St, Walpole, MA....508-660-1751
Bonanno, Paul/142 W Golf Ave, S Plainfield, NJ....908-756-8867
Bonavita, Donna/Four Vera Place, Montclair, NJ....201-744-7159
Bond, Dennis A/6481 Miriam Circle, E Petersburg, PA....717-569-5823
Bond, Higgins/304 Woodbine St, Teaneck, NJ....201-836-1396
Bone, Fred/28 Farm Court, New Britain, CT....203-827-8418
Bono, Peter/114 E 7th St, Clifton, NJ....201-340-1169
Bortman, Alan/355 Wood Rd, Briantree, MA....617-235-2077
Borzotta, Joseph/234 Garden St, Hoboken, NJ....201-420-0293
Botsis, Peter/1255 University Ave, Rochester, NY....716-288-7080
Botts, Steve/25-Q Sylvan Rd S, Westport, CT....203-226-4293
Bower, Steve/3000 Chestnut Ave #6, Baltimore, MD....301-243-0643
Bowers, David/309 Walnut Rd, Pittsburgh, PA....412-761-5666
Boyd, Lizi/229 Berkeley St #52, Boston, MA....617-266-3858
Boyer, Jeff/1325 18th St NW #908, Washington, DC....202-331-7722
Bracco, Anthony/214 65th St, W New York, NJ....201-861-9098
Bradbury, Robert & Assoc/26 Halsey Lane, Closter, NJ....201-768-6395
Bradshaw, James/97 Mt Tabor Way, Ocean Grove, NJ....908-775-2798
Bragg, Sholie/5 Oklahoma Ave, Wilmington, DE....302-761-9144
Brancato, Ron/333 N Plymouth Ave, Rochester, NY....716-262-4450
Brauckman, Krista/229 Berkeley #52, Boston, MA....617-266-3858
Bray, Mark/RD 1/Box 694/Huffs Chrch Rd, Alburtis, PA....215-845-3229
Bray, Robin, (Mr.)/7939 Norfolk Ave, Bethesda, MD....301-656-5722
Breeden, Paul M/PO Box 40A, Sullivan Harbor, ME....207-422-3007
Bremer/Keifer Studio/250 Alewife Ln, Suffield, CT....203-749-9680
Brenner, Meryl/16 Cady Ave, Somerville, MA....617-623-2237
Brent, Mike/597 Riverside Ave, Westport, CT....203-226-4724
Brettlinger, Nancy/2121 Wisconsin Ave NW, Washington, DC....202-965-7800
Brickman, Robin/32 Fort Hoosac Pl, Williamstown, MA....413-458-9853
Bridy, Dan Visuals Inc/625 Stanwix St #2402, Pittsburgh, PA....412-288-9362
Brier, David/38 Park Ave, Rutherford, NJ....201-896-8476
Brown, Carolyn/PO Box 33, Enosbury Falls, VT....802-933-7720
Brown, Leslie/477 Congress/Box 15490, Portland, ME....207-282-2238
Brown, Michael D/932 Hungerford Dr #24, Rockville, MD....301-762-4474
Brown, Remi/Box 186, Roselle Park, NJ....201-245-1218
Brown, Rick Illus/PO Box 341, Furlong, PA....215-794-8186
Brown, Ron Illus/126 Haverhill Rd, Topsfield, MA....508-887-3801
Brown, William L/6704 Westmoreland Ave, Takoma Park, MD....301-270-2014
Bru, Salvador/5130 Bradley Blvd, Chevy Chase, MD....301-654-4420
Bruemmer, Betsy/Box 1743, Edgartown, MA....508-627-9264
Brun, Robert/76 State St, Newburyport, MA....508-462-1948
Brunkus, Denise/111 Perryville Rd, Pittstown, NJ....908-735-2671
Bruno, Peggy/51 Grove St, Marshfield, MA....617-837-6896
Bry, Kimberly/127 Washington Cir, W Hartford, CT....203-236-8112
Bryant, Web/330 Ninth St SE, Washington, DC....202-546-1433
Bryce, William/15 Goodrich St, Pittsfield, MA....413-443-6713
Buccella, Bob/500 Kings Highway South, Cherry Hill, NJ....609-354-0110
Bucella, Martin/72 Martinique Dr, Cheektowaga, NY....716-668-0040
Buchanan, Steve/21 Sand Bank Rd, Watertown, CT....203-945-0285
Bullock, Wilbur/229 Berkeley #52, Boston, MA....617-266-3858
Bunnell, Deb Troyer/346 Lincoln St, Carlisle, PA....717-249-0937
Burchard, Susan Cronin/971 Main St, Hanover, MA....617-871-7805
Burger, Robert/145 Kingwood Stockton Rd, Stockton, NJ....609-397-3737
Burleson, Joe/6035 Blvd East, W New York, NJ....201-854-6029
Burroughs, Miggs/PO Box 6, Westport, CT....203-227-9667
Burrows, Bill & Assoc/3100 Elm Ave West, Baltimore, MD....301-889-3288
Buschini, Maryanne/238 W Highland Ave, Philadelphia, PA....215-242-8517
Bush, Lorraine/2025-A Franklin Pl, Wyomissing, PA....215-678-1252
Buszka, Kimberly/288 Chestnut Hill Ave #12, Brighton, MA....617-787-4245

Butcher, Jim/1357 E MacPhail Rd, Bel Air, MD 301-879-6380
Buterbaugh, Richard/2132 N Market St, Wilmington, DE....302-571-1124
Butler, Ralph/18521 Tarragon Way, Germantown, MD 301-587-1505
Butler, Susan Plante/2345 York Rd, Timonium , MD 301-560-1018
Buxton, John/4584 Sylvan Dr, Allison Oark, PA 412-486-6588
Byram, Stephen/318 73rd St, N Bergen, NJ....201-555-1212
Byrd, Bob/409 Warwick Rd, Haddonfield, NJ 609-428-9627

C

Cabib, Leila/8601 Buckhannon Dr, Potomac, MD....301-299-4158
Cable, Jerry/133 Kuhl Rd, Flemington, NJ 201-788-6750
Cage, Carter/80 Candlewood Dr, Murray Hill, NJ 201-464-2570
Calabro, Carol/1263 Massachusetts Ave #2, Arlington, MA....617-646-7961
Callahan, Donna/15 Connie Dr, Foxboro, MA....508-543-2705
Callahan, Kevin/26 France St, Norwalk, CT....203-847-2046
Callanan, Brian/5 Winston Pl, Yonkers, NY 914-779-4120
Calleja, Bob/490 Elm Ave, Bogota, NJ 201-488-3028
Callier, Gregory/45 17th Ave #5A, Newark, NJ 201-621-9385
Calver, Dave/70 Stoneham Dr, Rochester, NY....716-383-8996
Calvert, Jeff/9518 Whiskey Bottom Rd, Laurel, MD....301-236-4139
Camejo, John/9436 Fens Hollow, Laurel, MD....301-332-6528
Caminos, Jane/370 Newtonville, Newtonville, MA 617-964-1863
Campbell, Harry/194 Washington St #G, Jersey City, NJ....201-434-3651
Canger, Joseph/52 Horizon Dr, Edison, NJ 908-248-1487
Cannizzaro, Gregory, J/107 York Rd, Towson, MD....301-296-2402
Cannone, Gregory/1982 Lake Wood Rd, Toms River, NJ 908-349-4332
Canty, Thomas/178 Old Country Way, Braintree, MA....617-843-7262
Caporale, Wende L/Studio Hill Farm Rte 116, N Salem, NY 914-669-5653
Caputo, Vince/444 Bedford Rd, Pleasantville, NY....914-747-2220
Carallo, Annie/135 S Linwood Ave, Baltimore, MD 301-522-6060
Carbaga, Leslie/258 W Tulpehocken, Philadelphia, PA 215-438-9954
Carbone, Lou/286 Sylvan Rd, Bloomfield, NJ 201-338-8678
Cardella, Elaine/116 Clinton St, Hoboken, NJ 201-656-3244
Cardillo, James/49-D Village Green, Budd Lake, NJ 201-691-1530
Carleton, Kim/20 Yarmouth Rd, Norwood, MA 617-762-3228
Carlson, Frederick H/2335 Meadow Dr, Pittsburgh, PA 412-371-8951
Carlson, Jean Masseau/RR1/Box 303, Hinesburg, VT....802-482-2407
Carlson, Jonathan/1212 St Paul St, Baltimore, MD 301-625-5960
Carlson, Lee/1500 Massachusetts Ave NW #143, Washington, DC 202-429-9823
Carr, Bill/1035 69th Ave, Philadelphia, PA 215-276-1819
Carreiro, Ron/6 Hillside Dr, Plymouth, MA 508-224-9290
Carroll, William/316 Franklin St, Quincy, MA....617-479-4229
Carrozza, Cynthia/393 Beacon St, Boston, MA....617-437-7428
Carson, Jim/11 Foch St, Cambridge, MA....617-661-3321
Carson, Kathleen/8484 16th St #505, Silver Spring, MD 301-495-0759
Carter, Abby/823 Shore Rd, Cape Elizabeth, NJ 207-767-2328
Casilla, Robert/36 Hamilton Ave, Yonkers, NY 914-963-8165
Cassila, Robert/444 Bedford Rd, Pleasantville, NY....914-747-2220
Castellitto, Mark/126 Park Ave, Rutherford, NJ 201-935-2585
Catalano, Sal/114 Boyce Pl, Ridgewood, NJ 201-447-5318
Causey, Stephanie/7801 Archbold Terrace, Cabin John, MD 301-229-6727
Cayea, John/39 Lafayette St, Cornwall, NY....914-534-2942
Cellini, Joseph/415 Hillside Ave, Leonia, NJ 201-944-6519
Chadwick, Kevin/5416 30th Pl NW, Washington, DC....202-244-9588
Champagne, Marc/59 Chestnut Hill Ave, Brighton, MA....617-787-2631
Chandler, Fay M./1010 Memorial Dr #17E, Cambridge, MA 617-547-9013
Chandler, Jean/385 Oakwood Dr, Wyckoff, NJ 201-891-2381
Chandler, Karen/80 Lattingtown Rd, Locust Valley, NY....516-671-0388
Chapman, Linda/121 Bartlett Ave #3, Sharon Hill, PA 215-583-9806
Charles, Milton/199 Ravine Rd, Califon, NJ....201-832-7076
Chen, David/15013 Emory Lane, Rockville, MD 301-460-6575
Chen, Tony/241 Bixley Heath, Lynbrook, NY....516-596-9158
Chernishov, Anatoly/4 Willow Bank Ct, Mahwah, NJ....201-327-2377
Chesak, Lina/1206 Girard St NW, Washington , DC....202-234-4611
Chessare, Michele/25 Compass Ave, W Milford, NJ....201-728-9685
Chestnutt, David/7 Dublin Hill Dr, Greenwich, CT 203-869-8010
Chid/55 Desmond Ave, Bronxville, NY 914-793-6011
Chlumecky, Danielle/35 Middlesex Rd #12, Waltham, MA....617-899-5758
Christe, Dory (Ms)/3950 Brooklyn Ave, Baltimore, MD....301-355-5503
Chui Studio/2250 Elliot St, Merrick, NY....516-223-8474
Churchman, John/4 Howard St, Burlington, VT....802-863-4627
Cicha, Cheryl/, Boston, MA....617-555-1212
Cincotti, Gerald/42 Freeport Dr, Burlington, MA....617-229-4974
Clark, Bradley/36 Haggerty Hill Rd, Rhinebeck, NY 914-876-2615
Clark, Cynthia Watts/36 Haggerty Hill Rd, Rhinebeck, NY 914-876-2615
Clark, Patricia Cullen/6201 Benalder Dr, Bethesda, MD....301-229-2986
Clarke, Bob/55 Brooke Rd, Pittsford, NY 716-248-8683
Cleaver, Bill/7 Dublin Hill Drive, Greenwich, CT 203-869-8010
Clee, Suzanne K/7520 Crittenden St, Philadelphia, PA....215-247-8883
Cline, Rob/1140 Washington St #6, Boston, MA....617-266-3858
Cober, Alan E/95 Croton Dam Rd, Ossining, NY....914-941-8696
Cocozza, Chris/9 Woodbury Pl, Woodbury, CT....203-263-2061
Codd, Mary/65 Ashburton Ave, Providence, RI 401-273-9898
Cohen, Alan R/2828 N Howard St, Baltimore, MD 301-366-3855
Cohen, Gil/8-2 Aspen Way, Doylestown, PA....215-348-0779
Cohen, Santiago/705 Park Ave, Hoboken, NJ....201-420-7275
Cohen, Sharon/20200 Shipley Terrace #202, Germantown, MD....301-540-3466
Cohen, Susan D/84 1/2 Erie St, Jersey City, NJ 201-659-5472
Cole, Robin (Ms)/4 Marie Dr, Andover, MA....617-470-0609
Colleen/192 Southville RD, Southborough, MA 508-872-4549
Collette, Al/8 Covenger Dr, Medford, NJ 609-953-9470
Collyer, Frank/RR 1 Box 266, Stony Point, NY 914-947-3050
Commerford, Bill/55 Delle Ave, Boston, MA....617-445-5406
Condon, Ken/37 West St, Granby, MA 413-467-3792
Conge, Bob/28 Harper St, Rochester, NY....716-473-0291
Conner, Marsha/16 Douglas Pl, Verona, NJ 201-239-1408
Connolly, Jim/25 Cedar St, Hingham, MA 617-749-0825
Connolly, Karl S/217 W College Ave, Salisbury, MD....301-749-5698
Conrad, David/262 Main St, Watertown, MA 617-923-8129
Conrad, Melvin/1919 1/2 Market St 2nd Fl, Williamsport, PA....717-322-2002
Console, Carmen Jr/8 Gettysburg Dr, Voorhees, NJ....609-424-8735
Cook, William/3804 E Northern Pkwy, Baltimore, MD....301-426-1130
Cooper, Bob/301 Kettlerun Rd, Atco, NJ....609-767-0967
Copie/286 Oakwood Dr, Paramus, NJ....201-265-3405
Cordes, Kathy/, Baltimore, MD....301-467-8140
Corfield, Marie/48 Sylvan Place, Nutley, NJ 201-667-8071
Cornelius-Karp/26 E Maple Rd, Greenlawn, NY 516-466-4093
Cornell, Jeff/58 Noyes Rd, Fairfield, CT....203-259-7715
Correll, Cory/11511 Sullnick Way, Gaithersburg, MD....301-977-7254
Cosatt, Paulette/60 South St, Cresskill, NJ 201-871-3765
Costantino, Frank M./13B Pauline St, Winthrop, MA 617-846-4766
Costantino, Valerie/2037 New Hyde Park Rd, New Hyde Park, NY....516-358-9121
Costas, Laura/1650 Harvard St NW #718, Washington, DC....202-265-4499
Courtney, John P/779 Eleventh Ave, Patterson, NJ....201-345-7652
Covert, Susan/40 Matthew Dr, Fairport, NY....716-223-4765
Cowdrey, Richard/229 Berkeley St #52, Boston, MA....617-266-3858
Cox, Birck/325 N Pine, Lancaster, PA....717-396-9346
Cozzolino, Paul/211 Glen Gariff Rd, Massapequa Park, NY....516-795-2841
Craft, Kinuko/RFD #1 PO Box 167, Norfolk, CT 203-542-5018
Cramer, D L/10 Beechwood Dr, Wayne, NJ....201-628-8793
Crawford, Robert/123 Minortown Rd, Woodbury, CT....203-266-0059
Crofut, Bob/8 New St, Ridgefield, CT 203-431-4304
Croll, Carolyn/458 Newton Trnpk, Weston, CT 203-454-4687
Crompton, Jack/229 Berkeley #52, Boston, MA 617-266-3858
Crosman, Hilarie/120 Federal St, Salem, MA 508-745-0431
Cross, Peter/210 Cherry St, Katonah, NY....914-232-3975
Crouse, Danny/24 Appleton Rd, Glen Ridge, NJ 201-748-1650
Crowley, David/711 Washington St, Gloucester, MA....508-283-7866
Csatari, Joseph/Two Snapper Ave, South River, NJ....908-257-4660
Cuan, Sergio/92 Edgemont Pl, Teaneck, NJ 201-833-4337
Cunis, Peter/204 Park Ave #4, Hoboken, NJ 201-792-5164
Cunningham, Nancy/316 Regester St, Baltimore, MD....301-377-9254
Cunningham, Robert M/45 Cornwall Rd (Rt 45), Warren, CT 203-868-2702
Cusano, Steven R/80 Talbot Ct, Media, PA....215-565-8829
Cutler, Dave/656 Whispering Hills Dr, Chester, NY....914-469-4013

D

D'Allaird, John/411 Griffiths St, Syracuse, NY 315-425-7406
D'Entremont, John/355 Wood Rd, Braintree, MA 617-235-2077
D'zenis, Eric/7 Dublin Hill Dr, Greenwich, CT 203-869-8010
Dahm, Bob/166 Arnold Ave, Cranston, RI....401-781-5092
Daily, Don/57 Academy Rd, Bala Cynwyd, PA....215-664-5729
Dally, Lyman M/166 Beachwood Rd, Parsippany, NJ 201-887-1338
Daly, Tom/47 E Edsel Ave, Palisades Park, NJ....201-943-1837
Dameron, Ned/14 Manchester Pl #303, Silver Spring, MD 301-585-8512
Dano, Robert/129 Presidents Lane, Quincy, MA....617-773-9742
Darby, Janet/309 Walnut Rd, Pittsburgh, PA 412-761-5666
Darden, Howard/56 Roosevelt Ave, Butler, NJ....201-492-1273
Dare, Auston/20-C Foxwood Dr, Morris Plains, NJ....201-292-9608
Dargis, Julie/6907 Dartmouth Ave, College Park, MD 301-277-3056
Davidian, Anna/889 Worcester St, Wellesley, MA 617-655-6536
Davin-Hallet, Eleanor/73 Hunters Run, Pittsford, NY....716-385-4089
Davis, Gary/1 Cedar Pl, Wakefield, MA....617-245-2628
Davis, Glenn/223 Central St, Saugus, MA....617-231-3092

Davis, John/604 Ninth St, Carlstadt, NJ 201-460-7358
Davis, Susan/1107 Notley Dr, Silver Spring, MD 301-384-9426
Dawes, Joseph/20 Church Ct, Closter, NJ 201-767-8127
Dawson, John/116 Bedford Rd #1, Toronto , ON 416-926-0730
Dawson, Todd/3528 Greenly St, Wheaton, MD 301-933-7367
Deacon, Jim/36 Arnold St, Providence, RI 401-331-8742
DeAmicus, John/35 South Durst Dr, Milltown, NJ 908-249-4937
Dean, Glenn/RD #2 Box 788, Sussex, NJ 212-490-2450
Decandia, Albert/Box 8566, Haledon, NJ 201-942-9165
DeCerchio, Joseph/62 Marlborough Ave, Marlton, NJ 609-596-0598
DeGrandpre, Patty/27 Baker Ave, Beverly, MA 508-921-0410
Deigan, Jim/309 Walnut Rd, Pittsburgh, PA 412-761-5666
Delaney, John/14 Castle St, Saugus, MA 617-233-1409
DeLapine, Jim/398 31st St, Lindenhurst, NY 516-225-1247
Della-Piana, Elissa/201 Elm St, Medford, MA 671-395-2197
Dellicolli, Ronald E/1 Argilla Rd, Methuen, MA 617-437-9459
Delmonte, Steve/328 W Delavan Ave, Buffalo, NY 716-883-6086
DeLouise, Dan/177 N Cottage St, Valley Stream, NY 516-825-3015
DelRossi, Richard/8 Washington St, Hicksville, NY 516-939-0256
De Luz, Tony/49 Melcher St 3rd fl, Boston, MA 617-695-0006
Demarest, Robert/87 Highview Terr, Hawthorne, NJ 201-427-9639
Demers, Donald/PO Box 4009, Portsmouth, NH 207-439-1463
Demorat, Chuck/305 Cornelia Dr, Graham, NC 919-229-7359
De Muth, Roger T/4103 Chenango St, Cazenovia, NY 315-655-8599
Denham, Karl/155 Fifth St, Hoboken, NJ 201-792-6422
DePalma, Mary Newell/45 Bradfield Ave, Boston, MA 617-327-6241
Deponte, Fabio & Sara/PO Box 393/N Main St, Petersham, MA 508-724-8823
DeRosa, Dawn/25-Q Sylvan Rd S, Westport, CT 203-226-4293
Devaney, John/421 Broadway, Cambridge, MA 617-876-4046
Dever, Jeffrey L/7619 S Arbory Lane, Laurel, MD 301-776-2812
DeVita, Fred/5339 Randolph Rd #4, Rockville, MD 301-770-2237
DeVito, Grace/140 Hoyt St #4E, Stamford, CT 203-967-2198
DeVito, Joe/425 Lancaster Ct, Piscataway, NJ 908-699-1099
Dey, Lorraine/PO Box 268, Toms River, NJ 201-505-1670
Dezita, Fred/5339 Randolph Rd #4, Rockville, MD 301-770-2237
Dibner, Martin/Mayberry Hill, Casco, ME 207-627-4369
Diefendorf, Cathy/8 Cranberry Lane, Dover, MA 508-785-1513
Dillard, Sarah/31 Pleasant St, Charlestown, MA 617-241-0141
DiMartino, Paul/560 Mountain Ave, Washington Twnshp, NJ 212-764-5591
Dimensional Illustrators/362 2nd Street Pike, Southampton, PA 215-953-1415
Dininno, Steve/553 E Fulton St, Long Beach, NY (P 29) 516-431-1495
Dion, Madge/320 Palmer Terrace #1F, Mamaroneck, NY 914-698-1027
Dior, Jerry/9 Old Hickory Ln, Edison, NJ 908-561-6536
Dircks, David/16 Dunford St, Melville, NY 516-427-9377
DiSpenza, John/97 Forest Hill Rd, West Orange, NJ 201-325-3591
Dobrowolski, Chris/153 Pine Grove St, Needham, MA 617-444-7545
Dodge, Paul/731 N 24th St, Philadelphia, PA 215-232-6666
Dodson, Bert/RR 1/Box 1660, Bradford, VT 802-222-9384
Doggett, W Kirk/311 Walnut St, Wellesley, MA 617-431-7835
Donato, Michael Anthony/4082-A Woodbridge Ave, Edison, NJ 908-738-1339
Doney, Todd L W/18 Hillside Ave, Chatham, NJ 201-701-1747
Donnarumma, Dom/25 Stanwood Rd, New Hyde Park, NY 516-248-5113
Donnely, Brian/275 N Cottage St, Valley Stream, NY 516-872-9697
Dooling, Mike/731 N 24th St, Philadelphia, PA 212-232-6666
Dorsey, Bob/2133 Baird Rd, Penfield, NY 315-255-2367
Dow, Brian/115 Marshall St, Revere, MA 617-321-1315
Dowdle, Martha/474 Edinburgh Ct, Severna Park, MD 301-544-2969
Dreamer, Sue/345 Cross St, Hanson, MA 617-294-4508
Drescher, Joan/23 Cedar, Hingham, MA 617-749-5179
Dressel, Peggy/11 Rockaway Ave, Oakland, NJ 201-337-2143
Drinkwine, Sharon/229 Berkeley #52, Boston, MA 617-266-3858
Driver, Ray/26012 Brigadier Pl Unit E, Damacus, MD 301-972-0556
Drucker, Mort/42 Juneau Blvd, Woodbury, NY 516-367-4920
Drummey, Jack/8 Ninth St #313, Medford, MA 617-395-2778
Drummond, Deborah/67 Concord Rd, Sudbury, MA 508-443-3160
Drury, Christian Potter/61 Colonial Rd, Providence, RI 404-421-3406
Dudash, C Michael/PO Box 2803, Moretown, VT 802-496-6400
Dugan, Brian/544 W Meadow Ave, Rahway, NJ 201-499-8417
Dugan, Louise/5046 MacArthur Blvd, Washington, DC 202-966-7549
Duke, Chris/Maple Ave Box 471, Millbrook, NY 914-677-9510
Duke, W E/90 Elm St, Westfield, MA 413-562-8494
Dumville, Fritz/22 Edison Ave, Providence, RI 401-861-7629
Dunlavey, Rob/32 Mark Lee Rd, Needham, MA 617-449-7142
Dunne, Tom/16 Cherry St, Locust Valley, NY 919-644-1087
DuPont, Lane/20 Evergreen Ave, Westport, CT 203-222-1562
Durham, Bob/15 Warrenton Ave, Hartford, CT 203-523-4562
Durham, Ed/6308 Sword's Way, Bethesda, MD 301-493-4237
Dursee, Brian/514 Birch Ave, Westfield, NJ 908-233-8096
Dverin, Anatoly/229 Berkeley #52, Boston, MA 617-266-3858
Dvorak, Phillip/15 Warrenton Ave, Hartford, CT 203-523-4562
Dwingler, Randy/124 Median Dr, Wilmington, DE 302-478-6063
Dyen, Don/410 Parkview Way, Newtown, PA 215-968-9083
Dykes, John/17 Morningside Dr S, Westport, CT 203-222-8150

E

Eagle, Mike/7 Captains Ln, Old Saybrook, CT 203-388-5654
Earl, James/17 Parkview Dr, Hingham, MA 617-749-7982
Ebert, Len/Box 530/RD #2, Douglassville, PA 215-689-9872
Echevarria, Abe/Memory Ln Farm, Sherman, CT 203-355-1254
Eckstein, Bob/107 Cherry Lane, Medford, NY 516-654-0291
Edens, John/2464 Turk Hill Rd, Victor, NY 716-425-3441
Edwards, James/17 Rockview St, Boston, MA 617-522-2656
Egan, Bobbi/10 Myrtle St, White Plains, NY 914-761-8650
Eggleton, Bob/597 Smith St, Providence, RI 401-831-5030
Eichner, Thomas/4012 Southend Rd, Rockville, MD 301-871-1235
Einsel, Naiad/26 Morningside Dr S, Westport, CT 203-226-0709
Einsel, Walter/26 Morningside Dr S, Westport, CT 203-226-0709
Elliott, Elizabeth/532 20th St NW #809, Washington, DC 202-638-6009
Ellis, Jon/1622 Brownsville Rd, Langhorne, PA 215-750-6180
Ellson, Randy/Arctan/8 Prince St, Rochester, NY 716-244-6327
Elvidge, Ed/PO Box 709, SW Harbor, ME 207-244-5048
Emmett, Bruce/8 Gerard Ave, Bellport, NY 718-636-5263
Emmons, Barbara/19 Minjow St, Portland, ME 207-761-2472
Engeman, Tom/2801 Quebec St NW, Washington, DC 202-363-2623
Enos, Randall/11 Court of Oaks, Westport, CT 203-227-4785
Epstein, Aaron/2015 Aspen Dr, Plainsboro, NJ 609-275-1034
Epstein, Edward/PO Box 1089, Montpelier, VT 802-229-5123
Epstein, Len/720 Montgomery Ave, Narbeth, PA 215-664-4700
Epstein, Lorraine/21 Marianne Rd, Darien, CT 203-656-1185
Estey, Peg/27 Irving Terrace, Cambridge, MA 617-876-1790
Ettlinger, Doris/RD #2/Box 6, Hampton, NJ 908-537-6322
Eucalyptus Tree Studio/2221 Morton St, Baltimore, MD 301-243-0211
Evans, Leslie/17 Bay St, Watertown, MA 617-924-3058
Eveland, Russ/1103 Ralph Rd, Newark, DE 302-737-9102
Ewers, Joseph/220 Mill St, Holliston, MA 508-429-6375
Eynon, Debbie/118 Montgomery Ave #A3-3, Bala Cynwyd, PA 215-668-0986

F

Fabian, Steven/17 Central Ave, Mine Hill, NJ 201-989-0934
Fahey, Gilbert/60 Ridgewood St, Manchester, CT 203-647-8955
Fallin, Ken/25 Windsor Rd, Milton, MA 617-696-2677
Faraclas, Andrea/227 Chris Columbus Dr #335B, Jersey City, NJ 201-433-3459
Faria, Jeff/937 Garden St, Hoboken, NJ 201-656-3063
Farnham, Joe/25 Fuller St, Manchester, MA 508-688-3622
Farnsworth, Bill/PO Box 653, New Milford, CT 203-355-1649
Farrell, Marybeth/77 Dwight Pl, Engelwood, NJ 201-569-1655
Fauver, Chris/3929 Madison St, Hyattsville, MD 301-699-9227
Feeney, Betsy/444 Bedford Rd, Pleasantville, NY 914-747-2220
Feinen, Jeff/4702 Sawmill Rd, Clarence, NY 716-759-8406
Fellman, Nancy/126 Sumac St, Philadelphia, PA 215-483-3698
Ferris, Keith/50 Moraine Rd, Morris Plains, NJ 201-539-3363
Fiedler, Joseph D/500 Sampsonia Way, Pittsburgh, PA 412-322-7245
Field, Bob/336 Washington St, Brookline, MA 617-232-2230
Fifield, Lew/1300 Mt Royal Ave/Visual Comm, Baltimore, MD 301-669-9200
Figueroa, Rafael/176 Plainview Ave, Jersey City, NJ 201-451-3160
Fijal, Ted/121 Carriage Rd, Chicopee, MA 413-532-7334
Filippo, Judy/120 Brook St #1, Brookline, MA 617-731-4277
Filippucci, Sandra/Larchmont Acres E #614C, Larchmont, NY 212-477-8732
Finch, Sharon Roy/426 8th St NE, Washington, DC 202-546-1045
Fine, Howard/330 Rolling Rock Rd, Mountainside, NJ 908-522-1855
Finewood, Bill/605 S Main St, E Rochester, NY 716-377-2126
Finney, Lawrence/110 Mercer St #3D, Jersey City, NJ 201-432-8407
Fione, Dan/2276 Mt Carmel Ave, Glenside, PA 215-885-8227
Fiore, Peter/St Rd 2355-H, Matamoras, PA 717-491-5002
Fisch, Paul/5111 Coffee Tree Lane, N Syracuse, NY 315-451-8147
Fisher, Cynthia/RFD Box 87B, Charlemont, MA 413-625-8204
Fisher, Hyman W/121 E Northfield Rd, Livingston, NJ 201-994-9480
Fisher, Mark S/15 Colonial Dr, Westford, MA 508-392-0303
Fitzhugh, Gregg/3000 Chestnut Ave #6, Baltimore, MD 301-889-2733
Flat Tulip Studio/Rt 1 Box 146, Marietta, PA 717-426-1344
Fleischer, Pat/223 Katherine St, Scotch Plains, NJ 201-889-9059
Flickinger, Tracy/20 W Emerson St, Melrose, MA 617-662-8660
Flynn, Maura/8 George St, Manhasset, NY 516-627-6608

Fogletto, Ben/3137 Bay Ave, Ocean City, NJ 609-391-1537
Fondersmith, Mark/8 W Branch Ln, Baltimore, MD 301-385-3145
Ford, Pam/251 Greenwood Ave, Bethel, CT....203-797-8188
Forman, James/2 Central Pl, Lynbrook, NY....516-599-2046
Forte, Joseph/17 Parsonage Rd, E Setauket, NY....516-941-3641
Foster, Stephen Design/17 51st St #5, Weehawken, NJ....201-866-9040
Foster, Susan/4800 Chevy Chase Dr #500, Chevy Chase, MD....301-652-3848
Fournier, Walter/185 Forest St, S Hamilton, MA....508-468-2892
Fowler, Eric/411 Beatty St, Trenton, NJ 609-695-4305
Fox, Rosemarie/PO Box 186, Bearville, NY 914-679-6132
Foy, Lynne/243 Linwood Ave, Newton, MA 617-244-3768
Francis, John/2132 N Market St 3rd Fl, Wilmington, DE 302-655-9011
Francisco Adv & Design/126 Green Lane, Philadelphia, PA 215-482-6610
Franke, Phil/10 Nehring Ave, Babylon Village, NY 516-661-5778
Frankel, Adrian/315 Monroe St, Hoboken, NJ 201-656-4317
Freeman, Charles/192 Southville Rd, Southborough, MA....617-872-4549
Freeman, Mark/1146 19th St NW, Washington, DC....202-331-7722
Frick, Thomas/227 Doris Ave, Baltimore, MD....301-789-3045
Fricke, Bill/426 Adamston Rd, Bricktown, NJ 908-477-5482
Friederichs, Anni/10 Bay st #10, Westport, CT 203-544-8924
Friedman, Marvin/17 Montague Ave, W Trenton , NJ....609-883-1576
Frinta, Dagmar/2 College St, Providence, RI....401-331-3511
Frizzell, Mark/P O Box 3176 , Woburn, MA 617-933-0805
Fry, Leslie/567 St Paul St #5, Burlington, VT 802-862-4034
Fuchs, Bernie/3 Tanglewood Ln, Westport, CT....203-227-4644
Fuggetta, Richard/267 Central Ave, White Plains, NY....914-761-0214
Full Moon Creations/74 S Hamilton St, Doylestown, PA....215-345-1233
Furgalack, Roberta/10 Maize Dr, Charlestown, RI 401-364-3667

G

Gaadt, George/888 Thorn, Sewickley, PA 412-741-5161
Gabor, Tim/474 Elm St, Northampton, MA....413-585-0558
Gaines, Mark/179 S Harrison #504, E Orange, NJ 201-674-1669
Gallagher, Jim/169 Northfiled Rd, Bridgewater, NJ....908-722-5292
Gallagher, Matthew/1 Old Manor Rd, Holmdel, NJ 908-741-0157
Gallipoli, Wayne/12 Belmont St, Milford, CT 203-874-6992
Gallivan, Greta/11 North St #3, Marcellus, NY 315-673-9123
Gamache, John/192 Southville Rd, Southborough, MA....508-872-4549
Garbowski, Gene/8958 Watchlight Ct, Columbia, MD 301-596-1036
Garcia, Tom/597 Riverside Ave, Westport, CT 203-226-4724
Gardei, Dean/617 E 34th St, Baltimore, MD 301-235-3638
Gardner, Gail/227 Marlborough St, Boston, MA 617-266-8626
Gardner, Mike/21 Heather Road, Watertown, MA 617-924-4907
Garland, Michael/19 Manor Rd/RR #2, Patterson, NY....914-898-4347
Garland, Philip/717 Washington St, Newtonville, MA 617-332-6741
Garner, David/247 Broadway, Huntington, NY 212-265-6595
Garrett, Cynthia/1 Fitchburg St, Somerville, MA 617-628-2450
Gaszi, Edward/84 Evergreen Rd, New Egypt, NJ 609-758-9466
Gatto, Chris/PO Box 4041, Stamford, CT 203-264-2400
Gavin, Bill/268 Orchard St, Millis, MA....508-376-5727
Gay-Kassel, Doreen/24-A Chestnut Court, Princeton, NJ....609-497-0783
Gazsi, Ed/84 Evergreen, New Egypt, NJ....609-758-9466
Gebert, Warren/12 Stoneham Lane, New City, NY....914-354-2536
Geller, Andrea/45-B Hastings Ave, Rutherford, NJ 201-507-5134
Gensheimer, Frank/5 Lawrence St Bldg 15, Bloomfield, NJ 201-743-4305
Gensurowsky, Yvonne/2406 Yarmouth Ln, Crofton, MD....301-721-6938
Genzo, John Paul/802 Ravens Crest Dr, Plainsboro, NJ....609-275-5601
Geogriann, Margaret/4508 West Virginia Ave, Bethesda, MD....301-496-5566
Gerber, Mark & Stephanie/18 Oak Grove Rd, Brookfield, CT 203-775-3658
Gerlach, Cameron/3000 Chestnut Ave #113, Baltimore, MD 301-889-0406
Gervais, Stephen/183 Riverside Ave, Warwick, RI....401-737-8526
Geyer, Jackie/107 6th St #207 Fulton Bldg, Pittsburgh, PA....412-261-1111
Giana, Alan/19 Field Rock Rd, Farmington, CT 203-678-9239
Giardina, Laura/12 Buckingham Ct, Pomona, NY....914-354-0871
Giarnella, Andy/259 Main St, E Berlin, CT 203-828-8410
Giedd, Richard/101 Pierce Rd, Watertown, MA 617-924-4350
Giguere, Ralph/2220 Delancey Pl, Philadelphia, PA....215-968-3696
Gilbert, Douglas R/8 Lafayette St, Newburyport, MA....508-465-8285
Gilfoy, Bruce/568 Washington St, Wellesley, MA 617-235-8977
Gilligan, Sheila/185 Highland Ave, Somerville, MA 617-628-5144
Gilman, Mary/Star Rte 13-A, Wendell Depot, MA....508-544-7425
Gilmour, Joni/10 Dane St, Jamaica Plain, MA 617-524-6556
Gilroy, Robin/53 West St, Newton, MA....617-964-6128
Gino/7 Dublin Hill Dr, Greenwich, CT....203-869-8010
Ginzel, Katherine A/17 Allerton St, Plymouth, MA 508-746-1099
Giordano, Edward/59B St Andrews Blvd, Clifton, NJ....201-778-6379
Gist, Linda E/224 Madison Ave, Fort Washington, PA....215-643-3757
Giuliani, Alfred/11 Terhune Ave, Jersey City, NJ....201-432-0443
Giusti, Robert/340 Long Mountain Rd, New Milford, CT 203-354-6539
Gladden, Scott/444 Bedford Rd, Pleasantville, NY 914-747-2220
Glasbergen, Randy J/PO Box 611, Sherburne, NY 607-674-9492
Glazer, Art/2 James Rd, Mt Kisco, NY....914-666-4554
Glazer, Ted/28 West View Rd, Spring Valley, NY 914-354-1524
Glessner, Marc/24 Evergreen Rd, Somerset, NJ....908-249-5038
Glidden, Althea/726 Pacific St, Baltimore, MD 301-523-5903
Gnidziejko, Alex/Route 194, Alna, ME 207-586-5247
Goebel, Joe/72 High St, Topsfield, MA....508-887-3528
Gold, Al/450 Valley Rd, W Orange, NJ 201-673-9035
Gold, Marcy/155-L Friedman Rd, Monticello, NY....914-794-0359
Gold, Sandi/1756 Euclid St, Washington, DC....202-234-5680
Goldberg, Richard A./368 Congress St 5th Fl, Boston, MA 617-338-6369
Goldin, David/1477 Beacon St, Brookline, MA....617-731-0088
Goldinger, Andras/215 C St SE #310, Washington, DC....202-543-9029
Goldman, Marvin/RD 3 Gypsy Trail Rd, Carmel, NY....914-225-8611
Goode, Harley/30 Regina Dr, Monsey, NY 914-578-5677
Goodrich, Carter/137 Water St, Stonington, CT 203-535-1141
Gordley, Scott/229 Berkeley #52, Boston, MA 617-266-3858
Gorski, Peter/41 Elizabeth St, Peak's Island, ME....207-766-5593
Goryl, John/65 Robins Ave, Rockledge, PA 215-663-0128
Gothard, David/RD 4/Box 4301A, Bangor, ME....215-588-4937
Goudreau, Roc/1342 Berkshire Ave, Springfield, MA....413-543-6796
Graber, Jack/620 Union St, Schenectady, NY
(P 16,17) 518-370-0312
Grafica, Gergei/24 Roe park, Highland Falls, NY....914-446-2367
Grashow, James/14 Diamond Hill Rd, W Redding, CT....203-938-9195
Graves, David/R133-135 Wheeler St, Gloucester, MA....617-283-2335
Green, Howie/6 St James Ave, Boston, MA 617-542-6063
Green, Norman/11 Seventy Acres Rd, W Redding, CT 203-438-9909
Greene, Joel & Anne/70 Rocky Pond Rd, Boylston, MA 508-869-6440
Gregory, Lane/8 Cranberry Lane, Dover, MA....508-785-1513
Grewe, Nilou/4 Wakeman Pl, Larchmont, NY 914-834-6820
Griegg, Linda/509 Notley Rd, Silver Spring, MD....301-384-6340
Griesbach, Cheryl/41 Twinlight Terrace, Highlands, NJ....201-291-5945
Griesbach/Martucci/41 Twinlight Terrace, Highlands, NJ 908-291-5945
Griffo, Joseph/54 North Ave, New Rochelle, NY 914-633-5734
Grimes, Rebecca/936 Stone Rd, Westminster, MD....301-848-4472
Gross, Steve/434 E Front St, Plainfield, NJ 908-755-4738
Grossman, Andrew/3912 Ingomar St NW, Washington, DC 202-686-0480
Grote, Rich/21 Tyndale Rd, Hamilton Square, NJ 609-586-5896
Gruttola, John/4 School Ct, Coram, NY 516-696-7056
Guancione, Karen/262 DeWitt Ave, Belleville, NJ 201-450-9490
Gully, Bethany/791 Tremont St #W204, Boston, MA 617-437-7556
Gunn, Robert/229 Berkeley #52, Boston, MA 617-266-3858
Gunning, Kevin/37 Denison Rd, Middleton, CT....203-347-0688
Guran, Michael/1 Fitchburg St, Somerville, MA....617-666-8881
Gustafson, Dale/56 Fourbrooks Rd, Stamford, CT 203-322-5667
Guzzi, George/11 Randlett Pk, W Newton, MA 617-244-2932
Gyson, Mitch/4412 Colmar Gardens Dr E, Baltimore, MD....301-243-3430
Gyurcsak, Joe/Chestnut Willow #3A-6, Cranbury, NJ....609-426-4119

H

Haas, Shelly/50-A Village Green, Budd Lake, NJ 201-347-8544
Haber-Schaim, Tamar/1870 Beacon St/Bldg 6 #B1, Brookline, MA....617-738-8883
Haberman, Jim/12 Cleveland St #2, Arlington, MA 617-646-5906
Haefele, Steve/111 Heath Rd, Mahopac, NY....914-736-0785
Haffner, Marilyn/15 Seven Pines Ave, Cambridge, MA 617-547-2034
Hahn, Eileen/8 Hillwood Rd, East Brunswick, NJ 201-390-4188
Hallgren, Gary/98 Laurelton Dr, Mastic Beach, NY 516-399-5531
Hallman, Tom/38 S 17th St, Allentown, PA....215-776-1144
Halverson, Lydia/25-Q Sylvan Rd S, Westport, CT 203-226-4293
Hamilton, Ken/16 Helen Ave, West Orange, NJ....201-736-6532
Hamilton, Thomas/2276 Mt Carmel Ave, Glenside, PA....215-885-8227
Hamilton, William/81 Sand Rd, Ferrisburg, VT 802-877-6869
Hampshire, Michael/7 Dublin Hill Dr, Greenwich, CT....203-869-8010
Haney, William/674 S Branch River Rd, Somerville, NJ....908-369-8792
Hansen, Biruta/Sun Hill/RD1/Box 39G, Liverpool, PA 717-444-3682
Hansen, Ken/2 Fuller Ave, Swampscott, MA....617-598-0111
Hantel, Johanna/437 E Belvedere St #8F, Nazareth, PA....215-759-2025
Harden, Laurie/121 Banta Lane, Boonton Township, NJ 201-335-4578
Hardy, Jill/1662-D Beekman Pl NW, Washington, DC 202-667-4245
Hardy, Neil O/2 Woods Grove, Westport, CT....203-226-4446
Hardy-Faraci, Cheryl/59 Pitman, Wakefield, MA 617-245-5315
Harmon, Traci/3000 Chestnut Ave #6, Baltimore, MD 301-243-0643
Harrington, Glenn/329 Twin Lear Rd, Pipersville, PA 215-294-8104

Harrington, Sheila/2836 27th St NW, Washington, DC 202-328-3231
Harrington, Steve/597 Riverside Ave, Westport, CT 203-226-4724
Harris, Ellen/125 Pleasant St #602, Brookline, MA 617-739-1867
Harris, Peter/305 Union St, Franklin, MA 508-520-2400
Harsh, Fred/7 Ivy Hill Rd/Box 959, Ridgefield, CT 203-438-8386
Harty, Beth Rubin/4108 28th St, Mt Ranier, MD 301-927-0504
Harvey, Paul/475-B Commanche Ln, Stratford, CT 203-381-9836
Haselbacher, Nancy/109 Queensbury St, Boston, MA 617-424-8572
Hasto, Ray/34 1/2 State St, Pittsford, NY 716-385-6101
Hasz, Judith Ann/776 Warburton Ave #3A, Yonkers, NY 914-963-7019
Hatton, Enid/46 Parkway, Fairfield, CT 203-259-3789
Havice, Susan/6 Roundy Lane, Lynnfield, MA 617-334-3976
Hawkes, Kevin/2 Francis St, Belmont, MA 617-489-1878
Hazelton, Betsey/106 Robbins Dr, Carlisle, MA 508-369-5309
Healy, Deborah/72 Watchung Ave, Upper Montclair, NJ 201-746-2549
Hearn, Diane Dawson/22 Spring St, Pauling, NY 914-855-1152
Hearn, Walter/22 Spring St, Pauling, NY 914-855-1152
Heath, R Mark/4338 Roland Springs Dr, Baltimore, MD 301-366-4633
Heimann, Steve/PO Box 406, Oradell, NJ 201-345-9132
Heimbach, Gale/RD 1/Box 367/Washington St, Douglasville, PA 215-582-8026
Hein, Jean/2276 Mt Carmel Ave, Glenside, PA 215-885-8227
Heitmann, Bob/9071 Millcreek RD #116, Levittown, PA 215-946-1394
Henderson, Dave/32 James Rd/RR 5, Boonton Twnshp, NJ 201-402-1461
Henderson, Garnet/820 Hudson #2-7, Hoboken, NJ 201-653-3948
Hendrickson, Kathy/856 Springfield Ave, New Providence, NJ 201-665-2192
Hennessey, Glenn/2151 California St NW #40, Washington, DC 202-483-7883
Henrickson, Kathy/856 Springfield Ave, New Providence, NJ 201-665-1070
Henry, Doug/229 Berkeley #52, Boston, MA 617-266-3858
Henry-May, Rosemary/2625 Garfield St NW, Washington, DC 202-667-0455
Herring, Michael/RD 1 Box 205A, Cold Spring, NY 914-265-9476
Hess, Mark/88 Quicks Lane, Katonah, NY 914-232-5870
Hess, Richard/310 Litchfield Rd, Norfolk, CT 203-354-2921
Hess, Robert/63 Littlefield Rd, E Greenwich, RI 401-885-0331
Hidy, Lance/PO Box 806, Newburyport, MA 508-462-6567
Hierro, Claudia & Gregory/1099 Rosse Ave, New Milford, NJ 201-907-0423
Hildebrandt, Greg/120 American Rd, Morris Plains, NJ 201-292-6852
Hildebrandt, Tim/10 Jackson Ave, Gladstone, NJ 908-234-2149
Hill, Michael/2433 Maryland Ave, Baltimore, MD 301-366-8338
Hillios, Sonia/PO Box 90, Southampton, MA 413-527-4059
Hinlicky, Greg/PO Box 1521, Toms River, NJ 908-269-4867
Hobbs, Bob/515 Spring St, Newport, RI 401-848-5848
Hocking, Philip/1615 Manchester Lane NW, Washington, DC 202-882-8237
Hodgkinson, Geoffrey/192 Southville Rd, Southborough, MA 508-872-4549
Hoeffner, Deb/538 Cherry Tree Lane, Kinnelon, NJ 201-838-5490
Hoey, Peter/1730 16th St NW #5, Washington, DC 202-234-2110
Hoffman, Nancy/16 Ridge Dr, Berkeley Heights, NJ 908-665-2177
Hokanson, Lars/PO Box 199, Hopeland, PA 717-733-9066
Holas, Evzen/858 Broadway #2, Chelsea, MA 617-889-6167
Holder, John/128 Beechtree Dr, Broomall, PA 215-356-0362
Hopp, Andrea/301 High Mountain Ln, York Town, NY 914-767-7164
Hofkin, Bonnie/18 McKinley St, Rowayton, CT 203-866-3734
Houston, Greg/412 Lyman Ave, Baltimore, MD 301-323-7130
Hovey, Jack/717 Park Ave, Baltimore, MD 301-244-7205
Howard, Rob/55 Westland Terrace, Haverville, MA 508-372-8915
Howell, Van/PO Box 812, Huntington, NY 516-424-6499
Huehnergarth, John/196 Snowden Ln, Princeton, NJ 609-921-3211
Huelsman, Amy/24 S Calumet Ave, Hastings on Hudson, NY 914-478-0596
Huerta, Gerard/45 Corbin Dr, Darien, CT (P 21) **203-656-0505**
Huffaker, Sandy/23D Norwood Ct, Princeton, NJ 609-924-2883
Hughes, Neal/309 S Washington Ave, Moorestown, NJ 609-234-5322
Hughes, Stephanie/89 Oawton St, Brookline, MA 617-277-7676
Huling, Phil/938 Bloomfield St, Hoboken, NJ 201-795-9366
Hulsey, John/Rte 9D, Garrison, NY 914-424-3002
Hunt, Peter/Six Paag Lane, Little Spring, NJ 908-741-1465
Hurd, Jackie/71 Lockland Ave, Framingham, MA 608-879-6319
Hurd, Jane/4002 Virginia Pl, Bethesda, MD 301-229-7966
Hurd, Lauren/1715 Linden Ave, Baltimore, MD 301-377-9084
Hurwitz, Joyce/7314 Burdette Ct, Bethesda, MD 301-365-0340
Hutchison, Bruce/192 Southville Rd, Southboro, MA 508-872-4549
Huyssen, Roger/45 Corbin Dr, Darien, CT (P 21) **203-656-0200**
Hynes, Robert/5215 Muncaster Mill Rd, Rockville, MD 301-926-7813

IJ

Ingraham, Erick/66 Old Jaffrey Rd, Peterborough, NH 613-924-6785
Inouye, Carol/Gulf Schoolhouse Rd, Cornwallville, NY 518-634-7589
Iosa, Ann/7 Ivy Hill Rd/Box 959, Ridgefield, CT 203-438-8386
Ippolito, Frank/361 Devon St, Kearney, NJ 201-998-0581

Irish, Gary/45 Newbury St, Boston, MA 617-247-4168
Irwin, Virginia/37 Jamaica St #2, Jamaica Plain, MA 617-522-0736
Jackson, Robert R/816 Bainbridge St, Philadelphia, PA 215-627-8413
JAEL/PO Box 11178, Fairfield, NJ 201-808-4363
JAK Graphics Ltd/458 Newtown Trnpk, Weston, CT 203-454-4687
Jakubowski, Nancy/252 Doyle Ave, Providence, RI 401-331-7858
Janesko, Lou/10400 Connecticut Ave NW, Kensington, MD 301-933-5533
Jaquith, Diane/3 Newbury Terrace, Newton, MA 617-244-2256
Jareaux, Robin/28 Eliot St, Boston, MA 617-524-3099
Jauniskis, Ramune/20 Old Farm Rd, Dover, MA 508-785-2145
Jazwiecki, Leonard/66 Granby Heights, Granby, MA 413-256-0321
Jeffery, Lynn/RR4 Box 970, Stowe, VT 802-253-4767
Jennings, Beth/100 Prospect St #201, Jersey City, NJ 201-795-9483
Jerome, Karen A/633 Highland Ave, Needham, MA 617-444-8667
Jig, Harold/8421 Spruill Dr, Bowie, MD 301-262-7820
Johnson, Craig/63 Providence Ave. Doylestown, PA 215-348-2593
Johnson, D B/PO Box 360, Plainfield, NH 603-675-6113
Johnson, Glenn/76 Elm St #313, Boston, MA 617-522-0165
Johnson, Richard/PO Box 555, Cohasset, MA 617-749-7600
Johnson, Sarah/333 Wickenden St, Providence, RI 401-273-0903
Johnston-Carlson, Susan/36 Overlook Dr, Hackettstown, NJ 201-813-1113
Jonason, Dave/355 Epping Way, Annapolis, MD 301-849-8880
Jones, Barry/2725 Mary St, Easton, PA 215-253-3709
Jones, Don/695 Sayre Ave #22, Perth Amboy, NJ 908-324-1096
Jones, Jeffrey/17 Central Ave, Mine Hill, NJ 201-989-0934
Jones, John R/335 Town St, East Haddam, CT 203-873-9950
Jones, Keith R/844 Berkeley Ave, Trenton, NJ 609-695-7448
Jones, Robert/47 W Stewart, Lansdowne, PA 215-626-1245
Jones, Roger/34 Gorham St, Cambridge, MA 617-661-8645
Jordan, Laurie/7 Ivy Hill Rd/Box 959, Ridgefield, CT 203-438-8386
Jordan, Polly/29 Warren Ave, Somerville, MA 617-776-0329
Joudrey, Ken/530 Tanager Pl, Stratford, CT 203-378-5007
Joyce, Michael/1402 Beacon St, Brookline, MA 617-734-4424
Joyner, Eric/731 North 24th St, Philadelphia, PA 215-232-6666
Joyner, Ginny/PO Box 306, Winooski, VT 802-865-9565
Juhasz, Victor/576 Westminster Ave, Elizabeth, NJ 908-351-4227

K

Kabaker, Gayle/Normand RR# 1 Box 120, Ashfield, MA 413-625-2529
Kachik, John/3000 Chestnut Ave #6, Baltimore, MD 301-467-7916
Kaczman, James/7 Chester St, Watertown, MA 617-923-4605
Kalabokis, Peter/19 N Charlemont Ct, N Chelmsford, MA 508-251-3058
Kane, Kid/9 W Bridge St, New Hope, PA 215-862-0392
Kane, Michael/9 Holland Lane, Cranberry, NJ 609-448-0843
Kanturek, Les/63 Blumel Rd, Middletown, NY 914-692-0094
Kascht, John/635 A St NE, Washington, DC 202-546-9527
Kassel, Doreen/24-A Chestnut Ct, Princeton, NJ 609-497-0783
Kassler, Elizabeth/128 Prospect Ave, Dumont, NJ 201-385-3551
Kastner, John/158 Burwell Rd, Rochester, NY 716-328-3262
Kathan-Sayess, Shirley/205 Indian Meadow Dr, Northboro, MA 508-393-5108
Katsin, Nancy/229 Spring Garden Rd, Milford, NJ 201-995-2177
Kay, Patricia M/51 Linden Ave, Metuchen, NJ 908-549-7083
Kazi, Pat/2813 Rocks Rd, Jarrettsville, MD 301-838-9584
Keene, Donald/191 Clove Rd, New Rochelle, NY 914-636-2128
Kelley, Steve/3501 Windom Rd, Brentwood, MD 301-699-1766
Kelly, Sean/1622 19th St NW #3, Washington, DC 202-462-0606
Kemp, Dan/9543 Dublin Rd, Walkersville, MD 301-845-6107
Kerr, Tom/125 Bamm Hollow Rd, Middletown, NJ 201-922-6000
Ketler, Ruth Sofair/101 Bluff Terrace, Silver Spring, MD 301-593-6059
Keyes, Michael D/14 Lillian Ave, Providence, RI 401-467-6568
Kibiuk, Lydia V/8 F Cross Keys Rd, Baltimore, MD 301-433-1107
Kidd, Tom/59 Cross Brook Rd, New Milford, CT 203-355-1781
Kiernan, Jacquie/1 Rutgers Ct B3, Belleville, NJ 201-751-8717
Kilroy, John/28 Fairmount Way, Nantasket, MA 617-925-0582
King, Caryn/166 Ames St, Sharon, MA 617-784-2196
King, Manuel/20 Woodchuck Hill, Harvard, MA 508-456-3412
Kingsbery, Guy/305 High St, Milford, CT 203-878-8939
Kinstrey, Jim/1036 Broadway, W Longbranch, NJ 908-229-0312
Kirk Noll, Cheryl/19 Hooker St, Providence, RI 401-861-5869
Kirk, Betsy/310 St Dunstans Rd, Baltimore, MD 301-235-3154
Kiwak, Barbara/3000 Chestnut Ave #6, Baltimore , MD 301-243-0643
Klein, Kathryn/51 Melcher St, Boston, MA 617-350-7970
Kleinsteuber, Robert/38 Nina Court, Gaithersburg, MD 301-921-4253
Klim, Joseph/PO Box 463, Avon, CT 203-676-9933
Kline, Rob/229 Berkeley #52, Boston, MA 617-266-3858
Klopp, Karyl/5209 Eighth St/Cnstitutn Qtrs, Charlestown, MA 617-242-7463
Kluglein, Karen/37 Cary Rd, Great Neck, NY 212-684-2974

Knabel, Lonnie/34 Station St, Brookline, MA 617-566-4464
Knepp, Tim/3611 Laurel View Court, Laurel, MD 301-490-3115
Kocar, George F/, Boston, MA 617-555-1212
Koeppel, Gary/258 Chestnut Ave, Jamaica Plain, MA....617-522-3051
Kohl, Joe/522 Vine Ave, Toms River, NJ 908-349-4149
Korman, Ira/NJ 201-736-3022
Korvatin, Daniel/1702 Oak Court, Monmouth Junction, NJ....908-274-2363
Kossin, Sanford/143 Cowneck Rd, Port Washington, NY 516-883-3038
Koster, Aaron/2 Yeoman Way, Englishtown, NJ 908-536-2815
Kouw, Danny/1592 Panview Ave, Seaford, NY....516-221-5294
Kozlowski, Martin/141 Southside Ave 2nd Fl, Hastings, NY 914-478-7445
Kralyevich, Vincent/706 Hudson St, Hoboken, NJ 201-653-3277
Kraus, James/195 Canton St, Boston, MA 617-437-1945
Krause, Linda/390 Princeton Ave, Jersey City, NJ 201-451-5849
Krepel, Dick/288 Westbrook Rd, Essex, CT....203-767-2864
Krieger, Salem/91 Park Ave, Hoboken, NJ 201-963-3754
Krommes, Beth/RR 1/Box 116D, Rindge, NH....603-899-6061
Krosnick Studio/686 Undercliff Ave, Edgewater, NJ 201-224-5495
Krovatin, Dan/1702 Oak Ct, Monmouth Junction, NJ....201-274-2363
Krupinski, Loretta/6 Coach Dr, Old Lyme, CT....203-434-0075
Kseniak, Mark/12 Navesink Ave, Navesink, NJ....908-872-1559
Kubinyi, Laszlo/115 Evergreen Pl, Teaneck, NJ 201-833-4428
Kulczak, Frank/412 Diller Rd, Hanover, PA....717-637-2580
Kulhanek, Paul/167 Cherry St #177, Milford, CT....203-876-0697
Kunic, Diane/72 High St #2, Topsfield, MA 508-887-3528
Kupper, Ketti/3 Evergreen Ave, Wilton, CT 203-761-9454
Kutakoff, Lauren/47 Cobblewood Rd, Livingston, NJ 201-994-3569
Kyhos, Brian/4 Linwood Pl, Rochester, NY....716-454-2630
Kyle, Ron/186 Lincoln, Boston, MA 617-426-5942

L

La Grone, Roy E/25 Indiana Rd, Somerset, NJ 908-846-7959
Labrasca, Judy/7 Walcott Ave, Falmouth, ME....207-781-3858
Lacano, Frank/336 Sherwood Rd, Union, NJ....908-688-9251
Lackow, Andy/7004 Boulevard E #29C, Guttenberg, NJ 201-854-2770
LaCourse, Carol/Six Steppingstone Rd W, Durham, NH....603-659-6149
Laird, Thomas/128 South 2nd St, Philipsburg, PA....814-342-2935
Lamb, Greg/16 Greenough Ave, Jamaica Plain, MA 617-983-0875
Lambrenos, Jim/12 Salem Court, Atco, NJ 609-768-0580
Lang, Charles/33 Harbor St #2, Salem, MA....508-741-0029
Lang, Glenna/42 Stearns St, Cambridge, MA....617-661-7591
Langdon, John/4529 Pine St, Philadelphia, PA 215-476-4312
Langer, DC/662 Massachusetts Ave, Boston, MA 617-536-6651
Lanza, Barbara/PO Box 118, Pine Island, NY....914-258-4601
Laoang, Alfred/13416 Justice Rd, Rockville, MD....301-946-2530
Larrivee, Steven/1430 Pippin Orchard Rd, Cranston, RI 401-821-8417
Lawrence, Julie/174 Summit Ave #306, Summit, NJ....201-273-1934
Lawton, April/31 Hampshire Dr, Farmingdale, NY....516-454-0868
Layman, Linda J/9 Alan Rd, South Hamilton, MA 508-468-4297
Leaders, Marsha/20117 Laurel Hill Way, Germantown, MD 301-540-1652
Lebbad, James A/24 Independence Way, Titusville, NJ....212-645-5260
LeBlanc, Terry/425 Watertown St, Newton, MA....617-969-4886
Lee, Bryce/126 77th St, N Bergen, NJ....201-662-9106
Lee, Nan/Box 703, Easton, MD....301-822-8776
Lee, Robert/444 Bedford Rd, Pleasantville, NY....914-747-2220
Lee, Sue/52 JFK St, Cambridge, MA....617-864-1434
Lee, Tim/3985 Evans Rd, Atlanta, GA 404-938-8829
Lee, Victoria/D8 Holiday Estates, Jessup, MD 301-596-3532
Lee, Wangdon/1111 Park Ave #1218, Baltimore, MD....301-728-1616
Leeson, Carol Way/569 Barney's Joy Rd, S Dartmouth, MA....508-636-2404
Lefkowitz, Mark/94 Fox Meadow Lane, Dedham, MA....617-326-2615
Lefkowitz, Steve/2276 Mt Carmel Ave, Glenside, PA 215-885-8227
Lehew, Ron/17 Chestnut St, Salem, NJ 609-935-1422
Leigh, Tom/Rote Hill, Sheffield, MA....413-229-8258
Lemelman, Martin/1286 Country Club Rd, Allentown, PA....215-395-4536
Lemieux, Margo/22 Highland Ave, Mansfield, MA 508-339-7487
LeMoult, Dolph/597 Riverside Ave, Westport, CT 203-226-4724
Lenar, Loci B/17 Central Ave, Mine Hill, NJ 201-989-0934
Leonard, Martha/WV 304-233-0912
Leonard-Gibson, Barbara/3501 Toddsbury Lane, Olney, MD 301-570-9480
Lesh, David/18 McKinley St, Rowayton, CT 203-866-3734
Lesnick, H Robert/80 Merbrook Bend, Merion Station, PA 215-667-5395
LeVan, Susan/30 Ipswich St #211, Boston, MA 617-536-6828
Levee, Gayle/51 Century St, Medford, MA....617-396-9656
Levenson, Wendy/19 Flintlock Dr, Warren Town, NJ 908-647-0900
Levin, Mara/2 Beverly Cir, Holliston, MA....508-429-2790
Levine, Ned/301 Frankel Blvd, Merrick, NY....516-378-8122
Levinson, David/219-D Richfield Terr, Clifton, NJ 201-614-1627
Levinson, W Jason/11625 Sun Circle Way, Columbia, MD 301-854-0406
Levy, Pamela R/7 Trapelo St, Brighton, MA 617-254-5779
Levy, Robert S/1023 Fairway Rd, Franklin Square, NY 516-872-3713
Lewis, H. B./RD #2/48 Pequot Trail, Stonington, CT 203-535-3632
Lewis, Polly Krumbhaar/125 McClenaghan Mill Rd, Wynnewood, PA....215-649-1989
Leyonmark, Roger/229 Berkeley #52, Boston, MA 617-266-3858
Leyshon, Judy/5606 Sonoma Rd, Bethesda, MD 301-530-5070
Liberman, Joni Levy/14 Hill Park Terrace, Randolph, MA....617-986-4657
Lichtenfels, Lisa/146 Bay St, Springfield, MA....413-781-1359
Lies, Brian/9 Humboldt St, Cambridge, MA 617-876-0678
Life, Kay/419 Southwick Rd B7, Westfield, MA 413-562-6418
Light Flight/3000 Chestnut Ave #338, Baltimore, MD 301-235-1558
Lindsey, John/501A Gateway Ctr, Newton, MA....617-527-6790
Linnett, Charles/99 High St, Canton, MA....617-828-4972
Linstromberg, Ruth/41 Congress St #27, Nashua, NH 603-882-5021
Lipczenko, S Dimitri/3901 Tunlaw Rd NW #402, Washington, DC 202-338-1318
Lisi, Victoria Poyser/19 Krasky Lane, Bridgewater, CT 203-350-9404
Lisker, Emily/15 Island Pl, Woonsocket, RI 401-762-2502
Littmann, Barry/57 Overlook Dr, Hackettstown, NJ 201-850-4405
Littmann, Rosemary/299 Rutland Ave, Teaneck, NJ 201-833-2417
Lloyd, Mary Anne/11 Higgins St, Portland, ME 207-773-4987
LoBue, Keith/25-Q Sylvan Rd S, Westport, CT....203-226-4293
Loccisano, Karen/7 Ivy Hill Rd/Box 959, Ridgefield, CT 203-438-8386
Loew, David/6 Hickory Lane, Woodbury, CT....203-263-2253
Logan, Ron/PO Box 306, Brentwood, NY....516-273-4693
Lombardi, Judith/25-Q Sylvan Rd S, Westport, CT 203-226-4293
LoMele, Bachrun/100 Washington St, Hoboken, NJ....201-963-4572
Long, Bruce/112-H2 Frederick Ave, Rockville, MD....301-294-2252
Long, Paulette/728 Undercliff Ave, Edgewater, NJ 201-224-8106
Lorenz, Albert/49 Pine Ave, Floral Park, NY 516-354-5530
Loschiavo, Doree/2714 S Marvine St, Philadelphia, PA 215-336-1724
Löse, Hal/533 W Hortter St-Toad Hall, Philadelphia, PA (P 32)....215-849-7635
Love, Judith DuFour/68 Agassiz Ave, Belmont, MA....617-484-8023
Lowry, Rose/Appleton Rd RR 1, New Ipswich, NH 603-878-3202
Lozner, Ruth/9253 Three Oaks Dr, Silver Spring, MD....301-587-3125
Lubey, Dick/726 Harvard, Rochester, NY 716-442-6075
Lucas-Haji, Geri/2200 19th St NW, Washington, DC....202-387-9045
Lucier, Brian/158 Highland Ave, Athol, MA 508-249-6419
Lundgren, Timothy/4200 Torring Ford St, Torrington, CT 203-496-7439
Lumpkins, William Kurt/72 High St, Topsfield, MA 508-887-3528
Lyhus, Randy/4853 Cordell Ave #3, Bethesda, MD....301-986-0036
Lynch, Bob/2433 Maryland Ave, Bel Air, MD 301-836-9485
Lynch, Fred/123 Pinehurst Ave, Providence, RI 401-351-2699
Lynn, Kathy/1741 Bainbridge, Philadelphia, PA....215-545-5039
Lyons, Linda/515 Anderson Ave, Cliffside Park, NJ 212-216-8063

M

Maas, Julie/PO Box 252, Moody, ME....207-646-2764
Macanga, Steve/20 Morgantine Rd, Roseland, NJ....201-403-8967
MacArthur, Dave/147 E Bradford Ave #B, Cedar Grove, NJ 201-857-1046
Mackey, Greg/69 Fessenden St #2, Portland, ME 207-774-2420
Mackin & Dowd/2433 Maryland Ave, Baltimore, MD 301-366-8339
MacNeill, Scott/74 York St, Lambertville, NJ....609-397-4631
Maddalone, John/81 Lindberg Blvd, Bloomfield, NJ 201-338-1674
Maddocks, Bruce/39 Holman Rd, Auburndale, MA....617-332-7218
Maffia, Daniel/44 N Dean St, Englewood, NJ 201-871-0435
Magalos, Christopher/3308 Church Rd, Cherry Hill, NJ 609-667-7433
Magee, Alan/Route 68 Box 132, Cushing, ME 207-354-8838
Maharry, Carol/11 Chenin Run, Fairport, NY 716-223-8996
Mahoney, John/61 Dartmouth St, Boston, MA....617-267-8791
Mahoney, Katherine/60 Hurd Rd, Belmont, MA....617-489-0406
Maliki, Malik/79 Prince St, Rochester, NY 716-232-5113
Mandel, Saul/163 Maytime Dr, Jericho, NY 516-681-3530
Mann, Sheila/89-2 Staniford St, Auburndale, MA....617-969-2767
Manos, Jim/210 State Hwy 38, Maple Shade, NJ 609-235-2174
Manter, Barry/46 Eastern Promenade, Portland, ME....207-773-0790
Marchesi, Steve/7 Ivy Hill Rd/Box 959, Ridgefield, CT....203-438-8386
Marconi, Gloria/2525 Musgrove Rd, Silver Spring, MD 301-890-4615
Marek, Mark/42 Erie St, Dumont, NJ....201-384-1791
Marinelli, Jeff/99 Chapin St, Canandaigua, NY 716-394-2856
Marion, Kate/85 Columbus Ave, Greenfield, MA....413-774-4862
Mariuzza, Pete/146 Hardscrabble Rd, Briarcliff Manor, NY 914-769-3310
Marks, Laurie/1915 Walnut St, Philadelphia, PA....215-564-3494
Marovsis, Spyro/436 Dover St, Westbury, NY....516-997-7508
Marsella, Valerie/4 Briarwood Rd, Lincoln, RI....401-334-3113

Marshall, Pat/33325 M St NW 3rd Fl, Washington, DC................202-342-0222
Martin, Richard/485 Hilda St, East Meadow, NY 516-221-3630
Martin-Garvin, Dawne/Box 227, Monponsett, MA.....................617-293-3957
Maryanski, Ken/242 E Berkeley St, Boston, MA........................617-542-8748
Marzullo, Michael/2827 E Northern Parkway, Baltimore, MD.............301-426-7713
Mascio, Tony/4 Teton Ct, Voorhees, NJ.................................609-424-5278
Maslen, Barbara/RR 2/Box 697 Suffolk St Ext, Sag Harbor, NY.........516-725-3121
Masse, D D/81 Seward Lane, Aston, PA..................................215-494-7525
Masseau, Jean Carlson/RR 1 Box 303 Silver St, Hinesburg, VT.........802-482-2407
Masters, Rachel/PO Box 358, Watertown, MA............................617-969-6638
Matheis, Shelley/534 East Passaic Ave, Bloomfield, NJ................201-338-9506
Matsick, Anni/345 Oakley Dr, State College, PA.......................814-234-4752
Mattelson, Marvin/37 Cary Rd, Great Neck, NY.........................212-684-2974
Mattingly, David/1112 Bloomfield St, Hoboken, NJ.....................201-659-7404
Mattiucci, Jim/247 N Goodman St, Rochester, NY.......................716-271-2280
Mauro, Ray/228 Second St, Clifton, NJ................................201-546-8750
Max, Deborah Dudley/157 Newbrook Lane, Bay Shore, NY 516-968-5918
Mayforth, Hal/121 Rockingham Rd, Londonderry, NH....................603-432-2873
Mayo, Frank/265 Briar Brae Rd, Stamford, CT..........................203-322-3650
Mayo, Martin & Robert/9 Stanford Ave, Colonia, NJ 908-382-4730
Mazoujian, Charles/20 Brook Rd, Tenafly, NJ..........................201-569-8057
Mazut, Mark/PO Box M1573, Hoboken, NJ................................201-656-0657
Mazzini, John/68 Grey Ln, Levittown, NY..............................516-579-6518
McCloskey, Kevin/106 S Richmond St, Fleetwood, PA....................919-752-2476
McCollum, Rick/15 Dr Gillette Cir, Westport, CT......................203-227-4455
McCord, Kathleen/25-Q Sylvan Rd S, Westport, CT......................203-226-4293
McCracken, Steve/2743 Woodley Pl NW, Washington, DC 202-332-5857
McCurdy, Michael/66 Lake Buel Rd, Great Barrington, MA..............413-528-2749
McDermott, Michael/12 S Main St/PO Box 343, Stewartstown, PA........717-993-2746
McDonnell, Patrick/11 Laureldale Ave, Metuchen, NJ...................908-549-9341
McEntire, Fred/538 Long Rd, Pittsburgh, PA...........................412-731-3025
McGovern, Mike/27 Laurel Ave, Bradford, MA...........................508-373-4877
McGuire & McGuire/495 Old York #440, Jenkintown, PA..................215-886-4084
McGuire, Rebecca/34 E Gravers Ln, Philadelphia, PA...................215-248-1636
McIntosh, Jon C/17 Devon Rd, Chestnut Hill, MA.......................617-277-9530
McKee, Dianne/PO Box 102, Perkiomenville, PA.........................215-234-0377
McKie, Roy/164 Old Clinton Rd, Flemington, NJ........................908-788-7996
McLaughlin, Michael/158 Kelton St #8, Boston, MA.....................617-232-1692
McLellan, Anne C/285 Bennett St, Wrentham, MA........................508-384-7355
McLoughlin, Wayne/RR 1/ Box 818-A, Woodstock, VT.....................802-457-2752
McManus, Tom/31 The Crescent St, Montclair, NJ.......................212-725-1150
McMillan, Kenneth/702 ByBerry Rd, Philadelphia, PA 215-698-9785
McNally, Kathleen/21 North St, Saco, ME..............................207-282-2713
McNeel, Richard/530 Valley Rd #2G, Upper Montclair, NJ...............201-509-2255
McVicker, Charles/PO Box 183, Rocky Hill, NJ.........................609-924-2660
Medbery, Sherrell/18 Philadelphia Ave, Takoma Park, MD...............301-270-0314
Medeiros, John/273 Peckham St, Fall River, MA........................508-676-8752
Medici, Ray/16 Hawthorn St, Rosslindale, MA 617-323-0842
Meeker, Carlene/24 Shore Dr, Winthrop, MA............................617-846-5117
Meisel, Paul/51 Obtuse Rd S, Brookfield, CT..........................203-775-7859
Meisner, Arnold/, Peaks Island, ME...................................207-766-5091
Melius, John/3028 New Oak Ln, Bowie, MD..............................301-249-3709
Melvin, William Jr/211 Woodpecker Lane, Mt Holly, NJ.................609-267-3394
Menk, France/PO Box 350, Pound Ridge, NY.............................914-764-8583
Metcalf, Paul/Webber Rd/Box 35C, Brookfield, MA......................508-867-7754
Meyer, Glenn/PO Box 1663, Cranford, NJ...............................908-241-5009
Miceli, James/31 Homer St, Rochester, NY.............................716-461-0020
Milan, Bucky/Mill Town Road, Brewster, NY............................914-279-2840
Miles, Elizabeth/7 Ivy Hill Rd/Box 959, Ridgefield, CT 203-438-8386
Millet, Paula Shreve/2911 Overland Ave, Baltimore, MD................301-254-8655
Milnazik, Kim/73-2 Drexelbrook Dr, Drexel Hill, PA...................215-259-1565
Mineo, Andrea/12 Lincoln Blvd, Emerson, NJ...........................201-265-3886
Minisci, Diana/15 Warrenton Ave, Hartford, CT........................203-523-4562
Mintz, Margery/9 Cottage Ave, Somerville, MA.........................617-623-2291
Miserendino, Pete/1216 Kettletown Rd, Southbury, CT..................203-264-0908
Mistretta, Andrea/135 E Prospect St, Waldwick, NJ....................201-652-7531
Miyake, Yoshi/7 Ivy Hill Rd/Box 959, Ridgefield, CT 203-438-8386
Mladinich, Charles/7 Maspeth Dr, Melville, NY........................516-271-8525
Mock, Paul/27 Old Meeting House Green, Norton, MA....................508-285-8309
Modell, Frank/PO Box 8, Westport, CT.................................203-227-7806
Moede, Jade/96 S Main St, Lodi, NJ...................................201-778-4090
Molano, Gabriel/PO Box 482, Catskill, NY.............................518-945-2999
Moldoff, Kirk/18 McKinley St, Rowayton, CT...........................203-866-3734
Montana, Leslie/35 Lexington Ave, Montclair, NJ......................201-744-3407
Monteiro, Mary/32 Lyng St, N Dartmouth, MA...........................508-999-2880
Monteleone, Patrick/638 E State St, Trenton, NJ......................609-392-3232
Mooney, Gerry/2 Main St #3S, Dobbs Ferry, NY.........................914-693-8076
Moore, Jack/131 Cedar Lake West, Denville, NJ........................201-627-6931

Moore, Jo/1314 Kearney St NE, Washington, DC 202-526-2356
Morales, Manuel/PO Box 1763, Bloomfield, NJ..........................201-676-8187
Moran, Michael/21 Keep St, Madison, NJ...............................201-966-6229
Morecraft, Ron/97 Morris Ave, Denville, NJ...........................201-625-5752
Morozko, Bruce/111 First St, Jersey City, NJ.........................201-792-5974
Morris, Burton/270 Shady Ave #14, Pittsburgh, PA.....................412-441-2740
Morris, Marilyn/1852 Biltmore St NW, Washington, DC..................202-234-2286
Morrison, Bill/68 Glandore Rd, Westwood, MA..........................617-329-5288
Morrison, Pat/219 Rock Creek Church Rd N, Washington, DC 202-723-1824
Morrissey, Belinda/17 Casino Dr, Saratoga Springs, NY................201-836-7016
Morrissey, Pat/102 Maple Ave, Bellport, NY...........................516-286-5631
Morrow, Skip/Ware Rd/Box 123, Wilmington, VT.........................802-464-5523
Morton, Frank/18 High St, Oakland, ME................................207-465-3324
Moss, Donald/232 Peaceable St, Ridgefield, CT........................203-438-5633
Mowry, Scott/Box 644, Charlestown, MA................................617-242-2419
Mulholland, Kurt/4212 49th St NW, Washington, DC.....................202-244-4147
Muller, Bob/437 Prospect St, S Amboy, NJ.............................908-727-8629
Murakami, Maho/116 Brambach Rd, Scarsdale, NY 914-723-7145
Murphey, Peter/136 Mountain Ave, Malden, MA..........................617-324-6914
Murphy, Martha/9708 Robert Jay Way, Ellicott City, MD 301-750-7222
Murphy, Peter/136 Mountain Ave, Malden, MA...........................617-324-6914
Murray, John/337 Summer St, Boston, MA...............................617-426-0359
Musy, Mark/PO Box 755, Buckingham, PA................................215-794-8851
Myers, Lou/58 Lakeview Ave, Peekskill, NY............................914-737-2307
Myers, V Gene/41 Douglas Rd, Glen Ridge, NJ..........................201-429-8731

N

Nacht, Merle/374 Main St, Weathersfield, CT..........................203-563-7993
Naprstek, Joel/76 Park Place, Morris Plains, NJ......................201-285-0692
Nash, Bob/100 Grove St, Worcester, MA................................508-791-5530
Nash, Scott/15 Alden Rd, Dedham, MA..................................617-924-6050
Natale, Vince/47 Ethan Dr, Murray Hill, NJ...........................201-464-2677
Nees, Susan/4205 Morrison Ct, Baltimore, MD..........................301-355-0059
Neibart, Wally/1715 Walnut St, Philadelphia, PA 215-564-5167
Neider, Alan/283 Timberlane, Cheshire, CT............................203-878-9260
Newman, Barbara Johansen/45 South St, Needham, MA....................617-449-2767
Newman, Kevin /4 Larch Dr, Chester, NJ...............................908-879-7661
Newman, Robert/420 Springbrook Ln, Hatboro, PA.......................215-672-8079
Nez, John/7 Dublin Hill Dr, Greenwich, CT............................203-869-8010
Nicholson, Trudy/7400 Arden Rd, Cabin John, MD.......................301-229-0195
Niland, Brian/12 Columbine Rd, Paramus, NJ...........................201-265-6419
Niles, David/66 Third St, Dover, NH..................................603-742-6499
Nishimura, Masato/229 Berkeley #52, Boston, MA.......................617-266-3858
Noi Viva Design/220 Ferris Ave, White Plains, NY.....................914-946-1951
Noiset, Michelle/551 Tremont Ave, Boston, MA.........................617-542-2731
Norman, Helen/80 Main St, Dennisville, NJ............................609-861-2537
Norman, Marty/5 Radcliff Blvd, Glen Head, NY.........................516-671-4482
Northrup, Susan/14 Imperial Pl, Providence, RI.......................401-521-2389
Notarile, Chris/11 Hamilton Ave, Cranford, NJ........................201-272-1696
Nothwanger, Rosemary/7604 Shadywood Rd, Bethesda, MD.................301-469-7130
Novick, Dorothy Michele/5903 62nd Ave, Riverdale, MD.................301-277-3390
Noyes, David/506 Lebanon St, Melrose, MA.............................617-662-6009
Noyse, Janet/118 Woodland Rd, Wyncote, PA 215-572-6975
Nyman, Steven/10 Maywood Ct, Fairlawn, NJ............................201-797-1003

O

O'Leary, John/547 N 20th St, Philadelphia, PA........................215-561-7377
O'Malia, Carol/51 Dover Terrace, Westwood, MA 617-326-0908
O'Neill, Fran/PO Box 716, Boston, MA.................................617-267-9215
O'Rourke, Patricia/1469 Beacon St #12, Brookline, MA 617-787-9513
O'Shaughnessy, Stephanie/458 Newtown Trnpk, Weston, CT...............203-454-4687
Oesman, Carrie/34 Elizabeth Ave, Stanhope, NJ........................201-347-9066
Oh, Jeffrey/2635 Ebony Rd, Baltimore, MD.............................301-661-6064
Olivieri, Tom/256 Medford St 2nd Fl, Charlestown, MA.................617-241-5922
Olsen, Jimmy/50 New York Ave, Clark, NJ..............................908-388-0967
Olson, Victor/Fanton Meadows, West Redding, CT.......................203-938-2863
Olsson, David/1423 Quinnipiac Ave #514, New Haven, CT................203-469-1714
Oplinger, Barbara/46 Carlton St, Brookline, MA.......................617-277-5866
Orner, Eric/23 Bay St, Cambridge, MA.................................617-547-8371
Osser, Stephanie Fleischer/150 Winding River Rd, Needham, MA........617-237-1116
Ostergren, Sherri/75 Gardner St #15, Allston, MA.....................617-254-1254
Ostrokolowicz, Debra/6 Malden Dr, Webster, MA........................508-943-8451
Otnes, Fred/Chalburn Rd, West Redding, CT............................203-938-2829
Otto, Jeff/2276 Mt Carmel Ave, Glenside, PA..........................215-885-8227
Oughton, Taylor/Jamison, Bucks County, PA............................215-598-3246
Owens, Jim/3000 Chestnut Ave #108, Baltimore, MD.....................301-467-7588

P

Pagano, Richard/18 Cumberland St, West Babylon, NY 516-661-1459
Palladini, David/PO Box 494, Wainscott, NY.....................212-983-1362
Palmer, Carol/107 South St #203, Boston, MA.....................617-482-8938
Palmer, Jan/458 Newtown Trnpk, Weston, CT.....................203-454-4687
Palmer, Tom/40 Chicasaw Dr, Oakland, NJ.....................201-337-8638
Palombo, Lisa/226 Willow Ave, Hoboken, NJ.....................201-653-1501
Palulian, Dickran/18 McKinley St, Rowayton, CT 203-866-3734
Papadics, Joel/22 Scribner Pl, Wayne, NJ.....................201-956-7761
Pardo, Jose Angel/2803 Palisade Ave, Union City, NJ.....................201-867-5932
Parker, Earl/5 New Brooklyn Rd, Cedar Brook, NJ.....................609-567-2925
Parker, Edward/9 Carlisle St, Andover, MA.....................508-475-2659
Parmeter, Wayne/2505-A Concord Pike, Wilmington, DE 302-478-8506
Parsekian, John/5 Lawrence St/Bldg 15, Bloomfield, NJ.....................201-748-9717
Parson, Nan/597 Riverside Ave, Westport, CT.....................203-226-4724
Pasqua, Lou/309 Walnut Rd, Pittsburgh, PA.....................412-761-5666
Passalacqua, David/325 Versa Pl, Sayville, NY.....................516-589-1663
Pate, Rodney/7 Ivy Hill Rd/Box 959, Ridgefield, CT.....................203-438-8386
Paterson, James/2928 Mcgee Way, Olney, MD.....................301-774-8329
Patrick, Cyndy/71 Swan St #3, Everett, MA.....................617-387-4296
Patrick, Pamela/398-A Burrows Run, Chadds Ford, PA.....................215-444-5928
Pavey, Jerry/507 Orchard Way, Silver Spring, MD.....................301-384-3377
Pavia, Cathy/7 Ivy Hill Rd/Box 959, Ridgefield, CT.....................203-438-8386
Payne, Thomas/49 Sheridan Ave, Albany, NY.....................518-426-8816
Peck, Byron/1301 20th St NW #1005, Washington, DC.....................202-331-1966
Peck, Virginia/73 Winthrop Rd, Brookline, MA.....................617-232-1653
Pellaton, Karen/25-Q Sylvan Rd S, Westport, CT.....................203-226-4293
Pendola, Joanne/2 Sutherland Rd #34, Brookline, MA.....................617-566-4252
Pennor, Robert/928 Summit Rd, Cheshire, CT.....................203-758-4008
Pentleton, Carol/685 Chestnut Hill Rd, Chepachet, RI.....................401-568-0275
Perrin, Bryan/1364 Mercer St, Jersey City, NJ.....................201-432-1634
Perugi, Deborah/711 Boylston St, Boston, MA.....................617-421-9550
Phelps, Tim/504 Fairway Court, Towson, MD.....................301-955-3213
Phillips, Alan/2 Washington Sq #41, Larchmont, NY 914-834-4528
Phillips, David Illus/3000 Chestnut Ave #6, Baltimore, MD.....................301-467-7588
Pidgeon, Jean/38 W 25th St, Baltimore, MD.....................301-235-1558
Piejko, Alex/5796 Morris Rd, Marcy, NY 315-732-4852
Pierson, Huntley S/PO Box 14430, Hartford, CT 203-549-4863
Pierson, Mary Louise/RR 1/Box 68B, Thetford Ctr, VT.....................802-333-9996
Pietrobono, Janet/165 W 26th St, Bayonne, NJ.....................201-858-2394
Pinkney, Deborah/309 Walnut Rd, Pittsburgh, PA.....................412-761-5666
Pinkney, Jerry/41 Furnace Dock Rd, Croton-on-Hudson, NY 914-271-5238
Pippin, Matthew/128 Warren St, Lowell, MA.....................508-453-5583
Pirk, Kathy/5112 45th St NW, Washington, DC.....................202-363-5438
Pizzo, Robert/288 East Devonia Ave, Mt Vernon, NY.....................914-961-5020
Pizzo, Susan/288 E Devonia Ave, Mt Vernon, NY.....................914-644-4423
Plotkin, Barnett/126 Wooleys Ln, Great Neck, NY.....................516-487-7457
Pollack, Scott/78 Hidden Ridge Dr, Syosset, NY.....................212-517-3599
Polonsky, Gabriel/274 LaGrange St, Chestnut Hill, MA.....................617-965-3035
Pomerantz, Lisa/16 Kensington Dr, Easthampton, NJ.....................609-265-1588
Porter, John/7056 Carroll Ave, Takoma Park, MD.....................301-270-8990
Portwood, Andrew/18900 Germantown Rd, Germantown, MD.....................301-916-2175
Porzio, Ed/600 Governors Dr #20, Winthrop, MA 617-846-9456
Powell, Michael/813 E Haddonview, Westmont, NJ.....................609-854-7398
Pozefsky, Carol/6040 Boulevard E, W New York, NY.....................201-662-0111
Pratt, Wayne/PO Box 1421, Wilmington, VT.....................802-368-7207
Prendergast, Michael/12 Merrill St, Newburyport, MA.....................508-465-8598
Presley, Greg/20034 Frederick Rd #42, Germantown, MD.....................301-540-7877
Presnall, Terry/8 Cranberry Lane, Dover, MA.....................508-785-1513
Prey, Barbara Ernst/RD 1/Box 100A, Prosperity, PA.....................412-225-2996
Priest, Bob/42 Waltham St #410, Boston, MA.....................617-542-5321
Priestley, Russell T/241 W Emerson St, Melrose, MA.....................617-665-5892
Printz, Larry/1840 London Rd, Abington, PA.....................215-572-0331
Pritchard, Laura Robinson/8909 Carlisle Rd, Wynd Moor, PA 215-836-7062
Prokell, Jim/307 4th Ave #1100, Pittsburgh, PA.....................412-232-3636
Prosetti, Diane/10 Marne St, Newark, NJ.....................201-555-1212
Prosser, Les/3501 Windom Rd, Brenwood, MD.....................301-699-1766
Prowell, Denise/212 S 13th St #3, Allentown, PA.....................215-435-6329

QR

Quinn, Ger/7405 Arden Rd, Cabin Road, MD 301-229-8030
Quinn, Molly/229 Berkeley #52, Boston, MA.....................617-266-3858
Radiomayonnaise/96 Greenwood Place, Buffalo, NY 716-884-6007
Ramage, Alfred/5 Irwin St #7, Winthrop, MA.....................617-846-5955
Ramon, John/444 Bedford Rd, Pleasantville, NY 914-747-2220

Rankin, Mary/444 Bedford Rd, Pleasantville, NY 914-747-2220
Ransome, James/94 North St #4N, Jersey City, NJ..................201-659-3206
Raphael, Natalia/23 Parkton Rd #3, Jamaica Plain, MA 617-524-0121
Ravel, Ken/2 Myrtle Ave, Stoney Creek, PA..................215-779-2105
Rea, Ba/16 Thorton Rd, Scarborough, ME..................207-883-4712
Reed, Chris/17 Edgewood Rd, Edison, NJ..................908-548-3927
Reed, Dan/PO Box 2363, Providence, RI..................401-521-1395
Reeser, Tracy P (Mr)/254 Andover Rd, Glenmoore, PA..................215-649-8298
Regnier, Mark/59 Chestnut Hill Ave, Brighton, MA..................617-787-2631
Reiner, John/27 Watch Way, Lloyds Neck, NY 516-385-4261
Reinert, Kirk/1314 Hudson St #11, Hoboken, NJ..................201-420-8680
Reingold, Michael/310 Warwick Rd, Haddonfield, NJ..................609-354-1787
Reni/PO Box 186, Roselle Park, NJ..................908-245-1218
Reott, Paul/2701 Mckean St, Philadelphia, PA..................718-426-1928
Restivo, Jean/49 Belcourt Ave, N Providence, RI..................401-353-2260
Rheaume, Diane/PO Box 250, Hurlieville, NY..................914-434-2000
Rhodes, Nancy Muncie/146 Hathaway Rd, Dewitt, NY 315-446-8742
Riccio, Frank/279 Redding Rd, W Redding, CT..................203-938-9707
Rich, Anna M/1821 Chelsea St, Elmont, NY..................516-352-5025
Rich, Bob/15 Warrenton Ave, Hartford, CT..................203-523-4562
Richards, Kenn/3 Elwin Pl, East Northport, NY..................516-499-7575
Rickerd, Dave/22 Canvas Back Rd, Manalapan, NJ..................908-446-2119
Riley, Frank/108 Bamford Ave, Hawthorne, NJ..................201-423-2659
Riley, Kelly/213 Village St, Millis, MA..................508-376-5477
Riskin, Marty/12 Tidewinds Terrace, Marblehead, MA..................617-631-2073
Ritta, Kurt/66 Willow Ave, Hoboken, NJ..................201-792-7422
Ritter, Lisa/Dakin Farm Rd, Ferrisburg, VT..................908-788-3991
Roberts & Van Heusen/1153 Narragansett Blvd, Cranston, RI..................401-785-4490
Roberts, Cheryl/1153 Narragansett Blvd, Cranston, RI..................401-785-4490
Roberts, Paul/914 N Charles St #3D, Baltimore, MD..................301-783-8779
Roberts, Scott/2433 Maryland Ave, Baltimore, MD..................301-366-0737
Robertson, Paula Havey/65 Glenbrook Rd #7B, Stamford, CT..................203-327-4199
Robilotto, Philip/80-A Rt 9W, Glenmont, NY..................518-767-3196
Robins, Lili P/703 Forest Glen Rd, Silver Spring, MD..................301-593-8228
Robinson, Marcy/181 River Rd, Nutley, NJ..................201-667-3571
Rockwell, Richard/444 Bedford Rd, Pleasantville, NY..................914-747-2220
Roda, Bot/78 Victoria Ln, Lancaster, PA..................717-393-3831
Rodericks, Mike/129 Lounsbury Rd, Trumbull, CT..................203-268-1551
Roffo, Sergio/42 Shepard St #3, Boston, MA..................617-787-5861
Rogers, Glenda/1 Fayette Pk #100, Syracuse, NY..................315-478-4509
Rogerson, Zebulon W/1312 18th St NW 5th Fl, Washington, DC..................202-293-1687
Roldan, Jim/141 E Main St, E Hampstead, NH..................603-382-1686
Rom, Holly Meeker/4 Stanley Keys Ct, Rye, NY..................914-921-3155
Roman, Irena/369 Thom Clapp Rd Box 571, Scituate, MA..................617-545-6514
Romano, Al/150 Glenwood Dr, Guilford, CT..................203-453-9784
Roper, Robert/132 E Washington Lane, Philadelphia, PA..................215-438-1110
Rosen, Eileen/412 Anglesey Terrace, West Chester, PA..................215-524-8455
Rosenbaum, Harry/444 Bedford Rd, Pleasantville, NY..................914-747-2220
Rosenbaum, Jonathan/444 Bedford Rd, Pleasantville, NY..................914-747-2220
Rosenthal, Marc/#8 Route 66, Malden Bridge, NY..................518-766-4191
Ross, Barry/12 Fruit St, Northampton, MA..................413-585-8993
Ross, Larry/53 Fairview Ave, Madison, NJ..................201-377-6859
Rossi, Joseph/45 Lockwood Dr, Clifton, NJ..................201-278-5716
Rosso, David/316 Mountain Rd, Union City, NJ..................201-330-8463
Roth, Gail/7 Ivy Hill Rd/Box 959, Ridgefield, CT..................203-438-8386
Roth, Robert/148 Lakebridge Dr N, Kings Park, NY..................516-544-4232
Roth, Roger/RD 4/782 Old Rd, Princeton, NJ..................908-821-1678
Rothman, Sharon & Sol/112 Elmwood Ave, Bogota, NJ..................201-489-8833
Rowe, Charles/133 Aronimink Dr, Newark, DE..................302-738-0641
Ruff, Donna/15 Vincent Pl, Rowayton, CT..................203-866-8626
Runnion, Jeff/755 Salem St, Lynnfield, MA..................617-581-5066
Russill, Victoria/1620 Fuller St NW #203, Washington, DC..................202-462-0592
Russo, Anthony/373 Benefit St, Providence, RI..................401-351-1770
Rutt, Dick/6024 Wayne Ave #2-B, Philadelphia, PA..................215-844-3689
Ryan, Carol/14 Adams St, Port Washington, NY..................516-944-3953
Ryder, Jennifer/855 Beacon Street, Boston, MA..................617-437-9691

S

Saffioti, Lino/14 Pearlwood Dr, Huntington Sta, NY 516-673-3760
Safier-Kerzner, Sonia/9413 Locust Hill Rd, Bethesda, MD..................301-530-5167
Sahleanu, Valentine/72 High St #2, Topsfield, MA..................508-887-3528
Sahli, Barbara/8212 Flower Ave, Takoma Park, MD..................301-585-5122
Saint John, Bob/320 South St, Portsmouth, NH..................603-431-7345
Salamida, Dan/258 Third St, Hoboken, NJ..................201-420-0589
Salganik, Amy/527-A Allegheny Ave, Towson, MD..................301-821-6681
Sanders, Bruce/229 Berkeley #52, Boston, MA..................617-266-3858
Santoliquido, Delores/60 W Broad St #6H, Mt Vernon, NY 914-667-3199

Santore, Charles/138 S 20th St, Philadelphia, PA....................215-563-0430
Sarecky, Melody/1010 Vermont Ave #720, Washington, DC 202-347-5276
Sauk, Ed/1220 Keystone Rd, Chester, PA 215-494-6045
Saunders, Rob/34 Station St #1, Brookline, MA....................617-566-4464
Savadier, Elivia/45 Walnut Hill Rd, Chestnut Hill, MA 617-661-0951
Savidge, Robert T/1241 E St SE, Washington, DC....................202-547-5186
Scanlan, Peter/713 Willow Ave #5E, Hoboken, NJ 201-767-7342
Schall, Rene/5 Field Green Dr, Colchester, VT 802-878-1086
Scharf, Linda/240 Heath St #311, Boston, MA 617-738-9294
Schatell, Brian/180 Walnut St #B-31, Montclair, NJ....................201-746-7562
Schenker, Bob/31 W Circular Ave, Paoli, PA 215-688-8771
Scheuer, Lauren/122 Brooks St, Brighton, MA 617-782-5592
Schill, George/309 Walnut Rd, Pittsburgh, PA....................412-761-5666
Schill, Nancy/235 Channing Ave, Malvern, PA....................215-644-3426
Schiwall, Susan/2276 Mt Carmel Ave, Glenside, PA....................215-885-8227
Schiwall-Gallo, Linda/1342 Berkshire Ave, Springfield, MA....................413-543-6796
Schlemme, Roy/585 Centre St, Oradell, NJ 212-921-9732
Schneider, Frederick/15 Warrenton Ave, Hartford, CT 203-523-4562
Schoenberger, Carl/1925 16th St NW #701, Washington, DC....................202-483-3117
Schofield, Dennis/7013 Hegerman St, Philadelphia, PA....................215-624-8143
Schofield, Glen A/4 Hillside Ave, Roseland, NJ 201-226-5597
Schofield, Russ/5313 Waneta Rd, Bethesda, MD....................301-320-5008
Scholberg, Barbara/169 Laurelwood Dr, Hopedale, MA 508-473-7637
Schonbach Graphics/1851 Columbia Rd NW #603, Washington, DC 202-265-2240
Schooley, Greg,/207 Bellwood Circle, Mars, PA....................412-776-4156
Schorr, Kathy Staico/PO Box 142, Roxbury, CT 203-266-4084
Schorr, Todd/PO Box 142, Roxbury, CT....................203-266-4084
Schotte, Marilyn/7205 15th Ave, Takoma Park, MD 301-445-7114
Schottland, Miriam/2201 Massachucetts Ave NW, Washington, DC 202-328-3825
Schreck, John/174 Glengarry Rd, Fairfield, CT (P 35) 203-371-5869
Schreiber, Dana/36 Center St, Collinsville, CT....................203-693-6688
Schuh, Chris/414 Winter St, Holliston, MA....................508-429-6928
Schulenburg, Paul/11 Park St #4, Brookline, MA....................617-734-0548
Schultz, C G/1140 West Street Rd, West Chester, PA 215-793-3622
Schuster, David/3-A Winter St, Westborough, MA....................508-366-5021
Schwartz, Carol/8311 Frontwell Cir, Gaithersburg, MD....................301-926-4776
Schwartz, Joanna H/51 Woodland St #4, Newburyport, MA....................508-465-9635
Schwartz, Marty/18 Winfield Ct, East Norwalk, CT....................203-838-9935
Schwartz, Matt/42 Jefferson St, Cambridge, MA 617-661-4671
Schweigert, Carol/791 Tremont St #E406, Boston, MA....................617-262-8909
Scott, Margaret/1525 31st St NW, Washington, DC 202-965-0523
Scrofani, Joe/2 Akers Ave, Montvale, NJ....................201-391-3956
Seibert, Dave/16 Elmsgate Way, Rumford, RI 401-431-2077
Seidler, Mark/1024 Adams St, Hoboken, NJ 201-659-7711
Selby, Bob/159 Lyman St, Providence, RI....................401-725-3327
Selewacz, Mark/24 French St, Watertown, MA....................617-926-6331
Selwyn, Paul/68 Whiting Ln, W Hartford, CT 203-523-5752
Semler, Robert/308 Highland Terrace, Pitman, NJ 609-589-6495
Seppala, Mark/72 High St, Topsfield, MA 508-887-3528
Serafin, Marsha/25-Q Sylvan Rd S, Westport, CT....................203-226-4293
Sese, Maria/7501 Holiday Terrace, Bethesda, MD 301-405-4619
Sharpe, Jim/21 Ten O'Clock Ln, Weston, CT....................203-226-9984
Shaw, Barclay/170 East St, Sharon, CT 203-364-5974
Shaw, Fran/18 Imperial Place, Providence, RI 401-861-8002
Shaw, Kurt/2954 Sheridan Blvd, Pittsburgh, PA 412-771-7345
Sheehan, Tom/31 Marmion Rd, Melrose, MA 617-734-6038
Sheerin, Sean/106 Inman St #1, Cambridge, MA....................617-661-6972
Sherbo, Dan/4208 38th St NW, Washington, DC....................202-244-0474
Sherman, Gene/500 Helendale Rd, Rochester, NY 716-288-8000
Sherman, Linda/9825 Canal Rd, Gaithersburg, MD 301-590-0604
Sherman, Oren/30 Ipswich #301, Boston, MA....................617-437-7368
Sherman, Whitney/5101 Whiteford Ave, Baltimore, MD 301-435-2095
Shieldhouse, Stephanie/2904 Southern Ave, Baltimore, MD 301-254-7229
Shields, Sandra/62 Burton St, Bristol, RI 401-253-1922
Shiff, Andrew Z/153 Clinton St, Hopkinton, MA 508-435-3607
Shipman, Anne/43-C3 Jackson St, Essex Junctn, VT....................802-878-5073
Sickbert, Jo/7 Dublin Hill Dr, Greenwich, CT 203-869-8010
Siegel, Stuart/106 High Plain St, Walpole, MA....................508-668-5392
Sierra, Dorothea/192 Southville Rd, Southborough, MA 508-872-4549
Sikorski, Tony/2311 Clark Bldg, Pittsburgh, PA 412-391-8366
Simon, Dennis/16312 Yeoho Rd, Sparks, MD 301-329-3983
Simpson, Steve/104 Harvard Street, Newton, MA....................617-864-7360
Sinclair, Valerie/17 Bellwoods Pl, Toronto , ON....................416-594-3400
Singer, Gloria/14 Disbrow Ct, E Brunswick, NJ 908-257-4728
Sisti, Jerald/34 Wiedmann Ave, Clifton, NJ 201-478-7488
Skidmore, John/1112 Morefield Rd, Philadelphia, PA....................215-698-9114
Skinner, Cortney (Mr)/32 Churchill Ave, Arlington, MA....................617-648-2875
Sklut, Meryl/721 Pleasant Valley Way, W Orange, NJ 201-669-8078
Skypeck, George/2053-A Bedford Dr, Washington, DC 301-599-1018
Slamier, Marcia/4201 Cathedral Ave, Washington, DC....................202-244-7989
Slandorn, Peggy/RR1/Box 561A, Bloomsbury, NJ 201-479-6745
Sloan, Lois/3133 Conn Ave NW #615, Washington, DC....................202-387-3305
Slote, Elizabeth/9 Leonard Ave, Cambridge, MA....................617-868-0824
Smallwood, Steve/2417 3rd St Bsmt, Fort Lee, NJ....................201-585-7923
Smith, Douglas/73 Winthrop Rd, Brookline, MA 617-566-3816
Smith, Elwood H/2 Locust Grove Rd, Rhinebeck, NY 914-876-2358
Smith, Gail Hunter/PO Box 217, Barnegat Light, NJ 609-494-9136
Smith, Jeffrey/710 Lakeshore Drive, Hewitt, NJ....................201-853-2262
Smith, Marcia/112 Linden St, Rochester, NY....................716-461-9348
Smith, Monica/9 MacDonald Circle, Walpole, MA....................508-668-3027
Smith, Raymond/PO Box 6116, Hoboken, NJ 201-653-6638
Smith, Samantha Carol/3818 Greenmount Ave, Baltimore, MD............301-243-6184
Smith, Susan B/66 Clarendon #3, Boston, MA....................617-266-4441
Smith, Timothy A/PO Box 8784/JFK Station, Boston, MA 617-367-6472
Smith-Evers, Nancy/308 Washington St, Melrose, MA....................617-662-6390
Smola, Jim/94 Maple Hill Avr, Newington, CT 203-665-0305
Smolinski, Dick/25-Q Sylvan Rd S, Westport, CT 203-226-4293
Snure, Roger/Box 1294, Orleans, MA....................508-255-7069
Snyder, Emilie/50 N Pine St #107, Marietta, PA....................717-426-2906
Soileau, Hodges/350 Flax Hill Rd, Norwalk, CT....................203-852-0751
Sokolowski, Ted/RD #2 Box 408, Lake Ariel, PA 717-937-4527
Solari, Ed Jr/2276 Mt Carmel Ave, Glenside, PA....................215-885-8227
Sollers, Jim/2 Vickery St, Augusta, ME 207-626-3131
Soloto, Susan/1 Bridge St, Irvington, NY 914-591-6909
Somerville, Kevin/18 Lakeview St, River Edge, NJ....................201-488-1026
Sopin, Nan/9 Bradley Dr, Freehold, NJ....................908-462-7154
Sorensen, Robert/22 Strathmore Ave, Milford, CT....................203-874-6381
Soule, Robert Alan/15229 Baughman Dr, Silver Spring, MD 301-598-8883
Soyka, Ed/231 Lafayette Ave, Peekskill, NY....................914-737-2230
Spain, Valerie/83 Franklin St, Watertown, MA....................617-923-1989
Spanfeller, Jim/Mustato Rd, Katonah, NY....................914-232-3546
Sparacio, Mark & Erin/30 Rover Ln, Hicksville, NY 516-579-6679
Sparkman, Gene/PO Box 644, Sandy Hook, CT 203-426-0061
Sparks, Richard/2 W Rocks Rd, Norwalk, CT....................203-866-2002
Spear, Charles/456 Ninth St #2, Hoboken, NJ 201-798-6466
Spector, Joel/3 Maplewood Dr, New Milford, CT....................203-355-5942
Spellman, Susan/8 Cranberry Lane, Dover, MA....................508-785-1513
Speulda, William/363 Diamond Bridge Ave, Hawthorne, NJ 201-427-6661
Springer, Daniel/1156 Commonwealth Ave, Allston, MA 617-739-1482
Springer, Sally/317 S Lawrence Ct, Philadelphia, PA 215-925-9697
Sprouls, Kevin/1 Schooner Ln, Sweetwater, NJ....................609-965-4795
Squadroni, Tony/2276 Mt Carmel Ave, Glenside, PA 215-885-8227
St Jacques, Phillip/65 Hazel Ave, W Orange, NJ 201-731-6874
Staada, Glenn/490 Schooley Mt Rd, Hackettstown, NJ....................908-852-4949
Stabler, Barton/229 Spring Garden Rd, Milford, NJ 201-995-2177
Stackhouse, Donna/47-A Middle St, Portland, ME....................207-774-4977
Stafford, Rod/1491 Dewey Ave, Rochester, NY....................716-647-6200
Stahl, Benjamin F/18 Lowndes Ave, S Norwalk, CT....................203-838-5308
Stansbury Ronsaville Wood Inc/17 Pinwood St, Annapolis, MD............301-261-8662
Stanziani, Diane/210 Fountain St, Philadelphia, PA....................215-483-5317
Starr, Jim/110 W 25th St, Baltimore, MD 301-889-0703
Stasolla, Mario/37 Cedar Hill Ave, S Nyack, NY....................914-353-3086
Stavrinos, George/139 Lawrence Rd, Salem, NH 212-724-1557
Steadman, Evan T/18 Allen St, Rumson, NJ....................201-758-8535
Steadman, Lee/309 Walnut Rd, Pittsburgh, PA 412-761-5666
Steele, Mark/539 Tremont, Boston, MA....................617-424-0604
Steels, Richard/923 F St NW, Washington, DC....................202-667-2347
Steig, William/PO Box 8, Westport, CT 203-227-7806
Steinberg, James/17 Tudor St, Cambridge, MA....................617-876-9029
Steiner, Joan/Rd 1 Box 292, Craryville, NY....................518-966-8908
Stephens, Jean K/328 Brett Rd, Rochester, NY 716-288-8629
Sternberg, Debra/2151 California St NW #404, Washington, DC 202-483-7883
Steuer, Sharon/205 Valley Rd, Bethany, CT 203-393-3981
Stevens & Stevens/328 Brett Rd, Rochester, NY....................716-288-8629
Stewart, Edgar/59 Temple Pl #449, Boston, MA 617-482-4546
Stewart, Jonathan/1530 Spruce St, Philadelphia, PA....................215-546-3649
Still, Wayne Anthony/6819 Clearview St, Philadelphia, PA....................215-848-4292
Stillerman, Robbie/52 Prospect Ave, Sea Cliff, NY....................516-671-5815
Stirnweis, Shannon/31 Fawn Pl, Wilton, CT 203-762-7058
Stock, Jeffrey/33 Richdale Ave #105, Cambridge, MA....................617-868-8384
Storin, Joanne/145 Englewood Ave, Brookline, MA 617-731-6556
Stouffer, Stephanie/RR 1 Box 196, Belmont, VT 802-259-2686
Stout, Rex/10307 Procter St, Silver Spring, MD....................301-681-8344
Strauss, Pamela/97 Winthrop Rd, Brookline, MA 617-232-5847
Strawbridge, Drew/2276 Mt Carmel Ave, Glenside, PA 215-885-8227
Street, Janet/7 Berkshire Ave, Florence, MA 413-543-6796

Strode, Brad/236 Old Gradyville Rd, Glen Mills, PA....215-358-5088
Stroud, Steven/597 Riverside Ave, Westport, CT....203-226-4724
Stubbs, Elizabeth/27 Wyman St, Arlington, MA....617-646-0785
Studio 185/185 Forest St, S Hamilton, MA....508-468-2892
Sturrock, Walt/PO Box 734, Easton, PA....215-559-1256
Stutzman, Mark & Laura/100 G St, Mt Lake Park, MD....301-258-9383
Suchit, Stewart/88 summit Ave #2L, Jersey City, NJ....201-860-9177
Sullivan, Harriet/25-Q Sylvan Rd S, Westport, CT....203-226-4293
Sullivan, Richard/495 Hillside Ave, Needham Heights, MA....617-449-7901
Sullivan, Steve/72 Revere Dr, Ridgefield, CT....203-438-4969
Swan, Susan/83 Saugatuck Ave, Westport, CT (P 37)....203-226-9104
Sweeney, Jerry/339 Blvd of Allies, Pittsburg, PA....412-391-4471
Swenarton, Gordon/Lake Trial East, Morristown, NJ....908-953-0553
Symington, Gary/47 Middle Street, Portland, ME....207-774-4977
Syverson, Henry/PO Box 8, Westport, CT....203-227-7806
Szabo, Leslie/42 S Main St, S Norwalk, CT....203-838-2155
Szilagyi, Mary/56 Windle Park, Tarrytown, NY....914-631-8233

T

Taffet, Marc/1638 James St, Merrick, NY....516-623-2850
Tagel, Peggy/458 Newtown Trnpk, Weston, CT....203-454-4687
Talcott, Julia/38 Linden St #3, Brookline, MA....617-232-7306
Tarantolla, Daniel/3 Ernest Ct, Kings Park, NY....516-544-4387
Tarca, Lisa/27 Willis St #37, Framingham, MA....508-875-2047
Tarlow, Phyllis/42 Stafford Rd, New Rochelle, NY....914-235-9473
Tatore, Paul/10 Wartburg Pl, Valhalla, NY....914-769-1061
Tauss, Herb/S Mountain Pass, Garrison, NY....914-424-3765
Taylor, Dahl/508 Grand St, Troy, NY....518-274-6379
Taylor, Tim/PO Box 591, Roseland, NJ....201-228-6869
Tejeda, Linda/2 Copley Place 3rd Fl, Boston, MA....617-236-1422
Ten, Arnie/37 Forbus St, Poughkeepsie, NY....914-485-8419
Tennant, Craig/79 Chestnut Ave, Park Ridge, NJ....201-307-8869
Ternay, Bill/119 Birch Ave, Bala Cynwyd, PA....215-667-8626
Terreson, Jeffrey/206 Hack Green Rd, Pound Ridge, NY....914-764-4897
Thiel, Joseph/2253 Rogene Dr #101, Baltimore, MD....301-764-2123
Thiel, Libby/Route 2/Box 181C/Fenwick, Bryan's Road, MD....301-283-6347
Thomas, Chris/PO Box 1072, Southport, CT....203-255-9620
Thomas, Linda/169 Mason St #4A, Greenwich, CT....203-622-5925
Thomas, Rod/157 Langley Rd, Newton Centre, MA....617-244-2393
Thomas, Susan C/6804 Greenvale Parkway, Riverdale, MD....301-773-6671
Thompson, Arthur/39 Prospect Ave, Pompton Plains, NJ....201-835-3534
Thompson, Ellen/744 Watchung Ave #102, Plainfield, NJ....908-753-0597
Thompson, John M/118 Parkview Ave, Weehawken, NJ....201-865-7853
Thompson, John R/1124 Halesworth Dr, Potomac, MD....301-294-3085
Thompson, Richard/9309 Judge Place, Gaithersburg, MD....301-948-3732
Thompson, Willam/169 Norfolk Ave #9, Boston, MA....617-445-8009
Thornburgh, Bethann/1673 Columbia Rd NW #409, Washington, DC .202-667-0147
Thornley, Blair/60 Woodlawn St, Boston, MA....617-524-1808
Tiani, Alex/PO Box 4530, Greenwich, CT....203-661-3891
Tilden, David Anders/End of Wirt Way Box 2191, Duxbury, MA....617-934-0345
Tilney, Barnes/27 Glenville Ave, Allston, MA....617-782-5958
Timmons, Bonnie/100 West Highlands Ave, Philadelphia, PA....215-247-3556
Tinkelman, Murray/75 Lakeview Ave W, Peekskill, NY....914-737-5960
Todd, Barbara/251 Greenwood Ave, Bethel, CT....203-797-8188
Toelke, Cathleen/PO Box 487, Rhinebeck, NY....914-876-8776
Toelke, Ron/229 Berkeley #52, Boston, MA....617-266-3858
Torrisi, Gary/8 Cranberry Lane, Dover, MA....508-785-1513
Toth, Tibor/7939 Norfolk Ave, Bethesda, MD....301-656-5722
Trainor, Pete/1325 18th St NW #908, Washington, DC....202-331-7722
Trainor, Sandra/33 Montvale Ave #4, Woburn, MA....617-933-6196
Travis-Keene, Gayle/334 Swinton Way, Severne Park, MD....301-647-7220
Treatner, Meryl/239 Monroe St, Philadelphia, PA....215-627-2297
Trostli, Elisabeth/232 W Exchange St, Providence, RI....401-351-3429
Trusilo, Jim/309 Walnut Rd, Pittsburgh, PA....412-761-5666
Tseng, Jean & Mou-sein/458 Newtown Trnpk, Weston, CT....203-454-4687
Tsui, George/2250 Elliot St, Merrick, NY....516-223-8474
Tsui, Selena/2250 Elliot St, Merrick, NY....516-223-8474
Turci, Thomas P/41 Paul; Heights, Southington, CT....203-276-0458
Two-H Studio/45 Corbin Dr, Darien, CT (P 21)....203-656-0200
Tyrrell, Susan/124 Watertown St, Watertown, MA....617-923-9965
Tysko, Lisa/361 Nassau, Princeton, NJ....609-921-3610

UV

Ulrich, Christopher/232 W Exchange St, Providence, RI....401-272-2660
Ulrich, George/192 Southville Rd, Southborough, MA....617-872-4549
Undercuffer, Gary/1214 Locust St, Philadelphia, PA....215-545-3973
Underhill, Gary R/340 Franklin St, Bloomfield, NJ....201-429-1400
Ursino, John/372 Chestnut Hill Ave, Brookline, MA....617-782-1809
Vaccaro, Vic/1037 7th St, West Babylon, NY....516-888-2637
Valk, Tinam/2111 Henderson Ave, Silver Spring, MD....301-946-6583
Valla, Victor R/19 Prospect St, Falls Village, CT....203-824-5014
Valley, Gregg/128 Thomas Rd, McMurray, PA....412-941-4662
Van Dusen, Chris/37 Pearl St, Camden, ME....207-236-2961
Van Horn, Michael/RD 2/Box 442/Milan Hill Rd, Red Hook, NY....914-758-8407
Van Ryzin, Peter/652 Skyline Ridge Rd, Bridgewater, CT....203-350-6115
Van Seters, Kim/29 High St, Wayne, NJ....201-694-5502
Vance Wright Adams & Assoc/930 North Lincoln, Pittsburg, PA....412-322-1800
Vann, Bob/5306 Knox St, Philadelphia, PA....215-843-4841
Vartanoff, Ellen/4418 Renn St, Rockville, MD....301-460-7636
Vasconcellos, Daniel/4 Aubrey Terrace, Lynn, MA....617-599-9625
Vaughan, Martha/3751 W St NW, Washington, DC....202-333-1299
Vebell, Victoria/1 Cedar Spring Ln, Woodbury, CT....203-266-4007
Vella, Judy/404 Washington Ave, Linden, NJ....201-486-5430
Vella, Ray/345 Main St #7D, White Plains #7D, NY....914-997-1424
Veno, Joe/20 Cutler Rd, Hamilton, MA....508-468-3165
Verhoorn, Shirley/35 River St, Raynham, MA....508-823-2457
Verkoutern, Dana/11 Froude Circle, Cabin John, MD....301-320-6010
Vernaglia, Michael/1251 Bloomfield St, Hoboken, NJ....201-659-7750
Verougstraete, Randy/458 Newtown Trnpk, Weston, CT....203-454-4687
Vidinghoff, Carol/11 Lloyd Rd, Watertown, MA....617-924-4846
Viglione & Assoc, Dawn/384 Elm St, Monroe, CT....203-452-7962
Vincent, Kathy/19 Longview Rd, Port Washington, NY....516-883-9021
Vincenti, Anna Maria/P O Box 1123, Bethlehem, PA....215-865-0739
Vinsun, Lynda/15 Ballard St, Jamaica Plain, MA....617-524-3199
Viskupic, Gary/7 Westfield Dr, Center Port, NY....516-757-9021
Vissichelli, Joe/45 Queen St, Freeport, NY....516-872-3867
Vivilecchia, Lisa/3 Jefferson Ave, Everett, MA....617-389-1669
Volp, Kathleen/15 Waldo St, Somerville, MA....617-625-8355
Von Brincken, Maria/28 Village Rd, Sudbury, MA....508-443-4540
Von Eiff, Damon/2 W Argyle St, Rockville, MD....301-251-0381
Vorhies, Roger/RR 1/Box 398H/Plains Rd, Jericho, VT....802-899-3741
Vu, Anh/1729 Featherwood St, Silver Spring, MD....301-680-0421

W

Waites, Joan/4514 Avondale St, Bethesda, MD....301-657-4026
Walczak, Larry/803 Park Ave, Hoboken, NJ....201-798-6176
Waldman, Neil/47 Woodlands Ave, White Plains, NY....914-693-2782
Waldrep, Richard/2220 N Charles St, Baltimore, MD....301-243-0211
Walker, Brian/2004 Palamar Turn, Seabrook, MD....301-794-4574
Walker, Norman/37 Stonehenge Rd, Weston, CT....203-226-5812
Walker, S A/8 Gifford Ct, Salem, MA....508-745-6175
Walsh, Patrick J/2276 Mt Carmel Ave, Glenside, PA....215-885-8227
Ward, Ray/2276 Mt Carmel Ave, Glenside, PA....215-885-8227
Wasserboehr, Paul/72 High St #2, Topsfield, MA....508-887-3528
Wasserman, Amy/PO Box 1171, Framingham, MA....617-879-7679
Waterhouse, Charles/67 Dartmouth St, Edison, NJ....908-738-1804
Waters, Julian/9509 Aspenwood Pl, Gaithersburg, MD....301-977-5314
Watson, Karen/100 Churchill Ave, Arlington, MA....617-641-1420
Watts, Mark/2004 Par Dr, Warrington, PA....215-343-8490
Webber, Rosemary/644 Noank Rd, Mystic, CT (P 41)....203-536-3091
Wehrman, Richard/247 N Goodman St, Rochester, NY....716-271-2280
Weiland, Gary/7 Burr St, Jamaica Plain, MA....617-983-9251
Weisenbach, Stephen/200 Cedar Lane, Teaneck, NJ....201-836-1711
Weiss, Conrad/40 Mohawk Trail, W Milford, NJ....201-697-7226
Weiss, Richard/126 S 22nd St, Philadelphia, PA....215-567-3828
Weissman, Bari/41 Atkins St, Brighton, MA....617-783-0230
Welker, David/106 Mason Terrace, Boston, MA....617-738-6027
Welker, Gaylord/30 Summit Rd, Sparta, NJ....201-729-5134
Welkis, Allen/53 Heights Rd, Fort Salonga, NY....516-261-4160
Weller, Linda Boehm/7 Ivy Hill Rd/Box 959, Ridgefield, CT....203-438-8386
Wells, Carol/12122 Hooper Lane, Glen Arm, MD....301-592-5072
Welsh, Patrick/PO Box 463, Williamstown, NJ....609-728-0264
Westbrook, Eric C/2830 27th St NW, Washington, DC....202-328-8593
Westerfield, Bill/1133-A University Terrace, Linden, NJ....908-925-0695
Westlake, Laura/7 Dublin Hill Dr, Greenwich, CT....203-869-8010
Weston, Al/597 Riverside Ave, Westport, CT....203-226-4724
Whelan, Michael/23 Old Hayrake Rd, Danbury, CT....203-798-6063
White, Caroline/37 West St, Granby, MA....413-467-3792
Whiting, Ann/2627 Woodley Place NW, Washington, DC....202-462-1519
Whitney, Richard/Monadnock Studio/POB 427, Marlborough, NH....603-876-4353
Wielblad, Linda/22 Notre Dame Ave, Cambridge, MA....617-661-8504
Wiggins, Bryan/30 Victory Ave, S Portland, ME....207-767-4181
Wilcox, David/5955 Sawmill Rd, Doylestown, PA....201-832-7368

Wilkinson, Jeff/7011 Lachlan Circle, Baltimore, MD 301-828-0543
Willert, Beth Ann/4 Woodland Dr, Roselle, NJ 908-298-1237
Williams, Arlene/7401 Oak Crest Lane, Corksville, MD 301-498-6479
Williams, Donna/18 Battersea Lane, Ft Washington, MD 301-292-3611
Williams, Frank/731 North 24th St, Philadelphia, PA 215-232-6666
Williams, M David/8409 Cunningham Dr, Berwyn Heights, MD 301-345-4663
Williams, Marcia/84 Duncklee St, Newton Highlands, MA 617-332-5823
Williams, Ted/170 Elder Dr, Macedon, NY 315-986-3770
Williams, Toby/84 Franklin St, Watertown, MA 617-924-2406
Williges, Mel (Ms)/2 Hepworth Ct, W Orange, NJ 201-731-4086
Wilson, Barry/6541 1/2 Morton Pl Ne, Washington, DC 202-544-2728
Wilson, Mary Lou/247 N Goodman St, Rochester, NY 716-271-2280
Wilson, Patricia/71 Hobart St, Ridgefield Park, NJ 201-440-9034
Wilson, Phil/309 Walnut Rd, Pittsburgh, PA 412-761-5666
Wisnewski, Robert/36 E Madison Ave, Florham Park, NJ 201-377-4202
Wisniewski, David/12415 Chalford Lane, Bowie, MD 301-776-1006
Wissman, Ray/3823 Maple Grove Rd, Manchester, MD 301-239-3584
Witkowski, Robert T/PO Box 8701, Boston, MA 617-227-5095
Witschonke, Alan/68 Agassiz Ave, Belmont, MA 617-484-8023
Wolf, Elizabeth/3717 Alton Pl NW, Washington, DC 202-686-0179
Wolf-Hubbard, Marcie/1507 Ballard St, Silver Spring, MD 301-585-5815
Wolfe, Jean/222 Beach St, Malverne, PA 215-644-2941
Wolff, Punz/457 Herkimer Ave, Haworth, NJ 201-385-6028
Wombat Studio/10 Beechwood Dr, Wayne, NJ 201-628-8793
Woo, Karen/60 Lawton St, Brookline, MA 617-277-8598
Woolf, Anatal S/3000 Conn Ave NW #303, Washington, DC 202-667-9731
Wright, Amy/227 Old Mill Lane, Portsmouth, RI 401-849-4680
Wright, Bob Creative Group/247 N Goodman St, Rochester, NY 716-271-2280
Wright, Tom/9 W 29th St, Baltimore, MD 301-467-7300
Wu, Leslie/36 Harwood Lane, East Rochester, NY 716-385-3722
Wunsch, Marjory/16 Crescent St, Cambridge, MA 617-492-3839

Y

Yaccarino, Dan/124 Country Lane, Clifton, NJ 201-473-3666
Yaniv, Etty/50 Cedar Ct, Closter, NJ 201-784-8136
Yanson, John/733 15th St NW, Washington, DC 202-347-1511
Yavorsky Creative/2300 Walnut St #617, Philadelphia, PA 215-564-6690
Yeager, Alice/3157 Rolling Rd, Edgewater, MD 301-261-4239
Yealdhall, Gary/110 W 25th St, Baltimore, MD 301-889-5361
Yelenak, Andy/15 Warrenton Ave, Hartford, CT 203-523-4562
Yi, Kang/7 Trappers Way, Pomona, NY 914-354-7940
Young, Mary O'Keefe/28 Washington Ave, Irvington, NY 914-591-5481
Young, Michael/475 Shawmut Ave, Boston, MA 617-266-0343
Young, Robert Assoc/78 North Union St, Rochester, NY 716-546-1973
Young, Wally/7 Birch Hill Rd, Weston, CT 203-227-5672
Younger, Heidi/88 Summit Ave #2L, Jersey City, NJ 201-860-9177

Z

Zammarchi, Robert/Box 1147/32 Rugg Rd, Boston, MA 617-778-9513
Zappler, Nina/3153 Woodworth Rd, Waterloo, NY 315-789-5640
Zarins, Joyce Audy/19 Woodland St, Merrimac, MA 508-346-8994
Zaruba, Ken/967 Wambler Ln, Westminster, MD 301-876-8447
Zimmerman, Bruce/7805 Old Georgetown Rd, Bethesda, MD 301-656-2787
Zingone, Robin/32 Godman Rd, Madison, CT 212-288-8045
Zinn, Ron/117 Village Dr, Jerico, NY 516-933-2767
Zorad, Ivan/, Edison, NJ 201-985-8771
Zuba, Bob/105 W Saylor Ave, Plains, PA 717-824-5665
Zuban, Kevin/34 Idelwild Rd, Edison, NJ 908-949-8617
Zuckerman, Robert/100 Washington St, South Norwalk, CT 203-853-2670
Zwart, Lawrence Jan/PO Box 281, Rockport, ME 207-236-9028
Zwicker, Sara Mintz/98 Stetson St, Braintree, MA 617-848-8962
Zwingler, Randall/1106 Greenway Rd, Wilmington, DE 302-478-6063

SOUTHEAST

A

Adams, Dianne/129 Carlen Ave, Lexington, SC 803-957-7439
Adams, Rodney/847 S Church St, Burlington, NC 919-222-9333
Anderson, Robert/4209 Canal St, New Orleans, LA 504-486-9011
Anderson, Tim/, Winston-Salem, NC 919-377-9036
Anderton, John C/8714 Gateshead Rd, Alexandria, VA 703-360-3584
Andresen, Mark/6417 Gladys St, Metairie, LA 504-888-1644
Angelotta, Christine/6734 Kenyon Dr, Alexandria, VA 703-660-8427
Anthony, Tony/132 Rumson Rd, Atlanta, GA 404-237-9836
Architectural Art Inc/7700 Leesburg Pike Ste 401, Falls Church, VA 703-448-0704
Armstrong, Lynn/2510 Whisper Wind Ct, Roswell, GA 404-642-5512
Arroyo, Fian/7312 SW 80th St Plz #290, Miami, FL 305-663-1224
Artell, Michael/PO Box 1819, Covington, LA 504-626-3420
Arunski, Joe & Assoc/8600 SW 86th Ave, Miami, FL 305-473-4114
Attiliis, Andy/9710 Days Farm Dr, Vienna, VA 703-759-1519
August, Robert/666 Bantry Lane, Stone Mountain, GA 404-296-9666
Auth, Dennis/231 Pefley Dr, Norfolk, VA 804-497-3913
Azar, Joe/3935 N 4th St, Arlington, VA 703-527-1443
Azzinaro, Lewis/11872 St Trinians Ct, Reston, VA 703-620-5155

B

Bailey, R.C./255 Westward Dr, Miami Springs, FL 305-888-6309
Barbie, Michael/463 Old Post Rd, Niceville, FL 904-897-3441
Barklew, Pete/110 Alpine Way, Athens, GA 404-546-5058
Bennett, Gary/3304 Startan Ct, Louisville, KY 502-458-0338
Beyl, Charles E/510 N Alfred St, Alexandria, VA 703-549-7824
Birch, Candace/308 S Arrawana Ave, Tampa, FL 813-876-3634
Blakey, Paul/2910 Caribou Trail, Marietta, GA 404-977-7669
Bober, Kathleen/1408 N Fillmore St #12, Arlington, VA 703-528-1449
Bolling, Bob/2395 NE 185th St, N Miami Beach, FL 305-931-0104
Boone, Joe/ PW Inc/PO Box 99337, Louisville, KY 502-499-9220
Bowles, Aaron/1686 Sierra Woods Ct, Reston, VA 703-437-4102
Boyter, Charles/1135 Lanier Blvd NE, Atlanta, GA 404-727-5665
Brawner, Dan H/732 Richfield Dr, Nashville, TN 615-356-1244
Brennsteiner, Jim/13212 Pleasantview Lane, Fairfax, VA 703-803-8637
Bruce, Tim/5850 Brookway Dr, Winston-Salem, NC 919-767-8890
Bullock, Max/3064 Cedarwood Lane, Falls Church, VA 703-534-1441
Burns, John/Rte 1/Box 487A, Bluemont, VA 703-955-4786
Butler, Meryl/PO Box 991, Virginia Beach, VA 804-491-2280

C

Cable, Annette/21 Theatre Square #200, Louisville, KY 502-561-0737
Cable, Mark/600 E Main St, Louisville, KY 502-634-4911
Cain, Thomas/2161 Peachtree Rd NE #502, Atlanta, GA 404-355-2160
Carambat, David/PO Box 815, Abida Springs, LA 504-893-2432
Carey, Mark/3109 Pelham St, Chesapeake, VA 804-396-5768
Carter, Kip/225 Beaverdam Dr, Winterville, GA 404-542-5384
Carter, Tony/504 Baker Dr, Birmingham, AL 205-871-8010
Carter, Zane/1008 N Randolph St #100, Arlington, VA 703-836-2900
Cassady, Jack/Tampa, FL 813-960-9188
Castellanos, Carlos/20150-08 NE 3rd Court, Miami, FL 305-651-9524
Cathcart, Marilyn/6933 Columbia Ave, St Louis, MO 314-862-2644
Cavanagh, Tom/119 NW 93rd Terrace, Coral Sprngs, FL 305-753-1874
Chaffee, Doug/107 Shagbark Circle, Simponsville, SC 803-877-9826
Chau, Tung Wai/534 Richmar Dr, Nashville, TN 615-781-8607
Cheshire/Clemente Studios/16823 Francis West Ln, Dumfries, VA 703-221-8629
Clark, David/2101-B N Scott St, Arlington, VA 703-524-9076
Clegg, Dave/3571 Aaron Sosebee Rd, Cumming, GA 404-887-6306
CoConis, Ted/Airport Rd, Cedar Key, FL 904-543-5720
Collins, Samuel/PO Box 73004, Birmingham, AL 205-991-0557
Combs, R Mason/PO Box 573/Mile Branch, Pineville, KY 606-337-2012
Communication Arts/Bordeaux/129 E Pasagoula St, Jackson, MS 601-354-7955
Comport, Sally Wern/241 Central Ave, St Petersberg, FL 813-821-9050
Cooley, Rick L/Rt 1/ Box 155, Check, VA 703-651-4481
Cooper, Cheryl/525 22nd Ave N, St Petersburg, FL 813-822-5805
Correnti, Sandra/4 Meadow Dr, Bristol, VA 703-669-4924
Covington, Neverne/241-A Central Ave , St Petersburg, FL 813-822-1267
Cowan, Robert/528 Shelton Dr, Aberdeen, NC 919-944-1306
Craig, Robert E/2029 Mt Hope Church Rd, Whitsett, NC 919-697-2220
Crane, Gary/1511 W Little Creek Rd, Norfolk, VA 804-627-0717
Creative Group/1150 NW 72nd Ave #760, Miami, FL 305-591-7700
Crowther, Will/304 Hampton Dr, Dunnwoody, GA 404-393-8120
Cuevas, George/6337 SW 14th St, Miami, FL 305-264-7046
Curcio, Jeff/3520 S 6th St, Arlington, VA 703-920-7472

DEF

Dabagian, Marc/2614 Kingsley Rd, Raliegh, NC 919-847-0673
Dalton, Clay/939 Leeds Castle Way, Marietta, GA 404-425-1065
DeBro, James/2725 Hayden Dr, Eastpoint, GA 404-344-2971
Dekle, Merritt/310 W Lafayette St, Marianna, FL 904-526-3319
DeLahoussaye, Jeanne/816 Foucher, New Orleans, LA 504-581-2167
DeLoy, Dee/8166 Jellison St, Orlando, FL 407-273-8365
Diatz, Dianna/4629 Seminary Rd #301, Alexandria, VA 703-751-4064

Dillingham, Jerry/5952 Kenton Dr, Kernersville, NC....919-996-4059
Dixon, David/PO Box 454 B/ Rte 14, Gray, TN....615-283-0484
Dodson, Dale/1255 Richfield Dr, Rosewell, GA....404-526-5328
Dole, Algar/PO Box 1263, Harrisonburg, VA....703-896-6217
Dove Design Studio/2025 Rockledge Rd NE, Atlanta, GA....404-873-2209
Duckworth,Susie/2912 Kings Chapel Rd #7, Falls Church, VA....703-698-8987
Dunlap, Leslie/510 Robinson Court, Alexandria, VA....703-836-9067
Dupree, Melissa/1032 Jefferey Dr, Birmingham, AL....205-945-4916
Eddins, George/1249 East Blvd, Charlotte, NC....704-334-4543
Ehrenfeld, Jane/301 St George St, Farmville, VA....804-392-6190
Eldredge, Ernie/2683 Vesclub Cir, Birmingham, AL....205-822-3879
Ellis, Tim/2502 Hill-n-Dale, Greensboro, NC....919-288-6521
Ellistrations/PO Box 4567, Greensboro, NC....919-288-6521
Epperly's Art Studio/308 N Maple St, Graham, NC....919-227-2117
Faure, Renee/600 Second St, Neptune Beach, FL....904-246-2781
Findley, John/213 Elizabeth St, Atlanta, GA....404-659-7103
Firestone, Bill/4810 Bradford Dr, Alexandria, VA....703-354-0247
Fisher, Mike/411 Amethyst St, New Orleans, LA....504-288-4860
Floyd, Walt/1118 Rosedale Dr #4, Atlanta, GA....404-875-8061
Foster, Travis/313 Becklea Dr, Madison, TN....615-865-0811
Frank, Cheryll/2216 Eastgate Way, Tallahasse, FL....904-668-0909

G

Gaadt, David/2103 Tennyson Dr, Greensboro, NC....919-288-0953
Gabriele, Antonio J/931 Deep Lagoon Lane, Ft Myers, FL....305-433-3202
Garcia, Rick/620 NE 119th St, Miami, FL....407-784-6263
Gates, Donald/1552 Great Falls St, McLean, VA....703-442-4798
Gates, Kathleen/2019 Felix, Memphis, TN....901-725-4667
Gebhart, Bradley/13296B Blueberry Ln #202, Fairfax, VA....703-866-0531
Gignilliat, Elaine/747 Bayliss Dr, Marietta, GA....404-977-5635
Gilmore, Paulette/2860 Running Pump Ln, Herndon, VA....703-478-0349
Glasgow, Dale/4493 Andy Court, Woodbridge, VA....703-590-1702
Gonzalez, Thomas/755 Virginia Ave NE, Atlanta, GA....404-872-7980
Goris, Dennis/901 N Washington St, Alexandria, VA....703-739-0088
Gorman, Martha/3057 Pharr Ct Nrth NW #E6, Atlanta, GA....404-261-5632
Grandstaff, Chris/12704 Harbor View Ct, Woodbridge, VA....703-494-0422
Graphics Group/6111 PchtreeDunwdy Rd#G101, Atlanta, GA....404-391-9929
Graphics Illustrated/5720-E North Blvd, Raliegh, NC....919-878-7883
Greathead, Ian/1591 Sandpoint Dr, Atlanta, GA....404-640-6517
Griswold, Theophilus Britt/3807 Foxfield Lane, Fairfax, VA....703-830-7571
Guthrie, Dennis/1118 Franklin Ct, Atlanta, GA....404-325-6867

H

Hagen, David/14637 Stone Range Dr, Centreville, VA....703-830-4208
Hamilton, Laurie/4200 St Charles Ave, New Orleans, LA....504-891-3138
Hamilton, Marcus/12225 Ranburne Rd, Charlotte, NC....704-545-3121
Hanna, Kim/805 Jackson St, Falls Church, VA....703-532-2370
Harris, Leslie/1906 Wellbourne Dr NE, Atlanta, GA....404-872-7163
Harrison, Kenneth/4209 Canal St, New Orleans, LA....504-486-9011
Havaway, Jane/806 Briarcliff Rd, Atlanta, GA....404-872-7284
Heavner, Becky/202 E Raymond Ave, Alexandria, VA....703-683-1544
Heinly, John/5939 Ridge Ford Dr, Burke, VA....703-451-7263
Helms, John/4255 Arrowhead, Memphis, TN....901-363-6589
Henderling, Lisa/10076 Bay Harbor Terrace, Bay Harbor Isl, FL....305-866-3220
Herchak, Stephen/1735 St Julian Pl, Columbia, SC....803-799-1800
Herring, David/6246 Woodlake Dr, Atlanta, GA....404-945-8652
Hickey, John/3832 Abingdon Cir, Norfolk, VA....804-853-2956
Hickman, Stephen/105 S Jenkins St, Alexandria, VA....703-751-4070
Hicks, Richard Edward/3667 Vanet Rd, Chamblee, GA....404-457-8928
Hilfer, Susan/PO Box 50552, Columbia, SC....803-799-0689
Hinton, Patricia Gural/313 Sunset Ave, Louisburg, NC....919-496-6486
Hobson, Ken/209 Kirk Rd, Greensboro, NC....919-282-7789
Hodges, John/8 Sycamore Circle, Grenada, MS....601-226-7527
Hodges, Mike/3613 Noble Ave, Richmond, VA....804-321-0100
Holladay, Reggie/7395 NW 51st St, Lauderhill, FL....305-749-9031
Holz, Fred/8340 Greensboro Dr #51, McClean, VA....703-442-9323
Horn, Dave/42 Breckenridge Pkwy, Ashville, NC....704-645-6907
Howell, Troy/58 Dobson Lane, Falmouth, VA....703-373-5199
Humphrey, John J Jr/2241 Wrightsville Ave #0, Wilmington, NC....919-251-8222
Hyatt, Mitch/4171 Buckingham Ct, Marietta, GA....404-924-1241
Hyatt, Steven/4171 Buckingham Ct, Marietta, GA....404-924-1241

IJK

Image Electronic Inc/3525 Piedmont Rd NE #110, Atlanta, GA....404-262-7610
Irvin, Trevor/330 Southerland Terrace, Atlanta, GA....404-377-4754
James, Bill/15840 SW 79th Ct, Miami, FL....305-238-5709
Jamison, Alex/713 S Glebe Rd, Arlington, VA....703-486-2690
Jarvis, David/200 S Banana River Rd #1802, Coco Beach, FL....407-784-6263
Jepsen, Deirdre/Rte 1, Box 307E, Leesburg, VA....703-471-5468
Joffrion, Kathleen/4209 Canal St, New Orleans, LA....504-486-9011
Johnson, Pamela R/1415 N Key Blvd, Arlington, VA....703-525-5012
Jones, Jack/571 Dutch Valley Rd, Atlanta, GA....404-881-6627
Jones, Karen/3985 Evans Rd, Atlanta, GA....404-938-8829
Kanelous, George/2864 Lake Valencia Blvd E, Palm Harbor, FL....813-784-8528
Kasso, Larry/PO Box 40461, Baton Rouge, LA....504-295-1644
Katzowitz, Joel/3355 Atlanta Indstrl Dr, Atlanta, GA....404-641-9718
Kaufman, Robert J/3200 Libeth St, Charlotte, NC....704-568-3417
Kent, Derek/1081 Woodland Ave #4, Atlanta, GA....404-325-1565
Kettler, Al/1607 King St, Alexandria, VA....703-548-8040
Keys, Watt/612 E Tremont Ave, Charlotte, NC....704-332-6576
Kilgore, Susi/2905 Bay Villa, Tampa, FL....813-837-9759
Klioze, Marcia/2409 Andorra Pl, Reston, VA....703-620-4922
Krafcehk, Ken/815 S Lincoln St, Arlington, VA....703-553-0469
Kriese, Penny/6019 Waterbury Ct, Springfield, VA....703-644-8478
Kristoff, Dante/13835 Springstone Dr, Clifton, VA....703-818-2799

L

Lacz, John/2840 Somerset Dr, Ft Lauderdale, FL....305-525-4333
Laden, Nina/1517 McLendon Ave NE, Atlanta, GA....404-371-0052
Landis, Jeff/1372 50th Ave NE, St Petersburg, FL....813-525-0757
Lang, Cecily/250 E Royal Palm Rd #1A, Boca Raton, FL....407-392-5860
Lawling, Charlie/226 E Tremont Ave, Charlotte, NC....704-333-2070
Lee, Kelly/3511 N 22nd St, Arlington, VA....703-527-4089
Left, Stephen/1351 S Dixie Hwy #E8, Pompano Beach, FL....305-946-7485
Leiner, Alan/3265 Nocturne Rd, Venice, FL....813-493-6754
Leister, Bryan/202 E Raymond Ave, Alexandria, VA....703-683-1544
Lengyel, Kathy/2306 Jones Dr, Dunedin, FL....813-734-1382
Lester, Mike/8890 River Trace Dr, Duluth, GA....404-447-5332
Levine, Arlene/1107 S Peters #508, New Orleans, LA....504-522-1520
Lewczak, Scott/1600 E Jefferson Ct, Sterling, VA....703-435-5982
Lewis, Chris/755 Virginia Ave NE, Atlanta, GA....404-872-7980
Little, Pam/321 Niagara St, Orange City, FL....904-755-2919
Loehle, Don/2574 Sherbrooke Dr NE, Atlanta, CA....404-633-7145
Loehle, Richard/2608 River Oak Dr, Decatur, GA....404-325-9580
Long, Jim/4415 Briarwood Court N, Annandale, VA....703-354-8052
Lovell, Rick/2860 Lakewind Ct, Alpharetta, GA....404-442-3943
Lubsen, Laurie J Perkins/333 N Edison St, Arlington, VA....703-528-2667
Lukens, Jan/2354 Chaucer Lane, Winston-Salem, NC....919-788-5451
Lunsford, Annie/515 N Hudson St, Arlington, VA....703-527-7696

M

Maddox, Kelly/328 Greenwood Ave, Decatur, GA....404-377-0519
Madson, Steven/4129 Hampstead Lane, Woodbridge, VA....703-590-4341
Mahoney, Ron/2400 E Commercial Blvd #420, Ft Lauderdale , FL....412-261-3824
Majewski, Chuck/PO Box 95038, Madiera Beach, FL....813-367-3954
Marks, David/726 Hillpine Dr NE, Atlanta, GA....404-872-1824
Martin, Don/5110 S W 80th St, Miami, FL....305-665-2376
Martin, Lyn/PO Box 51972, Knoxville, TN....615-588-1760
Matthews, Lu/547 Mount Hermon Rd, Ashland, VA....804-798-9144
Mayberry, Douglas/1315 Oakhill Ave, Gulfport, MS....601-688-1884
Mayer, Bill/240 Forkner Dr, Decatur, GA....404-378-0686
McCall, Paul Illustraton/2403 Renseller Pl, Marietta, GA....404-953-1599
McGinness, Jim/3822 Jancie Rd, Fairfax, VA....703-691-0758
McGrail, Rollin/12470 West Hampton Circle, West Palm Beach, Fl....407-795-9525
McKeever, Michael/1240 NE 171 Terrace, N Miami Beach, FL....305-652-6668
McKelvey, David/3022 Huntshire Pl, Atlanta, GA....404-938-1949
McKissick, Randall/PO Box 21811, Columbia, SC....803-798-3688
McMahon, Mike/PO Box 1325, Charlotte, NC....704-372-6007
McManus, Eugenia/PO Box 39, Mayhew, MS....601-328-5534
Melrath, Susan/1211 Reading Terrace, W Palm Beach, FL....407-790-1561
Merrill, David/1067 Hwy 17 Bypass #L2, Mt Pleasant, SC....803-881-2869
Miller, A J/2207 Bay Blvd #201, Indian Rocks Bch, FL....813-596-6384
Miller-Sniady, Daphne/910 Enderby Dr, Alexandria, VA....703-548-0408
Mitchell, Bono/2118 N Oakland St, Alexandria, VA....703-276-0612
Mitchell, Charlie/1404 Regency Woods Dr, Atlanta, GA....404-634-0482
Mollica, Pat/20 Fourth St NW, Atlanta, GA....404-873-4693
Montgomery, Michael/7765 Fielder Rd, Jonesboro, GA....404-478-2929
Moore, Connie Illus/4242 Inverness Rd, Duluth, GA....404-449-9553
Moore, Cyd/3465 Fernway Dr, Montgomery, AL....205-281-4818
Moore, Larry/1635 Delaney St, Orlando, FL....407-648-0832
Moore, William "Casey"/4242 Inverness Rd, Duluth, GA....404-449-9553

Moses, David/3410 Renault St, Memphis, TN............................901-795-6157
Myers, Sherwood/9770 Sterling Dr, Miami, FL..........................305-238-0488

NO

Nelson, Merri/Rt 1/ Box 38, Purcellville, VA.............................703-478-8747
Neuhaus, David/2727 Duke St #709, Alexandria, VA 703-461-8710
Norvell, Jill/2123 Cabots Point Lane, Reston, VA.....................703-264-0600
O'Connor, John/2010 Scott Dr, Blacksburg, VA 703-953-2744
Of Mice & Graphics/3930 Hancock Circle, Atlanta, GA...............404-934-1249
Oliphant, Tim/200 MCHS Dr #2K, Lewisburg, TN......................615-359-7430
Olsen, Greg/666 Bantry Lane, Stone Mountain, GA...................404-296-9666
Overacre, Gary/3802 Vinyard Trace, Marietta, GA.....................404-973-8878
Ovies, Joe/3500 Piedmont St #430, Atlanta, GA........................404-462-1209

P

Pack, John/2342 N Fillmore St, Arlington, VA 703-243-4024
Pardue, Jack/2307 Sherwood Hall Ln, Alexandria, VA 703-765-2622
Parker, Suzy/1000 Wilson Blvd, Arlington, VA 703-276-3458
Parrish, George/919 Collier Rd NW, Atlanta, GA.......................404-266-0088
Pate, Martin/571 Dutch Valley Rd, Atlanta, GA.........................404-881-6627
Pawelka, Rick/5720 E North Blvd, Raleigh, NC.........................919-878-7883
Penca, Gary/8335 NW 20th St, Coral Springs, FL......................305-752-4699
Pentard, Alton/2911 Dumaine, New Orleans, LA.......................504-486-0633
Perry, Phil/968 Homewood Ct, Decatur, GA 404-634-2349
Pico, Steve/2433 Keene Park Dr, Largo, FL...............................813-446-5277
Pitt, Bob/503 Emory Circle, Atlanta, GA...................................404-378-0694
Polston, Deb/9165 Prestwick Club Dr, Duluth, GA.....................404-729-8916
Pomeroy, Bradley/4720 N 20th Rd #207, Arlington, VA...............703-920-7765
Poole, Colin/817 Mackall Ave, McLean, VA...............................703-893-0759
Powell, Rick/523 W 24th St, Norfolk, VA...................................804-622-2979
Primeau, Chuck/4960 Avenida Del Sol, Raleigh, NC 919-876-5529

R

Rabon, Elaine Hearn/573 Hill St, Athens, GA 404-353-8479
Rainock, Norman/10226 Purcell Rd, Glen Allen, VA 804-264-8123
Ramirez, Roberto/2718 W Mountain St #41, Kernersville, NC.....919-748-1768
Ramsey, Ted/1623 Stowe Rd, Reston, VA 703-481-9424
Rauchman, Bob/5210 SW 60th Place, Miami, FL.......................305-445-5628
Richards, Barbara/10607 Kennel Lane, Charlotte, NC 704-846-3944
Robinette, John/3745 Woodland, Memphis, TN.........................901-452-9853
Robinson, Mark/9050 Loreleigh Way, Fairfax, VA......................703-280-4123
Rogers, Nip/93 Ashby Ct, Marshall, VA 703-364-1247
Romeo, Richard/1066 NW 96th Ave, Ft Lauderdale, FL..............305-472-0072
Roolaart, Harry/PO Box 1325, Charlotte, NC............................704-372-6007
Rudnak, Theo/166 Beverly Rd NE, Atlanta, GA 404-876-4058

S

Saffold, Joe/719 Martina Dr NE, Atlanta, GA.............................404-231-2168
Salmon, Paul/5826 Jackson's Oak Ct, Burke, VA.......................703-250-4943
Sampson, Ronnie/1306 E Cary St, Richmond, VA 804-788-1358
Sams, B B/PO Box A, Social Circle, GA....................................404-464-2956
Sawyer, Peter A/7768 Clifton Rd, Fairfax, VA............................703-250-3117
Scheffer Studios/PO Box 2276, Clearwater, FL.........................813-736-6777
Schmidt, John F/7308 Leesville Blvd, Springfield, VA 703-750-0927
Schneider, Wendi/4209 Canal St, New Orleans, LA....................504-486-9011
Scott, Robert/4108 Forest Hill Ave, Richmond, VA.....................804-232-1627
Seif, Sue Solomon/4050 Innslake Dr, Glen Allen, VA.................804-747-9684
Selvage, Roger/2148 Cartwright Pl, Reston, VA.........................703-264-5325
Shelley, G A/3204 Winchelsea Dr, Charlotte, NC........................704-536-6510
Shelly, Ron/6396 Manor Lane, S Miami, FL...............................305-667-0154
Shepherd, Bob/8371 W Weyburn Rd, Richmond, VA...................804-230-0001
Short, Robbie/2903 Bentwood Dr, Marietta, GA.........................404-565-7811
Sipp, Geo/380 Garden Lane NW, Atlanta, GA............................404-876-0312
Sloan, Michael/PO Box 1397, Madison, TN...............................615-865-7018
Smith, Donald/PO Box 391, Athens, GA 404-543-5555
Smith, Terry E/813 Prince St #5, Alexandria, VA........................703-836-1810
Soper, Patrick/214 Stephens, Lafayette, LA..............................318-233-1635
Spence, Jim/4260 60th St, Vero Beach, FL...............................407-778-8859
Spetseris, Steve/571 Dutch Valley Road, Atlanta, GA.................404-881-6627
Spirduso, Kenneth/3811-9 Cornerwood Ln, Charlotte, NC...........704-366-4346
Spisak, Matt/968 Homewood Ct, Decatur, GA...........................404-634-2349
Stanton, Mark/67 Jonesboro St, McDonough, GA......................404-957-5966
Stanton, Reggie/411 Park Ave N #11, Winter Park, FL...............305-645-1661
Steadham, Richard/14085 Ryon Court, Woodbridge, VA 703-590-9464

Steiner, Peter/1948 Rockingham St, McLean, VA.......................703-237-9576
Stewart, Greg/Route 28, Knoxville, TN 615-577-3345
Stieferman, Guy/488 St Regis Pl, Cordova, TN..........................901-753-3729
Stone, David K/106 Stoneybrook, Chapel Hill, NC......................919-929-0853
Stork, Bill/7325 W Friendly Ave #D-1, Greensboro, NC..............919-299-3640
Story, Michael/PO Box 50492, Columbia, SC............................803-256-8813
Street, Renee & David/1414 S Pollard St, Arlington, VA..............703-521-6227
Streetworks Studio/1414 S Pollard St, Arlington, VA...................703-521-6227
Stevens, John/472 Brentwood Dr #11, Daytona Beach, FL 904-257-2622
Suplee, David/7328 Dartford Dr #9, McLean, VA........................703-848-4550

TUV

Tamara & Assoc/3565 Piedmont Rd #200, Atlanta, GA...............404-262-1209
Taylor, Creed/206 Media Bldg/VA Tech, Blacksburg, VA 703-961-5314
Teague, Tom/617 Hillcrest Drive SW, Vienna, VA.......................703-281-7036
Textured Graphics Studio/719 Martina Dr NE, Atlanta, GA...........404-231-2168
The Artsmith/440 College Ave/Box 391, Athens, GA...................404-543-5555
Thompson, Del/PO Box 7016 #225, Greenville, SC.....................803-232-5444
Tinney, Robert/PO Box 778, Washington, LA.............................318-826-3003
Tull, Bobbi/1210 N Chambliss St, Alexandria, VA.......................703-354-4322
Turner, Cynthia/3 Old Miller Pl, Santa Rosa Bch, FL...................904-231-4112
Turner, Jeanne/6900 Chestnut Ave, Falls Church, VA.................703-237-1108
Turner, Pete/938 Pamlico Dr, Cary, NC....................................919-467-8466
Ulan, Helen Cerra/4227 San Juan Dr, Fairfax, VA......................703-691-0474
Vaughn, Rob/600 Curtis Pkwy/Box 660706, Miami Springs, FL 305-885-1292
Vincent, Wayne/957 N Livingston St, Arlington, VA.....................703-532-8551
Vintson, Sherry/4860 Dover St NE, St Petersburg, FL.................813-822-2512
Vitsky, Sally/4116 Bromley Lane, Richmond, VA........................804-359-4726
Voide, Raymond H/3419 Braddock Dr, Woodbridge, VA...............703-878-2585

WXY

Wagner, Stephen R/Rt 1/Box 978, Washington, VA....................703-675-3046
Walsh, Pat/8801 McNair Dr, Alexander, VA...............................703-780-5578
Walsh, Taly/2481 Windbreak Dr, Alexandria, VA.........................703-765-6154
Walthall, Jeffrey/2031 Rockingham St, McLean, VA...................703-538-2738
Wariner, David/21 Theatre Square #200, Louisville, KY...............502-561-0737
Warnock, Ted/4141 N Henderson Rd #913, Arlington, VA............202-333-4147
Wasilowski, Bob/ 3258 Kinross Circle, Herndon, VA...................703-742-6658
Watts, David/1407 Brooks Ave, Raleigh, NC.............................919-783-5133
Webber, Warren/571 Dutch Valley Rd, Atlanta, GA.....................404-881-6627
Wetzel, Marcia/755 Virginia Ave NE, Atlanta, GA.......................404-872-7980
Whitver, Harry K/208 Reidhurst Ave, Nashville, TN....................615-320-1795
Wilgus, David/PO Box 971, Davidson, NC................................704-892-7738
Wilkinson, Joel/707 E McBee Ave, Greenville, SC......................803-235-4483
Williams, Tim/520 Country Glen Rd, Alpharetta, GA...................404-475-3146
Winkle, Mark/PO Box 25011, Durham, NC................................919-383-8449
Winslow, Terese/714 S Fairfax St, Alexandria, VA 703-836-9121
Woolridge, Anthony/5530 Ascot Ct #22, Alexandria, VA 703-578-0790
Xenakis, Thomas/523 W 24th St #25, Norfolk, VA......................804-622-2061
Yarnell, David Andrew/PO Box 286, Occoquan, VA....................703-690-2987
Young, Bruce/1262 Pasadena Ave NE, Atlanta, GA....................404-892-8509

MIDWEST

A

Ahearn, John D/151 S Elm, St Louis, MO 314-781-3389
AIR Studio/203 E Seventh St, Cincinnati, OH............................513-721-1193
Allen, David W/18108 Martin Ave #2F, Homewood, IL.................708-798-3283
Allen, Jim/Box 8454 , Moline, IL..309-799-3366
Allen, Rick/2216 E 32nd St, Minneapolis, MN............................612-721-8832
Ambre, Matt/3222 N Clifton #2F, Chicago, IL.............................312-935-5170
Anastas, Nicolette/307 N Michigan Ave #1008, Chicago, IL.........312-704-0500
Appleoff, Sandy/1809 Westport Rd, Kansas City, MO 816-753-5421
Archer, Doug/512 South Oak POB 307, Garnett, KS....................913-448-3841
Art Factory Ltd/925 Elmgrove, Elmgrove, WI.............................414-785-1940
Art Force Inc/21700 NW Hwy #570, Southfield, MI.....................313-569-1074
Artist Studios/666 Euclid Ave, Cleveland, OH............................216-241-5355
Atkinson, Steve/3340 W 127th St, Cleveland, OH.......................216-941-1058

B

Bachtell, Tom/202 South State, Chicago, IL 312-939-6603
Backderf, John/6730 Wallings Rd, Breckville, OH.......................216-561-7586

Backes, Nick/405 N Wabash #3203, Chicago, IL 312-329-1370
Backus, Michael/405 N Wabash #3203, Chicago, IL 312-329-1370
Balistreri Commercial Art/1410 E Pinedale Ct, Shorewood, WI 414-628-3724
Barrows, Scott/6S235 Steeple Run #203 A, Naperville, IL 708-355-4242
Barteck, Shelley/608 S 55th St, Omaha, NE 402-554-0656
Basham, Ray/9728 Watkins Rd SW, Patasklax, OH 614-461-1820
Beck, David M/5112 W Winona St, Chicago, IL 312-725-8474
Beck, Joan/2521 11th Ave S, Minneapolis, MN 612-870-7159
Bedrick, Jeffrey/490 Rockside Rd, Cleveland, OH 216-661-4222
Behm, Kim/1225 W 4th St, Waterloo, IA 319-234-7055
Behum, Cliff/26384 Aaron Ave, Euclid, OH 216-261-9266
Benton, Jim/3170 Middlebury, Birmingham, MI 313-644-5875
Berendsen, Bob/2233 Kemper Ln, Cincinnati, OH 513-861-1400
Berry, Jean/1489 W 95th St, Lenexa, KS 913-362-7800
Birkey, Randal/542 S Dearborn St 8th Fl, Chicago, IL 312-664-8009
Bischel, Mark/301 E Armour Blvd #315, Kansas City, MO 816-561-4473
Blanchette, Dan/400 N May St, Chicago, IL 312-829-3993
Bleck, Linda/2739 N Hampden Ct #15, Chicago, IL 312-281-0286
Blue Sky Pictures/1237 Chicago Rd, Troy, MI 313-583-2828
Bobnick, Richard/3412 Barbara Ln, Burnsville, MN 612-831-6313
Boehm, Roger C/529 South 7th St #539, Minneapolis, MN 612-332-0787
Bonk, Chris/908 W Euclid #104, Arlington Hghts, IL 708-577-5157
Bookwalter, Tom/11440 Oak Drive, Shelbyville, MI 616-672-5756
Borgert, Ted E./PO Box 1622, Cincinnati, OH (P 26) 513-721-8322
Borggren, Howard/333 N Michigan, Chicago, IL 312-368-4355
Boswick, Steven/331 Oak Circle, Wilmette, IL 718-251-1430
Bovy, Deb/1225 W 4th St, Waterloo, IA 319-234-7055
Bowman, Bob/163 Cedarwood Ct, Palatine, IL 708-966-2770
Boyer-Pennington, Lyn/4281 Baywood Dr, Traverse City, MI 616-938-1911
Brandtner, Al/1304 West Cornelia St 1st Fl, Chicago, IL 312-974-1154
Braught, Mark/629 Cherry St #18, Terre Haute, IN 812-234-6135
Brennan, Daniel/842 N Webster, Chicago, IL 312-822-0887
Britt, Tracy/68 E Franklin St, Dayton, OH 513-433-8383
Brooks, Dick/11712 N Michigan Rd #100, Zionsville, IN 317-873-1117
Bruning, Bill/1913 Park Ave, St Louis, MO 314-241-4014
Butler, Chris/405 N Wabash #1912, Chicago, IL 312-321-1336
Buttram, Andy/1636 Hickory Glen Dr, Miamisburg, OH 513-859-7428
Byer, Lou/3590 N Meridian St, Indianapolis, IN 315-925-8333

C

Call, Ken/1836 N Winchester, Chicago, IL 312-489-2323
Carloni, Kurt/4142 S Regal Manor Ct, New Berlin, WI 414-796-0886
Carr, Ted/43 E Ohio #1001, Chicago, IL 312-467-6865
Carroll, Justin/1913 Park Ave, St Louis, MO 314-241-4014
Carroll, Michael/538 Bellefort, Oak Park, IL 708-386-3197
Ceballos, John/68 E Franklin St, Dayton, OH 513-433-8383
Cedergren, Carl/225 Gramsie RD, St Paul, MN 612-481-1429
Centaur Studios/310 Mansion House Ctr, St Louis, MO 314-421-6485
Chapin, Patrick O/177 Westbridge Dr, Berea, OH 216-234-6890
Chickinelli, Mark/6348 Pierce St, Omaha, NE 206-282-5776
Christiansen, Lee/PO Box 3635, Minneapolis, MN 612-374-3169
Cigliano, Bill/1525 W Glenlake, Chicago, IL 312-973-0062
Clark, Sheree & Sayles, John/308 8th St, Des Moines, IA 515-243-2922
Clay, Steve/245 W North Ave, Chicago, IL 312-280-7945
Clifford, Keesler/6642 West H Ave, Kalamazoo, MI 616-375-0688
Clifford, Lawrence P/450 Reavis Pl, St Louis, MO 314-962-9822
Clubb, Rick/107 N Hale St #211, Wheaton, IL 708-665-1173
Clyne, Dan/307 N Michigan Ave #1008, Chicago, IL 312-704-0500
Cobane, Russell/8291 Allen Rd, Clarkston, MI 313-625-6132
Cochran, Bobbye/433 W Webster Ave, Chicago, IL 312-943-5912
Cohen, Jim/600 N McClurg Ct #3401A, Chicago, IL 312-266-9063
Cole, Grace/4342 N Clark, Chicago, IL 312-935-8605
Color Forms/407 E Fort St, Detroit, MI 313-961-7100
Communigrafix/5550 W Armstrong, Chicago, IL 312-774-3012
Conahan, Jim/822 Charles Ave, Naperville, IL 708-961-1478
Conely, Jim/PO Box 1315, Dayton, OH 513-252-1122
Connelly, Gwen/233 E Wacker Dr, Chicago, IL 312-943-4477
Connelly, Jim/4753 Byron Ctr SW, Wyoming, MI 616-532-6630
Conrad, Liz/11440 Oak Drive, Shelbyville, MI 616-672-5756
Cook, Esky/405 N Wabash #3203, Chicago, IL 312-329-1370
Cosgrove, Dan/405 N Wabash #2914, Chicago, IL 312-527-0375
Coulter, Marty/10129 Conway Rd, St Louis, MO 314-432-2721
Craig, John/RT 2 Box 81 Tower Rd, Soldiers Grove, WI 608-872-2371
Creative Source Inc/360 N Michigan Ave #805, Chicago, IL 312-649-9777
Crnkovich, Tony/5706 S Narragansett, Chicago, IL 312-586-9696
Csicsko, David/211 E Ohio #621, Chicago, IL 312-784-2343
Curran, Don/215 Parkland, St Louis, MO 314-965-8672

D

Dammer, Mike/350 W Ontario, Chicago, IL 312-943-4995
Davies, Paul/1208 E 98th Terr, Kansas City, MO 816-941-9313
Day, Rob/6095 Ralston Ave, Indianapolis, IN 317-253-9469
Dean, Mike/405 N Wabash #3203, Chicago, IL 312-329-1370
Dearth, Greg/4041 Beal Rd, Franklin, OH 513-746-5970
Derrick, Bill/3179 Autumn Trace Dr, St Louis, MO 314-739-1837
Derrick, Jenny/3179 Autumn Trace Dr, St Louis, MO 314-726-1803
Devarj, Silva/116 W Illinois, Chicago, IL 312-266-1358
DiCianni, Ron/340 Thompson Blvd, Buffalo Grove, IL 708-634-1848
Dickens, Holly/612 N Michigan #710, Chicago, IL 312-280-0777
Dinyer, Eric/5510 Holmes, Kansas City, MO 816-363-4795
Dolan, Paul/3834 N Kenmore, Chicago, IL 312-528-3526
Dougherty, Mike/110 E Sharon Rd, Glendale, OH 513-772-0650
Doughman, Terry/806 N 48 Ave #B, Omaha, NE 402-551-6930
Doyle, Pat/333 N Michigan Ave, Chicago, IL 312-263-2065
Duke, Lawrence/405 N Wabash #3203, Chicago, IL 312-329-1370
Dunlevy, Brad/3660 Jefferson, Kansas City, MO 816-931-8945
Durk, Jim/1853 Hastings Ave, Downer's Grove, IL 708-719-9779
Dye, Jennifer/1445 B Timber Trail, Akron, OH 216-928-7935
Dypold, Pat/429 West Superior #508, Chicago, IL 312-337-6919
Dzielak, Dennis/350 W Ontario #603, Chicago, IL 312-642-1241

E

Eberbach, Andrea/68 E Franklin St, Dayton, OH 513-433-8383
Edsey, Michael/6040 N Avondale, Chicago, IL 312-988-2703
Ehlert, Lois/839 N Marshall, Milwaukee, WI 414-276-8336
Eldridge, Gary/117 West Main St, Lowell, MI 616-897-6668
Ellis, Christy/914 N Winchester, Chicago, IL 312-342-6343
Ellithorpe, Chris/4207 N Kedvale #2D, Chicago, IL 312-283-4871
English, M John/6808 Orchard St, Liberty, MO 816-792-2530
English, Mark/512 Lakeside Ct, Liberty, MO 816-792-2530
Evans, Sid/1533 N Mohawk, Chicago, IL 312-421-2224

F

Fanning, Jim/10 E 66th St, Kansas City, MO 816-361-5191
Feldkamp-Malloy/180 N Wabash, Chicago, IL 312-263-0633
Ferraro, Sandra/6057 Hillside Ave, E Dr, Indianapolis, IN 317-255-6335
Flock, Mary/905 S Laflin #3, Chicago, IL 312-733-0459
Flood, Dick/1603 Sheridan Rd, Champaign, IL 217-352-8356
Fogle, David W/1257 Virginia Ave, Lakewood, OH 216-521-2854
Foley, Timothy/109 Straight St NW, Grand Rapids, MI 616-451-9539
Ford, Dan/8025 Watkins Dr, St Louis, MO 314-961-5554
Foster, Jack/650 N Willow, Elmhurst, IL 708-279-3040
Foster, Stephen/894 Grove St, Glencoe, IL 708-835-2315
Foty, Tom/3836 Shady Oak Rd, Minnetonka, MN 612-933-5570
Fredrickson, Mark/1913 Park Ave, St Louis, MO 314-241-4014
Frueh, Mark/405 N Wabash #2709, Chicago, IL 312-222-0337
Fuka, Ted/8037 S Kirkland Ave, Chicago, IL 312-585-2314

G

Gadecki, Ted/5048 N Glenwood, Chicago, IL 312-769-6566
Gauthier, Corbert/510 Marquette Ave #200, Minneapolis, MN 612-339-0947
Gelb, Jacki/3345 Seminary, Chicago, IL 312-988-2866
Gieseke, Thomas A/7909 W 61st St, Merriam, KS 913-677-4593
Gin, Byron/4 E Ohio #11, Chicago, IL 312-944-1130
Goldammer, Ken/120 W Illinois St #5W, Chicago, IL 312-878-7914
Gonnella, Rick/225 N Michigan #310, Chicago, IL 312-565-2580
Grace, Rob/7516 Lamar Ave #81, Prarie Village, KS 913-341-9135
Graef, Renee/403 W Washington Ave, Madison, WI 608-256-7796
Graham, Bill/116 W Illinois, Chicago, IL 312-467-0330
Grandpré, Mary/2216 E 32nd St, Minneapolis, MN 612-721-8832
Graning, Ken/1975 Cragin Dr, Bloomfield Hills, MI 313-851-3665
Grasch, Karen/405 N Wabash, Chicago, IL 312-822-9632
Graziano, Krafft & Zale/333 N Michigan #401, Chicago, IL 312-368-4355
Groff, David/2265 Avalon Ave, Kettering, OH 513-298-9719
Gsrmon, Van/1601 22nd St #201, W Des Moines, IA 515-246-6166
Gumble, Gary/803 Elmwood #3N, Evanston, IL 708-475-4712
Gustafson, Glenn/1300 Ivy Ct, Westmont, IL 708-810-9527

H

Hackett, Michael/20789 Millard, Taylor, MI 313-358-2660

Hagel, Mike/PO Box 610, Arlington Heights, IL................312-253-0638
Hagio, Kunio/680 N Lake Shore Dr #1020, Chicago, IL.........312-944-6655
Halbert, Michael/2419 Big Ben, St Louis, MO...................314-645-6480
Hamblin, George/944 Beach St, LaGrange Pk, IL...............708-352-1780
Hannan, Peter/1341 W Melrose, Chicago, IL....................312-883-9029
Hansen, Clint/405 N Wabash #1912, Chicago, IL................312-321-1336
Hanson, Eric/PO Box 3635, Minneapolis, MN....................612-374-3169
Hargreaves, Greg/1225 W 4th St, Waterloo, IA.................319-234-7055
Harman, Richard/207 S Cottonwood, Republic, MO...............417-732-2914
Harris, Jim/2310 E 101st Ave, Crown Point, IN................219-769-4460
Harris, John/3584 Normandy/1st fl, Shaker Hgts, OH...........216-838-1362
Harris, Scott/803 Greenleaf St, Evanston, IL.................312-440-2360
Harrison, William/324 W State St, Geneva, IL.................708-232-7733
Harritos, Peter/68 E Franklin St, Dayton, OH.................513-433-8383
Hatala, Dan/1225 W 4th St, Waterloo, IA......................319-234-7055
Hatcher, Lois/32 W 58th St, Kansas City, MO..................816-361-6230
Havlicek, Karel/405 N Wabash #3203, Chicago, IL..............312-329-1370
Hayes, Cliff/PO Box 1239, Chicago Hts, IL....................708-755-7115
Hayes, John/1121 W George St, Chicago, IL....................312-787-1333
Haynes, Bryan/2401 S 13th St, St Louis, MO...................314-771-0055
Haynes, Michael P./3070 Hawthorn Blvd, St Louis, MO..........314-772-3156
Hays, Michael/324 S Maple Ave, Oak Park, IL..................708-383-4229
Hockerman, Dennis/6024 W Chapel Hill Rd, Mequon, WI..........414-242-4103
Hodde, Julie/68 E Franklin St, Dayton, OH....................513-433-8383
Hodge, Gerald/1241 Bending Rd, Ann Arbor, MI.................313-764-6163
Hogenkamp-Bandle, Johnna/PO Box 16049, Shawnee Mission, KS...913-722-0687
Holladay Prints/5315 Tremont Ave #3, Davenport, IA...........319-386-5645
Holton, Susan V/1512 W Jonquil, Chicago, IL..................312-973-6429
Horn, Robert/405 N Wabash #2815, Chicago, IL.................312-644-0058
Howard, Deborah/PO Box 178 197, Toledo, OH...................419-335-3340
Hrabe, Curtis/2944 Greenwood Ave, Highland Park, IL..........708-432-4632
Hranilovich, Barbara/1200 N Jenison, Lansing, MI.............517-487-6474
Hullinger, C D/4436 South River Rd, West Lafayette, IN.......317-743-3690
Hunn, John/508 Sunnyside, St Louis, MO.......................314-968-1061
Hunt, Harlan/900 W Jackson #7W, Chicago, IL..................312-944-5680
Hunter, Steve/1225 W 4th St, Waterloo, IA....................319-234-7055

IJ

Illustrated Alaskan Moose/5 W Main St, Westerville, OH.......614-898-5316
Izold, Donald/20475 Bunker Hill Dr, Fairview Park, OH........216-333-9988
Jackson, Kelly/982 Paradrome St #2, Cincinnati, OH...........513-651-0258
Jackson-Zender Studio/1101 Southeastern Ave, Indianapolis, IN....317-639-5124
Jacobsen, Ken/5230 13th Ave S, Minneapolis, MN...............612-822-0650
James, Verzell/1521 W Sunnyside, Chicago, IL.................312-784-2352
Jarvis, Nathan Y/708-A Main St, Grand View, MO...............816-765-0617
Jay/17858 Rose St, Lansing, IL...............................708-474-9704
Jobst, T S/2351 Woodbrook Circle, Columbus, OH...............614-276-9921
Johannes, Greg/3713 N Racine #3 , Chicago, IL................312-528-7941
Johnson, BJ/540 N Lake Shore Dr #610, Chicago, IL............312-836-1166
Johnson, Diane/4609 N Claremont, Chicago, IL.................312-728-5874
Johnson, Rick/1212 W Chase, Chicago, IL......................708-790-1744
Johnson, Steve/440 Sheridan Ave South, Minneapolis, MN.......612-377-8728
Jones, Jan/2332 N Halstead, Chicago, IL......................312-929-1851
Jones, Mary/4511 N Campbell, Chicago, IL.....................312-769-1196
Jones, Michael Scott/400 W Erie #306, Chicago, IL............312-281-0462
Jonke, Tim/88 Jefferson Lane, Streamwood, IL.................708-213-3934
Juenger, Richard/1324 S 9th St, St Louis, MO.................314-231-4069
Juett, Christine/501 W 11th St, Traverse City, MI............616-929-4424

K

Kalisch, John W/1330 S 33rd St, Omaha, NE....................402-342-2572
Kasperski, Tom/1752 Atmore, St Louis, MO.....................314-522-3739
Kastaris, Rip/3301-A S Jefferson Ave, St Louis, MO...........314-773-2600
Kasun, Mike/2536 N 61st St, Milwaukee, WI....................414-444-5178
Kay, Michael/222 S Morgan #1A, Chicago, IL...................312-738-1835
Kecman, Milan/2730 Somia Dr, Cleveland, OH...................216-741-8755
Kelen, Linda/1922 W Newport, Chicago, IL.....................312-975-9696
Kennedy, Dean/1225 W 4th St, Waterloo, IA....................319-234-7055
Kessler Hartsock Assoc/5624 Belmont Ave, Cincinnati, OH......513-542-8775
Kessler, Clifford/6642 West H Ave, Kalamazoo, MI.............616-375-0688
Kilgore, Troy/PO Box 882, Bloomington, IN....................812-336-2362
Killeen, Tom/916 Olive #300, St Lousi, MO....................314-231-6800
Kirov, Lydia/4008 N Hermitage Ave, Chicago, IL...............312-248-8764
Klanderman, Leland/1913 Park Ave, St Louis, MO...............314-241-4014
Kleber, John/211 E Ohio #621, Chicago, IL....................312-784-2343
Klimt, Kathy/3415 N Hoyne, Chicago, IL.......................312-525-1837

Knutson, Doug/1225 W 4th St, Waterloo, IA....................319-234-7055
Kock, Carl/2076 N Elston, Chicago, IL........................312-342-8833
Kordic, Vladimir/35351 Grovewood Dr, Eastlake, OH............216-951-4026
Kortendick, Susan/2611 Eastwood, Evanston, IL................708-864-6062
Kotik, Kenneth/9 Last Chance Ct, St Peter, MO................314-441-1091
Krainik, David/4719 Center Ave, Lisle, IL....................708-963-4614
Kriegshauser, Shannon/12421 W Grafleman Rd, Hanna City, IL...309-565-7110
Kueker, Don /829 Ginger Wood Court, St Louis, MO.............314-225-1566
Kulov, Dean/733 W Irving Park Rd #2, Chicago, IL.............312-664-6040

L

Lackner, Paul/1225 W 4th St, Waterloo, IA....................319-234-7055
Ladden, Randee/1200 W Waveland, Chicago, IL..................312-327-8003
LaFever, Greg/68 E Franklin St, Dayton, OH...................513-433-8383
LaMantia, Joe/2507 Brewster Rd, Indianapolis, IN.............317-872-7856
Lambert, John/1911 E Robin Hood Ln, Arlington Heights, IL....708-392-6349
Lange, Denis K/1545 Country Rd #995, Ashland, OH.............419-289-0181
Langenderfer, Tim/631 Colona, Dayton, OH.....................513-298-5133
Langeneckert, Donald/4939 Ringer Rd, St Louis, MO............314-487-2042
Langeneckert, Mark/704 Dover Pl, St Louis, MO................314-752-0199
Larson, Seth/1315 Hathaway Ave, Lakewood, OH.................216-228-2172
Lattimen, Evan/4203 Holly, Kansas City, MO...................816-561-0103
Lawson, Robert/1523 Seminole St, Kalamazoo, MI...............616-345-7607
Lederman, Marsha/4 Alpine Ct, East Brunswick, NJ.............201-257-9324
Lee, Denis Charles/1120 Heatherway, Ann Arbor, MI............313-973-2795
Lee, Jared D/2942 Old Hamilton Rd, Lebanon, OH...............513-932-2154
Lesh, David/5693 N Meridan St, Indianapolis, IN..............317-253-3141
Letostak, John/7801 Fernhill Ave, Parma, OH..................216-885-1753
Lochray, Tom/3225 Oakland Ave, Minneapolis, MN...............612-823-7630
Loos, Jean/5539 Arnsby Pl, Cincinnati, OH....................513-561-8472
Lord, David/1449 N Pennsylvania, Indianapolis, IN............317-634-1244
Loveless, Jim/4137 San Francisco Ave, St Louis, MO...........314-533-7914

M

Mach, Steven/515 N Halstead, Chicago, IL.....................312-243-4239
MacNair, Greg/7515 Wayne, University City, MO................314-721-3781
Maggard, John/102 Marian Lane, Terrace Park, OH..............513-831-8801
Mahan, Benton/PO Box 66, Chesterville, OH....................419-768-2204
Mahler, Joseph/2507 Brewster Rd, Indianapolis, IN............317-872-7856
Mallet, Kim/301 E Armour Blvd #315, Kansas City, MO..........816-561-4473
Marlaire, Dennis/311 Kingston Dr, Frankfort, IL..............708-819-4750
Martin, Larry/68 E Franklin St, Dayton, OH...................513-433-8383
Mayerik, Val/20466 Drake Rd, Strongsville, OH................216-238-9492
Mayes, Kevin/1202 Tulsa St, Wichita, KS......................316-522-6742
Mayse, Steve/7515 Allman, Lenexa, KS.........................913-599-5440
McDermott, Teri/38W563 Koshare Trail, Elgin, IL..............708-888-2206
McElwain, Dianne/2507 Brewster Rd, Indianapolis, IN..........317-872-7856
McFarland, Tom F/7300 Belleview, Kansas City, MO.............816-363-5699
McKee-Anderson Group/919 Springer Dr, Lombard, IL............708-953-8706
McLean & Friends/25800 Northwestern Hwy, Southfield, MI......313-358-2660
McMahon, Mark/321 S Ridge Rd, Lake Forest, IL................708-295-2604
McNally, Jim/120 W Illinois, Chicago, IL.....................312-222-9504
McNicholas, Michael/7804 W College Dr, Palos Hts, IL.........708-361-2850
Meade, Roy/216 W Wayne St, Maumee, OH........................419-666-1168
Meadows, Laura/318 Sunnyside Ave, Waterloo, IA...............319-234-3392
Mendheim, Mike/6619 North Shore Dr, Chicago, IL..............312-338-0773
Meredith, Jane/333 E Ontario #4010B-B, Chicago, IL...........312-944-0731
Miller, Cindy/225 S Ashley, Ann Arbor, MI....................313-761-5600
Miller, Dave/727 Shady Oaks Ct, Elgin, IL....................312-476-4429
Miller, David/PO Box 474, Elkhart, IN........................219-295-1492
Miller, William (Bill)/1355 N Sandburg Ter #2002, Chicago, IL....312-787-4093
Mitchell, Kurt/3004 W 66th St, Chicago, IL...................312-476-4429
Molloy, Jack A/1645 Hennepin Ave South, Minneapolis, MN......612-374-3169
Moore, Stephen/1077 Country Creek Dr, Lebanon, OH............513-932-4295
Mora, Eddy/210 S Water St #44, Olathe, KS....................913-782-7983
Morgan, Leonard/730 Victoria Ct, Bowlingbrook, IL............708-739-7705
Muchmore, Pat/1225 W 4th St, Waterloo, IA....................319-234-7055
Mundy, C W/8609 Manderley Dr, Indianapolis, IN...............317-848-1330
Munger, Nancy/PO Box 125, Richland, MI.......................616-623-5458
Murakami, Tak/1535 E Juneway Terrace, Chicago, IL............312-764-7845
Murphy, Charles/4146 Pillsbury, Minneapolis, MN..............612-926-4123
Musgrave, Steve/213 W Institute Pl #502, Chicago, IL.........312-939-4717

N

Nagel, Mike/PO Box 610, Arlington Hts, IL....................312-253-0638

Neidigh, Sherry/325 W Huron #310, Chicago, IL................................312-787-6826
Nelson Studios/14849 W 95th St, Lenexa, KS.................................613-492-4444
Nelson, Diane/2816 Birchwood, Wilmette, IL..................................708-256-6200
Nelson, Fred/3 E Ontario #25, Chicago, IL....................................312-935-1707
Nichols, Gary/1449 N Pennsylvania St, Indianapolis, IN.................317-637-0250
Nighthawk Studio/1250 Riverbed Rd, Cleveland, OH.......................216-522-1809
Nixon, Tony/5552 Santa Fe, Overland, KS.....................................913-384-5444
Nobles, Kelly/2625 N Clark St, Chicago, IL....................................312-975-0536
Noche, Mario/1449 N Pennsylvania, Indianapolis, IN......................317-299-8221
Norcia, Ernest/3451 Houston Rd, Waynesville, OH..........................513-862-5761
Novak, Bob/6878 Fry Rd, Middlebury Hts, OH.................................216-234-1808
Noyes, Mary Albury/716 First St N #245, Minneapolis, MN...............612-338-1270
Nyberg, Tim/1012 Trillium Ln, Sister Bay, WI..................................414-854-4464

OP

O'Connell, Mitch/6425 N Newgard #3N, Chicago, IL.......................312-743-3848
O'Malley, Kathy/4510 N Paulina #1W, Chicago, IL..........................312-334-7637
Odyssey Artworx/1324-B Skyridge Dr, Crystal Lake, IL...................815-455-5554
Oliveros, Edmond/5800 Monroe St, Sylvania, OH...........................419-882-7131
Olson, Robert A/15215 Buchanan Ct, Eden Prairie, MN...................612-934-5767
Olson, Stan/PO Box 3635, Minneapolis, MN...................................612-374-3169
Ortman, John/535 N Michigan Ave, Chicago, IL..............................312-266-1417
Ostresh, Michael/2034 13th St, Granite City, IL..............................618-876-8861
Otto, Brian/2216 E 32nd St, Minneapolis, MN.................................612-721-8832
Palencar, John Jude/6763 Middlebrook Blvd, Middlebury, OH..........216-845-8163
Palnik, Paul/2357 Bixley Pk Rd, Bixley, OH....................................614-239-8710
Pappas, Chris/350 W Ontario #603, Chicago, IL..............................312-787-0455
Patterson/Thomas/1002 E Washington St, Indianapolis, IN...............317-638-1002
Pauling, Galen T/PO Box 3150, Southfield, MI.................................313-356-5614
Pauly, Thomas Allen/648 W Oakdale, Chicago, IL............................312-477-0440
Pepera, Fred/405 N Wabash #3203, Chicago, IL..............................312-329-1370
Perreault, Alison Marie/1121 Wellington Ave, Chicago, IL................213-935-5326
Petan, Greg J/253 E Delaware Pl, Chicago, IL.................................312-787-9490
Peterson, Bryan/207 E Buffalo #543, Milwaukee, WI........................414-291-0300
Peterson, Keith/7 W Campbell #2, Arlington Hghts, IL......................708-577-2279
Petrauskas, Kathy/1660 N Lasalle #2001, Chicago, IL.....................312-642-4950
Picasso, Dan/PO Box 3635, Minneapolis, MN.................................612-374-3169
Pitt Studios/1370 Ontario St #1430, Cleveland, OH.........................216-241-6720
Pitts, Ted/68 E Franklin St, Dayton, OH...513-433-8383
Pope, Giles/4222 Lindenwood, Matteson, IL...................................708-747-2056
Pope, Kevin/3735 Cleve Butcher Rd, Bloomington, IN......................812-824-6949
Post, Bob/2144 Lincoln Pk W, Chicago, IL......................................312-549-6725
Pozwozd, Sally/124 N Park, Westmont, IL.......................................708-969-5854
Prado, Hugo/3323 W Berteau Ave, Chicago, IL................................312-583-7627
Pranica, John/5702 W Henderson, Chicago, IL................................312-685-1207
Probert, Jean/317 W Old Watson, St Louis, MO...............................314-968-5076
Provenzano, Anthony/1046 Cora St, Des Plaines, IL.........................708-297-4560

QR

Quinn, Colleen/307 N Michigan Ave #1008, Chicago, IL...................312-704-0500
Racer-Reynolds Illust/120 W Illinois 5th Fl, Chicago, IL....................312-836-0099
RadenStudio/3016 Cherry, Kansas City, MO...................................816-756-1992
Rasmussen, Bonnie/8828 Pendleton, St Louis, MO..........................314-962-1842
Rawley, Don/7520 Blaisdell Ave S, Richfield, MN.............................612-866-1023
Rawson, Jon/1225 S Hamilton, Rockport, IL....................................815-838-4462
Redgrafix/19750 W Observatory Rd, New Berlin, WI.........................414-542-5547
Reed, Mike/1314 Summit Ave, Minneapolis, MN..............................612-374-3164
Regine, Elvira/445 East Ohio, Chicago, IL......................................312-943-7670
Renaud, Phill/2830 W Leland, Chicago, IL......................................312-583-2681
Reynolds, Bill/433 Thomas Ave South, Minneapolis, MN..................612-374-3169
Riedy, Mark/68 E Franklin St, Dayton, OH.....................................513-433-8383
Roberts, A Hardy/6512 Charlotte, Kansas City, MO..........................816-444-8210
Roberts, Michael/3406 Valley Ridge Rd #305, Middleton, WI............608-241-1557
Rockwell, Steven P/1613 Leytonstone Dr, Wheaton, IL.....................708-690-6979
Rogers, Buc/405 N Wabash #3203, Chicago, IL..............................312-329-1370
Rosco, Delro/405 N Wabash #3203, Chicago, IL..............................312-329-1370
Ross, Bill/11440 Oak Drive, Shelbyville, MI....................................616-672-5756
Rossi, Pam/908 Main St #3, Evanston, IL.......................................708-475-2533
Roth, Hy/1300 Ashland St, Evanston, IL...708-491-1937
Rownd, Jim/5230 13th Ave S, Minneapolis, MN...............................612-822-0650
Rybka, Stephen/3119 W 83rd St, Chicago, IL..................................312-737-1981

S

Sanford, John/5038 W Berteau, Chicago, IL....................................312-685-0656
Sapulich, Joe/8454 W 161st Pl, Tinley Park, IL................................708-532-8766

Schmelzer, J P/1002 S Wesley Ave, Oak Park, IL.............................708-386-4005
Schriner, John/1347 Glacier Lane N, Maple, MN.............................612-559-5529
Schroeppel, Rick/595 E Thornhill Dr #214, Carol Stream, IL............708-682-8212
Schuler, Mark/5410 W 68th St, Prairie Village, KS............................913-384-0646
Schweitzer, David/207 Buffalo St #543, Milwaukee, WI....................414-272-5666
Scibilia, Dom/8277 Broadview Rd, Broadview, OH...........................216-526-2036
Scott, Jerry/152 W Wisconsin Ave, Milwaukee, WI..........................414-271-5210
Selfridge, MC/817 Desplaines St, Plainfield, IL...............................815-436-7197
Sellars, Joseph/2423 W 22nd St, Minneapolis, MN..........................612-377-8766
Seltzer, Meyer Design & Illust/744 W Buckingham Pl, Chicago, IL.......312-348-2885
Sereta, Bruce/3010 Parklane Dr, Cleveland, OH..............................216-241-5355
Shaw, Ned/2770 N Smith Pike, Bloomington, IN...............................812-333-2181
Shay, RJ/3301 S Jefferson Ave, St Louis, MO.................................314-773-9989
Sheban, Chris/400 West Erie #300, Chicago, IL..............................312-549-1312
Sheldon, David/20 Lynnray Circle, Dayton, OH................................513-433-8383
Shuta, Joanne/700 3rd St S #301, Minneapolis, MN.........................612-343-0432
Sienkowski, Laurie/3660 Newcastle SE, Grand Rapids, MI...............616-247-0127
Signorino, Slug/3587 No Cross Trail, LaPort, IN...............................219-879-5221
Silcox, Juana/2507 Brewster Rd, Indianapolis, IN............................317-872-7856
Silvers, Bill/1496 Westford Ctr #212, Westlake, OH..........................516-422-1915
Sirrell, Terry/768 Red Oak Dr, Bartlett, IL.......................................708-213-9003
Sisson-Schlesser, Kathryn/707 W Wrightwood Ave, Chicago, IL........312-472-3877
Skeen, Keith D/3228 Prairie Dr, Deerfield, WI.................................608-423-3020
Skidmore Sahratian Inc/2100 W Big Beaver Rd, Troy, MI.................313-643-6000
Slack, Chuck/9 Cambridge Ln, Lincolnshire, IL...............................708-948-9226
Slonim, David/232 South Street, Chesterfield, IN.............................317-378-6511
Snodgrass, Steve/1919 N Sheffield, Chicago, IL..............................312-868-0900
Solovic, Linda/3509 Humphrey, St Louis, MO.................................314-773-7897
Songero, Jay/17858 Rose St, Lansing, IL.......................................708-849-5676
Soukup, James/Route 1, Seward, NE...402-643-2339
Speer, Terry/181 Forest St, Oberlin, OH...216-774-8319
Spiece, Jim/1811 Wood Haven #9, Ft Wayne, IN.............................219-747-3916
Staake, Bob/1009 S Berry Rd, St Louis, MO...................................314-961-2303
Stasiak, Krystyna/5421 N E River Rd #507, Chicago, IL...................312-380-4038
Stearney, Mark/405 N Wabash #2809, Chicago, IL..........................312-644-6669
Storyboard Studio/431 W Roscoe, Chicago, IL................................312-266-1417
Strandell Design Inc/218 E Ontario, Chicago, IL..............................312-661-1555
Streff, Michael/2766 Wasson Rd, Cincinnati, OH.............................513-731-0360
Stroster, Maria/2057 N Sheffield, Chicago, IL..................................312-525-2081
Styrkowicz, Tom/3801 Olentangy Blvd, Columbus, OH.....................614-261-6952
Sumichrast, Józef/465 Beverly, Lake Forest, IL...............................708-295-0255
Svolos, Maria/1936 W Estes, Chicago, IL.......................................312-338-4675
Swaford, Chris/Rt 2/Box 196-6, Billings, MO...................................417-744-4411
Swansen, Becky/815 N Marion, Oak Park, IL...................................312-383-0141
Swanson, James/815 North Marion, Oak Park, IL.............................708-383-0141
Syska, Richard/1905 W Foster, Chicago, IL.....................................312-728-2738

T

Tate, Clark/301 Woodford St, Gridley, IL...800-828-3008
Tate, Don/557 N Park Blvd, Glen Ellyn, IL.......................................708-469-0085
Taylor, David/1449 N Pennsylvania St, Indianapolis, IN....................317-634-2728
Taylor, Joseph/2117 Ewing Ave, Evanston, IL.................................708-328-2454
Theodore, Jim/17253 Pearl Rd, Cleveland, OH................................614-898-5316
Thiewes, Sam/111 N Andover Ln, Geneva, IL..................................708-232-0980
Thomas, Bob/68 E Franklin St, Dayton, OH.....................................513-433-8383
Thomas, Pat/711 Carpenter, Oak Park, IL.......................................708-383-8505
Thomas, Paul/4999 Orion Rd, Rochester, MI...................................313-656-2828
Thompson, John/1225 W 4th St, Waterloo, IA..................................319-234-7055
Thompson, Lowell/10 E Ontario #1104, Chicago, IL.........................312-664-1362
Thomssen, Kate/2216 E 32nd St, Minneapolis, MN..........................612-721-8832
Thornton, Shelley/1600 S 22nd St, Lincoln, NE...............................212-683-1362
Tipton, Bill/1762 Sparrow Pt Ln, Fenton, MO..................................314-343-9961
Tonkin, Thomas/25800 Northwestern Hwy, Southfield, MI................313-358-2660
Treadway, Todd/1225 W 4th St, Waterloo, IA...................................319-234-7055
Truxaw, Dick/7709 W 97th St, Overland Park, KS.............................319-383-1555
Tull, Jeff/3301-A S Jefferson Ave, St Louis, MO...............................314-773-2600
Turgeon, James/405 N Wabash #1413, Chicago, IL.........................312-644-1444

UV

Utley, Tom/490 Rockside Rd, Cleveland, OH...................................216-661-4222
Utterback, Bill/6105 Kingston Ave, Lisle, IL.....................................708-852-9764
Vaccarello, Paul/400 E Ohio #603, Chicago, IL...............................312-664-2233
Van Hamersfeld, Jon/916 Olive #300, St Louis, MO.........................314-231-6800
Van Kanegan, Jeff/Box 60-B RR1, Camp Point, IL...........................214-455-4171
Vanderbeek, Don/235 Monterey Ave, Dayton, OH............................513-293-5326
Vann, Bill Studio/1706 S 8th St, St Louis, MO.................................314-231-2322

Vanselow, Holly/2701 N Southport, Chicago, IL.................................312-975-5880
VanZanten, Hugh/536 W Grant #10, Chicago, IL 312-262-4954
Von Haeger, Arden/3301-A S Jefferson Ave, St Louis, MO..................314-773-2600
Voo, Rhonda/4 E Ohio #11, Chicago, IL...312-944-1130
Vuksanovich, Fran/3224 N Nordica, Chicago, IL 312-283-2138

W

Wald, Carol/217 Farnsworth Ave, Detroit, MI...................................313-832-5805
Walker, John/4423 Wilson Ave, Downer's Grove, IL..........................708-963-8359
Walker, Ken/19 W Linwood, Kansas City, MO 816-561-9405
Walsh, Cathy/225 W Huran #318, Chicago, IL.................................312-944-2985
Walter, Nancy Lee/PO Box 611, Elmhurst, IL 708-833-3898
Watford, Wayne/1913 Park Ave, St Louis, MO..................................314-241-4014
Watkinson, Brent/12904 Piccadilly Cir, Lenexa, KS............................913-888-2047
Wawiorka, Matt/1510 E Marion St, Shorewood, WI............................414-765-7531
Wells, Peter/, Milwaukee, WI...414-272-5525
Wesley, Carl/2401 Clinton Ave S #304, Minneapolis, MN......................612-871-4983
Westphal, Ken/7616 Fairway, Prairie Village, KS...............................913-381-8399
Whaley, Kevin/2216 E 32nd St, Minneapolis, MN..............................612-721-8832
Whitney, Bill/116 W Illinois 5th Fl, Chicago, IL.................................312-527-2455
Whitney, Jack/110 Garrell Ave, Bowling Green, OH............................419-475-6600
Whitney, Mike/7833 Kenridge Lane, St Louis, MO.............................314-968-1255
Wickart, Mark/6293 Surrey Ridge Rd, Lisle, IL..................................708-369-0164
Wickart, Terry/3881 64th St, Holland, MI 616-335-3511
Willey, Chris/3202 Windsor #2E, Kansas City, MO.............................816-483-1475
Williams, Gary/7045 california Ave, Hamond, IN................................219-844-8002
Williams, Gordon/1030 Glenmoor Ln, Glendale, MO 314-821-2032
Williams, Jim/225 N Michigan Ave #310, Chicago, IL..........................312-565-2580
Willson Graphics/100 E Ohio #314, Chicago, IL.................................312-642-5328
Willy, April Goodman/1512 Misty Ln, Indianapolis, IN..........................317-876-8910
Wilson, Donald/405 N Wabash #3203, Chicago, IL.............................312-329-1370
Wimmer, Chuck/7760 Oakhurst Circle, Cleveland, OH.........................216-526-2820
Winstein, Merryl/200 Oak St, St Louis, MO......................................314-968-2596
Wolf, Leslie/1812 Clayborne, Chicago, IL...312-935-1707
Woolery, Lee/2231 S Patterson Blvd, Dayton, OH..............................513-433-7912
Worcester, Mary/5230 13th Ave S, Minneapolis, MN 612-822-0650
Worman, Brian/4507 Glenway Ave, Cincinnati, OH.............................513-661-7881
Wright, Ted/1913 Park Ave, St Louis, MO..314-241-4014
Wrobel, Cindy/415 Alta Dena, St Louis, MO.....................................314-721-4467

YZ

Young & Laramore/310 E Vermont, Indianapolis, IN 317-264-8000
Youssi, John/17 N 943 Powers Rd, Gilberts, IL..................................708-428-7398
Zadnik, Pat/9215 Woods Way Dr, Kirtland, OH 216-256-6273
Zaresky, Don/41 Leonard Ave, Northfield Center, OH 216-467-5917
Zayell, Bonnie/1007 Gulf Rd, Elyria, OH..216-365-3477
Zimnicki Design/774 Parkview Ct, Roselle, IL....................................708-893-2666
Zumbo, Matthew/2105 N Summit #201, Milwaukee, WI.......................414-277-9541
Zumpfe, Rosemary/825 M St, Lincoln, NE..402-476-6480

S O U T H W E S T

AB

Abramson, Elaine/PO Box 330008, Ft Worth, TX 817-292-1855
Allen, Harrison/5811 Braes Heather, Houston, TX..............................713-729-3938
Andrew, Bill/1709 Dryden #709, Houston, TX...................................713-791-4924
Andrews, Chris/1515 N Beverly Ave, Tucson, AZ................................602-325-5126
Bailey, Craig/1508 Bayou Oak, Friendswood, TX...............................713-996-6984
Baker, David R/7254 Laurie Dr, Ft Worth, TX....................................817-429-4777
Bates, Greg/2811 McKinney #342, Dallas, TX...................................214-855-0055
Bleck, Cathie/1019 N Clinton, Dallas, TX...214-942-4639
Boatright, Phillip/7150 E Grand St #715, Dallas, TX............................214-324-3256
Brazeal, Lee Lee/9131 Westview, Houston, TX..................................713-445-8004
Brown, Charlie/1669 S Voss #392, Houston, TX.................................713-782-3447
Brown, Sue Ellen/3527 Oak Lawn Ave #269, Dallas, TX......................214-827-6140
Burns, Kevin/400 W Sam Houston Pkwy S #1137, Houston, TX 713-978-3343

C

Chambers, Lindy/RR 1 Box 7, Hockley, TX 713-467-6819
Chappell, Ellis/3525 Mockingbird Lane, Dallas, TX 214-521-5156
Chinchar, Alan/1718 Capstan, Houston, TX......................................713-480-3227
Cleveland, Thomas/15622 Canterbury Forrest, Tomball, TX...............713-370-8450

Collier, Steve/2001 Sul Ross, Houston, TX 713-522-0205
Collins, Rick/110 Clearview Dr #403, Friendswood, TX.......................713-996-5200
Connally, Connie/1107 Hilton, Richardson, TX..................................214-340-7818
Cooper, Karla Tuma/3333 Elm St #105, Dallas, TX............................214-871-1956
Cornelius, Ray-Mel/3521-C Dickerson, Dallas, TX.............................214-826-8988
Crampton, Michael/5429 Miller Ave, Dallas, TX.................................214-573-5626
Criswell, Ron/2929 Wildflower, Dallas, TX..214-620-9109
Cruz, Jose/4810 Cedar Springs #2210, Dallas, TX............................214-520-7004
Cumming, Moira/9754 Parkford Dr, Dallas, TX..................................214-343-8655
Curry, Tom/302 Lakehills Dr, Austin, TX...512-263-3407

DEF

Dean, Michael/2001 Sul Ross, Houston, TX......................................713-527-0295
Depew, Bob/2755 Rollingdale, Dallas, TX...214-241-9206
Dolphens, Tom/3525 Mockingbird Lane, Dallas, TX............................214-521-5156
Draper, Chad/413 N Tyler, Dallas, TX...214-526-4668
Drayton, Richard/PO Box 20053, Village of Oak Creek, AZ...................602-284-1566
Durbin, Mike/4034 Woodcraft, Houston, TX......................................713-667-8129
Engel, Norman/4316 Durango, Odessa, TX......................................915-368-7713
English, M John/3525 Mockingbird Lane, Dallas, TX...........................214-521-5156
Eubank, Mary Grace/6222 Northwood, Dallas, TX.............................214-692-7579
Evans, Eleanor/965 Slocum, Dallas, TX...214-760-8232
Falk, Rusty/707 E Alameda Dr, Tempe, AZ.......................................602-966-1626
Feiza, Anne/PO Box 131, Taos, NM..505-758-4930
Forbes, Bart/2706 Fairmount, Dallas, TX..214-748-8436
Ford, Cindy/2508 E 21 St, Tulsa, OK...918-743-3673

GH

Gamble, Kent/7010 Vicksburg, Lubbock, TX.....................................806-793-1389
Garns, G Allen/3314 East El Moro, Mesa, AZ....................................602-830-7224
Giangregorio, Laurie/6847 La Pasada, Hereford, AZ...........................602-378-3183
Gillespie, Mike/519 Gene Dr, Seagoville, TX.....................................214-287-8151
Gilliam, Charles/3903 San Ramon, Arlington, TX...............................817-861-1988
Girden, J M/2125 Cerrada Nopal E, Tucson, AZ.................................602-628-2740
Gormavay, Tom/1221 W Ben White Blvd, Austin, TX..........................512-326-8889
Graham, Jack/4160 N Craftsman Ct #202, Scottsdale, AZ 602-423-1500
Graves, Keith/809-A W 29th St, Austin, TX..512-478-3338
Griego, Tony/10609 W Seldon Lane, Peoria, AZ................................602-242-5492
Grimes, Don/3514 Oak Grove, Dallas, TX...214-526-0040
Hall, Bill/1235-B Colorado Ln, Arlington, TX......................................817-274-0817
Harr, Shane/637 Hawthorne, Houston, TX..713-523-8186
Harris, Jennifer/3333 Elm St #105, Dallas, TX...................................217-871-1956
Hartman, Daniel/409 W Hwy 3040 #602, Louisville, TX.......................214-315-1740
Haverfield, Mary/3333 Elm St #105, Dallas, TX.................................214-871-1956
Head, Ron/4835 LBJ Freeway, Dallas, TX..214-239-6529
High, Richard/4500 Montrose #D, Houston, TX..................................713-521-2772
Holden, William/2231 Nashua, Stafford, TX.......................................713-449-0765
Huey, Kenneth/5320 Richard Ave, Dallas, TX....................................214-821-3042

JKL

James, Marilyn/7 Dunlin Meadow, The Woodlands, TX.......................713-292-7529
Jenkins, Bill/3000 McKinney, Dallas, TX...214-744-4421
Jones, Marilyn/7 Dunlin Meadow Court, The Woodlands, TX................713-292-7529
Jones, Rusty/2312 Heatherworks Way, Carrollton, TX.........................214-306-3835
Kaplan, Kari/1507 W Lynn St, Austin, TX..512-476-6876
Karas, G Brian/4126 North 34th St, Phoenix, AZ................................602-956-5666
Kasnot, Keith/9228 N 29th St, Phoenix, AZ.......................................602-482-6501
Kenny, Kathleen/815 N First Ave #1, Phoenix, AZ..............................602-252-2332
Kenyon, Liz/4225 N 36th St #6, Phoenix, AZ.....................................602-954-8824
Kinkopf, Kathleen/, Dallas, TX..214-324-4801
Kirkman, Rick/PO Box 11816, Phoenix, AZ.......................................602-257-1634
Knox, David/2424 N Rose, Mesa, AZ...602-827-9339
Krejca, Gary/1203 S Ashe Ave, Tempe, AZ.......................................602-829-0946
Kriebel, Nancy/354 Los Lentes Rd NE, Los Lunas, NM........................505-865-6428
Kubricht, Mary Charles/637 Hawthorne, Houston, TX.........................713-522-1862
Lapsley, Bob/3707 Nottingham, Houston, TX.....................................713-667-4393
Lewis, Maurice/3704 Harper St, Houston, TX.....................................713-664-1807
Lindlof, Ed/603 Carolyn Ave, Austin, TX...512-472-0195
Lisieski, Peter/2921 N Pecan St, Nacogdoches, TX 409-564-4244

MNOP

MacFarland, Jean/126 Martinez St, Santa Fe, NM.............................505-983-2226
MacPherson, Kevin/4160 N Craftsman Ct #202, Scottsdale, AZ 602-423-1500
Maloney, Dave/637 Hawthorne, Houston, TX....................................713-522-1862

Martini, John/8742 Welles Dale, San Antonio, TX........512-699-9318
McClain, Lynn/8730 Vinewood, Dallas, TX 214-321-9374
McCullough, Greg/5203 Villa Del Mar Ave #104, Arlington, TX.......817-472-5173
McCullough, Lendy/111 E Santa Fe Ave #2, Santa Fe, NM 505-982-1964
McDonald, Mercedes/3232 McKinney #1260, Dallas, TX........214-855-0055
McElhaney, Gary/5205 Airport Blvd #201, Austin, TX........512-451-3986
McGar, Michael/3330 Irwindell Blvd, Dallas, TX........214-339-0672
Miller, Lyle/3100 Carlisle St #112, Dallas, TX........214-871-1195
Mosberg, Hilary/3232 McKinney #1260, Dallas, TX........214-855-0055
Nelson, John/936 W Catalina Dr, Phoenix, AZ........602-279-1131
Osiecki, Lori L/123 W 2nd St, Mesa, AZ........602-962-5233
Parker, Curtis/4160 N Craftsman Ct #202, Scottsdale, AZ........602-423-1500
Pendleton, Nancy/4160 N Craftsman Ct #202, Scottsdale, AZ........602-423-1500
Phillips, Barry/128 N Clark St, Burleson, TX........817-295-2007
Pietzsch, Steve/3057 Larry Drive, Dallas, TX 214-279-8851
Poli, Kristina/4211 Pebblegate Ct, Houston, TX........713-353-6910
Porea, Sean/22715 Imperial Valley #1702, Houston, TX........713-821-5159
Porfirio, Guy/2310 E 6th St, Tuscon, AZ........602-323-0518
Powell, Terry/8502-D Lyndon Ln, Austin, TX........512-335-0253
Pullen, John/3030 NW Expressway #400, Oklahoma City, OK........405-942-4868
Punchatz, Don Ivan/2605 Westgate Dr, Arlington, TX........817-469-8151

RS

Reed, Lynn Rowe/3333 Elm St #105, Dallas, TX........214-871-1956
Reed, William/2438 W 10th, Dallas, TX........214-333-2884
Reimisch, Robert/545 S 7th Ave, Yuma, AZ........602-783-7732
Ricks, Thom/6511 Adair Dr, San Antonio, TX 512-680-6540
Robins, Mike/637 Hawthorne, Houston, TX........713-522-1862
Rodriguez, Laura/5417 E 8th St, Tucson, AZ........602-625-7700
Rose, Lee/4250 TC Jester Blvd, Houston, TX........713-686-4799
Ross, Eileen/6736 N 11th St, Phoenix, AZ........602-234-1598
Salem, Kay/13418 Splintered Oak, Houston, TX........713-469-0996
Sanchez, Pat/8603 Baumgarten, Dallas, TX........214-328-2942
Senkarik, Mickey/PO Box 104, Helotes, TX........512-695-9327
Shaw, Robin/3730 Kirby #1150, Houston, TX........713-520-5715
Singleton, Bill/809 W Wedwick St, Tucson, AZ........602-294-1667
Sketch Pad/2605 Westgate Dr, Arlington, TX........817-469-8151
Skistmas, Jim/2730 N Stemmons Frwy #400, Dallas, TX........214-630-2574
Slattery, Jack/5911 Inwood #4, Houston, TX........713-785-6764
Smith, James Noel/1011 North Clinton, Dallas, TX 214-946-4255
Smithson, David/3760 E Presidio, Tucson, AZ........602-323-8651
Stribling-Sutherland, Kelly/933 East Harpole, Argyle, TX........214-855-0055

TVWY

Thelan, Mary/5907 Llano, Dallas, TX........214-827-8073
Tomas, Luis/419 E Continental Dr, Tempe, AZ........602-945-6515
Tracy, Libba/329 W Vernon Ave, Phoenix, AZ........602-254-8232
Turk, Stephen/3525 Mockingbird Lane, Dallas, TX........214-521-5156
VAS Communications/4800 N 22nd St, Phoenix, AZ........602-955-1000
Verzaal, Dale/2445 E Pebble Beach, Tempe, AZ........602-839-5536
Waltman, Lynne/PO Box 470889, Ft Worth, TX........817-738-1545
Walton, Paul R/8602 Santa Clara, Dallas, TX........214-327-7889
Warner, Michele/1011 North Clinton, Dallas, TX........214-946-4255
Washington, Bill/5114 Blanco Rd #1, San Antonio, TX 512-340-0021
Weakley, Mark/105 N Alamo #618, San Antonio, TX........512-222-9543
Williams, Michall Janes/546 S Country Club, Mesa, AZ........602-461-8220
Wilson, Raymond/2120 Arthur Dr, Ft Worth, TX........817-293-0093
Yost, Mo/2008 Laws St #1A, Dallas, TX........214-720-4024

ROCKY MTN

ABCD

Alavezos, Gus/2215 Ptarmigan, Colorado Springs, CO 719-528-6821
Alexander, Hugh/3655 S Verbena St #G201, Denver, CO........303-796-9208
Anderson, Jon/1465 Ellendale Ave, Logan, UT........801-752-8936
Arnold, Jean/1220 East 400 South, Salt Lake City, UT........801-582-4148
Botero, Kirk/396 Fifth St, Idaho Falls, ID........208-524-3959
Boyer, Gene/416 S Logan St, Denver, CO........303-778-7527
Christensen, James C/656 West 550 South, Orem, UT 801-224-6237
Colvin, Rob/1351 N 1670 W, Farmington, UT........801-451-6858
Dolack, Monte/132 W Front St, Missoula, MT........406-549-3248
Donahue, Michael/PO Box 26090, Colorado Springs, CO 719-591-1958
Donovan, David/437 Engel Ave, Henderson, NV........702-564-3598

FGH

Farley, Malcolm/6823 Swadley Ct, Arvada, CO 303-420-9135
French, Bob/8304 W 71st Ave, Arvada, CO........303-966-4768
Gordon, David/2040 Polk St, San Francisco, CA........415-681-6268
Hardiman, Miles/30 Village Dr, Littleton, CO........303-798-9143
Harris, Ralph/PO Box 1091, Sun Valley, ID........208-726-8077
Heiner, Joe & Kathy/850 N Grove Dr, Alpine, UT........801-756-6444
Hirokowa, Masami/3144 W 26th Ave, Denver, CO........303-458-1381
Ho, Quang/1553 Platte St #306, Denver, CO........303-477-4574
Hoffman, Kate/822 W Oak Street, Ft Collins, CO........303-493-1492
Hull, Richard/776 W 3500 South, Bountiful, UT........801-298-1632

KLMN

Kaemmer, Gary/1724 Ogden, Denver, CO........303-832-1579
Labadie, Ed/2309 Mt View #130, Boise, ID........208-377-2447
Lane, Tammy/PO Box 212, Aspen, CO........303-925-9213
Millard, Dennis/3345 S 300 W #A, Salt Lake City, UT........801-485-9782
Miller Group Ltd/250 Bell St #230, Reno, NV (P 34) **702-333-9009**
Morrison, Kathy/775 E Panama Dr, Littleton, CO........303-798-0424
Neeper Illustration & Concept Inc/737 Clarkson, Denver, CO 303-860-1857
Nelsen, Randy/15243 W Bayaud Ct, Golden, CO........303-278-9166
Nelson, Will/1517 W Hays, Boise, ID (P 38) **208-345-3131**
Norby, Carol H/192 South 600 East, Alpine, UT........801-756-1096

PRST

Peterson, Marty/918 55th St, Boulder, CO........303-499-0900
Price, Jeannette/1164 E 820 N, Provo, UT........801-377-3958
Ragland, Greg/2106 Lucky John Dr, Park City, UT........801-645-9232
Regester, Sheryl/PO Box 478, Silver Plume, CO........303-569-3374
Roush, Ragan/745 Poplar Ave, Boulder, CO........303-440-6582
Sauter, Ron/16738 E Crestline Ln, Denver, CO........303-680-5636
Strawn, Susan/1216 W olive St, Ft Collins, CO........303-493-0679
Sullivan, John/912 S Telluride St, Aurora, CO........303-671-9257
Twede, Brian L/435 S 300 E, Salt Lake City, UT........801-534-1459

UVWZ

Uhl, David/1501 Boulder, Denver, CO........303-860-7070
Valero, Wayne/11244 Corona Dr, North Glen, CO........303-452-3468
Van Schelt, Perry L/4495 Balsam Ave, Salt Lake City, UT........801-266-7097
Weller, Don/2240 Monarch Dr, Park City, UT........801-649-9859
Whitesides, Kim/PO Box 2189, Park City, UT........801-649-0490
Winborg, Larry/464 South, 275 East, Farmington, UT........801-451-5310
Zilberts, Ed/7249 S Perry Park Blvd, Larkspur, CO........303-220-5040

WEST COAST

A

Abe, George/2819 First Ave #240, Seattle,
WA (P 10) **206-443-0326**
Ace, Katherine/50 Claremont Ave, Orinda, CA 415-254-0705
Adaberry, Craig/1812 Wallam St, Los Angeles, CA........213-227-9224
Addad, Roland/2435 Polk St #21, San Francisco, CA........415-474-3763
Aguilar, Kevin/900 Oxford Dr, Redlands, CA........714-793-1126
Aizawa, Kaz/95 Hurlbut #11, Pasadena, CA........818-441-3306
Ajern, Larry/1212 22nd St, Sacramento, CA 916-442-5654
Akers, Deborah/21 Lafayette Cir #201, Lafayette, CA........415-283-7793
Alleman, Annie/1183 E Main St #E, El Cajon, CA........619-495-2554
Allen, Mark/9605 Sepulveda #5, Los Angeles, CA........818-894-9123
Allen, Pat/131 W Portola Ave, Los Altos, CA........416-941-3570
Allison, Gene/1232 Glen Lake Ave #314, Brea, CA........213-690-8382
Alvin, John/15942 Londelius, Sepulveda, CA........213-471-0232
Ambler, Barbara Hoopes/2769 Nipoma St, San Diego, CA........619-222-7535
Amit, Emmanuel/4322 Sunset Ave, Montrose, CA........213-249-1739
Anderson, Kevin/1267 Orkney Ln, Cardiff, CA........619-753-8410
Anderson, Sara/3131 Western Ave #51, Seattle, WA........206-285-1520
Anderson, Terry/5902 W 85th Pl, Los Angeles, CA........213-645-8469
Angel, Scott/21051 Barbados Circle, Huntington Bch, CA........714-557-5090
Ansley, Frank/801 Minnesota #14, San Francisco, CA........415-777-1941
Anthony, Mitchell/960 Maddux Dr, Palo Alto, CA........415-494-3240
Archey, Rebecca/80 Wellington/Box 307, Ross, CA........415-456-7711

Arkle, Dave/259 W Orange Grove, Pomona, CA...................................714-865-2967
Arruda, Richard/6010 Wilshire Blvd #505, Los Angeles, CA.................213-931-7449
Arshawsky, David/9401 Alcott St, Los Angeles, CA............................213-276-6058
Ash, Melissa/1329 Taylor St #4, San Francisco, CA............................415-563-0723
Atkins, Bill/PO Box 1091, Laguna Beach, CA....................................714-499-3857
Ayriss, Linda Holt/1700 E Beverly Dr, Pasadena, CA..........................818-798-1535

B

Babasin, Pierre/1207 Bunkerhill Dr, Roseville, CA..............................916-782-2956
Backus, Michael/286 E Montecito, Sierra Madre, CA...........................818-449-3840
Baker, Don/2819 First Ave #240, Seattle, WA (P 11) 206-443-0326
Banthien, Barbara/127 Leland, Tiburon, CA.....................................415-381-0842
Banyai, Istvan/13220 Valleyheart Dr #305, Studio City, CA..................818-906-7748
Barbaria, Steve/1990 Third St #400, Sacramento, CA.........................916-442-3200
Barbee, Joel/209 Avinada San Pablo, San Clemente, CA.....................714-498-0067
Barber, Karen/3444 21st St, San Francisco, CA.................................415-647-1256
Barnet, Nancy/8928 Shady Vista Ct, Elk Grove, CA.............................916-685-4147
Bartczak, Peter/PO Box 7709, Santa Cruz, CA..................................408-426-4247
Batcheller, Keith/1438 Calle Cecilia, San Dimas, CA...........................818-331-0439
Battles, Brian/6316 Dissinger Ave, San Diego, CA..............................619-267-3182
Bayless, Steve/2615 S King St/Box 207, Honolulu, HI..........................417-887-8007
Beach, Lou/1114 S Citrus Ave, Los Angeles, CA.................................213-934-7335
Becker, Cary/3443 Wade St, Los Angeles, CA...................................213-390-9595
Becker, Pamela/509 20th Ave, San Francisco, CA..............................415-387-8372
Beckerman, Carol/3950 Long Beach Blvd, Long Beach, CA....................213-595-5896
Beerworth, Roger/1723 S Crescent Hts Blvd, Los Angeles, CA...............213-933-9692
Bell, Karen/1700 Decker Canyon Rd, Malibu, CA................................213-457-2476
Benny, Mike/3704 Norris Ave, Sacramento, CA..................................916-447-8629
Bergendorff, Roger/17106 Sims St #A, Huntington Beach, CA................714-840-7665
Bettoli, Delana/737 Vernon Ave, Venice, CA.....................................213-396-0296
Biers, Nanette/123 Willow Ave, Corte Madera, CA...............................415-668-6080
Bilmes, Semyon/460 Rock St, Ashland, OR......................................503-488-0924
Bingham, Sid/2550 Kemper Ave, La Crescenta, CA.............................818-957-0163
Biomedical Illustrations/804 Columbia St, Seattle, WA.........................206-682-8197
Birnbaum, Dianne/17301 Elsinore Circle, Huntington Beach, CA.............714-847-7631
Bjorkman, Steve/2402 Michelson, Irvine, CA.....................................714-261-1411
Blackshear, Tom/1428 Elm Dr, Novato, CA.......................................415-897-9486
Blair, Barry/27461 Calle Arroyo #207, San Juan Capistrno, CA...............714-248-2527
Blank, Jerry/1048 Lincoln Ave, San Jose, CA....................................408-289-9095
Blechman, Laurel/7853 Mammoth Ave, Panorama City, CA...................818-785-7904
Blonder, Ellen/91 Woodbine Dr, Mill Valley, CA..................................415-388-9158
Boddy, William/609 N 10th St, Sacramento, CA.................................916-443-5001
Boge, Garrett/6606 Soundview Dr, Gig Harbor, WA.............................206-851-5158
Bohn, Richard/595 W Wilson St, Costa Mesa, CA...............................714-548-6669
Bolourchian, Flora/12485 Rubens Ave, Los Angeles, CA......................213-827-8457
Booth, George/950 Klish Way, Del Mar, CA.......................................203-227-7806
Booth, Margot/11604 104th Ave NE, Kirkland, WA..............................206-820-2047
Borders, Jane/3632 Kalsman Dr #2, Los Angeles, CA..........................213-836-7598
Bowles, Doug/716 Sanchez St, San Francisco, CA..............................415-285-8267
Bradley, Barbara/750 Wildcat Canyon Rd, Berkeley, CA.......................415-673-4200
Braun, Marty/271 Otsego Ave, San Francisco, CA...............................415-334-4106
Brice, Jeff/2819 First Ave #240, Seattle, WA (P 12) 206-443-0326
Bringham, Sherry/244 Ninth St, San Francisco, CA..............................415-621-2992
Broad, David/100 Golden Hinde Blvd, San Rafael, CA...........................415-479-5505
Brown, Bill & Assoc/1531 Pontius Ave #200, Los Angeles, CA...............213-652-9380
Brown, Bill Illus/4621 Teller #108, Newport Beach, CA..........................714-474-6002
Brown, Michael David/PO Box 45969, Los Angeles, CA........................213-379-7254
Brown, Rick/1502 N Maple, Burbank, CA...818-842-0726
Brown, Susan/2456 Riverplace, Los Angeles, CA...............................213-662-5035
Brownd, Elizabeth/6955 Fernhill Dr, Malibu, CA..................................213-457-4816
Browne, Rob/541 Winterberry Way, San Jose, CA..............................408-255-8843
Brugger, Bob/1132 Loma #4, Hermosa Beach, CA.............................213-372-0135
Buckley, Peggy/2250 Waimao Rd, Honolulu, HI.................................808-488-7647
Buechler, Barbara/13929 Marquessa Way #108A, Marina
Del Ray, CA...213-827-5106
Buerge, Bill/734 Basin Dr, Topanga, CA..213-455-3181
Bull, Michael/2350 Taylor, San Francisco, CA....................................415-776-7471
Burgio, Trish/8205 Santa Monica Blvd, Los Angeles, CA......................213-657-1469
Burns, Rhonda/6010 Wilshire Blvd #505, Los Angeles, CA....................213-931-7449
Burnside, John E/4204 Los Feliz Blvd, Los Angeles, CA.......................213-665-8913
Busacca, Mark/269 Corte Madera Ave, Mill Valley, CA..........................415-381-9048
Butler, Callie/2201 San Diguito Ave, Del Mar, CA................................619-755-5539

C

Cagle, Daryl...805-967-4529
Caldwell, Kirk/66 Broadway, San Francisco, CA.................................415-398-7553

Calsbeek, Craig/1316 3rd St Promenade, Santa Monica, CA.................213-394-6037
Camarena, Miguel/445 W Lexington Dr, Glendale, CA.........................818-246-8081
Cantor, Jeremy/1441 12th St #B, Manhattan Beach, CA......................213-545-9826
Cappello, Fred/58 Brookmont St, Irvine, CA......................................714-559-5050
Capstone Studios/3408 W Burbank Blvd, Burbank, CA........................818-985-8181
Carroll, Justin/1118 Chautauqua, Pacific Palisades, CA.........................213-459-3104
Case, Carter/3921 Palisades Place West, Tacoma, WA.........................206-566-9292
Casey, Sean/1705 Belmont Ave #300, Seattle, WA.............................206-329-4273
Ceccarelli, Chris/3427 Folsom Blvd, Sacramento, CA...........................916-455-0569
Chaffee, James/540 Colusa Way, sacramento, CA..............................916-344-1450
Chan, Ron/32 Grattan St, San Francisco, CA....................................415-681-0646
Chang, Warren/15120 Magnolia Blvd #211, Sherman Oaks, CA.............818-783-4573
Chase, Margo/2255 Bancroft Ave, Los Angeles, CA.............................213-668-1055
Chewning, Randy/13051 Springarden Ln, Westminster, CA....................213-433-7665
Chiodo, Joe/2556 Chicago St #40, San Diego, CA.............................619-275-6383
Chorney, Steven/18686 Cumnock Pl, Northridge, CA...........................818-366-7779
Chouinard, Roger/1233 S La Cienega Blvd, Los Angeles, CA.................213-855-8855
Christman, Michael/104 S El Molino, Pasadena, CA.............................818-793-1358
Christopher, Tom/6010 Wilshire Blvd #505, Los Angeles, CA.................213-931-7449
Chui, John/1962 San Pablo Ave #3, Berkeley, CA...............................415-841-2238
Chun, Milt/816 Queen St, Honolulu, HI...808-537-1406
Chung, Helen/94 Ocean Park #2, Santa Monica, CA...........................213-451-2078
Clark, Tim/8800 Venice Blvd, Los Angeles, CA..................................213-202-1044
Clarke, Greg/844 9th St #10, Santa Monica, CA.................................213-395-7958
Clemons, David/1425 East Orange Grove Blvd, Pasadena, CA..............818-797-8998
Coe, Wayne/12623 C Sherman Way, N Hollywood, CA.......................818-764-7918
Cohen, Elaine/2819 First Ave #240, Seattle, WA.................................206-443-0326
Cole, Dick/25 Hotaling Pl, San Francisco, CA....................................415-986-8163
Commander, Bob/8800 Venice Blvd, Los Angeles, CA..........................213-202-6765
Conrad, Jon/85 N Raymond, Pasadena, CA.....................................818-795-6460
Consani, Chris/2601 Walnut Ave, Manhattan Beach, CA......................213-546-6622
Cook, Anne/96 Rollingwood Dr, San Rafael, CA.................................415-454-5799
Coons, Byron/Pier 33 North, San Francisco, CA.................................415-956-4750
Cooper, Daniel E/17346 Chatsworth St #112, Granada Hills, CA............818-368-3919
Cormier, Wil/911 E Elizabeth St, Pasadena, CA.................................818-797-7999
Court, Rob/4621 Teller #108, Newport Beach, CA...............................714-474-6002
Creative Source/6671 W Sunset Blvd #1519, Los Angeles, CA..............213-462-5731
Criss, Keith/1005 Camelia St, Berkeley, CA......................................415-525-8703
Crowther, Katherine-Rose/332 Lennox #6, Oakland, CA.......................415-465-7134
Cuneo, John/120 Parnassus #1D, San Francisco, CA..........................415-664-3083
Curtis, Cheryl/821 Madison Ave, Escondido, CA.................................619-713-8443
Curtis, Todd/2032 14th St #7, Santa Monica, CA................................213-452-0738

D

Dalaney, Jack/3030 Pualei Circle #317, Honolulu, HI............................808-924-7450
Darold, Dave/PO Box 5000, Davis, CA..916-758-1379
Darrow, David R/9655 Derald Rd, Santee, CA....................................619-697-7408
Darrow, Whitney/950 Klish Way, Del Mar, CA....................................203-227-7806
DaVault, Elaine/4621 Teller #108, Newport Beach, CA..........................714-474-6002
Davidson, Kevin/505 S Grand St, Orange, CA....................................714-633-9061
Davis, David M/737 SE Sandy Blvd, Portland, OR...............................503-235-6878
Davis, Diane/4621 Teller #108, Newport Beach, CA.............................714-474-6002
Davis, Jeff/13343 Victory Blvd #12, Van Nuys, CA..............................818-764-5002
Day, Adrian/2022 Jones St, San Francisco, CA...................................415-928-0457
Day, Bruce/8141 Firth Green, Buena Park, CA....................................714-994-0338
Dayal, Antar/1596 Wright St, Santa Rosa, CA...................................707-544-1596
Deal, Jim/3451 24th Ave West #120, Seattle, WA...............................206-285-2986
Dean, Bruce/23211 Leonora Dr, Woodland Hills, CA............................818-716-5632
Dean, Donald/2560 Bancroft Way #14, Berkley, CA............................415-644-1139
DeAnda, Ruben/550 Oxford St #407, Chula Vista, CA..........................619-427-7765
Dearstyne, John/22982 LaCadena Dr, Laguna Hills, CA........................714-768-5619
Deaver, Georgia/123 Townsend #410, San Francisco, CA.....................415-974-6173
Dedini, Eldon/950 Klish Way, Del Mar, CA..203-227-7806
DeLeon, Cam/1440 Veteran Ave #366, Los Angeles, CA.......................213-477-0776
Dellorco, Chris/8575 Wonderland Ave, Los Angeles, CA.......................213-650-1370
Dennewill, Jim/5823 Autry Ave, Lakewood, CA..................................213-920-3895
Devaud, Jacques/1165 Bruin Tr/Box 260, Fawnskin, CA........................714-866-4563
Dickey, Burrell/4975 Elmwood Dr, San Jose, CA................................408-866-0820
Dietz, James/2203 13th Ave E, Seattle, WA......................................206-325-2857
Dietz, Mike/PO Box 3145, San Clemente, CA....................................714-496-3021
Diffenderfer, Ed/32 Cabernet Ct, Lafayette, CA..................................415-254-8235
Dillon, Tom/1986 Stonecroft Ct, Westlake Village, CA...........................805-495-5116
Dismukes, John Taylor/2820 Westshire Dr, Hollywood, CA....................213-467-2787
Doe, Bart/3300 Temple St, Los Angeles, CA.....................................213-383-9707
Doty, Eldon/3435 260th Ave NE, Redmond, WA................................206-868-9550
Dowlen, James/PO Box 475, Cotati, CA..707-579-1535
Downs, Richard/24294 Saradella Court, Murrieta, CA...........................714-677-3452

Duell, Nancy/1042 Oakwood Ave, Venice, CA 213-399-6903
Duffus, Bill/1745 Wagner, Pasadena, CA 818-792-7921
Dumaway, Suzanne Shimek/10333 Chrysanthemum Ln, L A, CA 213-279-2006
Durfee, Tom/25 Hotaling Pl, San Francisco, CA 415-781-0527

E

Eastman, Jody/3455 'D' St, LaVerne, CA 714-593-6501
Eastside Illustration/737 SE Sandy Blvd, Portland, OR 503-235-6878
Eckart, Chuck/PO Box 1090, Point Reyes Sta, CA 415-663-9016
Ecklund, Rae/14 Wilmot St, San Francisco, CA 415-923-0741
Eddington, Michael/14333 Van Nuys Blvd #29, Arletta, CA 818-899-7208
Edelson, Wendy/215 Second Ave S, Seattle, WA 206-728-1300
Eden, Terry/510 Emerson, Palo Alto, CA 415-326-5263
Egan, Tim/12200 Emelita St, N Hollywood, CA 818-995-4303
Ellescas, Richard/321 N Martel, Hollywood, CA 213-939-7396
Ellmore, Dennis/3245 Orange Ave, Long Beach, CA 213-424-9379
Elstad, Ron/18253 Solano River Ct, Fountain Valley, CA 714-964-7753
Endicott, James R/3509 N College, Newberg, OR 503-538-5466
Ericksen, Marc/1045 Sansome St #306, San Francisco, CA 415-362-1214
Erickson, Kernie/Box 2175, Mission Viejo, CA 714-831-2818
Erramouspe, David/8800 Venice Blvd, Los Angeles, CA 213-558-4914
Etow, Carole/18224 Herbold St, Northridge, CA 818-772-7501
Evans, Bill/101 Yesler #502, Seattle, WA 206-447-1600
Evans, Robert/1045 Sansome St #306, San Francisco, CA 415-397-5322
Evenson, Stan/445 Overland Ave, Culver City, CA 213-204-1771
Everitt, Betsy/2090 Broadway #805, San Francisco, CA 415-885-6734

F

Farrell, Rick/3918 N Stevens, Tacoma, WA 206-752-8814
Farris, Joe/950 Klish Way, Del Mar, CA 203-227-7806
Fennel Graphics/1530 Ellis St #411, Concorde, CA 415-671-7814
Fijosaki, Tuko/1260 Sundance, San Diego, CA 619-484-2211
Finger, John/1581 Boulevard Way, Walnut Creek, CA 415-945-0612
Fitting, Cynthia/2131 1/2 Pine St, San Francisco, CA 415-567-3353
Florczak, Robert/3408 W Burbank Blvd, Burbank, CA 818-985-8181
Forrest, William/817 12th St #2, Santa Monica, CA 213-458-9114
Fox, Mark/3006 Gough #102, San Francisco, CA 415-673-4811
Fraze, Jon/14160 Red Hill Ave #89, Tustin, CA 714-731-8493
Frazee, Marla/1199 N Holliston, Pasadena, CA 818-797-0612
French, Lisa/1069 Gardenia Ave, Long Beach, CA 213-599-0361
Friel, Bryan/5648 Case Ave #1, N Hollywood, CA 818-769-3140
Fulp, Jim/50 Divisadero St #50, San Francisco, CA 415-621-5462
Funkhouser, Kristen/716 Sanchez St, San Francisco, CA 415-285-8267

G

Galloway, Nixon/755 Marine Ave, Manhattan Beach, CA 213-545-7709
Garcia, Manuel/716 Sanchez St, San Francisco, CA 415-285-8267
Garner, Tracy/1830 S Robertson Blvd, Los Angeles, CA 213-204-1771
Garvie, Ben/1535 Green St #207, San Francisco, CA 415-441-1623
Garvie, Ben/6797 Lipmann Ave, San Diego, CA 619-452-0469
Gay, Garry/109 Minna St #567, San Francisco, CA 415-626-6005
Gayles, James/2200 Powell St/Twr 2 #325, Emeryville, CA 415-653-3753
Gellos, Nancy/20 Armour St, Seattle, WA 206-285-5838
Germain, Frank/2870 Calle Heraldo, San Clemente, CA 714-498-7234
Gerns, Laurie/6010 Wilshire Blvd #505, Los Angeles, CA 213-931-7449
Giambarba, Paul/5851 Vine Hill Rd, Sebastapol, CA 707-829-8895
Gin, Byron/190 Cervantes Blvd #7, San Francisco, CA 415-267-3087
Girvin, Tim Design/1601 Second Ave 5th Fl, Seattle, WA 206-623-7808
Gisko, Max/2629 Wakefield Dr, Belmont, CA 415-595-1893
Glass, Randy/2706 Creston Dr, Los Angeles, CA 213-462-2706
Gleeson, Tony/2525 Hyperion Ave #4, Los Angeles, CA 213-668-2704
Gleis, Linda/6671 Sunset Blvd #1519, Los Angeles, CA 213-461-6376
Glover, Gary/75 Brookview, Dana Point, CA 714-248-0232
Goddard, John/2774 Los Alisos Dr, Fallbrook, CA 619-728-5473
Goddard, Lon/190 Cervantes Blvd #7, San Francisco, CA 415-267-3087
Goethals, Raphaelle/1674 Rotary Dr, Los Angeles, CA 213-666-3189
Goldstein, Howard/7031 Aldea Ave, Van Nuys, CA 818-987-2837
Gomez, Ignacio/812 Kenneth Rd, Glendale, CA 818-243-2838
Gonzales, Danilo/1760 State St #21, S Pasadena, CA 818-441-2787
Gordon, Emily/2022 Jones St, San Francisco, CA 415-928-0457
Gottlieg, Dale/2821 Victor St, Belingham, WA 206-647-2598
Grant, Stan/432 Misson St #A, South Pasadena, CA 818-799-4697
Graphic Designers Inc/3325 Wilshire Blvd #610, Los Angeles, CA 213-381-3977
Gray, Steve/307 Bayview Dr, Manhattan Beach, CA 213-372-7844
Greenberg, Sheldon/218 Second Ave, San Francisco, CA 415-221-4970
Griffith, Linda/13972 Hilo Ln, Santa Ana, CA 714-832-8536
Grossman, Myron/12 S Fair Oaks Ave, Pasadena, CA 818-795-6992
Grove, David/382 Union St, San Francisco, CA 415-433-2100
Guidice, Rick/9 Park Ave, Los Gatos, CA 408-354-7787
Guitteau, Jud/2506 NE 49th St, Portland, OR 503-282-0445
Gunn, Robert/183 N Martell Ave #240, Los Angeles, CA 213-934-3395
Gunsaullus, Marty/716 Sanchez St, San Francisco, CA 415-285-8267
Gurvin, Abe/31341 Holly Dr, Laguna Beach, CA 714-499-2001

H

Haasis, Michael/941 N Croft Ave, Los Angeles, CA 213-654-5412
Hagner, Dirk/30723 Calla Chueca, San Juan Capistrano, CA 714-493-5596
Haig, Nancy A/2645 Sacramento #3A, San Francisco, CA 415-921-2415
Hale, Bruce/421 Bryant St, San Francisco, CA 415-882-9695
Hall, Patricia/5402 Ruffin Rd #103, San Diego, CA 619-268-0176
Hally, Greg/911 Victoria Dr, Arcadia, CA 818-574-0288
Hamagami, John/11409 Kingsland St, Los Angeles, CA 213-390-6911
Hamilton, Pamela/4900 Overland Ave #216, Culver City, CA 213-837-1784
Hammond, Cris/410 Johnson St, Sausalito, CA 415-332-7556
Hampton, Gerry Inc/PO Box 2792, Seal Beach, CA 714-840-8239
Handelsman, Bud/950 Klish Way, Del Mar, CA 619-259-5774
Hanna, Gary/3827 La Crescenta, La Cresenta, CA 818-249-1380
Hannah, Halsted (Craig)/2525 8th St #14, Berkeley, CA 415-841-2273
Hardesty, Debra S/1017 Vallejo Way, Sacramento, CA 916-446-1824
Harris, Michael/Future Fonts/5841 Columbus Ave, Van Nuys, CA 818-908-1237
Hasselle, Bruce/8691 Heil Rd, Westminster, CA 714-848-2924
Haydock, Robert/49 Shelley Dr, Mill Valley, CA 415-383-6986
Hays, Jim/3809 Sunnyside Blvd, Marysville, WA 206-334-7596
Hegedus, James C/11850 Otsego, N Hollywood, CA 818-985-9966
Heimann, Jim/1548 18th St, Santa Monica, CA 213-828-1041
Heinecke, Stu/9665 Wilshire Blvd #400, Los Angeles, CA 213-837-3212
Heinz, Michael/721 E Maxwell, Lathrop, CA 209-858-5220
Hendricks, Steve/1050 Elsiemae Dr, Boulder Creek, CA 408-338-6639
Hernandez, Oscar/5708 Case Ave #3, N Hollywood, CA 818-506-4541
Herrero, Lowell/433 Bryant St, San Francisco, CA 415-543-6400
Hershey, John/2350 Taylor St, San Francisco, CA 415-928-6553
Hewitson, Jennifer/859 Sandcastle Dr, Cardiff, CA 619-944-6154
Hienze, Mitchell/40751 Witherspoon Terrace, Fremont, CA 415-657-8124
Hilliard, Fred/5425 Crystal Springs Dr NE, Bainbridge Island, WA 206-842-6003
Hilton-Putnam, Denise/4758 Jean Dr, San Diego, CA 619-565-7568
Hinton, Hank/6118 W 6th St, Los Angeles, CA 213-938-9893
Hitch, Jeff/3001 Redhill Ave #6-210, Costa Mesa, CA 714-432-1802
Hobb, David/8818 Lamesa Blvd, Lamesa, CA 619-469-8106
Hodges, Ken/12401 Bellwood Rd, Los Alamitos, CA 213-431-4343
Hoff, Terry/1525 Grand Ave, Pacifica, CA 415-359-4081
Hogan, Jamie (Ms)/2858 Bush St, San Francisco, CA 415-929-0795
Hohman, Suzie/PO Box 594, Davis, CA 916-756-3016
Holder, Jimmy/920-K N 6th St, Burbank, CA 818-563-2162
Holmes, Matthew/126 Mering Ct, Sacramento, CA 916-484-6080
Homad, Jewell/1250 Long Beach Ave #309, Los Angeles, CA 213-627-6270
Hoover, Anne Nelson/8457 Paseo Del Ocaso, La Jolla, CA 714-454-4294
Hopkins, Chris/5408 135th Pl SW, Edmonds, WA 206-745-3397
Hopkins, Christopher/2932 Wilshire #202, Santa Monica, CA 818-985-8181
Hord, Bob/1760 Monrovia #B-9, Costa Mesa, CA 714-631-3890
Hosmer, Rick/720 West Mallon Ave #E, Spokane, WA 509-326-6769
Hovland, Gary/3408 Crest Dr, Manhattan Beach, CA 213-545-6808
Howe, Philip/540 1st Ave S, Seattle, WA 206-682-3453
Hubbard, Roger/19551 Green Mountain Dr, Newhall, CA 805-852-8875
Hudson, Dave/4621 Teller #108, Newport Beach, CA 714-474-6002
Hudson, Ron/725 Auahi St, Honolulu, HI 808-536-2692
Huhn, Tim/4718 Kester Ave #208, Sherman Oaks, CA 818-986-2352
Hull, John/2356 Fair Park Ave, Los Angeles, CA 213-254-4647
Hulsey, Kevin/3141 Hollywood Dr, Los Angeles, CA 818-501-7105
Hume, Kelly/912 S Los Robles, Pasadena, CA 818-793-8344
Humphries, Michael/11241 Martha Ann Dr, Los Alamitos, CA 213-493-3323
Hunt, Robert/107 Crescent Rd, San Anselmo, CA 415-824-1824
Hunt, Stan/950 Klish Way, Del Mar, CA 203-227-7806
Hunter, Alan/328-B Paseo De La Playa, Redondo Beach, CA 213-373-9468
Huston, Steve/85 N Raymond Ave #250, Pasadena, CA 818-578-0140
Huxtable, John/416 S 7th St, Burbank, CA 818-841-7114
Hyatt, John/80 Wellington Ave/Box 307, Ross, CA 415-456-7711

IJ

Ibusuki, James/2920 Rosanna St, Los Angeles, CA 818-244-1645
Irvine, Rex John/6026 Dovetail Dr, Agoura, CA 818-991-2522
Ishioka, Haruo/6010 Wilshire Blvd #505, Los Angeles, CA 213-931-7449

Ito, Joel/505 NW 185th St, Beaverton, OR....503-645-1141
Jacobs, Ellen Going/312 90th St, Daly City, CA....415-994-8800
Jacobsen, Gary/101 Yesler #502, Seattle, WA....206-441-0606
Jenkins, Mary/584 Hensley Ave #3, San Bruno, CA....415-589-2830
Jenks, Aleta/686 Mandana Blvd, Oakland, CA....415-444-4691
Jensen, David/1641 Merryton Ct, San Jose, CA....408-266-5645
Jew, Anson/PO Box 191006, Sacramento, CA....916-736-3183
Johnson, BE/297 Fairview St, Laguna Beach, CA....714-497-6717
Johnson, Iskra/1605 12th St, Seattle, WA....206-323-8256
Jones, Brent A/328 Hays St, San Francisco, CA....415-626-8337
Jones, Dan/716 Sanchez St, San Francisco, CA....415-285-8267
Jones, Steve/1081 Nowita Pl, Venice, CA....213-396-9111
Jordan, Dick/3500 Joy Lane, Shingle Springs, CA....916-677-2799
Jost, Larry/311 NW 77th St, Seattle, WA....206-328-1841
Joy, Pat/1259 Oak Dr, Vista, CA....619-726-2781
Joyner, Eric/425 The Alameda, San Anselmo, CA....415-459-1448
Judd, Jeff/827 1/2 N McCadden Pl, Los Angeles, CA....213-469-0333

K

Kaminski, Roberta-Anna/1802 Cnayon Terrace Ln, Folsom, CA....916-444-2840
Kanner, Catherine/717 Hampden Pl, Pacific Palisades, CA....213-393-7785
Kari, Morgan/22853 Mariano #226, Woodland Hills, CA....818-346-9167
Karwan, Johhny/190 Cervantes Blvd #7, San Francisco, CA....415-267-3087
Kato, R M/85 N Raymond #270, Pasadena, CA....818-356-9990
Keefer, Mel/415 Montana Ave #208, Santa Monica, CA....213-395-1147
Keeling, Gregg Bernard/5955 Harbor Dr, Oakland, CA....415-653-8518
Kenyon, Chris/14 Wilmot, San Francisco, CA....415-923-1363
Kilmer, David/1036 Hayes St, Irvine, CA....714-857-6979
Kimble, David/711 S Flower, Burbank, CA....213-849-1576
King, Heather/2622 1st Street #105, Napa, CA....707-226-1232
Kitchell, Joyce/2755 Eagle St, San Diego, CA....619-291-1378
Knutson, Kristin/210 NW 52nd St, Seattle, WA....206-784-5136
Koerber, Nora/1253 Boynton #12, Glendale, CA....818-507-0662
Koester, Michael/272 Gresham, Ashland, OR....503-488-0153
Koulian, Jack/442 W Harvard, Glendale, CA....818-956-5640
Kowalski, Mike/320 Pleasant St, Petaluma, CA....707-769-8613
Kratter, Paul/1128 Sanders Dr, Moraga, CA....415-339-0219
Krogle, Bob/25112 Carolwood St, El Toro, CA....714-951-6790
Kung, Lingta/8378 Denice Lane, West Hills, CA....818-348-3299
Kwan, Jonny/11944 Berrybrook Ct, Moorpark, CA....805-529-6561
Kylberg, Virginia/14 Midhill Dr, Mill Valley, CA....415-332-7443

L

Larson, Ron/940 N Highland Ave, Los Angeles, CA....213-465-8451
Lauderbaugh, Lindah/2002 N Bronson, Los Angeles, CA....213-467-5444
Lawrence, Scott/PO Box 3494, Santa Monica, CA....213-281-1919
Leary, Catherine/1125 S La Jolla Ave, Los Angeles, CA....213-937-8908
Leary, Pat/20707 Timberline, Walnut, CA....213-690-4867
Lee, Warren/88 Meadow Valley Rd, Corte Madera, CA....415-924-0261
Leech, Richard & Associates/725 Filbert St, San Francisco, CA....415-981-4840
Leeds, Beth Whybrow/1335 Main St #103, St Helena, CA....707-963-8426
Leedy, Jeff/190 Pelican Lane, Novato, CA....415-331-1354
Letter Perfect/6606 Soundview Dr, Gig Harbor, WA....206-851-5158
Levikova, Marina/3527 Summerfield Dr, Sherman Oaks, CA....213-285-8320
Levine, Bette/601 N Hayworth Ave, Los Angeles, CA....213-658-6769
Lewis, Dennis/6671 Sunset #1519, Los Angeles, CA....213-463-4490
Liao, Jeff/1630 Calle Vaquero #505, Glendale, CA....818-244-1511
Liao, Sharmen/914 Arroyo Terrace, Alhambra, CA....818-458-7699
Lindsay, Martin/4469 41st St, San Diego, CA....619-281-8851
Livermore, Joanie/1332o NW Marina Way, Portland, OR....503-285-8800
Livingston, Francis/3916 Sacramento St, San Francisco, CA....415-456-7103
Lloyd, Gregory/5534 Red River Dr, San Diego, CA....619-582-3487
Lobenberg, David/2612 J St #8, Sacramento, CA....916-447-1107
Lopez, Rafael/8100 Paseo del Ocaso, La Jolla, CA....619-454-0775
Loveless, Roger/1700 Yosemite #201D, Simi Valley, CA....805-522-0961
Lozano, Henry Jr/3205 Belle River Dr, Hacienda, CA....818-330-2095
Lugo, Lisette/301 S Spruce Ave, S San Francisco, CA....415-588-3375
Lulich, Ted/7033 SW Macadamia Ave #107, Portland, OR....503-245-1951
Lundgren-Ellis, Alvalyn/1343 Thayer Ave, Los Angeles, CA....818-707-0635
Lutzow, Jack A/240 Dolores St #321, San Francisco, CA....415-863-6628
Lyons, Steve/320 Cypress Dr, Fairfax, CA....415-459-7560
Lytle, John/PO Box 5155, Sonora, CA....209-928-4849

M

M Design/2819 First Ave, Seattle, WA....206-443-0326
Machat, Mike/4426 Deseret Dr, Woodland Hills, CA....818-702-9433
MacLeod, Lee/301 Congress Pl, Pasadena, CA....818-799-1775
Magovern, Peg/Pier 33 North, San Francisco, CA....415-956-4750
Mahoney, Jennifer/1099 Folsom St, San Francisco, CA....415-626-7272
Mahoney, Patricia/1414-A 20th Ave, San Francisco, CA....415-661-5915
Majlessi, Heda/1707 Boyleson #207, Seattle, WA....206-323-2694
Manchess, Greg/3217 N 25th St, Takoma, WA....513-433-8383
Manning, Michele/894 Chestnut St, San Francisco, CA....415-771-3088
Marsh, Cynthia/4434 Matilija Ave, Sherman Oaks, CA....818-789-5232
Marshall, Craig/404 Crescent Ave, San Francisco, CA....415-641-1010
Martin, Greg J/3604 Rosemary Ave, Glendale, CA....818-957-5266
Martin, Gregory S/1307 Greenlake Dr, Cardiff, CA....619-753-4073
Martin, Henry/950 Klish Way, Del Mar, CA....203-227-7806
Mason, Hatley N III/817 24th St, Sacramento, CA....916-446-6037
Mathers, Petra/1621 NE Knott St, Portland, OR....503-282-7089
Matthew, David/1145 Columbine Ave, Sunnyvale, CA....408-248-8732
Mattos, John/1546 Grant Ave, San Francisco, CA....415-397-2138
Maydak, Michael S/7310 Joshua Circle, Pleasanton, CA....415-484-4461
Mayeda, Kaz/243 Bickwell #A, Santa Monica, CA....213-452-0054
Mazzetti, Alan/375-A Crescent Ave, San Francisco, CA....415-541-0238
McAllister, Chris/716 Sanchez St, San Francisco, CA....415-285-8267
McCandlish, Mark/PO Box 4053, Big Bear Lake, CA....714-982-1428
McClure, Royce/7316 Pyramid Dr, Los Angeles, CA....213-651-3706
McConnell, Jim/10921 Live Oak Blvd, Live Oak, CA....916-695-1355
McDougall, Scott/712 N 62nd St, Seattle, WA....206-783-1403
McElroy, Darlene/1381 Warner #B, Tustin, CA....714-760-9631
McGinty, Mick/PO Box 687, N Hollywood, CA....818-985-8181
McGowan, Daniel/6318 15th Ave NE, Seattle, WA....206-526-8927
McGraw, Kim/405 S Beverly Dr, Beverly Hills, CA....213-556-0500
McKiernan, James E/2501 Cherry Ave #310, Signal Hill, CA....213-427-1953
McLennan, Connie/1325 Howe Ave #207, Sacramento, CA....916-929-0408
McMahon, Bob/6820 Independence Ave #31, Canoga Park, CA....818-999-4127
Mercado, Vernon/374-A Second Ave, San Francisco, CA....415-386-5469
Merritt, Norman/621 Paseo De Los Reyes, Redondo Beach, CA....213-378-4689
Metz Air Art/2817 E Lincoln Ave, Anaheim, CA....714-630-3071
Meyer, Gary/21725 Ybarra Rd, Woodland Hills, CA....818-992-6974
Meyers, Kristine Everett/5262 Butterwood Cir, Orangevale, CA....916-989-2420
Mezzapelle, Bruno/251 Kearny St #511, San Francisco, CA....415-441-4384
Miller, Gregory/7317 Loch Aleme Ave, Pico Rivera, CA....213-948-2915
Miller, Warren/950 Klish Way, Del Mar, CA....203-227-7806
Mills, Diane Bogush/PO Box 162430, Sacramento, CA....916-454-9286
Millsap, Darrel/1744 6th Ave, San Diego, CA....619-543-0122
Mitchell, Briar Lee/6749 Babcock Ave, North Hollywood, CA....818-982-8594
Mitoma, Tim/4865 Doyle St #9, Emeryville, CA....415-547-1343
Moch, Paul/1414 Oakland Blvd #4, Walnut Creek, CA....415-932-5815
Moline-Kramer, Bobbie /20901 Abalar St, Woodland Hills, CA....818-884-1361
Mollering, David/2250 Caminito Pescado #3, San Diego, CA....619-225-0752
Monahan, Leo/721 S Victory Blvd, Burbank, CA....818-843-6115
Montoya, Ricardo/5416 Agnes Pl, Riverside, CA....714-533-0507
Morrow, JT/220 Cavanaugh Way, Pacifica, CA....415-355-7899
Morse, Bill/173 18th Ave, San Francisco, CA....415-221-6711
Mortensen, Cristine/140 University Ave #102, Palo Alto, CA....415-321-4787
Mortensen, Gordon/140 University Ave #102, Palo Alto, CA....415-321-4787
Mouri, Gary/25002 Reflejo, Mission Viejo, CA....714-951-8136
Moyna, Nancy/1125 6th St #4, Santa Monica, CA....213-458-1291
Mukai, Dennis/CA....213-452-9060
Murphy, Michael/2630 Washington St, Alameda, CA....415-523-8796
Murray, Joe/14531 Big Basin Way, Saratoga, CA....408-867-7520
Muzick, Terra/1805 Pine St #21, San Francisco, CA....415-346-6141

N

Nagata, Mark/1660 11th Ave, San Francisco, CA....415-661-7528
Nagle, Candace/230 S Oakland Ave #C, Pasadena, CA....818-793-0342
Nahas, Margo Zafer/1233 S La Cienega Blvd, Los Angeles, CA....213-855-8855
Nakamura, Joel/221 W Maple Ave, Morovia, CA....818-795-6460
Navarro, Arlene & Larry/1921 Comstock Ave, Los Angeles, CA....213-201-4744
Neila, Anthony/14 Patricia Ln, Mill Valley, CA....415-383-7580
Nelson, Craig/11943 Nugent Dr, Granada Hills, CA....818-363-4494
Nelson, Mike/1836 Woodsdale Ct, Concord, CA....707-746-0800
Nelson, R Kenton/12 South Fair Oaks Ave, Pasadena, CA....818-792-5252
Nelson, Susan/2363 N Fitch Mtn Rd, Healdsburg, CA....707-431-7166
Nelson, Will/716 Montgomery St, San Francisco, CA (P 38)....415-433-1222
Nethery, Susan/1548 18th St, Santa Monica, CA....213-828-1931
Nicholson, Norman/132 Leona Ct, Alamo, CA....415-837-0695
Nielson, Anne/Ave of The Oaks, Canyon Country, CA....805-251-8791
Nikosey, Tom/188 Dapplegrey Rd, Canoga Park, CA....213-937-2994

Nishimura, Masato/39571 Holmstead Ave, North Branch, MN..............612-674-8039
Noble, Larry/PO Box 229, Crestline, CA.................................714-338-5218
Norman, Gary/7825 Manchester Ave #8, Playa Del Rey, CA.................213-578-2191
Nugent, Denise/PO Box 61, Burton, WA....................................206-463-5412
Nunez, Manuel/1018 W 13th St, San Pedro, CA 213-832-2471
Nye, Linda S/2482 Alto Cerro Cir, San Diego, CA 619-272-1305

O

O'Brien, Kathy/401 Alameda del Prado, Navato, CA 415-883-2964
O'Malley, Peg/275 25th Ave, San Francisco, CA 415-725-5231
O'Mary, Tom/8418 Menkar Rd, San Diego, CA 619-578-5361
O'Neil, Sharron/409 Alberto Way #6, Los Gatos, CA 408-354-3816
Oakley, Kevin/1123 N Glen Oaks, Burbank, CA 818-443-6162
Obrero, Rudy/3400 Barham, Los Angeles, CA 213-850-5700
Oden, Richard/PO Box 415, Laguna Beach, CA 714-760-7001
Olson, Rik/749 Circle Court, San Francisco, CA 415-589-4392
Oppenheimer, Jennie/85 Liberty Ship Way #112, Sausalito, CA...........415-331-0834
Orvidas, Ken/832 Evelyn Ave, Albany, CA 415-525-6626
Osborn, Jacqueline/710 Palo Alto, Palo Alto, CA 415-326-2275
Osborn, Stephen/710 Palo Alto, Palo Alto, CA 415-326-2275

P

Pace, Julie/915 Allendale, Los Angeles, CA............................213-931-3630
Padilla, Anthony/624 La Paloma Ave, Alhambra, CA......................818-289-1932
Palay/Beaubois/124 University #200, Palo Alto, CA 415-322-8456
Palermo, David/3359 Calle San Tiheo, Carlsbad, CA.....................619-452-0600
Paluso, Christopher/3217 Sweetwater Springs #89, Rancho
San Diego, CA...619-670-4907
Pansini, Tom/16222 Howland Ln, Huntington Bch, CA.....................714-847-9329
Paris Productions/2207 Garnet, San Diego, CA..........................619-272-4992
Parkinson, Jim/6170 Broadway Terrace, Oakland, CA 415-547-3100
Passey, Kim/115 Hurlbut #17, Pasadena, CA.............................818-441-4384
Pavesich, Vida/1152 Arch St, Berkeley, CA.............................415-528-8233
Peck, Everett/716 Sanchez St, San Francisco, CA.......................415-285-8267
Pederson, Sharleen/101 California St #1107, Santa Montica, CA.........213-306-7847
Peringer, Stephen/17808 184th Ave NE, Woodinville, WA.................206-788-5767
Perini, Ben/1113 Clayton Ct, Novato, CA 415-892-6535
Petersen, Jeff/2956 Nicada Dr, Los Angeles, CA........................213-470-0140
Peterson, Barbara/2629 W Northwood, Santa Ana, CA.....................714-546-2786
Peterson, Eric/270 Termino Avenue, Long Beach, CA.....................213-438-2785
Phillips, Laura/1770 E Sonoma St, Altadena, CA........................818-794-6138
Pickard, Morgan/4621 Teller 3108, Newport Beach, CA 714-474-6002
Pierazzi, Gary/331 Leland Ave, Menlo Park, CA 415-854-8765
Pina, Richard/600 Moulton #401, Los Angeles, CA.......................213-227-5213
Platz, Henry III/15922 118th Pl NE, Bothell, WA.......................206-488-9171
Podevin, J F/5812 Newlin Ave, Whittier, CA 213-945-9613
Ponte, Don/845 Broadway, Sonoma, CA...................................707-935-6335
Porcuna, Ramon/3183 Wayside Plaza #218, Walnut Creek, CA 415-932-4739
Pound, John/5587 Noe Ave, San Diego, CA...............................707-445-3769
Powers, Teresa/14380 Foothill Blvd #6, Sylmar, CA.....................818-362-7205
Pryor, Robert/2153 Charlemagne, Long Beach, CA........................213-597-6161
Przewodek, Camille/4029 23rd St, San Francisco, CA....................415-826-3238
Puchalski, John/1311 Centinela Ave, Santa Monica, CA 213-828-0841
Putnam, Jamie/882 S Van Ness Ave, San Francisco, CA...................415-641-0513
Pyle, Charles S/946 B St, Petaluma, CA................................707-765-6734

R

Rabin, Cheryl/1562 44th Ave, San Francisco, CA........................415-665-9057
Raess Design/424 N Larchmont Blvd, Los Angeles, CA 213-461-9206
Read, Elizabeth/2000 Vallejo St #19, San Francisco, CA 415-929-7323
Renwick/183 N Martell Ave #240, Los Angeles, CA.......................213-934-3395
Renz, Mike/2223 Franklin Ave East, Seattle, WA........................206-323-9257
Rhodes, Barbara/2402 Sonora Ct, Carlsbad, CA 619-729-4228
Richardson, Nelva/2619 American River Dr, Sacramento, CA 916-482-7438
Richter, Mische/950 Klish Way, Del Mar, CA............................619-259-5774
Rictor, Lew/3 Damon Ct, Alameda, CA...................................415-769-7130
Rieser, William/2906 Hermosa View Dr, Hermosa Beach, CA 213-318-1837
Rinaldi, Linda/5717 Chicopee, Encino, CA..............................818-881-1578
Roady, Suzanne/244 9th St, San Francisco, CA..........................415-621-2992
Robertson, Chris/PO Box 84391, Los Angeles, CA 213-207-5712
Robles, Bill/3443 Wade St, Los Angeles, CA............................213-390-9595
Rogers, Mike/8000 Owensmouth St #9, Canoga Park, CA 818-344-8609
Rogers, Paul/1207 N Holliston Ave, Pasadena, CA.......................213-874-0343
Rosco, Delro/1420 E 4th St, National City, CA.........................213-464-1575
Rosenberg, Kenneth/9710 E Lennon Ave, Arcadia, CA 818-574-1631

Rother, Sue/19 Brookmont Circle, San Anselmo, CA 415-454-3593
Ruddell, Gary/183 N Martell Ave #240, Los Angeles, CA 213-934-3395
Russo, Dave/613-D Fell St, San Francisco, CA..........................415-431-8080

S

Sakahara, Dick/28826 Cedarbluff Dr, Rancho Palos Verdes, CA 213-541-8187
Salentine, Katherine/2022 Jones St, San Francisco, CA.................415-928-0457
Salk, Larry/5455 Wilshire Blvd #1212, Los Angeles, CA 213-934-1975
Salvati, Jim/1091 Wesley Ave, Pasadena, CA............................818-441-2544
Sano, Kazuhiko/105 Stadium Ave, Mill Valley, CA.......................415-381-6377
Saputo, Joe/4024 Jasper Rd, Springfield, OR 503-746-1737
Sarn/1201 Howard St, San Francisco, CA................................415-928-1602
Sassooni, Maral/1416 Queens Rd, West Hollywood, CA....................213-656-9323
Sava, Judy/813 R St, Sacramento, CA...................................916-444-7844
Sawyer, Scott/1535 Green St #207, San Francisco, CA 415-441-1623
Scanlon, Dave/1600 18th St, Manhattan Beach, CA.......................213-545-0773
Schaefer, Robert/6010 Wilshire Blvd #505, Los Angeles, CA 213-931-7449
Schftenaar, Johanna/2457 Wellsley Ave, Los Angeles, CA 213-479-6014
Schields, Gretchen/4556 19th St, San Francisco, CA....................415-558-8851
Schmidt, Eric/1852 Kirkby Rd, Glendale, CA............................818-507-0263
Schneider, Doug/4201 Cleveland #12, San Diego, CA.....................619-692-0545
Schroeder, Mark/Pier 33 North, San Francisco, CA......................415-421-3691
Schumaker, Ward/466 Green St #203, San Francisco, CA..................415-398-7295
Scoggins, Timothy/207 N Juanita #5, Redondo Beach, CA 213-543-3569
Scribner, Jo Anne L/3314 N Lee, Spokane, WA...........................509-484-3208
Seckler, Judy/12 S Fair Oaks Ave, Pasadena, CA........................818-508-8778
Shachat, Andrew/119 Felix St #12, Santa Cruz, CA 408-458-0566
**Sharp, Bruce/2819 First Ave #240, Seattle,
WA (P 13)**...**206-443-0326**
Shed, Greg/716 Sanchez St, San Francisco, CA..........................415-285-8267
Shek, W E/1315 Ebener St #4, Redwood City, CA.........................415-363-0687
Shepherd, Roni/1 San Antonio Pl, San Francisco, CA....................415-421-9764
Shields, Bill/14 Wilmot, San Francisco, CA............................415-346-0376
Shigley, Neil/3478 Monroe Ave, Lafayette, CA..........................415-284-7210
Short, Kevin/PO Box 4037, Mission Viejo, CA...........................714-472-1035
Siboldi, Carla/20 W Bellevue Ave, San Mateo, CA.......................415-344-1459
Sigala, Anthony/1681 Amberwood Dr #209, S Pasadena, CA................818-799-1448
Sigwart, Forrest/1033 S Orlando Ave, Los Angeles, CA..................213-655-7734
Silberstein, Simon/1131 Alta Loma Rd #516, W Hollywood, CA 213-652-5226
Siu, Peter/559 Pacific Ave #6, San Francisco, CA......................415-398-6511
Skaar, Al/2819 First Ave #240, Seattle, WA............................206-443-0326
Sloan, Rick/9432 Appalachian Dr, Sacramento, CA 916-364-5844
Smith, J J/4239 1/2 Lexington Ave, Los Angeles, CA....................213-668-2408
Smith, J Randall/130 Maple St #10, Auburn, CA.........................916-823-5535
Smith, Jere/2819 First Ave #240, Seattle, WA..........................206-443-0326
Smith, John C/101 Yesler #502, Seattle, WA............................206-441-0606
Smith, Terry/14333 Tyler St, Sylmar, CA...............................818-362-3599
Smollin, Mark/2112 Queensberry Rd, Pasadena, CA.......................818-798-5999
Snyder, Teresa & Wayne/25727 Mountain Dr, Arlington, WA 206-435-8998
Solie, John/202 W Channel Rd, Santa Monica, CA........................213-454-8147
Solvang-Angell, Diane/425 Randolph Ave, Seattle, WA 206-324-1199
South, Randy/3731 Cahuenga Blvd W, Studio City, CA....................818-766-3877
Spear, Jeffrey A/1228 11th St #201, Santa Monica, CA..................213-395-3939
Spear, Randy/4532 Toucan St, Torrance, CA.............................213-370-6071
Speidel, Sandra/14 Wilmot, San Francisco, CA..........................415-923-1363
Spellman, David/2345 Martin Ave #122, Los Angeles, CA 213-257-6098
Spencer, Joe/11201 Valley Spring Ln, Studio City, CA 818-760-0216
Steam/Dave Willardson/, Glendale, CA..................................818-242-5688
Stearwalt, Terri/275 S Marengo Ave #312, Pasadena, CA.................818-795-3413
Steele, Robert Gantt/14 Wilmot, San Francisco, CA 415-923-0741
Stein, Mike/4340 Arizona, San Diego, CA...............................619-295-2455
Steine, Debra/6561 Green Gables Ave, San Diego, CA....................619-698-5854
Steirnagle, Michael/8100 Paseo del Ocaso, La Jolla, CA................619-454-7280
Stepp, Don/275 Marguerita Ln, Pasadena, CA............................818-799-0263
Stermer, Dugald/1844 Union St, San Francisco, CA......................415-921-8281
Stevenson, Dave/522 Colonial Circle, Vacaville, CA....................707-477-5720
Stewart, Barbara/1640 Tenth Ave #5, San Diego, CA.....................619-238-0083
Stramler, Gwyn/24294 Saradella Ct, Murrieta, CA.......................714-677-3452
Stuart, Walter/716 Sanchez St, San Francisco, CA......................415-285-8267
Stubbs, Barbara/8447 Mica Way, Citrus Hts, CA.........................916-722-9982
Sullivan, Donna/5959 Riverside Blvd #13, Sacramento, CA 916-786-3800
Sullivan, Melinda May/834 Moultrie St, San Francisco, CA..............415-648-2376
Suma, Doug/605 Third St #204, San Francisco, CA.......................415-777-2120
Suvityasiri, Sarn/1811 Leavenworth St, San Francisco, CA..............415-928-1602
Svoboda, John/3211-B S Shannon, Santa Ana, CA.........................714-979-8992
Swendsen, Paul/4630 Fulton St, San Francisco, CA......................415-668-1077
Swimm, Tom/33651 Halyard Dr, Laguna Niguel, CA........................714-496-6349

Syme, Hugh/3408 W Burbank Blvd, Burbank, CA (P 18)....818-985-8181
Syntax International/1790 5th St, Berkeley, CA....415-849-0560

T

Tachiera, Andrea/7416 Fairmount Ave, El Cerrito, CA....415-525-3484
Tanenbaum, Robert/5505 Corbin Ave, Tarzana, CA....818-345-6741
Tank, Darrell/716 Montgomery St, San Francisco, CA (P 39)....415-433-1222
Tarleton, Suzanne/1740 Stanford St, Santa Monica, CA....213-859-7563
Tarrish, Laura/123 Townsend St #215, San Francisco, CA....415-442-1866
Taylor, C Winston/17008 Lisette St, Granada Hills, CA....818-363-5761
Taylor, George/95 Hurlbut #2, Pasadena, CA....818-799-3435
Teach, Buzz/1874 27th St, Sacramento, CA....916-454-3556
Teebken, Tim/1618 W Lomita Blvd #5, Harbor City, CA....213-325-8789
Tenud, Tish/3427 Folsom Blvd, Sacramento, CA....916-455-0569
Tessler, John/614 N 10th St #200, Sacramento, CA....916-442-4600
Thayn, Ellayn/PO Box 8505, Victorville, CA....619-241-9794
The Committee/4741 Laurel Canyon Blvd, N Hollywood, CA....818-902-1440
Thomas, Mary Ann/18620 Hatteras St #222, Tarzana, CA....818-705-0289
Thompson, Brian/183 E Palm, Altadena, CA....818-798-5901
Thon, Bud/410 View Park Ct, Mill Valley, CA....415-332-5319
Thornton, Blake/18780 Melvin Ave, Sonoma, CA....707-935-9716
Thornton, Sandra/3129 Root Ave, Carmichael, CA....916-489-2877
Tiessen, Ken/311 Quincy Ave, Long Beach, CA....213-438-1346
Tilley, Debbie/2821 Camino Del Mar #78, Del Mar, CA....619-481-3251
Tillingerhast, David/2112 Queensberry Rd, Pasadena, CA....818-791-8088
Tilly, Debra/2051 Shadetree, Escondido, CA....619-432-6282
Tom, Katherine/1810 Sunset Ave, Santa Barbara, CA....805-687-0249
Tomita, Tom/3568 E Melton, Pasadena, CA....818-796-4213
Tosch, Jamie S/8732 Fair Oaks Blvd #44, Carmichael, CA....916-944-2097
Truesdale Art & Design/5482 Complex St #112, San Diego, CA....619-268-1026
Tsuchiya, Julie/Pier 1/LOPR, San Francisco, CA....415-986-5365
Tucker, Ezra/1865 Old Mission Dr, Solvang, CA....818-905-0758
Turchyn, Sandie/156 N Hamel Dr, Beverly Hills, CA....213-652-9561
Turner, David/3970 Atlantic #206, Long Beach, CA....213-490-9558

UV

Unger, Joe/17120 NE 96th St, Redmond, WA....206-883-1419
Unger, Judy/14160 Oro Grande St, Sylmar, CA....818-362-6470
Unruh, Jack/716 Montgomery St, San Francisco, CA....415-433-1222
Uyehara, Elizabeth/1020 Westchester Pl, Los Angeles, CA (P 40)....213-731-4168
Van Der Palen/3443 Wade St, Los Angeles, CA....212-390-9595
Van Overloop, Chris J/1714 Capitol Ave, Sacramento, CA....916-444-2840
Vance, Steve/1955 Vero Gordo St, Los Angeles, CA....213-662-3441
Vandervoort, Gene/3201 S Ramona Dr, Santa Ana, CA....714-549-3194
Varah, Monte/18052 Rayen St, North Ridge, CA....818-886-2820
Vibbert, Carolyn/3911 Bagley Ave N, Seattle, WA....206-634-3473
Vigon, Jay/708 S Orange Grove Ave, Los Angeles, CA....213-937-0355
Von Schmidt, Eric/1852 Kirkby Rd, Glendale, CA....818-507-0263
Voo, Rhonda/8800 Venice Blvd, Los Angeles, CA....213-859-1532
Voss, Tom/7584 Charmant Dr #2121, San Diego, CA....619-457-2055

W

Wack, Jeff/3614 Berry Dr, Studio City, CA....818-508-0348
Waldron, Sarah/3690 Primrose Ave, Santa Rosa, CA....707-778-0848
Walstead, Curt/398 Via Colinas, Westlake Village, CA....818-595-2981
Walters, Steve/6010 Wilshire Blvd #505, Los Angeles, CA....213-931-7449
Walton, Brenda/910 2nd Ave 2nd FL, Sacramento, CA....916-448-4998
Warnick, Elsa/812 SW St Clair #7, Portland, OR....503-228-2659
Warren Illus/396 Imperial Way #103, Daly City, CA....415-994-8800
Washington, Romeo/1567 19th Ave #2, San Francisco, CA....415-282-4847
Waters Art Studio/1820 E Garry St #207, Santa Ana, CA....714-250-4466
Watson, Richard Jesse/PO Box 1470, Murphys, CA....209-728-2701
Watts, Stan/28310 Foothill Dr, Agoura Hills, CA....805-499-4747
Weber, Robert/950 Klish Way, Del Mar, CA....619-259-5774
Weiss, Stacy/19551 Turtle Ridge Lane, Northridge, CA....213-939-9797
Welch, Michael/1312 25th St, Sacramento, CA....916-446-5691
Welch, W John/2020 Santa Clara Ave #204, Alameda, CA....415-523-9054
Werner, Jerry/PO Box 8000, Black Butte, OR....503-595-2038
Westlight/2223 S Carmelina Ave, Los Angeles, CA (P 19)....800-872-7872
Weston, Will/135 S LaBrea, Los Angeles, CA....213-854-3666
Wetmore, Barry/1840 Hanscom Dr, S Pasadena, CA....213-254-5438
Wexler, Ed/4701 Don Pio Dr, Woodland Hills, CA....818-505-7121
Wheaton, Liz/80 Wellington Ave/Box 307, Ross, CA....415-456-7711
White, Charlie III/1725 Berkeley St, Santa Monica, CA....213-453-4418
Wicks, Ren/3443 Wade St, Los Angeles, CA....213-390-9595
Willardson + Assoc/103 W California, Glendale, CA....818-242-5688
Williams, John C/5100 N Muscatel Ave, San Gabriel, CA....818-286-7949
Williams, Wayne/15423 Sutton St, Sherman Oaks, CA....213-937-2882
Wilson, Gahan/950 Klish Way, Del Mar, CA....619-259-5774
Wilson, Rob/4729 Eighth Ave, Sacramento, CA....916-451-0449
Wilson, Rowland/7501 Solano St, Rancho La Costa, CA....619-944-3631
Wilton, Nicholas/85 Liberty Ship Way #112, Sausalito, CA....415-331-0834
Wilton/Oppenheimer/85 Liberty Ship Way, Sausalito, CA....415-331-0834
Wiltse, Kris/2819 First Ave #240, Seattle, WA....206-443-0326
Winston, Jeannie/8800 Venice Blvd, Los Angeles, CA....213-558-0141
Winterbauer, Michael James/1220 Lyndon St #22, S Pasadena, CA....818-578-1253
Winters, Greg/2139 Pinecrest Dr, Altadena, CA....818-798-7666
Witus, Edward/634 W Knoll Dr, Los Angeles, CA....213-828-6521
Wolf, Paul/900 1st Ave S #208, Seattle, WA....206-623-1459
Wolfe, Bruce/206 El Cerrito Ave, Piedmont, CA....415-655-7871
Wolin, Ron/4501 Firmament, Encino, CA....213-214-6207
Woodman, Bill/950 Klish Way, Del Mar, CA....619-259-5774
Woodward, Teresa/544 Paseo Miramar, Pacific Palisades, CA....213-459-2317
Wray, Greg/824 E Providencia Ave, Burbank, CA....818-845-2375
Wright, Carol/2500 Angie Way, Rancho Cordova, CA....916-635-4705
Wright, Jonathan/2110 Holly Dr, Los Angeles, CA....213-461-1091

XYZ

Xavier, Roger/3227 Dal Amo Blvd, Lakewood, CA....213-531-9631
Yamada, Kenny/2330 Haste St #306, Berkeley, CA....415-841-4415
Yenne, Bill/111 Pine St, San Francisco, CA....415-989-2450
Yeomans, Jeff/3838 Kendall, San Diego, CA....619-274-2855
Yoshiyama, Glenn/2819 First Ave #240, Seattle, WA....206-443-0326
Zaslavsky, Morris/228 Main St #6, Venice, CA....213-399-3666
Zick, Brian/3251 Primera Ave, Los Angeles, CA....213-876-0402
Ziemienski, Dennis/414 First St East, Sonoma, CA....707-935-0357
Zinc, Debra/Pier 33 North, San Francisco, CA....415-956-4750
Zito, Andy/135 S La Brea Ave, Los Angeles, CA....213-931-1181

INTERNATIONAL

Andic, Mike/PO Box 500, Woodstock , ON....519-439-4661
Broda, Ron/361 Dundas St, London, ON....519-672-2538
Cantin, Charles/809 Cartier, Quebec , QC....418-524-1931
Dionisi, Sandra/859 King St W, Toronto, ON....416-867-1771
Frampton, Bill/49 Henderson, Toronto , ON....416-535-1931
MacLeod, Ainslie/33 Long Acre, London, England WC2,....071-240-1812
Gabbana, Marc/1540 Westcott Rd, Windsor, ON....519-948-7705
Hammond, Franklin/1179-A W King St #310, Toronto , ON....416-533-4434
Heda, Jackie/3 Playter Blvd #3, Toronto , ON....416-463-8692
Jamison, Diane/2 Berkeley St #206, Toronto , ON....416-369-9442
Johnston, WB/572 Mountain Ave, Winnipeg , MB....204-582-1686
Jones, Danielle/55 W Charles St #1003, Toronto, ON....416-968-6277
Krb, Vladimir/PO Box 2955/Drumheller Sta, Alberta , AB....403-823-6385
Kunz, Anita/230 Ontario St, Toronto, ON....416-364-3846
Kurisu, Jane/97 Air Drie Rd, Toronto, ON....416-424-2524
Levine, Ron/1619 Williams St #202, Montreal, QU....212-727-1967
Liss, Julius/446 Lawrence Ave W, Toronto, ON....416-784-1416
MacDougall, Rob/2049 Lakeshore Rd W, Oakville , ON....416-847-7663
Miller, Jean/350 Esna Park Dr, Markham, ON....416-883-4114
Olthuis, Stan/524 Queen St E, Toronto , ON....416-860-0300
Ormond, Rick/42 Portland Crscnt, Newmarket , ON....416-961-4098
Pariseau, Pierre Paul/9067 Place do Montgoitier, Montreal, QU....514-388-7192
Pastucha, Ron/336 McNeans Ave, Winnipeg , MB....204-222-3178
Reed, Barbara/37 Strathmore Blvd, Toronto , ON....416-461-9793
Rubess, Balvis/260 Brunswick Ave, Toronto , ON....416-927-7071
Sekeris, Pim/570 Milton St #10, Montreal , QU....514-844-0510
Shumate, Michael/198 Chelsea Rd, Kingston , ON....613-384-5019
Snider, Jackie/RR 7/Hwy 30, Brighton , ON....613-475-4551
Tughan, James/1179-A King St W #310, Toronto, ON....416-535-9149
Van Ginkel, Paul/40 Edgehart Estates Rd NW, Calgary, AB....403-241-0516

PHOTOGRAPHERS

NYC

A

Abatelli, Gary/80 Charles St #3W....212-924-5887
Abramowitz, Ellen/166 E 35th St #4H....212-686-2409
Abramowitz, Jerry/680 Broadway....212-420-9500
Abramson, Michael/15 Renwick St....212-941-1970
Accornero, Franco/620 Broadway....212-674-0068
Acevedo, Melanie/244 W 11th St #2F....212-243-5333
Adam & Adams Photo/7 Dutch St....212-619-2171
Adamo, Jeff/50 W 93rd St #8P....212-866-4886
Adams, Eddie/80 Warren St #14....212-406-1166
Adams, Steven/344 W 38th St....212-594-6979
Addio, Edward/151 W 19th St 10th Fl....212-206-1686
Adelman, Barbara Ellen/5 E 22nd St #25A....212-353-8931
Adelman, Bob/151 W 28th St....212-736-0537
Adelman, Menachem Assoc/45 W 17th St 5th Fl....212-675-1202
Adler, Arnie/70 Park Terrace W....212-304-2443
Afanador, Reuven/342 W 84th St....212-724-4590
Agor, Alexander/108-28 Flatlands 7 St, Brooklyn....718-531-1025
Aharoni, Oudi/704 Broadway....212-777-0847
Aich, Clara/218 E 25th St....212-686-4220
Aiosa, Vince/5 W 31st St....212-563-1859
Albert, Jade/59 W 19th St #3B....212-242-0940
Alberts, Andrea/121 W 17th St....212-242-5794
Alcorn, Richard/160 W 95th St #7A....212-866-1161
Alexander, Robert/560 W 43rd St #12A....212-231-9248
Alexanders Studio/500 Seventh Ave 18th Fl....212-560-2178
Alexanders, John W/308 E 73rd St....212-734-9166
Allbrition, Randy/212 Sullivan St....212-529-1228
Allison, David/42 E 23rd St....212-460-9056
Alper, Barbara/202 W 96th St....212-316-6518
Alpern/Lukoski/149 W 12th St....212-645-8148
Altamari, Christopher/56 W 22nd St....212-645-8484
Amato, Paul/881 Seventh Ave #405....212-541-4787
Amrine, Jamie/30 W 22nd St....212-243-2178
Anders, Robert/724 Beverly Rd, Brooklyn....718-438-8746
Andrews, Bert/50 W 97th St....212-662-6732
Anik, Adam/111 Fourth St #1-I....212-529-2359
Anthony, Don/79 Prall Ave, Staten Island....718-317-6340
Antonio/Stephen Photo/5 W 30th St 4th Fl....212-629-9542
Apoian, Jeffrey/66 Crosby St....212-431-5513
Apple, Richard/80 Varick St #4B....212-966-6782
Arago, Chico/One Fifth Ave....212-982-2661
Aranita, Jeffrey/60 Pineapple St, Brooklyn....718-625-7672
Arbus, Amy/60 E 8th St #19H....212-353-9418
Ardito, Peter/64 N Moore St....212-941-1561
Aref, Jaramay/601 W 26th St....212-727-1996
Aresu, Paul/568 Broadway #608....212-334-9494
Arky, David/140 Fifth Ave #2B....212-242-4760
Arlak, Victoria/40 East End Ave....212-879-0250
Arma, Tom/38 W 26th St....212-243-7904
Arndt, Dianne/400 Central Park West....212-866-1902
Arslanian, Ovak/344 W 14th St....212-255-1519
Ashe, Bill/534 W 35th St....212-695-6473
Ashworth, Gavin/110 W 80th St....212-874-3879
Astor, Joseph/154 W 57th St....212-307-2050
Attoinese, Deborah/11-42 44th Dr, L I City....718-729-5614
Aubry, Daniel/365 First Ave....212-598-4191
Auster, Evan/215 E 68th St #3....212-517-9776
Auster, Walter/18 E 16th St....212-627-8448
Ava, Beth/87 Franklin St....212-966-4407
Avedis/130 E 65th St....212-472-3615
Avedon, Richard/407 E 75th St....212-879-6325
Axon, Red/17 Park Ave....212-532-6317
Azzato, Hank/348 W 14th St 3rd Fl....212-929-9455
Azzi, Robert/116 E 27th St....212-481-6900

B

Baasch, Diane/41 W 72nd St #11F....212-724-2123
Babchuck, Jacob/132 W 22nd St 3rd Fl....212-929-8811
Babushkin, Mark/110 W 31st St....212-239-6630
Back, John/15 Sheridan Sq....212-243-6347
Bahrt, Irv/310 E 46th St....212-661-5260
Baiano, Salvatore/160 Fifth Ave #818....212-633-1050
Bailey, Richard/96 Fifth Ave....212-255-3252
Baillie, Allan & Gus Francisco/220 E 23rd St 11th Fl....212-683-0418
Bakal-Schwartzberg/40 E 23rd St....212-254-2988
Baker, Chuck/1630 York Ave....212-517-9060
Baker, Gloria/415 Central Park West....212-222-2866
Baker, Joe/35 Wooster St....212-925-6555
Bakerman, Nelson/220 E 4th St #2W....212-777-7321
Baldwin, Joel/350 E 55th St....212-308-5991
Baliotti, Dan/19 W 21st St....212-627-9039
Ballerini, Albano/231 W 29th St....212-967-0850
Bancroft, Monty/161 W 15th St....212-807-8650
Barash, Howard/349 W 11th St....212-242-6182
Baratta, Nicholas/450 W 31st St....212-947-7445
Barba, Dan/305 Second Ave #322....212-420-8611
Barber, James/873 Broadway....212-598-4500
Barbieri, Gianpaolo....212-370-4300
Barcellona, Marianne/175 Fifth Ave #2422....212-463-9717
Barclay, Bob Studios/5 W 19th St 6th Fl....212-255-3440
Barkentin, George/15 W 18th St....212-243-2174
Barnett, Nina/295 Park Ave S Pnthse B....212-979-8008
Barnett, Peggy/26 E 22nd St....212-673-0500
Barns, Larry/21 W 16th St....212-242-8833
Barr, Neal/222 Central Park South....212-765-5760
Barr, Paula/144 E 24th St....212-473-4191
Barrett, John E/215 W 95th St....212-864-6381
Barrick, Rick/12 E 18th St 4th Fl....212-741-2304
Barrows, Wendy Photography/205 E 22nd St #4H....212-685-0799
Bartlett, Chris/21 E 37th St #2R....212-213-2382
Barton, Paul/111 W 19th St #2A....212-691-1999
Basile, Joseph/448 W 37th St....212-564-1625
Basilion, Nicholas/150 Fifth Ave #532....212-645-6568
Baumann, Jennifer/682 Sixth Ave....212-633-0160
Baumann, Michael/206 E 26th St....212-532-6696
Baumel, Ken/234 Fifth Ave #3251....212-929-7550
Bean, John/5 W l9th St....212-242-8106
Bechtold, John/117 E 31st St....212-679-7630
Beck, Arthur/119 W 22nd St....212-691-8331
Becker, Jonathan/451 West 24th St....212-929-3180
Beebe, Rod/1202 Lexington Ave #205....212-996-8926
Beechler, Greg/200 W 79th St PH #A....212-580-8649
Begleiter, Steven/38 Greene St....212-334-5262
Behl, David/13-17 Laight St 2nd Fl....212-226-4968
Belinsky, Jon/134 W 26th St #777....212-627-1246
Bell, Hugh/873 Broadway....212-260-2260
Beller, Janet/225 Varrick St....212-727-0188
Belott, Robert/236 W 26th St....212-924-1503
Belushin, Blandon/56 W 22nd St....212-691-0301
Benedict, William/530 Park Ave....212-832-3164
Benn, Mitchell/75 Bank St....212-255-8686
Benson, Harry/181 E 73rd St....212-249-0284
Benson, Mary Anne/160 Fifth Ave #817....212-243-6811
Bercow, Larry/344 W 38th St....212-629-9000
Berenholtz, Richard/600 W 111th St #6A....212-222-1302
Berger, Joseph/121 Madison Ave #3B....212-685-7191
Bergman, Beth/150 West End Ave....212-724-1867
Bergreen, John Studio/31 W 21st St #5RW....212-366-6316
Berkwit, Lane (Ms)/262 Fifth Ave....212-889-5911
Berman, Howard/5 E 19th St #303....212-473-3366
Berman, Malcolm/446 W 25th St....212-727-0033
Bernson, Carol/PO Box 2244 Styvsnt Sta....212-473-3884
Bernstein, Audrey/33 Bleecker St....212-353-3512
Bernstein, Bill/38 Greene St....212-334-3982
Bernstein, Steve/47-47 32nd Place, Long Island City....718-786-8100
Bersell, Barbara/12 E 86th St....212-734-9049
Bessler, John/503 Broadway 5th Fl....212-941-6179
Bester, Roger/55 Van Dam St 11th Fl....212-645-5810
Betz, Charles/138 W 25th St 10th Fl....212-675-4760
Bevilacqua, Joe/202 E 42nd St....212-490-0355
Biddle, Geoffrey/5 E 3rd St....212-505-7713
Bies, William/21-29 41st St #1A, LI City....718-278-0236
Bijur, Hilda/190 E 72nd St....212-737-4458
Biondo, Michael/23 Second Ave....212-226-5299
Birdsell, Doreen/297 Third Ave....212-213-4141

Bisbee, Terry/290 W 12th St	212-242-4762
Bischoff, Beth/448 W 37th St	212-714-1751
Bishop, David/251 W 19th St	212-929-4355
Blachut, Dennis/145 W 28th St 8th Fl	212-947-4270
Blackburn, Joseph M/568 Broadway #800	212-966-3950
Blackman, Barry/150 Fifth Ave #220	212-627-9777
Blackman, Jeffrey/2323 E 12th St, Brooklyn	718-769-0986
Blackstock, Ann/484 W 43rd St #22S	212-695-2525
Blake, Jeri/227 E 11th St	212-473-2739
Blake, Rebecca/584 Broadway #310	212-925-1290
Blakeman, Barry/150 Fifth Ave #220	212-627-9777
Blanch, Andrea/434 E 52nd St	212-888-7912
Blanchard, Sharland/45 W 85th St #4A	212-874-3388
Blechman, Jeff/591 Broadway	212-226-0006
Blecker, Charles/350 Bleecker St #140	212-242-8390
Blell, Dianne/125 Cedar St	212-732-2990
Blinkoff, Richard/147 W 15th St 3rd Fl	212-620-7883
Block, Helen/385 14th St, Brooklyn	718-788-1097
Block, Ira Photography/215 W 20th St	212-242-2728
Block, Ray/458 W 20th St #4D	212-691-9375
Bloom, Teri/300 Mercer St #6C	212-475-2274
Blosser, Robert/741 West End Ave #3C	212-662-0107
Blum, Frederick/111 E 14th St	212-969-8695
Boas, Christopher/20 Bond St	212-982-8576
Bobbe, Leland/51 W 28th St	212-685-5238
Bocconi, Joseph/310 W 4th St	212-645-4157
Bodi Studios/340 W 39th St	212-947-7883
Bogertman, Ralph Inc/34 W 28th St	212-889-8871
Boisseau, Joseph/3250 Hering Ave #1, Bronx	212-519-8672
Bolesta, Alan/11 Riverside Dr #13SE	212-873-1932
Boljonis, Steven/555 Ft Washington Ave #4A	212-740-0003
Bonomo, Louis/118 W 27th St #2F	212-242-4630
Boon, Sally/108 Bowery	212-334-9160
Borderud, Mark/12 W 27th St	212-828-4949
Bordnick, Barbara/39 E 19th St	212-533-1180
Borham, Bruce/155 Ave of Americas #10	212-645-9339
Bosch, Peter/477 Broome St	212-925-0707
Boszko, Ron/140 W 57th St	212-541-5504
Bottomley, Jim/125 Fifth Ave	212-677-9646
Bourbeau, Katherine/484 W 43rd St	212-268-1595
Bowditch, Richard/175 Fifth Ave #2613	212-564-5413
Brady, Steve/292 Lafayette St #5E	212-941-6093
Brakha, Moshe/77 FIfth Ave #17D	212-645-7946
Brandt, Peter/73 Fifth Ave #6B	212-242-4289
Bratton Felder Photo/420 E 86th St	212-517-3938
Braun, Yenachem/666 West End Ave	212-873-1985
Braverman, Alan/139 Fifth Ave	212-674-1925
Bredel, Walter/21 E 10th St	212-228-8565
Breitrose, Howard/443 W 18th St	212-242-7825
Brello, Ron/400 Lafayette St	212-982-0490
Brenner, George/15 W 24th St #3E	212-691-7436
Breskin, Michael/133 Second Ave	212-979-8245
Brett, Clifton/242 W 30th St	212-947-0139
Brewster, Don/235 West End Ave	212-874-0548
Brey, Albert/312 W 90th St #4A	212-874-8163
Bridges, Kiki/147 W 26th St 3rd Fl	212-807-6563
Brill Studio/270 City Island Ave, City Island	212-885-0802
Brill, James/108 Fifth Ave #17C	212-645-9414
Britton, Peter/315 E 68th St	212-737-1664
Brizzi, Andrea/405 W 23rd St	212-627-2341
Brochmann, Kristen/236 W 27th St	212-989-6319
Brody, Bob/5 W 19th 2nd Fl	212-741-0013
Bronstein, Steve/5 E 19th St #303	212-473-3366
Brooke, Randy/179 E 3rd St	212-677-2656
Brosan, Roberto/873 Broadway	212-473-1471
Brown, Cynthia/448 W 37th St	212-564-1625
Brown, Nancy/6 W 20th St 2nd Fl	212-924-9105
Brown, Owen Studio/224 W 29th St #PH	212-947-9470
Brucker, Andrew/225 Central Park W	212-724-3236
Bruderer, Rolf/435 E 65th St	212-684-4890
Bruno Burklin/873 Broadway	212-420-0208
Brunswick, Cecile/127 W 96th St	212-222-2088
Bryan-Brown, Marc/4 Jones St #4	212-691-6045
Bryce, Sherman E/60 E 8th St #19D	212-580-9639
Bryson, John/12 E 62nd St	212-755-1321
Bucci, Andrea/287 E 3rd St	212-260-1939
Buceta, Jaime/56 W 22nd St 6th Fl	212-807-8485
Buck, Bruce/39 W 14th St	212-645-1022
Buckler, Susanne/344 W 38th St	212-279-0043
Buckley, Dana/156 Waverly Pl	212-206-1807
Buckmaster, Adrian/332 W 87th St	212-799-7318
Buckner, Bill/131 W 21st St	212-366-1859
Buonnano, Ray/237 W 26th St	212-675-7680
Burnette, David/13-17 Laight St	212-683-2002
Burnie, Ellen Forbes/19 Hubert St	212-219-1091
Burns, Tom/534 W 35th St	212-927-4678
Burquez, Felizardo/22-63 38th St #1, Astoria	718-274-6139
Buss, Gary/250 W 14th St	212-645-0928
Butera, Augustus/300 Riverside Dr #11F	212-864-7772
Butler, Robert/400 Lafayette St	212-982-8051
Butts, Harvey/77 Fifth Ave #8B	212-459-4689
Buzoianu, Peter/32-15 41st St, Long Island City	718-278-2456
Byers, Bruce/11 W 20th St 5th Fl	212-242-5846

C

Cadge, Jeff/344 West 38th St #10B	212-563-0547
Cailor/Resnick/237 W 54th St 4th Fl	212-977-4300
Cali, Deborah/333 W 86th St	212-873-8800
Callis, Chris/91 Fifth Ave	212-243-0231
Camera Communications/110 Greene St	212-925-2722
Camp, E J (Ms)/20 E 10th St	212-475-6267
Campbell, Barbara/138 W 17th St	212-929-5620
Campbell, Kelly/954 Lexington Ave #231	212-879-6170
Campos, John/411 W 14th St 2nd Fl	212-675-0601
Canady, Philip/1411 Second Ave	212-737-3855
Cannon, Gregory/876 Broadway 2nd Fl	212-228-3190
Cantor, Phil/75 Ninth Ave 8th Fl	212-243-1143
Caplan, Skip/124 W 24th St	212-463-0541
Cardacino, Michael/20 Ridge Rd, Douglaston	212-947-9307
Carloh/81 Perry St #4B	212-431-4100
Carlson, Jay/9 E 19th St	212-473-5130
Carlson-Emberling Studio/9 E 19th St	212-473-5130
Carroll, Robert/270 Park Ave S	212-477-4593
Carron, Les/15 W 24th St 2nd Fl	212-255-8250
Carson, Donald/115 W 23rd St	212-807-8987
Carter, Dwight/120 W 97th St #14C	212-932-1661
Casarola, Angelo/165 W 18th St 3rd Fl	212-620-0620
Casey/10 Park Ave #3E	212-684-1397
Cashin, Art/5 W 19th St	212-255-3440
Castelli, Charles/41 Union Sq W #425	212-620-5536
Caulfield, Patricia/115 W 86th St #2E	212-362-1951
Cavanaugh, Ken/6803 Ft Hamilton Pkwy, Brooklyn	718-745-6983
Caverly, Kat/504 W 48th St	212-757-8388
Cearley, Guy/460 Grand St #10A	212-979-2075
Celnick, Edward/36 E 12th St	212-420-9326
Cementi, Joseph/133 W 19th St 3rd Fl	212-924-7770
Cempa, Andrew/301 E 50th St #12	212-935-4787
Cenicola, Tony Studio/325 W 37th St 11th Fl	212-695-0773
Chakmakjian, Paul/35 W 36th St 8th Fl	212-563-3195
Chalfant, Todd/85 E 10th St #5C	212-260-3726
Chalk, David/215 E 81st St	212-744-6005
Chalkin, Dennis/5 E 16th St	212-929-1036
Chan, John/225 E 49th St	212-755-3816
Chan, Michael/22 E 21st St	212-460-8030
Chaney, Scott/36 W 25th St 11th Fl	212-924-8440
Chanteau, Pierre/80 Warren St	212-227-4931
Chapman, Mike/543 Broadway 8th Fl	212-966-9542
Charles, Frederick/254 Park Ave S #7F	212-505-0686
Charles, Lisa/119 W 23rd St #500	212-807-8600
Chauncy, Kim/123 W 13th St	212-242-2400
Checani, Richard/333 Park Ave S	212-674-0608
Chelsea Photo/Graphics/641 Ave of Americas	212-206-1780
Chen, Paul Inc/133 Fifth Ave	212-674-4100
Chernin, Bruce/330 W 86th St	212-496-0266
Chestnut, Richard/236 W 27th St	212-255-1790
Chiba/303 Park Ave S #412	212-674-7575
Chin, Ted/118 W 27th St 3rd Fl	212-627-7296
Chin, Walter/160 Fifth Ave #914	212-924-6760
Christensen, Paul H/286 Fifth Ave	212-279-2838
Chrynwski, Walter/154 W 18th St	212-675-1906
Cipolla, Karen/103 Reade St 3rd Fl	212-619-6114
Cirone, Bettina/211 W 56th St #14K	212-262-3062
Clarke, Kevin/900 Broadway 9th Fl	212-460-9360
Clarke, Scott/210 E 36th St	212-481-9592
Claxton, William/108 W 18th St	212-206-0737

Clayton, Tom/568 Broadway #601 212-431-3377
Clementi, Joseph Assoc/133 W 19th St 3rd Fl 212-924-7770
Clough, Terry/147 W 25th St 212-255-3040
Cobb, Jan/5 W 19th St 3rd Fl 212-255-1400
Cobin, Martin/145 E 49th St 212-758-5742
Cochnauer, Paul/1186 Broadway #833 212-532-9033
Cochran, George/381 Park Ave S 212-689-9054
Cohen, James/36 E 20th St 4th Fl 212-533-4400
Cohen, Lawrence Photo/247 W 30th St 212-967-4376
Cohen, Marc David/5 W 19th 212-741-0015
Cohen, Steve/37 W 20th St #304 212-727-3884
Cohn, Ric/137 W 25th St #1 212-924-4450
Colabella, Vincent/304 E 41st St 212-949-7456
Coleman, Bruce/381 Fifth Ave 2nd Fl 212-683-5227
Coleman, Gene/250 W 27th St 212-691-4752
Colen, Corrine/519 Broadway 212-431-7425
Colletti, Steve/200 Park Ave #303E 212-972-2218
Collins, Arlene/64 N Moore St #3E (P 65) 212-431-9117
Collins, Benton/873 Broadway 212-254-7247
Collins, Chris/35 W 20th St 212-633-1670
Collins, Joe J/208 Garfield Pl, Brooklyn 718-965-4836
Collins, Ken/14 E 17th St 212-563-6025
Collins, Sheldon/27 W 24th St 212-242-0076
Colliton, Paul/310 Greenwich St 212-242-6287
Colombo, Michel/119 W 23rd St 212-727-9238
Colton, Robert/1700 York Ave 212-831-3953
Conn, John/1639 Plymouth Ave #2 212-931-9051
Contarsy, Ron/297 W 96th St 212-678-0660
Cook, Irvin/534 W 43rd St 212-925-6216
Cook, Rod/29 E 19th St 212-995-0100
Cooke, Colin/380 Lafayette St 212-254-5090
Cooper, Bill/118 E 28th St 212-213-4433
Cooper, Martha/310 Riverside Dr #805 212-222-5146
Corbett, Jane/303 Park Ave S #512 212-505-1177
Corbo, Sal/18 E 18th St 212-242-3748
Cordoza, Tony/15 W 18th St 212-243-8441
Corman, Richard/385 West End Ave 212-799-2395
Cornish, Dan/594 Broadway #1204 212-226-3183
Corporate Photographers Inc/45 John St 212-964-6515
Corti, George/10 W 33rd St 212-239-4490
Cosimo/43 W 13th St 212-206-1818
Costa, Herman/213 W 80th St 212-595-0309
Coupon, William/170 Mercer St 212-941-5676
Couzens, Larry/16 E 17th St 212-620-9790
Cowley, Jay/225 E 82nd St 212-988-3893
Cox, David/25 Mercer St 3rd Fl 212-925-0734
Cox, Rene/395 South End Ave 212-321-2749
Crampton, Nancy/35 W 9th St 212-254-1135
Crawford, Nelson/10 E 23rd #600 212-475-7808
Cronin, Casey/115 Wooster St 212-334-9253
Crum, John R Photography/124 W 24th St 212-463-8663
Cuesta, Michael/37 W 20th St #606 212-929-5519
Cuington, Phyllis/36 W 25th St 11th Fl 212-691-1901
Culberson, Earl/5 E 19th St #303 212-473-3366
Cunningham, Peter/53 Gansevoort St 212-633-1077
Curatola, Tony/18 E 17th St 212-243-5478
Cutler, Craig/39 Walker St 212-966-1652
Czaplinski, Czeslaw/90 Dupont St, Brooklyn 718-389-9606

D

D'Addio, James/12 E 22nd St #10E 212-533-0668
D'Amico, John/3418 Ave "L", Brooklyn 718-377-4246
D'Antonio, Nancy/303 W 92nd St 212-666-1107
D'Innocenzo, Paul/568 Broadway #604 212-925-9622
Daley, James D/568 Broadway 212-925-7192
Daly, Jack/247 W 30th St 212-695-2726
Dantuono, Paul/433 Park Ave So 212-683-5778
Dantzic, Jerry/910 President St, Brooklyn 718-789-7478
Datoli, Michael/121 W 17th St #4C 212-691-5851
Dauman, Henri/4 E 88th St 212-860-3804
David, Gabrielle/4024 6th Ave, Brooklyn 718-856-2315
Davidian, Peter/588 Broadway #1203 212-941-8077
Davidson, Bruce/79 Spring St 212-475-7600
Davis, Darien/254 Park Ave S #9-O 212-995-5783
Davis, David Photo/477 W 143rd St #4C 212-234-9429
Davis, Dick/400 E 59th St 212-751-3276
Davis, Don/61 Horatio St 212-989-2820
Dawes, Chris/666 Greenwich St 212-924-2255
Day, Lee/55 Hudson St 212-619-4117
De Olazabal, Eugenia/828 Fifth Ave 212-980-8075
Decanio, Steve/448 W 37th St #11C 212-594-0593
DeGrado, Drew/250 W 40th St 5th Fl 212-302-2760
DeLeon, Katrina/286 Fifth Ave #1206 212-279-2838
DeLeon, Martin/286 Fifth Ave #1206 (P 58) 212-714-9777
DeLessio, Len/121 E 12th St #4F 212-353-1774
DeMarchelier, Patrick/162 W 21st St 212-924-3561
DeMelo, Antonio/126 W 22nd St 212-929-0507
DeMilt, Ronald/873 Broadway 2nd Fl 212-228-5321
Denker, Deborah/460 Greenwich St 212-219-9263
Denner, Manuel/249 W 29th St 4th Fl 212-947-6220
Dennis, Lisl/135 E 39th St 212-532-8226
DePaul, Raymond/529 W 42nd St #6M 212-967-0831
DePra, Nancy/15 W 24th St 212-242-0252
Derr, Stephen/420 W 45th St 4th Fl 212-246-5920
DeSanto, Thomas/116 W 29th St 2nd Fl 212-967-1390
DeToy, Ted/511 E 78th St 212-988-1869
Deutsch, Jack/310 E 46th St 212-799-7179
DeWys, Leo/1170 Broadway 212-689-5580
Di Chiaro, Dennis/46 W 37th St 212-268-9270
Dian, Russell/432 E 88th St #201 212-722-4348
Diaz, Jorge/142 W 24th St 12th Fl 212-925-0102
Diaz/Schneider Studio /318 W 39th St 212-695-3620
Dillon, Jim/39 W 38th St 12th Fl 212-849-8158
DiMicco/Ferris Studio/40 W 17th St #2B 212-627-4074
DiVito, Michael/320 7th Ave #1, Brooklyn 718-788-4816
Dodge, Jeff/133 Eighth Ave 212-620-9652
Doerzbacher, Cliff/12 Cottage Ave, Staten Island 718-981-3144
Doherty, Marie/43 E 22nd St 212-674-8767
Dole, Jody (Mr)/95 Horatio St 212-691-9888
Dorf, Myron Jay/205 W 19th St 3rd Fl 212-255-2020
Dorot, Didier/48 W 21st St 9th Fl 212-206-1608
Dorrance, Scott/12 w 27th St 212-675-5235
Dorris, Chuck/492 Broome St 212-334-9282
Doubilet, David/1040 Park Ave #6J 212-348-5011
Drabkin, Si Studios Inc/40-10 Littleneck Pkwy, Littleneck 718-279-4512
Dresner, Harvey/302-46 46th Ave, Bayside 718-225-2332
Dressler, Marjory/4 E Second St 212-254-9758
Drew, Rue Faris/177 E 77th St 212-794-8994
Drivas, Joseph/15 Beacon Ave, Staten Island 718-667-0696
Dubler, Douglas/162 E 92nd St 212-410-6300
Duchaine, Randy/200 W 18th St #4F 212-243-4371
Ducote, Kimberly/445 W 19th St #7F 212-989-3680
Dugdale, John/59 Morton St 212-691-5264
Duke, Dana/620 Broadway 212-260-3334
Duke, Randy/2825 Grand Concourse, Bronx 212-364-2584
Duke, William/155 Chambers St 212-285-2404
Dunkley, Richard/648 Broadway #506 212-979-6996
Dunn, Phoebe/19 W 21st St #901 212-627-4060
Dunning, Hank/50 W 22nd St 212-675-6040
Dunning, Robert/57 W 58th St 212-688-0788
Duomo Photo Inc/133 W 19th St 212-243-1150

E

Eagan, Timothy/319 E 75th St 212-969-8988
Eberstadt, Fred/791 Park Ave 212-794-9471
Eccles, Andrew/305 Second Ave #346 212-353-0477
Eckerie, Tom/32 Union Sq E #707 212-677-3635
Eckstein, Ed/234 Fifth Ave 5th Fl 212-685-9342
Edahl, Edward/236 W 27th St 212-929-2002
Eddy, Jean/PO Box 2994/Rockefeller Ctr 516-483-3745
Edgeworth, Anthony/130 Madison Ave 4th Fl 212-679-6031
Edinger, Claudio/456 Broome St (P 68) 212-219-8619
Edwards, Harvey/420 E 54th St #21E 516-261-5239
Eggers, Claus/900 Broadway 212-473-0064
Eguiguren, Carlos/196 W Houston St 212-727-7550
Ehrenpreis, Dave/2 W 31st St #405 212-947-3535
Eisenberg, Steve/448 W 37th St 212-563-2061
Eisner, Sandra/873 Broadway 2nd Fl 212-727-0669
Ekmekji, Raffi/377 Park Ave S 212-696-5577
Elbers, Johan/18 E 18th St 212-929-5783
Elgort, Arthur/136 Grand St 212-219-8775
Elios-Zunini Studio/142 W 4th St 212-228-6827
Elmore, Steve/60 E 42nd St #411 212-472-2463
Elness, Jack/236 W 26th St 212-242-5045

Emberling, David/9 E 19th St	212-473-5130
Emerson, John/48 W 21st St 10th Fl	212-741-3818
Emil, Pamela/327 Central Park West	212-749-4716
Emrich, Bill/448 W 19th St Penthse A	212-889-7482
Endress, John Paul/254 W 31st St	212-736-7800
Enfield, Jill/211 E 18th St	212-777-3510
Engel, Mort Studio/260 Fifth Ave 4th Fl	212-769-6826
Englander, Maury/43 Fifth Ave	212-242-9777
Engle, Mort Studio/260 Fifth Ave	212-889-8466
Englehardt, Duk/80 Varick St #4E	212-226-6490
Englert, Michael/142 W 24th St	212-243-3446
Epstein, Mitch/353 E 77th St	212-517-3648
Epstein, Paula/146 Sullivan St #5	212-777-5177
Epstein, S Karin/610 West End Ave	212-496-5592
Essel, Robert/39 W 71st St #A	212-877-5228
Estevez, Herman/480 Broadway	212-941-0330
Estrada, Sigrid/902 Broadway	212-673-4300
Everly, Bart/228 Seventh Ave 2nd Fl	212-989-3869

F

Famighetti, Thomas/40 W 24th St	212-255-8334
Farber, Enid/PO Box 1770/Church St Sta	201-451-6744
Farber, Robert/207-A 62nd St	212-486-9090
Faria, Rui/304 Eighth Ave #3	212-929-2993
Farrell, Bill/343 E 30th St #17C	212-683-1425
Farrell, John/189 Second Ave	212-460-9001
Farwell, Linda/55 East End Ave	212-988-6015
Favero, Jean P/208 Fifth Ave #3E	212-683-9188
Feibel, Theodor/102-10 66th Rd #15C, Forest Hills	718-897-2445
Feinstein, Gary/19 E 17th St	212-242-3373
Feintuch, Harvey/1440 E 14th St, Brooklyn	718-339-0301
Fellerman, Stan/152 W 25th St	212-243-0027
Fellman, Sandi/548 Broadway	212-925-5187
Ferguson, Phoebe/289 Cumberland St, Brooklyn	718-643-1675
Ferich, Lorenz/516 E 78th St #D	212-517-6838
Ferorelli, Enrico/50 W 29th St	212-685-8181
Ferrante, Terry/555 Third Ave	212-683-7967
Ferrari, Maria/37 W 20th St #1207	212-924-1241
Ferri, Mark/463 Broome St	212-431-1356
Fery, Guy/31 W 21st St	212-255-4646
Feurer, Hans/160 Fifth Ave	212-924-6760
Fields, Bruce/71 Greene St	212-431-8852
Filari, Katrina/286 Fifth Ave	212-279-2838
Fineman, Dana/40 W 24th St	212-627-0631
Finkelman, Allan/118 E 28th St #608	212-684-3487
Finlay, Alastair/13-17 Laight St 5th Fl	212-334-8001
Firman, John/434 E 75th St	212-794-2794
Fischer, Carl/121 E 83rd St	212-794-0400
Fischer, Ken/121 E 83rd St	212-794-0400
Fisher, Jon/236 W 27th St 4th Fl	212-206-6311
Fisher, Steven/233 W 99th St	212-666-0121
Fishman, Chuck/473 Broome St	212-941-8582
Fishman, Robert/153 W 27th St #502	212-620-7976
Fitz, Mike/160 Fifth Ave #912	212-243-6995
Fiur, Lola Troy/360 E 65th St	212-861-1911
Flatow, Carl/20 E 30th St	212-683-8688
Floret, Evelyn/3 E 80th St	212-472-3179
Floyd, Bob/PO Box 216	212-684-0795
Flying Camera/114 Fulton St	212-619-0808
Flynn, Matt/99 W 27th St	212-627-2985
Flynn, Richard/306 W 4th St	212-243-0834
Fogliani, Tom/84 Thomas St 5th Fl	212-766-8809
Forastieri, Marili/426 W Broadway #6G	212-431-1840
Ford, Charles/32 E 22nd St	212-460-5320
Forelli, Chip/529 W 42nd St #3R	212-564-1835
Fornuff, Doug/323 Park Ave South	212-529-4440
Forrest, Bob/273 Fifth Ave 3rd Fl	212-288-4458
Foto Shuttle Japan/47 Greene St	212-966-9641
Foulke, Douglas/140 W 22nd St	212-243-0822
Fox, Howard/12 E 86th St #1522	212-517-3700
Fox, Jeffrey/6 W 20th St	212-620-0147
Foxx, Stephanie/274 W 71st St	212-580-9158
Frailey, Stephen/11 Charlton St	212-741-2630
Frajndlich, Abe/30 E 20th St #605	212-995-8648
Frame, Bob/225 Lafayette #503	212-431-6707
Frampton, Jerald/23-25 Astoria Blvd, Long Island City	718-726-1373
Francais, Isabelle/873 Broadway	212-678-7508

Francekevich, Al/73 Fifth Ave	212-691-7456
Frances, Scott/175 Fifth Ave #2401	212-529-6642
Francisco, Gus/220 E 23rd St	212-683-0418
Francki, Joe/420 E 54th St #21E	212-838-3170
Frank, Dick/11 W 25th St	212-242-4648
Frankian, Paul/59 W 19th St #X	212-675-1654
Fraser, Douglas/9 E 19th St	212-777-8404
Fraser, Rob/211 Thompson St #1E	212-677-4589
Frazier, David/7 Second Ave	212-459-4491
Fredericks, Bill/124 W 24th St #6B	212-463-0955
Freed, Leonard/79 Spring St	212-966-9200
Freidman, Lee/76 E 1st St	212-529-4544
Freithof, Wolfgang/628 Broadway #401	212-274-8300
Freni, Al/381 Park Ave S #809	212-679-2533
Friedman, Benno/26 W 20th St	212-255-6038
Friedman, Jerry/873 Broadway	212-505-5600
Friedman, Lee/76 E 1st St	212-529-4544
Friedman, Steve/545 W 111th St	212-864-2662
From, Anita/1114 Sixth Ave	212-703-1407
Froomer, Brett/7 E 20th St	212-533-3113
Fruitman, Sheva/28 Grove St	212-727-9829
Funk, Mitchell/500 E 77th St	212-988-2886
Furones, Claude Emile/40 Waterside Plaza	212-683-0622
Fusco, Paul/79 Spring St	212-966-9200

G

Gaffney, Joe/118 E 93rd St #5A	212-534-3985
Galante, Dennis/133 W 22nd St 3rd Fl	212-463-0938
Galante, Jim/678 Broadway	212-529-4300
Galipo, Frank/257 Park Ave S 9th Fl	212-995-8720
Gall, Sally/266 W 11th St	212-242-1458
Gallucci, Ed/568 Broadway #602	212-226-2215
Galton, Beth/236 W 26th St	212-242-2266
Gang, Julie/14 Jay St	212-925-3351
Ganges, Halley/35 W 36th St	212-868-1810
Garik, Alice/ Photo Comm/173 Windsor Pl, Brooklyn	718-499-1456
Garn, Andrew/85 E 10th St #5D	212-353-8434
Geaney, Tim/648 Broadway #1009	212-677-7913
Geller, Bonnie/57 W 93rd St	212-864-5922
Gelsobello, Paul/245 W 29th St #1200	212-947-0317
Generico, Tony/130 W 25th St	212-627-9755
Gentieu, Penny/87 Barrow St	212-691-1994
George, Michael/525 Hudson St	212-627-5868
Gershman, Neil/135 W 29th St	212-629-5877
Gerstein, Jesse/249 W 29th St	212-629-4688
Gescheidt, Alfred/175 Lexington Ave	212-889-4023
Getlen, David/60 Gramercy Park	212-475-6940
Ghergo, Christina/160 Fifth Ave #817	212-243-6811
Gianni, Fabrizio/245 E 58th St	212-752-8174
Gibbons, George/292 City Islnd Ave, Bronx	212-885-0769
Gigli, Ormond/327 E 58th St	212-758-2860
Gilbert, Gil/29 E 22nd St	212 254-3096
Gilbert, Thom/438 W 37th St	212-563-3219
Gillardin, Andre/6 W 20th St	212-675-2950
Giordano, John A/60 E 9th St #538	212-477-3273
Giovanni, Raeanne/311 E 12th St	212-673-7199
Giraldo, Anita/83 Canal #611	212-431-1193
Givotovsky, Andrei/105 E 10th St	212-777-8028
Gladstone, Gary/237 E 20th St #2H	212-777-7772
Glancz, Jeff/822 Greenwich St #2A	212-741-2504
Glassman, Keith/365 First Ave 2nd Fl	212-353-1214
Glaviano, Marco/222 Central Park S #41	212-307-7794
Glinn, Burt/41 Central Park W	212-877-2210
Globus Brothers Photography/44 W 24th St (P 56)	**212-243-1008**
Gloos, Conrad/155 W 68th St	212-724-1536
Goble, Brian/80 Varick St #6A	212-219-0887
Godlewski, Stan/1317 Laight St	212-941-1230
Goff, Lee/32 E 64th St	212-223-0716
Gold, Bernie/873 Broadway #301	212-677-0311
Gold, Charles/56 W 22nd St	212-242-2600
Goldberg, Les/147 W 22nd St	212-242-3825
Goldman, Michael/177 Hudson St	212-966-4997
Goldman, Richard/36 W 20th St	212-675-3033
Goldman, Susan/380 Lafayette St 5th Fl	212-674-8298
Goldring, Barry/568 Broadway #608	212-334-9494
Goldsmith, Lynn/241 W 36th St	212-736-4602
Goldstein, Art/66 Crosby St	212-966-2682

Goll, Charles R/404 E 83rd St 212-628-4881
Golob, Stanford/10 Waterside Plaza 212-532-7166
Goltz, Jason/16 First Ave 212-677-0929
Gonzalez, Luis/85 Livingston St, Brooklyn 718-834-0426
Goodman, Michael/71 W 23rd St 3rd Fl 212-727-1760
Gordon, Andrew/48 W 22nd St 212-807-9758
Gordon, Anthony/155 Wooster St 212-529-3711
Gordon, Joel/112 Fourth Ave 4th Fl 212-254-1688
Gordon, T S/153 W 18th St 212-978-4056
Gorin, Bart/1160 Broadway 212-683-3743
Gotman, John/111 W 24th St 212-255-0569
Gottfried, Arlene/523 E 14th St 212-260-2599
Gottlieb, Dennis/137 W 25th St 212-620-7050
Gould, Jeff/98-41 64th Rd, Rego Park 718-897-0610
Gove, Geoffrey/117 Waverly Pl 212-260-6051
Gozo Studio/40 W 17th St 212-620-8115
Graff, Randolph/160 Bleecker St 212-254-0412
Graflin, Liz/111 Fifth Ave 12th Fl 212-529-6700
Grand, Paul/1800 Ocean Pkwy, Brooklyn 718-375-0138
Grant, Joe/447 W 36th St 6th Fl 212-947-6807
Grant, Robert/62 Greene St 212-925-1121
Graves, Tom/136 E 36th St (P 77) 212-683-0241
Gray, Darren R/60 W 13th St #13C 212-886-1833
Gray, Katie/145 Hudson St 212-226-0223
Gray, Robert/160 West End Ave 212-721-3240
Green-Armytage, Stephen/171 W 57th St #7A 212-247-6314
Greenberg, David/54 King St 212-316-9196
Greenberg, Joel/265 Water St 212-285-0979
Greene, Jim/20 W 20th St #703 212-741-3764
Greene, Joshua/448 W 37th St #8D 212-243-2750
Greene, Richard/56 W 22nd St 212-242-5282
Greenfield, Lois/52 White St 212-925-1117
Greenfield-Sanders, Timothy/135 E 2nd St 212-674-7888
Gregoire, Peter/448 W 37th St 212-967-4969
Gregory, John/39 E 19th St 6th Fl 212-529-9424
Gregory, Kevin/237 W 26th St 212-807-9859
Greyshock, Caroline/578 Broadway #707 212-266-7563
Griffiths, Philip Jones/79 Spring St 212-966-9200
Grill, Tom/30 Irving Place 212-353-8600
Grimes, Tom/930 Columbus Ave 212-316-3741
Grinaldi, Michael/45 Tudor City Pl #1410 212-599-1266
Groen, Michael/119 W 23rd St #1002 212-929-1620
Gross, David/922 Third Ave #3R 212-688-4729
Gross, Garry/235 W 4th St 212-807-7141
Gross, Geoffrey/40 W 27th St 12th Fl 212-685-8850
Gross, Pat/315 E 86th St #1S East 212-427-9396
Grossman, David M/211 E 7th St, Brooklyn (P 78) 718-438-5021
Grossman, Eugene/310 Greenwich St #22H 212-962-6795
Grossman, Henry/37 Riverside Dr 212-580-7751
Grotell, Al/170 Park Row #15D 212-349-3165
Gruen, John/20 W 22nd St 212-242-8415
Guatti, Albano/250 Mercer St #C403 212-674-2230
Gudnason, Torkil/58 W 15th St 212-929-6680
Guice, Brad Studio/6 N Moore St 212-206-0966
Gurney, Manning/25 W 38th St 3rd Fl (P 79) 212-391-0965
Gurovitz, Judy/207 E 74th St 212-988-8685
Guyaux, Jean-Marie/29 E 19th St 212-529-5395
Guzman/31 W 31st St 212-643-9375

H

Haar, Thomas/463 West St 212-929-9054
Haas, Ken Inc/15 Sheridan Square 212-255-0707
Haber, Graham/344 W 38th St 212-268-4148
Hagen, Boyd/448 W 37th St #6A 212-244-2436
Haggerty, David/17 E 67th St 212-879-4141
Hagiwara, Brian/504 La Guardia Pl 212-674-6026
Haimann, Todd/26 W 38th St 212-391-0810
Halaska, Jan/PO Box 6611 FDR Sta 718-389-8923
Haling, George/231 W 29th St #302 212-736-6822
Hall, Barnaby/347 W 36th St #17PH 212-967-2912
Hamilton, Joe/15-22 Central Ave, Far Rockaway 718-868-4501
Hamilton, Keith/749 FDR Dr #6D 212-982-3375
Hamilton, Mark/119 W 23rd St 212-242-9814
Hammond, Francis/24 Wycoff St, Brooklyn 718-935-9038
Hammond, Maury/9 E 19th St 212-460-9990
Hampton Studios/515 Broadway #4A 212-431-4320
Hamsley, David/47 W 90th St 212-580-8667
Handelman, Dorothy/10 Gay St 212-242-3058
Hansen, Barbara/2278 Bronx Park East #F13, Bronx 212-798-6013
Hansen, Constance/31 W 31st St 9th Fl 212-643-9375
Hanson, Kent/147 Bleecker St #3R (P 82) 212-777-2399
Harbutt, Charles/1 Fifth Ave 212-645-4274
Hardin, Ted/454 W 46th St #5A-N 212-307-6208
Harrington, Grace/312 W 48th St 212-246-1749
Harris, Jeff/16 W 19th St 7th Fl 212-334-0125
Harris, Michael/18 W 21st St 212-255-3377
Harris, Ronald G/119 W 22nd St 212-255-2330
Harrison, Howard/150 W 22nd St 2nd Fl 212-989-9233
Hartmann, Erich/79 Spring St 212-966-9200
Haruo/126 W 22nd St 212-505-8800
Harvey, Ned/164 W 25th St 11th fl 212-807-7043
Hashi Studio/49 W 23rd St 3rd Fl 212-675-6902
Hashimoto/153 W 27th St #1202 212-645-1221
Hathon, Elizabeth/8 Greene St 212-219-0685
Hausman, George/1181 Broadway 6th Fl 212-686-4810
Haviland, Brian/34 E 30th St 4th Fl 212-481-4132
Hayes, Kerry/35 Taft Ave, Staten Island 212-925-3021
Hayward, Bill/21 E 22nd St 212-979-7352
Hecker, David/568 Broadway 212-925-1233
Heiberg, Milton/71 W 23rd St 5th Fl 212-741-6405
Heiges, Jeff/6750 Fifth Ave, Brooklyn 718-833-3212
Heinlein, David/56 W 22nd St 212-645-1158
Heir, Stewart/30 W 22nd St 5th Fl East 212-633-2187
Heisler, Gregory/568 Broadway #800 212-777-8100
Helburn, Bill/161 E 35th St 212-683-4980
Hellerman, William/31 Linden St, Brooklyn 718-443-2611
Hellerstein, Stephen A/56 W 22nd St 12th Fl 212-645-0508
Helms, Bill/1175 York Ave 212-759-2079
Hemsay, Yvonne/4520 Henry Hudson Pkwy, Riverdale 212-549-0095
Henze, Don Studio/39 W 29th St 4th Fl 212-689-7375
Heron, Michal (Ms)/28 W 71st St 212-787-1272
Herr, H Buff/56 W 82nd St 212-595-4783
Hess, Brad/5 W 29th St 9th fl 212-684-3131
Heuberger, William/140 W 22nd St 212-242-1532
Heyert, Elizabeth/251 W 30th St #12AW 212-594-1008
Heyman, Ken Photo/37 Bank St 212-627-2028
Hilaire, Max/218 E 27th St 212-889-1685
Hill, Mark/119 W 23rd St #1003 212-727-1528
Hill, Pat/37 W 26th St 212-532-3479
Hill, Steve/220 E 25th St #4D 212-683-1642
Hill, Timothy/336 Clinton Ave, Brooklyn 718-783-3896
Himmel, Lizzie/218 E 17th St 212-777-6482
Hine, Skip/117 E 24th St #4B 212-529-6100
Hing/ Norton Photography/24 W 30th St 8th Fl 212-683-4258
Hiro/50 Central Park West 212-580-8000
Hirsch, Butch/107 W 25th St 212-929-3024
Hirst, Michael/1150 Sixth Ave 212-941-6318
Hll, Timothy/336 Clinton Ave, Brooklyn 718-783-3896
Hochman, Allen Studio/9-11 E 19 St 212-777-8404
Hochman, Richard/210 Fifth Ave 212 532-7766
Hodgson, David/550 Riverside Dr 212-864-6941
Hoffman, Ethan/95 Van Dam St 212-645-4274
Holbrooke, Andrew/50 W 29th St 212-889-5995
Holdeier, John/37 W 20th St #606 212-620-4260
Holderer, John/37 W 20th St #606 212-620-4260
Holdorf, Thomas/132 W 22 St 3rd Fl 212-727-7981
Holland, Robin/430 Greenwich St 212-431-5351
Hollyman, Stephanie/85 South St 212-825-1828
Hollyman, Tom/300 E 40th St #19R 212-867-2383
Holub, Ed/83 Canal St #309 212-431-2356
Holz, George/400 Lafayette 212-505-5607
Hom, Frank/601 W 26th St #13A 212-979-5533
Hooper, Thomas/126 Fifth Ave #5B 212-691-0122
Hopkins, Douglas/PO Box 185 212-243-1774
Hopkins, Stephan/475 Carlton Ave, Brooklyn 718-783-6461
Hopson, Gareth/22 E 21st St 212-535-3800
Hori, Richard/119 W 23rd St #400 212-645-8333
Horowitz, Irwin/1200 Broadway #5A 212-889-8098
Horowitz, Ross M/206 W 15th St 212-206-9216
Horowitz, Ryszard/137 W 25th St 212-243-6440
Horst/188 E 64th St #1701 212-751-4937
Horvath, Jim/95 Charles St 212-741-0300
Houze, Philippe Louis/123 Prince St 212-614-0435
Howell, Josephine/127 Pacific St, Brooklyn 718-858-2451
Huang, Ken/287 Avenue C 212-982-6976

Huibregtse, Jim/54 Greene St 212-925-3351
Hume, Adam/231 E 76th St Box 30 212-794-1754
Huntzinger, Bob/76 Ninth Ave 212-929-9001
Hurwitz, Harrison/14 Horatio St #2E 212-989-4113
Huston, Larry/40 E 21st St 212 777-7541
Huszar, Steven/377 Park Ave South 212-532-3772
Hyman, Barry/319 E 78th St #3C 212-879-3294
Hyman, Paul/124 W 79th St 212-255-1532

I

Ianuzzi, Tom/141 Wooster St #6A (P 85) 212-563-1987
Icaza, Iraida/412 E 50th St 212-688-8137
Ichi/303 Park Ave S #506 212-254-4810
Ihara/568 Broadway #507 212-219-9363
Ikeda, Shig/636 Sixth Ave #4C 212-924-4744
Image Makers/310 E 23rd St #9F 212-533-4498
Imperatori, Gabriella/438 Broome St 212-941-0010
Ing, Francis/112 W 31st St 5th Fl 212-279-5022
Intrater, Roberta/1212 Beverly Rd, Brooklyn 718-462-4004
Iooss, Walter/344 W 72nd St 212-601-3232
Irwin, William/70 Remsen St #9B, Brooklyn 718-237-2598
Isaacs, Norman/277 W 11th St 212-243-5547
Ishimuro, Eisuke/130 W 25th St 10th Fl 212-255-9198
Ivany, Sandra/6 W 90th St #6 212-580-1501
Ivy, Lawrence/504 E 54th St 212-475-6696
Izu, Kenro/140 W 22nd St 212-254-1002

J

J & M Studio/107 W 25th St #3A 212-627-5460
Jackson, Martin/217 E 85th St #110 215-271-5149
Jacobs, Marty/34 E 23rd St 5th Fl 212-475-1160
Jacobs, Robert/448 W 37th St 212-967-6883
Jacobson, Jeff/230 Hamilton Ave, Staten Island 718-720-0533
James, Don/PO Box 901, Brooklyn 718-797-9850
Jawitz, Louis H/13 E 17th St #PH 212-929-0008
Jeffery, Richard/119 W 22nd St 212-255-2330
Jeffrey, Lance/30 E 21st St #4A 212-674-0595
Jenkinson, Mark/142 Bleecker St Box 6 212-529-0488
Jenssen, Buddy/34 E 29th St 212-686-0865
Joel, Seth/515 Broadway 212-925-1373
Joern, James/125 Fifth Ave 212-260-8025
Joester, Steve/15 W 26th St 5th Fl 212-545-9255
Johansky, Peter/27 W 20th St 212-242-7013
Jones, Carolyn/167 Spring St 212-431-9696
Jones, Chris/240 E 27th St 212-685-0679
Jones, Spencer/23 Leonard St #5 212-941-8165
Jones, Steve Photo/120 W 25th St #3E 212-929-3641
Joseph, Meryl/158 E 82nd St 212-861-5057

K

Kachaturian, Armen/330 Broome St 212-334-0986
Kahan, Eric/36 W 20th St 3rd Fl 212-243-9727
Kahlil, Sean/200 E 37th St 4th Fl 212-686-5084
Kahn, R T/156 E 79th St 212-988-1423
Kalinsky, George/4 Pennsylvania Plaza 212-563-8095
Kalleberg, Garrett/520 E 5th St #2B 212-674-2716
Kamper, George Productions Ltd/15 W 24th St
(P 86,87) 212-627-7171
Kamsler, Leonard/140 Seventh Ave 212-242-4678
Kan Photography/153 W 27th St #406 212-645-2684
Kana, Titus/876 Broadway 212-473-5550
Kanakis, Michael/144 W 27th St 10th Fl 212-807-8232
Kane, Art/568 Broadway 212-925-7334
Kane, Peter T/236 W 26th St #502 212-924-4968
Kaniklidis, James/1270 E 18th St, Brooklyn 718-338-0931
Kaplan, Alan/7 E 20th St 212-982-9500
Kaplan, Michael/171 W 23d St #3A 212-741-3271
Kaplan, Peter B/7 E 20th St #4R 212-995-5000
Kaplan, Peter J/924 West End Ave 212-222-1193
Karales, James H/147 W 79th St 212-799-2483
Karia, Bhupendra/9 E 96th St #15B 212-860-5479
Kasten, Barbara/251 W 19th St #8C 212 627-5229
Kasterine, Dmitri/237 Lafayette St 212-226-0401
Katchian, Sonia/44 W 54th St 212-586-5304
Katrina/286 Fifth Ave #1206 212-279-2838

Katvan, Moshe/40 W 17th St 212-242-4895
Katz, Baruch/121 W 27th St #1205 212-645-6085
Katz, Paul/65-61 Saunders St #1L, Queens 718-275-3615
Katzenstein, David/21 E 4th St 212-529-9460
Kaufman, Curt/215 W 88th St 212-873-9841
Kaufman, Elliott/255 W 90th St 212-496-0860
Kaufman, Jeff/27 W 24th St 212-627-1878
Kaufman, Mickey/144 W 27th St 212-255-1976
Kaufman, Ted/121 Madison Ave #4E 212-685-0349
Kawachi, Yutaka/33 W 17th St 2nd Fl 212-929-4825
Kaye, Nancy/77 Seventh Ave #7U 818-886-1180
Kayser, Alex/211 W Broadway 212-431-8518
Keeve, Douglas/50 Ave A 212-777-5405
Keller, Tom/440 E 78th St 212-472-3667
Kelley, Charles W Jr/649 Second Ave #6C-30 212-686-3879
Kelley, David/265 W 37th St #23E 212-869-7896
Kellner, Jeff/16 Waverly Pl 212-475-3719
Kennedy, Donald J/521 W 23rd St 10th Fl 212-206-7740
Kent, Karen/29 John St 212-962-6793
Kerbs, Ken/100 Dean St #1, Brooklyn 718-858-6950
Keyser, James/630 Hudson St 212-243-6405
Khornak, Lucille/425 E 58th St 212-593-0933
Kilkelly, James/40 W 73rd St #2R 212-873-6820
King, Wm Douglas/1766 E 32nd St, Brooklyn 718-998-8351
Kingsford, Michael Studio/874 Broadway 212-475-0553
Kinmonth, Rob/3 Rutherford Pl 212-475-6370
Kirk, Barbara/447 E 65th St 212-734-3233
Kirk, Charles/276 Winchester Ave, Staten Island 212-677-3770
Kirk, Malcolm/12 E 72nd St 212-744-3642
Kirk, Russell/31 W 21st St 212-206-1446
Kitchen, Dennis/80 Fourth Ave 3rd fl 212-674-7658
Kittle, Kit/511 E 20th St 212-995-8866
Klauss, Cheryl/463 Broome St 212-431-3569
Klein, Arthur/35-42 80th St, Jackson Heights 718-278-0457
Klein, Matthew/104 W 17th St #2E 212-255-6400
Klein, Steven/145 E 36th St #2 212-481-3860
Kohli, Eddy/160 Fifth Ave #914 212-924-6760
Kojima, Tak/25 W 23rd St 2nd Fl 212-243-2243
Kolansky, Palma/55 Vandam St #15 212-727-7300
Konstantin Photography/306 W 57th St 212-765-8973
Kopelow, Paul/135 Madison Ave 14th Fl 212-689-0685
Kopin, Therese/228 E 25th St 212-684-2636
Kopitchinski, Reuben/98 Riverside Dr 212-724-1252
Korsh, Ken/118 E 28th St 212-685-8864
Kosoff, Brian/28 W 25th St 6th Fl 212-243-4880
Koudis, Nick/40 E 23rd St 2nd Fl 212-475-2802
Kouirinis, Bill/381 Park Ave S #710 212-696-5674
Kovner, Richard/80 East End Ave #10A 212-775-7989
Kozan, Dan/127 W 25th St 12th fl 212-691-2288
Kozlowski, Mark/48 Fourth St, Troy 212-684-7487
Kozyra, James/568 Broadway 212-431-1911
Kramer, Daniel/110 W 86th St 212-873-7777
Kramer, Nathaniel/730 Park Ave 212-737-6098
Krasner/Trebitz/PO Box 1548 Cooper Sta 212-777-2132
Kratochvil, Antonin/448 W 37th St #6G 212-947-1589
Kraus, Brian/126 W 22nd St 212-691-1813
Krein, Jeffrey/119 W 23rd St #800 212-741-5207
Krementz, Jill/228 E 48th St 212-688-0480
Krinke, Michael/107 W 25th St #3A 212-627-5460
Kroll, Eric/118 E 28th St #1005 212-684-2465
Kron, Dan/154 W 18th St 212-463-9333
Krongard, Steve/212-A E 26th St 212-689-5634
Kuczera, Mike/20 W 22nd St #817 212-620-8112
Kudo/39 Walker St 212-966-1856
Kuehn, Karen/49 Warren St 212-406-3005
Kugler, Dennis/43 Bond St 212-677-3826
Kuhn, Ann Spanos/1155 Broadway 212-595-7611
Kunze, George/601 Tenth Ave 212-268-4456
Kupinski, Steven/36 E 20th St 212-982-3230

L

LaChappelle, David/613 E 6th St #4A 212-529-7020
Lachenauer, Paul/876 Broadway 212-529-7059
Lacombe, Brigitte/30 E 81st St 212-472-9660
Lacy, John/24746 Rensselaer, Oak Park, MI 313-548-3842
Lafontaine, Marie Josee/160 Fifth Ave #914 212-924-6760
LaMoglia, Anthony/63 Eighth Ave #3B, Brooklyn 718-636-9839

LaMonica, Chuck/20 Mountain Ave, New Rochelle	212-727-7884
Lane, Morris/212-A E 26th St	212-696-0498
Lang, Rob/243 West End Ave	212-595-2217
Lange, George/817 West End Ave	212-666-1414
Langley, David/536 W 50th St	212-581-3930
Lanting, Ted/61 Horatio St	212-206-1263
Laperruque, Scott/157 Chambers St 12th Fl	212-962-5200
Larrain, Gilles/95 Grand St	212-925-8494
Larson, Susan/56 W 22nd St	212-929-8980
Laszlo Studio/11 W 30th St 2nd fl	212-736-6690
Laszlo, Hege/179 E 80th St	212-737-1620
Lategan, Barry/502 LaGuardia Pl	212-228-6850
Lattari, Tony/448 W 37th St #7A	212-947-7488
Laubmeyer, Klaus/874 Broadway	212-598-4066
Laurance, Bruce Studio/253 W 28th St 5th Fl	212-947-3451
Laure, Jason/8 W 13th St 11th Fl	212-691-7466
Laurence, Mary/PO Box 1763	212-903-4025
Lavoie, Raymond/1371 First Ave #1R	212-472-7596
Lawrence, Christopher/12 E 18th St	212-807-8028
Lawrence, David/160 Ave of Americas 2nd Fl	212-274-0710
Lax, Ken/239 Park Ave S	212-228-6191
Layman, Alex/142 W 14th St 6th Fl	212-989-5845
LeBaube, Guy/310 E 46th St	212-986-6981
Ledbetter, Anthony Rush/333 E 14th St #11K	212-533-5949
Lederman, Ed/166 E 34th St #12H	212-685-8612
LeDuc, Grant/41 E 7th St #22	212-869-3050
Leduc, Lyle/320 E 42nd St #1014	212-697-9216
Ledzian, Mark/245 W 29th St	212-563-4589
Lee, Jung (Ms)/132 W 21st St 3rd Fl	212-807-8107
Lee, Vincent/155 Wooster St #3F	212-254-7888
Lee, Wellington/381 Park Ave S #617	212-696-0800
Lefkowitz, Jay Alan/5 E 16th St	212-929-1036
Legrand, Michel/152 W 25th St 12th Fl	212-807-9754
Lehman, Amy/210 E 75th St	212-535-7457
Leibovitz, Annie/55 Vandam St 14th Fl	212-807-0220
Leicmon, John/200 W 15th St	212-675-3219
Leighton, Thomas/321 E 43rd St PH #12	212-370-1835
Lein, Kevin/83 Leonard St 3rd Fl (P 88)	**212-966-2764**
Lenaas, John/27 W 76th St	212-799-4379
Lenore, Dan/249 W 29th St #2N	212-967-7115
Leo, Donato/866 Ave of Americas	212-685-5527
Leonian, Phillip/220 E 23rd St	212-989-7670
Lerner, Richard/20 W 20th St #501	212-627-2070
Lesinski, Martin/40 W 17th St #2B	212-463-7857
Lesnick, Steve/27 W 24th St 10th Fl	212-929-1078
Leung, J Ming/60 Pineapple St #6B, Brooklyn	718-522-1894
Leven, Barbara/48 W 21st St 12th fl	212-645-4828
Levin, James/1570 First Ave #3D	212-734-0315
Levine, Jonathan/366 Broadway	212-791-7578
Levine, Nancy/41 Fifth Ave #3D	212-473-0015
Levinson, Ken/35 East 10th St	212-254-6180
Levy, Peter/119 W 22nd St	212-691-6600
Levy, Richard/5 W 19th St	212-243-4220
Lewin, Gideon/25 W 39th St	212-921-5558
Lewin, Ralph/156 W 74th St	212-580-0482
Lewis, Robert/333 Park Ave S 4th Fl	212-475-6564
Lieberman, Nathaniel/353 E 77th St	212-517-3648
Liebman, Phil/315 Hudson	212-269-7777
Lindner, Steven/18 W 27th St 3rd Fl	212-683-1317
Lippman, Marcia/220 E 63rd St	212-832-0321
Lisi-Hoeltzell Ltd/156 Fifth Ave	212-255-0303
Little, Christopher/4 W 22nd St	212-691-1024
Lloyd, Harvey/310 E 23rd St	212-533-4498
Lock, Al/438 Broome St #1N	212-886-1851
Loete, Mark/33 Gold St #405	212-571-2235
Loew, Anthony/503 Broadway	212-226-1999
Logan, Kevin/119 W 23rd St #803	212-206-0539
Logozio, Lou/48 W 21st St	212-741-3818
Lombardi, Frederick/180 Pinehurst Ave	212-568-0740
Lomeo, Angelo/336 Central Park W	212-663-2122
Lonninge, Lars/121 W 19th St	212-627-0100
Loomis, Just/160 Fifth Ave #914	212-924-6760
Loppacher, Peter/39 Jane St	212-929-1322
Lorenz, Robert/80 Fourth Ave	212-505-8483
Loughborough, John/169 W 85th St #4A	212-874-7396
Louise, Stephanie/160 Fifth Ave #914	212-924-6760
Love, Robin/676 Broadway 4th Fl	212-777-3113
Lowe, Jacques/138 Duane St	212-227-3298

Lubianitsky, Leonid/1013 Ave of Americas	212-391-0197
Lucka, Klaus/101 Fifth Ave 2nd Fl	212-255-2424
Luftig, Allan/873 Broadway	212-533-4113
Lulow, William/126 W 22nd St	212-675-1625
Lupino, Stephan/543 Broadway #4	212-334-6474
Luppino, Michael/126 W 22nd St 6th Fl	212-633-9486
Luria, Dick/5 E 16th St 4th Fl	212-929-7575
Luttenberg, Gene/7608 Hewlett St, New Hyde Park	212-620-8112
Lyon, Mark/145 W 58th St	212-333-2631
Lypides, Chris/119 W 23rd St	212-741-1911

M

Maas, Rita/40 W 27th St 12th fl	212-447-0410
Maass, Rob/166 E 7th St	212-473-5612
Macdonald, Keith/117 E 31st St	212-447-0711
Macedonia, Carmine/866 Ave of Americas	212-889-8520
Mackiewicz, Jim/160 Fifth Ave #908	212-989-8438
MacLaren, Mark/430 E 20th St	212-674-0155
MacWeeney, Alen Inc/171 First Ave	212-473-2500
Madere, John/75 Spring St 5th Fl	212-966-4136
Magni, Tiziano/145 E 36th St #2	212-481-3860
Mahdavian, Daniel/PO Box 1850 Canal St Sta	212-226-6265
Mahshie, Jason/452 W 19th St #1C	212-627-7395
Maisel, David/16 E 23rd St 3rd Fl	212-228-2288
Maisel, Jay/190 Bowery	212-431-5013
Malignon, Jacques/34 W 28th St	212-532-7727
Maloof, Karen/110 W 94th St #4C	212-678-7737
Mandarino, Tony/114 E 32nd St	212-686-2866
Manella, Robert/132 W 21st St	212-645-6419
Mangia, Tony/11 E 32nd St #3B	212-889-6340
Mani, Monsor/40 E 23rd St	212-947-9116
Manna, Lou/347 E 53rd St #6D	212-683-8689
Manno, John/20 W 22nd St #802	212-243-7353
Marchese, Jim/200 W 20th St	212-242-1087
Marco, Phil/104 Fifth Ave 4th Fl	212-929-8082
Marcus, Barry/23 Second Ave	212-420-9443
Marcus, Helen/120 E 75th St	212-879-6903
Maresca, Frank/236 W 26th St	212-620-0955
Margerin, Bill/41 W 25th St	212-645-1532
Marshall, Elizabeth/200 Central Pk S #31A	212-463-7884
Marshall, Jim Studio/20 Jay St, Brooklyn	718-797-9449
Marshall, Lee/201 W 89th St	212-799-9717
Martin, Bard/142 W 26th St	212-929-6712
Martin, Gene/157 E 72nd St #10A	212-861-0811
Martin, Gregg/169 Columbia Hts, Brooklyn	718-522-3237
Martinez, Oscar/303 Park Ave S #408	212-673-0932
Marvullo Photomontage/141 W 28th St #502	212-564-6501
Marx, Richard/130 W 25th St	212-929-8880
Marzelli, Michael/78 Fifth Ave	212-727-8700
Masca/109 W 26th St	212-929-4818
Mason, Donald/111 W 19th St #2E	212-675-3809
Massey, Philip/475 W 186th St	212-928-8210
Masullo, Ralph/111 W 19th St	212-727-1809
Masunaga, Ryuzo/119 W 22nd St 5th Fl	212-807-7012
Mathews, Barbara Lynn/16 Jane St	212-691-0823
Mathews, Bruce Photo/95 E 7th St	212-529-7909
Matsuo, Toshi/105 E 29th St	212-532-1320
Matthews, Cynthia/200 E 78th St	212-288-7349
Matura, Ned/119 W 23rd St #1002	212-463-9692
Maucher, Arnold/154 W 18th St	212-206-1535
Mauro, Aldo/496 LaGuardia Pl #524	212-989-4989
Maynard, Chris/297 Church St	212-255-8204
Mazzeo, Michael/37 W 20th St #606	212-627-3766
McCabe, David/39 W 67th St #1403	212-874-7480
McCabe, Robert/117 E 24th St	212-677-1910
McCarthy, Jo Anna/535 Greenwich St	212-675-2757
McCarthy, Margaret/31 E 31st St	212-696-5971
McCartney, Susan/902 Broadway #1608	212-533-0660
McDermott, Brian/48 W 21st St	212-675-7273
McGlenn, David/18-23 Astoria Blvd, LI City	718-626-9427
McGloughlin, James/148 W 24th St 5th Fl	212-206-8207
McGlynn, David/18-23 Astoria Blvd, Long Island City	718-626-9427
McGoon, James/317 E 18th St	212-779-3905
McGrath, Norman/164 W 79th St #16	212-799-6422
McLaughlin, Glenn/6 W 20th St 2nd Fl	212-645-7028
McLoughlin, James Inc/148 W 24th St 5th Fl	212-206-8207
McNally, Brian T/234 E 81st St #1A	212-744-1263

McNally, Joe/305 W 98th St #6D S....212-219-1014
McNamara, Jeff/280 Lafayette....212-966-4325
McQueen, Mark/265 E 7th St....212-995-8965
McPherson, Andrew/160 Fifth Ave #914....212-924-6760
Mead, Chris/108 Reade St....212-619-5616
Megna, Richard/210 Forsyth St....212-473-5770
Meisel, Steven/303 Park Ave S #409....212-777-7130
Melford, Michael/13 E 47th St 5th Fl....212-473-3095
Mella, Michael/217 Thompson St....212-777-6012
Mellon/69 Perry St....212-691-4166
Memo Studio/39 W 67th St #1402....212-787-1658
Mena, Marcos/49 W 44th St....212-921-0739
Menashe, Abraham/306 E 5th St #27 (P 95)....212-254-2754
Menda, George/568 Broadway #403....212-431-7440
Menken, Howard Studios/119 W 22nd St....212-924-4240
Mensch, Barbara/274 Water St....212-349-8170
Meola, Eric/535 Greenwich St....212-255-5150
Merle, Michael G/54 W 16th St....212-741-3801
Mervar, Louis/36 W 37th St....212-868-0078
Messin, Larry/64 Carlyle Green, Staten Island....718-948-7209
Metz, Simon/56 W 22nd St....212-807-6106
Metzner, Sheila/310 Riverside Dr #20....212-863-1222
Meyer, Kip/80 Madison Ave #7E....212-683-9039
Meyer, Rich/13 Laight St....212-226-7560
Meyer-Bosse, Hilmar/487 W Broadway....212-979-1616
Meyerowitz, Joel/151 W 19th St....212-242-0740
Micaud, Christopher/143 Ave B....212-473-7266
Michals, Duane/109 E 19th St....212-473-1563
Michelson, Eric T/101 Lexington Ave #4B....212-683-6259
Mieles, Peter/20 Ave D #11I....212-475-6025
Milbauer, Dennis/15 W 28th St....212-532-3702
Milisenda, John/424 56th St, Brooklyn....718-439-4571
Miller, Bert/30 Dongan Pl....212-567-7947
Miller, Bill Photo/239 Park Ave S #5C....212-777-3304
Miller, Donald L/295 Central Park W (P 96,97)....212-496-2830
Miller, Eileen/28 W 38th St....212-944-1507
Miller, Myron/23 E 17th St....212-242-3780
Miller, Rex/34-28 29th St, Astoria....718-392-3263
Miller, Sue Ann/115 W 27th St 9th Fl....212-645-5172
Milne, Bill/140 W 22nd St....212-255-0710
Mincey, Dale/50 Grand St #5F....212-713-5129
Ming Studio/60 Pineapple St #6B, Brooklyn....212-254-8570
Minh Studio/200 Park Ave S #1507....212-477-0649
Minks, Marlin/34-43 82nd St, Jackson Hts....718-507-9513
Mistretta, Martin/220 W 19th St 11th Fl....212-675-1547
Mitchell, Andrew/220 Berkeley Pl, Brooklyn....718-783-6727
Mitchell, Benn/119 W 23rd St....212-255-8686
Mitchell, Diane/175 W 73rd St....212-877-7624
Mitchell, Jack/356 E 74th St....212-737-8940
MKM Studios, Inc/117 E 31st St....212-447-0711
Molkenthin, Michael/135 W 26th St #6....212-727-2788
Montezinos, Joseph/142 W 26th St....212-645-4385
Moore, Carla/11 W 19th St....212-633-0300
Moore, Chris/20 W 22nd St #810....212-242-0553
Moore, Jimmy/38 E 19th St....212-674-7150
Moore, Robert/11 W 25th St....212-691-4373
Moore, Truman/873 Broadway 4th Fl....212-533-3655
Moran, Nancy/143 Greene St....212-505-9620
Morello, Joe/40 W 28th St....212-684-2340
Morgan, Jeff/27 W 20th St #604....212-924-4000
Morissa/37 W 20th St #1201....212-741-2620
Morosse, Mark/122 Montague St #5, Brooklyn....212-642-5264
Morris, Bill/34 E 29th St 6th Fl....212-685-7354
Morris, Leonard/200 Park Ave S #1410....212-473-8485
Morrison, Ted/286 Fifth Ave....212-279-2838
Morsch, Roy/1200 Broadway #2B....212-697-5537
Morsillo, Les/13 Laight St....212-219-8009
Morton, Keith/39 W 29th St 11th Fl....212-889-6643
Moscati, Frank/1181 Broadway....212-686-4810
Moskowitz, Sonia/5 W 86th St #18B....212-877-6883
Mougin, Claude/227 W 17th St....212-691-7895
Mroczynski, Claus/529 W 42nd St #2L....212-947-2767
Mucchi, Fabio/5 W 20th St....212-620-0167
Mucci, Tina/119 W 23rd St #902....212-206-9402
Mullane, Fred/116 E 27th St 8th Fl....212-580-4045
Muller, Rick/23 W 31st St #3....212-967-3177
Muller, Rudy/318 E 39th St....212-679-8124
Mundy, Michael/220 E 5th St #1E....212-529-7114
Munro, Gordon/381 Park Ave S....212-889-1610
Munson, Russell/458 Broadway 5th Fl....212-226-8875
Murphy, Arthur A/421 E 64th St #6F....212-628-1332
Myers, Gary/105 W 70th St #1F....212-787-2712
Myers, Robert J/407 E 69th St....212-249-8085
Myriad Communications Inc/208 W 30th St....212-564-4340

N

Nadelson, Jay/116 Mercer St....212-226-4266
Nahem, Richard/21 W 16th St....212-206-0039
Nahoum, Ken/95 Greene St PH-E....212-219-0592
Naideau, Harold/233 W 26th St....212-691-2942
Nakamura, Tohru/112 Greene St....212-334-8011
Nakano, George/8 1/2 MacDougal Alley....212-228-9370
Namuth, Hans/20 W 22nd St....212-691-3220
Nanfra, Victor/222 E 46th St....212-687-8920
Naples, Elizabeth/210 Fifth Ave....212-889-1476
Nault, Corky/251 W 19th St....212-807-7310
Nedboy, Robin/335 W 38th St....212-563-1924
Needham, Steven Mark/111 W 19th St 2nd Fl....212-206-1914
Neil, Joseph/150 Fifth Ave #319....212-691-1881
Neleman, Hans/348 W 14th St....212-645-5832
Nelken, Dan Studio/43 W 27th St....212-532-7471
Nesbit, Charles/62 Greene St....212-925-0225
Neumann, Peter/30 E 20th St 5th Fl....212-420-9538
Neumann, William/119 W 23rd St #206....212-691-7405
Neve, Roger/88 Lexington Ave....212-684-5180
Newler, Michael/135 W 29th St 4th Fl....212-643-0022
Newman, Arnold/39 W 67th St....212-877-4510
Newton, Philip/311 E 12th St....212-353-2467
Ney, Nancy/108 E 16th St 6th Fl....212-260-4300
Nguyen, Minh/200 Park Ave S....212-477-0649
Niccolini, Dianora/2 W 32nd St #200....212-564-4953
Nicholas, Peter/29 Bleecker St....212-529-5560
Nicholson, Nick/121 W 72nd St #2E....212-362-8418
Nicks, Dewy/361 W 36th St #9B....212-563-2971
Nicolaysen, Ron/448 W 37th St #12A....212-947-5167
Niederman, Mark/119 W 25th St....212-255-9052
Niefield, Terry/12 W 27th St 13th Fl....212-686-8722
Nielsen, Anne/288 W 12th St....212-463-0712
Nisnevich, Lev/133 Mulberry St....212-219-0535
Nivelle, Serge/145 Hudson St 14th Fl....212-226-6200
Niwa-Ogrudek Ltd/17 W 17th St....212-645-8008
Nons, Leonard/5 Union Sq West....212-741-3990
Noren, Catherine/15 Barrow St....212-627-7805
Norvila, Algis/963 Lorimer St, Brooklyn....718-388-0516
Nystrom, Dick/158 Spring St....212-431-6793

O

O'Brien, Michael/145 E 36th St #2....212-481-3860
O'Bryan, Maggie/344 E 9th St....212-777-8574
O'Connor, David/153 E 26th St #7B....212-689-5892
O'Connor, Thom/74 Fifth Ave....212-620-0723
O'Neill, Michael/134 Tenth Ave....212-807-8777
O'Rourke, J Barry/578 Broadway #707....212-226-7113
Obremski, George/1200 Broadway #2A....212-684-2933
Ochi, Toru/70 W 95th St #4B....212-865-1865
Ockenga, Starr/68 Laight St....212-431-5158
Oelbaum, Zeva/600 W 115th St #84L....212-864-7926
Ogilvy, Stephen/35 W 36th St....212-643-9330
Ohringer, Frederick/514 Broadway....212-737-6487
Okenfels III, Frank/245 E 30th St....212-683-1304
Olivo, John/545 W 45th St....212-765-8812
Olman, Bradley/15 W 24th St 11th Fl....212-243-0649
Ommer, Uwe/84 Riverside Dr....212-496-0268
Oner, Matt/231 E 14th St #4R....212-529-2844
Opton, Suzanne/312 E 9th St #6....212-353-8100
Oringer, Hal/568 Broadway #503....212-219-1588
Ort, Samuel/3323 Kings Hwy, Brooklyn....718-377-1218
Ortner, Jon/64 W 87th St (P 44,45)....212-873-1950
Oshimoto, Ryuichi/286 Fifth Ave....212-279-2838
Otfinowski, Danuta/165 W 20th St....212-243-6625
Otsuki, Toshi/241 W 36th St....212-594-1939
Owens, Sigrid/221 E 31st St....212-686-5190

P

Paccione/73 Fifth Ave	212-691-8674
Padys, Diane/11 Worth St 4th Fl	212-941-8532
Page, Lee/310 E 46th St	212-286-9159
Pagliuso, Jean/12 E 20th St	212-674-0370
Pagnano, Patrick/217 Thompson St	212-475-2566
Palmisano, Giorgio/309 Mott St #4A	212-431-7719
Palubniak, Jerry/144 W 27th St	212-645-2838
Palubniak, Nancy/144 W 27th St	212-645-2838
Pappas, Tony/73-37 Austin St, Forest Hills	718-261-6898
Paras, Michael/668 Ave of Americas 2nd Fl (P 50)	**212-243-8546**
Parker, Bo/448 W 37th St	212-564-1131
Parks, Claudia/210 E 73rd St #1G	212-879-9841
Passmore, Nick/150 W 80th St	212-724-1401
Pastor, Mariano/54 W 21st St	212-645-7115
Pateman, Michael/155 E 35th St	212-685-6584
Peden, John/155 W 19th St 6th Fl	212-255-2674
Pederson/Erwin/76 Ninth Ave 16th Fl	212-929-9001
Pelaez, Jose Luis/568 Broadway #103	212-995-2283
Pellesier, Sam/22 W 21st St	212-242-7222
Pemberton, John/377 Park Ave S 2nd Fl	212-532-9285
Penn, Irving/89 Fifth Ave 11th Fl	212-880-8426
Penny, Donald Gordon/505 W 23rd St #PH	212-243-6453
Peoples, Joe/11 W 20th St 6th Fl	212-633-0026
Peress, Gilles/72 Spring St	212-966-9200
Perkell, Jeff/36 W 20th St 6th fl	212-645-1506
Perry, Linda/PO Box 340398/Ryder Sta, Brooklyn	718-376-0763
Perweiler, Gary/873 Broadway	212-254-7247
Peterson, Grant/568 Broadway #1003	212-475-2767
Peticolas, Kip/210 Forsyth St	212-473-5770
Petoe, Denes/39 E 29th St	212-213-3311
Pettinato, Anthony/42 Greene St	212-226-9380
Pfeffer, Barbara/40 W 86th St	212-877-9913
Pfizenmaier, Edward/42 E 23rd	212-627-5659
Philipeaux, Eddy Jean/POB 2994 Rockefeller Ctr Sta	212-468-2889
Philippas, Constantine/446 E 20th St #9E	212-674-5248
Phillips, James/82 Greene St	212-219-1799
Picayo, Jose/32 Morton St	212-989-8945
Pich, Tom/310 E 65th St	212-288-3376
Piel, Denis/458 Broadway 9th Fl	212-925-8929
Pierce, Richard/241 W 36th St #8F	212-947-8241
Pilgreen, John/140 E 13th St 2nd Fl	212-982-4887
Pilossof, Judd/142 W 26th St	212-989-8971
Pinderhughes, John/122 W 26th St 12th Fl	212-989-6706
Pioppo, Peter/50 W 17th St	212-243-0661
Piscioneri, Joe/333 Park Ave S	212-473-3345
Pite, Jonathan/244 E 21st St #7	212-777-5484
Pix Elation/230 Park Ave #2525	212-581-6470
Pizzarello, Charlie/15 W 18th St	212-243-8441
Plessner, W/121 W 27th St #502	212-645-2121
Plotkin, Bruce/3 W 18th St 7th Fl	212-691-6185
Pobereskin, Joseph/139 Lincoln Pl, Brooklyn (P 51)	**212-619-3711**
Pobiner, Ted Studios Inc/381 Park Ave S	212-679-5911
Pohl, Birgit/PO Box 2206	212-420-0350
Poli, Bruce/110 Christopher St #55	212-242-6853
Polsky, Herb/1024 Sixth Ave	212-730-0508
Popper, Andrew J/330 First Ave	212-982-9713
Porges, Danny/37 W 39th St #1002	212-391-4117
Portnoy, Neal/1 Hudson St	212-362-5053
Porto, Art/333 Park Ave S 2nd Fl	212-353-0488
Porto, James/87 Franklin St	212-966-4407
Poster, James Studio/210 Fifth Ave #402	212-206-4065
Pottle, Jock/301 W 89th St #15	212-874-0216
Powers, Guy/534 W 43rd St	212-563-3177
Prezant, Steve Studios/666 Greenwich St #720	212-727-0590
Pribula, Barry/59 First Ave	212-777-7612
Price, Clayton J/205 W 19th St	212-929-7721
Price, David/4 E 78th St	212-794-9040
Priggen, Leslie/215 E 73rd St	212-772-2230
Prozzo, Marco/270 Bowery	212-966-8917
Pruitt, David/PO Box 832/Madison Sq Station	212-979-2921
Pruzan, Michael/1181 Broadway 8th Fl	212-686-5505
Psihoyos, Louis/521 W 23rd St	212-242-9090
Pugliese, Lara/354 Butler St, Brooklyn	718-636-8498
Puhlmann, Rico/530 Broadway 10th Fl	212-941-9433
Putnam, Quentin/1141 Brooklyn Ave, Brooklyn	718-693-7567

R

Raab, Michael/831 Broadway	212-533-0030
Raboy, Marc/205 W 19th St	212-242-4616
Rajs, Jake/252 W 30th St #10A	212-947-9403
Rapoport, David/55 Perry St #2D	212-691-5528
Rappaport, Sam/515 Ave I #3H, Brooklyn	718-253-5175
Rattner, Robert/106-15 Jamaica Ave, Richmond Hill	718-441-0826
Ratzkin, Lawrence/740 West End Ave	212-222-0824
Ravid, Joyce/12 E 20th St	212-477-4233
Ray, Bill/350 Central Park West (P 101)	**212-222-7680**
Raymond, Lilo/212 E 14th St	212-362-9546
Rea, Jimmy/512 Broadway	212-627-7903
Reeks, Deck/145 W 58th St	212-459-9816
Regan, Ken/6 W 20th St 8th Fl	212-989-2004
Regen, David/227 E 11th St #3D	212-222-0532
Reichert, Robert/149 W 12th St	212-645-9515
Reinhardt, Mike/881 Seventh Ave #405	212-541-4787
Rentmeester, Co/4479 Douglas Ave, Riverdale	212-757-4796
Reznicki, Jack/568 Broadway #704	212-925-0771
Rezny, Aaron/119 W 23rd St	212-691-1894
Rezny, Abe/28 Cadman Plz W/Eagle Wrhse, Brooklyn Heights	212-226-7747
Rhodes, Arthur/325 E 64th St	212-249-3974
Richardson, Alan/568 Broadway #604	212-966-4366
Richman, Susan/119 W 25th St 11th fl	212-929-8801
Ricucci, Vincent/109 W 27th St 10th Fl	212-807-8295
Ries, Henry/204 E 35th St	212-689-3794
Ries, Stan/48 Great Jones St	212-533-1852
Riggs, Cole/39 W 29th St	212-481-6119
Riggs, Robert/502 Laguardia Pl	212-254-7352
Riley, David & Carin/152 W 25th St	212-741-3662
Riley, Jon/12 E 37th St	212-532-8326
Rivelli, William/303 Park Ave S #508	212-254-0990
Roberts, Grant/120 Eleventh Ave	212-242-2000
Roberts, Mathieu/122 E 13th St #3A	212-460-5160
Robinson, CeOtis/4-6 W 101st St #49A	212-663-1231
Robinson, Herb/11 W 25th St	212-627-1478
Robinson, James/155 Riverside Dr	212-580-1793
Robison, Chuck/21 Stuyvesant Oval	212-777-4894
Robledo, Maria/43 W 29th St	212-213-1517
Rodamar, Richard/370 Ninth St, Brooklyn	718-965-2758
Rodin, Christine/38 Morton St	212-242-3260
Rohr, Robert/325 E 10th St #5W	212-674-1519
Rolo Photo/214 W 17th St	212-691-8355
Rosa, Douglas/151 W 19th St 6th Fl	212-727-2422
Rose, Uli/975 Park Ave #8A	212-988-8890
Rosenberg, Ken/514 West End Ave	212-362-3149
Rosenthal, Barry/205 W 19th St	212-645-0433
Rosenthal, Ben/20 E 17th St	212-807-7737
Rosenthal, Marshall M/231 W 18th St	212-807-1247
Ross, Ken/80 Madison Ave 7th Fl	212-213-9205
Ross, Mark/345 E 80th St	212-744-7258
Ross, Steve/10 Montgomery Pl, Brooklyn	718-783-6451
Rossi, Emanuel/78-29 68th Rd, Flushing	718-894-6163
Rossignol, Lara/425 W 23rd St #17A	212-243-2750
Rossum, Cheryl/310 E 75th St	212-628-3173
Roth, Seth/137 W 25th St	212-620-7050
Rothaus, Ede/34 Morton St	212-989-8277
Rozsa, Nick/325 E 64th St	212-734-5629
Rubenstein, Raeanne/8 Thomas St	212-964-8426
Rubin, Al/250 Mercer St #1501	212-674-4535
Rubin, Daniel/126 W 22nd St 6th Fl	212-989-2400
Rubin, Susan/327 E 14th St	212-460-5695
Rubinger, Diane/36 W 35th St	212-714-0955
Rubyan, Robert/270 Park Ave S #7C	212-460-9217
Rudnick, James/799 Union Street, Brooklyn (P 111)	**212-466-6337**
Rudolph, Nancy/35 W 11th St	212-989-0392
Rugen-Kory/27 W 20th St #603	212-242-2772
Ruggeri, Francesco/71 St Marks Pl #9	212-505-8477
Rumbough, Stan/154 W 18th St #8A	212-206-0183
Russell, Dawn/222 E 21st St	212-228-2963
Russo, Gary/309 E 8th St #2A	212-228-1736
Ryan, Will/16 E 17th St 2nd Fl	212-242-6270
Rysinski, Edward/109 W 27th St 2nd Fl	212-807-7301
Ryuzo/119 W 22nd St 5th Fl	212-807-7012

S

Sabal, David/20 W 20th St #501 212-242-8464
Sacha, Bob/370 Central Park W 212-749-4128
Sahaida, Michael/5 W 19th St 5th Fl 212-924-4545
Sahihi, Ashkan/301 E 12th St 212-533-4026
Sailors, David/123 Prince St 212-505-9654
Sakas, Peter/400 Lafayette St 212-254-6096
Salaff, Fred/322 W 57th St 212-246-3699
Saltiel, Ron Cameron/78 Fifth Ave 7th Fl 212-627-0003
Salvati, Jerry/206 E 26th St 212-696-0454
Salzano, Jim/29 W 15th St 212-242-4820
Samardge, Nick/302 W 86th St 212-226-6770
Sander, J T/107 E 88th St #3F 212-996-6189
Sanders, Chris/130 W 23rd St #2 212-645-6111
Sandone, A J/132 W 21st St 9th Fl 212-807-6472
Sanford, Tobey/888 Eighth Ave #166 212-245-2736
Santos, Antonio/202 E 21st St 212-477-3514
Sarapochiello, Jerry/47-A Beach St 212-219-8545
Sartor, Vittorio/10 Bleecker St #1-D 212-674-2994
Sato Photo/152 W 26th St 212-741-0688
Satterwhite, Al/80 Varick St #7B 212-219-0808
Saunders, Daryl-Ann/254 Park Ave S #3M 212-242-0942
Savides, Harris/648 Broadway #1009 212-260-6816
Saville, Lynn/440 Riverside Dr #45 212-932-1854
Sawyer, David/270 Park Ave S #3A 212-473-2577
Saylor, H Durston/219 W 16th St #4B 212-620-7122
Scalora, Suza/3 W 30th St 212-643-0058
Scanlan, Richard/1601 Third Ave #31D 212-996-4571
Scarlett, Nora/37 W 20th St 212-741-2620
Scavullo, Francesco/212 E 63rd St 212-838-2450
Schecter, Lee/13-17 Laight St 3rd Fl 212-431-0088
Schein, Barry/118-60 Metropolitan Ave, Kew Gardens 718-849-7808
Schenk, Fred/112 Fourth Ave 212-677-1250
Schenk, Tom/311 Greenwich St 212-587-3445
Schiavone, Carmen/271 Central Park West 212-496-6016
Schierlitz, Tom/544 E 27th St 212-595-1699
Schild, Irving/34 E 23rd St 212-475-0090
Schiller, Judy/328 W 19th St 212-924-7612
Schinz, Marina/222 Central Park S 212-246-0457
Schlachter, Trudy/160 Fifth Ave 212-741-3128
Schneider, Josef/119 W 57th St 212-265-1223
Schneider, Peter/31 W 21st St 212-366-6242
Schreck, Bruno/873 Broadway #304 212-254-3078
Schuld, Karen/77 Bleecker St #120 212-674-0031
Schulze, Fred/38 W 21st St 212-242-0930
Schupf, John/568 Broadway #106 212-226-2250
Schwartz, Marvin/223 W 10th St 212-929-8916
Schwartz, Sing-Si/15 Gramercy Park S 212-475-9222
Schwerin, Ron/889 Broadway 212-228-0340
Sclight, Greg/322 Second Ave 3rd Fl 212-736-2957
Scruggs, Jim/32 W 31st St #3 212-629-6495
Secunda, Shel /112 Fourth Ave 3rd Fl 212-477-0241
Seesselberg, Charles/236 W 27th St 10th Fl 212-807-8730
Seghers, Carroll/441 Park Ave S 212-679-4582
Seidman, Barry/85 Fifth Ave 212-255-6666
Seitz, Sepp/12 E 22nd St #9F 212-505-9917
Selby, Richard/113 Greene St 212-431-1719
Seliger, Mark/251 W 19th St 212-633-0848
Seligman, Paul/163 W 17th St 212-242-5688
Selkirk, Neil/515 W 19th St 212-243-6778
Seltzer, Abe/443 W 18th St 212-807-0660
Seltzer, Kathleen/25 E 4th St 212-475-0314
Serling, Peter/157 W 74th St 212-496-9824
Sewart, David Harry/100 Chambers St 212-619-7783
Shaffer, Stan/2211 Broadway 212-580-5522
Shapiro, Pam/11 W 30th St 2nd Fl 212-967-2363
Sherman, Guy/108 E 16th St 6th Fl 212-675-4983
Shiki/119 W 23rd St #1009 212-929-8847
Shipley, Christopher/41 Fifth Ave #4D 212-529-2988
Shiraishi, Carl/137 E 25th St 11th Fl 212-679-5628
Shorr, Kathy/137 Duane St 212-349-6577
Shung, Ken/220 E 49th St 212-807-1449
Silbert, Layle/505 LaGuardia Pl 212-677-0947
Silva-Cone Studios/260 E 36th St 212-279-0900
Silver, Larry/236 W 26th St 212-807-9560
Silverman, Ellen/126 W 25th St 212-627-5911
Simko, Robert/395 South East Ave #28E 212-912-1192
Simon, Peter Angelo/520 Broadway #702 212-925-0890
Simone, Luisa/222 E 27th St #18 212-679-9117
Simons, Chip/165 Ave A #5 212-228-7459
Simpson, Coreen/599 West End Ave 212-877-6210
Simpson, Jerry/244 Mulberry St 212-941-1255
Simson, Emily/102 E 30th St 5th Fl 212-689-6423
Singer, Michelle/251 W 19th St #5C 212-969-9522
Sinnott, Joseph/1251 Bay Rudge Pkwy #4, Brooklyn 718-680-7615
Sint, Steven/45 W 17th St 5th Fl 212-463-8844
Sit, Danny/280 Park Ave S #11J 212-979-5533
Skalski, Ken L/873 Broadway 212-777-6207
Skelley, Ariel/80 Varick St #6A 212-226-4091
Skinner, Marc/216 Van Buren St, Brooklyn 718-455-7749
Sklar, Lori/117/01 Park Lane S #83D, Kew Gardens 212-431-7652
Skogsbergh, Ulf/5 E 16th St 212-255-7536
Skolnick-Chany/106 E 19th St 212-254-3409
Skolnik, Lewis/135 W 29th St 212-239-1455
Slade, Chuck/12 E 14th St #4B 212-807-1153
Slavin, Fred/43 W 24th St 8th Fl 212-627-2652
Slavin, Neal/62 Greene St 212-925-8167
Sleppin, Jeff/3 W 30th St 212-947-1433
Slotnick, Jeff/225 Lafayette St 212-966-5162
Small, John/400 Second Ave 212-645-4720
Smilow, Stanford/333 E 30th St/Box 248 212-685-9425
Smith, Jeff/30 E 21st St 212-674-8383
Smith, Michael/140 Claremont Ave #5A 212-724-2800
Smith, Rita/666 West End Ave #10N 212-580-4842
Smith, Sean/80 Varick St #6A 212-366-5182
Smith, William E/498 West End Ave 212-877-8456
Snider, Lee/221 W 82nd St #9D 212-873-6141
Snyder, Norman/98 Riverside Dr #16C 212-219-0094
SO Studio Inc/34 E 23rd St 212-475-0090
Sobel, Jane/2 W 45th St #1200 212-382-3939
Sochurek, Howard/680 Fifth Ave 212-582-1860
Solomon, Chuck/114 Horatio St 212-645-4853
Solomon, Paul/440 W 34th St #13E 212-760-1203
Solowinski, Ray/154 W 57th St #826 212-757-7940
Soluri, Michael/95 Horatio St #633 212-645-7999
Somekh, Ric/13 Laight St 212-219-1613
Soot, Olaf/419 Park Ave S 212-686-4565
Sorce, Wayne/20 Henry St #5G, Brooklyn 718-237-0497
Sorensen, Chris/PO Box 1760 212-684-0551
Sorokin, Lauren/866 Broadway 212-777-0971
Sotres, Craig/440 Lafayette St 6th Fl 212-979-6161
Spatz, Eugene/264 Sixth Ave 212-777-6793
Specht, Diane/167 W 71st St #10 212-877-8381
Speier, Leonard/190 Riverside Dr 212-595-5480
Speliotis, Steven/114 E 13th St #5D 212-529-4765
Spelman, Steve/260 W 10th St 212-242-9381
Spinelli, Frank/12 W 21st St 12th Fl 212-243-8318
Spinelli, Paul/1619 Third Ave #21K 212-410-3320
Spiro, Ed/340 W 39th St 212-947-7883
Spreitzer, Andy/225 E 24th St 212-685-9669
Springston, Dan/135 Madison Ave/Penthouse So 212-689-0685
St Denis, Pauline/150 E 18th St 212-677-2197
St John, Lynn/308 E 59th St 212-308-7744
Staedler, Lance/154 W 27th St 212-243-0935
Stahman, Robert/1200 Broadway #2D 212-679-1484
Standart, Joe/5 W 19th St 5th Fl 212-924-4545
Stanton, William/160 W 95th St #9D 212-662-3571
Stark, Philip/245 W 29th St 15th Fl 212-868-5555
Starkoff, Robert/140 Fifth Ave 212-741-0669
Steedman, Richard C/214 E 26th St 212-684-7878
Steele, Bill/534 W 43rd St 212-563-3177
Steele, Kim/640 Broadway #7W 212-777-7753
Steigman, Steve/5 E 19th St #303 212-627-3400
Steinbrenner, Karl/225 E 24th St 3rd Fl 212-779-1120
Steiner, Charles/61 Second Ave 212-777-0813
Steiner, Christian/300 Central Park West 212-724-1990
Stember, John/881 Seventh Ave #1003 212-757-0067
Stephanie Studios/277 W 10th St #2D 212-929-1029
Stephens, Greg/450 W 31st St 10th Fl 212-643-9477
Stern, Anna/261 Broadway #3C 212-349-1134
Stern, Bert/66 Crosby St 212-925-5909
Stern, Bob/12 W 27th St 212-889-0860
Stern, Cynthia/515 Broadway #2B 212-925-2677
Stern, John/201 E 79th St #15C 212-477-0656

Stern, Laszlo/11 W 30th St 2nd Fl.................................212-239-6600
Sternfeld, Joel/353 E 77th St..212-517-3648
Stettner, Bill/118 E 25th St...212-460-8180
Stevenson, Monica/360 W 36th St.................................212-594-5410
Stewart, David Harry/100 Chambers St........................212-619-7783
Stewart, John/80 Varick St...212-966-6783
Stiles, James/413 W 14th St..212-627-1766
Stinnett, Taryn/305 2nd Ave #324.................................212-533-0613
Stone, Erika/327 E 82nd St...212-737-6435
Stroili, Elaine/416 E 85th St #3G...................................212-879-8587
Strongin, Jeanne/61 Irving Pl..212-473-3718
Stuart, John/80 Varick St #4B..212-966-6783
Stupakoff, Otto/80 Varick St..212-334-8032
Sugarman, Lynn/40 W 22nd St......................................212-691-3245
Summerline, Sam/237 Park Ave #2100..........................212-551-1446
Sun Photo/29 E 22nd St #2-N...212-505-9585
Sussman, Daniel/369 Seventh Ave 3rd Fl......................212-947-5546
Sussman, David/138 W 25th St......................................212-675-5863
Svensson, Steen/52 Grove St...212-242-7272
Swedowsky, Ben/381 Park Ave S...................................212-684-1454
Swick, Danille/276 First Ave #11A..................................212-777-0653
Sylvestre, Lorraine/175 Fifth Ave #2583........................212-675-8134
Symons, Abner/27 E 21st St 10th Fl...............................212-777-6660

T

Tannenbaum, Ken/16 W 21st St.....................................212-675-2345
Tanous, Dorothy/652 Hudson St #3W............................212-255-9409
Tara Universal Studios/34 E 23rd St..............................212-260-8280
Tardio, Robert/19 W 21st St...212-463-9085
Taufic, William/166 W 22nd St.......................................212-620-8143
Taylor, Curtice/29 E 22nd St #2S...................................212-473-6886
Taylor, Jonathan/5 W 20th St 2nd Fl..............................212-741-2805
Tcherevkoff, Michel/873 Broadway (P 126,127)............212-228-0540
Teare, Nigel/38 W 26th St..212-243-3015
Teboul, Daniel/146 W 25th St..212-645-8227
Tegni, Ricardo/100 E Mosholu Pkwy S #6F...................212-367-8972
Temkin, Jay/64-21 Douglaston Pkwy, Douglaston..........718-229-9212
Temogen/102-01 101st Ave, Ozone Park........................718-805-1057
Ten West Productions/10 W 18th St...............................212-929-4899
Tessler, Stefan/115 W 23rd St.......................................212-924-9168
Thomas, Mark/141 W 26th St 4th Fl...............................212-741-7252
Thompson, Kenneth/220 E 95th St.................................212-348-3530
Thomson, Walter/311 Smith St, Brooklyn.......................718-797-3818
Tighe, Michael/110 E 1st St #12.....................................212-254-4252
Tillinghast, Paul/20 W 20th St 7th Fl..............................212-741-3764
Tillman, Denny/39 E 20th St...212-674-7160
Timpone, Robert/126 W 22nd St....................................212-989-4266
Togashi/36 W 20th St..212-929-2290
Tornberg-Coghlan Assoc/6 E 39th St.............................212-685-7333
Toto, Joe/13-17 Laight St...212-966-7626
Tracy, Charles/568 Broadway...212-219-9880
Tran, Clifford/17 W 20th St 6W #C..................................212-675-8492
Trzeciak, Erwin/145 E 16th St..212-254-4140
Tullis, Marcus/13 Laight St 3rd fl....................................212-966-8511
Tully, Roger/344 W 38th St #10D....................................212-947-3961
Tung, Matthew/78 Fifth Ave 7th Fl..................................212-741-0570
Turbeville, Deborah/160 Fifth Ave #914.........................212-924-6760
Turin, Miranda/71 W 10th St #2......................................212-979-9712
Turner, Pete Photography/154 W 57th St.......................212-765-1733
Tweedy-Holmes, Karen/180 Claremont Ave #51.............212-866-2289
Tweel, Ron/241 W 36th St..212-563-3452
Tyler, Mark/233 Broadway #822.....................................212-962-3690

UV

Uher, John/529 W 42nd St..212-594-7377
Umans, Marty/29 E 19th St...212-995-0100
Unangst, Andrew/381 Park Ave S...................................212-889-4888
Ursillo, Catherine/1040 Park Ave....................................212-722-9297
Vaccaro, Nick/530 Laguardia Pl #4.................................212-477-8620
Vaeth, Peter/295 Madison Ave..212-685-4700
Vail, Baker Photography Inc/111 W 24th St....................212-463-7560
Valente, Jerry/193 Meserole Ave, Brooklyn...................718-389-0469
Valeska, Shonna/140 E 28th St......................................212-683-4448
Van De Heyning, Sam/318 E 18th St..............................212-982-2396
Van Der Heyden, Frans/60-66 Crosby St #4D.................212-226-8302
Van Dommele, Rudolph/210 E 36th St #6C.....................212-481-9592

Vanglintenkamp, Rik/377 Rector Pl................................212-945-1917
Varriale, Jim/36 W 20th St..212-807-0088
Vega, Julio/428 W 26th St...212-645-1867
Vega, Luis/1551 Glover St, Bronx...................................212-829-7868
Veldenzer, Alan/160 Bleecker St....................................212-420-8189
Vera, Cesar/284 Lafayette St #5A..................................212-941-8594
Veretta Ltd/318 W 39th St PH..212-563-0650
Veronsky, Frank/1376 York Ave......................................212-744-3810
Vest, Michael/343 E 65th St #4RE..................................212-532-8331
Vhandy Productions/401 E 57th St.................................212-759-6150
Vickers & Beechler/200 W 79th St PH #A.......................212-580-8649
Vickers, Camille/200 W 79th St PH #A............................212-580-8649
Vidal, Bernard/450 W 31st St #9C...................................212-629-3764
Vidol, John/37 W 26th St...212-889-0065
Viesti, Joe/PO Box 20424, Cherokee Sta.......................212-734-4890
Vine, David/873 Broadway 2nd Fl...................................212-505-8070
Visual Impact Productions/15 W 18th St 10th Fl.............212-243-8441
Vitale, Peter/157 E 71st St..212-249-8412
Vogel, Allen/348 W 14th St...212-675-7550
Vogel, Rich/119 W 23rd St #800......................................415-435-9207
Volckening, William/13 Sterling Pl, Brooklyn, NY............718-789-5107
Volkmann, Roy/260 Fifth Ave..212-889-7067
Volpi, Rene/121 Madison Ave #11-I................................212-532-7367
Von Briel, Rudi/PO Box 2017..212-288-7512
Von Hassell, Agostino/277 W 10th St PH-D....................212-242-7290
Vos, Gene/9-W Park Ave S..212-714-1155

W

Wagner, Daniel/12 E 32nd St 4th Fl................................212-481-0786
Wagner, David A/568 Broadway #103.............................212-925-5149
Wahlund, Olof/7 E 17th St...212-929-9067
Waine, Michael/873 Broadway..212-533-4200
Waldo, Maje/PO Box 1156 Cooper Sta...........................212-353-9868
Waldron, William/463 Broome St....................................212-226-0356
Wallace, Randall/43 W 13th St #3F.................................212-242-2930
Wallach, Louis/417 Lafayette St......................................212-925-9553
Walsh, Bob/401 E 34th St...212-684-3015
Waltzer, Bill/110 Greene St #96......................................212-925-1242
Waltzer, Carl/873 Broadway #412...................................212-475-8748
Walz, Barbra/143 W 20th St..212-242-7175
Wan, Stan/310 E 46th St...212-986-1555
Wang, Harvey/574 Argyle Rd, Brooklyn..........................718-282-2800
Wang, John Studio Inc/30 E 20th St................................212-982-2765
Wang, Tony Studio Inc/118 E 28th St #908.....................212-213-4433
Warchol, Paul/133 Mulberry St.......................................212-431-3461
Ward, Bob Studio/151 W 25th St....................................212-473-7584
Warwick, Cyndy/144 E 22nd St.......................................212-420-4760
Watanabe, Nana/130 W 25th St 10th Fl..........................212-741-3248
Watson, Albert M/777 Washington St..............................212-627-0077
Watson, Michael/133 W 19th St 2nd Fl...........................212-620-3125
Watt, Elizabeth/141 W 26th St..212-929-8504
Watts, Cliff/650 Amsterdam Ave.....................................212-362-3354
Watts, Judy/311 E 83rd St #5C.......................................212-439-1851
Waxman, Dani/242 E 19th St..212-995-2221
Wayne, Meri/134 E 22nd St #503....................................212-979-7707
Weaks, Dan/5 E 19th St #303..212-473-3366
Webb, Alex/79 Spring St..212-966-9200
Weber, Bruce/135 Watts St...212-685-5025
Weckler, Chad/210 E 63rd St..212-355-1135
Weidlein, Peter/122 W 26th St..212-989-5498
Weinberg, Carol/40 W 17th St...212-206-8200
Weinstein, Michael/508 Broadway...................................212-925-2612
Weinstein, Todd/47 Irving Pl...212-254-7526
Weiss, David/15 W 24th St..212-924-1030
Weiss, Mark/262 Mott St...212-941-9866
Weiss, Michael Photo/10 W 18th St 2nd Fl....................212-929-4073
Welles, Harris/84 Forsyth St...212-226-1961
West, Bonnie/636 Ave of Americas #3C..........................212-929-3338
Westheimer, Bill/167 Spring St #3W...............................212-431-6360
Wexler, Jayne/24 Prince St...212-334-0229
Wexler, Mark/484 W 43rd St...212-564-7733
Wheatman, Truckin/251 W 30th St #4FW........................212-239-1081
Whipple, George III/301 E 73rd St..................................212-219-0202
Whitaker, Ross/206 W 15th 4th Fl...................................212-727-0044
White, Bill/34 W 17th St..212-243-1780
White, David/31 W 21st St...212-727-3454
White, James/666 Greenwich St.....................................212-924-2255

White, John/11 W 20th St 6th Fl	212-691-1133
White, Steven/666 Greenwich St	212-924-2255
White, Timothy/448 W 37th St #7C	212-971-9039
Whitehurst, William/32 W 20th St	212-206-8825
Whitely Presentations/60 E 42nd St #419	212-490-3111
Whitman, Robert/1181 Broadway 7th Fl	212-213-6611
Whyte, Douglas/519 Broadway	212-431-1667
Wick, Kevin/484 E 24th St, Brooklyn	718-858-6989
Wick, Walter/560 Broadway #404	212-966-8770
Wien, Jeffrey/29 W 38th St	212-354-8024
Wien, Jeffrey/890 Broadway	212-243-7028
Wier, John Arthur/36 W 25th St 11th fl	212-691-1901
Wiesehahn, Charles/249 W 29th St #2E	212-563-6612
Wilby, Dan/45 W 21st St 5th Fl	212-929-8231
Wilcox, Shorty/DPI/19 W 21st St #901	212-627-4060
Wildes, Brett/156 Chambers St 4th Fl	212-431-3496
Wilkes, John/42 E 23rd St 6th Fl	212-475-0794
Wilkes, Stephen/48 E 13th St	212-475-4010
Wilks, Harry/234 W 21st St	212-929-4772
Williamson, Richie/514 W 24th St	212-807-0816
Wills, Bret/38 Greene St	212-925-2999
Wilson, Mike/441 Park Ave S	212-683-3557
Wing, Peter/56-08 138th St, Flushing	718-762-3617
Winstead, Jimmy/453 Washington Ave, Brooklyn	718-789-2997
Wisenbaugh, Jean/41 Union Sq W #1228	212-929-5590
Wohl, Marty/40 E 21st St 6th Fl	212-460-9269
Wojcik, James/256 Mott St	212-431-0108
Wolf, Bruce/136 W 21st St 8th Fl	212-633-6660
Wolf, Henry/167 E 73rd St	212-472-2500
Wolf, Robert/359 W 48th St #2A	212-581-4030
Wolff, Brian R/560 W 43rd St #5K	212-465-8976
Wolfson, Robert/236 W 26th St	212-924-1510
Wolfson, Steve and Jeff/13-17 Laight St 5th Fl	212-226-0077
Wong, Daniel Photography/395 Broadway #4C	212-966-3230
Wong, Leslie/303 W 78th St	212-595-0434
Wood, Susan/641 Fifth Ave	212-371-0679
Woods, Patrick/41-15 45th St #5N, Sunnyside	718-786-5742
Wormser, Richard L/800 Riverside Dr	212-928-0056
Wright, Roy/353 E 77th St	212-517-3648
Wylie, Bill/146 W 17th St	212-627-1007
Wyman, Ron/36 Riverside Dr	212-799-8281
Wynn, Dan/170 E 73rd St	212-535-1551
Wyville, Mark/24-40 31st Ave, Long Island City	718-204-2816

YZ

Yalter, Memo/14-15 162nd St, Whitestone	718-767-3330
Yamashiro, Tad/224 E 12th St	212-473-7177
Yee, Tom/141 W 28th St	212-947-5400
Yoav/4523 Broadway	212-942-8185
Young, Donald/166 E 61st St Box 148	212-593-0010
Young, James/56 W 22nd St	212-477-6413
Young, Ken/333 Park Ave S 2nd fl #18	212-475-0071
Young, Rick/27 W 20th St #1003	212-929-5701
Youngblood, Lee/200 W 70th St #8F	212-595-7913
Yuen, Dan/PO Box 0070/Prince St Sta	212-925-4746
Zager, Howard/245 W 29th St	212-239-8082
Zan/108 E 16th St 6th Fl	212-477-3333
Zander, George/141 W 28th St	212-971-0874
Zander, Peter/312 E 90th St #4A	212-534-3125
Zanetti, Gerry/536 W 50th St	212-767-1717
Zapp, Carl/119 W 22nd St #2	212-924-4240
Zegre, Francois/11 W 20th St	212-627-8726
Zehnder, Bruno/PO Box 5996	212-840-1234
Zeray, Peter/113 E 12th St	212-674-0332
Zimmerman, David/36 W 20th St 10th Fl	212-206-1000
Zimmerman, Marilyn/100 W 25th St 4th Fl	212-206-1000
Zingler, Joseph/18 Desbrosses St	212-226-3867
Zoiner, John/12 W 44th St	212-972-0357
Zwiebel, Michael/42 E 23rd St	212-477-5629

NORTHEAST

A

Abarno, Richard/PO Box 540, Carolina, RI	401-364-2037

Abbey Photographers/268 Broad Ave, Palisades Park, NJ	201-947-1221
Abbott, James/303 N 3rd St 1st Fl, Philadelphia, PA	215-925-9706
Abdelnour, Doug/Rt 22 PO Box 64, Bedford Village, NY	914-234-3123
Abel, Jim/216 Towd Pt Rd, South Hampton, NY	516-287-4357
Abel, Pat/23 N Wycome Ave, Landsdowne, PA	215-928-0499
Abell, Ted/51 Russell Rd, Bethany, CT	203-777-1988
Abend, Jay/18 Central St, Southborough, MA	508-624-0464
Abraham, Jack/229 Inza St, Highland Park, NJ	201-572-6093
Abramson, Dean/PO Box 610, Raymond, ME	207-655-7386
Abstract Studios/9723 Baltimore Blvd #1, College Park, MD	301-441-4600
Accame, Deborah/5161 River Rd Bldg 2B, Bethesda, MD	301-652-1303
Adamczyk, Wes/260-262 North Ave, Dunellen, NJ	908-968-4060
Adams Studio Inc/1523 22nd St NW Courtyard, Washington, DC	202-785-2188
Adams, John P/78 Beane Lane, Newington, NH	603-436-0039
Adams, Jon/PO Box 2, Jenkintown, PA	215-886-6658
Adams, Neill/2305 Coleridge Dr, Silver Spring, MD	301-206-5104
Addis, Kory/144 Lincoln St #4, Boston, MA	617-451-5142
Adsit-Pratt, Diane/RD1/Box 220, Blairstown, NJ	908-459-5815
Afterglow Studios/165B New Boston St, Woburn, MA	617-938-6960
Agalias, George/25 Washington Valley Rd, Watchung, NJ	212-874-7615
Agelopas, Mike/2510 N Charles St, Baltimore, MD	301-235-2823
Ahrens, Gene/544 Mountain Ave, Berkeley Heights, NJ	201-464-4763
Aiello, Frank/35 S Van Brunt St, Englewood, NJ	201-894-5120
Akis, Emanuel/145 Lodi St, Hackensack, NJ	201-342-8070
Aladdin Studio/9 Columbine Dr, Nashua, NH	603-883-1011
Albee, Larry/PO Box 501, Kennet Square, PA	215-388-6741
Albers, Debra/9153 Brookville Rd, Silver Spring, MD	301-588-5703
Albert, Sharon/PO Box 370, Newton High, MA	617-964-2826
Albrizio, Linda/112 Center Ave, Chatham, NJ	201-635-2276
Alcarez, Mark/86 Bartlett St, Charlestown, MA	617-451-2629
Alejandro, Carlos Photography/8 E 37th St, Wilmington, DE	302-762-8220
Alexander, Bruce/127 Harantis Lake Rd, Chester, NH	603-887-2530
Alexander, Jules/9 Belmont Ave, Rye, NY	914-967-8985
Alexanian, Nubar/11 Sumner St, Gloucester, MA	508-281-6152
Allen, Bryan/40 Budd St, Morristown, NJ	201-540-9551
Allen, C J/67 Brookside Ave/Box 1137, Boston, MA	617-524-1925
Allen, Carole/11 Crescent St, Keene, NH	603-357-1375
Allsopp, Jean Mitchell/16 Maple St/RR 2/PO Box 224, Shirley, MA	617-425-2296
Alonso, Manuel/One Circle West, Stamford, CT	203-359-2838
Althaus, Mike/5161 River Rd Bldg 2B, Bethesda, MD	301-652-1303
Altman, Steve/46 Prescott #1, Jersey City, NJ	201-434-0022
Ambrose, Ken/129 Valerie Court, Cranston, RI	401-826-0606
Ames, Thomas Jr/85 Mechanic St, Lebanon, NH	603-448-6168
Amicucci, Nick/55 Fourth Ave, Garwood, NJ	908-789-1669
Amranand, Ping/4502 Saul Rd, Kensington, MD	301-564-0938
Amstock/12 Appleton Terrace, Watertown, MA	617-926-4749
Ancker, Clint/3 Hunter Trl, Warren, NJ	908-356-4280
Ancona, George/Crickettown Rd, Stony Point, NY	914-786-3043
Andersen-Bruce, Sally/19 Old Mill Rd, New Milford, CT	203-355-1525
Anderson, Lee/2828 10th St NE, Washington, DC	202-547-1989
Anderson, Monica/11 Ranelegh Rd, Boston, MA	617-787-5510
Anderson, Richard Photo/2523 N Calvert St, Baltimore, MD	301-889-0585
Anderson, Ronald N/898 New Mark Esplanade, Rockville, MD	301-294-3218
Anderson, Theodore/235 N Madison St, Allentown, PA	215-437-6468
Andersson, Monika L/11 Ranelegh Rd, Brighton, MA	617-787-5510
Andrews Studios/RD 3/Box 277, Pine Bush, NY	914-744-5361
Andris-Hendrickson Photography/408 Vine St, Philadelphia, PA	215-925-2630
Angier, Roswell/65 Pleasant St, Cambridge, MA	617-354-7784
Ankers Photo/316 F St NE, Washington, DC	202-543-2111
Ansin, Mikki/2 Ellery Square, Cambridge, MA	617-661-1640
Anstett, Carol Gaegler/136 Spring Towne Circle, Parkville, MD	301-529-3341
Anthony, Greg/107 South St, Boston, MA	617-423-4983
Anyon, Benjamin/206 Spring Run Ln, Downington, PA	215-363-0744
Aperture PhotoBank/180 Lincoln St, Boston, MA	617-451-1973
Appleton, Hal/Kingston, Doug/6 Stickney Terrace, Hampton, NH	603-926-0763
Arbor Studios/56 Arbor St, Hartford, CT	203-232-6543
Arce Studios/48 S Main St, S Norwalk, CT	203-866-8845
Arkadia Photography/72 Cedar Hill Rd, Marlborough , MA	508-481-7650
Armen, James/P O Box 586, Belmont, MA	617-923-1908
Armor, Jan Douglas/2701 E Main Rd, Portsmouth, RI	401-683-3754
Armstrong, Christine/4701 Bel Air Rd, Baltimore, MD	301-488-5603
Armstrong, James/125 Russelville Rd, Easthampton, MA	413-572-1078
Aronson Photographics/1168 Commonwealth Ave, Boston, MA	617-731-6900
Arruda, Gary/17 Clinton Dr, Hollis, NH	603-889-3722
Arruda, Robert/329 Lamartine St, Boston, MA	617-482-1425
Asterisk Photo/2016 Walnut St, Philadelphia, PA	215-972-1543
Atlantic Photo/Boston/669 Boylston St, Boston, MA	617-267-7480
Augenstein, Ron/509 Jenne Dr, Pittsburgh, PA	412-653-3583

Austin, Miles/26 Sandra Cir, Westfield, NJ....908-232-1155
Avanti Studios/46 Waltham St, Boston, MA....617-574-9424
Avarella, Russell/35-02 Berdan Ave, Fair Lawn, NJ....201-796-5588
Avatar Studio/1 Grace Dr, Cohasset, MA....617-383-1099
Avics Inc/116 Washington Ave, Hawthorne, NJ....201-444-8118
Avid Productions Inc/10 Terhune Place, Hackensack, NJ....201-343-1060
Avis, Paul/300 Bedford, Manchester, NH....603-627-2659
Azel, Robert/RR 1/Box 924, E Stoneham, ME....207-928-2325

B

B & H Photographics/2035 Richmond, Philadelphia, PA....215-425-0888
Bacharach Inc/44 Hunt St, Watertown, MA....617-924-6200
Baehr, Sarah/708 South Ave, New Canaan, CT....203-966-6317
Baer, Rhoda/3006 Military Rd NW, Washington, DC....202-364-8480
Baitz, Otto/130 Maple Ave #9B1, Red Bank, NJ....908-530-8809
Baker, Bill Photo/1045 Pebble Hill Rd RD3, Doylestown, PA....215-348-9743
Bakhtiar, Sherry/7927 Iverness Ridge Rd, Potomac, MD....301-299-2671
Baldwin, Steve/8 Eagle St, Rochester, NY....716-325-2907
Bale, J R/1283 Cambridge Ave, Plainfield, NJ....908-561-9762
Baleno, Ralph/192 Newtown Rd, Plainview, NY....516-293-3399
Banville, Andre/Chevalier Ave, Greenfield, MA....413-773-7513
Barao, S J/580 Arcade Ave, Seekonk, MA....508-336-5015
Bard, M/Box 126AA/Lily Pond Rd, Parksville, NY....914-292-5972
Barker, Robert/35 Buffalo Dr, Rochester, NY....719-383-8850
Barlow, Len/8 Gloucester St, Boston, MA....617-266-4030
Barnes, Christopher/122 Winnisimmet St, Chelsea, MA....617-884-2745
Barocas, Melanie Eve/78 Hart Rd, Guilford, CT....203-457-0898
Baron, Greg/35 E Stewart Ave, Lansdowne, PA....215-626-8677
Barone, Christopher/381 Wright Ave, Kingston, PA....717-287-4680
Barrett, Bob/323 Springtown Rd, New Paltz, NY....914-255-1591
Barron, David M/247 Dutton Rd, sudbury, MA....508-443-7423
Barros, Ricardo/67 Delaware Ave, Lambertville, NJ....609-397-8336
Barrow, Pat/10 Post Office Rd, Silver Spring, MD....301-588-3131
Barrow, Scott/44 Market St, Cold Spring, NY....914-265-4242
Barth, Stephen/37 S Clinton St, Doylestown, PA (P 59)....215-340-0900
Bartlett, Linda/3316 Runnymede Pl NW, Washington, DC....202-362-4777
Bartz, Michael A/723 Greenleaf St, Allentown, PA....215-434-1117
Basch, Richard/2627 Connecticut Ave NW, Washington, DC....202-232-3100
Baskin, Gerry/12 Union Park St, Boston, MA....617-482-3316
Bassett, Betsy/ 123 Washington Ave, Newton, MA....617-332-8072
Bates, Carolyn/174 Battery St, Burlington, VT....802-862-5386
Bavendam, Fred/PO Box 276, E Kingston, NH....603-642-3215
Beach, Jonathan/116 Townline Rd, Syracuse, NY....315-455-8261
Beall, Gordon/PO Box 528, Glen Echo, MD....301-229-0142
Bean, Jeremiah/122 E Westfield Ave, Roselle Park, NJ....908-789-2200
Beards, James/45 Richmond St, Providence, RI....401-273-9055
Beardsley, John/322 Summer St 5th Fl, Boston, MA....617-482-0130
Beatty, Alex/32 Lincoln Ave, Lynnfield, MA....617-334-4069
Beauchesne Photo/4 Bud Way/Vantage Pt III/#2, Nashua, NH....603-880-8686
Beck, Richard/116 Manor Dr, Red Bank, NJ....908-747-8948
Becker, Art/2617 Peach St, Erie, PA....814-453-4198
Becker, Tim/266 Burnside Ave, E Hartford, CT....203-528-7818
Beckerman, Arnold/Star Route 70, Great Barrington, MA....413-229-8619
Beebe, Jay/186 Atlantic Ave, Marblehead, MA....617-631-2730
Beigel, Daniel/1615 St MArgarets Rd, Annapolis, MD....301-974-1234
Bell, David/2705 W 17th St, Erie, PA....814-833-1657
Bell, Mike/630 N Second St, Philadelphia, PA....215-925-2084
Bender, Frank/2215 South St, Philadelphia, PA....215-985-4664
Benedetto, Angelo/825 S 7th St, Philadelphia, PA....215-627-1990
Bennett, Robert J/310 Edgewood St, Bridgeville , DE....302-337-3347
Bennett, William/128 W Northfield Rd, Livingston, NJ....201-992-7967
Benoit, David/31 Blackburn Ctr, Gloucester , MA....508-281-3079
Benson, Gary/PO Box 29, Peapack, NJ....908-234-2216
Benvenuti, Judi/12 N Oak Ct, Madison, NJ....201-377-5075
Berenson, Barry/21-D Marion Rd, Salem, MA....508-745-8567
Bergman, LV & Assoc/East Mountain Rd S, Cold Spring, NY....914-265-3656
Bergold Jr., James/410 Gravel Hill Rd, Kinnelon, NJ....201-492-8578
Berinstein, Martin/215 A St 6th Fl, Boston, MA....617-268-4117
Berndt, Jerry/41 Magnolia Ave, Cambridge, MA....617-354-2266
Berner, Curt/211 A St, Boston, MA....617-269-1698
Bernstein, Daniel/7 Fuller St, Waltham, MA....617-894-0473
Berry, Michael/838 S Broad St, Trenton, NJ....609-396-2413
Bertling, Norbert G Jr/2125 N Charles St, Baltimore, MD....301-727-8766
Bethoney, Herb/23 Autumn Circle, Hingham, MA....617-740-2290
Bevan, Pat/200 Fort Meade Rd #907, Laurel, MD....301-498-7808
Bezushko, Bob/1311 Irving St, Philadelphia, PA....215-735-7771
Bezushko, George/1311 Irving St, Philadelphia, PA....215-735-7771
Bibikow, Walter/76 Batterymarch St, Boston, MA....617-451-3464
Biegun, Richard/56 Cherry Ave, West Sayville, NY....516-567-2645
Bilyk, I George/314 E Mt Airy Ave, Philadelphia, PA....215-242-5431
Bindas, Jan Jeffrey/205 A St, Boston, MA....617-268-3050
Bingham, Jack/66 Third St, Dover, NH....603-742-7718
Binzen, Bill/49 Weatogue Rd, Salisbury, CT....203-824-0093
Birn, Roger/150 Chestnut St, Providence, RI....401-421-4825
Bishop, Jennifer/2732 St Paul St, Baltimore, MD....301-366-6662
Blackfan Studio/266 Meetinghouse Rd, New Hope, PA....215-862-3503
Blair, Jonathan/2301 N Grant Ave, Wilmington, DE....302-652-4122
Blair, Randall/3939 McKinley St NW, Washington, DC....202-364-1019
Blake, Mike/35 Drummer Rd, Acton, MA....617-264-9099
Blakely, Peter/RR 2/ Box 185, Antrim, NH....603-588-6336
Blakeslee-Lane Studios/916 N Charles St, Baltimore, MD....301-727-8800
Blank, Bruce/228 Clearfield Ave, Norristown, PA....215-539-6166
Blate, Samuel R/10331 Watkins Mill Dr, Gaithersburg, MD....301-840-2248
Blevins, Burgess/601 N Eutaw St #713, Baltimore, MD....301-685-0740
Blizzard, William/PO Box 302, Vorhees, NJ....609-784-4406
Bloomberg, Robert/4 Pleasant St, Danbury, CT....203-794-1764
Bloomenfeld, Richard/200-19 E 2nd St, Huntington Sta, NY....516-424-9492
Blouin, Craig/PO Box 892, Henniker, NH....603-428-3036
Boehm, J Kenneth/96 Portland Ave, Georgetown, CT....203-544-8524
Bogacz, Mark F/11 Pondview Place, Tyngsboro, MA....617-649-3886
Bogart, Del/211 Conanicus Ave, Jamestown, RI....401-423-1709
Bognovitz, Murray/4980 C Wyaconda Rd, Rockville, MD....301-984-7771
Bohm, Linda/7 Park St, Montclair, NJ....201-746-3434
Boisvert, Paul/229 Loomis St, Burlington, VT....802-862-7249
Bolster, Mark/502 W North Ave, Pittsburgh, PA....412-231-3757
Bolton, Bea/186 Lincoln, Boston, MA....617-423-2050
Bonito, Arthur/5 Nolans Point Rd, Lake Hopatcong, NJ....201-663-1555
Bonjour, Jon/496 Congress St, Portland, ME....207-773-5398
Bookbinder, Sigmund/Box 833, Southbury, CT....203-264-5137
Booker, David/8 Lum Lane, Newark, NJ....201-465-0944
Borg, Erik/RR #3/Drew Lane, Middlebury, VT....802-388-6302
Borkoski, Matthew/305 Ladson Rd, Silver Spring, MD....301-681-3051
Borkovitz, Barbara/2844 Wisconsin Ave NW , Washington, DC....202-338-2533
Born, Flint/163 Summer St, Somerville, MA....617-666-3483
Borris, Daniel/126 11th St SE, Washington, DC....202-546-3193
Boston Photographers/56 Creighton St, Boston, MA....617-491-7474
Botelho, Tony/505 Greenwich Ave, W Warwick, RI....401-828-0567
Bova, David/123 Dayton St, Danvers, MA....508-750-4346
Bowen, Dave/PO Box 937, Wellsboro, PA....717-326-1212
Bowl, Greg Studio/409 W Broadway, S Boston, MA....617-268-1210
Bowman, Gene/86 Lackawanna Ave, West Paterson, NJ....201-256-9060
Bowman, Jo/1102 Manning St, Philadelphia, PA....215-625-0200
Bowman, Ron/PO Box 4071, Lancaster, PA....717-898-7716
Bowne, Bob/708 Cookman Ave, Asbury Park, NJ....908-988-3366
Boxer, Jeff Photography/520 Harrison Ave, Boston, MA....617-266-7755
Boyer, Beverly/17 Llanfair Rd, Ardmore, PA....215-649-0657
Brack, Dennis/318 Third St Rear NE, Washington, DC....202-547-1176
Bradley, Dave/840 Summer St, Boston, MA....617-268-6644
Bradley, Roy/113 S Brandywine, Schenectady, NY....518-377-9457
Bradtke, Andrew/1611 Wilson Place, Silver Spring, MD....301-588-8724
Branner, Debra/4528 Maryknoll Rd, Pikesville, MD....301-486-4665
Branner, Phil/578 Woodbine Ave, Towson, MD....301-486-5150
Brassard, Paul/44 Spring St, Adams, MA....413-743-2265
Braverman, Ed/337 Summer St, Boston, MA....617-423-3373
Bravo, David/33 Hubbell St, Bridgeport, CT....203-384-8524
Brega, David/PO Box 13, Marshfield Mills, MA....617-555-1212
Brennan, James/231 Curtis Corner Rd, Peace Dale, RI....401-789-7170
Brenner, Jay/24 S Mall St, Plainview, NY....516-752-0610
Breslin, Daniel/1480 Pleasant Valley Wy #42, W Orange, NJ....201-736-4585
Bress, Pat/7324 Arrowood Rd, Bethesda, MD....301-469-6275
Briel, Petrisse/107 South St 2nd Fl, Boston, MA....617-338-6726
Briglia, Thomas/PO Box 487, Linwood, NJ....609-748-0864
Brignoli, Frank & Christine/PO Box 778, E Dennis, MA....508-385-8191
Brignolo, Joseph B/Oxford Springs Rd, Chester, NY....914-496-4453
Brilliant, Andy/107 South St #203, Boston, MA....617-482-8938
Brink, Fred/94 Harvard Ave, Brookline, MA....617-566-5223
Brittany Photo/217 N Wood Ave, Linden, NJ....908-925-0055
Britz Fotograf/2619 Lovegrove St, Baltimore, MD....301-338-1820
Broock, Howard/432 Sharr Ave, Elmira, NY....607-733-1420
Brown, Christopher/, Boston, MA....617-555-1212
Brown, Constance/PO Box 2346, Providence, RI....401-274-2712
Brown, Dorman/POB 0700/Coach Rd #8B, Quechee, VT....802-296-6902
Brown, Gerald/1929 Chestnut St, Harrisburg, PA....713-236-4698
Brown, Martin/Cathance Lake, Grove Post Office, ME....207-454-7708

Brown, Nan/12 Spaulding St, Boston, MA................617-522-3344
Brown, Porter/1213 Swingingdale Dr, Silver Spring, MD................301-384-3055
Brown, Skip/6514 75th St, Cabin John, MD................301-320-0752
Brown, Stephen R/1882 Columbia Rd NW, Washington, DC................202-667-1965
Brownell, David/PO Box 60, Andover, NH................603-735-6640
Brownell, William/1411 Saxon Ave, Bay Shore, NY................516-665-0081
Brt Photographic Illustrations/911 State St, Lancaster, PA................717-393-0918
Bruce, Brad/PO Box 151, Beaver Falls, PA................412-846-2776
Brundage, Kip/66 Union St, Belfast, ME................207-338-5210
Bruno Photo/326 A Street, Boston, MA................617-451-6152
Bryn, Deborah/PO Box 504, Waterford, NY................518-235-4656
Bubbenmoyer, Kevin/RD #2 Box 110, Orefield, PA................215-395-9167
Bubriski, Kevin/817 Main St, Bennington, VT................802-442-4516
Buchanan, Robert Photography/466 Lakeview Ave, Valhalla, NY................914-948-9260
Buckley Assoc/3190 Vaughan St, Portsmouth, NH................603-431-9313
Buckman, Sheldon/17 Kiley Dr, Randolph, MA................617-986-4773
Buff, Cindy/580 Patten Ave #55, Long Branch, NJ................201-870-3223
Bulkin, Susan/5453 Houghton Place, Philadelphia, PA................215-483-4881
Bulvony, Matt/2715 Sarah St, Pittsburgh, PA................412-431-5344
Burak, Chet/130 Taunton Ave, E Providence, RI................401-431-0625
Burdick, Gary Photography/9 Parker Hill, Brookfield, CT................203-775-2894
Burger, Oded/9 Wickford Rd, Framingham, MA................508-788-0677
Burke, Bill/6 Melville Ave, Dorchester, MA................617-265-3070
Burke, John/60 K St, Boston, MA................617-269-6677
Burke, John & Judy/116 E Van Buren Ave, New Castle, DE................302-322-8760
Burke, Robert/35 Darrow Dr, Catonsville, MD................301-744-4314
Burns, Steve/30 Westwood Ave/POB 175,
Westwood, NJ (P 61) **201-358-1890**
Burrell, Fred/25 Shadyside Ave, Nyack, NY................914-358-4902
Burris, Ken/PO Box 592, Shelburne, VT................802-985-3263
Burwell/Burwell/6925 Willow St NW, Washington, DC................202-882-1337
Buschner Studios/450 West Metro Park, Rochester, NY................716-475-1170
Butler, Herbert/200 Mamaroneck Ave, White Plains, NY................914-683-1767
Butler, Jeff/106 Wood St, Rutherford, NJ................201-460-1071
Buxbaum, Jack/33 Queen Ave, New Castle, DE................302-656-5121
Byron, Pete/75 Mill Rd, Morris Plains, NJ................201-538-7520

C

Cacicedo, Kathy/53 Briarwood Dr E, Berkeley Heights, NJ................908-665-7892
Caffee, Chris/216 Blvd of Allies, Pittsburg, PA................412-642-7734
Cafiero, Jeff/410 Church Ln, North Brunswick, NJ................908-297-8979
Caggiano, Angelo/214 S 17th St, Philadelphia, PA................215-433-8312
Cali, Guy/Layton Rd, Clarics Summit, PA................717-587-1957
Callaghan, Charles/54 Applecross Circle,
Chalfont, PA (P 64) **215-822-8258**
Campbell, Tyler/PO Box 373, Chestertown, MD................301-778-4938
Canavino, Kay/1 Fitchburg St, Somerville, MA................617-625-1115
Canner, Larry/413 S Ann St, Baltimore, MD................301-276-5747
Cantor-MacLean, Donna/2828 10th St NE, Washington, DC................202-789-1200
Capobianco, Ron/10 Arlington Lane, Bayville, NY................516-628-2670
Capone, Frank/230-D Ferry St, Easton, PA................215-252-4100
Carbone, Fred/1041 Buttonwood St, Philadelphia, PA................215-236-2266
Carrino, Nick/710 S Marshall St, Philadelphia, PA................215-925-3190
Carroll, Hanson/11 New Boston Rd, Norwich, VT................802-649-1094
Carroll, Mary Claire/POB 67, Richmond, VT................802-434-2312
Carroll, Michael Photo/25 Main St, Pepperell, MA................508-433-6500
Carstens, Don/2121 N Lovegrove St, Baltimore, MD................301-385-3049
Carter, J Pat/3000 Chestnut Ave #116, Baltimore, MD................301-243-6074
Carter, John/111 Orange St, Wilmington, DE................302-652-4353
Carter, Philip/PO Box 479, Bedford Hills, NY................914-232-5882
Casciano, Jerry/59 Rivington Ave, W Long Branch, NJ................908-389-8941
Castalou, Nancy/RD 2/ Box 145, Valatie, NY................518-758-9565
Castle, Ed/4242 East West Highway #509, Chevy Chase, MD................301-585-9300
Cataffo, Linda/PO Box 460, Palisades Park, NJ................201-694-5047
Catalano, Adrian/219 5th St, Cambridge, MA................617-868-5352
Catania, Vin/77 King Philip St, S Weymouth, MA................617-337-3435
Cateriniccio, Russell Paul/1974 St George Ave #4, Rahway, NJ................908-499-7162
Caudill, Dennis/1814 Lancaster St, Baltimore, MD................301-563-0906
Caughey, Bern/59 Pond St, Cohasset, MA................617-357-3165
Cavallo, Frank/666 Anderson Ave, Cliffside, NJ................201-941-9522
Cavanaugh, James/On Location/PO Box 158, Tonawanda, NY................716-633-1885
Cerniglio, Tom/1115 E main St, Rochester, NY................716-654-8561
Chachowski, Hank/119 N Fifth Ave, Manville, NJ................201-722-0948
Chadbourne, Bob/595-603 Newbury St, Boston, MA................617-262-3800
Chandoha, Walter/RD 1 PO Box 287, Annandale, NJ................908-782-3666
Chao, John/Bayview Business Pk, Gilford, NH................603-293-2727
Chaplain, Ira/44 Brimmer St, Boston, MA................617-227-5662

Chaplin, June/230 Dunkirk Rd, Baltimore, MD................301-377-2742
Chapman, Kathy/322 Summer St 5th Fl, Boston, MA................617-482-9502
Charland, Robert/840 Summer St, Boston, MA................617-268-4599
Chase, Richard/70 Central St, Acton, MA................508-263-0368
Chase, Thomas W/PO Box 1965, Rochester, NH................603-875-2808
Chatwin, Jim/5459 Main St, Williamsville, NY................716-634-3436
Chauve, Karyn/75 Highland Rd, Glenn Cove, NY................516-676-0365
Cherin, Alan/907 Penn Ave, Pittsburgh, PA................412-261-3755
Child, Andrew/12205 Village Sq Terr #202, Rockville, MD................301-251-0720
Chiusano, Michael/39 Glidden St, Beverly, MA................508-927-7067
Chomitz, Jon/3 Prescott St, Somerville, MA................617-625-6789
Choroszewski, Walter J/1310 Orchard Dr/S Branch, Somerville, NJ................908-369-3555
Christian, Douglas/443 Albany St, Boston, MA................617-482-6206
Christoph/149 Broadway, Greenlawn, NY................516-757-0524
Christopoulos Photography/45 Lee St, Pawtucket, RI................401-722-0350
Chromographics/9 May St, Beverly, MA................508-927-7451
Ciaglia, Joseph/2036 Spruce St, Philadelphia, PA................215-985-1092
Ciuccoli, Stephen/575 Broad St #528, Bridgeport, CT................203-333-5228
Clancy, Paul/95 Chestnut St, Providence, RI................401-421-8025
Clare, William/416 Bloomfield Ave, Montclair, NJ................201-783-0680
Clark, Conley/9003 Linton St, Silver Spring, MD................301-445-4650
Clark, Leigh/1359 Beacon St, Brookline, MA................617-566-1612
Clark, Michael/PO Box 423, Stowe, VT................802-253-7927
Clarke, Jeff/266 Pine St, Burlington, VT................802-863-4393
Clarkson, Frank/PO Box 148, Portsmouth, NH................603-427-0006
Clary, Jim/1090 Eddy St, Providence, RI................401-941-8100
Cleff, Bernie Studio/715 Pine St, Philadelphia, PA................215-922-4246
Clegg, Cheryl/27 Dry Dock Ave, Boston, MA................617-423-6317
Clemens, Clint/345 Summer St, Boston, MA................617-482-3838
Clemens, Peter/153 Sidney St, Oyster Bay, NY................516-922-1759
Clements/Howcroft/59 Wareham St, Boston, MA................617-423-3516
Clermont, Paula/10A Anderson Circle, Londonderry, NH................603-432-3634
Clifford, Joan/38 Hudson St, Quincy, MA................617-328-4623
Clifford, Len/RD Box 1628, Columbia, NJ................201-475-4021
Clineff, Kindra/16 Hillside Ave, Winchester, MA................617-756-0020
Clymer, Jonathan/180-F Central Ave, Englewood, NJ................201-568-1760
Coan, Stephen/750 South 10th St, Philadelphia, PA................215-923-3183
Cobos, Lucy/PO Box 8491, Boston, MA................617-876-9537
Coffee Pond Productions/72 Lincoln St #14, Newton High, MA................617-965-2323
Cohen, Daniel/744 Park Ave, Hoboken, NJ................201-659-0952
Cohen, Evan/323 N Paca St, Baltimore, MD................301-539-0111
Cohen, Marc Assoc/23 Crestview Dr, Brookfield, CT................203-775-1102
Cohen, Stuart/PO Box 2007, Salem, MA................617-631-7150
Collegeman, Stephen R/7812 Temple St, Hyattsville, MD................301-422-2790
Collins & Collins/PO Box 10736, State College, PA................814-234-2916
Colorworks Inc/14300 Cherry Lane Ct #106, Laurel Center, MD................301-490-7909
Colucci, Joe/Box 2069/86 Lackawanna Ave, W Patterson, NJ................201-890-5770
Colwell, David/3405 Keats Terrace, Ijamsville, MD................301-865-3931
Comb, David/107 South St 2nd Fl, Boston, MA................617-426-3644
Comella, Jeff/12 Pecan Dr, Pittsburgh, PA (P 66)................**412-795-2706**
Comet, Renee/410 8th St NW, Washington, DC................202-347-3408
Comick, Joe/11428 Mapleview Dr, Silver Spring, MD................301-946-0860
Conaty, Jim/Hanscom Fld E/Bldg #1724, Bedford, MA................617-469-6990
Conboy, John/1225 State St, Schenectady, NY................518-346-2346
Confer, Holt/2016 Franklin Pl, Wyomissing, PA................215-678-0131
Congalton, David/206 Washington St, Pembroke, MA................617-826-2788
Conner, Marian/456 Rockaway Rd #15, Dover, NJ................201-328-1823
Connor, Donna/272 Fourth Ave, Sweetwater, NJ................609-965-3396
Connors, Gail/9 Alpen Green Ct, Burtonsville, MD................301-890-9645
Contrino, Tom/22 Donaldson Ave, Rutherford, NJ................212-947-4450
Conway Photography/PO Box 165, Charlestown, MA................617-242-0064
Cooke, Doug/210 South St, Boston, MA................617-482-6154
Coolidge, Jeffrey/322 Summer St, Boston, MA................617-338-6869
Coonan, Steve/3921 Old Town Rd, Huntingtown, MD................301-855-1441
Cooper, John F/571 Central Ave #120, Murray Hill, NJ................201-273-0368
Cooper, Jon/4050 Washington St, Boston, MA................617-666-3453
Cooperman, Bill/7030 Powder Valley Rd, Zionsville, PA................215-965-2733
Corbett Jr, J D/Box 1219, Browns Mill, NJ................609-893-3516
Corcoran, John/310 Eighth St, New Cumberland, PA................717-774-0652
Cordingley, Ted/31 Blackburn Center, Gloucester, MA................617-283-2591
Cornell, Linc/31 Farm Hill Rd, Natick, MA................508-650-1612
Cornicello, John/317 Academy Terr, Linden, NJ................201-925-6675
Cornwell, Carol/10 Jordan Mill Ct, Whitehall, MD................301-343-1391
Corporate Graphics/Oxford/28 Corporate Cir, Albany, NY................518-452-8410
Corsiglia, Betsy/PO Box 934, Martha's Vineyard, MA................508-693-5107
Cortesi, Wendy/3034 'P' St NW, Washington, DC................202-965-1204
Cosloy, Jeff/35 Morrill St, W Newton, MA................617-965-5594
Coughlin, Suki/Main St/Box 1498, New London, NH................603-526-4645

Courtney, David M/36 Tremont St, Concord, NH....603-228-8412
Coxe, Dan/16 Bassett St, Providence, RI....401-331-5961
Coxe, David/, Cambridge, MA....617-547-4957
CR 2/36 St Paul St, Rochester, NY....716-232-5140
Crabtree, Shirley Ann/1 Prospect St #2A, New Rochelle, NY....914-636-5494
Crane, Tom/113 Cumberland Pl, Bryn Mawr, PA....215-525-2444
Cranna, Greig/55 Pemberton St, Cambridge, MA....617-868-8808
Crawford, Carol/14 Fortune Dr Box 221, Billerica, MA....617-663-8662
Creamer, Robert/2220 Eutaw Pl, Baltimore, MD....301-728-1586
Creative Image Photo/325 Valley Rd, West Orange, NJ....201-325-2352
Creative Images/122 Elmcroft Rd, Rochester, NY....716-482-8720
Creative Photography/Bustleton & Tyson Aves, Philadelphia, PA....215-332-8080
Croes, Larry/256 Charles St, Waltham, MA....617-894-4897
Crossan, Eric/473 Blackbird Landing Rd, Townsend, DE....302-834-7474
Crossley, Dorothy/Mittersill Rd, Franconia, NH....603-823-8177
Cullen, Betsy/125 Kingston St, Boston, MA....617-542-0965
Cunningham, Chris/9 East St, Boston, MA....617-542-4640
Curtis, Jackie/Alewives Rd, Norwalk, CT....203-866-9198
Curtis, John/50 Melcher St, Boston, MA....617-451-9117
Cury, Valerie/2153 California St NW #404, Washington, DC....202-332-3403
Cushner, Susie/354 Congress St, Boston, MA....617-542-4070
Czamanske, Marty/61 Commercial St, Rochester, NY....716-546-1434
Czepiga, David/101 Fitzrandolph Ave, Hamilton, NJ....609-396-2976

D

D'Amico, Sam/142 Worden Ave, Hopelawn, NJ....201-442-8246
D'Angelo, Andy/620 Centre Ave, Reading, PA....215-376-1100
Dai, Ping/30 Park St, Wakefield, MA....617-246-4704
Daigle, James/460 Harrison Ave, Boston, MA....800-992-9347
Dalia, Gerald/26 Park Place, Morristown, NJ....201-267-2217
Dalton, Douglas/236 Armington St, Cranston, RI....401-781-4099
Danello, Peter/386 Kerrigan Blvd, Newark, NJ....201-371-5899
Daniels, Craig/2103 St Paul St, Baltimore, MD....301-467-7536
Daniels, Mark/8413 Piney Branch Rd, Silver Spring, MD....301-587-1727
Dannenberg, Mitchell/261 Averill Ave, Rochester, NY....716-473-6720
Darling, Paul/418 County Rd, Barrington, RI....401-245-8330
Davidson, Heather/RD 2/Box 215, Rock Hall, MD....301-639-7368
Davis, Harold/299 Pavonia Ave, Jersey City, NJ....800-759-2583
Davis, Howard/19 E 21st St, Baltimore, MD....301-625-3838
Davis, James/159 Walnut St, Montclair, NJ....201-747-6972
Davis, Neal Assoc/42 Breckenridge, Buffalo, NY....716-881-4047
Davis, Pat Photo/14620 Pinto Ln, Rockville, MD....301-424-0577
Davis, Rick/210 Carter Dr #9/Matlack Ind, West Chester, PA....215-436-6050
Davis, Rita G/26 Ryder Ave, Dix Hills, NY....516-595-9368
Day, Joel/421 Walnut St, Lancaster, PA....717-291-7228
De Lorenzo, Bob/211 Steward St, Trenton, NJ....609-586-2421
De Lucia, Ralph/120 E Hartsdale Ave, Hartsdale, NY....914-472-2253
De Maio, Joe/529 Main St, Charlestown, MA....617-242-2000
De Simone, Bill/43 Irving St, Cambridge, MA....617-491-4583
De Zanger, Arie/, Sugarloaf, NY....914-469-4498
Dean, Floyd/2-B S Poplar St, Wilmington, DE....302-655-7193
Dean, John/2435 Maary land Ave, Baltimore, MA....301-243-8357
Debas, Bruno/49 Melcher St, Boston, MA....617-451-1394
Dee, Monica/208 Willow Ave #403, Hoboken, NJ....201-963-6086
Deering, William/700 Nottingham Rd, Wilmington, DE....302-888-2267
DeFilippis, Robert/70 Eighth St, Woodridge, NJ....201-896-9241
Degginger, Phil/189 Johnson Rd, Morris Plains, NJ....201-455-1733
Degrado, Drew/37 Midland Ave, Elmwood Park, NJ....201-797-2890
Delaney, Ray/403 Charles St, Providence, RI....401-331-9450
Delano, Jon/227 Christopher Columbus Dr, Jersey City, NJ....201-309-2110
Delbert, Christian/19 Linell Circle, Billerica, MA....617-273-3138
DeLellis, R A/43 Merrimack St, Lawrence, MA....508-681-0588
Delevingne, Lionel/123 Audubon Rd, Leeds, MA....413-586-3424
Delmas, Didier/1 Mill St, Burlington, VT....802-862-0120
DeMichele, Bill/40 Broadway, Albany, NY....518-436-4927
Dempsey-Hart, Jonathan/60 K Street, Boston, MA....617-268-0777
Dempster, David/5 Pirates Ln, Gloucester, MA....508-281-5118
Denison, Bill/302 Thornhill Rd, Baltimore, MD....301-323-1114
Denuto, Ellen/24 Mill St, Patterson, NJ....212-517-0296
Derenzis, Philip/421 N 23rd St, Allentown, PA (P 270)....215-776-6465
Desroches, David/443 Albany St #403, Boston, MA....617-482-0300
Devenny, Joe/RFD 1/Box 147, Waldoboro, ME....207-549-7693
Deveraux, Joanne/123 Oxford St, Cambridge, MA....617-876-7618
DeVito, Mary/2528 Cedar Ave, Ronkonkoma, NY....516-981-4547
DeVito, Michael Jr/40-A N Village Ave, Rockville Ctr, NY....212-243-5267
DeWaele, John/14 Almy St, Lincoln, RI....401-726-0084
Dey, Kinsley/78 Mill Run West, Hightstown, NJ....609-426-9762
Dibble, Warren/373 Commonwealth Ave #504, Boston, MA....617-236-1606
Dickenson, Townsend P/208 Flax Hill Rd #60, Norwalk, CT....203-853-4834
Dickstein, Bob/101 Hillturn Lane, Roslyn Heights, NY....516-621-2413
Diebold, George/416 Bloomfield Ave, Montclair, NJ....212-645-1077
Dietz, Donald/PO Box 177, Dorchester, MA....617-265-3436
DiGiacomo, Melchior/32 Norma Rd, Harrington Park, NJ....201-767-0870
Dillard, Ted/16 Ayer Rd/Box 112, Harvard, MA....508-456-8779
Dillon, Emile Jr/PO Box 39, Orange, NJ....201-675-5668
Dillon, George/210 South St, Boston, MA....617-482-6154
DiMaggio, Joe/512 Adams St, Centerport, NY....516-271-6133
DiMarco, Salvatore C Jr/1002 Cobbs St, Drexel Hill, PA....215-789-3239
DiMartini, Sally/1 Oyster lane, E Hampton, NY....516-329-1236
DiMarzo, Bob/92 Prince St, Boston, MA....617-720-1113
Di Meo, Martha/69 Laconia Rd, Cranston, RI....401-722-1460
Dinet Associates/5858 Molloy Rd #100, Syracuse, NY....315-455-6673
Dinn, Peter/52 Springtree Lane, S Berwick, ME....207-384-2877
Disario, George/50 Washington St, Newburyport, MA....508-465-2218
Distefano, Paul/, Hasbrouck Heights, NJ....201-471-0368
Distler, Dan/618 Allen St, Syracuse, NY....315-475-1938
Dodge, Brooks/PO Box 247/Eagle Mtn Rd, Jackson, NH....603-383-6830
Dodson, George/692 Gennessee St, Annapolis, MD....301-261-2099
Dolgin, Marcia/Box 127, Sharon, MA....617-784-4454
Donnelly, Gary/137 S easton Rd, Glenside, PA....215-576-6223
Donovan, Bill/165 Grand Blvd, Scarsdale, NY....914-472-0938
Dorfmann, Pam/5161 River Rd Bldg 2B, Bethesda, MD....301-652-1303
Dorman-Brown Photo/POB 700/Coach Rd #8B, Quechee, VT....802-296-6902
Dosch, Patrick/5 Concord Ave #64, Cambridge, MA....617-492-4777
Douglass, Jim Photogroup/5161 River Rd Bldg 2A, Bethesda, MD....301-652-1303
Dovi, Sal/2935 Dahlia St, Baldwin, NY....516-379-4273
Dow, Jim/95 Clifton St, Belmont, MA....617-484-4624
Dow, Norman/52 Concord Ave, Cambridge, MA....617-492-1236
Dowling, John/521 Scott Ave, Syracuse, NY....315-446-8189
Dragan, Dan/PO Box 2, N Brunswick, NJ....908-566-3431
Dratch, Howard/2173 Stoll Rd, Saugerties, NY....914-246-5213
Dreyer, Peter H/916 Pleasant St #11, Norwood, MA....617-762-8550
Druse, Ken/105 Cambridge Pl, Brooklyn, NY....718-230-0184
Dubroff, Richard/1900 Tatnall St, Wilmington, DE....302-655-7718
Duffy, Daniel/50 Croydon Rd, Worcester, MA....508-853-9116
Dugas, Rich/6 Laurel Lane, N Smithfield, RI....401-765-1863
Dunham, Tom/335 Gordon Rd, Robinsville, NJ....609-259-6042
Dunn, Jeffrey/32 Pearl St, Cambridge, MA....617-864-2124
Dunne, Paul/28 Southpoint Dr, S Sandwich, MA....508-420-5511
Dunoff, Rich/1313 Delmont Ave, Havertown, PA....215-642-6137
Dunwell, Steve/20 Winchester St, Boston, MA (P 67)....617-423-4916
Dupont, Iris/7 Bowdoin Ave, Dorchester, MA....617-436-8474
Durrance, Dick/Dolphin Ledge, Rockport, ME....207-236-3990
Durvin, Bill/135 Webster St, Pawtucket, RI....401-728-0091
Dutkovic, Bill/160 William Pitt Way, Pittsburgh, PA....412-826-5235
Dweck, Aboud/2300 Walnut St #626, Philadelphia, PA....215-564-9325
Dwiggins, Gene/204 Westminster Mall, Providence, RI....401-421-6466
Dworsky, Jeff/PO Box 32, Stonington, ME....207-367-5546
Dyekman, James E/14 Cherry Hill Circle, Ossining, NY....914-941-0821
Dyer, Ed/414 Brandy Lane, Mechanicsburg, PA....717-737-6618

E

Earle, John/PO Box 63, Cambridge, MA....617-628-1454
Eastern Light Photo/113 Arch St, Philadelphia, PA....215-238-0655
Eastwood, Henry C/800 3rd St NE, Washington, DC....202-543-9229
Edelman, Harry/2790 McCully Rd, Allison Park, PA....412-486-8822
Edenbaum, Josh/232 W Exchange St, Providence, RI....401-943-5568
Edgar, Andrew/135 McDonough St, Portsmouth, NH....603-436-4221
Edgerton, Brian/Box 364/11 Old Route 28, Whitehouse, NJ....908-534-9400
Edson, Franz Inc/26 Watch Way, Huntington, NY....516-692-4345
Edson, Steven/25 Otis St, Watertown, NY....617-357-8032
Edwards, Robert/9302 Hilltop Ct, Laurel, MD....301-490-9659
Egan, Jim/Visualizations/150 Chestnut St, Providence, RI....401-331-6220
Ehrlich, George/PO Box 186, New Hampton, NY....914-355-1757
Eich, Ed/10 Chapman Ave, Andover, MA....508-470-1424
Eisenberg, Leonard J/85 Wallingford Rd, Brighton, MA....617-787-3366
El-Darwish, Mahmoud/6925-A Willow St NW, Washington, DC....202-291-5424
Elder, Tommy/40 Stowe St, Concord, MA....508-369-1658
Electro/Grafiks/1238 Callow Hill St #404, Philadelphia, PA....215-923-6440
Elkins, Joel/8 Minkel Rd, Ossining, NY....914-941-0168
Elson, Paul/8200 Blvd East, North Bergen, NJ....201-662-2882
Emmott, Bob/700 S 10th St, Philadelphia, PA....215-925-2773
Ennis, Phil/98 Smith St, Freeport, NY....516-379-4273

Enos, Chris/1 Fitchburg St, Somerville, MA....617-625-8686
Epstein, Alan Photography/295 Silver St, Agawam, MA....413-789-3320
Epstein, Robert/6677 MacArthur Blvd, Bethesda, MD....301-320-3946
Epstein, William/Box 9067, N Bergen, NJ....201-662-7983
Erle, Steve/87 Gainsborough St, Boston, MA....617-357-3042
Esposito, Anthony Jr/48 Old Amity Rd, Bethany, CT....203-393-2231
Esposito, James/220 Little Falls Rd, Cedar Grove, NJ....201-239-1887
Esto Photo/222 Valley Pl, Mamaroneck, NY....914-698-4060
Evans, John C/223 Fourth Ave #1712, Pittsburgh, PA (P 69)....412-281-3663
Everett Studios/22 Barker Ave, White Plains, NY....914-997-2200
Everett, Michael/1744 Kalorama Rd NW, Washington, DC....202-234-2349
Everson, Martha/219 Fisher Ave, Brookline, MA (P 70,71)....617-232-0187
Ewing Galloway/100 Merrick Rd, Rockville Centre, NY....516-764-8620
Eyle, Nicolas Edward/205 Onondaga Ave, Syracuse, NY....315-422-6231

F

F-90 Inc/60 Sindle Ave, Little Falls, NJ....201-785-9090
Falkenstein, Roland/142 North Bread St, Philadelphia, PA....215-592-7138
Falocco, John/1 Forest Dr, Warren, NJ....908-769-9044
Fanelli, Chip/10 Nevada Ave, Somerville, MA....617-623-8374
Faraghan, George/940 N Delaware Ave, Philadelphia, PA....215-928-0499
Farkas, Alan/114 St Paul St #2, Rochester, NY....716-232-1124
Farley, G R/701 John St, Utica, NY....315-894-4438
Farrer, Herman/1305 Sheridan St NW, Washington, DC....202-723-7979
Farris, Mark/8804 Monard Dr, Silver Spring, MD....301-588-6637
Fatone, Bob/166 W Main St, Niantic, CT....203-739-2427
Fatta, Carol Photography/25 Dry Dock Ave, Boston, MA....617-423-6638
Faulkner, Robert I/14 Elizabeth Ave, East Brunswick, NJ (P 72)....201-390-6650
Fay Foto/45 Electric Ave, Boston, MA....617-267-2000
Feeney, Sandra/10 Cooke St, Providence, RI....401-272-8269
Feil, Charles W III/36 Danforth St, Portland, ME....207-773-3754
Feiling, David/1941 Teall Ave, Syracuse, NY....315-437-7059
Feingersh, Jon/18533 Split Rock Ln, Germantown, MD....301-428-9525
Feinstein, Claire/201 Tilton Rd #13-A, Northfield, NJ....609-383-8622
Felber, Richard/8 Ore Hill Rd, S Kent, CT....203-927-4016
Felker, Richard/RR 1/Box 200-B, Pembroke, ME....207-726-5890
Fell, Derek/PO Box 1, Gardenville, PA....215-766-2858
Fellows, Dick/401 N 21st St, Philadelphia, PA....215-977-7788
Fennell, Mary/57 Maple Ave, Hastings on Hudson, NY....914-478-3627
Feraulo, Richard/760 Plain St, Marshfield, MA....617-837-9563
Ferreira, Al/237 Naubuc Ave, East Hartford, CT....203-569-8812
Ferrino, Paul/PO Box 3641, Milford, CT....203-878-4785
Fetter, Frank/232 Spring St, Red Bank, NJ....201-530-8613
Fetters, Paul/3333 K St NW #50, Washington, DC....202-342-0333
Ficara, Sal/300 W Main St, Stamford, CT....203-327-4535
Ficksman, Peter/468 Fore St, Portland, ME....207-773-3555
Fields, Tim/916 Dartmouth Glen Way, Baltimore, MD....301-323-7831
Filipe, Tony/PO Box 1107, Block Island, RI....401-728-2339
Findlay, Christine/Hwy 36 Airport Plaza, Hazlet, NJ....908-264-2211
Fine, Jerome/4594 Brookhill Dr N, Manlius, NY....315-682-7272
Finlayson, Jim/PO Box 337, Locust Valley, NY....516-676-5816
Finnegan, Michael/PO Box 901, Plandome, NY....516-676-0653
Fiore, Anthony/600 Cooper Center W, Pennsauken, NJ....609-662-1884
Fisher, Al/601 Newbury St, Boston, MA....617-536-7126
Fisher, Patricia/2234 Cathedral Ave NW, Washington, DC....202-232-3781
Fitch, Roberrt/725 Branch Ave, Providence, RI....401-521-5959
Fiterman, Al/1415 Bayard St, Baltimore, MD....301-625-1265
Fitton, Larry/2029 Maryland Ave, Baltimore, MD....301-727-0092
Fitzhugh, Susan/3406 Chestnut Ave, Baltimore, MD....301-243-6112
Flanigan, Jim/1325 N 5th St #F4, Philadelphia, PA....215-236-4448
Fleming, Daniel/1140 Washington St, Boston, MA....617-426-9340
Fleming, Kevin/1669 Chinford Trail, Annapolis, MD....301-268-4484
Flesch, Patrice/46 McBride St, Jamaica Plains, MA....617-522-7199
Fleshner, Ed/11 Exchange Pl, Portland, ME....207-797-5982
Fletcher, John C/64 Murray Hill Terrace, Bergenfield, NJ....201-387-2171
Fletcher, Sarah/389 Charles St, Providence, RI....401-751-3557
Flint, Stan/2315 Maryland Ave, Baltimore, MD....301-837-9923
Flowers, Morocco/520 Harrison Ave, Boston, MA....617-426-3692
Floyd Dean Inc/2-B S Poplar St, Wilmington, DE....302-655-7193
Flynn, Bryce/14 Perry Dr Unit A, Foxboro, MA....508-543-3020
Fogle, John/25 Vine St, Marblehead, MA....617-631-4238
Foley, Paul/791 Tremont #E110, Boston, MA....617-266-9336
Foote, James/22 Tomac Ave, Old Greenwich, CT....203-637-3228
Forbes, Fred/1 South King St, Gloucester City, NJ....609-456-1919
Forbes, Peter/3833 Rexmere Rd, Baltimore, MD....301-889-5420
Ford, Sandra Gould/7123 Race St, Pittsburgh, PA....412-731-7039
Ford, Tim/121 W Lanvale St, Baltimore, MD....301-383-8070
Fordham, Eric S/282 Moody St, Waltham, MA....617-647-7927
Forster, Daniel/124 Green End Ave, Middletown, RI....401-847-4866
Fortin, Paul/318 W Washington St, Hanson, MA....617-447-2614
Forward, Jim/56 Windsor St, Rochester, NY....716-423-0820
Foster, Cynthia/143 Riverview Ave, Annapolis, MD....301-224-4746
Foster, Frank/PO Box 518, W Harwich, MA....617-536-8267
Foster, Nicholas/143 Claremont Rd, Bernardsville, NJ....908-766-7526
Fota, Gregory M/1935 Fernway Ave, Bethlehem, PA....215-865-9851
Foti, Arthur/8 W Mineola Ave, Valley Steam, NY....516-872-0941
Fournier, John/P O Box 121, Block Island, RI....401-466-2523
Fox, Debi/5161 River Rd Bldg 2B, Bethesda, MD....301-652-1303
Fox, Jon Gilbert/RR 1/Box 307G, Norwich, VT....802-649-2828
Fox, Peggy/701 Padonia Rd, Cockeysville, MD....301-252-0003
Fracassa, Glen/272 W Exchange St #200, Providence , RI....401-751-5882
Francisco, Thomas/21 Quine St, Cranford, NJ....201-272-1155
Francois, Emmett W/208 Hillcrest Ave, Wycoff, NJ....201-652-5775
Francouer, Norm/144 Moody St, Waltham, MA....617-891-3830
Frank, Carol/1032 N Calvert St, Baltimore, MD....301-244-0092
Frank, Diane/208 North Ave West, Cranford, NJ....908-276-2229
Frank, Laurence/219 Henry St, Stamford, CT....203-975-7720
Frank, Richard/48 Woodside Ave, Westport, CT....203-227-0496
Frankel, Felice/202 Ellington Rd, Longmeadow, MA....413-567-0222
Fraser, Renee/1260 Boylston St, Boston, MA....617-646-4296
Frederick, Leigh/333 Robinson Lane, Wilmington, DE....302-428-6109
Fredericks, Michael Jr/RD 2 Box 292, Ghent, NY....518-672-7616
Freeman, Charles Photo/3100 St Paul St, Baltimore, MD....301-243-2416
Freer, Bonnie/265 S Mountain Rd, New City, NY....212-535-3666
Freeze Frame Studios/255 Leonia Ave, Bogota, NJ....201-343-1233
Freid, Joel Carl/1501 14th St NW, Washington, DC....800-869-7413
French, Larry/162 Linden Lane, Princeton, NJ....609-924-2906
French, Russell/496 Congress St, Portland, ME....207-874-0011
Freund, Bud/1425 Bedford St #9C, Stamford, CT....203-359-0147
Friedman, Rick/133 Beaconsfield Rd, Brookline, MA....617-734-8125
Fries, Janet/4439 Ellicott St NW, Washington, DC....202-362-4443
Friscia, Santa/395 Carriage Shop Rd, E Falmouth, MA....508-548-7995
Frog Hollow Studio/Box 897, Bryn Mawr, PA....215-353-9898
Fuchs, Betsy/75 Sumner St, Newton Ctr, MA....617-332-6363
Furman, Michael/115 Arch St, Philadelphia, PA....215-925-4233
Furst, Arthur/4 Noon Hill Ave, Norfolk, MA....508-520-1703

G

G/Q Studios/1217 Spring Garden St, Philadelphia, PA....215-236-7770
Gabrielsen, Kenneth/11 Tuttle St #15, Stamford, CT (P 74)....203-964-8254
Gadomski, Michael P/RD 1/Box 201-B, Greentown, PA....717-676-3998
Gale, Howard & Judy/712 Chestnut St, Philadelphia, PA....215-629-0506
Gale, John & Son/712 Chestnut St, Philadelphia, PA....215-629-0506
Gallery, Bill/86 South St, Boston, MA (P 46,47)....617-542-0499
Gallo, Peter/1238 Callowhill St #301, Philadelphia, PA....215-925-5230
Gans, Hank/RR 1/Box 2564, Wells, ME....207-646-9871
Gans, Harriet/50 Church Lane, Scarsdale, NY....914-723-7017
Ganson, John/14 Lincoln Rd, Wayland, MA....508-358-2543
Ganton, Brian/882 Pompton Ave, Cedar Grove, NJ....201-857-5099
Garaventa, John/105 Constock Rd, Manchester, CT....203-647-1579
Garber, Bette S/3160 Walnut St, Thorndale, PA (P 271)....215-380-0342
Garber, Ira/150 Chestnut St, Providence, RI....401-274-3723
Garcia, Richard/30 Kimberly Pl, Wayne, NJ....201-956-0885
Gardner, Charles/12 N 4th St, Reading, PA....215-376-8086
Garfield, Peter/7370 MacArthur Blvd, Glen Echo, MD....301-229-6800
Garnier, William/155 New Boston St, Woburn, MA....617-933-4301
Gates, Ralph/364 Hartshorn Dr Box 233, Short Hills, NJ....201-379-4456
Gawrys, Anthony P/163 Lowell St, Peabody, MA....508-531-5877
Gee, Elizabeth/186 Rte 24/RFD #1, Mendham, NJ....201-543-2447
Geer, Garry/183 St Paul St, Rochester, NY (P 75)....716-232-2393
Geiger, Michael/PO Box 146, Tillson, NY....914-658-3106
Generalli, Janet/21 Russell St, Brookline, MA....617-566-0782
Gensheimer, Rich/2737 E 41st St, Erie, PA....814-825-5822
George, Fred/737 Canal St/Bldg #35/2nd Fl, Stamford, CT....203-348-7454
George, Walter Jr/20 Main St, Clinton, NJ....908-735-7013
Geraci, Steve/106 Keyland Ct, Bohemia, NY....516-567-8777
Germer, Michael/27 Industrial Ave, Chelmsford, MA....508-250-9282
Getgen, Linda/201 North St, Hingham, MA....617-749-7815
Getzoff, Joseph/1 Ellis Rd, W Caldwell, NJ....201-226-5259

Giandomenico, Bob/13 Fern Ave, Collingswood, NJ ... 609-854-2222
Giese, Al/RR 1/Box 302, Poundridge, NY ... 914-764-5512
Giglio, Harry/925 Penn Ave #305, Pittsburgh, PA ... 412-261-3338
Gilbert, Mark/12 Juliette St, Boston, MA ... 617-265-1038
Giles, Frank/182 Main St #35, Burlington, VT ... 802-658-3615
Gillette, Guy/133 Mountaindale Rd, Yonkers, NY ... 914-779-4684
Gilligan Group/Rte 517/Crossrds Ctr, Hackettstown, NJ ... 908-813-0901
Gilstein, Dave/25 Amflex Dr, Cranston, RI ... 401-946-6100
Giraldi, Frank/42 Harmon Pl, N Haledon, NJ ... 201-423-5115
Glasofer, David/176 Main St, Metuchen, NJ ... 908-549-1845
Glass, Mark/814 Garden St, Hoboken, NJ ... 201-798-0219
Glass, Peter/15 Oakwood St, East Hartford, CT ... 203-528-8559
Glick, Robert/3 Dohrmann Ave, Teaneck, NJ ... 201-836-3911
Gluck, Mike/2 Bronxville Rd, Bronxville, NY ... 914-961-1677
Goell, Jon/535 Albany St, Boston, MA (P 76) ... 617-423-2057
Goembel, Ponder/666 Easton Rd, Reigelsville, PA ... 215-749-0337
Gold, Gary D/One Madison Pl, Albany, NY ... 518-434-4887
Goldblatt, Steven/32 S Strawberry St, Philadelphia, PA ... 215-925-3825
Goldenberg, Barry/70 Jackson Dr/Box 412, Cranford, NJ ... 908-276-1510
Goldman, Mel/329 Newbury St, Boston, MA ... 617-536-0539
Goldman, Rob/15 South Grand Ave, Baldwin, NY ... 516-223-4018
Goldsmith, Bruce/1 Clayton Ct, Park Ridge, NJ ... 201-391-4946
Goldstein, Alan/10 Post Office Rd B-3, Silver Spring, MD ... 301-589-1690
Goldstein, Robert/PO Box 1127, Dennis, MA ... 508-385-5030
Good, Richard/5226 Osage Ave, Philadelphia, PA ... 215-472-7659
Goodman, Howard/PO Box 453, Peekskill, NY ... 914-737-1162
Goodman, John/337 Summer St, Boston, MA ... 617-482-8061
Goodman, John D/5 East Rd, Colchester, VT ... 802-878-0200
Goodman, Lou Photography/322 Summer St, Boston, MA ... 617-542-8254
Goodman/Van Riper Photo/3502 Quesada St NW, Washington, DC ... 202-362-8103
Goodwin, Scott/109 Broad St, Boston, MA ... 617-451-8161
Gorany, Hameed/413 Beacon Hill Terrace, Gaithersburg, MD ... 301-840-0012
Gorchev & Gorchev/11 Cabot Rd, Woburn, MA ... 617-933-8090
Gordon, David A/1413 Hertel Ave, Buffalo, NY ... 716-833-2661
Gorodnitzki, Diane/Main St/Box 357, Sagaponack, NY ... 516-537-1788
Gorrill, Robert B/PO Box 206, North Quincy, MA ... 617-328-4012
Gothard, Bob/1 Music St, W Tisbury, MA ... 508-693-1060
Gottheil, Philip/1278 Lednam Ct, Merrick, NY ... 516-378-6802
Gottlieb, Steve/3601 East-West Hwy, Chevy Chase, MD ... 301-951-9648
Gozbekian, Leo/117-A Gayland St, Watertown, MA ... 617-923-1666
Graham, Jim/720 Chestnut St, Philadelphia, PA ... 215-592-7272
Graham, Steffi/5726 Cross Country Blvd, Baltimore, MD ... 301-664-8493
Grant, Gail/7006 Valley Ave, Phildelphia, PA ... 215-482-9857
Grant, Jarvis/1650 Harvard St NW #709, Washington, DC ... 202-387-8584
Grant/Miller/5 Lake St, Morris, NY ... 607-263-5060
Graphic Accent/446 Main St PO Box 243, Wilmington, MA ... 508-658-7602
Grassl, Jennie Lawton/5 Sycamore St, Cambridge, MA ... 617-876-1321
Gray, Sam/17 Stilling St, Boston, MA ... 617-237-2711
Grayson, Jay/9 Cockenoe Dr, Westport, CT ... 203-222-0072
Green, Elisabeth/52 Springtree Lane, S Berwick, ME ... 207-384-2877
Green, Jeremy/1720 Lancaster St, Baltimore, MD ... 301-732-5614
Greenaway, Malcolm/642 Corn Neck Rd, Block Island, RI ... 401-466-2122
Greenberg, Chip/325 High St, Metuchen, NJ ... 908-548-5612
Greenberg, Steven/560 Harrison Ave, Boston, MA ... 617-423-7646
Greene, Joe/Box 148, Allston, MA ... 617-338-1388
Greenfield, David/56 Fordham Dr, Matawan, NJ ... 201-747-2662
Greenhouse, Richard/7532 Heatherton Ln, Potomac, MD ... 301-365-3236
Greenlar, Michael/305 Hillside St, Syracuse, NY ... 315-454-3729
Gregg, Sandy/PO Box 5027, North Branch, NJ ... 908-231-9617
Gregory, Mark/10615 Duvall St, Glenn Dale, MD ... 301-262-8646
Greniers Commercial Photo/127 Mill St, Springfield, MA ... 413-532-9406
Griebsch, John/25 N Washington St, Rochester, NY ... 716-546-1303
Griffin, Arthur/22 Euclid Ave, Winchester, MA ... 617-729-2690
Griffiths-Belt, Annie/1301 Noyes Dr, Silver Spring, MD ... 301-495-3127
Griggs, Dennis/Box 44A/Foreside Rd, Topsham, ME ... 207-725-5689
Grohe, Stephen F/451 D St #809, Boston, MA ... 617-426-2290
Gruol, Dave/92 Western Ave, Morristown, NJ ... 201-267-2847
Guarinello, Greg/252 Highwood St, Teaneck, NJ ... 201-384-2172
Gude, Susann/Slip 1-A/Spruce Dr, E Patchogue, NY ... 516-654-8093
Guidera, Tom III/403 N Charles St #200, Baltimore, MD ... 301-752-7676
Gummerson, Anne/225 W 25th St, Baltimore, MD ... 301-235-8325
Gunderson, Gary/PO Box 397, Danbury, CT ... 203-792-2273
Guynup, Sharon/813 Willow Ave, Hoboken, NJ ... 201-798-0781

H

H/O Photographers/197 Main St, Hartford, VT ... 802-295-6321
Hagan, Robert/PO Box 6625, Providence, RI ... 401-421-4483
Hagerman, Ron/389 Charles St, Providence, RI (P 80) ... 401-272-1117
Hahn, Bob/3522 Skyline Dr, Bethlehem, PA ... 215-868-0339
Hales, Mick/PO Box 157/Glenwood Farm, Cold Spring, NY ... 914-265-4483
Hall, Gary Clayton/PO Box 838, Shelburne, VT ... 802-985-8380
Hallinan, Peter J/PO Box 183, Boston, MA ... 617-924-1539
Halsman, Irene/297 N Mountain Ave, Upper Montclair, NJ ... 201-746-9155
Halstead, Dirck/3332 P St NW, Washington, DC ... 202-338-2028
Haman, Stuart/13 Dorset Hill Ct, Owings Mill, MD ... 301-356-2048
Hambourg, Serge/Box 753, Crugers, NY ... 212-866-0085
Hambright/Hoachlander Assoc/414 11th St SE, Washington, DC ... 202-546-1717
Hamburg, Karen/218 Cedar Ave, Blackwood, NJ ... 609-232-0737
Hamerman, Don/19 Bellmere Ave, Stamford, CT (P 81) ... 212-627-5474
Hamilton, Bruce/444 Western Ave, Brighton, MA ... 617-783-9409
Hamlin, Elizabeth/434 Franklin St, Cambridge, MA ... 617-876-6821
Hamor, Robert/2308 Columbia Cir, Merrimack, NH ... 603-424-6737
Handler, Lowell/147 Main St, Coldspring, NY ... 914-265-4023
Hansen-Mayer Photography/281 Summer St, Boston, MA ... 617-542-3080
Hansen-Sturm, Robert/334 Wall St, Kingston, NY ... 914-338-8753
Hanstein, George/389 Belmont Ave, Haledon, NJ ... 201-790-0505
Harholdt, Peter/4980C Wyaconda Rd, Rockville, MD ... 301-984-7772
Haritan, Michael/1701 Eben St, Pittsburgh, PA ... 412-343-2112
Harkey, John/90 Larch St, Providence, RI ... 401-831-1023
Harkins, Kevin F/219 Appleton St, Lowell, MA ... 508-452-9704
Harp, David/6027 Pinehurst Rd, Baltimore, MD ... 301-433-9242
Harrington, Blaine III/2 Virginia Ave, Danbury, CT ... 203-798-2866
Harrington, John/455 Old Sleepy Hollow Rd, Pleasantville, NY ... 914-939-0702
Harrington, Phillip A/Wagner Ave/ PO Box 10, Fleischmann's, NY ... 914-254-5227
Harris, Brownie/POB 164/McGuire Lane, Croton-on-Hudson, NY ... 914-271-6426
Harris, Eunice & Leonard/19 Clarendon Ave, Providence, RI ... 401-331-9784
Harrison, Jim/One Thompson Square, Charleston, MA ... 617-242-4314
Hart, Russell/49 Monroe Ave, Larchmont, NY ... 914-833-1516
Harting, Christopher/327 Summer St, Boston, MA ... 617-451-6330
Hartlove, Chris/802 Berry St, Baltimore, MD ... 301-889-7293
Harvey, Milicent/49 Melcher St, Boston, MA ... 617-482-4493
Hathaway, Dwayne/404 W Baltimore St #8, Baltimore, MD ... 301-659-0282
Hatos, Kathleen/3418 Keins St, Philadelphia, PA ... 215-425-3960
Hausner, Clifford/37-14 Hillside Terrace, Fairlawn, NJ ... 201-791-7409
Hayes, Barry/53 Main St, St Johnsbury, VT ... 802-748-8916
Hayes, Calvin/2125 N Charles St, Baltimore, MD ... 301-685-0646
Hayman, Jim Studio/100 Fourth Ave, York, PA ... 717-843-8338
Hayward, Matthew/1168 Commonwealth Ave, Boston, MA ... 617-666-0555
Haywood, Alan/39 Westmoreland Ave, White Plains, NY ... 914-946-1928
Hazlegrove, Cary/PO Box 442/One Main St, Nantucket, MA ... 508-228-3783
Heard, Gary/274 N Goodman St, Rochester, NY ... 416-271-6780
Heath, Penny/Rt 1/Box 94, Redwood, NY ... 315-482-5636
Heayn, Mark/17 W 24th St, Baltimore, MD ... 301-235-1608
Heerlein, Karen/200 Wiliams St, Port Chester, NY ... 914-937-7042
Height, Edward/58 White Birch Dr, Rockaway, NJ ... 201-627-9212
Heilman, Grant/506 W Lincoln Ave, Lititz, PA ... 717-626-0296
Heinz, F Michael Photography/10 Perry Ave, Norwalk, CT ... 203-847-6820
Heist, Scott/616 Walnut St, Emmaus, PA ... 215-965-5479
Helldorfer, Fred/1 Sassasfras Ct, Voorhees, NJ ... 609-772-1039
Helmar, Dennis/416 W Broadway, Boston, MA ... 617-269-7410
Henderson, Elizabeth/107 South St, Boston, MA ... 617-695-1313
Herity, Jim/601 Riverside Ave, Westport, CT ... 203-454-3979
Herko, Robert/121 Hadley St, Piscataway, NJ ... 908-563-1613
Herrera, Frank/318 Kentucky Ave SE, Washington, DC ... 301-229-7930
Hess, Allen/17 Sandpiper Lane, Pittsford, NY ... 716-381-9796
Hewett, Ian/124 Webster Ave, Jersey City, NJ ... 201-216-9388
Hewitt, Malcolm/323 Newbury St, Boston, MA ... 617-262-7227
Hickey, Bill/54 Summit Ave, Westwood, NJ ... 201-666-3861
Hickman, Louis/Box 5358, Plainfield, NJ ... 908-561-2696
Higgins & Ross/281 Princeton St, N Chelmsford, MA ... 508-454-4248
Highsmith, Carol/3299 K St NW #404, Washington, DC ... 202-347-0910
Hill, Britian (Ms)/Pleasnat Pond Rd/Box 238, Francestown, NH ... 603-547-8873
Hill, John T/388 Amity Rd, New Haven, CT ... 203-393-0035
Hill, Jon/159 Burlington St, Lexington, MA ... 617-862-6456
Hill, Rob/Hoagland Rd, Blairstown, NJ ... 908-459-4667
Hilliard, Bruce/125 Walnut St, Watertown, MA ... 617-923-0916
Hilliard, Henry/14 Harvard Ave 3rd Fl, Boston, MA ... 617-789-4415
Hinton, Ron/1 Fitchburg St C318, Somerville, MA ... 617-666-3565
Hirsch, Linda/7 Highgate Rd, Wayland, MA ... 508-653-0161
Hirshfeld, Max/1027 33rd St NW, Washington, DC ... 202-333-7450
Hitchcox, Glen/7 Blauvelt St, Nanuet, NY (P 83) ... 914-623-5859
Hoachlander, Anice/1001 Sigsbee Pl NE, Washington, DC ... 202-269-0587
Hodges, Sue Anne/87 Gould Rd, Andover, MA ... 617-475-2007

Hoffman, Dave/PO Box 1299, Summit, NJ 908-277-6285
Hollander, David/147 S Maple Ave/Box 443, Springfield, NJ 201-467-0870
Holmes, Greg/2007 Hickory Hill Ln, Silver Spring, MD 301-460-3643
Holoquist, Marcy/2820 Smallman St, Pittsburgh, PA....412-261-4142
Holt, John/25 Dry Dock Ave, Boston, MA....617-426-4658
Holt, Walter/PO Box 936, Media, PA 215-565-1977
Holt/Aiguier Photography/535 Albany St, Boston, MA 617-338-7674
Holtz, Ron/9153 Brookville Rd, Silver Spring, MD 301-589-7900
Homan, Mark/1916 Old Cuthbert Rd #B24, Cherry Hill, NJ 609-795-6763
Hone, Stephen/859 N 28th St, Philadelphia, PA....215-765-6900
Hood, Sarah/1924 37th St NW, Washington, DC....202-337-2585
Hopkins, Tom/15 Orchard Park, Box 7A, Madison, CT 203-245-0824
Horizon Aerial/6 Lakeside Ave, Nashua, NH....603-889-8318
Hornick/Rivlin Studio/25 Dry Dock Ave, Boston, MA....617-482-8614
Horowitz, Abby/915 N 28th St, Philadelphia, PA 215-925-3600
Horowitz, Ted/214 Wilton Rd, Westport, CT (P 48,49) ...203-454-8766
Horsman, Bill/248 Moss Hill Rd, Boston, MA....617-522-4545
Hotshots/35 Congress St/PO Box 896, Salem, MA....617-744-1557
Houck, Julie/21 Clinton St, S Portland, ME....207-767-3365
Houser, Robert/PO Box 299, Litchfield, CT 203-567-4241
Houston, Robert/1512 E Chase St, Baltimore, MD 301-327-2632
Howard, Jerry/317 N Main, Natick, MA 617-653-7610
Howard, Peter/7 Bright Star Ct, Baltimore, MD....301-866-5013
Howard, Richard/45 Walnut St, Somerville, MA....617-628-5410
Hoyt, Russell/171 Westminister Ave, S Attleboro, MA....508-399-8611
Hoyt, Wolfgang/222 Valley Pl, Mamaroneck, NY....914-698-4060
Hubbell, William/99 East Elm St, Greenwich, CT....203-629-9629
Huber, William Productions/49 Melcher, Boston, MA 617-426-8205
Huet, John/27 Dry Dock Ave 7th Fl, Boston, MA....617-423-6317
Hundertmark, Charles/6264 Oakland Mills Rd, Sykesville, MD 301-242-8150
Hungaski, Andrew/Merribrook Lane, Stamford, CT....203-327-6763
Hunsberger, Douglas/115 W Fern Rd, Wildwood Crest, NJ 609-522-6849
Hunt, Barbara/12017 Nebel St, Rockville, MD 301-468-1613
Hunter, Allan/56 Main St 3rd Fl, Milburn, NJ 201-467-4920
Hurwitz, Joel/PO Box 1009, Leominster, MA 617-537-6476
Husted, Dan/143 Sagamore Rd, Milburn, NJ....201-761-1348
Hutchings, Richard/24 Pinebrook Dr, Larchmont, NY 914-834-9633
Hutchins Photography/309 Main St, Watertown, MA 617-926-8880
Hutchinson, Clay/Viewfinder Pub/Box 41, Old Chatham, NY 518-794-7767
Hutchinson, Gardiner/PO Box 41, Old Chatham, NY....518-794-7767
Hutnak, Gene/269 Greenville Ave, Johnston, RI 401-232-5090
Huyler, Willard/107 Jerome St, Roosevelt Plns, NJ....908-245-1081
Hyde, Dana/PO Box 1302, South Hampton, NY 516-283-1001
Hyon, Ty/65 Drumhill Rd, Wilton, CT 203-834-0870

IJ

Iafrate, Doreen/8 Blackstone Valley Pl #201, Lincoln, RI 401-333-2886
Iannazzi, Robert F/450 Smith Rd, Rochester, NY....716-624-1285
Ibberson, Chris/35 W William St, Corning , NY....607-937-5487
Ide, Roger/529 Main St, Charlestown, MA 617-242-7872
Iglarsh, Gary/2229 N Charles St, Baltimore, MD 301-235-3385
Image Designs/345 Cornwall Ct, Katonah, NY 914-232-8231
Image Photographic Svcs/622 Thomas Blvd, E Orange, NJ....201-675-6555
Image Source Inc/PO Box 1929, Wilmington, DE 302-658-5897
Images Commercial Photoy/360 Sylvan Ave, Englewood Cliffs, NJ....201-871-4406
Impact Multi Image Inc/117 W Washington 2nd fl, Pleasantville, NJ....609-484-8100
Impact Studios/1084 N Delaware Ave,
Philadelphia, PA (P 54) 215-426-3988
Insight Photo/55 Gill Lane #5, Iselin, NJ....908-283-4727
IntVeldt, Gail/5510 Corral Lane, Frederick, MD....301-473-4531
Iverson, Bruce/7 Tucker St #65, Pepperell, MA 617-433-8429
Jackson, Cappy/1034 Monkton Rd, Monkton, MD....301-343-1313
Jackson, Glenwood/3000 Chestnut Ave #10, Baltimore, MD....301-366-0049
Jackson, Martin/314 Catherine St #401, Philadelphia, PA....215-271-5149
Jackson, Philip/534 E Second St, Plainfield, NJ....800-878-5999
Jackson, Reggie/135 Sheldon Terr, New Haven, CT 203-787-5191
Jacobs, Kip/208 E Miami Ave, Cherry Hill, NJ 609-427-0019
Jacoby, Edward/108 Mt Vernon, Boston, MA....617-723-4896
Jagger, Warren/150 Chestnut St Box 3330, Providence, RI....401-351-7366
Jakubek, Alan/P O Box 562, Winooski, VT 802-863-8299
Jamison, Jon/247 Bly Rd, Schenectady, NY 518-869-6211
Jaramillo, Alain/613 N Eautaw St, Baltimore, MD 301-727-2220
Jarvis, Guy/109 Broad St, Boston, MA 617-482-8998
Jaynes, Claude/122 Waverly St, Everett, MA 617-389-4703
Jeffries, William C/232 Market St, Middletown, PA 717-944-5694
Jenkins, Hank/234 Arlington Ave, Paterson, NJ 201-956-7244
Jenkins, John/1900 N Tatnall St, Wilmington, DE 302-658-5897
Jesudowich, Stanley/200 Henry St, Stamford, CT....203-359-8886
Joachim, Bruno/326 A Street, Boston, MA 617-451-6156
Joel, Yale/Woodybrook Ln, Croton-On-Hudson, NY....914-271-8172
Johnson, April L/3 Rowe Ave, Rockport, MA....617-298-5448
Johnson, Cynthia/316 10th St NE, Washington, DC....202-546-9864
Johnson, Stella/137 Langdon Ave, Watertown, MA 617-923-1263
Jones, Alexander/1243-A Maryland Ave NE, Washington, DC....202-832-1225
Jones, Isaac/3000 Chestnut Ave, Baltimore, MD 301-889-5779
Jones, Lou/22 Randolph St, Boston, MA....617-426-6335
Jones, Marvin T/5203 14th St NW, Washington, DC 202-726-4066
Jones, Peter/43 Charles St, Boston, MA....617-227-6400
Jones, Tom Photo/89 Pleasant St, Brunswick, ME 207-725-5238
Joseph, Ed/3081 Cypress Ct, Monmouth Junctn, NJ 908-329-6825
Joubert, Larry/728 Auburn St #G4, Whitman, MA 617-447-1178
Judice, Ed/83 W Main St, Orange, MA....508-544-2739
Juracka, Frank/179 Widmer Rd, Wappingers Falls, NY....914-297-2074

K

Kaetzel, Gary/PO Box 3514, Wayne, NJ....201-696-6174
Kagan, BC/43 Winter St 4th Fl, Boston, MA 617-482-0336
Kalfus, Lonny/226 Hillside Ave, Leonia, NJ 201-944-3909
Kalischer, Clemens/Main St, Stockbridge, MA....413-298-5500
Kalish, JoAnne/512 Adams St, Centerport, NY 516-271-6133
Kalisher, Simpson/North St, Roxbury, CT 203-354-8893
Kaminsky, Saul/36 Sherwood Ave, Greenwich, CT 203-869-3883
Kan, Dennis/PO Box 248, Clarksburg, MD....301-428-9417
Kane, John/POB 731, New Milford, CT....203-354-7651
Kane, Martin/401 Sharpless St, West Chester, PA....215-696-0206
Kannair, Jonathan/91 Quaker Lane, Bolton, MA 508-779-2266
Kaplan, Barry/5 Main St, Wickford, RI 212-254-8461
Kaplan, Carol/20 Beacon St, Boston, MA....617-720-4400
Karlin, Lynn/RD Box 12, Harborside, ME....207-326-4062
Karlsson, Bror/543 Park St, Montclair, NJ 201-783-6491
Karnow, Catherine/1707 Columbia Rd #518, Washington, DC 202-332-5656
Karosis, Rob/855 Islington St, Portsmouth, NH....603-436-8876
Karten, Roy/803 Malcolm Dr, Silver Spring, MD....301-445-0751
Kaskons, Peter/Westech Ind Park, Tyngsboro, MA....508-649-7788
Kasper, Ken/1232 Cobbs St, Drexel Hill, PA....215-789-7033
Katz, Bruce/2700 Connecticut Ave NW #103B, Washington, DC 202-332-5848
Katz, Dan/36 Aspen Rd, W Orange, NJ 201-731-8956
Katz, Geoffrey/156 Francestown Rd, New Boston, NH....603-487-3819
Katz, Philip/286 Meetinghouse Rd, New Hope, PA....215-862-3503
Kauffman, Bob/28 Hemlock Dr, Farmingdale, NY 516-454-9637
Kauffman, Kenneth/915 Spring Garden St, Philadelphia, PA....215-649-4474
Kaufman, Robert/58 Roundwood Rd, Newton Upper Falls, MA....617-964-4080
Kawalerski, Ted/7 Evergreen Way, North Tarrytown, NY 212-242-0198
Kawamoto, Noriko/9727 Softwater Way, Columbia, MD 301-953-0467
Keating, Roger/102 Manatee Rd, Hingham, MA....617-749-5250
Keeley, Chris/4000 Tunlaw Rd NW #1119, Washington, DC 202-337-0022
Keiser, Anne B/3760 39th St #f144, Washington, DC 202-966-6733
Keith, David/96 Reservation Rd, Sunderland, MA 413-665-7944
Keller & Peet Assoc/107 Park Ave, Arlington, MA....617-646-1311
Kelley, Edward/20 White St, Red Bank, NJ....908-747-0596
Kelley, Patsy/70 Atlantic Ave/PO Box 1147, Marblehead, MA 617-639-1147
Kelly, Joanne/92 Marlborough #1, Boston, MA....617-266-5690
Kelly/Mooney Photography/87 Willow Ave, North Plainfield, NJ 908-757-5924
Kenik, David Photography/16 Atlantic Ave, W Warwick, RI 401-823-3080
Kennedy, Thomas/4002 Laird Pl, Chevy Chase, MD 202-857-7458
Kenner, Ray/401 W Redwood #506, Baltimore , MD 410-837-4742
Kernan, Sean/School St, Stony Creek, CT....203-481-4478
Kerper, David/1018 E Willow Grove Ave, Philadelphia, PA 215-836-1135
Kim, Chang/9425 Bethany Pl, Gaithersburg, MD....301-840-5741
Kimball, Sandra/409 W Broadway, Boston, MA 617-268-1980
King, Joseph/5 Michael Dr, Lincoln, RI....401-272-9560
Kingdon, David/40 Church St, Fair Haven, NJ 201-741-6621
Kinney, Barbara/2025 Kalorama Rd NW #3, Washington, DC....202-387-6629
Kinum, Drew/Glen Avenue, Scotia, NY....518-382-7566
Kipperman, Barry/529 Main St, Charlestown, MA....617-241-7323
Kirkman, Tom/58 Carley Ave, Huntington, NY 212-628-0973
Kirschbaum, Jed/102 N Wolfe St, Baltimore, MD....301-332-6940
Kitman, Carol/147 Crescent Ave, Leonia, NJ 201-947-2969
Kittle, James Kent/49 Brinckerhoff Ln, New Canann, CT....203-966-2442
Klapatch, David/2049 Silas Deane Hwy, Rocky Hill, CT 203-563-3834
Klebau, James/5806 Maiden Lane, Bethesda, MD 301-320-2666
Klein, Robert D/273 Rock Rd, Glen Rock, NJ 201-445-6513
Kleinschmidt, Carl/408 Cobble Creek Curve, Newark, DE....302-733-0456
Kligman, Fred/2323 Stewart Rd, Silver Spring, MD 301-589-4100

Klim, Greg/14 Nichols Rd, Needham , MA	617-327-3980
Kline, Andrew/, Montpelier, VT	802-229-4924
Klinefelter, Eric/10963 Hickory Ridge Rd, Columbia, MD	301-964-0273
Klonsky, Arthur/RR1/Box 235, Londonderry, VT	802-824-4135
Knapp, Stephen/74 Commodore Rd, Worcester, MA	617-757-2507
Knowles, Robert M/525 Ellendale Ave #PH, Rye Brook, NY	914-934-2619
Knudsen, Rolf/155 Brookside Ave #6, West Warwick, RI	401-826-1945
Koby-Antupit Photographers/8 JFK St, Cambridge, MA	617-547-7552
Korona, Joseph/25 Foxcroft Rd, Pittsburgh, PA	412-279-9200
Koslowski, Wayne/1195 Westfield Ave, Rahway, NJ	908-381-8189
Kovner, Mark/14 Cindy Lane, Highland Mills, NY	914-928-6543
Kowerski, Marty/530 Pine Hill Rd, Lilitz, PA	717-627-7722
Kramer, Arnold/1839 Ingleside Terr NW, Washington, DC	202-667-9385
Kramer, Phil/122 W Church St, Philadelphia, PA	215-928-9189
Kramer, Rob/409 W Broadway, Boston, MA	617-269-9269
Krasner, Stuart/7837 Muirfield Ct, Potomac, MD	301-983-1599
Kremer, Glenn/374 Congress St, Boston, MA	617-482-7158
Kress, Michael/5709 Lenox Rd, Bethesda, MD	301-229-1900
Krist, Bob/333 S Irving, Ridgewood, NJ	201-585-9464
Krogh, Peter Harold/3301 Oberon St, Kensington, MD	301-933-2468
Krohn, Lee/RR1/Box 1205, Manchester, VT	802-362-4824
Krubner, Ralph/4 Juniper Court, Jackson, NJ	201-364-3640
Kruper, Alexander Jr/70 Jackson Dr Box 152, Cranford, NJ	908-709-0220
KSN Images/475 Linden Lane #203, Media, PA	215-565-7268
Kucine, Cliff/85 York St #3, Portland, ME	207-773-2568
Kugielsky, Joseph/15 Bridal Path Trail, Newtown, CT	203-426-7123
Kusnetz, Shelley/142 Randolph Pl, W Orange, NJ	201-736-4362

L

LaBadessa, Teresa/219 Commonwealth Ave, Newton, MA	508-785-0467
LaBua, Frank/37 N Mountain Ave, Montclair, NJ	212-967-7576
Labuzetta, Steve/180 St Paul St, Rochester, NY	716-546-6825
Lamar Photographics/147 Spyglass Hill Dr, Ashland, MA	508-881-2512
Lambert, Elliot/167 Langley Rd, Newton, MA	617-965-5496
Lambert, Katherine/6856 Eastern Ave NW #209, Washington, DC (P 53)	**202-882-8383**
Landsman, Gary D/12115 Parklawn Dr Bay-S, Rockville, MD	301-468-2588
Landsman, Meg/27 Industrial Ave, Chelmsford, MA	508-250-9282
Landwehrle, Don/9 Hother Ln, Bayshore, NY	516-665-8221
Lane, Whitney/109 Somerstown Rd, Ossining, NY	914-762-5335
Langone, James A/36 Loring St, Springfield, MA	413-732-1174
Lanman, Jonathan/63 South St, Hopkinton, MA	508-435-2194
Lapides, Susan Jane/451 Huron Ave, Cambridge, MA	617-864-7793
LaRaia, Paul/171 Sterling Ave, Jersey City, NJ	201-332-7505
Larrimore, Walter/2245 Southland Rd, Baltimore, MD	301-281-1774
Larson, Al/760 Bartlett Rd, Middle Island, NY	516-924-8729
Lauber, Christopher/609 Crescent Dr, Bound Brook, NJ	908-271-4077
Laundon, Samuel A/144 Moody St, Waltham, MA	617-899-2037
Lautman, Robert & Andrew/4906 41 St NW, Washington, DC	202-966-2800
Lauver, David A/29 S Market St, Selinsgrove, PA	717-374-0515
Lavery, Dean/RD4/Box 270C, McKee City, NJ	609-641-3284
Lavine, David S/4016 The Alameda, Baltimore, MD	301-467-0523
Lavoie, George/227 N Brow St, E Providence, RI	401-438-4344
Lawfer, Larry/27 Dry Dock Ave, Boston, MA	617-439-4309
Lawrence, Stephanie/3000 Chestnut Ave #217, Baltimore, MD	301-235-2454
Leach, Peter/802 Sansom, Philadelphia, PA	215-574-0230
Leaman, Chris/42 Old Lancaster Rd, Malvern, PA	215-647-8455
Leatherman, William/173 Massachusetts Ave, Boston, MA	617-536-5800
LeBlond, Jerry/7 Court Sq, Rutland, VT	802-773-4205
Lee, John/IBM Americas Grp/Rt 9, N Tarrytown, NY	914-332-2864
Lee, Raymond/PO Box 9743, Baltimore, MD	301-323-5764
Leeming Studios Inc/222 Richmond St, Providence, RI	401-421-1916
Lefcourt, Victoria/3207 Coquelin Terr, Chevy Chase, MD	301-652-1658
Leifer, David/251 Kelton St, Boston, MA	617-277-7513
Lemay, Charles J/PO Box 6356, Manchester, NH	603-669-9380
Leney, Julia/PO Box 434, Wayland, MA	508-653-4139
Lennon, Jim/24 South Mall, Plainview, NY	516-752-0610
Lent, Michael/421 Madison St, Hoboken, NJ	201-798-4866
Leomporra, Greg/RTE 130 & Willow Drive, Cinnaminson, NJ	609-829-6866
Leonard, Barney/134 Cherry Lane, Wynnewood, PA	215-649-5588
Lepist, Enn/E Park Rd/Gldn Apts, Hyde Park, NY	914-229-7972
Lerat, Andree/241 Perkins St #H202, Boston, MA	617-738-9553
Leslie, Barbara/81 Grant St, Burlington, VT	802-864-0060
Lesser, John/881 Hampton Way, Williamstown, NJ	609-728-3840
Lester, Terrell/RR1/Box 469, Deer Isle, ME	207-348-6253
Leung, Jook /35 S Van Brunt St, Englewood, NJ (P 89)	**201-894-5881**
Levart, Herb/566 Secor Rd, Hartsdale, NY	914-946-2060
Leveille, David/27-31 St Bridget's Dr, Rochester, NY	716-423-9474
Levin, Aaron M/3000 Chestnut Ave #102, Baltimore, MD	301-467-8646
Levin, Rosalind/1 Wall St, Fort Lee, NJ	201-944-6014
Levin, Ted/RR 1 Box 313A/Bloodbrk Rd, Fairlee, VT	802-333-9804
Levine, Allen/2 Merry Lane, East Hanover, NJ	201-884-1154
Levine, Mimi/8317 Woodhaven Blvd, Bethesda, MD	301-469-6550
Levy, Seymour/10 Chestnut St, Needham, MA	617-444-4218
Lewis Studios/344 Kaplan Dr, Fairfield, NJ	201-227-1234
Lewis, Ronald/PO Box 489, East Hampton, NY	516-329-1886
Lewis, Ross/47 North Drive, E Brunswick, NJ	201-828-2225
Lewis, Steve/63 Endicott Street, Boston, MA	617-723-8801
Lewiton, Marvin/18 West St, Arlington, MA	617-646-9608
Lewitt, Peter/39 Billings Park, Newton, MA	617-244-6552
Ley, Russell/103 Ardale St, Boston, MA	617-325-2500
L I Image Works/14-20 Glenn St, Glenn Cove, NY	516-671-9661
Lidington, John/2 C St, Hull, MA	617-925-2969
Lieberman, Allen/RR 3/ Box 37, Cranbury, NJ	609-799-4448
Lieberman, Fred/2426 Linden Ln, Silver Spring, MD	301-565-0644
Lightstruck Studio/613 N Eutaw St, Baltimore, MD	301-727-2220
Liller, Tamara/700 7th St SW #418, Washington, DC	202-488-3710
Lilley, Weaver/2107 Chancellor St, Philadelphia, PA	215-567-2881
Lillibridge, David/Rt 4 Box 1172, Burlington, CT	203-673-9786
Linck, Tony/2100 Linwood Ave, Fort Lee, NJ	201-944-5454
Lincoln, Denise/30 St John Pl, Westport, CT	203-226-3724
Lincoln, James/19 Newtown Trnpke, Westport, CT	203-226-3724
Line, Craig/PO Box 11, Marshfield, VT	802-426-3592
Linehan, Clark/31 Blackburn Ctr, Gloucester, MA	808-281-3903
Lippenholz, Richard/10524 Lakespring Way , Cockeysville, MD	301-628-0935
Lipshutz, Ellen/Buckhill Farm Rd, Arlington, VT	802-375-6316
Litoff, Walter/2919 Union St, Rochester, NY	716-232-6140
Littell, Dorothy/74 Lawn St, Boston, MA	617-739-5196
Littlehales, Breton/9520 Seminole St, Silver Spring, MD	202-291-2422
L M Associates/20 Arlington, Newton, MA	617-232-0254
Lobell, Richard/536 West Chester St, Long Beach, NY	516-431-8899
Lockwood, Lee/27 Howland Rd, West Newton, MA	617-965-6343
Lodriguss, Jerry/20 Millbank Lane, Voorhees, NJ	609-770-8246
Lokmer, John/PO Box 2782, Pittsburgh, PA	412-765-3565
Long Shots/4421 East West Hwy, Bethesda, MD	301-654-0279
Longcor, W K/Bear Pond, Andover, NJ	201-398-2225
Longley, Steven/2224 North Charles St, Baltimore, MD	301-467-4185
Lord, Jim/PO Box 879, Fair Lawn, NJ	201-796-5282
Lorusso, Larry/1 Main St, Whitinsville, MA	508-234-2900
Lovering, Talbot/P.O. Box 513, Lincoln, MA	617-566-6010
Lovett, Kevin/79 Toby St, Providence, RI	401-861-2556
Lowe, Shawn Michael/2 Horizon Rd #1205, Ft Lee, NJ	201-224-0982
Lowe, Thom/1420 E Front St, Plainfield, NJ	908-769-8485
Lowry, Laurence/47 Moynihan Rd, S Hamilton, MA	508-468-2562
Loy, John/1611 Shipley Rd, Wilmington, DE (P 91)	**302-762-3812**
Lukowicz, Jerome/122 Arch St, Philadelphia, PA	215-922-7122
Lundell, Jim/266 Lake St, Haverhill, MA	508-372-3390
Lynch, Ron/124 Bloomfield St, Hoboken, NJ	201-963-3476
Lynch, Tim/160 Merrimack St, Lowell, MA	508-970-1000

M

Macchiarulo, Tony/748 Post Rd E, Westport, CT	203-221-7830
Machalaba, Robert/4 Brentwood Dr, Livingston, NJ	201-992-4674
MacHenry, Kate/5 Colliston Rd #6, Brookline, MA	617-277-5736
Maciel, Chris/RD2 Box 176 Riley Rd, New Windsor, NY	914-564-6972
MacKenzie, Maxwell/2641 Garfield St NW, Washington, DC	202-232-6686
Mackey, Doc/North St Church, Georgetown, MA	508-352-7055
MacLean, Alex/25 Bay State Rd, Boston, MA	617-536-6261
Macomber, Peter/100 Oak St, Portland, ME	207-772-1208
MacWright, Jeff/RD 4/248 East Main, Chester, NJ	908-879-4545
Macys, Sandy (Mr)/552 RR 1, Waitsfield, VT	802-496-2518
Madwed, Steven/1125 Post Rd, Fairfield, CT	203-255-4002
Maggio, Chris/180 St Paul St, Rochester, NY	716-454-3929
Maglott, Larry/249 A St, Boston, MA (P 92,93)	**617-482-9347**
Magno, Thomas/19 Peters St, Cambridge, MA	617-492-5197
Magro, Benjamin/2 Mechanic St, Camden, ME	207-236-4774
Mahoney, Bob/347 Cameo Circle, Liverpool, NY	315-652-7870
Malin, Marc/121 Beach St 7th Fl, Boston, MA	617-734-4916
Malitsky, Ed/337 Summer St, Boston, MA	617-451-0655
Maloney, Michael J/76 Lyall St, Boston, MA	617-469-3666
Maltinsky Photo/1140 Washington St, Boston, MA	617-426-2128
Malyszko, Michael/90 South St, Boston, MA	617-426-9111
Mandel, Mitchell T/213 S 17th St, Allentown, PA	215-434-1897

Mandelkorn, Richard/309 Waltham St, W Newton, MA	617-332-3246
Manheim, Michael Philip/PO Box 35, Marblehead, MA	617-631-3560
Manley, Fletcher/PO Box 25, S Londonderry, VT	802-824-6148
Mann, Richard J/PO Box 2712, Dix Hills, NY	516-754-8496
Manning, Ed/875 E Broadway, Stratford, CT	203-375-3384
Manville, Ron/163 Exchange St #303, Pawtucket, RI	401-722-3313
Marchese, Frank/56 Arbor St, Hartford, CT	203-232-4417
Marchese, Vincent/PO Box AZ, Paterson, NJ	201-278-2225
Marcotte, Denise/303 Broadway, Cambridge, MA	617-864-8406
Marcus, Fred/10 Crabapple Dr, Roslyn, NY	516-621-3260
Marcus, Joe/100 W Milton St, Easton , PA	215-258-1407
Mares, Manuel/185 Chestnut Hill Ave, Brighton, MA	617-782-4208
Margel, Steve/215 First St, Cambridge, MA	617-547-4445
Margolis, David/682 Howard Ave, New Haven, CT	203-777-7288
Margolis, Paul/109 Grand Ave, Englewood, NJ	201-569-2316
Margolycz, Jerry/316 Summer St, Boston, MA	617-338-5633
Marinelli, Jack/673 Willow St, Waterbury, CT	203-756-3273
Marinelli, Mary Leigh/4 Salton Stall Pkwy, Salem, MA	508-745-7035
Markel, Brad/639 'E' St NE, Washington, DC	202-544-2332
Markowitz, Joel/2 Kensington Ave, Jersey City, NJ	202-451-0413
Marsel, Steve/215 First St, Cambridge, MA	617-547-4445
Marshall, Alec/1 Midland Gardens, Bronxville, NY	914-779-0022
Marsico, Dennis/110 Fahrenstock, Pittsburgh, PA	412-781-6349
Martin Paul Ltd/247 Newbury St, Boston, MA	617-536-1644
Martin, Bruce/266-A Pearl St, Cambridge, MA	617-492-8009
Martin, Butch/715 Hussa St, Linden, NJ	201-486-3049
Martin, Jeff/6 Industrial Way W, Eatontown, NJ	908-289-0888
Martin, Marilyn/130 Appleton St #2I, Boston, MA	617-262-5507
Martin, Michael P/220 E Preston Ave, Wildwood Crest, NJ	609-729-0838
Martin-Elson, Patricia/120 Crooked Hill Rd, Huntington, NY	516-427-4799
Martson, Sven/228 Dwight St, New Haven, CT	203-777-1535
Masiello, Ralph/75 Webster St, Worcester, MA	508-752-9871
Mason, Donald W/10 E 21st St, Baltimore, MD	301-244-0385
Mason, Phil/15 St Mary's Ct, Brookline, MA	617-232-0908
Mason, Tom/117 Van Dyke Rd, Hopewell, NJ	609-466-0911
Massar, Ivan/296 Bedford St, Concord, MA	617-369-4090
Masser, Randy/15 Barnes Terrace, Chappaqua, NY	914-238-8167
Mastalia, Francesco/326 Montgomery St 4th Fl, Jersey City, NJ	212-772-8449
Mastri, Len/1 Mill St, Burlington, VT	802-862-4009
Matkins, Leo/904 N Van Buren St, Wilmington, DE	302-655-4542
Matt, Phil Studio/PO Box 10406, Rochester, NY	716-461-5977
Mattei, George Photography/179 Main St, Hackensack, NJ	201-342-0740
Mattingly, Brendan/4404 Independence St, Rockville, MD	301-933-3942
Maughart, Brad/13 Church St, Framingham, MA	508-875-4447
Mauro, George/9 Fairfield Ave, Little Falls, NJ	201-890-0880
Mauss, Peter/222 Valley Pl, Mamaroneck, NY	914-698-4060
Mavodones, Bill/46 Waltham St #105, Boston, MA	617-423-7382
May, Bill/PO Box 1567, Montclair, NJ	201-624-6782
Mayernik, George/41 Wolfpit Ave #2N, Norwalk, CT	203-846-1406
Mayor, Michael/246 Wanaque Ave, Pompton Lakes, NJ	201-839-9007
Mazzoleni, Deborah/3801 Old Columbia Pike, Baltimore , MD	301-461-4492
Mazzone, James/1201 82nd St, N Bergen, NJ	201-861-8992
McBreen, Edward/6727 Harbison Ave, Philadelphia , PA	215-331-5149
McCarthy, William/55 Winter St, Auburn, ME	207-782-2904
McCary, Joe/8804 Monard Dr, Silver Spring, MD	301-588-6637
McClintock, Robert/11 Main St, Brattleboro, VT	802-257-1100
McConnell & McConnell/, , NY	516-883-0058
McConnell, Jack/182 Broad St, Old Wethersfield, CT	203-563-6154
McConnell, Russ/8 Adler Dr, E Syracuse, NY	315-433-1005
McCormack, Richard/459 Farimount Ave, Jersey City, NJ	201-435-8718
McCormick & Nelson, Inc/34 Piave St, Stamford, CT	203-348-5062
McCormick, Ed/55 Hancock St, Lexington, MA	617-862-2552
McCoy, Dan/Box 573, Housatonic, MA	413-274-6211
McDonald, Jean Duffy/14 Imperial Pl #504, Providence, RI	401-274-2292
McDonald, Kevin R/319 Newtown Turnpike, Redding, CT (P 94)	**203-938-9276**
McDonough, Doug/1612 olton St, Baltimore, MD	301-669-6696
McDowell, Bill/56 Edmonds St, Rochester, NY	716-442-8632
McElroy, Philip/23 Main St, Watertown, MA	617-924-0470
McFarland, Nancy & Lowell/3 Tuck Lane, Westport, CT	203-227-6178
McGovern, Michael/502 Worcester St, Baltimore, MD	301-825-0978
McGrail, John/6576 Senator Ln, Bensalem, PA	215-750-6070
McKaig, Chandler Jr/1819 Lovering Ave, Wilmington, DE	302-658-8147
McKean, Thomas R/1418 Monk Rd, Gladwyne, PA	215-642-1412
McKiernan, Scott/560 Harrison Ave, Boston, MA	617-545-0008
McMullen, Mark/25 Monroe St, Albany, NY	518-426-9284
McMullin, Forest/183 St Paul St, Rochester, NY	716-262-3944
McNamara, Casey/109 Broad St, Boston, MA	617-542-5337
McNeely, Robert/2425 Ontario Rd NW #1, Washington, DC	202-387-4352
McNeill, Brian/840 W Main St, Lansdale, PA	215-368-3326
McNiss, Chase/2308 Columbia Circle, Merrimack, NH	603-429-1489
McQueen, Ann/791 Tremont St #W401, Boston, MA	617-267-6258
McWilliams, Jack/15 Progress Ave, Chelmsford, MA	508-256-9615
Meacham, Josep/601 N 3rd St, Philadelphia, PA	215-925-8122
Meadowlands Photo/259 Hackensack St, East Rutherford, NJ	201-933-9121
Mecca, Jack/RD 6/Box 369B, Branchville, NJ	201-702-7438
Mednick, Seymour/316 S Camac, Philadelphia, PA	215-735-6100
Medvec, Emily/151 Kentucky Ave SE, Washington, DC	202-546-1220
Meech, Christopher/456 Glenbrook Rd, Stamford, CT	203-348-1158
Mehling, Joseph/P.O. Box 235, S Strafford, VT	802-765-4297
Mehne, Ralph/1501 Rose Terrace, Union, NJ	908-686-0668
Meiller, Henry Studios/1026 Wood St, Philadelphia, PA	215-922-1525
Melino, Gary/25 Bright Water Dr, Warwick, RI	508-379-0166
Mellor, D W/1020 Mt Pleasant Rd, Bryn Mawr, PA	215-527-9040
Melo, Michael/RR1/Box 20, Winterport, ME	207-223-8894
Melton, Bill/180 Zachary Rd, Manchester, NH	603-668-0110
Melton, Janice Munnings/692 Walkhill St, Boston, MA	617-298-1443
Mendelsohn, David/15 Tall Pines Rd, Durham, NH	603-942-7622
Mendez, Manny/150 Adams St, Newark, NJ	201-344--4440
Mendlowitz, Benjamin/Rte 175/Box 14, Brooklin, ME	207-359-2131
Mercer, Ralph/451 D St 9th Fl, Boston, MA (P 55)	**617-951-4604**
Merchant, Martin/22 Barker Ave, White Plains, NY	914-997-2200
Merrick, Tad/64 Main St, Middlebury, VT	802-388-9598
Merritt Communications/152 N Main St, Natick, MA	508-651-3340
Merz, Laurence/215 Georgetown Rd, Weston, CT	203-222-1936
Mesmer, Jerry/1523 22nd St NW/Courtyard, Washington, DC	202-785-2188
Messina, Sebastian/65 Willard Ave, Bloomfield, NJ	201-548-6000
Metzger, Lise/2032 Belmont Rd #301, Washington, DC	202-462-5904
Michaels, John - MediaVisions/17 May St, Clifton, NJ	201-772-0181
Milens, Sanders H/38 Mt Philo Rd POB 805, Shelburne, VT	802-388-9598
Miles, Damian/6 S Broad St, Ridgewood, NJ	201-447-4220
Miles, William A/374 Congress St #304, Boston, MA	617-426-6862
Miljakovich, Helen/114 Seventh Ave #3C	212-242-0646
Millard, Howard/220 Sixth Ave, Pelham, NY	914-738-3689
Miller, David Photo/5 Lake St, Morris, NY	607-263-5060
Miller, Don/60 Sindle Ave, Little Falls, NJ	201-785-9090
Miller, J T/12 Forest Edge Dr, Titusville, NJ	609-737-3116
Miller, John L/223 West Fell St, Summit Hill, PA	717-645-3661
Miller, Melabee/29 Beechwood Pl, Hillside, NJ	908-527-9121
Miller, Michael S/32 Main St, Englishtown, NJ	908-446-1331
Miller, Myra/10500 Rockville Pk #121, Rockville, MD	301-564-9288
Miller, Peter/RD 1/Box 1515 , Waterbury, VT	802-244-5339
Miller, Roger/1411 Hollins St Union Sq, Baltimore, MD	301-566-1222
Millman, Lester Jay/PO Box 61H, Scarsdale, NY	914-946-2093
Milovich, Dan/590 Summit Dr, Carlisle, PA	717-249-0045
Mindell, Doug/811 Boylston St, Boston, MA	617-262-3968
Mink, Mike/180 St Paul St 5th Fl, Rochester, NY	716-325-4865
Miraglia, Elizabeth/50 Fairview Ave #3A, Norwalk, CT	203-852-9926
Mirando, Gary Photography/27 Cleveland St, Valhalla, NY (P 98)	**914-997-6588**
Mitchell, Jane/354 Salem, Wakefield, MA	617-245-9878
Mitchell, Les/RD #4/Box 93 Pittenger Pnd Rd, Freehold, NJ	908-462-2451
Mitchell, Mike/1501 14th St NW #301, Washington, DC	202-234-6400
Mitchell, Richard/51 Bristol St, Boston, MA	617-350-3115
Mogerley, Jean/1262 Pines Lake Dr W, Wayne, NJ	201-839-2355
Molinaro, Neil R/15 Walnut Ave, Clark, NJ	908-396-8980
Monroe, Robert/Kennel Rd, Cuddebackville, NY	914-754-8329
Montgomery, Darrow/724 Ninth St NW, Washington, DC	202-347-7534
Moore, Cliff/30 Skillman Ave, Rocky Hill, NJ	609-921-3754
Mopsik, Eugene/230 Monroe St, Philadelphia, PA	215-922-3489
Morelli, Mark/44 Roberts Rd, Cambridge, MA	617-547-0409
Morgan, Bruce/315 W Sunrise Hwy, Freeport, NY	516-546-2034
Morgan, Hank/14 Waterbury Ave, Stamford, CT	203-325-3120
Morgan, Rosalind/RFD 2/Box 135, Houlton, ME	207-532-7286
Morley, Bob/186 Lincoln St #202, Boston, MA	617-482-7279
Morrion, Marybeth/345 Cornwall Ct, Katonah, NY	914-232-8231
Morrow, Christopher W/PO Box 208, Arlington, MA	617-648-6770
Morse, Timothy/148 Rutland St, Carlisle, MA	508-369-8036
Moshe, Danny/PO Box 2701, Kensington, MD	301-890-9469
Mottau, Gary/17 Irving Place, Holliston, MA	508-429-8645
Moulthrop, David H/RFD 3 Box 2, Great Barrington, MA	413-528-3593
Moyer, Stephen/911 State St, Lancaster, PA	717-393-0918
Mullen, Stephen/825 N 2nd St, Philadelphia, PA	215-574-9770
Mulligan, Joseph/239 Chestnut St, Philadelphia, PA	215-592-1359
Murphy, Bill/875 Central Ave, Albany, NY	518-489-3861
Murray, Chris/110 Brenner Dr, Congers, NY	914-268-5531

Murray, Dan/840 Summer St, Boston, MA 617-268-6713
Murray, Matt/PO Box 53605, Philadelphia, PA....215-430-8136
Murray, Ric/232 W Exchange St, Providence, RI 401-751-8806
Murry, Peggy/1913 VWaverly St, Philadelphia, PA 215-735-4834
Muskie, Stephen O/23 Lookout Hill, Peterborough, NH 603-924-6541
Musto, Tom/225 S Main St, Wilkes-Barre, PA....717-822-5798
Mutschler, Bob/177 Main St #183, Ft Lee, NJ 201-869-8507
Mydans, Carl/212 Hommocks Rd, Larchmont, NY 212-841-2345
Myers Studios Inc/5775 Big Tree Rd, Orchard Park, NY....716-662-6002
Myers, Barry/407 Thayer Ave, Silver Spring, MD 301-585-8617
Myers, Gene/250 N Goodman St, Rochester, NY (P 57)....716-244-4420
Myers, Steve/PO Box J, Almond, NY....607-276-6400
Myron/127 Dorrance St, Providence, RI 401-421-1946

N

Nadel, Lee/10 Loveland Rd, Brookline, MA 617-451-6646
Nagler, Lanny/56 Arbor St, Hartford, CT....203-233-4040
Nathan, Simon/175 Prospect St #21D, E Orange, NJ....201-675-5026
Navin, Christopher/8 Prospect St, Grafton, MA....508-839-3227
Neelon, Michael N/349 Lincoln St, Hingham, MA 617-740-2066
Nelder, Oscar/93 Hardy St/Box 661, Presque Isle, ME 207-769-5911
Nelson, Michael/5 Academy Ave, Cornwall-on-Hudson, NY 914-534-4563
Nemerofsky, Jesse/307 Pocasset Ave, Providence, RI....401-943-9099
Nerney, Dan/5 Vincent Pl, Rowayton, CT....203-853-2782
Nettis, Joseph/1534 Sansom St 2nd Fl, Philadelphia, PA 215-563-5444
Neudorfer, Brien/46 Waltham St, Boston, MA....617-451-9211
Neumayer, Joseph/Chateau Rive #102, Peekskill, NY....914-739-3005
Newman, Alan & Mark O'Neill/65 Commerce Rd, Stamford, CT 203-327-6225
Newton, Christopher/119 Indian Pond Rd, Kingston, MA....617-585-4838
Ngo, Meng H/21 Village Commons, Fishkill, NY 914-897-2836
Nible, Rick/408 Vine St 4th Fl, Philadelphia, PA 215-625-0638
Nicoletti, Vincent/280 Granatan Ave, Mt Vernon, NY....914-668-2199
Nighswander, Tim/315 Peck St, New Haven, CT 203-789-8529
Nikas, Greg/Drawer 690, Ipswich, MA 508-356-0018
Niles, James/238 Sixth St #One, Jersey City, NJ 201-659-2408
Noble Inc/2313 Maryland Ave, Baltimore, MD 301-235-5235
Nochton, Jack/1238 W Broad St, Bethlehem, PA....215-691-2223
Noel, Peter/99 Rear Washington St 2nd Fl, Melrose, MA....617-322-7629
Noon, Liz/110 Mill St, Newton, MA....617-965-2931
Nordell, John/12 Grove St, Boston, MA....617-723-5484
Norris, Robert/RFD 1 Box 4480, Pittsfield, ME 207-487-5981
North Light Photo/332 Dante Ct, Holbrook, NY 516-585-2900
North, Robert/85 Main St/Box 6, Windsor, VT....802-674-2602
Northlight Visual Comm Group Inc/21 Quine St, Cranford, NJ 201-272-1155
Norton, Dick/10 Thatcher St #110, Boston, MA 617-523-4720
Nowitz, Richard/10844 Brewer House Rd, Rockville, MD....301-816-2372
Nute, Edward/20 Middle St, Plymouth, MA....508-746-9120
Nutu, Dan/170 Varick Rd, Newton, MA....617-332-0713

O

O'Byrne, William/Box 517, Boothbay Harbor, ME....207-633-5623
O'Clair, Dennis/75 Stuart Ave, Amityville, NY 516-598-3546
O'Connell, Bill/791 Tremont St, Boston, MA....617-437-7556
O'Connor, Patrick/44 Front St, Worcester, MA 508-798-8399
O'Donnell, John/116 Mile Square Rd, Yonkers, NY....914-968-1786
O'Donoghue, Ken/8 Union Park St, Boston, MA 617-542-4898
O'Grady, Paul/270 Norfolk St, Canmbridge, MA 617-868-0086
O'Hagan, J Barry/455 Chestnut St, N Andover , MA....508-683-0408
O'Hare, Richard/POB 273, Clifton Heights, PA....215-626-1429
O'Neil, Julie/5 Craigie Cir #7, Cambridge, MA 617-547-5168
O'Neill, James/1543 Kater St, Philadelphia, PA....215-545-3223
O'Neill, Martin/1914 Mt Royal Terr 1st Fl, Baltimore, MD....301-225-0522
O'Neill, Michael Photo/162 Lakefield Rd, E Northport, NY....516-754-0459
O'Shaughnessy, Bob/23 Dry Dock Ave, Boston, MA 617-345-0727
O'Shaughnessy, Leslie/1 Fieldstone Dr, Hollis, NH 603-465-2488
O'Toole, Terrence/104 Union Park St, Boston, MA 617-426-6357
Obermeyer, Eva/2 Union Ave, Irvington, NJ 201-374-6856
Odor, Lou/288 Kerrigan Blvd, Newark, NJ 201-371-2669
Ogden, Sam/273 Summer St, Boston, MA 617-426-1021
Oglesbee, Brian/126 N Main St, Wellsville, NY 716-593-6803
Ohlmeyer, Herb/165G Overmount St, W Paterson, NJ....201-878-7773
Okada, Tom/229 Weston Rd, Wellesley, MA....617-237-7119
Olbrys, Anthony/41 Pepper Ridge Rd, Stamford, CT....203-322-9422
Oliver/McConnell Photo/406 S Franklin St, Syracuse, NY....315-428-0344
Olivera, Bob/108 Chestnut St, Rehoboth, MA 508-252-9617
Oliwa, Bill/516 Locust Ave, Hillside, NJ 201-688-7538
Olmstead Studio/118 South St, Boston, MA 617-542-2024
Olsen, Dan/303 Congress St 4th Fl, Boston, MA....617-951-0765
Olsen, Peter/1415 Morris St, Philadelphia, PA....215-465-9736
Orabona, Jerry/107 Main St, Sayreville, NJ....201-613-1141
Orkin, Pete/80 Washington St, S Norwalk, CT 203-866-9978
Orrico, Charles/72 Barry Ln, Syosset, NY 516-364-2257
Ostrowski, Stephen/RD 1 Box 1544, Charlotte, VT....802-425-2349
Ostrowski, Waldemar/386 Brook Ave, Passaic Park, NJ....201-471-3033
Ours, Mary Noble/3402 Prospect St NW, Washington, DC....202-338-8870
Ouzer, Louis/120 East Ave, Rochester, NY....716-454-7582
Owen, Edward/443 Eye St NW, Washington, DC 202-842-2257
Owens, John/451 D St #810, Boston, MA 617-330-1498

P

P & R Associates/3382 Springfield Rd, Summit, NJ....201-273-1978
Paige, Peter/269 Parkside Rd, Harrington Park, NJ....201-767-3150
Painter, Joseph/205 Fairmont Ave, Philadelphia, PA....215-592-1612
Palette Studios/399 Market St, Philadelphia, PA 215-440-0500
Palmer, Gabe/Fire Hill Farm, West Redding, CT 203-938-2514
Palmiere, Jorge/316 F St NE #21, Washington, DC 202-546-7380
Pamatat, Ken/165 West Ave, Rochester, NY....716-235-1222
Panioto, Mark/95 Mohawk Ln, Wethersfield, CT....203-529-9016
Panorama International/Box 63, West Newton, MA....617-969-0879
Pantages, Tom/3 Raymond St, Gloucester, MA....617-525-3678
Pape, Maria/35 Woodway Rd, Stamford, CT 203-329-3035
Pappas, Ernest/Box 385, Hibernia, NJ 201-627-3453
Paredes, Cesar/332 Clarksville Rd, Princeton, NJ 609-799-1404
Parker, Charles A/5 Elm St, Woodstock, VT....802-457-1113
Parker, James/PO Box 4542, Annapolis, MD 301-528-1099
Parks, Melanie/5 Broadview Lane, Red Hook, NY 914-758-0656
Parragos, Dimitrios/107 Fredrich Ave, Babylon, NY....516-669-5895
Parrot Productions/3730 Zuck Rd, Erie, PA 814-833-8739
Parsons, Andrew/59 Wareham, Boston, MA....617-542-9071
Paskevich, John/1500 Locust St #3017, Philadelphia, PA....215-735-9868
Pasley, Richard/90 Hamilton St, Cambridge, MA....617-864-8386
Patel, Ghanshyam/130 Thorne St, Jersey City, NJ....201-653-5839
Patterson, David/3299 K St NW, Washington, DC....202-347-0910
Paul, Donna/146 W Concord St, Boston, MA 617-247-0034
Paul, Martin/37 Winchester St, Boston, MA....617-451-1818
Paul, Richard/2011 Noble St, Pittsburgh, PA....412-271-6609
Pavlovich, James/49 Worcester St, Boston, MA....617-266-9723
Pawlick, John/22 Erie St, Boston, MA 617-964-1930
Paxenos, Dennis F/2125 Maryland Ave #103, Baltimore, MD 301-837-1029
Payne, Cymie/87 Cherry St, Cambridge, MA....617-868-0758
Payne, John/43 Brookfield Pl, Pleasantville, NY 914-747-1282
Peabody, Richard/20120 Lavender Pl, Germantown, MD 301-353-0371
Pearse, D/223 Parham Rd, Springfield, PA 215-328-3179
Pease, Greg/23 E 22nd St, Baltimore, MD (P 99) 410-332-0583
Peck, Daniel/7199 Chesapeake Ave, Silver Spring, MD....301-587-1714
Peckham, Lynda/65 S Broadway, Tarrytown, NY 914-631-5050
Peet, George/107 Park Ave, Arlington, MA 617-876-3855
Pehlman, Barry/542 Merioneth Dr, Exton, PA 215-524-1444
Peirce, George E/133 Ramapo Ave, Pompton Lakes, NJ....201-831-8418
Peirce, Michael/242 E Berkeey St 5th Fl, Boston, MA....617-491-0643
Pellegrini, Lee/381 Newtonville Ave, Newtonville, MA....617-964-7925
Peluso, Frank/15 Caspar Berger Rd, Whitehouse Station, NJ 908-534-9637
Pendergrast, Mark/RD 2/Box 1412, Stowe, VT....802-253-4159
Penneys, Robert/12 E Mill Station, Newark, DE....302-733-0444
Penni, Jay/15A St Mary's Court, Brookline, MA 617-232-7281
Perlman, Ilene/483 Hope St, Providence, RI 401-273-8087
Perlmutter, Steven/282 Shelton Rd, Monroe, CT 203-789-8493
Perluck, David/122 Chestnut St, Providence, RI 401-831-5796
Pernold, Marianne/PO Box 722, Rye, NH....603-431-8814
Perron, Robert/119 Chestnut St, Branford, CT 203-481-2004
Persons Photography/478 Hanover St, Manchester, NH 603-669-5771
Peters, Michael/102 Chestnut St, Kearny, NJ 201-998-0175
Peterson, Brent/73 Maple Ave, Tuckahoe, NY....212-573-7195
Peterson, Bruce/465-D Medford St, Charlestown, MA....617-241-8228
Petrakes, George/242 E Berkeley, Boston, MA 617-695-0556
Petronio, Frank/214 Andrews St #4C, Rochester, NY 716-454-3804
Petty, David/15 Union St/Stone Mill Bldg, Lawrence, MA....508-794-0404
Philips, Jaye R/2 Crescent Hill Ave, Arlington, MA....617-646-8491
Photo Craft/202 Perry Pkwy, Gaithersburg, MD 301-417-9507
Photo Dimensions/12 S Virginia Ave, Atlantic City, NJ 609-344-1212
Photo Synthesis/216 Blvd of Allies, Pittsburgh, PA....412-642-7734
Photo-Colortura/PO Box 1749, Boston, MA....617-522-5132

Photogenics/52 Garden St, Cambridge, MA....617-876-6540
Photographers & Co/113 S Brandywine Ave, Schenectady, NY....518-377-9457
Photographic House/158 W Clinton St, Dover, NJ....201-366-3000
Photographic Illustration Ltd/7th & Ranstead, Philadelphia, PA....215-925-7073
Photographie/630 N 2nd St, Philadelphia, PA....215-925-2084
Phototech/9 Church St, Waltham, MA....617-899-4141
Photown Studio/190 Vandervoort St, North Tonawanda, NY....716-693-2912
Photoworks/211 Glenridge Ave, Montclair, NJ....201-509-8840
Piaget, John/540 Nepperhan Ave, Yonkers, NY....914-376-7401
Picarello, Carmine/12 S Main St, S Norwalk, CT....203-866-8987
Pickerell, Jim H/110 Frederick Ave E Bay, Rockville, MD....301-251-0720
Pickett, John/109 Broad St, Boston, MA....617-542-7308
Picone, Paul Kevin/162 Western Ave, Gloucester , MA....508-281-1725
Picture That Inc/880 Briarwood, Newtown Square, PA....215-353-8833
Picturesques Studios/1879 Old Cuthbert Rd, Cherry Hill, NJ....609-354-1903
Picturewise/10 Terhune Pl, Hackensack, NJ....201-343-1060
Pierce, Barbara/P.O. Box 196, Pittsford, VT....802-747-3070
Pierlott, Paul/PO Box 1321, Merchantville, NJ....609-665-6392
Pietersen, Alex/67 N The Village Green, Budd Lake, NJ (P 100)....201-347-7504
Pinkerton, Margo Taussig/RR1/Box 81, Canaan, NH....603-523-4202
Piperno, Lauren/215 E Dean St, Freeport, NY....718-935-1550
Pivak, Kenneth/605 Pavonia Ave, Jersey City, NJ....201-656-0508
Plank, David/Cherry & Carpenter Sts, Reading, PA....215-376-3461
Plessner, Vic/52 Ridgefield Ave , Ridgefield, NJ....201-440-8317
Plouffe, Reid/PO Box 5142, Portsmouth, NH....603-431-2891
Poggenpohl, Eric/12 Walnut St, Amherst, MA....413-256-0948
Pohuski, Michael/36 S Paca St #314, Baltimore, MD....301-962-5404
Polansky, Allen/1431 Park Ave, Baltimore, MD....301-383-9021
Polatty, Bo/4309 Wendy Court, Monrovia, MD....301-865-5728
Polcou, Duane/288 Abbey Dr, Somerset, NJ....201-805-0608
Pollard, Duncan/33 Knowlton St, Somerville, MA....617-666-1173
Pollard, Pat/24 Spring Lane, Farmington, CT....203-677-9557
Pollock, Steven/7th & Ranstead Sts, Philadelphia, PA....215-925-7073
Polss, Madeline/124 W 38th St, Wilmington, DE....302-762-2453
Polumbaum, Ted/326 Harvard St, Cambridge, MA....617-491-4947
Poor, Suzanne/280 Bloomfield Ave, Verona, NJ....201-857-5161
Pope-Lance, Elton/125 Stock Farm Rd, Sudbury, MD....508-443-4393
Porcella, Phil/337 Summer St, Boston, MA....617-423-2002
Potter, Anthony/509 W Fayette St, Syracuse, NY....315-428-8900
Powell, Bolling/1 Worcester Square, Boston, MA....212-627-4392
Pownall, Ron/1 Fitchburg St, Somerville, MA....617-354-0846
Preisler, Don/8563 Greenbelt Rd #204, Greenbelt, MD....301-552-3567
Pressman, Herb/57 West St, Portland, ME....207-879-2608
Prezio, Franco/606 Allen Ln, Media, PA....215-565-6919
Price, Donald/2849 Kennedy Blvd, Jersey City, NJ....201-420-7255
Price, Greg/PO Box 665, Cranford, NJ....908-245-1711
Prieur, Kevin/79 Milk St #1108, Boston, MA....617-292-6411
Prince, James/329 Mercer St, Stirling, NJ....908-580-9080
Procopio, Richard/PO Box 422, Rockport, ME....207-596-6379
Profetti, Diane/10 Marne St, Newark, NJ....201-344-1699
Profetto, Joe Jr./566 Delsea Dr, Vineland, NJ....609-696-3771
Proud, Barbara/1815 Lovering Ave, Wilmington, DE....302-429-9345
Proulx, Robert/194 Main St, Woonsocket, RI....401-769-8348
Przyborowski, Thomas/47 Stanton St, Clark, NJ....201-381-2964
Putnam, Sarah/8 Newell St, Cambridge, MA....617-547-3758

QR

Quin, Clark/241 A Street, Boston, MA....617-451-2686
Raab, Timothy/163 Delaware Ave, Delmar, NY....518-439-2298
Rabdau, Yvonne/RR2 Box 590 Kelly Ct, Stormville, NY....914-221-4643
Rabinowitz, Barry/515 Willow St, Waterbury, CT....203-574-1129
Radcliffe, Tom/7002 Carroll Ave, Tokoma Park, MD....301-270-2340
Raducanu, Constantin/5-B Jefferson , Bala Cynwyd, PA....215-667-0726
Rae, John/148 Worchester St, Boston, MA....617-266-5754
Raiche Photography/305 Stark Ln, Manchester, NH....603-623-7912
Ralston, Peter/60 Ocean St, Rockland, ME....207-594-9209
Ramos & Harris Photo/21 Chauncey Ave, E Providence, RI....401-434-0534
Ramsdale, Jack/945 North 5th, Philadelphia, PA....215-238-1436
Ranck, Rosemary/323 W Mermaid Ln, Philadelphia, PA....215-242-3718
Rand, Howard/131 Sedgefield, N kingstown, RI....401-294-3581
Randall Photography/209 4th St, Providence, RI....401-273-6418
Rapp, Frank/327 A St, Boston, MA....617-542-4462
Rauch, Bonnie/Crane Rd, Somers, NY....914-277-3986
Ray, Dean/2900 Chestnut Ave, Baltimore, MD....301-243-3441
Raycroft, Jim/326 A Street #C, Boston, MA....617-542-7229
Raymond, Charlotte/P.O. Box 4000, Princeton, NJ....609-921-4983
Rea, Mark/12 Cottage St, Watertown, MA....617-923-3058
Reed, Tom/9505 Adelphi Rd, Silver Spring, MD....301-439-2912
Reichel, Lorna/PO Box 63, E Greenbush, NY....518-477-7822
Reilly, Kevin D/1931 Spring Garden St, Philadelphia, PA....215-988-1737
Reis, Jon Photography/141 The Commons, Ithaca, NY....607-272-1966
Rembold, Jon A/15823 Easthaven Ct, Bowie, MD....301-805-0975
Renard, Jean/142 Berkeley St, Boston, MA....617-266-8673
Renckly, Joe/1200 Linden Pl, Pittsburgh, PA....412-323-2122
Resnick, Seth/28 Seaverns Ave #8, Boston, MA (P 102,103)....617-983-0291
Ressmeyer, Roger/61 Hill St #400, South Hampton, NY....516-283-6183
Retallack, John/207 Erie Station Rd, West Henrietta, NY....716-334-1530
Revette, David Photography Inc/111 Sunset Ave, Syracuse, NY....315-422-1558
Riccitelli, Bruce/PO Box 1387, Union, NJ....908-688-2129
Rice, Peter/326 A St 5th Fl, Boston, MA....617-338-6652
Richards, Christopher/12 Magee Ave, Stamford, CT....203-964-0235
Richards, Mark/58 Falcon St, Needham, MA (P 105)....617-449-7135
Richards, Toby/1 Sherbrooke Dr, Princeton Junction, NJ....609-275-1885
Richardson, Jonathan R/PO Box 305, Andover, MA....508-975-7722
Richmond, Jack/374 Congress St #506, Boston, MA....617-482-7158
Riemer, Ken/180 St Paul St, Rochester, NY....716-232-5450
Riley, George/Sisquisic Trail PO Box 102, Yarmouth, ME....207-846-5787
Riley, Laura/Hidden Spng Fm PO Box 186, Pittstown, NJ....908-735-7707
Ritter, Frank/2414 Evergreen St, Yorktown Hts, NY....914-962-5385
Rivera, Tony/28 Dutch Lane, Ringoes, NJ....908-788-3991
Rixon, Mike/1 Meadow Lane, Bow, NH....603-228-2362
Rizzi, Leonard F/5161 River Rd Bldg 2B, Bethesda, MD....301-652-1303
Rizzo, John/146 Halstead St, Rochester, NY....716-288-1102
Robb, Steve/535 Albany St, Boston, MA....617-542-6565
Roberts, Michael J/126 Washington St, Providence, RI....401-751-7579
Roberts, Terrence/1909 N Market St, Wilmington, DE....302-658-8854
Robins, Susan/124 N Third St, Philadelphia, PA....215-238-9988
Robinson, George A/33 Kilburn St, Burlington, VT....802-862-6902
Robinson, Mike/2413 Sarah St, Pittsburgh, PA....412-431-4102
Rocheleau, Paul/Canaan Rd, Richmond, MA....413-698-2676
Rockhill, Morgan/204 Westminster St, Providence, RI....401-274-3472
Roe, Bobby/335 S 18th St, Allentown, PA....215-433-2053
Rogers, Paul/RFD 4 Box 460, Stowe, VT....802-253-4549
Romanoff, Mark/8 Wessex Rd, Silver Spring, MD....301-585-6627
Romanos, Michael/30 Stanton Rd, Brookline, MA....617-277-3504
Ronay, Vivian R/3419 Quebec St NW, Washington, DC....202-362-1460
Roos, Warren/135 Somerset St, Portland, ME....207-773-3771
Roper, Bob Photo/518 Catherine St, Philadelphia, PA....215-440-9009
Rörström, John/13 Summit St, E Hampton, CT (P 108)....203-267-7255
Rose, Edward/2880 Diamond Hill Rd, Cumberland, RI....401-334-4169
Roseman, Shelly/1238 Callowhill St, Philadelphia, PA....215-922-1430
Rosen, Morton/122 Main St, Sayville, NY....516-589-5337
Rosenblatt, Jay/360 Glenwood Ave, E Orange, NJ....201-414-8833
Rosenblum, Bruce/181 W 16th St, Bayonne, NJ....201-436-7141
Rosenthal, Karin/150 Irving St, Watertown, MA....617-923-2307
Rosenthal, Stephen/59 Maple St, Auburndale, MA....617-244-2986
Rosier, Gerald/PO Box 470, Framingham, MA....617-881-2512
Rosner, Stu/One Thompson Sq, Charlestown, MA....617-242-2112
Ross, Alex F/1622 Chestnut St, Philadelphia, PA....215-576-7799
Ross, Carolyn/107 South St #501, Boston, MA....617-482-6115
Ross, Doug/610 Eighth Ave, E Northport, NY....516-754-0387
Rossi, Dave/121 Central Ave, Westfield, NJ....908-232-8300
Rossotto, Frank/184 E Main St, Westfield, NY....716-326-2792
Roth, Eric/337 Summer St, Boston, MA....617-338-5358
Rothstein, Gary/55 Valley Rd, New Rochelle, NY....914-235-6938
Rotman, Jeffrey L/14 Cottage Ave, Somerville, MA....617-666-0874
Rowan, Norm R/106 E 6th St, Clifton, NJ....201-340-2284
Rowan, Scott/1 Quail Hill Ln, Downingtown, PA....215-269-9583
Rowin, Stanley/791 Tremont St #W515, Boston, MA (P 109)....617-437-0641
Rowland, Elizabeth A/209 Autumn Dr, Exton, PA....215-363-0763
Roystos, Richard/76 Van Derveer Rd, Freehold, NJ....201-462-5420
Rubenstein, Len/87 Pine St, Easton, MA....508-238-0744
Rubino, Larry/364 Glenwood Ave, E Orange, NJ....201-744-0999
Rubinstein, Len/, Boston, MA....617-238-0744
Rudock, Bill/63 West Lane, Sayville, NY....516-567-2985
Ruggeri, Lawrence/10 Old Post Office Rd, Silver Spring, MD....301-588-3131
Ruggieri, Ignazio/86 Lackawanna Ave, W Paterson, NJ....201-785-2247
Ruiz, Felix/72 Smith Ave, White Plains, NY....914-949-3353
Ruiz, Robert/818 E Highland Dr, Buffalo, NY....716-837-1428
Rummel, Hal/36 S Paca St #515, Baltimore, MD....301-244-8517
Rumph, Charles/3328 N St NW, Washington, DC....202-338-4431

Runyon, Paul/113 Arch St, Philadelphia, PA ... 215-238-0655
Rusnak, John/9303 Sutton Pl, Silver Spring, MD ... 301-587-2746
Russ, Clive/1311 North St, Walpole, MA ... 508-668-2536
Russell Studios/103 Ardale, Boston, MA ... 617-325-2500
Russo, Angela/9 Appleton St, Boston, MA ... 617-338-6640
Russo, Rich/11 Clinton St, Morristown, NJ ... 201-538-6954
Ryan, Michael/50 Melcher St, Boston, MA ... 617-236-1920
Ryder, Scott/409 W Broadway, Boston, MA ... 617-269-5864
Ryerson, Kathleen & Gordon/92 Heritage Lane, Hamburg, NJ ... 201-827-6728

S

Sabol, George Jeremy/2B Park Ave, Englishtown, NJ ... 908-446-4944
Sagala, Steve/350 Route 46, Rockaway, NJ ... 201-625-0484
Sakmanoff, George/323 Newbury St, Boston, MA ... 617-262-7227
Salamon, Londa/2634 Parrish, Philadelphia, PA ... 215-765-6632
Salamone, Anthony/17 Anthol St, Brighton, MA ... 617-254-5427
Salant, Robin/317 Elm St, Westfield, NJ ... 908-654-6847
Salomone, Frank/296 Brick Blvd, Bricktown, NJ ... 908-920-1525
Samara, Thomas/713 Erie Blvd West, Syracuse, NY ... 315-476-4984
Samia Photography/2828 10th St NE, Washington, DC ... 202-635-0096
Samu, Mark/39 Erlwein Ct, Massapequa, NY ... 516-795-1849
Samuels Studio/8 Waltham St, PO Box 201, Maynard, MA ... 508-897-7901
Sanderson, John/2310 Pennsylvania Ave, Pittsburgh, PA ... 412-263-2121
Sanford, Eric/110 Shaw St, Manchester, NH ... 603-624-0122
Santaniello, Angelo/20 Passaic St, Garfield, NJ ... 201-473-1141
Santos, Don/175-A Boston Post Rd, Waterford, CT ... 203-443-5668
Santos, Randy/1438 Fenwick Ln, Silver Spring, MD ... 301-589-2400
Sapienza, Louis A/1344 Martine Ave, Plainfield, NJ ... 908-756-9200
Saraceno, Paul/Box 277, Groton, MA ... 508-448-2566
Sargent, William/PO Box 331, Woods Hole, MA ... 508-548-2673
Sasso, Ken/116 Mattabaffet Dr, Meriden, CT ... 203-235-1421
Sauter, Ron Photo/183 St Paul St, Rochester, NY ... 716-232-1361
Savage, Sally/99 Orchard Terrace, Piermont, NY ... 914-359-5735
Sawa, Joji/2 Fenwick Rd, Winchester, MA ... 617-721-0196
Saydah, Gerard/PO Box 210, Demarest, NJ ... 201-768-2582
Sayers, Jim/325 Valley Rd, West Orange, NJ ... 201-325-2352
Scalera, Ron/8 Rosenbrook Dr, Lincoln Park, NJ ... 201-694-0234
Scarpetta, Tony/443 Albany St #305, Boston, MA ... 617-350-8640
Schaeffer, Bruce/631 N Pottstown Pike, Exton, PA ... 215-363-5230
Schafer, Jim/109 Forest Hills Rd, Pittsburgh, PA ... 412-371-2491
Schamp, J Brough/3616 Ednor Rd, Baltimore, MD ... 301-235-0840
Scheller, George/PO Box 402, Hackettstown, NJ ... 201-852-4670
Schenk, Andy/28 Mulberry Ln, Colts Neck, NJ ... 908-946-9459
Scherer, Jim/35 Kingston St, Boston, MA ... 617-338-5678
Scherlis, James/3900 N Charles St #904, Baltimore, MD ... 301-235-4528
Scherzi, James/5818 Molloy Rd, Syracuse, NY ... 315-455-7961
Schill, William Sr/ PO Box 25, Haddon Heights, NJ ... 609-547-0148
Schindler, Allen/129 Westover Ave, W Caldwell, NJ ... 201-403-8919
Schlanger, Irv/946 Cherokee Rd, Huntington Valley, PA ... 215-663-0663
Schlegel, Robert/2 Division St #10-11, Somerville, NJ ... 908-231-1212
Schleipman, Russell/298-A Columbus Ave, Boston, MA ... 617-267-1677
Schlowsky, Bob/73 Old Rd, Weston, MA ... 617-899-5110
Schmitt, Steve/33 Sleeper St #106, Boston, MA ... 617-426-0858
Schoen, Robert/241 Crescent St, Waltham, MA ... 617-647-5546
Schoon, Tim/PO Box 7446, Lancaster, PA ... 717-291-9483
Schroeder, H Robert/PO Box 7361, W Trenton, NJ ... 609-883-8643
Schroers, Kenneth/188 Highland Ave, Clifton, NJ ... 201-472-8395
Schulmeyer, LT Photo/40 W Chesapeake Ave, Towson, MD ... 301-337-8725
Schultz, Jurgen/Rt 100 N/Box 19, Londonderry, VT ... 802-824-3475
Schwab, Hilary/4614 Maple Ave, Bethesda, MD ... 301-656-7930
Schwartz, Jon C/1109 C St NE, Washington, DC ... 202-546-4129
Schwartz, Linda Photo/One Franklin Dr, Mays Landing, NJ ... 609-625-7617
Schwartz, Robin/11 North Shore Tr, Sparta, NJ ... 201-729-7020
Schwarz, Ira/2734 Cortland Pl NW, Washington, DC ... 202-232-2054
Schweikardt, Eric/PO Box 56, Southport, CT ... 203-221-7132
Schwoerer, Eliott/778 Oak Ave, Maywood, NJ ... 201-843-6884
Scott, Jesse/114 Broughton Ave, Bloomfield, NJ ... 201-338-1548
Seckinger, Angela/11231 Bybee St, Silver Spring, MD ... 301-649-3138
Seidel, Joan/337 Summer St, Boston, MA ... 617-357-8674
Selig, Mark/45 Electric Ave, Boston, MA ... 617-267-2000
Seng, Walt/810 Penn Ave #400, Pittsburgh, PA ... 412-391-6780
Serbin, Vincent/304 Church Rd, Bricktown, NJ ... 201-477-5620
Severi, Robert/813 Richmond Ave, Silver Spring, MD (P 112,113) ... 301-585-1010
Sewall & Co, James/PO Box 433, Old Town, ME ... 207-827-4456
Shafer, Bob/3554 Quebec St N W, Washington, DC ... 202-362-0630
Shaffer, Nancy/PO Box 333, Lincroft, NJ ... 201-846-6304
Shaffer-Smith Photo/56 Arbor St, Hartford, CT ... 203-236-4080
Shambroom, Eric/383 Albany St, Boston, MA ... 617-423-0359
Shanley, James G/8 West St, Stoneham, MA ... 617-279-9060
Shapiro, Betsy/7 E Burn St, Brighton, MA ... 617-783-2889
Sharp, Barry/30 Tower Hill Rd, N Kingston, RI ... 401-295-1686
Sharp, Steve/153 N 3rd St, Philadelphia, PA ... 215-925-2890
Shaw Studios/836 Richie Highway, Severne Park, MD ... 301-647-1200
Shawn, John/129 Sea Girt Ave, Manasguan, NJ ... 908-223-1190
Shearn, Michael/214 S 12th St, Philadelphia, PA ... 215-232-6666
Sheldon, John/PO Box 548, Hartford, VT ... 802-295-6321
Shepherd, Francis/PO Box 204, Chadds Ford, PA ... 215-347-6799
Sher, Fred/210 Kinderkamack Rd, Oradell, NJ ... 201-599-1213
Sherer, Larry/3000 Chestnut Ave #343D, Baltimore, MD ... 301-235-8443
Sherman, Stephen/49 Melcher St 5th Fl, Boston, MA (P 115) ... 617-542-1496
Sherriff, Bob/963 Humphrey St, Swampscott, MA ... 617-599-6955
Shields, Rob/830 Eddy St, Providence, RI ... 401-461-8848
Shinnick, John/3224 Kennedy Blvd, Jersey City, NJ ... 201-420-1056
Shive, James/316 Tall Oak Rd, Edison, NJ ... 201-906-9623
Shoemake, Allan Hunter/56 Main St, Millburn, NJ ... 201-467-4920
Shooters Photo/PO Box 7822, York, PA ... 717-764-4446
Shopper, David/409 W Broadway #219, Boston, MA ... 617-268-2044
Shotwell, John/241 A Street, Boston, MA ... 617-357-7456
Shupe, Greg/483 Water St, Framingham, MA ... 508-877-7700
Siciliano, Richard/809 Albany St, Schenectady, NY ... 518-370-4417
Sidney, Rhoda/59 E Linden Ave B7, Englewood, NJ ... 201-568-3919
Sieb, Fred/Box480/Birch Hill, North Conway, NH ... 603-356-5879
Siegel, Hyam Photography/PO Box 356, Brattleboro, VT ... 802-257-0691
Siegel, Marjorie/, Boston, MA ... 617-731-2855
Sigall, Dana/348 Congress St, Boston, MA (P 116,117) ... 617-357-5140
Signal Stock/54 Applecross, Chalfont, PA ... 215-997-2311
Silk, Georgiana B/190 Godfrey Rd E, Weston, CT ... 203-226-0408
Silver Light Studio/735 Sumner Ave, Springfield, MA ... 413-737-2003
Silver, David/165 Front St, Chicopee, MA ... 413-594-8353
Silver, Walter S/107 South St #203, Boston, MA ... 617-426-4743
Silverman, Jeff/1 East Front St, Keyport, NJ ... 908-264-3939
Silverman, Paul/49 Ronald Dr, Clifton, NJ ... 201-472-4339
Silverstein, Abby/3315 Woodvalley Dr, Baltimore, MD ... 301-486-5211
Silverstein, Roy/1604 Gary Rd, East Meadow, NY ... 516-481-3218
Silvia, Peter/20 Burdick Ave, Newport, RI ... 401-841-5076
Simeone, J Paul/116 W Baltimore Pike, Media, PA ... 215-566-7197
Simian, George/566 Commonwealth Ave, Boston, MA ... 617-267-3558
Simmons, Erik Leigh/60 K Street, Boston, MA (P 52) ... 617-268-4650
Simon, David/97 Wayne St, Jersey City, NJ ... 201-795-9326
Simon, Peter S/RFD 280, Chilmark, MA ... 508-645-9575
Simons, Stuart/71 Highland St, Patterson, NJ ... 201-278-5050
Simpson, John WH/ 98 Linden Lane, Princeton, NJ ... 609-924-8996
Sinclair, Dan/150 Preble St, Portland, ME ... 207-772-6161
Sinclair, Jodie/109 Broad St, Boston, MA ... 617-482-0328
Singer, Arthur/Sedgewood RD 12, Carmel, NY ... 914-225-6801
Singer, Jay/20 Russell Park Rd, Syosset, NY ... 516-935-8991
Siteman, Frank/136 Pond St, Winchester, MA ... 617-729-3747
Sitkin, Marc/15 Warrenton Ave, Hartford, CT ... 203-523-4562
Skalkowski, Bob/310 Eighth St, New Cumberland, PA ... 717-774-0652
Skibee, John/4 Bud Way, Nashua, NH ... 603-880-8686
Skoogfors, Leif/415 Church Rd #B2, Elkins Park, PA ... 215-635-5186
Slezinger, Natan/1191 Chestnut St, Newton, MA ... 617-964-0700
Sloan Photo/182 High St, Waltham, MA ... 617-542-3215
Sloan, Jim/12017 Nevel St, Rockville, MD ... 301-732-7940
Sloane, Jim/12017 Nevel St, Rockville, MD ... 301-881-9330
Smalley, James C/7 Jackson Rd, Scituate, MA ... 617-545-1664
Smalling, Walter Jr/1541 8th St NW, Washington, DC ... 202-234-2438
Smaltz, Richard/PO Box 535 Rt 318, W Middlesex, PA ... 412-528-1234
Smith, Bill Photo/20 Newbury St, Boston, MA ... 617-267-4026
Smith, Brian/7 Glenley Terrace, Brighton, MA ... 617-782-5560
Smith, Dana/140 Ohio St, New Bedford, MA ... 508-998-8547
Smith, David A/PO Box 338, Lebanon, CT ... 203-642-6460
Smith, David K/731 Harrison Ave, Boston, MA ... 617-424-1555
Smith, David L/420 Goldway, Pittsburgh, PA ... 412-687-7500
Smith, Gary & Russell/65 Washington St, S Norwalk, CT ... 203-866-8871
Smith, Gene/876-K N Lenola Rd, Moorestown, NJ ... 609-722-5225
Smith, George E/408 St Lawrence Dr, Silver Spring , MD ... 301-593-9618
Smith, Gordon E/65 Washington St, S Norwalk, CT ... 203-866-8871
Smith, Greg/1827 Belmont Rd NW, Washington, DC ... 202-328-9282
Smith, Hugh R/2515 Burr St, Fairfield, CT ... 203-255-1942
Smith, Philip W/1589 Reed Rd #2A, W Trenton, NJ ... 609-737-3370
Smith, Rodney/Lawrence Lane, Palisades, NY ... 914-359-3814

Smith, Stuart/68 Raymond Lane, Wilton, CT............................203-762-3158
Smyth, Kevin/23 Walnut Ave, Clark, NJ....................................908-388-8831
Snitzer, Herb/64 Roseland St, Cambridge, MA.........................617-497-0251
Socolow, Carl/2714 Dickinson Ave, Camp Hill, PA.....................717-763-7760
Solaria Studio/190 Tuckerton Road, Indian Mills, NJ..................609-268-0045
Solomon, Alan/Rt 33, Chatam, NY..518-392-5220
Solomon, Daryl/8 Illingworth Ave, Tenafly, NJ...........................201-871-3236
Solomon, Ron/149 W Montgomery St, Baltimore, MD..................301-539-0403
Soorenko, Barry/5161 River Rd Bldg 2B, Bethesda, MD.............301-652-1303
Sortino, Steve/2125 N Charles St, Baltimore, MD......................301-625-2125
Spahr, David/170 Water St, Hallowell, ME.................................207-623-5067
Spartana, Stephen/19 S Strickler St, Baltimore, MD..................301-945-2173
Spaulding, Matt/49 Dartmouth, Portland, ME.............................207-772-4725
Spectrum Photography/1 Dundee Park, Andover, MA..................508-470-2009
Speedy, Richard/1 Sherbrooke Dr, Princeton Junction, NJ..........609-275-1885
Spence, George A/15 Scott Ct, Ridgefield Park, NJ....................201-641-2032
Spencer, Dave/PO Box 726, Hanson, MA...................................617-447-0918
Spencer, Michael/735 Mt Hope Ave, Rochester, NY....................716-475-6817
Spencer, Stephen/145 Crary St, Providence, RI.........................401-751-1925
Sperduto, Stephen/18 Willett Ave, Port Chester, NY..................914-939-0296
Spiegel, Ted/RD 2 Box 353 A, South Salem, NY.........................914-763-3668
Spiro, Don/137 Summit Rd, Sparta, NJ......................................212-484-9753
Spozarsky, Michael/5 Academy St, Newton, NJ.........................201-579-1385
Sprecher, Allan/1428 E Baltimore St, Baltimore, MD.................301-235-5004
St Pierre, Joe/135 McDonough St #27, Portsmouth, NH.............603-436-6070
Staccioli, Marc/167 New Jersey Ave, Lake Hopatcong, NJ..........201-663-5334
Stanley, James G/8 West St, Stoneham, MA..............................617-279-9060
Stapleton, John/3407 Widener Rd, Philadelphia, PA...................215-233-3864
Starosielski, Sergei/181 Doty Circle, W Springfield, MA.............413-733-3530
Stayner & Stayner/3060 Williston Rd, S Burlington, VT..............802-865-3477
Stearns, Stan/1814 Glade Ct, Annapolis, MD............................301-268-5777
Stein, Geoffrey R/348 Newbury St, Boston, MA........................617-536-8227
Stein, Howard/200 William St, Port Chester, NY.......................914-939-0242
Stein, Jonathan/579 Sagamore Ave, Portsmouth, NH.................603-436-6365
Stein, Larry/51 Union St, Worcester, MA..................................508-754-1470
Stein, Martin/157 Highland Ave, Winthrop, MA.........................617-539-0070
Steiner, Peter Photo/183 St Paul St 3rd Fl,
Rochester, NY (P 118,119).................................**716-454-1012**
Steinkamp, Susan V/1013 Independence SE, Washington, DC.....202-544-4886
Stevenson, Jeff/496 Congress St, Portland, ME.........................207-773-5175
Stewart, Tom/205 Johnson Point Rd, Penobscot,
ME (P 120,121)..**207-326-9370**
Stier, Kurt/451 "D" St, Boston, MA..617-330-9461
Still, John/17 Edinboro St, Boston, MA.....................................617-451-8178
Stillings, Jamey/87 N Clinton Ave 5th Fl, Rochester, NY............716-232-5296
Stiltz, Thomas/8210 Thornton Rd, Baltimore, MD.....................301-337-5565
Stockfield, Bob/3000 Chestnut Av #114/Mill Ctr, Baltimore, MD...301-235-7007
Stockwell, Thomas/20 Blue Bell Rd, Worcester, MA...................508-853-1000
Stone, Parker II/6632 Temple Dr, E Syracuse, NY.....................315-463-0577
Stone, Steven/20 Rugg Rd, Allston, MA (P 123).......**617-782-1247**
Stratos, Jim/128 Pine St, Peekskill, NY....................................212-695-5674
Strauss, Diane/1666 32nd St NW, Washington, DC....................202-965-1733
Strohmeyer, Damian/14 Daniel St, Arlington, MA......................617-648-6543
Stromberg, Bruce/PO Box 2052, Philadelphia, PA.....................215-735-3520
Stuart, Stephen Photography/10 Midland Ave, Port Chester, NY...914-939-0302
Stuck, John D/RD 1 Box 234, Selinsgrove, PA...........................717-374-8898
Studio Assoc/30-6 Plymouth St, Fairfield, NJ............................201-575-2640
Studio Capricorn/109 Higginson Ave, Lincoln, RI......................401-726-8450
The Studio Inc/938 Penn Ave, Pittsburgh, PA...........................412-889-5422
Studio Tech/35 Congress St Box 390, Salem, MA......................617-745-5070
Stultz, Natalie/B5 Meadowbrook Joy Dr, S Burlington, VT..........802-863-1640
Suarez, Ileana/6901 Bergenkine Ave, Gutenberg, NJ.................201-869-8910
Sued, Yamil/425 Fairfield Ave Bldg 4, Stamford, CT..................203-324-0234
Sullivan, Sharon/325 1/2 4th St, Jersey City, NJ.......................212-545-7965
Susoeff, Bill/1063 Elizabeth Dr, Bridgeville, PA........................412-941-8606
Suter, John/1118 Commonwealth Ave #5A, Boston, MA.............617-735-0812
Sutphen, Chazz/22 Crescent Beach Dr, Burlington, VT..............802-862-5912
Sutter, Frederick/6123 Blue Whale Ct, Waldorf, MD..................301-843-7510
Sutton, Humphrey/38 E Brookfield Rd, N Brookfield, MA............508-867-4474
Swann Niemann Photography/9 W 29th St, Baltimore, MD.........301-467-7300
Swanson, Dick/6122 Wiscasset Rd, Bethesda, MD....................202-965-1185
Swartley, Lowell/28 W Broad St, Souderton, PA........................215-721-7118
Sweeney Jr, Gene/1200 Monkton Rd, Monkton, MD...................301-343-1609
Sweet, Ozzie/Sunnyside Acres, Francestown, NH......................603-547-6611
Swett, Jennifer/PO Box 102, N Sutton, NH...............................603-927-4648
Swisher, Mark/3819 Hudson St, Baltimore, MD.........................301-732-7788
Swoger, Arthur/61 Savoy St, Providence, RI.............................401-331-0440
Szabo, Art/156-A Depot Rd, Huntington, NY..............................516-549-1699

T

Tack, Charles/11345 Sunset Hills Rd, Reston, VA......................703-471-1511
Tadder, Morton/1010 Morton St, Baltimore, MD........................301-837-7427
Tagg, Randall/18 Broxbourne Dr, Fairport, NY
(P 124,125)..**716-425-3139**
Taglienti, Maria/294 Whippany Rd, Whippany, NJ......................201-428-4477
Tango, Rick/7 Deer Run, Bethel, CT...203-748-1652
Tarantola, Kathy/109 Broad St, Boston, MA.............................617-423-4399
Tardi, Joseph/125 Wolf Rd #108, Albany, NY............................518-438-1211
Tardiff, Gary/355 Wood Rd #230, Braintree, MA.......................617-848-6904
Tarsky, Jeffrey/75 Haynes Rd, Newton, MA..............................617-965-6970
Tartaglia, Vic/42 Dodd St, Bloomfield, NJ.................................201-429-4983
Taylor, Ed/668 Front St, Teaneck, NJ......................................201-836-8345
Taylor, Robert/55 Lane Rd, Fairfield, NJ...................................201-227-5000
Teatum, Marc/28 Goodhue St, Salem, MA................................508-745-2345
Teitelbaum, Phyliss/917 Lamberton Dr, Silver Spring, MD..........301-649-1449
Tenin, Barry/PO Box 2660 Saugatuck Sta, Westport, CT............203-226-9396
Tepper, Peter/183 Bennett St, Bridgeport, CT..........................203-367-6172
Tesch, Geoffrey/639 Boughton Hill Rd, Honeoye Falls, NY.........716-624-4096
Tesi, Mike/12 Kulick Rd, Fairfield, NJ.......................................201-575-7780
Texter, Jay/PO Box 78, Souderton, PA.....................................215-821-0963
Thauer, Bill/542 Higgens Crowell Rd, W Yarmouth, MA.............508-362-8222
Thayer, Mark/25 Dry Dock Ave, Boston, MA.............................617-542-9532
Thellman, Mark/PO Box 1209, Merchantville, NJ.......................609-488-9093
Thiebauth, Jeffrey/57 Pine Circle, S Weymouth, MA.................617-335-2686
Thomas, Edward/140-50 Huyshope Ave, Hartford, CT................203-246-3293
Thomas, Melvin III/75 Prospect St #7C, E Orange, NJ...............201-678-9655
Thomas, Ted/PO Box 2051, Teaneck, NJ..................................201-837-6682
Thompson, Eleanor/PO Box 1304, Weston, CT..........................203-226-8659
Thompson, S./333 Pemberton Browns Mills Rd, New Lisbon, NJ...609-893-2726
Thuss, Bill/407 Main St, Rockland, ME.....................................207-596-0603
Titcomb, Jeffery/423 W Broadway, South Boston, MA................617-269-8777
Tkatch, James/2307 18th St NW, Washington, DC.....................202-462-2211
Tolbert, Brian/911 State St, Lancaster, PA...............................717-393-0918
Tollen, Cynthia/50 Fairmont St, Arlington, MA..........................617-641-4052
Tong, Darren/28 Renee Terrace, Newton, MA...........................617-527-3304
Tornallyay, Martin/77 Taft Ave, Stamford, CT...........................203-357-1777
Total Concept Photo/95-D Knickerbocker Ave, Bohemia, NY......516-567-6010
Tracy, Don/1133 E Oxford St, Philadelphia, PA.........................215-426-5154
Trafidlo, James F/17 Stilling St, Boston, MA.............................617-338-9343
Traub, Willard/PO Box 2429, Framingham, MA..........................508-872-2010
Traver, Joseph/187 Hodge Ave, Buffalo, NY.............................716-884-8844
Treiber, Peter/917 Highland Ave, Bethlehem, PA......................215-867-3303
Tretick, Stanley/4365 Embassy Park Dr NW, Washington, DC......202-537-1445
Tribulas, Michael/1879 Old Cuthbert Rd #14, Cherry Hill, NJ......609-354-1903
Tritsch, Joseph/507 Longstone Dr, Cherry Hill, NJ....................609-424-0433
Troeller, Linda/718 Polk Ave, Lawrenceville, NJ........................609-396-2660
Troha, John/9030 Saunders Lane, Bethesda, MD.......................301-469-7440
Trola, Bob/1216 Arch St 2nd Fl, Philadelphia, PA......................215-977-7078
Trottier, Charles/PO Box 581, Burlington, VT............................802-862-1881
Trueworthy, Nance/PO Box 8353, Portland, ME.........................207-774-6181
Truslow, Bill/855 Islington St, Portsmouth, NH..........................603-436-4600
Trzoniec, Stanley/58 W Main St, Northboro, MA........................617-393-3800
Tsufura, Satoru/48 Bently Rd, Cedar Grove, NJ........................201-239-4870
Tuemmler, Stretch/45 Casco, Portland, ME..............................207-871-0350
Turner, Steve/286 Compo Rd South, Westport, CT....................203-454-3999
Turpan, Dennis P/25 Amsterdam Ave, Teaneck, NJ...................201-837-4242

U

Uksaker, Michael/275 Park Ave, E Hartford, CT........................203-282-0341
Ultimate Image/Photo/PO Box 22, Lawton, PA..........................717-934-2226
Umstead, Dan/7475 Morgan Road 7-6, Liverpool, NY................315-457-0365
Urban, John/144 Lincoln St, Boston, MA...................................617-426-4578
Urban, Peter/71 Wachusett St, Jamaica Plain, MA....................617-983-9169
Urbina, Walt/7208 Thomas Blvd, Pittsburgh, PA........................412-242-5070
Urdang, Monroe/461-A Oldham Ct, Ridge, NY...........................516-744-3903
Ury, Randy/PO Box 7312, Portland, ME....................................207-871-0291
Usher III, Aaron/1080 Newport Ave, Pawtucket, RI...................401-725-4595
Ushkurnis, Jim/387 Park Ave, Worcester, MA...........................508-795-1333
Uzzle, Burk/737 N 4th St, Philadelphia, PA...............................215-629-1202

V

Vadnai, Peter/180 Valley Rd, Katonah, NY...............................914-232-5328
Valentino, Thom/25 Navaho St, Cranston, RI............................401-946-3020

Valerio, Gary/278 Jay St, Rochester, NY....716-352-0163
Van Der Wal, Onne/PO Box 609, Newport, RI....401-846-9552
Van Gorder, Jon/63 Unquowa Rd, Fairfield, CT....203-255-6622
Van Lockhart, Eric/145 Cross Ways Park W, Woodbury, NY....516-364-3000
Van Petten, Rob/109 Broad St, Boston, MA....617-426-8641
Van Schalkwyk, John/50 Melcher St, Boston, MA....617-542-4825
Van Valkenburgh, Larry/511 Broadway, Saratoga Springs, NY....518-583-3676
Vandall, D C/PO Box 515, Worchester, MA....508-852-4582
Vanden Brink, Brian/PO Box 419, Rockport, ME....207-236-4035
Vandermark, Peter/523 Medford St, Charlestown, MA....617-242-2277
Vanderwarker, Peter/28 Prince St, West Newton, MA....617-964-2728
VanderWiele, John/75 Boulevard, Pequannock, NJ....201-694-2095
Vangha, Ruhi/PO Box 344, Wayne, PA....215-293-1315
Vasquez, George/249 8th St, Boston, MA....617-482-2882
Vaughan, Ted/351 Doe Run Rd, Manheim, PA....717-665-6942
Vazquez, Claudio/2726 Brandwine St NW, Washington, DC....202-543-7782
Vecchio, Dan/204 Forest Hill Dr, Syracuse, NY....315-437-9019
Vecchione, Jim/9153 Brookville Rd, Silver Springs, MD....301-589-7900
Veerasarn, Oi/2707 Adams Hill Rd NW, Washington, DC....202-387-8667
Vendikos, Tasso/141 Hawthorne St, Massapequa Park, NY....516-541-1635
Ventura, Michael/5016 Elm St, Bethesda, MA....301-654-6205
Verheeck, Al/160 Birchwood Rd, Paramus, NJ....201-652-4291
Vericker, Joe/111 Cedar St 4th Fl, New Rochelle, NY....914-632-2072
Verno, Jay/101 S 16th St, Pittsburgh, PA....412-381-5350
Vidor, Peter/48 Grist Mill Rd, Randolph, NJ....201-267-1104
Vieira, Jacque/15 Bitterweet Dr, Seekonk, MA....508-399-7272
Visual Productions/2121 Wisconsin Ave NW #470, Washington, DC....202-337-7332
Von Falken, Sabine V/Rt 183, Glendale, MA....413-298-4933
Von Hoffmann, Bernard/2 Green Village Rd, Madison, NJ....201-377-0317
Voscar The Maine Photographer/PO Box 661, Presque Isle, ME....207-769-5911

W

Waggaman, John/RD 5/ Box 240, Williamsport, PA....800-336-6062
Wagner, William/208 North Ave West, Cranford, NJ....908-276-2229
Walch, Robert/724 Cherokee St, Bethlehem, PA....215-866-3345
Walker, Robert/13 Thorne St, Jersey City, NJ....201-659-1336
Wallen, Jonathan/41 Lewis Pkwy, Yonkers, NY....914-476-8674
Walling, Kit/1741 Johnson Ave NW, Washington, DC....202-483-7194
Walp's Photo Service/182 S 2nd St, Lehighton, PA....215-377-4370
Walsh, Dan/409 W Broadway, Boston, MA....617-268-7615
Walters, Day/PO Box 5655, Washington, DC....202-362-0022
Walther, Michael/2185 Brookside Ave, Wantagh, NY....516-783-7636
Wanamaker, Roger/PO Box 2800, Darien, CT....203-655-8383
Ward, Jack/221 Vine St, Philadelphia, PA....215-627-5311
Ward, Michael/916 N Charles St, Baltimore, MD....301-727-8800
Ward, Tony/704 South 6th St, Philadelphia, PA....215-238-1208
Wargo, Matt/1424 S Broad St, Philadelphia, PA....215-468-5842
Waring, Nicholas/E 5808 63rd Ave, Riverdale, MD (P 128)....301-864-8115
Warinsky, Jim/224 W Hudson Ave, Englewood, NJ....212-206-6448
Warner, Roger/409 W Broadway, S Boston, MA....671-268-8333
Warniers, Randall/35 Cleveland St, Arlington, MA....617-643-0454
Warren, Bob/1511 Gilford Ave, Baltimore, MD....301-539-2807
Warren, Murray/415 Route 17, Upper Saddle River, NJ....201-327-4832
Warunek, Stan/205 Gill Ave, Dupont, PA....717-654-0421
Washnik, Andrew/145 Woodland Ave, Westwood, NJ....201-664-0441
Wasserman, Cary/Six Porter Rd, Cambridge, MA....617-492-5621
Watkins, Charles/75 E Wayne Ave #W-311, Silver Springs, MD....301-587-9284
Watkins, Norman/3000 Chestnut Ave #213, Baltimore, MD....301-467-3358
Watson, H Ross/Box 897, Bryn Mawr, PA....215-353-9898
Watson, Linda M/38 Church St/Box 14, Hopkinton, MA....508-435-5671
Watson, Tom/2172 West Lake Rd, Skaneateles, NY....315-685-6033
Wawrzonek, John/70 Webster St, Worcester, MA....508-798-6612
Way, James/622-R Main St, Reading, MA....617-944-3070
Weber, Kevin/138 Longview Dr, Baltimore, MD....301-747-8422
Wee, John/115 Pius St, Pittsburg, PA (P 129)....412-381-6826
Weems, Al/14 Imperial Pl #504, Providence, RI....401-455-0484
Weidman, H Mark/2112 Goodwin Lane, North Wales, PA....215-646-1745
Weigand, Tom/707 North 5th St, Reading, PA....215-374-4431
Weiner, Jeff/163 N Main St, Port Chester, NY....914-939-8324
Weinrebe, Steve/, Philadelphia, PA....215-625-0333
Weinrich, Ken/21 Oriole Terrace, Newton, NJ....201-579-6784
Weisenfeld, Stanley/135 Davis St, Painted Post, NY....607-962-7314
Weiss, Michael/212 Race St, Philadelphia, PA....215-629-1685
Weitz, Allan/147 Harbinson Pl, E Windsor, NJ....609-443-5549
Weller, Bruce/3000 Chestnut Ave #11, Baltimore, MD....301-235-4200
Wells, Heidi/1284 Beacon St #607, Brookline, MA....617-232-7417
Welsch, Ms Ulrike/4 Dunns Lane, Marblehead, MA....617-631-1641
Wendler, Hans/RD 1 Box 191, Epsom, NH....603-736-9383
Werner, Perry/259 Continental Ave, River Edge, NJ....201-967-7306
West, Judy/8 Newcomb St, Boston, MA....617-442-9343
Westphalen, James/20 Forest Ave, Brookhaven, NY....516-286-0987
Westwood Photo Productions/PO Box 859, Mansfield, MA....617-339-4141
Wexler, Ira/4911 V St NW, Washington, DC....202-337-4886
Wheat, Frank/225 W 25th St, Baltimore, MD....301-889-1780
Wheeler, Ed/1050 King of Prussia Rd, Radnor, PA....215-964-9294
Wheeler, Nick/414 Concord Rd, Weston, MA....617-891-5525
Whitcomb, David/212 E Cross St, Basltimore , MD....301-727-7507
White, Andrew/5727 29th Ave, Hyattsville, MD....301-559-7718
White, Frank/18 Milton Pl, Rowayton, CT....203-866-9500
White, Sharon/107 South St, Boston, MA....617-423-0577
Whitenack, Ernie/PO Box 332, Newton, MA....617-964-3326
Whitman, Edward/613 N Eutaw St, Baltimore, MD....301-727-2220
Whittemore, Patrick/7 Union Park St, Boston, MA....617-695-0584
Wieland, Mark/12115 Parklawn Dr Bay-S, Rockville, MD....301-468-2588
Wierzbowski, Joe/91 Main St W, Rochester, NY....716-546-8381
Wilcox, Jed/PO Box 1271, Newport, RI....401-847-3853
Wild, Terry/RD 3/Box 68, Williamsport, PA....717-745-3257
Wiley, John Jay/208-A W Wayne Ave, Wayne, PA....215-337-9668
Wilkins, Doug/33 Church St, Canton, MA....617-828-2379
Wilkinson, Peter/1944 Warwick Ave, Warwick, RI....401-738-5059
Willet, Don/4712 Kenwood Ave, Baltimore, MD....301-668-4647
Williams, Calvin/2601 Madison Ave #503, Baltimore , MD....301-728-1483
Williams, Jay/9101 W Chester Pike, Upper Darby, PA....215-789-3030
Williams, Lawrence S/9101 W Chester Pike, Upper Darby, PA....215-789-3030
Williams, Woodbridge/PO Box 11, Dickerson, MD....301-972-7025
Willson, Hub/1228 Turner St, Allentown, PA....215-434-2178
Wilson, John G/2416 Wynnefield Dr, Havertown, PA....215-446-4798
Wilson, Kevin/11231 Bybee St, Silver Spring, MD....301-649-3151
Wilson, Robert L/PO Box 1742, Clarksburg, WV....304-623-5368
Windman, Russell/348 Congress St, Boston, MA....617-357-5140
Winstead, Gene/300 Observer Highway #602, Hoboken, NJ....201-714-9245
Wise, Harriet/242 Dill Ave, Frederick, MD....301-662-6323
Wiseman, Pat/93 Prince Ave, Marstons Mills, MA....508-420-3395
Witbeck, David/77 Ives St, Providence, RI (P 130)....401-274-9118
Wittkop, Bill/346 Main St, Chatham, NJ....201-635-1825
Wojnar, Lee/326 Kater St, Philadelphia, PA....215-922-5266
Wojnarowicz, Mitch/22 Clarne Ave, Amsterdam, NY....518-843-2886
Wolff, Tom/2102 18th St NW, Washington, DC....202-234-7130
Woloszyn, Gustav/1111 E Elizabeth Ln, Linden, NJ....908-925-7399
Wood, Richard/169 Monsgnr O'Brien Hwy, Cambridge, MA....617-661-6856
Woodard, Steve/2003 Arbor Hill Ln, Bowie, MD....301-249-7705
Woolf, John/58 Banks St, Cambridge, MA....617-876-4074
Wooloff, Warren/20602 West St, Wrentham, MA....508-883-8783
Wrenn, Bill/41 Wolfpit Ave, Norwalk, CT....203-845-0939
Wright, Jeri/PO box 7, Wilmington, NY....518-946-2658
Wright, Ralph/43 Forest Park Dr, Nashua, NH....603-882-1519
Wu, Ron/179 St Paul St, Rochester, NY....716-454-5600
Wurster, George/128 Berwick, Elizabeth, NJ....908-352-2134
Wyatt, Ronald/846 Harned St #1A, Perth Amboy, NJ....908-442-7527
Wychunis, Tony/128 Osborne St, Philadelphia, PA....215-482-4927
Wyland, Katharine/24 Montague Ave #3, W Trenton, NJ....609-771-3705
Wyman, D Jake/PO Box M85, Hoboken, NJ....201-420-8462
Wyman, Ira/14 Crane Ave, West Peabody, MA....508-535-2880
Wyner,Kenneth/7012 Westmoreland Ave, Takma Park, MD....202-269-6284

YZ

Yablon, Ron/834 Chestnut St #PH 105, Philadelphia, PA....215-923-1744
Yamashita, Michael/25 Roxiticus Rd, Mendham, NJ....201-543-4473
Yellen, Bob/833 Second Ave, Toms River, NJ....908-341-6750
Z, Taran/528 F St Terrace SE, Washington, DC....202-543-5322
Zabek, V J/50A Joy St, Boston, MA....617-227-3123
Zaccardi, Grace/2523 N Calvert St, Baltimore, MD....301-889-1121
Zaporozec, Terry (Mr)/43 Johnson Rd, Hackettstown, NJ....908-637-6720
Zappa, Tony/143 Parkway Dr, Roslyn Heights, NY....516-484-4907
Zaslow, Francine/791 Tremont St #W406, Boston, MA....617-437-0743
Zickl & Butcher/46 Lincoln St, Jersey City, NJ....201-656-5680
Zito, Roy/PO Box 1123, Fairlawn, NJ....201-796-0104
Zmiejko, Tom/PO Box 126, Freeland, PA....717-636-2304
Zubkoff, Earl/2426 Linden Lane, Silver Spring, MD....301-585-7393
Zucker, Gale/PO Box 2281/Short Beach, Branford, CT....203-488-0499
Zugcic, Joseph/20 Union Hill Rd, Morganville, NJ....908-536-3288
Zullinger, Carson/1909 N Market St, Wilmington, DE....302-654-3905
Zungoli, Nick/Box 5, Sugar Loaf, NY....914-469-9382

Zurich, Robert/445 Highway 35, Eatontown, NJ 908-389-9010
Zutell, Kirk/911 State St, Lancaster, PA....717-393-0918

SOUTHEAST

A

Adcock, James/3108 1/2 W Leigh St #8, Richmond, VA....804-358-4399
Adcock, Susan/PO Box 349, Pegram, TN....615-646-4114
Alderman Company/325 Model Farm Rd, High Point, NC....919-889-6121
Alexander, Rick & Assoc/212 S Graham St, Charlotte, NC....704-332-1254
Allard, William Albert/Rt 689/PO Box 148, Batesville, VA....804-823-5951
Allen, Bob/710 W Lane St, Raleigh, NC....919-833-5991
Allen, Don/1787 Shawn Dr, Baton Rouge, LA....504-925-0251
Allen, Erich/602 Riverside Ave, Kingsport, TN....615-246-7262
Allen, Michael/PO Box 11510, Nashville, TN....615-754-0059
Alston, Cotten/Box 7927-Station C, Atlanta, GA....404-876-7859
Alterman, Jack/285 Meeting St, Charleston, SC....803-577-0647
Alvarez, Jorge/3105 W Granada, Tampa, FL....813-831-6765
American Image/4303 Granada St, Alexandria, VA....703-360-7507
Ames, Kevin/1324 Brainwood Ind Ct, Atlanta, GA....404-325-6736
Anderson, Suzanne Stearns/3355 Lenox Rd NE #200, Atlanta, GA....404-261-0439
Arruza, Tony/250 Edmor Rd, West Palm Beach, FL....407-832-5978
Atlantic Photo/319 N Main St, High Point, NC....919-884-1474
Axion Inc/120 South Brook St, Louisville, KY....502-584-7666
Ayres, Jim/2575 Oakhill Dr, Marietta, GA....404-578-9857
Azad/246 NW 69th St, Boca Raton, FL....407-362-9352

B

Bachmann, Bill/PO Box 950833, Lake Mary, FL....407-322-4444
Baker, I Wilson/1094 Morrison Dr, Charleston, SC....803-577-0828
Balbuza, Joseph/25 NE 210 St, Miami, FL....305-652-1728
Ball, Roger/1402-A Winnifred, Charlotte, NC....704-335-0479
Baptie, Frank/1426 9th St N, St Petersburg, FL....813-823-7319
Barley, Bill/PO Box 280005, Columbia, SC....803-755-1554
Barnes, Billy E/313 Severin St, Chapel Hill, NC....919-942-6350
Barnes, William/8A Forrest Lake Shopping Ctr, Columbia, SC....803-782-8088
Barr, Ian/2640 SW 19th St, Fort Lauderdale, FL (P 134)....305-584-6247
Barreras, Anthony/1231-C Booth St NW, Atlanta, GA....404-352-0511
Barrs, Michael/6303 SW 69th St, Miami, FL....305-665-2047
Bartlett & Assoc/2309 Silver Star Rd, Orlando, FL....407-295-0818
Bassett, Donald/9185 Green Mdows Way, Palm Bch Gardens, FL....407-694-1109
Bateman, John H/3500 Aloma Ave W #18, Winter Park, FL....407-671-2516
Beck, Charles/2721 Cherokee Rd, Birmingham, AL....205-871-6632
Beck, G & Assoc/2135 J Deforr Hill Rd, Atlanta, GA....404-352-8385
Becker, Joel/5121 Virginia Bch Blvd #E3, Norfolk, VA....804-461-7886
Belk, Michael/1708 Peachtree St NW #203, Atlanta, GA....404-874-6304
Belloise, Joe/3569 Cocoplum Circle, Coconut Creek, FL....305-941-9895
Bennett, Robert/6194 Deer Path Court, Manassas, VA....703-361-7705
Bentley, Gary/921 W Main St, Hendersonville, TN....615-822-7770
Berg, Audrey & Fronk, Mark/7655 Fullerton Rd, Springfield, VA....703-455-7343
Bergeron, Joe/516 Natchez, New Orleans, LA....504-522-7503
Bernstein, Alan/6766 NW 43rd Pl, Coral Springs, FL....306-753-1071
Bertsch, Werner J/441 NE 4th Ave #3, Fort Lauderdale, FL (P 135)....305-463-1912
Beswick, Paul/4479 Westfield Dr, Mableton, GA....404-944-8579
Bewley, Glen/428 Armour Circle, Atlanta, GA....404-872-7277
Bilby, Glade/1715 Burgundy, New Orleans, LA....504-866-0031
Biver, Steven/2402 Mt Vernon Ave, Alexandria, VA....703-548-1188
Blankenship, Bob Photo/1 Newport Place NW, Atlanta, GA....404-351-8938
Blanton, Jeff/5515 S Orange Ave, Orlando, FL (P 136)....407-851-7279
Blount, Ron/4118 S 36th St, Arlington, VA....703-671-8160
Boatman, Mike/3430 Park Ave, Memphis, TN....901-324-9337
Boblett, Ben/4801 N 20th St, Arlington, VA....703-243-7152
Bollman, Brooks/1183 Virginia Ave NE, Atlanta, GA....404-876-2422
Bondarenko, Marc/212 S 41st St, Birmingham, AL....205-933-2790
Booth's Studio/1747 Independence Blvd #E10, Sarasota, FL....813-359-3456
Borchelt, Mark/4398-D Eisenhower Ave, Alexandria, VA....703-751-2533
Borum, Michael/625 Fogg St, Nashville, TN....615-259-9750
Bose, Patti/1413 Haven Dr, Orlando, FL....407-895-3005
Bostick, Rick/489 Semoran Blvd #109, Casselberry, FL....407-331-5715
Boughton, Mark/302 King Rd, Fairview, TN....615-799-2143
Bowie, Ed/312 W Vermillion, Lafayette, LA....318-234-0576
Boxer, Bill/118-35 Canon Blvd #C104, Newport News, VA....804-873-3686
Boyd, Richard/PO Box 5097, Roanoke, VA....703-366-3140
Boyle, Jeffrey/8725 NW 18th Terrace #215, Miami, FL....305-592-7032
Bradshaw, David/9 West Main St, Richmond, VA....804-225-1883
Branan, Tom/P O Box 4075, Ocala, FL....904-351-1405
Brasher/Rucker Photography/3373 Park Ave, Memphis, TN....901-324-7447
Braun, Bob/PO Box 547755, Orlando, FL....407-425-7921
Braun, Paulette/1500 N Orange #42, Sarasota, FL....813-366-6284
Bridgeforth, Lauri/129 S Loudon St #201, Winchester, VA....703-665-9484
Bridges, Bob/205 Wolverine Rd, Cary, NC....919-469-3359
Brill, David/Route 4, Box 121-C, Fairbourn, GA....404-461-5488
Brinson, Rob/PO Box 93372, Atlanta, GA....404-874-2497
Brooks, Charles/800 Luttrell St, Knoxville, TN....615-525-4501
Broomell, Peter/1 South Third St, Amelia Island, FL....904-261-8557
Brown, Billy/2700 Seventh Ave S, Birmingham, AL (P 137)....205-251-8327
Brown, Charlie/5649-H General Washington Dr, Alexandria, VA....703-354-6688
Brown, Doug/2900-A Jefferson Davis Hwy, Alexandria, VA....703-684-8778
Brown, George/961 3rd St NW, Atlanta, GA....404-875-3238
Brown, Richard Photo/PO Box 830, Asheville, NC....704-253-1634
Bryant, Scott/11089 Stagestone Way, Manassas , VA....703-551-2311
Bryson, Stephen/PO Box 8702, Atlanta, GA....404-248-9773
Buchman, Tim/212 S Graham St, Charlotte, NC....704-332-1254
Bumpus, Ken/1770 W Chapel Dr, Deltona, FL....904-789-3080
Burgess Photography, Lee/1359 Chesterfield Dr, Clearwater, FL....813-586-3022
Burgess, Robert/6238 27th St N, Arlington, VA....703-533-7741
Burnette, David/1915 N Upton St, Arlington, VA....703-527-2388
Burns, Jerry/331-B Elizabeth St, Atlanta, GA (P 133)....404-522-9377
Busch, Scherley/4186 Pamona Ave, Miami, FL....305-661-6605
Byrd, Syndey/7932 S Clairborne #6, New Orleans, LA....504-865-7218

C

Calahan, Walter P/4656 S 34th St #B2, Arlington, VA (P 62,63)....703-998-8380
Calamia, Ron & Assoc/8140 Forshey St, New Orleans, LA....504-482-8062
Cameron, Larry/1314 Lincoln St #301, Columbia, SC....803-799-7558
Carlton, Chuck/120 S Brook St , Louisville, KY....502-584-7666
Carnes, John/103 White Bridge Rd, Nashville, TN....615-356-3275
Carolina Photo Grp/120 W Worthington Ave, Charlotte, NC....704-334-7874
Carpenter, Michael/7704 Carrleigh Pkwy, Springfield, VA....703-644-9666
Carriker, Ronald/565 Alpine Rd, Winston Salem, NC....919-765-3852
Caswell, Sylvia/PO Box 9890, Birmingham, AL....205-252-2252
Caudle, Rod Studio/248 Holland Rd, Powder, GA....404-424-3730
Cavedo, Brent/714 Cleveland St, Richmond, VA....804-355-2777
Cerny, Paul/5200 Wood St, Zephyr Hills, FA....813-782-4386
Cerri, Robert/1465 NE 121st St #B302, N Miami, FL....305-895-1500
Chalfant, Flip/1867 Windemere DR NE, Atlanta, GA....404-881-8510
Chamowitz, Mel/3931 N Glebe Rd, Arlington, VA....703-536-8356
Chapple, Ron/501 N College, Charlotte, NC....704-377-4217
Chernush, Kay/3855 N 30th St, Arlington, VA....703-528-1195
Chesler, Donna & Ken/6941 NW 12th St, Plantation, FL....305-581-6489
Choiniere, Gerin/1424 N Tryon St, Charlotte, NC....704-372-0220
Clark, Marty/1105 Peachtree St NE, Atlanta, GA....404-873-4618
Clark, Robert/1237-F Gadsen St, Columbia, SC....803-779-1907
Clayton, Al/141 The Prado NE, Atlanta, GA....404-577-4141
Clayton, Julie Ann/8123-B Northboro Ct, W Palm Beach, FL....407-642-4971
Cody, Dennie/5880 SW 53rd Terrace, Miami, FL....305-666-0247
Colbroth, Ron/8610 Battailles Ct, Annandale, VA....703-978-5879
Coleman, Michael J/Torpedo Factory Art Ctr/#328, Alexandria, VA....703-548-2353
Compton, Grant/7004 Sand Nettles Dr, Savannah, GA....912-897-3771
Contorakes, George/7160 SW 47th St, Miami, FL....305-661-0731
Conway, Tim/1227 Meigs St, Augusta, GA....404-733-5832
Cook, Jamie/1740 Defoor Pl, Atlanta, GA....404-351-1883
Cook, Tony/PO Box 290260, Tampa, FL....813-985-8902
Copeland, Jim/2135-F Defoor Hills Rd, Atlanta, GA....404-881-0221
Cornelia, William/PO Box 5304, Hilton Head Island, SC....803-671-2576
Cornelius, John/915 W Main St, Abington, MA....703-628-1699
Corry, Leon/4072 Park Ave, Miami, FL....305-667-7147
Cosby-Bowyer Inc/209 N Foushee St, Richmond, VA....804-643-1100
Coste, Kurt/929 Julia, New Orleans, LA....504-523-6060
Cravotta, Jeff/PO Box 9487, Charlotte, NC....704-377-4912
Crawford, Dan/RT 9/ Box 546-D, Chapel Hill, NC....919-968-4290
Crawford, Pat/918 Lady St, Columbia, SC....803-799-0894
Crewe, Coates/1331 Hagood Ave, Columbia, SC....803-771-7432
Crocker, Will/1806 Magazine St, New Orleans, LA....504-522-2651
Cromer, Peggo/1206 Andora Ave, Coral Gables, FL....305-667-3722
Crosby, David/229 Trade Ave, Hickory, NC....704-327-6575

Crum, Lee/1536 Terpsichore St, New Orleans, LA....504-529-2156
Crum, Robert/3402 El Prado, Tampa, FL....813-839-3719
Culpepper, Mike Studios Inc/PO Box 1371, Columbus, GA....404-323-5703
Cutrell, Gary/317 Draper St, Warner Robins, GA....912-929-3191

D

Dakota, Irene/2121 Lucerne Ave, Miami Beach, FL....305-674-9975
Dakota, Michael/808 NW 8th St Rd, Miami, FL....305-325-8727
Dale, John/576 Armour Circle NE, Atlanta, GA....404-872-3203
Daniel, Ralph/1305 University Dr NE, Atlanta, GA....404-872-3946
David, Alan/416 Armour Circle NE, Atlanta, GA....404-872-2142
Davidson, Cameron/5316 Admiralty Ct, Alexandria, VA....703-922-3922
Dawson, Bill/289 Monroe, Memphis, TN....901-522-9171
Deal Bowie & Assoc/809 W University, Lafayette, LA....318-234-0576
Degast, Robert/PO Box 282, Wachapreague, VA....804-787-8060
Deits, Katie/2001 Bomar Dr #4, N Palm Beach, FL (P 138)....407-775-3399
DeKalb, Jed/PO Box 22884, Nashville, TN....615-331-8527
Demolina, Raul/3903 Ponce De Leon, Coral Gables, FL....305-448-8727
Design & Visual Effects/1228 Zonolite Rd, Atlanta, GA....404-872-3283
Desrocher, Jack/Rt 3/Box 611, Eureka Springs, AR....501-253-6615
DeVault, Jim/2400 Sunset Pl, Nashville, TN....615-269-4538
Dewein, Norman/691 Ringgold Rd, Clarksville, TN....615-648-0293
Diaz, Rick/4884 SW 74th Ct, Miami, FL....305-264-9761
Dickerson, John/1895 Annwicks Dr, Marietta, GA....404-977-4138
Dickey, Bo/PO Box 20151, Atlanta, GA....404-875-0290
Dickinson, Dick/1781 Independence Blvd #1, Sarasota, FL....813-355-7688
Dietrich, David/8453 NW 70th St, Miami, FL....305-594-5902
Dixon, Tom/3404-D W Windover Ave, Greensboro, NC....919-294-6076
Dobbs, David/812 Larry Ln, Decatur, GA....404-325-2426
Doby III, Welton B/816 N St Asaph St, Alexandria, VA....703-684-3813
Dorin, Jay/10076 Bay Harbor, Harris Bay Harbor Is, FL....305-866-3888
Doty, Gary/PO Box 23697, Ft Lauderdale, FL....305-928-0645
Douglas, Keith/405 NE 8th St, Ft Lauderdale, FL....305-763-5883
Dressler, Brian/300-A Huger St, Columbia, SC....803-254-7171
Dry, Dan/897 Starks Bldg, Louisville, KY....502-581-0661
Duncan, Thom/PO Box 726, Falls Church, VA....703-532-1444
Durbak, Dave/14280 Carlson Circle, Tampa, FL....813-855-8051
Duvall, Joe/1601 Philadelphia Ave, Orlando, FL....407-671-0421
Duvall, Thurman III/1021 Northside Dr NW, Atlanta, GA....404-875-0161

E

Eastep, Wayne/4512 Ascot Circle S, Sarasota, FL....813-355-9605
Eastmond, Peter/PO Box 856 E, Barbados,W Indies,....809-429-7757
Easton, Steve/5937 Ravenswood Rd #H-19, Ft Lauderdale, FL....305-983-6611
Edwards, Jim/416 Armour Circle NE, Atlanta, GA....404-875-1005
Eighme, Bob/1520 E Sunrise Blvd, Ft Lauderdale, FL....305-527-8445
Elkins, John/Northgate Mall #223, Durham, NC....919-286-4049
Elliot, Tom/19756 Bel Aire Dr, Miami, FL....305-251-4315
Ellis, Gin/1203 Techwood Dr, Atlanta, GA....404-892-3204
Elmore, James/4807 5th St W, Bradenton, FL....813-755-0546
Ely, Scott Rex/816 N St Asaph St, Alexandria, VA....703-683-3773
Engelman, Suzanne/1621 Woodbridge Lk Cir, W Palm Beach, FL....407-969-6666
Epley, Paul/3110 Griffith St, Charlotte, NC....704-332-5466
Erickson, Jim/117 S West St, Raleigh, NC....919-833-9955
Escher, Mark/428 Armour Circle NE, Atlanta, GA (P 132)....404-874-3272
Esplinoza, Patrick/153 Patchen Dr #28, Lexington, KY....606-269-2378
Evenson, Thomas/Bruce Studio/79-25 4th St N, St Petersburg, FL....813-577-5626

F

Fedusenko, David/4200 NW 79th Ave #2A, Miami, FL....305-599-2364
Fineman, Michael/7521 SW 57th Terrace, Miami, FL....305-666-1250
Fisher, Kurt/280 Elizabeth St #A-105, Atlanta, GA....404-525-1333
Fisher, Ray/10700 SW 72nd Ct, Miami, FL....305-665-7659
Flynn, Rusty/379 W Michigan St #200, Orlando, FL....407-843-6767
Foley, Roger/325 N Manchester St, Arlington, VA....703-524-6274
Forer, Dan/1970 NE 149th St, North Miami, FL....305-949-3131
Fortenberry, Mark/128 Wonderwood Dr, Charlotte, NC....704-365-4774
Fotoworks/1419 W Waters Ave #118, Tampa, FL....813-935-5103
Fowley, Douglas/103 N Hite Ave, Louisville, KY....502-897-7222
Frasier, Richard/2857 Nutley St, Fairfax, VA (P 73)....703-385-3761
Frazier, Jeff/1025 8th Ave S, Nashville, TN....615-242-5642
Frazier, Steve/2168 Little Brook Lane, Clearwater, FL....813-736-4235
Freeman, Tina/POB 30308, New Orleans, LA....504-523-3000
Frink, Stephen/PO Box 2720, Key Largo, FL....305-451-3737
Fulton, George/1237-F Gadsden St, Columbia, SC....803-779-8249

G

G L Studios/103 W Intendencia, Pensicola, FL....904-433-2400
Gamand, Philippe/2636 Key Largo Lane, Fort Lauderdale, FL....305-583-7262
Gandy, Skip/302 East Davis Blvd, Tampa, FL....813-253-0340
Gardella Photography & Design/781 Miami Cr NE, Atlanta, GA....404-231-1316
Garner Studios/1114 W Peachtree St, Atlanta, GA....404-875-0086
Garrett, Kenneth/PO Box 208, Broad Run, VA....703-347-5848
Garrison, Gary/1052 Constance St, New Orleans, LA....504-588-9422
Gefter, Judith/1725 Clemson Rd, Jacksonville, FL....904-733-5498
Gelberg, Bob/7035-E SW 47th St, Miami, FL....305-665-3200
Gemignani, Joe/13833 NW 19th Ave, Miami, FL....305-685-7636
Geniac, Ruth/13353 Sorrento Dr, Largo, FL....813-595-2275
Genser, Howard/837 E New York Ave, Deland, FL....904-734-9688
Gentile, Arthur Sr/7335 Connan Lane, Charlotte, NC....704-846-3793
Gerlich, Fred S/1220 Spring St NW, Atlanta, GA (P 139)....404-872-3487
Gillian, John/14378 SW 97th Lane, Miami, Fl....305-251-4784
Glaser, Ken & Assoc/923-D Metairie Rd, New Orleans, LA....504-895-7170
Gleasner, Bill/132 Holly Ct, Denver, NC....704-483-9301
Glover, Robert/709 Second Ave, Nashville, TN....612-726-0790
Golden, Jon/PO Box 2826, Charlottesville, VA....804-971-8100
Gomez, Rick/2545 Tigertail Ave, Miami, FL....305-856-8338
Gooch, Mark/PO Box 55744, Birmingham, AL....205-328-2868
Good, Jay/20901 NE 26th Ave, N Miami Beach, FL....305-935-4884
Gordon, Lee/1936 Church St, West Palm Beach, FL....407-686-6360
Gornto, Bill/590 Ponce De Leon Ave, Atlanta, GA....404-876-1331
Grace, Arthur/4044 N Vacation Ln, Arlington, VA....703-524-3097
Graham, Curtis/648 First Ave S, St Petersburg, FL....813-821-0444
Graham, Michael/771 NW 122nd St, North Miami, FL....305-687-5446
Granberry Studios/578 Montgomery Ferry Dr, Atlanta, GA....404-874-2426
Grant, Peter/3414 Wilson Blvd, Arlington, VA....703-525-0389
Greenberg, Bob/15505 Bull Run Rd #253, Miami Lakes, FL (P 140)....305-433-8888
Greentree, Neil/3431 Carlin Springs Rd, Falls Church, VA....703-379-1121
Griffiths, Simon/2003 Fairview Rd, Raleigh, NC....919-829-9109
Grigg, Roger Allen/PO Box 52851, Atlanta, GA....404-876-4748
Groendyke, Bill/6344 NW 201st Ln, Miami, FL....305-625-8293
Grove, Bob/210 N Lee St #208 2nd Fl Rear, Alexandria, VA....703-548-3972
Gual, Tomas/1916 Loiza St 2nd Fl, Santurce, PR....809-728-6532
Guggenheim, David/167 Mangum St, Atlanta, GA....404-577-4676
Guider, John/517 Fairground Ct, Nashville, TN....615-255-4495
Guillermety, Edna/3133 Lakestone Dr, Tampa, FL....813-962-1748
Gupton, Charles/5720-J North Blvd, Raleigh, NC....919-850-9441
Guravich, Dan/PO Box 891, Greenville, MS....601-335-2444

H

Hackney, Kerry/8171 NW 67th St, Miami, FL....305-592-3664
Haggerty, Richard/656 Ward St, High Point, NC....919-889-7744
Hall, Don/2922 Hyde Park st, Sarasota, FL....813-365-6161
Hall, Ed/7010 Citrus Point, Winter Park, FL....407-657-8182
Hall, Keith/4607 N Lois Ave #C, Tampa, FL....813-875-6629
Hallinan, Dennis/P O Box 1783, Winter Haven, FL....813-293-7942
Hamel, MIke/7110 SW 63rd Ave, Miami, FL....305-665-8583
Hamilton, Tom/2362 Strathmore Dr, Atlanta, GA....404-266-0177
Hannau, Michael/3800 NW 32nd Ave, Miami, FL....305-633-1100
Hansen, Eric/3005 7th Ave S/Box 55492, Birmingham, AL....205-251-5587
Harbison, Steve/1516 Crestwood Dr, Greeneville, TN....615-638-2535
Hardy, Frank/1003 N 12th Ave, Pensacola, FL....904-438-2712
Harkins, Lynn S/1900 Byrd Ave #101, Richmond, VA....804-285-2900
Harkness, Chris/1412 Fairway Dr, Tallahassee, FL....904-224-9805
Harrison, Michael/1124-A S Mint St, Charlotte, NC....704-334-8008
Hathcox, David/5730 Arlington Blvd, Arlington, VA....703-845-5831
Haviland, Patrick/413 W 10th St #4C, Charlotte, NC....704-376-7574
Hayden, Kenneth/1318 Morton Ave, Louisville, KY....502-583-5596
Heger, Jeff/2406 Nemeth Ct, Alexandria, VA....703-765-1552
Heinen, Ken/4001 Lorcom Lane, Arlington, VA....703-528-0186
Heller, David/202 West Jean St, Tampa, FL....813-251-7326
Henderson, Collins & Muir Photo/6005 Chapel Hill Rd, Raleigh, NC....919-851-0458
Henderson, Eric/1200 Foster St NW, Atlanta, GA....404-352-3615
Hendley, Arington/454 Irwin St NE, Atlanta, GA....404-577-2300
Henley, John/1910 E Franklin St, Richmond, VA....804-649-1400
Henry, Benton/Rt 1/ Box 6C, Latta, SC....803-752-2097
Heston, Ty/4505 131st Ave N #18, Clearwater, FL....813-573-4878

Heyl, Steven/P O Box 150, Leesburg, VA................................703-771-9355
Higgins, Neal/2300 Peachtree Rd NW, Atlanta, GA....................404-355-3240
Hill, Dan/9132 O'Shea Ln, W Springfield, VA.............................703-451-4705
Hill, Jackson/2032 Adams St, New Orleans, LA..........................504-861-3000
Hill, Tom/207 E Parkwood Rd, Decatur, GA................................404-377-3833
Hillyer, Jonathan/450-A Bishop St, Atlanta, GA..........................404-351-0477
Hoflich, Richard/544 N Angier Ave NE, Atlanta, GA.....................404-584-9159
Hogben, Steve/3180 Oakcliff Indus St, Atlanta, GA......................404-266-2894
Holland, Ralph/3706 Alliance Dr, Greensboro, NC.......................919-855-6422
Holland, Robert/14602 SW 82nd Ct, Miami, FL............................305-255-6758
Hood, Robin/1101 W Main St, Franklin, TN..................................615-794-2041
Hope, Christina/2720 3rd St S, S Jacksonville Bch, FL................904-246-9689
Horan, Eric/PO Box 6373, Hilton Head Island, SC.......................803-842-3233
Hosack, Loren/509 Inlet Rd, North Palm Bch, FL.........................407-848-0091
Humphries, Gordon & Vi/Boozer Shopping Ctr, Columbia, SC....803-772-3535
Hunter, Bud/1911 27th Ave S, Birmingham, AL...........................205-879-3153
Hunter, Fil/2402 Mt Vernon Ave, Alexandria, VA.........................703-836-2910

IJ

Isaacs, Lee/629 22nd Ave S, Birmingham, AL.............................205-591-1191
Isgett, Neil/4303-D South Blvd, Charlotte, NC............................704-376-7172
Jackson Photographics, R/520 N Willow Ave, Tampa, FL.............813-254-6806
Jacques, Ronny/2055 Sun Home St, Sarasota, FL.......................813-923-5208
Jamison, Chipp/2131 Liddell Dr NE, Atlanta, GA
(P 141)..404-873-3636
Jann, Gail/US 19/Box 41, Byson City, NC.....................................704-488-8576
Jarrett Photo/1210 Spring St NW, Atlanta, GA.............................404-892-6547
Jautz, Ron/PO Box 566, Alexandria, VA.......................................703-548-5578
Jeffcoat, Russell/1201 Hagood Ave, Columbia, SC......................803-799-8578
Jeffcoat, Wilber L/1864 Palomino Cir, Sumter, SC......................803-773-3690
Jimison, Tom/5929 Annunciation, New Orleans, LA.....................504-891-8587
Johns, Douglas/2535 25th Ave N, St Petersburg, FL...................813-321-7235
Johnson, Dennis/10909 Santa Clara Dr, Fairfax, VA....................703-385-7032
Johnson, Everette/5024 Williamsburg Blvd, Arlington, VA...........703-536-8483
Johnson, George L Photo Inc/16603 Round Oak Dr, Tampa, FL....813-963-3222
Johnson, Silvia/6110 Brook Dr, Falls Church, VA.........................703-532-8653
Jones, David/319-F South Westgate Dr, Greensboro, NC.............919-294-9060
Jones, Samuel A/131 Pineview Rd, West Columbia, SC...............803-791-4896
Jureit, Robert A/916 Aguero Ave, Coral Gables, FL.....................305-667-1346
Jurgens, Daniel/202 S 22nd St, Tampa, FL..................................813-248-3636

K

Kaplan, Al/PO Box 611373, North Miami, FL................................305-891-7595
Kaplan, Martin & Laura/PO Box 7206, McLean, VA......................703-893-1660
Kappiris, Stan/PO Box 14331, Tampa, FL.....................................813-289-4651
Katz, Arni/PO Box 724507, Atlanta, GA.......................................404-953-1168
Kaufman, Len/740 Tyler St, Hollywood, FL...................................305-920-7822
Kearney, Mitchell/301 E 7th St, Charlotte, NC.............................704-377-7662
Kennedy, Chuck Group /2745-B Hidden Lake Blvd,
Sarasota, FL (P 142).......................................813-951-0393
Kennedy, M Lewis/2700 7th Ave S, Birmingham, AL...................205-252-2700
Kenner, Jack/PO Box 3269, Memphis, TN...................................901-527-3686
Kent, David/7515 SW 153rd Ct #201, Miami, FL..........................305-382-1587
Kern Photography/1243 N 17th Ave, Lake Worth, FL...................407-582-2487
Ketchum, Larry/530 Pylon Dr, Raleigh, NC..................................919-856-1860
King, J Brian/1267 Coral Way, Miami, FL.....................................305-856-6534
King, Tom/7401 Chancery Lane, Orlando, FL...............................407-856-0618
Kinney, Greg/238 Burlington Pl, Nashville, TN.............................615-297-8084
Kinsella, Barry/1010 Andrews Rd, West Palm Beach, FL............407-832-8736
Kirby, Jim/2057Swans Neck Way, Reston, VA.............................703-476-9828
Klemens, Susan/5803 Queens Gate Ct, Alexandria, VA..............703-960-5085
Kling, David Photography/502 Armour Circle, Atlanta, GA...........404-881-1215
Knapp, Bevil/118 Beverly Dr, Metairie, LA...................................504-831-1496
Knibbs, Tom/5907 NE 27th Ave, Ft Lauderdale, FL.....................305-491-6263
Knight, Steve/1212 E 10th St, Charlotte, NC...............................704-334-5115
Kogler, Earl/PO Box 3578, Longwood, FL....................................407-331-4035
Kohanim, Parish/1130 W Peachtree NW, Atlanta, GA.................404-892-0099
Kollar, Robert E/1431 Cherokee Trail #52, Knoxville, TN............615-573-8191
Koplitz, William/729 N Lime Ave, Sarasota, FL............................813-366-5905
KPC Photo/PO Box 32188, Charlotte, NC (P 143)..........704-358-5855
Krafft, Louise/1008 Valley Dr, Alexandria, VA..............................703-998-8648
Kreider, R C/13105 Pennerview Ln, Fairfax, VA...........................703-631-7257

L

LaCoe, Norm/PO Box 855, Gainesville, FL..................................904-466-0226

Lafayette, James/181 Club Course Dr/Sea Pines, Hilton Head, SC......803-785-3201
Lai, Bill/PO Box 13644, Atlanta, GA...404-982-9008
Lair, John/1122 Roger St, Louisville, KY.......................................502-589-7779
Lane, M/2200 Sunderland Rd #133K, Winston-Salem, NC..........919-768-0803
Langone, Peter/516 NE 13th St, Ft Lauderdale, FL.....................305-467-0654
Lanpher, Keith/865 Monticello Ave, Norfolk, VA...........................804-627-3051
Larimer, Richard/209 N Foushee, Richmond, VA.........................804-643-1100
Larkin, Paul/710 Tenth St, Atlanta, GA..404-432-6309
Lathem & Associates Photo/559 Dutch Valley Rd NE, Atlanta, GA......404-873-5858
Latil, Michael/816 N St Asaph St, Alexandria, VA.......................703-548-7645
Lauzon, Denis/5170 NE 12th Ave, Ft Lauderdale, FL..................305-771-0077
Lavenstein, Lance/348 Southport Cir #103, Virginia Beach, VA....804-499-9959
Lawrence, David/PO Box 835, Largo, FL......................................813-586-2112
Lawrence, John R/Box 330570, Coconut Grove, FL.....................305-447-8621
Lawrence, Mark M/PO Box 23950, Ft Lauderdale, FL..................305-565-8866
Lawson, Slick/3801 Whitland Ave, Nashville, TN.........................615-383-0147
Lazzo, Dino/PO Box 452606, Miami, FL......................................305-856-1148
Lee, Chung P/7820 Antiopi St, Annandale, VA............................703-560-3394
Lee, George/423 S Main St, Greenville, SC.................................803-232-4119
Leggett, Albert/1415 Story Ave, Louisville, KY............................502-584-0255
Leo, Victor/121 W Main St, Louisville, KY....................................502-589-2423
Lesser, Eric/616-C W Hill Ave , Knoxville, TN.............................615-524-7457
Lex, Debra/132 NW 98th Terrace, Plantation, FL.........................305-285-0999
Lightbenders/11450 SW 57th St, Miami, FL................................305-595-6174
Lightscapes Photo/7655 Fullerton Rd, Springfield, VA.................703-455-7343
Lipson, Stephen/15455 SW Terrace, Miami, FL..........................305-662-8656
Little, Chris/PO Box 467221, Atlanta, GA....................................404-641-9688
Long, Lewis/3130 SW 25th St, Miami, FL....................................305-448-7667
Loumakis, Constantinos/826 SW 13th St, Ft Lauderdale, FL.......305-525-7367
Lowery, Ron/409 Spears Ave, Chattanooga, TN..........................615-265-4311
Lubin, Jeff/6641 Backlick Rd, Springfield, VA..............................703-569-5086
Lucas, Steve/16100 SW 100th Ct, Miami, FL..............................305-238-6024
Luege, Alexander/5290 SW 5th St, Miami, FL.............................305-445-5795
Luttrell, David/5117 Kesterwood Dr, Knoxville,
TN (P 144)...615-688-1430
Luzier, Winston/1122 Pomelo Ave, Sarasota, FL.........................813-952-1077
Lynch, Warren/1324 E Washington St, Louisville, KY...................502-587-7722

M

Macuch, Rodger/1133 Spring St, Atlanta, GA..............................404-876-7002
Magee, Ken/7928 Ferara Dr, New Orleans, LA............................504-889-3928
Malles, Ed/1013 S Semoran Blvd, Winter Park, FL......................407-679-4155
Malyana/Box 530606, Miami, FL...305-866-5343
Mann, James/1007-B Norwalk, Greensboro, NC.........................919-288-2508
Mann, Rod/5082 Woodleigh Rd, Knotts Island, NC......................919-429-3009
Maratea, Ronn/4338 Virginia Beach Blvd, Virginia Beach, VA.....804-340-6464
Marciak, Alex/4938-D Eisenhower Ave, Alexandria, VA..............703-461-0047
Marcus, Joel/2250 ULmerton Rd East #15, Clearwater, FL........813-573-0575
Markatos, Jerry/Rt 2 Box 419/Rock Rest Rd, Pittsboro, NC........919-542-2139
Marquet, Carolou/4628 N 21st St, Arlington, VA..........................703-243-5354
Marquez, Toby/1709 Wainwright Dr, Reston, VA..........................703-471-4666
Martin, Fred/110 Country View Dr, Simpsonville, SC...................803-297-0010
Martineau, Gerald/300 S Harrison St, Arlington, VA....................703-931-8561
Mason, Chuck/8755 SW 96th St, Miami, FL................................305-270-2070
Masson, Lisa/3122 S Abingdon St, Arlington, VA.........................703-379-1401
May, Clyde/1037 Monroe Dr NE, Atlanta, GA..............................404-873-4329
Mayor, Randy/2007 Fifteenth Ave S, Birmingham, AL.................205-933-2818
Mazey, Jon/2724 NW 30th Ave, Ft Lauderdale, FL......................305-731-3300
McBride, Tal/3510 Lorcom Ln, Arlington, VA................................703-525-8331
McCannon, Tricia/416 Armour Cir NE, Atlanta, GA......................404-873-3070
McCarthy, Tom/8960 SW 114th St, Miami, FL.............................305-233-1703
McClure, Dan/320 N Milledge, Athens, GA..................................404-354-1234
McCord, Fred/2720 Piedmont Rd NE, Atlanta, GA.......................404-262-1538
McElhinney, Susan/3526 N Third St, Arlington, VA......................703-527-8293
McGee, E Alan/1816-E Briarwd Ind Ct, Atlanta, GA.....................404-633-1286
McGowan, Pat/14035 NW 1st Ave, Miami, FL.............................305-685-2095
McGurkin, Douglas/5600 Glenridge Dr #B-55, Atlanta, GA.........404-252-7108
McIntyre, William/3746 Yadkinville Rd, Winston-Salem, NC........919-922-3142
McKenzie & Dickerson/133 W Vermont Ave/Box 152, Sthrn Pines, NC...919-692-6131
McLaren, Lynn/PO Box 2086, Beaufort, SC.................................803-524-0973
McLaughlin, Ken/623 7th Ave S, Nashville, TN............................615-256-8162
McNabb, Tommy/4015 Brownsboro Rd, Winston-Salem, NC........919-625-3014
McNamee, Win/467 N Thomas St, Arlington, VA..........................703-553-6027
McNeely, Burton/PO Box 338, Land O'Lakes, FL........................813-996-3025
McQuerter, James/4518 S Cortez, Tampa, FL.............................813-839-8335
McVicker, Sam/PO Box 880, Dunedin, FL....................................813-734-9660
Meacham, Ralph/Rt 6 Garrison Rd, Franklin, TN.........................615-794-1988

Meredith, David/2900 NE 30th St #2H, Ft Lauderdale, FL 305-564-4579
Michaels, Gary/4190 Braganza Rd, Coconut Grove, FL 305-661-6202
Mikeo, Rich/2189 N Powerline Rd, Pompano Beach, FL 305-960-0485
Miller, Brad/3645 Stewart, Coconut Grove, FL 305-666-1617
Miller, Bruce/9401 61st Court SW, Miami, FL 305-666-4333
Miller, Randy/6666 SW 96th St, Miami, FL 305-667-5765
Milligan, Mark/8022 Stillbrook Rd, Manassas, VA 703-791-2175
Millington, Rod/PO Box 49286, Sarasota, FL 813-388-1420
Mills, Henry/5514 Starkwood Dr, Charlotte, NC 704-535-1861
Mims, Allen/107 Madison Ave, Memphis, TN 901-527-4040
Minardi, Mike/PO Box 14247, Tampa, FL 813-251-1696
Mitchell, Deborah Gray/7000 NE 4th Ct, Miami, FL
(P 145)...**305-757-4233**
Molina, Jose/3250 SW 24th St, Miami, FL 305-443-1617
Molony, Bernard/PO Box 15081, Atlanta, GA 404-457-6934
Montage Studio/422 E Howard Ave, Decatur, GA 404-377-7715
Moore, George Photography/1301 Admiral St, Richmond, VA 804-355-1862
Moore, Leslie/8551 NW 47th Ct, Fort Lauderdale, FL 305-742-4074
Moore, Mark/3803 W Gray, Tampa, FL 813-874-0410
Moore, Rick/955 Church St, Mobile, AL 205-432-8689
Moreland, Mike/PO Box 250388, Atlanta, GA 404-993-6059
Morgan, Frank/400 35th St, Virginia Beach, VA 804-422-9328
Morgan, Red/13885 Columbine Ave, W Palm Beach, FL 407-793-6085
Morris, Paul /PO Box 530894, Miami Shores, FL 305-757-6700
Mouton, Girard M III/3535 Buchanan St, New Orleans, LA 504-288-4338
Muldez, Richard/122 Executive Blvd #105, Chesapeake, VA 804-490-6640
Murphy, Lionel Jr/4317 Iola Dr, Sarasota, FL 813-925-1212
Murphy, Michael/3200 S Westshore Blvd, Tampa, FL 813-831-1210
Murray, Steve/1520 Brookside Dr #3, Raleigh, NC 919-828-0653
Myers, Fred/114 Regent Ln, Florence, AL 205-766-4802
Myhre, Gordon/PO Box 1226, Ind Rocks Beach, FL 813-238-0360

N

Narod, Bob/12213 Sugar Creek Ct, Hendron, VA 703-444-1964
Nemeth, Judy/930 N Poplar St, Charlotte, NC 704-375-9292
Neubauer, John/1525 S Arlington Ridge Rd, Arlington, VA 703-920-5994
Nicolay, David/4756 W Napolean #3, Metarie, LA 504-888-7510
Nilsen, Audrey/630 Fog St, Nashville, TN 312-561-8044
Noa, Orlando/885 W 32nd St, Hialeah, FL 305-822-3320
Nodine, Dennis/PO Box 30353, Charlotte, NC 704-373-3374
Noel, Rip/707 Maryville Pke, Knoxville, TN 615-573-6635
Norling Studios Inc/221 Swathmore Ave/Box 7167, High Point, NC......919-434-3151
Norris, Robert Photo/224 Lorna Square, Birmingham, AL 205-979-7005
Norton, Mike/4917 W Nassau, Tampa, FL 813-876-3390
Novak, Jack/3701 S George Mason Dr/C-2 No, Falls Church, VA.........703-931-8600
Novak, Lou/PO Box 561652, Miami, FL 305-253-0942
Novicki, Norb/6800 North West 2nd St, Margate, FL 305-971-8954

O

O'Connor, Michael/9041 Froude, Surfside, FL 305-861-3746
O'Kain, Dennis/102 W Main, Lexington, GA 404-743-3140
O'Sullivan, Brian/1401 SE 8th St, Deerfield Beach, FL 305-429-0712
Oesch, James/3706 Ridge Rd, Annadale, VA 703-941-3600
Olive, Tim/754 Piedmont Ave NE, Atlanta, GA 404-872-0500
Olivier, Rick/225 N Peters St #3, New Orleans, LA 504-522-7646
Olsen, Larry/4544 Eisenhowr Ave, Alexandria, VA 703-751-8051
Olson, Carl/3325 Laura Way, Winston, GA 404-949-1532
Oquendo, William/4680 SW 27th Ave, Ft Lauderdale, FL 305-981-2823
Osborne, Mitchel L/920 Frenchman St, New Orleans, LA 504-949-1366
Ottman, Matthew/4410 Providence Ln #8, Winston-Salem, NC 919-998-0408

P

Paganelli, Manuello/6003-E Curtier Dr, Alexandria, VA 703-719-9567
Parker, Phillip M/385 S Main St, Memphis, TN 901-529-9200
Parrish, David/PO Box 208, Springfield, TN 615-384-2664
Parsley, Keith/801-K Atando Ave, Charlotte, NC 704-331-0812
Patterson, Pat/233 Rose Haven Dr, Raleigh, NC 919-787-4260
Payne, Steve/1524 Virginia St E, Charleston, WV 304-343-7254
Pearce, Frank/215-A Pine Knoll Dr, Greenville, SC 803-292-9016
Peeler, Alan/2175 Madison Ave, Memphis, TN 901-272-1769
Pelosi & Chambers/684 Greenwood Ave NE, Atlanta, GA 404-872-8117
Peters, J Dirk/PO Box 15492, Tampa, FL 813-888-8444
Petrey, John/670 Clay St/Box 2401, Winter Park, FL 407-645-1718
Phillips, David/20 Topsail Tr, New Port Richey, FL 813-849-9458
Photo-Synthesis/1239 Kensington Rd, McLean, VA............................703-734-8770

Photographic Group/7407 Chancery Ln, Orlando, FL 407-855-4306
Photographic Ideas/701 E Bay St/Box 1216, Charleston, SC...............803-577-7020
Photography Unlimited/3662 S West Shore Blvd, Tampa, FL 813-839-7710
Picture Credits/2820 Dorr Ave #210, Fairfax, VA 703-876-9588
Pierson, Art/1107 Lincoln Ave, Falls Church, VA 703-237-5937
Pinckney, Jim/PO Box 22887, Lake Buena Vista, FL 407-239-8855
Pinnacle Studios/2420 Schirra Pl, Highpoint, NC 919-886-6565
Pishnery, Judy/405 Cherokee Pl, Atlanta, GA...................................404-525-4829
Pittenger, Kerry/100 Northeast 104th St, Miami Shores, FL 305-756-8830
Plachta, Greg/721 N Mangum, Durham, NC 919-682-6873
Pocklington, Mike/9 W Main St, Richmond, VA 804-783-2731
Ponzoni, Bob/703 Westchester Dr, High Point, NC 919-885-8733
Posey, Mike/3524 Canal St, New Orleans, LA 504-488-8000
Poucel, Guilermo/4500 S Four Mile Run Dr #610, Arlington, VA 703-820-1370
Premier Photo Group/8171 NW 67th St, Miami, FL 305-592-3664
Prism Studios/1027 Elm Hill Pike, Nashville, TN 615-255-1919
Profancik, Larry/2101 Production, Louisville, KY 502-499-9220
Pruett, Charlie/12213 Sugar Creek Court, Herndon, VA 707-444-1964
Pryor, Maresa/1122 Pamelo Ave, Sarasota, FL 813-952-1077
Purin, Thomas/14190 Harbor Lane, Lake Park, FL 407-622-4131
Putnam, Don/623 7th Ave So, Nashville, TN 615-242-7325

R

Ramos, Victor/8390 SW 132 St, Miami, FL 305-255-3111
Randolph, Bruce/132 Alan Dr, Newport News, VA 804-877-0992
Rank, Don/2265 Lawson Way, Atlanta, GA 404-452-1658
Ratcliffe, Rodney/206 Rogers St NE #11, Atlanta, GA 404-373-2767
Rathe, Robert A/8451-A Hilltop Rd, Fairfax, VA 703-560-7222
Raymond, Tom/3211-A Hanover Dr, Johnson City, TN 615-928-2700
Redel, Tim/5055 Seminary Rd #723, Alexandria, VA 703-931-7527
Regan, Mark/10904 Barton Hill Court, Reston, VA 703-620-5888
Richards, Courtland William/PO Box 59734, Birmingham, AL...............205-871-8923
Richardson, Lynda/POB 8296, Richmond, VA (P 107).....**804-272-0965**
Richardson/Wright/POB 8296, Richmond, VA (P 107).....**804-272-0965**
Rickles, Tom/5401 Alton Rd, Miami, FL 305-866-5762
Riggall, Michael/403 8th St NE, Atlanta, GA.....................................404-872-8242
Riley, Richard/34 N Ft Harrison, Clearwater, FL 813-446-2626
Rippey, Rhea/PO Box 50093, Nashville, TN (P 146)......**615-646-1291**
Rob/Harris Productions/PO Box 15721, Tampa, FL 813-258-4061
Rodgers, Ted/544 Plasters Ave, Atlanta, GA 404-892-0967
Rodriguez, Richard/2728 N Washington Blvd, Arlington, VA................703-820-8452
Rogers, Brian/689 Antone St NW, Atlanta, GA 404-355-8069
Rogers, Chuck/2480 Briarcliff Rd #306/4, Atlanta, GA 404-633-0105
Rogers, Tommy/3694 Niagara Dr, Lexington, KY 606-271-5091
Rosen, Olive/3415 Arnold Ln, Falls Church, VA 703-560-5557
Royals, Ron/2295 Pine Burr Dr, Kernersville, NC 919-869-3878
Rubio, Manny/1203 Techwood Dr, Atlanta, GA 404-892-0783
Runion, Britt/7409 Chancery Ln, Orlando, FL 407-857-0491
Russell, John Photo/PO Box 2141, High Point, NC 919-887-1163
Rutherford, Michael W/623 Sixth Ave S, Nashville, TN 615-242-5953

S

Salerno, Lawrence/4201 W Cypress, Tampa, FL 813-876-7580
Salmon, George/10325 Del Mar Circle, Tampa, FL.............................813-961-8687
Salter, Jeff/4215 Bethel Church Rd #B12, Columbia, SC 803-787-8620
Sanacore, Steve/87 Westbury Close, West Palm Beach, FL 407-795-1510
Sanchez, Robert/10089 SW 26th St, Miami, FL 305-687-8008
Sandlin, Mark/45 Little Rd, Sharpsburg, GA 404-251-5207
Sansone, Carla A/5401 Robline Dr, Metairie, LA 504-588-5339
Santos, Roberto/15929 NW 49th Ave, Hialeah, FL 305-621-6047
Savage, Chuck/113 S Jefferson St, Richmond, VA 804-780-0304
Saylor, Ted/2312 Farwell Dr, Tampa, FL 813-879-5636
Schaedler, Tim/PO Box 1081, Safety Harbor, FL 813-796-0366
Schatz, Bob/112 Second Ave N, Nashville, TN (P 147) ..**615-254-7197**
Schenck, Gordon H/PO Box 35203, Charlotte, NC.............................704-332-4078
Schenker, Richard/7401 Clearview, Tampa, FL 813-885-5413
Schermerhorn, Tim/3408 Langdale Dr, High Point, NC 919-887-6644
Schettino, Carmen/5638 Country Lakes Dr,
Sarasota, FL (P 148)...**813-351-4465**
Schiavone, George/7340 SW 48th St #102, Miami, FL 305-662-6057
Schiff, Ken/4884 SW 74th Ct, Miami, FL 305-667-8685
Schneider, John/4203 Hewitt St #14G, Greensboro, NC 919-855-0261
Schulke, Debra/6770 SW 101st St, Miami, FL 305-667-0961
Schulke, Flip/14730 SW 158th St, Miami, FL 305-251-7717
Schumacher, Karl/6254 Park Rd, McLean, VA 703-241-7424
Scott, Bill/PO Box 6281, Charlotte, NC 704-534-0421

Scott, James/210 N Fillmore St, Arlington, VA 703-522-8261
Seifried, Charles/Rt 3 Box 162, Decatur, AL 205-355-5558
Seitz, Arthur/1905 N Atlantic Blvd, Ft Lauderdale, FL 305-563-0060
Sharpe, David/816 N St Asaph St, Alexandria, VA 703-683-3773
Shea, David/217 Florida Blanca Pl, Ft Walton Beach, FL 904-244-0666
Sheffield, Scott/1126 North Blvd, Richmond, VA 804-358-3266
Sheldon, Mike/RR 3/Box 365, Waynesville, NC 704-648-0508
Sherman, Ron/PO Box 28656, Atlanta, GA (P 149) 404-993-7197
Shoffner, Charles/PO Box 3232, Charlottesville, VA 804-978-1277
Shone, Phil/544 Plasters Ave, Atlanta, GA 404-487-5766
Shrout, Bill/Route 1 Box 317, Theodore, AL 205-973-1379
Silla, Jon/400 S Graham St, Charlotte, NC 704-377-8694
Silver Image Photo/5128 NW 58th Ct, Gainesville, FL 904-373-5771
Sink, Richard/1225 Cedar Dr, Winston Salem, NC 919-784-8759
Sisson, Barry/6813 Bland St, Springfield, VA 703-569-6051
Smart, David/PO Box 11743, Memphis, TN 901-685-1431
Smeltzer, Robert/29 Stone Plaza Dr, Greenville, SC 803-235-2186
Smith, Clark/618 Glenwood Pl, Dalton, GA 404-226-2508
Smith, Deborah/1007-13 Norwalk St, Greensboro, NC 919-292-1190
Smith, Ramsey/720-C Hembree Pl, Roswell, GA 404-664-4402
Smith, Randy/4450 S Tiffany Dr, West Palm Beach, FL 407-697-9122
Smith, Richard & Assoc/1007 Norwalk St #B, Greensboro, NC 919-292-1190
Smith, Richard Photo/1625 NE 3rd Ct, Ft Lauderdale, FL 305-523-8861
Snow, Chuck/2700 7th Ave S, Birmingham, AL 205-251-7482
Southern Exposures/4300 NE 5th Terrace, Oakland Park, Fl 305-565-4415
Sparkman, Clif/161 Mangum St SW #301, Atlanta, GA 404-588-9687
Sparks, Don/770 Claughton Isl Dr #1112, Miami, FL 904-261-0365
Speidell, Bill/1030 McConville Rd, Lynchburg, VA 804-237-6426
Spelios, James S/1735 Brantley Rd #507, Ft Myers, FL 813-939-3304
Spence, Christopher/3368 NW 64th St, Ft Lauderdale, FL 305-979-8295
St John, Chuck/2724 NW 30th Ave, Ft Lauderdale, FL 305-731-3300
St John, Michael/PO Box 1202, Oldsmar, FL 813-872-0007
Stansfield, Ross/4938-D Eisenhower Ave, Alexandria, VA 703-370-5142
Staples, Neil/5092 NE 12th Ave, Ft Lauderdale, FL 305-680-9043
Starling, Robert/PO Box 25827, Charlotte, NC 704-568-7611
Starr, Steve/2425 Inagua Ave, Cocanut Grove, FL 305-856-5801
Staub, Pat/529 N College St, Charlotte, NC 704-377-2153
Steckbeck, Mark/47 Bentley Dr, Sterling, VA 703-430-4757
Stein, Art/2419 Mt Vernon Ave, Alexandria, VA 703-684-0675
Stein, Leslie/9931 NW 11th St, Plantation, FL 305-424-1656
Stern, John/1240 Center Pl, Sarasota, FL 813-388-3244
Stevenson, Aaron/707 Jackson Ave, Charlotte, NC 704-332-3147
Stewart, Harvey & Co Inc/836 Dorse Rd, Lewisville, NC 919-945-2101
Stickney, Christopher/321 10th Ave N, St Petersburg, FL 813-821-3635
Stoppee Photographics Group/13 W Main St, Richmond, VA 804-644-0266
Stover, David/3132 Ellwood Ave , Richmond, VA 804-355-0565
Stratton, Jimi/670 11th St NW, Atlanta, GA 404-876-1876
Strode, William A/1008 Kent Rd, Goshin, KY 502-228-4446
Sumner, Bill/3400 Pan Am Dr, Coconut Grove, FL 303-856-5958
Suraci, Carl/216 Hillsdale Dr, Sterling, VA 703-620-6645
Swann, David/PO Box 7313, Atlanta, GA 404-873-3003
Sweetman, Gary Photo/2904 Manatee Ave W, Bradenton, FL 813-748-4004

TUV

Taft, Jerry/8880 Old King's Rd S #24E, Jacksonville, FL 904-731-5887
Taylor, John Michael/2214-B E 7th St, Charlotte, NC 704-347-8822
Taylor, Randy/555 NE 34th St #701, Miami, FL 305-573-5200
Telesca, Chris/PO Box 51449, Raleigh, NC 919-846-0101
Tenney, Michael/PO Box 37287, Charlotte, NC 704-372-7700
Terranova, Michael/1135 Cadiz St, New Orleans, LA 504-899-7328
Tesh, John/904-A Norwalk St, Greenboro, NC 919-299-1400
Tetro, Jim/1921 Woodford Rd, Vienna, VA 703-847-9650
Thiel, Erhard/7637 Webbwood Ct, Springfield, VA 703-569-7579
Thomas, J Clark/235 Lauderdale Rd, Nashville, TN 615-269-7700
Thomas, Jay/2955 Cobb Pkwy #195, Atlanta, GA 404-432-1735
Thomas, Larry/1212 Spring St, Atlanta, GA 404-881-8850
Thomas, Norm/ PO Box 468, Mayo, FL 904-294-2911
Thompson & Thompson/5180 NE 12th Ave, Ft Lauderdale, FL 305-772-4411
Thompson, Darrell/124 Rhodes Dr, Marietta, GA 404-641-2020
Thompson, Ed C/2381 Drew Valley Rd, Atlanta, GA 404-636-7258
Thompson, Michael Photography/PO Box 110, Talking Rock, GA 404-692-5876
Thompson, Rose/4338 NE 11th Ave, Oakland Park, FL 305-563-7937
Thompson, Thomas L/731-B Highland Ave, Atlanta, GA 404-892-3499
Thomson, John Christian/3820 Hardy St, Hattiesburg, MS 601-264-2878
Tilley, Arthur/290 Heaton Park Dr, Decatur, GA 404-371-8086
Tobias, Jerry/2117 Opa-Locka Blvd, Miami, FL 305-685-3003
Toth, Craig/1420 E River Dr, Margate, FL 305-974-0946
Townsend, Jill Perry/9745 Vale Rd, Vienna, VA 202-429-5609
Traves, Stephen/360 Elden Dr, Atlanta, GA 404-255-5711
Tropix /PO Box 6398, West Palm Beach, FL 407-790-2790
Trufant/Dobbs/1902 Highland Rd, Baton Rouge, LA 504-344-9690
Truman, Gary/PO Box 7144, Charleston, WV 304-755-3078
Tucker, Mark/114 Third Ave North, Nashville, TN 615-254-6802
Turnau, Jeffrey/4950 SW 72nd Ave #114, Miami, FL 305-666-5454
Tuttle, Steve/12 Fort Williams Pkwy, Alexandria, VA 703-751-3452
Uzzell, Steve/1419 Trap Rd, Vienna, VA 703-938-6868
Uzzle, Warren/5201 William & Mary Dr, Raleigh, NC 919-266-6203
Valada, M C/2192 Oakdale Rd, Cleveland, OH 216-397-9308
Van Camp, Louis/713 San Juan Rd, New Bern, NC 919-633-6081
Van de Zande, Doug/307 W Martin St, Raleigh, NC 919-832-2499
Vance, David/150 NW 164th St, Miami, FL 305-354-2083
Vaughn, Marc/11140 Griffing Blvd, Biscayne Park, FL 305-895-5790
Verlent, Christian/PO Box 530805, Miami, FL 305-751-3385
Victor, Ira/2026 Prairie Ave, Miami Beach, FL 305-532-4444
Viola, Franklin/9740 Coleman Rd, Roswell, GA 404-594-1086
Visual Art Studios/3820 Hardy St, Hattiesburg, MS 601-264-2878
Vogtner, Robert A/PO Box 9163, Mobile, AL 205-694-8725
Vullo, Phillip Photography/565 Dutch Valley Rd NE, Atlanta, GA 404-874-0822

WYZ

Wagoner, Mark/12-H Wendy Ct Box 18974, Greensboro, NC 919-854-0406
Walker, Reuel Jr/PO Box 5421, Greenville, SC 803-834-9836
Walker, Wes/301 Calvin St, Greenville, SC 803-242-9108
Wallace, Doyle/2408 Summit Springs Dr, Dunwoody, GA 404-448-8300
Walpole, Gary/193 Pine St, Memphis, TN 901-726-1155
Walters, Tom/3108 Airlie St, Charlotte, NC 704-537-7908
The Waterhouse/PO Box 2487, Key Largo, FL 800-451-3737
Webb, Jon/2023 Kenilworth Ave, Louisville, KY 502-587-7722
Webster & Co/2401 Euclid Ave, Charlotte, NC 704-522-0647
Weinlaub, Ralph/1100 S Dixie Hwy W, Pompano Beach, FL 305-941-1368
Weinmiller Inc/201 W Moorehead St, Charlotte, NC 704-377-1595
Welsh, Kelley/11450 SE 57th St, Miami, FL 305-595-6174
Wheless, Rob/3039 Amwiler Rd #114, Atlanta, GA 404-729-1066
Whipps, Dan/816 N St Asaph St, Alexandria, VA 703-684-3808
White, Drake/PO Box 40090, Augusta, GA 404-733-4142
Whitehead, Dennis R/1410 N Nelson St, Arlington, VA 703-524-6814
Whitman, Alan/724 Lakeside Dr, Mobile, AL 205-661-0400
Whitman, John/604 N Jackson St, Arlington, VA 703-524-5569
Wien/Murray Studio/2480 W 82nd St #8, Hialeah, FL 305-828-7400
Wiley & Flynn/379 W Michigan Ave #200, Orlando, FL 407-843-6767
Willard, Jean/684 Greenwood Ave, Atlanta, GA 404-872-8117
Williams, Jimmy/3801 Beryl Rd, Raleigh, NC 919-832-5971
Williams, Ron/105 Space Park Dr #A, Nashville, TN 615-331-2500
Williams, Sonny/555 Dutch Valley Rd NE, Atlanta, GA 404-892-5551
Willis, Joe/105 Lake Emerald Dr #314, Ft Lauderdale, FL 305-485-7185
Willison, Dusty/4302 SW 70th Tr, Davey, FL 305-474-3271
Wilson, Andrew/1640 Smyrna-Roswell Rd SE, Smyrna, GA 404-436-7553
Winner, Alan/PO Box 695249, Miami, FL 305-653-6778
Wolf, David/1770 Quail Ridge Rd, Raleigh, NC 919-782-8395
Wolf, Lloyd/5710 First St, Arlington, VA 703-671-7668
Wood, James/PO Box 510129, Melbourne Beach, FL 407-725-4581
Wood, Michael/470 Woods Mill Rd NW, Gainesville, GA 404-536-9006
Woodbury, Mark & Assoc/6801 NW 9th Ave #102, Ft Lauderdale, FL 305-977-9000
Woodson, Richard/PO Box 12224, Raliegh, NC 919-833-2882
Wright, Christopher/404 East Davis Blvd, Tampa, FL 813-251-5206
Wright, Tim/4920 Cleveland St #104, Virginia Bch, VA (P 106) 804-272-0965
Wrisley, Bard/PO Box 1021, Dahlonega, GA 404-524-6929
Yankus, Dennis/223 S Howard Ave, Tampa, FL 813-254-4156
Young, Chuck/1199-R Howell Mill Rd, Atlanta, GA 404-351-1199
Zeck, Gerry/1939 S Orange Ave, Sarasota, FL 813-366-9804
Zillioux, John/9127 SW 96th Ave, Miami, FL 305-270-1270
Zimmerman, Mike/7821 Shalimar, Mira Mar, FL 305-963-6240
Zinn, Arthur/2661 S Course Dr, Pompano Beach, FL 305-973-3851

MIDWEST

A

Abel Photographics/7035 Ashland Dr, Cleveland, OH 216-526-5732
Abramson, Michael Photo/3312 W Belle Plaine, Chicago, IL 312-267-9189
Adamo, Sam/490 Parkview Dr, Seven Hills, OH 216-447-9249

Adams Group/703 E 30th St #17, Indianapolis, IN 317-924-2400
Adams, Steve Studio/3101 S Hanley, Brentwood, MO 314-781-6676
Adcock, Gary/70 W Huron St #1009, Chicago, IL 312-943-6917
AGS & R Studios/314 W Superior, Chicago, IL 312-649-4500
Alan, Andrew/20727 Scio Church Rd, Chelsea, MI....313-475-2310
Albright, Dave/200 S Main, Northville, MI 313-473-2556
Alexander Glass Ingersol/3000 South Tech, Miamisburg, OH....513-885-2008
Alexander, Mark/412 Central Ave, Cincinnati, OH....413-651-5020
Allan-Knox Studios/450 S 92nd St, Milwaukee, WI 414-774-7900
Allen, Carter/8081 Zionsville Rd/POB 68520, Indianapolis, IN 317-872-7720
Alpert, Paul/1703 Simpson #5, St Louis, MO 314-664-0705
Altman, Ben/1420 W Dickens Ave, Chicago, IL 312-944-1434
Amenta/555 W Madison #3802, Chicago, IL 312-248-2488
American Images/104 E 2nd St, Marshfield, WI....715-387-8682
Anderson, Craig/105 7th St, W Des Moines, IA 515-279-7766
Anderson, Rob/900 W Jackson, Chicago, IL 312-942-0551
Anderson, Whit/650 West Lake St, Chicago, IL....312-933-7644
Andre, Bruce/436 N Clark, Chicago, IL....312-661-1060
Andrew, Larry/1632 Broadway, Kansas City, MO....816-471-5565
Anmar Photography/3310 Jamieson, St Louis, MO 314-644-1010
Ann Arbor Photo/670 Airport Blvd, Ann Arbor, MI 313-995-5778
Arciero, Anthony/70 E Long Lake Rd, Bloomfield Hills, MI 313-645-2222
Armour, Tony/1035 West Lake, Chicago, IL....312-733-7338
Arndt, David M/4620 N Winchester, Chicago, IL....312-334-2841
Arndt, Jim/400 First Ave N #510, Minneapolis, MN 612-332-5050
Arsenault, Bill/1244 W Chicago Ave, Chicago, IL 312-421-2525
Ascherman, Herbert Jr/1846 Coventry Vllg , Cleveland Hghts, OH......216-321-0055
Atevich, Alex/325 N Hoyne Ave, Chicago, IL (P 159) ...312-942-1453
Atkinson, David/14 North Newstead, St Louis, MO....314-535-6484
Au, King/108 3rd St #218, Des Moines, IA....515-243-2218
Audio Visual Impact Group/100 West Erie, Chicago, IL....312-664-6247
Ayala/320 E 21 St, Chicago, IL 312-326-0728

B

Baer Studio/5807 Capri Ln, Morton Grove, IL 708-966-4759
Baer, Gordon/18 E 4th St #903, Cincinnati, OH 513-381-4466
Bagnoli, Susan/74-24 Washington Ave, Eden Prairie, MN....612-944-5750
Bahm, Dave/711 Commercial, Belton, MO....816-331-0257
Baker, Gregory/4630 Charles St, Rockford, IL (P 160)....815-398-1114
Baker, Jim/1632 Broadway, Kansas City, MO....816-471-5565
Baker, Stephen/7075 W 21st St, Indianapolis, IN....317-243-8090
Balogh, Jim/6114 Park Ave, St Louis, MO 314-781-4231
Balterman, Lee/910 N Lake Shore Dr, Chicago, IL 312-642-9040
Baltz, Bill/3615 Superior Ave, Cleveland, OH....216-431-0979
Banna, Kevin/617 W Fulton St #2, Chicago, IL 312-845-9650
Banner & Burns Inc/452 N Halstead St, Chicago, IL 312-644-4770
Bannister, Will/849 W Lill Ave #K, Chicago, IL 312-327-2143
Barkan Keeling Photo/905 Vine St, Cincinnati, OH 513-721-0700
Barlow Photography Inc/1115 Olivette Exec Pkwy, St Louis, MO....314-994-9990
Barnett, Jim/5580 N Dequincy St, Indianapolis, IN....317-257-7177
Baron, Jim/812 Huron St #314, Cleveland, OH....216-781-7729
Barrett, Bob Photo/3733 Pennsylvania, Kansas City, MO 816-753-3208
Barton, Mike/5019 Nokomis Ave S, Minneapolis, MN....612-831-9557
Bartone, Tom/436 N Clark St, Chicago, IL....312-836-0464
Bartz, Carl Studio Inc/1307 Washington St #706, St Louis, MO 314-231-8690
Basdeka, Pete/1254 N Wells, Chicago, IL....312-944-3333
Bass, Alan/824 North Racine #1, Chicago, IL....312-666-6111
Battrell, Mark/1611 N Sheffield, Chicago, IL (P 158)....312-642-6650
Baver, Perry L/2923 W Touhy, Chicago, IL 312-674-1695
Bayles, Dal/4431 N 64th St, Milwaukee, WI....414-464-8917
Beasley, Michael/1210 W Webster, Chicago, IL....312-248-5769
Beaugureau Studio/704 N Sylviawood, Park Ridge, IL....708-696-1299
Beaulieu, Allen/400 N First Ave #604, Minneapolis, MN....612-338-2327
Beck, Bruce/1980 Stonington Ct, Rochester Hills, MI....313-652-0550
Beck, Peter/718 Washington Ave N #605, Minneapolis, MN....612-338-5712
Beckett Photography/117 S Morgan, Chicago, WI 312-733-6550
Bednarski, Paul S/981 Beaconsfield, Grosse Pt, MI....313-882-0427
Behr Images/6717 Odana Rd, Madison, WI....608-833-4994
Bellville, Cheryl Walsh/2823 8th St S, Minneapolis, MN....612-333-5788
Belter, Mark/640 N LaSalle St #555, Chicago, IL 312-337-7676
Benda, Tom/20555 LaGrange, Frankfurt, IL 815-469-3600
Bender + Bender/281 Klingel Rd, Waldo, OH....614-726-2470
Benkert, Christine/27 N 4th St #501, Minneapolis, MN....612-340-9503
Bennet, Patrick/330 E 47th St, Indianapolis, IN....317-283-7530
Benoit, Bill/1708 1/2 Washington, Wilmette, IL 708-251-7634
Bentley, David/208 West Kinzie, Chicago, IL 312-836-0242
Benyas-Kaufman Photo/8775 W 9 Mile Rd, Oak Park, MI 313-548-4400
Bergerson, Steven/3349 45th Ave S, Minneapolis, MN 612-724-0720
Berglund, Peter/718 Washington Ave N, Minneapolis, MN....612-371-9318
Bergos, Jim Studio/122 W Kinzie St, Chicago, IL....312-527-1769
Berkman, Elie/125 Hawthorn Ave, Glencoe, IL 708-835-4158
Berlin Chic Photo/1708 W School Rd 3rd Fl, Chicago, IL 312-327-2266
Berlow, Marc Photography/867 Tree Ln #105, Prospect Hts, IL....312-787-6528
Berr, Keith/1220 W 6th St #608, Cleveland, OH....216-566-7950
Berthiaume, Tom/1008 Nicollet Mall, Minneapolis, MN (P 176) 612-338-1999
Bevacqua, Alberto/720 N Wabash, Chicago, IL 312-458-1760
Bidak, Lorne/827 Milwaukee Ave, Chicago, IL....312-733-3997
Bieber, Tim/3312 W Belle Plaine, Chicago, IL 312-463-3590
Biel Photographic Studios/2289-91 N Moraine Blvd, Dayton, OH....513-298-6621
Bierwagen, Ottmar/50 Woodycrest Ave, Toronto, ON 416-463-6560
Bilsley, Bill/613 Mariner Dr, Elgin, IL....708-931-7666
Bishop, Robert/5622 Delmar St #103 West, St Louis, MO....314-367-8787
Bjornson, Howard/300 N Ashland, Chicago, IL....312-243-8200
Blackburn, Charles A/1100 S Lynndale Dr, Appleton, WI 414-738-4080
Blahut, Joseph/2400 Lakeview #906, Chicago, IL....312-525-2946
Blakeley, Pamela/876 Castelgate, Lake Forest, IL 708-234-3256
Block, Ernie/1138 Cambridge Cir Dr, Kansas City, KS....913-321-3080
Block, Stuart/1242 W Washington Blvd, Chicago, IL 312-733-3600
Bock, Edward/400 N First Ave #207, Minneapolis, MN 612-332-8504
Bond, Paul/1421 N Dearborn #302, Chicago, IL 312-280-5488
Borde, Richard & Dawn/5328 29th Ave S, Minneapolis, MN 612-729-1913
Bornefeld, William/586 Hollywood Pl, St Louis, MO 314-962-5596
Boschke, Les/806 North Peoria, Chicago, IL 312-666-8819
Bosek, George/1301 S Wabash 2nd Fl, Chicago, IL 312-939-0777
Bosy, Peter/120 North Green, Chicago, IL 312-243-9220
Boucher, Joe/5765 S Melinda St, Milwaukee, WI 414-281-7653
Bowen, Paul/Box 3375, Wichita, KS 316-263-5537
Brackenbury, Vern/1516 N 12th St, Blue Springs, MO....816-229-6703
Braddy, Jim/PO Box 11420, Chicago, IL....312-337-5664
Bradley, Rodney/329 10th Ave SE, Cedar Rapids, IA....319-365-5071
Brandenburg, Jim/708 N 1st St, Minneapolis, MN 612-341-0166
Brandt & Assoc/Rt 7/Box 148, Barrington Hills, IL 708-428-6363
Braun Photography/3966 W Bath Rd, Akron, OH 216-666-4540
Brayne, TW/326 W Kalamazoo Ave, Kalamazoo, MI....616-375-4422
Brettell, Jim/2152 Morrison Ave, Lakewood, OH....216-228-0890
Brimacombe, Gerald/7212 Mark Terrace, Minneapolis, MN....612-941-5860
Briskey, Bob/508 N Hoyne St, Chicago, IL 312-226-5055
Broderson, Fred/935 W Chestnut, Chicago, IL 312-226-0622
Brody, David & Assoc/6001 N Clark, Chicago, IL 312-761-2735
Brody, Jerry/70 W Hubbard, Chicago, IL....312-329-0660
Brosilow, Michael/480 Menomonee, Chicago, IL 312-266-1136
Brown, Alan J/815 MAin St, Cincinnati, OH 513-421-5588
Brown, Ron/1324 N Street, Lincoln, NE 402-476-1760
Brown, Steve/107 W Hubbard, Chicago, IL....312-467-4666
Browne, Warren/1012 W Randolph St, Chicago, IL 312-733-8134
Bruno, Sam/1630 N 23rd, Melrose Park, IL 708-345-0411
Bruton, Jon/3838 W Pine Blvd, St Louis, MO 314-533-6665
Brystrom, Roy/6127 N Ravenswood, Chicago, IL 312-973-2922
Bukva, Walt/10464 W 400 N, Michigan City, IN....219-872-9469
Bundt, Nancy/1908 Kenwood Parkway, Minneapolis, MN....612-377-7773
Burjoski, David/511 West Dr, St Louis, MO....314-725-4060
Burress, Cliff/5420 N Sheridan, Chicago, IL....312-651-3323
Burris, Zack/407 N Elizabeth, Chicago, IL....312-666-0315
Buschauer, Al/728 S Northwest Hwy, Barrington, IL 708-382-8484
Bush, Tim/617 W Fulton St, Chicago, IL 708-654-4373

C

C-H Studios/517 S Jefferson 7th Fl, Chicago, IL 312-922-8880
Cabanban, Orlando/531 S Plymouth Ct, Chicago, IL 312-922-1836
Cable, Wayne/2212 N Racine, Chicago, IL....312-525-2240
Cain, C C/420 N Clark, Chicago, IL....312-644-2371
Cairns, Robert/2076 N Elston Ave #301, Chicago, IL....312-384-3114
Camacho, Mike/124 W Main St, West Dundee, IL 708-428-3135
Camera Works Inc/1260 Carnegie Ave, Cleveland, OH 216-687-1788
Camerawork, Ltd/400 S Greens St #203, Chicago, IL....312-666-8802
Campbell, Bob/722 Prestige, Joliet, IL....815-725-1862
Candee, Michael Studios/1212 W Jackson Blvd, Chicago, IL....312-226-3332
Caporale, Michael/6710 Madison Rd, Cincinnati, OH 513-561-4011
Carell, Lynn/3 E Ontario #25, Chicago, IL 312-935-1707
Carney, Joann/401 N Racine, Chicago, IL 312-829-2332
Carosella, Tony/4138-A Wyoming, St Louis, MO....314-664-3462
Carter, David/2901 N Lincoln, Chicago, IL 312-929-0306

Carter, Mary Ann/5954 Crestview, Indianapolis, IN....317-255-1351
Casalini, Tom/10 1/2 Main St, Zionsville, IN....317-873-5229
Cascarano, John/657 W Ohio, Chicago, IL....312-733-1212
Cedrowski, Dwight/981 Beaconsfield, Detroit, MI....313-971-3107
Ceolla, George/5700 Ingersoll Ave, Des Moines, IA....515-279-3508
Chadwick Taber Inc/617 W Fulton, Chicago, IL....312-454-0855
Chambers, Tom/153 W Ohio, Chicago, IL....312-227-0009
Chapman, Cam/126 W Kinzie, Chicago, IL....312-222-9242
Chare, Dave/1045 N Northwest Hwy, Park Ridge, IL....708-696-3188
Charlie Company/2148 Lakeside, Cleveland, OH....216-566-7464
Charlton, James/11518 N Pt Washington Rd, Mequon, WI....414-241-8634
Chauncey, Paul C/388 N Hydraulic, Wichita, KS....316-262-6733
Cherup, Thomas/PO Box 84, Dearborn Hts, MI....313-561-9376
Chicago Photographers/430 West Erie St, Chicago, IL....312-944-4828
Chobot, Dennis/2857 E Grand Blvd, Detroit, MI....313-875-6617
Christman, Gerald/985 Ridgewood Dr, Highland Park, IL....708-433-2279
Church, Dennis/301 S Bedford St #6, Madison, WI....608-255-2726
Clark, Junebug/36264 Freedom Rd, Farmington, MI (P 161)....313-478-3666
Clark, Thom/1927 W Farwell, Chicago, IL....312-338-5829
Clarke, Jim/3721 Grandel Sq, St Louis, MO....314-652-6262
Classic Visions Photography/4725 West North Ave, Milwaukee, WI....414-447-7800
Clawson, David/6800 Normal Blvd, Lincoln, NE....402-489-1302
Clawson, Kent/2530 West Wilson Ave, Chicago, IL....312-583-0001
Clayton, Curt/2655 Guoin, Detroit, MI....313-567-3897
Clemens, Jim/1311 Gregory, Wilmette, IL....708-256-5413
Click/ Chicago/213 W Institute Pl #503, Chicago, IL....312-787-7880
Cloudshooters/Aerial Photo/4620 N Winchester, Chicago , IL....312-334-2841
Coats & Greenfield Inc/2928 Fifth Ave S, Minneapolis, MN....612-827-4676
Cocose, Ellen/445 E Ohio #222, Chicago, IL....312-527-9444
Coffey, Mark/77 W Huron St #1712, Chicago, IL....312-883-4652
Coha, Dan/9 W Hubbard, Chicago, IL....312-664-2270
Coil, Ron Studio/15 W Hubbard St, Chicago, IL....312-321-0155
Color Associates/10818 MW Industrial Blvd, St Louis, MO....800-456-SEPS
Comess, Herb/540 Custer St, Evanston, IL....312-791-3152
Commercial Images Group/15339 Center St, Harvey, IL....708-333-1047
Compton, Ted/112 N Washington, Hinsdale, IL....312-654-8781
Condie, Thomas M/535 N 27th St, Milwaukee, WI....414-342-6363
Conison, Joel Photography/18 W 7th St, Cincinnati, OH....513-241-1887
Conner/Nichols Photo/520 Virginia Ave, Indianapolis, IN....317-634-8710
Cool, Nick/1892 N Lincoln Ave, Salem, NY....216-332-1509
Copeland, Burns/6651 N Artesian, Chicago, IL....312-465-3240
Cote, Eaton/26 Spring Ave, Waukon, IA....319-568-2253
Cowan, Ralph/604 Division Rd, Valparaiso, IN....219-462-0199
Cox, D E/Detroit/22111 Cleveland #211, Dearborn, MI....313-561-1842
CR Studio/1859 W 25th St, Cleveland, OH....216-861-5360
Crane, Arnold/666 N Lake Shore Dr, Chicago, IL....312-337-5544
Crane, Michael/1717 Wyandotte St, Kansas City, MO....816-221-9382
Croff, Will/1100 S Lynndale, Appleton, WI....414-738-4080
Crofoot, Ron/6140 Wayzata Blvd, Minneapolis, MN....612-546-0643
Crofton, Bill/326R Linden Ave, Wilmette, IL....708-256-7862
Cromwell, Patrick/1739 Coolidge, Berkley, MI....313-543-5610
Crosby, Paul/1083 Tenth Ave SE, Minneapolis, MN....612-378-9566
Cross, Emil/1886 Thunderbird, Troy, MI....313-362-3111
Crowther Photography/1108 Kenilworth Ave, Cleveland, OH....216-566-8066
Culbert-Aguilar, Kathleen/1338 W Carmen, Chicago, IL....312-561-1266
Culp, John L Jr/1133 E 45th St, Chicago, IL....312-285-5570
Curtis, Lucky Photography/1540 N North Park Ave, Chicago, IL....312-787-4422

D

D'Orio, Tony/1147 W Ohio, Chicago, IL....312-421-5532
Dacuisto, Todd/840 N Old World 3rd St, Milwaukee, WI....414-272-8772
Dale, LB/7015 Wing Lake Rd, Birmingham, MI....313-851-3296
Dapkus, Jim/Westfield Photo/Rte 1 Box 247, Westfield, WI....608-296-2623
Davito, Dennis/638 Huntley Heights, Manchester, MO....314-394-0660
Deahl, David/70 W Hubbard, Chicago, IL....312-644-3187
Debacker, Michael/231 Ohio, Wichita, KS....316-722-3075
DeBolt, Dale/120 West Kinzie St, Chicago, IL....312-644-6264
DeLaittre, Bill/7661 Washington Ave S, Edina, MN....612-941-4884
Delich, Mark/304 W 10th St #200, Kansas City, MO....816-474-6699
DeNatale, Joe/2129 W North Ave, Chicago, IL....312-489-0089
Denning, Warren/231 Ohio, Wichita, KS (P 162)....316-262-4163
Design Photography Inc/2001 Hamilton Ave, Cleveland, OH....216-687-0099
Dieringer, Rick/19 W Court St, Cincinnati, OH (P 163)....513-621-2544
Dinerstein, Matt/606 W 18th St, Chicago, IL....312-243-4766
Ditlove, Michel/18 W Hubbard, Chicago, IL....312-644-5233
Ditz, Michael/2292 Cole St, Birmingham, MI....313-642-8884
Donner, Michael/5534 S Dorchester, Chicago, IL....312-241-7896
Donofrio, Randy/6459 S Albany, Chicago, IL....312-737-0990
Dovey, Dean/1917 N Milwaukee, Chicago, IL....312-292-1737
Doyle, Tim/1550 E 9 Mile Rd, Ferndale, MI....313-543-9440
Drea, Robert/1909 S Halstead, Chicago, IL....312-472-6550
Drew, Terry-David/452 N Morgan #2E, Chicago, IL....312-829-1630
Drickey, Pat/1412 Howard St, Omaha, NE....402-344-3786
Drier, David/804 Washington St #3, Evanston, IL....708-475-1992
Dublin, Rick/414 Third Ave W, Minneapolis, MN....612-332-8924
DuBroff, Don/2031 W Cortez, Chicago, IL....312-252-7390
DuFresne, Gilmore/PO Box 291, Maryville, MO....816-582-7545

E

Eagle, Lin/1725 W North Ave, Chicago, IL....312-276-0707
Ebel, Bob Photography/1376 W Carroll, Chicago, IL....312-222-1123
Ebenoh, Tom/7050 Justamere Hill, Hause Springs, MO....314-671-0439
Eckhard, Kurt/1306 S 18th St, St Louis, MO....314-241-1116
Edwards, Bruce/930 S park Ave, Winthrop Harbor, IL....708-746-5168
Edwards, Thomas/PO Box 1193, Milwaukee, WI....414-258-6331
Eggebenn, Mark/1217 Center Ave, Dostburg, WI....414-564-2344
Einhorn, Mitchell/311 N Des Plaines #603, Chicago, IL....312-944-7028
Eisner, Scott Photography/1456 N Dayton, Chicago, IL....312-642-2217
Elacy, John/24746 Renssalaer, Oak Park, MI....313-548-3842
Elan Photography/1130 S Wabash #203, Chicago, IL....312-431-0746
Eliasen, Steve/100 S Lyndale Dr, Appleton, WI....414-738-4080
Elledge, Paul/1808 W Grand Ave, Chicago, IL....312-733-8021
Elmore, Bob and Assoc/315 S Green St, Chicago, IL....312-641-2731
Englehard, J Versar/1156 West Grand, Chicago, IL....312-787-2024
Eshelman, Charlie/59 W Hubbard, Chicago, IL....312-527-1330
ETM Studios/130 S Morgan, Chicago, IL....312-666-0660
Evans, Patricia/1153 E 56th St, Chicago, IL....312-288-2291
Ewert, Steve/17 N Elizabeth, Chicago, IL....312-733-5762

F

Faitage, Nick Photography/1914 W North Ave, Chicago, IL....312-276-9321
Farber, Gerald/4925 Cadieux, Detroit, MI....313-885-4300
Farmer, Terry/524 S 2nd St #510, Springfield, IL....217-785-0975
Faverty, Richard/1019 W Jackson, Chicago, IL....312-633-0566
Feferman, Steve/462 Fern Dr, Wheeling, IL....708-459-3695
Fegley, Richard/777 North Michigan Ave #706, Chicago, IL....312-337-7770
Feher, Michael/1818 Chouteau, St Louis, MO....314-231-9200
Feld, D K/675 Morningside Ct, Chicago, IL....708-529-2288
Feldman, Stephen L/2705 W Agatite, Chicago, IL....312-539-0300
Ferderbar Studios/62 W Huron, Chicago, IL....312-642-9296
Ferguson, Ken/400 North May, Chicago, IL....312-829-2366
Ferguson, Scott/710 North Tucker, St Louis, MO....314-241-3811
Fetters, Grant/173 W Clay St, Meuskegon, MI....616-722-4723
Ficht, Bill/244 Blue Spruce La, Aurora, IL....708-851-2185
Finlay & Finlay Photo/141 E Main St, Ashland, OH....419-289-3163
Firak Photography/1043 West Grand St, Chicago, IL....312-421-2225
Fish, Peter Studio/1151 West Adams, Chicago, IL....312-829-0129
Fitzsimmons, J Kevin/2380 Wimbledon Rd, Columbus, OH....614-457-2010
Fleck, John/9257 Castlegate Dr, Indianpolis, IN....317-849-7723
Fleming, Larry/PO Box 3823, Wichita, KS....316-267-0780
Fletcher, Mike/7467 Kingsbury, St Louis, MO....314-721-2279
Flood, Kevin/1329 Macklind St, St Louis, MO....314-647-2485
Floyd, Bill/404 North Way, Chicago, IL....312-243-1611
Fong, John/13 N Huron St, Toledo, OH....419-243-7378
Fontayne Studios Ltd/4528 W Oakton, Skokie, IL....708-676-9872
Foran, Bob/3930 Varsity Dr, Ann Arbor, MI....313-973-0960
Ford, Madison/2616 Industrial Row, Troy, MI....313-280-0640
Forrest, Michael/2150 Plainfield Ave NE, Grand Rapids, MI....616-361-2556
Forsyte, Alex/1180 Oak Ridge Dr, Glencoe, IL....708-835-0307
Forth, Ron/1507 Dana St, Cincinnati, OH....513-841-0858
Fortier, Ron/613 Main #301, Rapid City, SD....605-341-3739
Foto-Graphics/2402 N Shadeland Ave, Indianapolis, IN....317-353-6259
Fox Commercial Photo/119 W Hubbard, Chicago, IL....312-664-0162
Fox, Fred & Sons/2746 W Fullerton, Chicago, IL....312-342-3233
Francis, Dan/4515 Delaware St N, Indianapolis, IN....317-283-8244
Frantz, Ken/706 N Dearborn, Chicago, IL....312-951-1077
Franz, Bill/820 E Wisconsin, Delavan, WI....414-728-3733
Freeman, George/1061 W Balmoral, Chicago, IL....312-275-1122
Frerck, Robert/4158 N Greenview 2nd Fl, Chicago, IL....312-883-1965
Frey, Jeff Photography Inc/405 E Superior St, Duluth, MN (P 164)....218-722-6630

Frick, Ken Photographer/66 Northmoor Pl, Columbus, OH 614-263-9955
Friedman & Karant Studios/400 North May St, Chicago, IL....................312-527-1880
Friedman, Susan J/400 North May St, Chicago, IL 312-733-0891
Fritz, Tom/2930 W Clybourn, Milwaukee, WI 414-344-8300
Futran, Eric/3454 N Bell, Chicago, IL (P 165) 312-525-5020

G

Gabriel Photo/160 E Illinois, Chicago, IL 312-743-2220
Gale, Bill/3041 Aldrich Ave S, Minneapolis, MN....................612-827-5858
Galloway, Scott/2772 Copley Rd, Akron, OH 216-666-4477
Gardiner, Howard/9 E Campbell #1, Arlington Hts, IL 708-392-0766
Gargano, Pat/3200 Coral Park Dr, Cincinnati, OH....................513-662-2780
Garmon, Van/312 Eighth St #720, Des Moines, IA 515-247-0001
Gates, Bruce/356 1/2 S Main St, Akron, OH....................216-535-2221
Gaymont, Gregory/1812 N Hubbard St, Chicago, IL 312-421-3146
Gerlach, Monte/705 S Scoville, Oak Park, IL....................708-848-1193
Getsug, Don/1255 South Michigan Ave, Chicago, IL 312-939-1477
Giannetti, Joseph/119 4th St N #501, Minneapolis, MN 612-339-3172
Gillette, Bill/2917 Eisenhower, Ames, IA 515-294-4340
Gilo, Dave/121 N Broadway, Milwaukee, WI 414-273-1022
Gilroy, John Photography/2407 West Main St, Kalamazoo, MI (P 166)....................616-349-6805
Girard, Connie/609 Renolda Woods Ct, Dayton, OH 513-294-2095
Girard, Jennifer/1455 W Roscoe, Chicago, IL....................312-929-3730
Glass, Greg/3000 South Tech, Miamisburg, OH 513-885-2008
Glendinning, Peter/106 W Allegan #508, Lansing, MI 517-484-6200
Glenn, Eileen/407 N Elizabeth Pl #101, Chicago, IL....................312-666-7300
Gluth, Bill/173 E Grand Ave, Fox Lake, IL 312-834-4798
Goddard, Will/PO Box 8081, St Paul, MN....................612-488-5359
Goff, D R/66 W Wittier St, Columbus, OH (P 157)....................614-443-6530
Goldberg, Lenore/210 Park Ave, Glencoe, IL 708-835-4226
Goldstein, Steven/343 Copper Lakes Blvd, St Louis, MO 314-227-8797
Goodwin, Andy/220 Pottawatamie, New Lenox, IL....................818-485-8822
Goss, James M/1737 McGee St, Kansas City, MO....................816-471-8069
Goss, Michael/2444 W Chicago Ave, Chicago, IL 312-235-4800
Gould, Christopher/224 W Huron, Chicago, IL....................312-944-5545
Gould, Ron/1609 N Wolcott, Chicago, IL....................312-235-0157
Graham, Stephen/1120 W Stadium #2, Ann Arbor, MI 313-761-6888
Graham-Henry, Diane/613 W Belden, Chicago, IL 312-327-4493
Grajczyk, Chris/126 North 3rd St #405, Minneapolis, MN 612-333-6265
Grande, Ruth/8081 Zionsville Rd, Indianapolis, IN 317-872-7220
Gray, Walter/1035 W Lake, Chicago, IL....................312-733-3800
Grayson, Dan/831 W Cornelia, Chicago, IL 312-477-8659
Gregg, Rene/4965 McPherson, St Louis, MO 314-361-1963
Griffith, Sam/345 N Canal, Chicago, IL....................312-648-1900
Grippentrag, Dennis/70 E Long Lake Rd, Bloomfield Hills, MI 313-645-2222
Groen, John/676 N LaSalle, Chicago, IL 312-266-2331
Grondin, Timothy/815 Main St, Cincinnati, OH....................513-421-5588
Grubman, Steve/456 N Morgan, Chicago, IL....................312-226-2272
Grunewald, Jeff/161 W Harrison St, Chicago, IL....................312-663-5799
GSP/156 N Jefferson, Chicago, IL....................312-944-3000
Gubin, Mark/2893 S Delaware Ave, Milwaukee, WI 414-482-0640
Guenther, Stephen/807 Church St, Evanston, IL....................708-328-4837
Guerry, Tim/711 S Dearborn #304, Chicago, IL....................312-294-0070
Gyssler, Glen/221 E Cullerton, Chicago, IL 312-842-2202

H

Haberman, Mike/529 S 7th St #427, Minneapolis, MN 612-338-4696
Hadley, Alan/140 First Ave NW, Carmel, IN....................317-846-2259
Haefner, Jim/1407 N Allen, Troy, MI 313-583-4747
Hafencher, Lou/2462 E Oakton, Arlington Hghts, IL 708-593-7977
Haines, W C (Bill)/3101 Mercier Ste 484, Kansas City, MO 816-531-0561
Halbe, Harrison/710 N Tucker Blvd #218, St Louis, MO....................314-621-0505
Hall, Brian/900 W Jackson Blvd #8W, Chicago, IL 312-226-0853
Haller, Pam/935 W Chestnut, Chicago, IL 312-243-4462
Halsey, Daniel/12243 Nicollet Ave S, Minneapolis, MN 612-894-2722
Hamill, Larry/77 Deshler, Columbus, OH (P 156) 614-444-2798
Hammarlund, Vern/135 Park St, Troy, MI 313-588-5533
Handley, Robert E/1920 E Croxton, Bloomington, IL....................309-828-4661
Hanselman, Linda/PO Box 8072, Cincinnati, OH....................513-321-8469
Harbron, Patrick/366 Adelaide St E #331, Toronto, ON 416-462-0128
Harding Studio/2076 N Elston, Chicago, IL....................312-252-4010
Harlan, Bruce/52922 Camellia Dr, South Bend, IN....................219-239-7350
Harrig, Rick/3316 South 66th Ave, Omaha, NE....................402-397-5529
Harris, Bart/70 W Hubbard St, Chicago, IL 312-751-2977
Hart, Bob/1457 S Michigan, Chicago, IL....................312-939-8888
Hartjes, Glenn/1100 S Lynndale, Appleton, WI 414-738-4080
Hauser, Marc/1810 W Cortland, Chicago, IL....................312-486-4381
Hawker, Chris/119 N Peoria, Chicago, IL 312-829-4766
Hayes, Robert Cushman/7350 Gracely Dr, Cincinnati, OH 513-941-2447
Hedrich, Sandi/10-A W Hubbard, Chicago, IL....................312-527-1577
Hedrich-Blessing/11 W Illinois St, Chicago, IL 312-321-1151
Henebry, Jeanine/1154 Locust Rd, Wilmette, IL 708-251-8747
Henning, Paul/PO Box 92397, Milwaukee, WI....................414-765-9441
Hermann, Dell/676 N LaSalle, Chicago, IL....................312-664-1461
Hernandez, Rick/1952 Hazelwood Ave SE, Warren, OH 216-369-2847
Hertzberg, Richard/432 N Clark St, Chicago, IL 312-836-0464
Hill, John/4234 Howard, Western Springs, IL....................708-246-3566
Hill, Roger/4040 W River Dr, Comstock Park, MI....................616-784-9620
Hillery, John/PO Box 2916, Detroit, MI....................313-345-9511
Hirneisen, Richard/306 S Washington St #218, Royal Oak, MI 313-399-2410
Hirschfeld, Corson/316 W Fourth St, Cincinnati, OH....................513-241-0550
Hix, Steve/517 Southwest Blvd, Kansas City, MO....................816-421-5114
Hodes, Charles S/233 E Erie, Chicago, IL....................312-951-1186
Hodge, Adele/405 N Wabash Ave #805, Chicago, IL 312-828-0611
Hodges, Charles/539 W North Ave, Chicago, IL....................312-664-8179
Hofer, Charles/2134 North St, Peoria, IL....................309-676-6676
Holographics Design System/1134 W Washington, Chicago, IL....................312-226-1007
Holzemer, Buck/3448 Chicago Ave, Minneapolis, MN 612-824-3874
Hopkins, William/445 W Erie, Chicago, IL 312-787-2032
Horstman, Mike/700 Forest Edge Dr, Vernon Hills, IL 708-634-4505
Hoskins, Sarah/1206 Isabella, Wilmette, IL 708-256-5724
Houghton, Michael/Studiohio/55 E Spring St, Columbus, OH 614-224-4885
Howrani, Armeen/2820 E Grand Blvd, Detroit, MI....................313-875-3123
Hurling, Robert/325 W Huron, Chicago, IL....................312-944-2022
Hutson, David/8120 Juniper, Prairie Village, KS....................913-383-1123
Hyman, Randy/7709 Carnell Ave, St Louis, MO....................314-821-8851

I

Iacono, Michael/412 Central Ave, Cincinnati, OH....................513-621-9108
Iann-Hutchins/2044 Euclid Ave, Cleveland, OH....................216-579-1570
Image Productions/115 W Church, Libertyville, IL 708-680-7100
Image Studios/1100 S Lynndale Dr, Appleton, WI 414-738-4080
Imagematrix/2 Garfield Pl, Cincinnati, OH....................513-381-1380
Imagination Unlimited/1280 East Miner, Des Plaines, IL....................708-803-0199
Imbrogno, James/935 West Chestnut St #03, Chicago, IL....................312-644-7333
Ingram, Russell/2334 W 116th Pl, Chicago, IL....................312-238-4114
Ingve, Jan & Assoc/1185 Sterling Ave #115, Palatine, IL....................708-381-3456
International Photo Corp/1035 Wesley, Evanston, IL....................708-475-6400
Irving, Gary/PO Box 38, Wheaton, IL....................708-653-0641
Isenberger, Brent/108 3rd St #360, Des Moines, IA....................515-243-2376
Itahara, Tets/676 N LaSalle, Chicago, IL 312-649-0606
Iwata, John/325 W New York Ave, Oshkosh, WI 414-426-1487
Izquierdo, Abe/213 W Institute #208, Chicago, IL 312-787-9784
Izui, Richard/315 W Walton, Chicago, IL 312-266-8029

J

Jackson, David/1021 Hall St, Grand Rapids, MI 616-243-3325
Jacobson, Scott/3435 N County Rd #18, Plymouth, MN 612-546-9191
Jacquin Enterprise/1219 Holly Hills, St Louis, MO 314-832-4221
James, Phillip MacMillan/2300 Hazelwood Ave, St Paul, MN....................612-777-2303
Jelen, Tom/PO Box 115, Arlington Heights, IL (P 167)....................708-506-9479
Jenkins, David/1416 S Michigan Ave, Chicago, IL 312-229-2299
Jensen, Michael/1101 Stinson Blvd NE, Minneapolis, MN 612-379-1944
Jilling, Helmut/3420-A Cavalier Trail, Cuyahoga Falls, OH 216-928-1330
Jochim, Gary/1324 1/2 N Milwaukee, Chicago, IL....................312-252-5250
Joel, David Photo Inc/1515 Washington Ave, Wilmette, IL (P 168)....................708-256-8792
Johnson, Dave/15840 Forrer, Detroit, MI 313-589-0066
Johnson, Donald/2807 Brindle, Northbrook, IL 708-480-9336
Johnson, Jim/802 W Evergreen, Chicago, IL 312-943-8864
Jolly, Keith/32049 Milton Ave, Madison Hts, MI....................313-588-6544
Jones, Brent/9121 S Merrill Ave, Chicago, IL 312-933-1174
Jones, Dawson Inc/23 N Walnut St, Dayton, OH (P 169)....................513-859-7799
Jones, Dick/325 W Huron St, Chicago, IL 312-642-0242
Jones, Duane/5605 Chicago Ave S, Minneapolis, MN 612-823-8173
Jones, Harrison/113 North May St, Chicago, IL....................312-421-6400
Jones, Mark/718 Washington Ave N, Minneapolis, MN 612-338-5712
Jordan, Jack/840 John St, Evansville, IN....................812-423-7676
Jordano, Dave/1335 N Wells, Chicago, IL....................312-280-8212

Joseph, Mark/1007 N La Salle, Chicago, IL....312-951-5333
Joyce, Todd/7815 Lake St, Cincinnati, OH....513-421-1209
Justice Patterson Studio/7609 Production Dr, Cincinnati, OH....513-761-4023

K

Kalman & Pabst Photo Group/400 Lakeside Ave NW, Cleveland, OH..216-574-9090
Kalyniuk, Jerry/4243 N Winchester, Chicago, IL....312-666-5588
Kansas City Photographic/1830 Main St, Kansas City, MO....816-221-2710
Kaplan, Dick/708 Waukegan, Deerfield, IL....708-945-3425
Kaplan, Matthew/5452 N Glenwood, Chicago, IL....312-769-5903
Karant, Barbara/400 N May St, Chicago, IL....312-527-1880
Katz, Sue/2828 N Burling #406, Chicago, IL....312-549-5379
Katzman, Mark/710 N Tucker St #512, St Louis, MO....314-241-3811
Kauck, Jeff/1050 E McMillan , Cincinnati, OH....513-751-8515
Kauffman, Kim/444 Lentz Court, Lansing, MI....517-371-3036
Kazu Studio/1211 West Webster, Chicago, IL....312-348-5393
Kean, Christopher/3 S Prospect/Pickwick Bldg, Park Ridge, IL....312-559-0880
Keefer, KC/2308 Hecker Ave, Rockford, IL....815-968-5584
Keeling, Robert/900 West Jackson Blvd #7W, Chicago, IL....312-944-5680
Keeven, Pam/2838 Salena, St Louis, MO....314-773-3587
Keisman & Keisman/518 W 37th St, Chicago, IL....312-268-7955
Kelly, Tony/1131 Main St, Evanston, IL....708-864-0488
Kelsch, R R/4999 Madison Rd, Cincinnati, OH....513-271-9017
Keltsch, Steve/9257 Castlegate Dr, Indianapolis, IN....317-849-7723
Kern, C S/220 N Walnut St, Muncie, IN....317-288-1454
Ketchum, Art/1524 Peoria, Chicago, IL....312-733-7706
Kildow, William/1743 West Cornelia, Chicago, IL....312-248-9159
Kimbal, Mark/23860 Miles Rd, Cleveland, OH....216-587-3555
Kinast, Susan/1504 S Fremont, Chicago, IL....312-337-1770
King, Jay Studios/1629 North Milwaukee, Chicago, IL....312-327-0011
Kingsbury, Andrew/700 N Washington #306, Minneapolis, MN....612-340-1919
Kitahara, Joe/304 W 10th St, Kansas City, MO....816-474-6699
Kloc, Howard/520 W Eleven Mile Rd, Royal Oak, MI....313-541-1704
Klutho, David E/3421 Meramec St, St Louis, MO....314-352-4534
Knepp Studio/1742 McKinley St, Mishawaka, IN....219-259-1913
Knize, Karl/1920 N Seminary, Chicago, IL....312-477-1001
Koechling, William/1307 E Harrison, Wheaton, IL....708-665-4419
Kogan, David/1242 W Washington Blvd, Chicago, IL (P 170)....312-243-1929
Kolesar, Jerry Photographics/679 E Mandoline, Madison Hts, MI....313-589-0066
Kompa, Jeff/25303 Lorain Rd, N Olmstead, OH....216-777-1611
Kondas, Thom Assoc/1529 N Alabama St, Indianapolis, IN....317-637-1414
Kondor, Linda/2141 West Lemoyne, Chicago, IL....312-642-7365
Korab, Balthazar/PO Box 895, Troy, MI....313-641-8881
Krajcirovic, Maria/1133 W Maple Ave, Evanson, IL....708-864-1803
Krantz, Jim/5017 S 24th St, Omaha, NE....402-734-4848
Krantzen Studios/100 S Ashland, Chicago, IL....312-942-1900
Krejci, Donald/3121 W 25th St, Cleveland, OH....216-831-4730
Krueger, Dick/2147 W Augusta Blvd, Chicago, IL....312-384-0008
Kufrin, George/535 N Michigan #1407, Chicago, IL....312-787-2854
Kuhlmann, Brian/10542 Byfield, St Louis, MO....314-867-5117
Kuhule, Craig/30 Tenth St, Toledo, OH....419-242-9170
Kulp, Curtis/1255 S Michigan, Chicago, IL....312-786-1943
Kusel, Bob/2156 W Arthur, Chicago, IL....312-465-8283

L

Lacey, Ted/4733 S Woodlawn, Chicago, IL....312-624-2419
Lachman, Cary/1927 Grant St, Evanston, IL....708-864-0861
Lafavor, Mark/1008 Nicollet Mall, Minneapolis, MN (P 177)....612-338-1999
Lallo, Ed/7329 Terrace, Kansas City, MO....816-523-6222
Lambert, Bill/2220 Hassell #308, Hoffeman Estates, IL....312-519-0189
Lancaster, Bill/114 E Front St #208, Traverse City, MI....616-929-2619
Landau, Allan/1147 West Ohio, Chicago, IL....312-942-1382
Landis, Mike/1030 N Crooks Rd #O, Clawson, MI....313-435-5420
Lane, Jack Studio/815 N Milwaukee Blvd, Chicago, IL....312-733-3937
Lange, Jim Design/320 N Michigan #901, Chicago, IL....312-606-9313
Lanza, Scott/3200 S 3rd St, Milwaukee, WI....414-482-4114
LaRoche, Andre/32588 Dequindre, Warren, MI....313-978-7373
Larsen, Kim/Soren Studio/114 W Kinzie, Chicago, IL....312-527-0344
LaTona, Tony/1317 E 5th, Kansas City, MO....816-474-3119
Lause, Lew/127 Prospect St, Marion, OH....614-383-1155
Lauth, Lyal/833 W Chicago Ave 6th Fl, Chicago, IL....312-829-9800
Leavenworth Photo Inc/929 West St, Lansing, MI....517-482-4658
Leavitt, Debbie/2029 W Armitage, Chicago, IL....312-235-6777
Leavitt, Fred/916 Carmen, Chicago, IL....312-784-2344
Lecat, Paul/820 N Franklin, Chicago, IL....312-664-7122
Lee, David/Bloomington, IL (P 171)....309-825-1646
Lee, Robert Photo/1512 Northlin Dr, St Louis, MO....314-965-5832
LeGrand, Peter/413 Sandburg, Park Forest, IL....708-747-4923
Lehn, John & Associates/2601 E Franklin Ave, Minneapolis, MN....612-338-0257
Leick, Jim/1709 Washington Ave, St Louis, MO....314-241-2354
Leinwohl, Stef/1462 W Irving Park Rd, Chicago, IL....312-975-0457
Leonard, Steve/825 W Gunnison, Chicago, IL....312-275-8833
Leslie, William F/53 Tealwood Dr, Creve Coeur, MO....314-993-8349
Levey, Don/15 W Delaware Pl, Chicago, IL....312-329-9040
Levin, Daniel/2530 Superior Ave 4th Fl, Cleveland, OH....216-781-0600
Levin, Jonathan/1035 W Lake St, Chicago, IL....312-226-3898
Lewandowski, Leon/210 N Racine, Chicago, IL....312-467-9577
Lightfoot, Robert/311 Good Ave, Des Plaines, IL....708-297-5447
Likvan Photo/107 S Wapella Ave, Mt Prospect, IL....708-394-2069
Linc Studio/1163 Tower, Schaumberg, IL....708-882-1311
Lindblade, George R/PO Box 1342, Sioux City, IA....712-255-4346
Lindwall, Martin/234 E Maple Ave, Mundelein, IL....708-566-1578
Lipman, Michael/216 N Clinton St, Chicago, IL....312-454-1414
Lipschis, Helmut Photography/2053 N Sheffield, Chicago, IL....312-935-7886
Liss, Leroy/6243 N Ridgeway Ave, Chicago, IL....312-539-4540
Lohbeck, Stephen/710 North Tucker, St Louis, MO....314-231-6038
Love, Ken/6911 N Mcalpin Ave, Chicago, IL....312-775-5779
Lowry, Miles/222 S Morgan #3B, Chicago, IL....312-666-0882
Lubeck, Larry/405 N Wabash Ave, Chicago, IL....312-726-5580
Lucas, John V/4100 W 40th St, Chicago, IL....312-927-4500
Lucas, Joseph/701 Euclid Ave, Island Park, IL....708-432-1705
Ludwigs, David/3600 Troost St, Kansas City, MO....816-531-1363
Luke, John/1100 S Lynndale Dr, Appleton, WI....414-738-4080
Lyles, David/855 W Blackhawk St, Chicago, IL....312-642-1223

M

Maas, Curt/5860 Merle Hay Rd/Box 127, Johnston, IA....515-270-3732
MacDonald, Al/32 Martin Lane, Elk Grove, IL....708-437-8850
MacDonald, Neil/1515 W Cornelia, Chicago, IL....312-525-5401
Mack, Richard/2331 Hartzell, Evanston, IL....708-869-7794
Mactavish, Arndt/4620 N Winchester, Chicago, IL....312-334-2841
Magin, Betty/412 Spring Valley Ct, Chesterfield, MO....314-878-5388
Maguire, Jim/144 Lownsdale, Akron, OH....216-630-9050
Maki & Smith Photo/6156 Olson Mem Hwy, Golden Valley, MN....612-541-4722
Malinowski, Stan/1150 N State #312, Chicago, IL....312-951-6715
Manarchy, Dennis/229 W Illinois, Chicago, IL....312-828-9117
Mandel, Avis/1550 N Lakeshore Dr #10G, Chicago, IL (P 172,173)....312-642-4776
Mankus, Gary/835 N Wood St #101, Chicago, IL....312-421-7747
Mar, Jan/343 Harrison St, Oak Park, IL....708-524-1898
Marden Photo/PO Box 20574, Indianapolis, IN....317-251-8373
Marianne Studio/117 S Jefferson, Mt Pleasant, IA....319-986-6573
Marienthal, Michael/1832 S Halsted, Chicago, IL....312-226-5505
Marovitz, Bob/3450 N Lake Shore Dr, Chicago, IL....312-975-1265
Marshall, Don Photography/415 W Huron, Chicago, IL....312-944-0720
Marshall, Paul/208 W Kinzie, Chicago, IL....312-222-9002
Martin, Barbara E/46 Washington Terrace, St Louis, MO....314-361-0838
Martone Inc/209 S Main St 5th Fl, Akron, OH....216-434-8200
Marvy, Jim/41 Twelfth Ave N, Minneapolis, MN....612-935-0307
Masheris, R Assoc Inc/1338 Hazel Ave, Deerfield, IL....708-945-2055
Mathews, Bruce/1014 NE 97th , Kansas City, MO....816-373-2920
Matlow, Linda/300 N State St #3926, Chicago, IL....312-321-9071
Matusik, Jim/2223 W Melrose, Chicago, IL....312-327-5615
Mauney, Michael/1405 Judson Ave, Evanston, IL....708-869-7720
May, Ron/PO Box 8359, Ft Wayne, IN....219-483-7872
May, Sandy/18 N 4th St #506, Minneapolis, MN....612-332-0272
McAlpine, Scott/110 S Elm St, N Manchester, IN....219-982-8822
McCabe, Mark/1301 E 12th St, Kansas City, MO....816-474-6491
McCaffery, Randy/3309 Industrial Pkwy, Jeffersonville, NY....812-284-3456
McCall, Paul/1844 Rutherford, Chicago, IL....312-622-4880
McCann, Larry/666 W Hubbard, Chicago, IL....312-942-1924
McCann, Michael/15416 Village Woods Dr, Eden Prairie, MN (P 175)....612-949-2407
McCay, Larry Inc/3926 N Fir Rd #14, Mishawaka, IN....219-259-1414
McClelan, Thompson/206 S First St, Champaign, IL....217-356-2767
McGee, Alan/3050 Edgewood St, Portage, IN....219-762-2805
McHale Studios Inc/2827 Gilbert Ave, Cincinnati, OH....513-961-1454
McKay, Doug/512 S Hamley, St Louis, MO....314-863-7167
McKellar, William/1643 N Milwaukee Ave, Chicago, IL....312-235-1499
McKinley, William/113 North May St, Chicago, IL....312-666-5400
McMahon, David/800 Washington Ave N #309, Minneapolis, MN....612-339-9709

McMahon, Franklin/1319 Chestnut, Wilmette, IL....708-256-5528
McNichol, Greg/1222 West Elmdale, Chicago, IL....312-973-1032
Mead, Robert/711 Hillgrove Ave, La Grange, IL....312-354-8300
Media Works/PO Box 3581, Evansville, IN....812-425-0553
Meleski, Mike/725 W Randolph, Chicago, IL....312-707-8500
Melkus, Larry/679-E Mandoline, Madison Hts, MI....313-589-0066
Meoli, Rick/710 N Tucker #306, St Louis, MO....314-231-6038
Meyer, Aaron/1302 W Randolph, Chicago, IL....312-243-1458
Meyer, Fred/415 N Dearborn, Chicago, IL....312-527-4873
Meyer, Gordon/216 W Ohio, Chicago, IL....312-642-9303
Meyer, Robert/208 W Kinzie St, Chicago, IL....312-467-1430
Michael, William/225 W Hubbard, Chicago, IL....312-644-6137
Micus Photo/517 S Addison, Villa Park, IL....708-941-8945
Mignard Associates/1950-R South Glenstone, Springfield, MO....417-881-7422
Mihalevich, Mike/9235 Somerset Dr, Overland Park, KS....913-642-6466
Miller Photo/7237 W Devon, Chicago, IL....312-631-1255
Miller, Buck/PO Box 33, Milwaukee, WI....414-672-9444
Miller, Frank/6016 Blue Circle Dr, Minnetonka, MN....612-935-8888
Miller, Jon/11 W Illinois, Chicago, IL....312-738-1816
Miller, Pat/420 N Fifth St #840, Minneapolis, MN....612-339-1115
Miller, Spider/833 North Orleans, Chicago, IL....312-944-2880
Mills, Gary/PO Box 260, Granger, IN....219-277-8844
Mitchell, John Sr/2617 Greenleaf, Elk Grove, IL....708-956-8230
Mitchell, Rick/652 W Grand, Chicago, IL....312-829-1700
Mitzit, Bruce/Architectural Photo/1205 Sherwin, Chicago, IL....312-508-1937
Mooney, Kevin O/511 N Noble, Chicago, IL....312-738-1816
Moore, Bob c/o Mofoto Grphcs/1007 Washington Ave, St Louis, MO....314-231-1430
Moore, Dan/1029 N Wichita #9, Wichita, KS....316-264-4168
Morrill, Dan/1811 N Sedgewick, Chicago, IL....312-787-5095
Morton & White/7440 Pingue Dr, Worthington, OH....614-885-8687
Moshman Photography/2700 Central Park Ave, Evanston, IL....708-869-6770
Moss, Jean/1255 S Michigan Ave, Chicago, IL....312-786-9110
Mottel, Ray/760 Burr Oak Dr, Westmont, IL....708-323-3616
Moustakas, Daniel/1255 Rankin, Troy, MI....313-589-0100
Moy, Clinton Photography/4815 W Winnemar, Chicago, IL....312-666-5577
Moy, Willie/364 W Erie, Chicago, IL....312-943-1863
Mueller, Linda/1900 Delmar, St Louis, MO....314-621-2400
Muresan, Jon/6018 Horger St, Dearborne, MI....313-581-5445
Murphey, Gregory/2615 N Wilton, Chicago, IL....312-327-4856
Musich, Jack/325 W Huron, Chicago, IL....312-644-5000
Mutrux, John L/5217 England, Shawnee Missn, KS....913-722-4343

N

Nagel, Ed/943 W Superior St, Chicago, IL....312-733-4337
Nathanson, Neal/7531 Cromwell, St Louis, MO....314-727-7244
Nawrocki, William S/332 S Michigan Ave, Chicago, IL....312-427-8625
Nelson, Tom/800 Washington Ave N #301, Minneapolis, MN....612-339-3579
Nelson-Curry, Loring/420 N Clark, Chicago, IL....312-644-2371
Neumann, Robert/101 S Mason St, Saginaw, MI....616-784-7111
New View Photo/5275 Michigan Ave, Rosemont, IL....708-671-0300
Newmann, Jeffrey/9960 Mt Eaton, Wadsworth, OH....216-336-4790
Niedorf, Steve/700 Washington Ave N #304, Minneapolis, MN....612-332-7124
Nielen, Audrey/33 East Cedar #11E, Chicago, IL....312-787-8226
Nielsen, Ron/1313 W Randolph #326, Chicago, IL....312-226-2661
Nienhuis, John/3623 N 62nd St, Milwaukee, WI....414-442-9199
Njaa, Reuben/5929 Portland Ave S, Minneapolis, MN....612-866-9906
Nobart Inc/1133 S Wabash Ave, Chicago, IL....312-427-9800
Nolan, Tim/2548 Shirley, St Louis, MO....314-388-4125
Norman, Rick/1051 S Freemont, Springfield, MO....417-865-0772
Norris, James/2301 N Lowell, Chicago, IL....312-342-1050
Northlight Studio/1539 E 22nd St, Cleveland, OH....216-621-3111
Novak, Ken/2483 N Bartlett Ave, Milwaukee, WI....414-962-6953
Novak, Sam/650 West Lake St, Chicago, IL....312-707-9111
Nozicka, Steve/405 N Wabash #3203, Chicago, IL....312-329-1370
Nugent Wenckus Inc/110 Northwest Hwy, Des Plaines, IL....312-694-4151

O

O'Barski, Don/17239 Parkside Ave, S Holland, IL....708-596-0606
O'Keefe, JoAnne/2963 Pacific, Omaha, NE....402-341-4128
Oakes, Kenneth Ltd/902 Yale Ln, Highland Park, IL....708-432-4809
Oberle, Frank/6633 Delmar, St Louis, MO....314-721-5838
Oberreich, S/1930 N Alabama St, Indianapolis, IN....317-923-1980
Officer, Hollis/905 E 5th St, Kansas City, MO....816-474-5501
Olausen, Judy/213 1/2 N Washington Ave, Minneapolis, MN....612-332-5009
Olberding, David/2141 Gilbert Ave, Cincinnati, OH....513-221-7036
Ollis, Karen/1547 Superior Ave E, Cleveland, OH....216-781-8646
Olsson, Russ/215 W Illinois, Chicago, IL....312-329-9358
Ontiveros, Don/1837 West Evergreen, Chicago, IL....312-342-0900
Oscar & Assoc/63 E Adams, Chicago, IL....312-922-0056
Oxendorf, Eric/1442 N Franklin Pl Box 92337, Milwaukee, WI....414-273-0654

P

Palmisano, Vito/7346 W Pensacola, Norridge, IL....708-453-2308
Panama, David/1100 N Dearborn, Chicago, IL....312-642-7095
Parallel Productions Inc/1008 Nicollet Mall, Minneapolis, MN (P 176,177)....612-338-1999
Parker, Norman/710 N 2nd St #300N, St Louis, MO....314-621-8100
Parks, Jim/210 W Chicago, Chicago, IL....312-321-1193
Paszkowski, Rick/7529 N Claremont #1, Chicago, IL....312-761-3018
Paternite, David/1245 S Clevelnd-Massilon Rd #3, Akron, OH....216-666-7720
Paulson, Bill/5358 Golla Rd, Stevens Point, WI....715-344-8484
Payne-Garrett Photo/5301 Michigan Ave, Chicago, IL....312-671-0300
Pease, Scott/2020 Euclid Ave 4th Fl, Cleveland, OH....216-621-3318
Pech, Ted/10818 Midwest Industrial Blvd, St Louis, MO....800-456-7377
Perkins, Ray/222 S Morgan St, Chicago, IL....312-421-3438
Perman, Craig/1645 Hennepin #311, Minneapolis, MN....612-338-7727
Perno, Jack/1956 W Grand, Chicago, IL....312-829-5292
Perry, Eric/2616 Industrial Row, Troy, MI....313-280-0640
Perspective Inc/2322 Pennsylvania St, Fort Wayne, IN....219-424-8136
Peterson, Jan/325 16th St, Bettendorf, IA....319-355-5032
Peterson, Richard Photo/1200 7th St N #101, Minneapolis, MN....612-943-2404
Petroff, Tom/19 W Hubbard, Chicago, IL....312-836-0411
Petrovich, Steve/679-E Mandoline, Madison Hts, MI....313-589-0066
Phillips, David R/1230 W Washington Blvd, Chicago, IL....312-733-3277
Philpott, Keith/13736 W 82nd St, Lenexa, KS....913-492-0715
Photo Concepts/23042 Commerce Dr #2001, Farmington Hills, MI....313-477-4301
Photo Enterprises/2134 North St, Peoria, IL....309-676-6676
Photo Group/1945 Techny Rd, Northbrook, IL....708-564-9220
Photo Ideas Inc/804 W Washington Blvd, Chicago, IL....312-666-3100
Photo Images/1945 Techny #9, Northbrook, IL....708-272-3500
Photo Reserve/2924 N Racine St, Chicago, IL....312-871-7371
Photocraft/220 N Walnut St, Muncie, IN....317-288-1454
Photographic Arts/624 W Adams, Chicago, IL....312-876-0818
Photographic Illustration/404 Enterprise Dr, Westerville, OH....614-888-8682
Pictorial/8081 Zionsville Rd, Indianapolis, IN....317-872-7220
Pierce, Rod/917 N Fifth St, Minneapolis, MN....612-332-2670
Pieroni, Frank/2432 Oak Industrial Dr NE, Grand Rapids, MI....616-459-8325
Pintozzi, Peter/110 W Kinzie, Chicago, IL....312-828-9777
Pioneer Hi-Bred Internat'l/5860 Merle Hay Rd/Box 127, Johnston, IA....515-270-3732
Pitt, Tom/1201 W Webster, Chicago, IL....312-281-5662
Pohlman Studios Inc/535 N 27th St, Milwaukee, WI....414-342-6363
Pokempner, Marc/1453 W Addison, Chicago, IL....312-525-4567
Polaski, James/216 W Ohio 3rd Fl, Chicago, IL....312-944-6577
Poli, Frank/158 W Huron, Chicago, IL....312-944-3924
Polin, Jack Photography/7306 Crawford, Lincolnwood, IL....708-676-4312
Pomerantz, Ron/363 West Erie, Chicago, IL....312-787-6407
Poon On Wong, Peter/420 5th St N #810, Minneapolis, MN....612-340-0798
Pope, Kerig/414 N Orleans, Chicago, IL....312-222-8999
Poplis, Paul/3599 Refugee Rd Bldg B, Columbus, OH....614-231-2942
Portney, Michael/4975 Gateshead, Detroit, MI....313-881-0378
Portnoy, Lewis/5 Carole Lane, St Louis, MO....314-567-5700
Powell, Jim/326 W Kalamazoo, Kalamazoo, MI....616-381-2302
Powers, Pat/240 Mosley Ave, Lansing, MI....517-484-5880
Price, Paul/2292 Cole St, Birmingham, MI....313-642-8884
Primary Image/515 28th St #109, Des Moines, IA....515-283-2102
Proctor, T Shaun/409 N Racine, Chicago, IL (P 178)....312-829-5511
Przekop, Harry Jr Commercial Photo/950 W Lake St, Chicago, IL....312-829-8201
Puffer, David/213 W Institute, Chicago, IL....312-266-7540
Puza, Greg/PO Box 1986, Milwaukee, WI....414-444-9882
Pyrzynski, Larry/2241 S Michigan, Chicago, IL....312-472-6550

QR

Quinn, James/518 S Euclid, Oak Park, IL....708-383-0654
Quist, Bruce/1370 N Milwaukee, Chicago, IL....312-252-3921
Rack, Ron/1201 Main St 1st Fl, Cincinnati, OH....513-421-6267
Radencich, Michael/3016 Cherry, Kansas City, MO....816-756-1992
Radlund & Associates/4704 Pflaum Rd, Madison, WI....608-222-8177
Railsback, Kevin/Box 239, Shellsburg, IA....319-436-2813
Randall, Bob/2340 W Huron, Chicago, IL....312-235-4613
Randolph, Jon/1434 W Addison, Chicago, IL....312-248-9406
Reames-Hanusin Studio/3306 Commercial Ave, Northbrook, IL....708-564-2706
Reed, Dick/1330 Coolidge, Troy, MI....313-280-0090

Regina, Elvira/201 E Chestnut #16A, Chicago, IL....312-943-7670
Reid, Ken/1651 W North Ave, Chicago, IL....312-733-2121
Reiss, Ray/2144 N Leavitt, Chicago, IL....312-384-3245
Remington, George/1455 W 29th St, Cleveland, OH....216-241-1440
Renerts, Peter Studio/633 Huron Rd, Cleveland, OH....216-781-2440
Renken, Roger/PO Box 11010, St Louis, MO....314-394-5055
Reuben, Martin/1231 Superior Ave, Cleveland, OH....216-781-8644
Ricco, Ron/117 W Walker St 4th Fl, Milwaukee, WI....414-645-6450
Rice, Ted/2599 N 4th St, Columbus, OH....614-263-8656
Rich, Larry/29731 Everett, Southfield, MI....313-557-7676
Richland, Kathy/839 W Wrightwood, Chicago, IL....312-935-9634
River, Milissa/2500 Lakeview, Chicago, IL....312-929-5031
Robert, Francois/740 N Wells, Chicago, IL....312-787-0777
Robinson, David/1147 W Ohio, Chicago, IL....312-942-1650
Roessler, Ryan/2413 N Clyborn Ave, Chicago, IL....312-951-8702
Rogowski, Tom/214 E 8th St, Cincinnati, OH (P 179)....513-621-3826
Rohman, Jim/2254 Marengo, Toledo, OH....419-865-0234
Rollo, Jim/1830 Main St, Kansas City, MO....816-221-2710
Romine, Mark/227 Fairway Dr, Bloomington, IL....309-662-4258
Rosmis, Bruce/833 North Orleans, Chicago, IL....312-787-9046
Rossi Studio/4555 Emery Ind Pkwy #105, Cleveland, OH....216-831-0688
Rothrock, Douglas/368 West Huron, Chicago, IL....312-951-9045
Rottinger, Ed/5409 N Avers, Chicago, IL....312-583-2917
Rovtar, Ron/49 Walhalla Rd, Columbus, OH....614-261-6083
Rowley, Joe/401 N Racine, Chicago, IL....312-829-2332
Rubin, Laurie/1111 W Armitage, Chicago, IL....312-348-6644
Rush, Michael/415 Delaware, Kansas City, MO....816-471-1200
Russetti, Andy/1260 Carnegie St, Cleveland, OH....216-687-1788
Rustin, Barry/934 Glenwood Rd, Glenview, IL....708-724-7600
Rutt, Don/324 Munson St, Traverse City, MI....616-946-2727
Rutten, Bonnie/414 Sherburne Ave, St Paul, MN....612-224-5777
Ryan, Gary/415 W Nine Mile Rd, Ferndale, MI....313-398-0850

S

Sacco Photography Ltd/2035 W Grand Ave, Chicago, IL....312-243-5757
Sacks, Andrew/20727 Scio Church Rd, Chelsea, MI (P 154,155)....313-475-2310
Sacks, Ed/Box 7237, Chicago, IL....312-871-4700
Sadin, Abby/1420 W Dickens Ave, Chicago, IL....312-404-0133
Saks Photo/9257 Castlegate Dr, Indianapolis, IN....317-849-7723
Sala, Don/3342 Cumberland Trail, Olympia Trail, IL....708-747-6964
Salisbury, Mark/161 W Harrison 12th Fl, Chicago, IL....312-922-7599
Salter, Tom/685 Pallister, Detroit, MI....313-874-1155
Saltzman, Ben/700 N Washington, Minneapolis, MN....612-332-5112
Sanders, Kathy/411 South Sangamon, Chicago, IL....312-829-3100
Sanderson, Glenn/1002 Pine St, Green Bay, WI....414-437-6200
Sandoz Studios/118 W Kinzie, Chicago, IL....312-527-1800
Santow, Loren/2537 West Leland, Chicago, IL....312-509-1121
Sapecki, Roman/56 E Oakland Ave, Columbus, OH....614-262-7497
Sarnacki, Michael/912 Hilldale Dr, Royal Oak, MI....313-541-2210
Sauer, Neil W/2844 Arsenal, St Louis, MO....314-664-4646
Schabes, Charles/1220 W Grace St, Chicago, IL....312-787-2629
Schanuel, Tony/10901 Oasis Dr, St Louis, MO (P 180)....314-849-3495
Schaugnessy, MacDonald/1221 Jarvis, Elk Grove Village, IL....708-437-8850
Schewe, Jeff/624 West Willow, Chicago, IL....312-951-6334
Schlissman, Paul/PO Box 412, Deerfield, IL (P 181)....708-945-0768
Schmidt, Jerry/Rt 4/Box 882W, Warrensburg, MO....816-429-2305
Schneck, Alan/132 W Stevenson Dr, Glendale Heights, IL....708-665-2623
Schnepf, James/W277 N2730 Trillium Lane, Pewaukee, WI....414-691-3980
Schoenbach, Glenn/329 Enterprise Ct, Bloomfield Hills, MI....313-335-5100
Scholtes, Marc/726 Central Ave NE, Minneapolis, MN....612-378-1888
Schramm, Ron/7061 N Ridge, Chicago, IL....312-973-0246
Schrempp, Erich/723 W Randolph, Chicago, IL....312-454-3237
Schridde, Charles Photography Inc/600 Ajax Dr, Madison Hts, MI....313-589-0111
Schube-Soucek/1735 Carmen Dr, Elk Grove Village, IL....708-439-0640
Schuemann, Bill/1591 S Belvoir Blvd, South Euclid, OH....216-382-4409
Schuessler, Dave/40 E Delaware, Chicago, IL....312-787-6868
Schuette, Bob/207 E Buffalo #645, Milwaukee, WI....414-347-1113
Schulman, Bruce/1102 W Columbia, Chicago, IL....312-917-6420
Schulman, Lee/669 College Ave/Box 09506, Columbus, OH....614-235-5307
Schultz Assoc, Carl/740 W Washington, Chicago, IL....312-454-0303
Schultz, Tim/935 W Chestnut, Chicago, IL....312-733-7113
Schwartz, Linda/2033 N Orleans, Chicago, IL....312-327-7755
Scott, Denis/216 W Ohio St, Chicago, IL....312-467-5663
Secreto, Jim/2140 Austin, Troy, MI....313-689-0480
Segal, Doug Panorama/230 N Michigan Ave, Chicago, IL....312-236-8545
Segal, Mark/230 N Michigan Ave, Chicago, IL....312-236-8545
Segielski, Tony/1886 Thunderbird, Troy, MI....313-362-3111
Sereta, Greg/2440 Lakeside Ave, Cleveland, OH....216-861-7227
Severson, Kent/529 S 7th St #637, Minneapolis, MN....612-375-1870
Sexton, Ken/118 W Kinzie, Chicago, IL....312-854-0180
Seymour, Ronald/314 W Superior, Chicago, IL....312-642-4030
Shafer, Ronald/1735 N Paulina #305, Chicago, IL....312-342-9209
Shaffer, Mac/526 E Dunedin Rd, Columbus, OH....614-268-2249
Shambroom, Paul/1607 Dupont Ave N, Minneapolis, MN....612-521-5835
Shanoor Photo/116 W Illinois, Chicago, IL....312-266-0465
Shaw, George/1032 N Crooks Rd #L, Clawson, MI....313-435-4665
Shay, Arthur/618 Indian Hill Rd, Deerfield, IL....708-945-4636
Sheagren, Joel/529 S Seventh St #415, Minneapolis, MN....612-371-9516
Shelli, Bob/PO Box 2062, St Louis, MO....314-664-7793
Shepherd, Clark/461 E College St, Oberlin, OH....216-775-4825
Sheppard, Richard/421 N Main St, Mt Prospect, IL....708-259-3565
Shigeta-Wright Assoc/1546 N Orleans St, Chicago, IL....312-642-8715
Shippert, Philip/1049 N Paulina, Chicago, IL....312-235-1500
Shirmer, Bob/11 W Illinois St, Chicago, IL....312-321-1151
Shotwell, Chuck/2111 N Clifton, Chicago, IL....312-929-0168
Shoulders, Terry/676 N LaSalle, Chicago, IL....312-642-6622
Siede/Preis Photo/1526 N Halsted, Chicago, IL....312-787-2725
Sierecki, John/56 East Oak St, Chicago, IL....312-664-7824
Sigman, Gary/2229 W Melrose St, Chicago, IL....312-871-8756
Silker, Glenn/5249 W 73rd St #A, Edina, MN....612-835-1811
Sills, Casey/411 N Lasalle, Chicago, IL....312-670-3660
Simeon, Marshall/1043 W Randolph St, Chicago, IL....312-243-9500
Simmons, Howard D/2033 W North Ave, Chicago, IL....312-278-2033
Sindelar, Dan/2517 Grove Springs Ct, St Louis, MO....314-846-4775
Singer, Beth/25741 River Dr, Franklin, MI....313-626-4860
Sinkler, Paul/420 5th St N #516, Minneapolis, MN....612-343-0325
Sinklier, Scott/5860 Merle Hay Rd/Box 127, Johnston, IA....515-270-3732
Skalak, Carl/47-46 Grayton Rd, Cleveland, OH....216-676-6508
Skrebneski, Victor/1350 N LaSalle St, Chicago, IL....312-944-1339
Sky View Aerial Photo/220 S Robert St #201, St Paul, MN....612-290-9766
Sladcik, William/215 W Illinois, Chicago, IL....312-644-7108
Smetzer, Donald/2534 N Burling St, Chicago, IL....312-327-1716
Smith, Bill/600 N McClurgh Ct #802, Chicago, IL....312-787-4686
Smith, Crain/POB 30043, Cleveland, OH....216-661-0636
Smith, Doug Photo/2911 Sutton, St Louis, MO....314-645-1359
Smith, Richard/PO Box 455, Round Lake, IL....708-546-0977
Smith, Richard Hamilton/PO Box 14208, St Paul, MN....612-645-5070
Smith, Robert/496 W Wrightwood Ave, Elmhurst, IL....708-941-7755
Snook, J J/118 W Ohio, Chicago, IL....312-495-3939
Snook, Jim/1433-G W Fullerton, Addison, IL....708-495-3939
Snow, Andy/322 S Patterson Blvd, Dayton, OH....513-461-2930
Snyder, Don/3700 Superior Ave, Cleveland, OH....216-881-5955
Snyder, John/811 W Evergreen, Chicago, IL....312-440-1053
Soluri, Tony/1147 W Ohio, Chicago, IL....312-243-6580
Sorokowski, Rick/1015 N Halsted, Chicago, IL....312-280-1256
Spahr, Dick/1133 E 61st St, Indianapolis, IN....317-255-2400
Spectra Studios/213 W Institute #512, Chicago, IL....312-787-0667
Spencer, Gary/3546 Dakota Ave S, Minneapolis, MN....612-929-7803
Spingola, Laurel/1233 W Eddy, Chicago, IL....312-883-0020
Spitz, Robert/804 Milford St, Evanston, IL....708-869-4992
Stage Three Productions/32588 Dequindre, Warren, MI....313-978-7373
Stansfield, Stan/215 W Ohio, Chicago, IL....312-337-3245
Starkey, John/551 W 72nd St, Indianapolis, IN....317-254-0700
Starmark Photo/706 N Dearborn, Chicago, IL....312-944-6700
Stealey, Jonathan/PO Box 611, Findlay, OH....419-423-1149
Steele, Charles/1130 S Wabash Ave #200, Chicago, IL....312-922-0201
Stegbauer, Jim/421 Transit, Roseville, MN....612-333-1982
Stein, Frederic/955 West Lake St, Chicago, IL....312-226-7447
Steinberg, Mike/633 Huron Rd, Cleveland, OH....216-589-9953
Stenberg, Pete Photography/225 W Hubbard, Chicago, IL....312-644-6137
Stenbroten, Scott/107 W Van Buren #211, Chicago, IL....312-929-4677
Stewart, Ron/314 E Downer Pl, Aurora, IL....708-897-4317
Stone, Tony Worldwide/233 East Ontario, Chicago, IL....312-787-7880
Stornello, Joe/4319 Campbell St, Kansas City, MO....816-756-0419
Straus, Jerry/247 E Ontario, Chicago, IL....312-787-2628
Strauss, Sara/134 Upland Ave, Youngstown, OH....216-794-5881
Stroud, Dan/1414 Illinois St, Midland, MI....517-636-9483
Strouss, Sarah/524 Warner Rd, Hubbard, OH....216-568-0203
Struse, Perry L Jr/232 Sixth St, West Des Moines, IA....515-279-9761
Stump, Art/1920 N Dayton, Chicago, IL....312-477-5569
Summers Studio/153 W Ohio, Chicago, IL....312-527-0908
Sundlof, John/1324 Isabella St, Wilmette, IL....708-256-8877
Sutter, Greg/3030-C Laura Lane, Middleton, WI....608-831-5523

Swanson, Michael/215 W Ohio, Chicago, IL.............................312-337-3245
Sykaluk, John/2500 North Main St, Rockford, IL
(P 183)..**815-968-3819**

T

Taber, Gary/305 S Green St, Chicago, IL..............................312-726-0374
Talbot, Mark/1725 North Ave, Chicago, IL............................312-276-1777
Taxel, Barney/4614 Prospect Ave, Cleveland, OH................216-431-2400
Taylor, Dale E/2665-A Scott Ave, St Louis, MO....................314-652-9665
Technigraph Studio/1212 Jarvis, Elk Grove Village, IL..........708-437-3334
Tepporton, Earl/8701 Harriet Ave S, Minneapolis, MN..........612-887-7852
Teri Studios/700 W Pete Rose Way, Cincinnati, OH.............513-784-9696
Teufen, Al/620 E Smith Rd, Medina, OH..............................216-723-3237
The Picture Place/3721 Grandel Sq, St Louis, MO................314-652-6262
The Studio, Inc/4239 N Lincoln, Chicago, IL.........................312-348-3556
Thill, Nancy/537 South Dearborn, Chicago, IL......................312-939-7770
Thoen, Greg/14940 Minnetonka Indust Rd, Minnetonka, MN.............612-938-2433
Thomas, Bill/Rt 4 Box 387, Nashville, IN..............................812-988-7865
Thomas, Tony/676 N Lasalle St 6th Fl, Chicago, IL...............312-337-2274
Thornberg, Russell/PO Box 101, Akron, OH 216-928-8621
Tillis, Harvey S/1050 W Kinzie, Chicago, IL..........................312-733-7336
Tirotta, John/920 E Wayne St, South Bend, IN.....................219-234-4244
Tolbert, R V/21015 Clare Ave, Maple Hts, OH......................216-663-9214
Tolchin, Robert/1057 Kenton Rd, Deerfield, IL......................708-945-9477
TPS Studio/4016 S California, Chicago, IL.............................312-847-1221
Tracy, Janis/213 W Institute Pl, Chicago, IL..........................312-787-7166
Trantafil, Gary/222 S Morgan, Chicago, IL............................312-666-1029
Traversie, Jim/23 N Walnut St, Dayton, OH (P 169) **513-859-7799**
Trotter, Jim/12342 Conway Rd, St Louis, MO.......................314-878-0777
Tucker, Bill/114 W Illinois, Chicago, IL..................................312-321-1570
Tucker/Thompson Photo/613 Second Ave SE, Cedar Rapids, IA..........319-366-7791
Tushas, Leo/111 N Fifth Ave #309, Minneapolis, MN 612-333-5774
Tweton, Roch/524 Hill Ave, Grafton, ND................................701-352-1513
Tytel, Jeff/59 W Hubbard, Chicago, IL..................................312-329-0222

UV

Uhlmann, Gina/1611 N Sheffield, Chicago, IL........................312-642-6650
Umland, Steve/600 Washington Ave N, Minneapolis, MN.................612-332-1590
Upitis, Alvis/620 Morgan Ave S, Minneapolis, MN.................612-374-9375
Uttermohlen, Mary Lou/860 Dennison Ave, Columbus, OH............614-297-7639
Van Allen, John/U of Iowa Fndtn/Alumni Ctr, Iowa City, IA 319-354-9512
Van Antwerp, Jack/1220 W Sixth St #704, Cleveland, OH 216-621-0515
Van Inwegen, Bruce/1422 W Belle Plaine,
Chicago, IL (P 184,185)..**312-477-8344**
Van Marter, Robert/1209 Alstott Dr S, Howell, MI
(P 186)...**517-546-1923**
Vandenberg, Greg/161 W Harrison 12th Fl, Chicago, IL 312-939-2969
Vander Lende, Craig/129 S Division St, Grand Rapids, MI 616-235-3233
Vander Veen, David/5151 N 35th St, Milwaukee, WI................414-527-0450
VanKirk, Deborah/855 W Blackhawk St, Chicago, IL...............312-642-3208
Variakojis, Danguole/5743 S Campbell, Chicago, IL...............312-776-4668
Vaughan, Jim/321 S Jefferson, Chicago, IL............................312-663-0369
Vedros, Nick/215 W 19th St, Kansas City, MO 816-471-5488
Ventola, Giorgio/230 W Huron, Chicago, IL...........................312-951-0880
Vergos Studio/122 W Kinzie 3rd Fl, Chicago, IL.....................312-527-1769
Viernum, Bill/1629 Mandel Ave, Westchester, IL....................708-562-4143
Villa, Armando/1872 N Clybourne, Chicago, IL......................312-472-7003
Visser, James Photography/4274 Shenandoah Ave,
St Louis, MO (P 187)...**314-771-6857**
Visual Data Systems Inc/5617 63rd Pl, Chicago, IL................312-585-3060
Vizanko Advertising Photo/11511 K-Tel Drive, Minnetonka, MN.........612-933-1314
Vollan, Michael/175 S Morgan, Chicago, IL...........................312-644-1792
Von Photography/685 W Ohio, Chicago, IL.............................312-243-8578
Voyles, Dick & Assoc/2822 Breckenridge Ind Ctr, St Louis, MO 314-968-3851
Vuksanovich/318 N Laflin St, Chicago, IL..............................312-664-7523
Vyskocil, Debbie/PO Box 395, Summit, IL..............................708-496-8057

W

Wagenaar, David/1035 W Lake St, Chicago, IL 312-942-0943
Waite, Tim/717 S Sixth St, Milwaukee, WI..............................414-643-1500
Wakefield, John/5122 Grand Ave, Kansas City, MO 816-531-8448
Walker, Jessie Assoc/241 Fairview, Glencoe, IL.....................708-835-0522
Wallace, David/1100 S Lynndale Dr, Appleton, WI..................414-738-4080
Wans, Glen/325 W 40th, Kansas City, MO..............................816-931-8905
Ward, Les/21477 Bridge St #C & D, Southfield, MI 313-350-8666

Warkenthien, Dan/117 South Morgan, Chicago, IL.................312-666-6056
Warren, Lennie/800 West Huron, Chicago, IL.........................312-666-0490
Watts, Dan/245 Plymouth, Grand Rapids, MI.........................616-451-4693
Weber, J Andrew/303 S Donald Ave, Arlington Hts, IL............708-255-2738
Weddle, Ben/218 Delaware St #108, Kansas City,
MO (P 152,153)...**816-421-2902**
Wedlake, James/750 Jossman Rd, Ortonville, MI...................313-627-2711
Weidemann, Skot/6621-B Century Ave, Middleton, WI...........608-836-5744
Weiland, Jim/1100 S Lynndale Dr, Appleton, WI.....................414-739-7824
Weiner, Jim/540 N Lakeshore Dr, Chicago, IL........................312-644-0040
Weinstein, John/2413 N Clybourn Ave, Chicago, IL................312-509-1003
Weinstein, Phillip/343 S Dearborn, Chicago, IL......................312-922-1945
Weispfenning, Donna/2425 Franklin E #401, Minneapolis, MN..........612-333-1453
Welzenbach, John/2011 W Fullerton Ave, Chicago, IL............312-772-2011
Wengroff, Sam/3325-D North Racine, Chicago, IL..................312-248-6623
West, Mike/300 Howard Ave, Des Plaines, IL.........................708-699-7886
West, Stu/212 Third Ave N #320, Minneapolis, MN.................612-375-0404
Westerman, Charlie/630 W Oakdale, Chicago, IL...................312-248-5709
White, Bob/201 Ward St, Energy, IL......................................618-942-4531
Whitford, T R/1900 Delmar #2, St Louis, MO.........................314-621-2400
Whitmer, Jim/125 Wakeman, Wheaton, IL 708-653-1344
Wicks, L Photography/1235 W Winnemac Ave, Chicago, IL 312-878-4925
Wiegand, Eric/2339 Ferndale, Sylvan Lake, MI......................313-682-8746
Wilker, Clarence/2021 Washington Ave, Lorain, OH...............216-244-5497
Wilkes, Mike/2530 Superior, Cleveland, OH...........................216-781-0605
Willette, Brady T/1030 Nicollett Mall #203, Minneapolis, MN 612-338-6727
Williams, Alfred G/Box 10288, Chicago, IL.............................312-947-0991
Williams, Barry/18 W Northwood Ave, Columbus, OH.............614-291-9774
Williams, Basil/4068 Tanglefoot Terrace, Bettendorf, IA..........319-355-7142
Williams, Bob/32049 Milton Ave, Madison Heights, MI............313-588-6544
Williams, James Photo/119 N 4th St #503, Minneapolis, MN..........612-332-3095
Wilson, Jack/212 Morgan St, St Louis, MO............................314-241-1149
Wilson, Malcolm/2619 Glendora Ave, Cincinnati , OH............513-569-8313
Wirthlin, Walter/PO Box 660, Osage Beach, MO....................314-348-3058
Witte, Scott J/219 N Milwaukee St, Milwaukee, WI.................414-233-4430
Woburn & Ken Carr/4715 N Ronald St, Harwood Heights, IL.........708-867-5445
Woehrle, Mark/3150 North Lindberg, St Louis, MO.................314-298-1727
Wojnowski, Tom/5765 Burger St, Dearborn Hts, MI................313-561-0043
Wolf, Bobbe/1101 W Armitage, Chicago, IL...........................312-472-9503
Wolff, Ed/11357 S Second St, Schoolcraft, MI.......................616-679-4702
Wolford, Rick/2300 E Douglas, Wichita, KS...........................316-264-3013
Wood, Merrell/4449 Royal Ridge Way, Kettering, OH..............513-299-2531
Wooden, John/219 N 2nd St J#306, Minneapolis, MN.............612-339-3032
Woodward, Greg/811 W Evergreen #204, Chicago, IL............312-337-5838
Worzala, Lyle/8164 W Forest Preserve #1, Chicago, IL...........312-434-7156

YZ

Yamashiro, Paul Studio/1500 N Halstead, Chicago, IL...........312-321-1009
Yapp, Charles/723 Randolph, Chicago, IL.............................312-558-9338
Yarrington, Todd/897 Ingleside Ave, Columbus, GA...............614-297-0498
Yates, Peter/1208 Bydding Rd, Ann Arbor, MI
(P 188)...**313-995-0839**
Yaworski, Don/600 White Oak Ln, Kansas City, MO...............816-455-4814
Yazback Photo/PO Box 5146, Mishanaka, IN.........................219-256-1546
Yeager, Alton E/648 W 35th St, Chicago, IL...........................312-523-5788
Zaitz, Dan/1950 West Thomas, Chicago, IL...........................312-276-3569
Zake, Bruce/633 Huron Rd 3rd Fl, Cleveland, OH
(P 189)...**216-694-3686**
Zamiar, Thomas/210 W Chicago, Chicago, IL........................312-787-4976
Zann, Arnold/502 N Grove Ave, Oak Park, IL.........................708-386-2864
Zarlengo, Joseph/419 Melrose Ave, Boardman, OH...............216-782-7797
Zena Photography/633 Huron Rd SE 5th Fl, Cleveland, OH 216-621-6366
Zimion/Marshall Studio/1043 W Randolph, Chicago, IL...........312-243-9500
Zorn, Jim/1880 Holste Rd, Northbrook, IL...............................708-498-4844
Zukas, R/311 N Desplaines #500, Chicago, IL.......................312-648-0100

S O U T H W E S T

A

Abraham, Joe/11944 Hempstead Rd #C, Houston, TX............713-460-4948
Abrial, Larry/1240 N Cowan #256, Louisville, TX....................214-219-6921
Aker/Burnette Studio/4710 Lillian, Houston, TX......................713-862-6343
Alexander, Laury/516 111th St NW #3, Albuquerque, NM 505-843-9165
Alford, Jess/1800 Lear St #3, Dallas, TX (P 196)..........**214-421-3107**

Allen, Jim Photo/5600 Lovers Ln #212, Dallas, TX.................214-351-3200
Allred, Mark/904-B W 12th St, Austin, TX 512-472-2972
Anderson, Derek Studio/3959 Speedway Blvd E, Tucson, AZ 602-881-1205
Anderson, Randy/1606 Lewis Trail, Grand Prairie, TX 214-660-1071
Angle, Lee/1900 Montgomery, Fort Worth, TX............................817-737-6469
Ashe, Gil/Box 686, Bellaire, TX...713-668-8766
Ashley, Constance/2024 Farrington St, Dallas, TX......................214-747-2501
Associated Photo/2344 Irving Blvd, Dallas, TX..........................214-630-8730
Austin, David/2412 Fifth Ave, Fort Worth, TX...........................817-335-1881

B

Badger, Bobby/1355 Chemical, Dallas, TX...............................214-634-0222
Bagshaw, Cradoc/PO Box 9511, Santa Fe, NM..............................505-473-2811
Baker, Bobbe C/1119 Ashburn, College Station, TX......................409-696-7185
Baker, Jeff/6161 Premier Dr, Irving, TX 214-550-7992
Baker, Nash/2208 Colquitt, Houston, TX (P 197)...........**713-529-5698**
Baldwin/Watriss Assoc/1405 Branard St, Houston, TX 713-524-9199
Bardin, Keith Jr/PO Box 191241, Dallas, TX.............................214-686-0611
Barker, Kent/2919 Canton St, Dallas, TX................................214-760-7470
Baxter, Scott/PO Box 25041, Phoenix, AZ.................................602-254-5879
Beebower Brothers/9995 Monroe #209, Dallas, TX.........................214-358-1219
Bennett, Sue/PO Box 1574, Flagstaff, AZ.................................602-774-2544
Bennett, Tony R/PO Box 568366, Dallas, TX..............................214-747-0107
Benoist, John/PO Box 20825, Dallas, TX.................................214-692-8813
Berman, Bruce/140 N Stevens #301, El Paso, TX..........................915-544-0352
Berrett, Patrick L/2521 Madison NE, Albuquerque, NM....................505-881-0935
Berry, George S Photography/Rt 2 Box 325B, San Marcos, TX.............512-396-4805
Bissell, Gary/120 Paragon #217, El Paso, TX............................915-833-1942
Blue, Janice/1708 Rosewood, Houston, TX................................713-522-6899
Bock, Ken/PO Box 568108, Dallas, TX....................................214-692-7355
Bondy, Roger/309 NW 23rd St, Oklahoma City, OK.........................405-521-1616
Booth, Greg/1322 Round Table, Dallas, TX...............................214-688-1855
Bowman, Matt/8602 Santa Clara, Dallas, TX..............................214-637-0211
Bradley, Matt/15 Butterfield Ln, Little Rock, AR.......................501-224-0692
Bradshaw, Reagan/4101 Guadalupe, Austin, TX............................512-458-6101
Brady, Steve/5250 Gulfton #2G, Houston, TX.............................713-660-6663
Britt, Ben/2401 S Ervay #205, Dallas, TX 214-428-2822
Brousseau, Jay/2608 Irving Blvd, Dallas, TX (P 199)...**214-638-1248**
Brown, David Photo/280 Edgewood Ct, Prescott, AZ.......................602-445-2485
Buffington, David/2401 S Ervay #105, Dallas, TX........................214-428-8221
Bumpass, R O/1222 N Winnetka, Dallas, TX...............................214-742-3414
Burkey, J W/1526 Edison St, Dallas, TX.................................214-746-6336

C

Cabluck, Jerry/Box 9601, Fort Worth, TX................................817-336-1431
Caldwell, Jim/101 W Drew, Houston, TX..................................713-527-9121
Campbell, Doug/5617 Matalee, Dallas, TX................................214-823-9151
Cannedy, Carl/3333 Elm St, Dallas, TX..................................214-748-1048
Capps, Robbie/5729 Goliad, Dallas, TX..................................214-827-9339
Captured Image Photography/5131 E Lancaster, Fort Worth, TX...........817-457-2302
Cardellino, Robert/315 Ninth St #2, San Antonio, TX...................512-224-9606
Carey, Robert "Lobster"/2318 E Roosevelt, Phoenix, AZ 602-267-8845
Carr, Fred/2331-D Wirtcrest, Houston, TX...............................713-680-2465
Chehabi, Saad/5028 Airline, Dallas, TX.................................214-526-4989
Chenn, Steve/6301 Ashcroft, Houston, TX
(P 200,201)...**713-271-0631**
Chisholm, Rich & Assoc/6813 Northampton Way, Houston, TX 713-957-1250
Clair, Andre/11415 Chatten Way, Houston, TX 713-465-5507
Clark, H Dean/18405 FM 149, Houston, TX................................713-469-7021
Clifford, Geoffrey C/4719 Brisa Del Norte, Tucson, AZ.................602-577-6439
Clintsman, Dick/3001 Quebec #102, Dallas, TX...........................214-630-1531
Cobb, Lynn/PO Box 16521, Santa Fe, NM..................................505-473-3094
Cohen, Stewart Charles/2401 S Ervay #206, Dallas, TX..................214-421-2186
Cole, Ralph Inc/PO Box 2803, Tulsa, OK (P 202)......**918-585-9119**
Cooke, Richard & Mary/209 E Ben White Blvd #110, Austin, TX 512-444-6100
Cotter, Austin/1350 Manufacturing #211, Dallas, TX....................214-742-3633
Cowlin, James/PO Box 34205, Phoenix, AZ................................602-264-9689
Craig, George/314 E 13th St, Houston, TX (P 203)........**713-862-6008**
Crittendon, James/5914 Lake Crest, Garland, TX.........................214-226-2196
Crossley, Dave/1412 W Alabama, Houston,
TX (P 204) **713-523-5757**
Crossley/Pogue/1412 W Alabama, Houston,
TX (P 204) **713-523-5757**
Cruff, Kevin/2328 E Van Buren, Phoenix, AZ.............................602-225-0029
Crump, Bill/1357 Chemical, Dallas, TX..................................214-630-7745
Cutter, Stephen/1535 E Dolphin Ave, Mesa, AZ...........................602-962-4359

D

Davey, Robert/PO Box 2421, Prescott, AZ................................602-445-1160
Davidson, Josiah/PO Box 607, Cloudcroft, NM............................800-537-7810
Davis, Mark/8718 Boundbrook Ave, Dallas, TX............................214-348-7679
Dawson, Greg/2211 Beall St, Houston, TX (P 205) **713-862-8301**
Debenport, Robb/2412 Converse, Dallas, TX..............................214-631-7606
Debold, Bill/TX...512-837-6294
Dolin, Penny Ann/, Scottsdale, AZ......................................602-228-3015
Drews, Buzzy/1555 W Mockingbird #202, Dallas, TX.......................214-351-9968
Driscoll, W M/PO Box 8463, Dallas, TX..................................214-363-8429
DuBose, Bill/6646 E Lovers Lane #603, Dallas, TX......................214-781-6147
Duering, Doug/2610 Catherine, Dallas, TX...............................214-946-6597
Duncan, Nena/306 Shady Wood, Houston, TX...............................713-782-3130
Duran, Mark/66 East Vernon, Phoenix, AZ................................602-279-1141
Durham, Thomas/PO Box 4665, Wichita Falls, TX..........................817-691-4414
Dyer, John/107 Blue Star, San Antonio, TX..............................512-223-1891
Dykinga, Jack/3808 Calle Barcelona, Tucson, AZ.........................602-326-6094

EF

Easley, Ken/2810 S 24th St #109, Phoenix, AZ...........................602-244-9727
Edens, Swain/1905 N St Marys St, San Antonio, TX.......................512-226-2210
EDS Photography Services/Mail Code CY-01-68, Plano, TX.................214-612-5791
Edwards, Bill/3820 Brown, Dallas, TX...................................214-521-8630
Enger, Linda/915 S 52nd St #5, Tempe, AZ...............................602-966-5776
Ewasko, Tommy/5645 Hillcroft #202, Houston, TX.........................713-784-1777
Fantich, Barry/PO Box 70103, Houston, TX...............................713-520-5434
Farris, Neal/500 Expostion #104, Dallas, TX...........................214-821-5612
Faye, Gary/2421 Bartlett, Houston, TX..................................713-529-9548
Findysz, Mary/3550 E Grant, Tucson, AZ.................................602-325-0260
Fontenot, Dallas/6002 Burning Tree Dr, Houston, TX 713-988-2183
Ford, Bill/3501 N MacArthur Blvd #421, Irving, TX......................214-255-5312
Foxall, Steve Photography Inc/6132 Belmont Ave,
Dallas, TX (P 207)...**214-824-1977**
Frady, Connie/2808 Fifth Ave, Fort Worth, TX...........................817-927-7589
Francis, Pam/2700 Albany #303, Houston, TX.............................713-528-1672
Freeman, Charlie/3333-A Elm St, Dallas, TX.............................214-742-1446
Fry, John/5909 Goliad, Dallas, TX......................................214-821-1689
Fuller, Timothy Woodbridge/135 1/2 S Sixth Ave, Tucson, AZ............602-622-3900

G

Gaber, Brad/4946 Glen Meadow, Houston, TX 713-723-0030
Galloway, Jim/2335 Valdina St, Dallas, TX..............................214-954-0355
Garacci, Benedetto/7315 Ashcroft #102, Houston, TX.....................713-771-3209
Gary & Clark Photographic Studio/2702 Main, Dallas, TX................214-939-9070
Gatz, Larry/5250 Gulfton #3B, Houston, TX..............................713-666-5203
Gayle, Rick/2318 E Roosevelt, Phoenix, AZ..............................602-267-8845
Geffs, Dale/15715 Amapola, Houston, TX.................................713-777-2228
Gerczynski, Tom/2211 N 7th Ave, Phoenix, AZ............................602-252-9229
Germany, Robert/2739 Irving Blvd, Dallas, TX...........................214-747-4548
Gilmore, Dwight/2437 Hillview, Fort Worth, TX..........................817-536-4825
Gilstrap, L C/132 Booth Calloway, Hurst, TX............................817-284-7701
Giordano, Michael/PO Box 15497, San Antonio, TX........................512-734-5552
Glentzer, Don Photography/3814 S Shepherd Dr, Houston, TX.............713-529-9686
Golfoto Inc/224 North Independence, Enid, OK...........................405-234-8284
Gomel, Bob/10831 Valley Hills, Houston, TX.............................713-988-6390
Goodman, Robert/2025 Levee, Dallas, TX.................................214-653-1120
Grass, Jon/3141 Irving #209, Dallas, TX................................214-634-1455
Green, Mark/2406 Taft St, Houston, TX (P 208,209)....**713-523-6146**
Greenberg, Chip/2521 Madison NE, Albuquerque, NM 505-884-1012
Greshon, Daniel/2314 Converse, Houston, TX............................713-524-9992
Grider, James/732 Schilder, Fort Worth, TX.............................817-732-7472
Guerrero, Charles/8301 Shoal Creek Blvd, Austin, TX...................512-467-2797

H

Hagler, Skeeter/PO Box 628, Red Oak, TX................................214-576-5620
Hale, Butch Photography/1319 Conant, Dallas, TX 214-637-3987
Halpern, David/7420 E 70th St, Tulsa, OK...............................918-252-4973
Ham, Dan/PO Box 5149, Taos, NM...505-758-1463
Hamblin, Steve/4718 Iberia, Dallas, TX 214-630-2848
Hamburger, Jay/1817 State St, Houston, TX..............................713-869-0869
Hamilton, Jeffrey Muir/6719 Quartzite Canyon Pl, Tucson, AZ 602-299-3624
Hand, Ray/10921 Shady Trail #100, Dallas, TX
(P 210,211) **214-351-2488**

Handel, Doug/3016 Selma, Dallas, TX	214-446-2236
Harness, Brian/1402 S Montreal Ave, Dallas, TX	214-330-4419
Hart, Len/2100 Wilcrest #102, Houston, TX	713-974-3265
Hart, Michael/7320 Ashcroft #105, Houston, TX (P 212,213)	**713-271-8250**
Hartman, Gary/911 South St Marys St, San Antonio, TX	512-225-2404
Hatcok, Tom/113 W 12th St, Deer Park, TX	713-479-2603
Hawks, Bob/1345 E 15th St, Tulsa, OK	918-584-3351
Hawn, Gray Photography/PO Box 16425, Austin, TX	512-328-1321
Haynes, Mike/10343 Best Dr, Dallas, TX	214-352-1314
Hedrich, David/4006 South 23rd St #10, Phoenix, AZ	602-220-0090
Heiner, Gary/2039 Farrington, Dallas, TX	214-760-7471
Heinsohn, Bill/5455 Dashwood #200, Bellaire, TX	713-666-6515
Heit, Don/8502 Eustis Ave, Dallas, TX	214-324-0305
Henry, Steve/7403 Pierrepont Dr, Houston, TX	713-937-4514
Hoke, Doug/805 NW 49th St, Oklahoma City, OK (P 214)	**405-840-1256**
Hollenbeck, Phil/2833 Duval Dr, Dallas, TX (P 194)	**214-331-8328**
Holley, Tom/2709-E Pam Am NE , Albuquerque, NM	505-345-1660
Horst, Taylor/2521 Madison NE, Albuquerque, NM	505-881-7901
Huber, Phil/13562 Braemar Dr, Dallas, TX	214-243-4011

JK

Jenkins, Gary/2320 Indian Creek, Irving, TX	214-952-8868
Jennings, Steve/PO Box 52813, Tulsa, OK	918-745-0836
Jew, Kim/1518 Girard NE, Albuquerque, NM	505-255-6424
Johnson, Ed/8560 Park Lane #79, Dallas, TX	214-361-7621
Johnson, Michael/830 Exposition #215, Dallas, TX	214-828-9550
Johnson, Norman/2015 7th St NW #A-2, Albuquerque, NM	505-842-9411
Jolly, Randy/801 E Campbell Rd #110, Richardson, TX	214-644-8542
Jones, Aaron/PO Box 5799, Santa Fe, NM	505-988-5730
Jones, C Bryan/2900 N Loop W #1130, Houston, TX	713-956-4166
Jones, Jerry/5250 Gulfton #4A, Houston, TX	713-668-4328
Jones, Will/4602 E Elwood St #13, Phoenix, AZ	602-968-7664
Kaluzny, Zigy/4700 Strass Dr, Austin, TX	512-452-4463
Kasie Photos/2123 Avignon, Carrollton, TX	214-492-7837
Katz, John/5222 Red Field, Dallas, TX	214-637-0844
Kellis, Shawn/3433 W earll Dr, Phoenox, AZ	602-272-7777
Kendrick, Robb/2700 Albany #303, Houston, TX	713-528-4334
Kennedy, David Michael/PO Box 254, Cerrillos, NM	505-473-2745
Kenny, Gill/6541 N Camina Catrina, Tucson, AZ	602-577-1232
Kern, Geof/1337 Crampton, Dallas, TX	214-630-0856
King, Jennifer/4031 Green Bush Rd, Katy, TX	713-392-8784
Kirkland, Bill/PO Box 801001, Dallas, TX	214-741-7673
Kirkley, Kent/4906 Don St, Dallas, TX	214-688-1841
Klumpp, Don/804 Colquitt, Houston, TX	713-521-2090
Kneten, Rocky/2425 Bartlett, Houston, TX	713-528-5235
Knowles, Jim/6102 E Mockingbird Ln #499, Dallas, TX	214-699-5335
Knudson, Kent/PO Box 10397, Phoenix, AZ	602-277-7701
Korab, Jeanette/9000 Directors Row, Dallas, TX	214-337-0114
Kretchmar, Phil Photography/233 Yorktown, Dallas, TX	214-744-2039
Kroninger, Rick/PO Box 15913, San Antonio, TX	512-733-9931
Kuntz, Bryan Photography/7700 Brenwick #5A, Houston, TX	713-667-4200
Kuper, Holly/5522 Anita St, Dallas, TX	214-827-4494

LM

Lacker, Pete/235 Yorktown St, Dallas, TX	214-748-7488
Larsen, Peter/2410 Farrington, Dallas, TX	214-630-3500
Latorre, Robert/2336 Farrington St, Dallas, TX	214-630-8977
Laybourn, Richard/4657 Westgrove, Dallas, TX	214-931-9984
Lettner, Hans/830 North 4th Ave, Phoenix, AZ	602-258-3506
Lewis, Barry/2401 S Ervay #306, Dallas, TX	214-421-5665
Loper, Richard/1000 Jackson Blvd, Houston, TX	713-529-9221
Lorfing, Greg/1900 W Alabama, Houston, TX	713-529-5968
Loven, Paul/1405 E Marshall, Phoenix, AZ	602-253-0335
Luker, Tom/PO Box 6112, Coweta, OK	918-486-5264
Mader, Bob/2570 Promenade Center N, Richardson, TX	214-690-5511
Magee, Mike/1325 Conant St, Dallas, TX	214-638-6868
Mageors & Rice Photo Service Inc/240 Turnpike Ave, Dallas, TX	214-941-3777
Manley, Dan/1350 Manufacturing #213, Dallas, TX	214-748-8377
Mann, Chris/2001 S Ervay #100, Dallas, TX	214-426-1810
Manning, John/1240 Hanna Creek, DeSoto, TX	214-224-6787
Manske, Thaine/7313 Ashcroft #216, Houston, TX	713-771-2220
Maples, Carl/1811 Cohn, Houston, TX	713-868-1289
Markham, Jim/2739 S E Loop 410, San Antonio, TX	512-648-0403
Markow, Paul/2222 E McDowell Rd, Phoenix, AZ	602-273-7985

Marks, Stephen/4704-C Prospect NE, Albuquerque, NM	505-884-6100
Marshall, Jim/382 N First Ave, Phoenix, AZ	602-258-4213
Matthews, Michael/2727 Cancun, Dallas, TX	214-306-8000
Maxham, Robert/223 Howard St, San Antonio, TX	512-223-6000
Mayer, George H/1356 Chemical, Dallas, TX (P 215)	**214-424-4409**
McClain, Edward/756 N Palo Verde, Tucson, AZ	602-326-1873
McCormick, Mike/5950 Westward Ave, Houston, TX	713-988-0775
McCoy, Gary/2700 Commerce St, Dallas, TX	214-320-0002
McKenzie, David/4707 Red Bluff, Austin, TX	512-453-1965
McNee, Jim/PO Box 741008, Houston, TX	713-796-2633
Means, Lisa/5915 Anita, Dallas, TX	214-826-4979
Meckler, Steven/121 S 4th Ave, Tucson, AZ	602-792-2467
Meredith, Diane/6203 Westcott, Houston, TX	713-862-8775
Messina, John/4440 Lawnview, Dallas, TX	214-388-8525
Meyerson, Arthur/4215 Bellaire Blvd, Houston, TX	713-660-0405
Meyler, Dennis/1903 Portsmouth #25, Houston, TX (P 216)	**713-520-1800**
Mills, Jack R/PO Box 32583, Oklahoma City, OK	405-787-7271
Moberley, Connie/215 Asbury, Houston, TX	713-864-3638
Molen, Roy/3302 N 47 Pl, Phoenix, AZ	602-840-5439
Monteaux, Michele/5 Vista Grande Dr, Santa Fe, NM	505-982-5598
Moore, Terrence/PO Box 41536, Tucson, AZ	602-623-9381
Moot, Kelly/2331-D Wirtcrest Ln, Houston, TX	713-683-6400
Morgan, Paul/3408 Main St, Dallas, TX	214-741-3908
Morris, Garry/9281 E 27th St, Tucson, AZ	602-795-2334
Morris, Mike/4003 Gilbert #6, Dallas, TX	214-528-3600
Morrison, Chet Photography/2917 Canton, Dallas, TX	214-939-0903
Morrow, James R/PO Box 2718, Grapevine, TX	214-402-9960
Muir, Robert/Box 42809 Dept 404, Houston, TX	713-784-7420
Murdoch, Lane/1350 Manufacturing #205, Dallas, TX	214-651-0200
Murphy, Dennis/101 Howell St, Dallas, TX	214-651-7516
Myers, Jeff/5250 Gulfton #4 Suite A, Houston, TX	713-661-9532
Myers, Jim/165 Cole St, Dallas, TX	214-698-0500

NOP

Neely, David/412 Briarcliff Lane, Bedford, TX	817-498-6741
Netzer, Don/1345 Conant, Dallas, TX	214-869-0826
Neubauer, Larry/11716 Terry Dr, Balch Springs, TX	214-284-2480
Newby, Steve/4501 Swiss, Dallas, TX	214-821-0231
Noble, Jeff/688 West 1st St #5, Tempe, AZ	602-968-1434
Norrell, J B/7315 Ashcroft #110, Houston, TX	713-981-6409
Norton, Michael/3427 E Highland Ave, Phoenix, AZ (P 195)	**602-840-9463**
Nufer, David/405 Montano NE #1, Albuquerque, NM	505-345-9500
O'Dell, Dale/2040 Bissonet, Houston, TX (P 217)	**713-521-2611**
Olvera, James /235 Yorktown St, Dallas, TX	214-760-0025
Pantin, Tomas/1601 E 7th St #100, Austin, TX	512-474-9968
Papadopolous, Peter/PO Box 474, Ranchos de Taos, NM	505-758-0789
Paparazzi/2917 Canton St, Dallas, TX	214-939-0091
Parrish, John/1218 Manufacturing, Dallas, TX	214-742-9457
Parsons, Bill/518 W 9th St, Little Rock, AR	501-372-5892
Patrick, Richard/215-B W 4th St , Austin, TX	512-472-9092
Payne, Al /830 North 4th Ave, Phoenix, AZ	602-258-3506
Payne, C Ray/2737 Irving Blvd, Dallas, TX	214-638-1355
Payne, Richard/1601 S Shepard #282, Houston, TX	713-524-7525
Payne, Tom/2425 Bartlett, Houston, TX	713-527-8670
Perlstein, Mark/1844 Place One Ln, Garland, TX	214-690-0168
Peterson, Bruce Photo/2430 S 20th St, Phoenix, AZ	602-252-6088
Pettit, Steve/206 Weeks, Arlington, TX	817-265-8776
Pfuhl, Chris/PO Box 542, Phoenix, AZ	602-253-0525
Phelps, Greg/2360 Central Blvd, Brownsville, TX	512-541-4909
Photo Group/2512 East Thomas #2, Phoenix, AZ	602-381-1332
Photo Media, Inc/2805 Crockett, Fort Worth, TX	817-332-4172
Pierson, Sam/1019 Forest Home Dr, Houston, TX	713-497-3176
Pledger, Nancy/2124 Farrington #300, Dallas, TX	214-761-9545
Pogue, Bill/1412 W Alabama, Houston, TX (P 204)	**713-523-5757**
Porter, Albert/7215 Wild Valley, Dallas, TX	214-349-2230
Post, Andy/4748 Algiers #300, Dallas, TX	214-634-4490
Poulides, Peter/PO Box 202505, Dallas, TX	214-902-8800
Probst, Kenneth/3527 Oak Lawn Blvd #375, Dallas, TX	214-522-2031

QR

Quilia, Jim/3125 Ross, Dallas, TX	214-276-9956
Rahn, Reed/610 W 11th St, Tempe, AZ	602-829-7455
Ralph, Michael/10948 Pelham, El Paso, TX	915-595-3787
Raphaele Inc/616 Hawthorne, Houston, TX	713-524-2211

Rascona, Donna & Rodney/4232 S 36th Place, Phoenix, AZ 602-437-0866
Raymond, Rick Photography/382 North First Ave, Phoenix, AZ 602-581-8160
Records, Bill/505 W 38, Austin, TX 512-458-1017
Redd, True/2328 Farrington, Dallas, TX...214-638-0602
Reedy, Mark/1512 Edison #100, Dallas, TX 214-748-1777
Reens, Louis/4814 Sycamore, Dallas, TX...214-827-3388
Reese, Donovan/3007 Canton, Dallas, TX 214-748-5900
Reinig, Tom/2720 N 68th St#5426, Scottsdale, AZ 602-966-4199
Reisch, Jim/235 Yorktown St, Dallas, TX...214-748-0456
Robbins Jr, Joe D/7700 Renwick #5, Houston, TX.............................713-667-5050
Robbins, Joe/7700 Renwick #5A, Houston, TX 713-667-5050
Robson, Howard/3807 E 64th Pl, Tulsa, OK 918-492-3079
Roe, Cliff/26734 InterstHwy N, Spring, TX.......................................713-367-2520
Rose, Kevin/1513 Reisen Dr, Garland, TX 214-495-3004
Rubin, Janice/705 E 16th St, Houston, TX.......................................713-868-6060
Running, John/PO Box 1237, Flagstaff, AZ......................................602-774-2923
Rusing, Rick/1555 W University #106, Tempe, AZ.............................602-967-1864
Russell, Gail/PO Box 241, Taos, NM..505-776-8474
Russell, Nicholas/849-F Harvard, Houston, TX 713-864-7664
Ryan, Tom/2919 Canton St, Dallas, TX 214-651-7085

S

Samaha, Sam/1526 Edison, Dallas, TX 214-630-1369
Sanders, Chuck/715 W 13th St, Tempe, AZ 602-820-3179
Savant, Joseph/4756 Algiers St, Dallas, TX......................................214-951-0111
Savins, Matthew/101 Howell St, Dallas, TX.......................................214-651-7516
Saxon, John/1337 Crampton, Dallas, TX 214-630-5160
Scheer, Tim/1521 Centerville Rd, Dallas, TX 214-328-1016
Scheyer, Mark/3317 Montrose #A1003, Houston, TX 713-861-0847
Schlesinger, Terrence/PO Box 32877, Phoenix, AZ 602-957-7474
Schmidt, David/74 W Culver, Phoenix, AZ...602-258-2592
Schneps, Michael/4311 Benning, Houston, TX....................................713-668-4600
Schuster, Ellen/3719 Gilbert, Dallas, TX...214-526-6712
Scott, Ron/1000 Jackson Blvd, Houston, TX......................................713-529-5868
Seeger, Stephen/2931 Irving Blvd #101, Dallas, TX 214-634-1309
Segrest, Jerry Photography/1707 S Arvay, Dallas, TX 214-426-6360
Segroves, Jim/170 Leslie, Dallas, TX...214-827-5482
Sellers, Dan/1317 Conant, Dallas, TX...214-631-4705
Shands, Nathan/1107 Bryan, Mesquite, TX.......................................214-285-5382
Shaw, Robert/1723 Kelly SE, Dallas, TX 214-428-1757
Shield-Marley, DeAnne/101 S Victory #1315, Little Rock, AR...............501-372-6148
Siegel, Dave/224 N 5th Ave, Phoenix, AZ 602-257-9509
Sieve, Jerry/PO Box 1777, Cave Creek, AZ 602-488-9561
Simon, Frank/4030 N 27th Ave #B, Phoenix, AZ (P 218).............................**602-279-4635**
Simpson, Micheal/1415 Slocum St #105, Dallas, TX 214-761-0000
Sims, Jim/2811 McKinney #224, Dallas, TX 214-855-0055
Sims, John/336 Melrose #14A, Richardson, TX..................................214-231-6065
Sloan-White, Barbara/1001 Missouri, Houston, TX 713-529-4055
Smith, Dan/2700 Flora St, Dallas, TX...212-819-0466
Smith, Ralph/2211 Beall, Houston, TX...713-862-8301
Smith, Seth/2401 S Ervay #204, Dallas, TX.......................................214-428-4510
Smith/Garza Photography/PO Box 10046, Dallas, TX..........................214-941-4611
Smothers, Brian/834 W 43rd St, Houston, TX....................................713-695-0873
Snedeker, Katherine/, Dallas, TX..214-745-1250
Sperry, Bill/3300 E Stanford, Paradise Valley, AZ 602-955-5626
St Angelo, Ron/PO Box 161702, Las Colinas, TX...............................817-481-1833
St Gil & Associates/PO Box 820568, Houston, TX...............................713-347-3337
Staarjes, Hans/20 Lana Lane, Houston, TX..713-621-8503
Stewart, Craig/1900 W Alabama, Houston, TX....................................713-529-5959
Stiller, Rick/1311 E 35th St, Tulsa, OK..918-749-0297
Storr, Jay/PO Box 7190, Houston, TX 713-861-6111
Studio 3 Photography/2804 Lubbock, Fort Worth, TX..........................817-923-9931
Suddarth, Robert/3402 73rd St, Lubbock, TX.....................................806-795-4553
Summers, Chris/2437 Bartlett St, Houston, TX....................................713-524-7371
Swindler, Mark/206 Santa Rita, Odessa, TX 915-332-3515

TUV

Talley, Paul/4756 Algiers St, Dallas, TX..214-951-0039
Thatcher, Charles/403 W Mockingbird Lane, Dallas, TX......................214-643-9444
The Quest Group/3007 Paseo, Oklahoma City, OK 405-946-1757
Thompson, Dennis/15 E Brady, Tulsa, OK 918-743-5595
Threadgill, Toby/1345 Chemical, Dallas, TX.......................................214-638-1661
Timmerman, Bill/844 S Edward Dr #1, Tempe, AZ...............................602-968-9474
Tomlinson, Doug/9307 Mercer Dr, Dallas, TX......................................214-321-0600
Trotto, John Photo Inc/4006 S 23rd St #10, Phoenix, AZ 602-268-2020
Tunison, Richard/7829 E Foxmore Lane, Scottsdale, AZ 602-998-4708
Turner, Danny/4228 Main St, Dallas, TX...214-760-7472
Urban, Linda/2931 Irving Blvd #101, Dallas, TX..................................214-634-9009
Vandivier, Kevin/904 E 44th St, Austin, TX...512-450-1506
VanOverbeek, Will/305 E Sky View, Austin, TX....................................512-454-1501
Vantage Point Studio/1109 Arizona Ave, El Paso, TX...........................915-533-9688
Vener, Ellis/2926 Helena St, Houston, TX..713-523-0456
Viewpoint Photographers/9034 N 23rd Ave #11, Phoenix, AZ 602-245-0013
Vine, Terry/5455 Dashwood #200, Houston, TX...................................713-664-2920
Vracin, Andrew/4609 Don, Dallas, TX..214-688-1841

WZ

Walker, Balfour/1838 E 6th St, Tucson, AZ...602-624-1121
Webb, Drayton/5455 Dashwood #300, Belaire, TX 713-660-7497
Weeks, Christopher/1260 E 31st Pl, Tulsa, OK....................................918-749-8289
Wellman, Jeffrey B/415 Sunset St, Santa Fe, NM................................505-989-9231
Wells, Craig/537 W Granada, Phoenix, AZ..602-252-8166
Welsch, Diana/1505 Forest Trail, Austin, TX..512-469-0958
Werre, Bob/2437 Bartlett St, Houston, TX (P 219)........**713-529-4841**
Wheeler, Don/1933 S Boston Ave/Studio C, Tulsa, OK 918-587-3808
White, Frank Photo/1109 E Freeway, Houston, TX 713-223-1110
Whitlock, Neill/122 E 5th St, Dallas, TX...214-948-3117
Williams, Laura/223 Howard, San Antonio, TX......................................512-223-6000
Williams, Oscar/8535 Fairhaven, San Antonio, TX 512-690-8807
Williamson, Thomas A/10830 N Central Expy #201, Dallas, TX 214-373-4999
Willis, Gordon/3910 Buena Vista #23, Dallas, TX..................................214-520-7035
Wolenski, Stan/2919 Canton, Dallas, TX...214-749-0749
Wolfhagen, Vilhelm/4916 Kelvin, Houston, TX......................................713-522-2787
Wollam, Les/5215 Goodwin Ave, Dallas, TX...214-760-7721
Wood, Keith Photography Inc/1308 Conant St, Dallas, TX (P 192,193)..............................**214-634-7344**
Wristen, Don/2025 Levee St, Dallas, TX 214-748-5317
Zabel, Ed/PO Box 58601, Dallas, TX..214-748-2910
Zemnick, Mark/3202 Westbell #2202, Phoenix, AZ 602-866-8711

ROCKY MTN

AB

Adams, Butch Photography/1414 S 700 W, Salt Lake City, UT 801-973-0939
Aiuppy, Larry/PO Box 26, Livingston, MT...406-222-7308
Alaxandar/1201 18th St #240, Denver, CO 303-298-7711
Alston, Bruce/PO Box 2480, Steamboat Springs, CO............................303-879-1675
Appleton, Roger/3106 Pennsylvania, Colorado Springs, CO 719-635-0393
Archer, Mark/228 S Madison St, Denver, CO..303-399-5272
Bailey, Brent P/PO Box 70681, Reno, NV 702-826-4104
Bartek, Patrick/PO Box 26994, Las Vegas, NV 702-368-2901
Bator, Joe/8245 Yarrow St, Arvada, CO...303-425-0833
Bauer, Erwin A/Box 543, Teton Village, WY..307-733-4023
Beebe, Kevin/2460 Eliot St, Denver, CO...303-455-3627
Beery, Gale/150 W Byers, Denver, CO 303-777-0458
Berchert, James H/2886 W 119th Ave, Denver, CO................................303-466-7414
Berge, Melinda/1280 Ute Ave, Aspen, CO...303-925-2317
Biggs, Deborah/8335 E Fairmont #11-207, Denver, CO.........................719-388-5846
Birnbach, Allen/3600 Tejon St, Denver, CO..303-455-7800
Blake, John/4132 20th St, Greeley, CO 303-330-0980
Bosworth/Graves Photo Inc/1055 S 700 W, Salt Lake City, UT 801-972-6128
Brock, Sidney/3377 Blake St #102, Denver, CO 303-296-9462
Burggraf, Chuck/2941 W 23rd Ave, Denver, CO.....................................303-480-9053
Busath, Drake/701 East South Temple St, Salt Lake City, UT 801-364-6645
Bush, Michael/2240 Bellaire St, Denver, CO 303-377-1057

C

Cambon, Jim/216 Racquette Dr, Denver, CO...303-221-4545
Captured Light Imagery/4817 S 1740 EA 6, Salt Lake City, UT..............801-277-0265
Cava, Greg Photography/2912 S Highland #J, Las Vegas, NV (P 237)...............................**702-735-2282**
Chesley, Paul/Box 94, Aspen, CO 303-925-1148
Coca, Joe/213 1/2 Jefferson St, Ft Collins, CO 303-482-0858
Collector, Stephen/4209 26th St, Boulder, CO 303-442-1386
Cook, James/PO Box 11608, Denver, CO..303-433-4874
Coppock, Ron/1764 Platte St, Denver, CO...303-477-3343
Cronin, Bill/2543 Xavier, Denver, CO 303-458-0883
Cruz, Frank/1855 Blake St #5E, Denver, CO..303-297-1007

D

Daly, Glenn/155 Lone Pine Rd, Aspen, CO 303-925-2224
DeHoff, RD/632 N Sheridan, Colorado Springs, CO 303-635-0263
DeLespinasse, Hank/2300 E Patrick Ln #21, Las Vegas, NV 702-798-6693
DeMancznk, Phillip/5635 Riggins Ct #15, Reno, NV 702-826-5533
DeSciose, Nick/2700 Arapahoe St #2, Denver, CO 303-296-6386
DeVore, Nicholas III/1280 Ute, Aspen, CO 303-925-2317
Dickey, Marc/PO Box 4705, Denver, CO 303-449-6310
Douglass, Dirk/2755 S 300 W #D, Salt Lake City, UT 801-485-5691
DuBois, F.E./The Bench, Fallon, NV 702-867-2551

EFG

Elder, Jim/PO Box 1600, Jackson Hole, WY 307-733-3555
Fader, Bob/14 Pearl St, Denver, CO 303-744-0711
Farace, Joe Photo/14 Inverness #B100, Englewood, CO 303-799-6606
Feld, Stephen/9480 Union Sq #208, Sandy, UT 801-571-1752
Frazier, Van/2770 S Maryland Pkwy, Las Vegas, NV 702-735-1165
Gallian, Dirk/PO Box 4573, Aspen, CO 303-925-8268
Goetze, David/3215 Zuni, Denver, CO 303-458-5026
Gorfkle, Gregory D/16544 SE 28th St, Bellevue, WA 206-746-3312
Graf, Gary/1870 S Ogden St, Denver, CO 303-722-0547

HJ

H B R Studios/3310 South Knox Court, Denver, CO 303-789-4307
Harris, Richard/935 South High, Denver, CO 303-778-6433
Havey, James/1836 Blake St #203, Denver, CO 303-296-7448
Hazen, Ryne/172 West 36th St, Ogden, UT 801-621-6400
Heaton, Grant/156 W Utopia Ave, Salt Lake City, UT 801-467-0101
Herridge, Brent/736 South 3rd West, Salt Lake City, UT 801-363-0337
Hiser, David C/1280 Ute Ave, Aspen, CO 303-925-2317
Holdman, Floyd/1908 Main St, Orem, UT 801-224-9966
Hunt, Steven/2098 E 25 S, Layton, UT 701-544-4900
Huntress, Diane/3337 W 23rd Ave, Denver, CO
(P 247) **303-480-0219**
Johnson, Jim Photo/16231 E Princeton Circle, Denver, CO 303-680-0522
Johnson, Ron/2460 Eliot St, Denver, CO 303-458-0288

KL

Kay, James W/PO Box 81042, Salt Lake City, UT 801-583-7558
Kelly, John P/PO Box 1550, Basalt, CO 303-927-4197
Kitzman, John/3060 22nd St, Boulder, CO 303-440-7623
Koropp, Robert/901 E 17th Ave, Denver, CO 303-830-6000
Krause, Ann/PO Box 4165, Boulder, CO 303-444-6798
Laidman, Allan/110 Free Circle Ct A102, Aspen, CO 303-925-4791
Laszlo, Larry/420 E 11th Ave, Denver, CO 303-832-2299
Lee, Jess/6799 N Derek Ln, Idaho Falls, ID 208-529-4535
LeGoy, James M/PO Box 21004, Reno, NV 702-322-0116
Levy, Patricia Barry/3389 W 29th Ave, Denver, CO 303-458-6692
Lichter, Michael/3300 14th St, Boulder, CO 303-449-3906
Lissy, David/14472 Applewood Ridge Rd, Golden,
CO (P 250) **303-277-0232**
Lokey, David/PO Box 7, Vail, CO 303-949-5750
Lotz, Fred/4220 W 82nd Ave, Westminster, CO 303-427-2875

M

Mahaffey, Marcia/283 Columbine #135, Denver, CO 303-778-6316
Mangelsen, Tom/POB 241185/ 8206 J St, Omaha, NE 800-228-9686
Markus, Kurt/237 1/2 Main St, Kalispell, MT 406-756-9191
Marlow, David/111-R Atlantic Ave, Aspen, CO 303-925-8882
Martin, Hughes/1408 Willow Ln, Park City, UT 801-649-1471
Masamori, Ron/5051 Garrison St, Wheatridge, CO 303-423-8120
McDonald, Kirk/350 Bannock, Denver, CO 303-733-2958
McDowell, Pat/PO Box 283, Park City, UT 801-649-3403
McManemin, Jack/568 S 400 W, Salt Lake City, UT 801-359-3100
McRae, Michael/925 SW Temple, Salt Lake City, UT 801-328-3633
Messineo, John/PO Box 1636, Fort Collins, CO 303-482-9349
Miles, Kent/465 Ninth Ave, Salt Lake City, UT
(P 252) **801-364-5755**
Milmoe, James O/14900 Cactus Cr, Golden, CO 303-279-4364
Milne, Lee/3615 W 49th Ave, Denver, CO 303-458-1520
Mitchell, Paul/1517 S Grant, Denver, CO 303-722-8852

NOP

Neligh, Dave/PO Box 811, Denver, CO 303-534-9005
Ng, Ray/1855 Blake St, Denver, CO (P 255) **303-292-0112**
Noble, Chris/8415 Kings Hill Dr, Salt Lake City, UT 801-942-8335
Oswald, Jan/921 Santa Fe, Denver, CO 303-893-8038
Outlaw, Rob/PO Box 1275, Bozeman, MT 406-587-1482
Patryas, David/3200 Valmont Rd #1, Boulder, CO 303-444-7372
Paul, Ken/1523 E Montane Dr E, Genesee, CO 303-526-1162
Peck, Michael/2046 Arapahoe St, Denver, CO 303-296-9427
Peregrine Studio/1541 Platte St, Denver, CO 303-455-6944
Perkin, Jan/428 L St, Salt Lake City, UT 801-355-0112
Phillips, Ron/6682 S Sherman St, Littleton, CO 303-730-8567
Powell, Todd/PO Box 2279, Breckenridge, CO 303-453-0469
Preston, Greg/3111 S Valley View A117, Las Vegas, NV 702-873-0094
Purlington, Camille/8221 S Race St, Littleton, CO 303-797-6523

QR

Quinney, David Jr/423 E Broadway, Salt Lake City, UT 801-363-0434
Radstone, Richard/4055 Spencer #235, Las Vegas, NV 702-364-2004
Rafkind, Andrew/1702 Fairview Ave, Boise, ID 208-344-9918
Ramsey, Steve/4800 N Washington St, Denver, CO. 303-295-2135
Redding, Ken/PO Box 717, Vail, CO. 303-476-2446
Rehn, Gary/860 Toedtli Dr, Boulder, CO 303-499-9550
Reynolds, Roger/3310 S Knox Ct, Englewood, CO 303-789-4307
Rose, Jan J/17 East 2200 South, Bountiful, UT 801-292-8518
Rosen, Barry/1 Middle Rd, Englewood, CO 303-758-0648
Rosenberg, David/1545 Julian SE, Denver, CO 303-893-0893
Rosenberger, Edward/2248 Emerson Ave, Salt Lake City, UT.. 801-355-9007
Russell, John/PO Box 4739, Aspen, CO 303-920-1431

S

Saehlenou, Kevin/3478 W 32nd Ave, Denver, CO 303-455-1611
Sallaz, William R/3512 W 96th St Circle, Westminster, CO 406-466-7321
Saviers, Trent/2606 Rayma Ct, Reno, NV 702-747-2591
Schlack, Greg/1510 Lehigh St, Boulder, CO 303-499-3860
Schmiett, Skip/740 W 1700 S #10, Salt Lake City, UT 801-973-0642
Schoenfeld, Michael/PO Box 876, Salt Lake City, UT 801-532-2006
Shattil, Wendy/PO Box 67422, Denver, CO 303-721-1991
Shivdasani, Suresh/PO Box 2710, Sun Valley, ID 208-622-3494
Smith, David Scott/1437 Avenue E, Billings, MT
(P 259) **406-259-5656**
Smith, Derek/568 South 400 West, Salt Lake City,
UT (P 230) **801-363-1061**
Sokol, Howard/3006 Zuni St, Denver, CO 303-433-3353
St John, Charles/1760 Lafayette St, Denver, CO. 303-860-7300
Staver, Barry/5122 S Iris Way, Littleton, CO 303-973-4414
Stewart, Sandy/26406 Columbine Glen, Golden, CO 303-278-8039
Stoecklein, David/PO Box, Ketchum, ID 208-726-5191
Sunlit Ltd/1523 E Montane Dr, Genesse, CO 303-526-1162
Swartz, William/6801 S Emporia #103, Greenwood Village, CO 303-790-4545

T

Tanner, Scott/2755 South 300 West #D, Salt Lake City, UT 801-466-6884
Tejada, David X/1553 Platte St #205, Denver, CO
(P 260,261) **303-458-1220**
Tharp, Brenda/PO Box 4412, Denver, CO 303-980-0639
Till, Tom/PO Box 337, Moab, UT 801-259-5327
Tobias, Philip/3614 Morrison Rd, Denver, CO 303-936-1267
Travis, Tom/1219 S Pearl St, Denver, CO 303-377-7422
Tregeagle, Steve/2994 S Richards St #C, Salt Lake City, UT 801-484-1673

VWY

Van Hemert, Martin/9837 Stonehaven, South Jordan, UT 801-569-1847
Walker, Rod/PO Box 2418, Vail, CO. 303-926-3210
Wayda, Steve/5725 Immigration Canyon, Salt Lake City, UT.. 801-582-1787
Weeks, Michael/PO Box 6965, Colorado Springs, CO 719-632-2996
Wellisch, Bill/2325 Clay St, Denver, CO 303-455-8766
Welsh, Steve/1191 Grove St, Boise, ID 208-336-5541
Wheeler, Geoffrey/721 Pearl St, Boulder, CO 303-449-2137
White, Stuart/1812 3rd Ave N, Great Falls, MT 406-761-6666
Yarborough, Carl/PO Box 4739, Aspen, CO 303-920-1431

WEST COAST

A

Abecassis, Andree L/756 Neilson St, Berkeley, CA 415-526-5099
Abraham, Russell/60 Federal St #303, San Francisco, CA 415-896-6400
Abramowitz, Alan/PO Box 45121, Seattle, WA 206-621-0710
Ackroyd, Hugh S/Box 10101, Portland, OR 503-227-5694
Adams, Michael/PO Box 4217, Mission Viejo, CA 714-583-8651
Adamstein, Jerome/2601 Broadmoor Dr #84, Palm Springs, CA....619-321-2260
Addor, Jean-Michel/1456 63rd St, Emeryville, CA 415-653-1745
Adler, Bob/33 Ellert St, San Francisco, CA....415-695-2867
Agee, Bill & Assoc/715 Larkspur Box 612, Corona Del Mar, CA 714-760-6700
Aguilera-Hellweg, Max/1316 1/2 Westerley Terrace, L A, CA....213-965-0899
Ahrend, Jay/1046 N Orange Dr, Hollywood, CA 213-462-5256
Aldridge, Wayne/330 SE Union Ave, Portland, OR 503-236-5517
All Sports Photo USA/6160 Fairmont Ave #H, San Diego, CA 319-280-3595
Allan, Larry/3503 Argonne St, San Diego, CA....619-270-1850
Allen, Charles/537 S Raymond Ave, Pasadena, CA 818-795-1053
Allen, Judson Photo/839 Emerson, Palo Alto, CA 415-324-8177
Allison, Glen/1910 Griffith Park Blvd, Los Angeles, CA....213-666-0883
Ambrosio, Joe/8230 Beverly Blvd #3, Los Angeles, CA....213-655-1505
Amdal, Philip/916 W Raye, Seattle, WA 206-282-8666
Andelotte, John/15747 East Valley Blvd, City of Industry, CA....818-961-2118
Andersen, Kurt/250 Newhall, San Francisco, CA....415-641-4276
Anderson, Karen/1170 N Western Ave, Los Angeles, CA 213-461-9100
Anderson, Rick/8871-B Balboa Ave, San Diego, CA....619-268-1957
Ansa, Brian/2605 N Lake Ave, Altadena, CA 818-797-2233
Apton, Bill/1060 Folsom St, San Francisco, CA....415-861-1840
Arend, Christopher/5401 Cordova St Ste 204, Anchorage, AK 907-562-3173
Armas, Richard/6913 Melrose Ave, Los Angeles, CA....213-931-7889
Arnold, Robert /1379 Natoma, San Francisco, CA 415-621-6161
Arnone, Ken/3886 Ampudia St, San Diego, CA....619-298-3141
Aron, Jeffrey/17801 Sky Park Cir #H, Irvine, CA 714-250-1555
Aronovsky, James/POB 83579, San Diego, CA 619-232-5855
Arrabito, Jim/PO Box 916, Everett, WA....206-339-3637
Arzola, Frank/4903 Morena Blvd #1201, San Diego, CA....619-483-3810
Atherly, Robbin/1000 Brannan, San Francico, CA 415-626-1100
Atiee, James/922 N Formosa Ave, Hollywood, CA 213-850-6112
Atkinson Photo/4320 Viewridge Ave #C, San Diego, CA....619-565-0672
Avery, Franklin/PO Box 15458, San Francisco, CA....415-986-3701
Avery, Ron/11821 Mississippi Ave, Los Angeles, CA 213-477-1632
Ayres, Robert Bruce/8609 Venice Blvd, Los Angeles, CA 213-837-8190

B

Bacon, Garth/18576 Bucknall Rd, Saratoga, CA 408-866-5858
Bagley, John/730 Clemintina, San Francisco, CA 415-861-1062
Baker, Bill/265 29th St, Oakland, CA 415-832-7685
Baker, Frank/21462 La Capilla, Mission Viejo, CA....714-472-1163
Balderas, Michael/5837-B Mission Gorge Rd, San Diego, CA....619-563-7077
Baldwin, Doug/216 S Central Ave, Glendale, CA....818-547-9268
Banko, Phil/1249 First Ave S, Seattle, WA 206-621-7008
Banks, Ken/135 N Harper Ave, Los Angeles, CA 213-930-2831
Bardin, James/111 Villa View Dr, Pacific Palisades, CA....213-689-4566
Bare, John/3001 Red Hill Ave #4-102, Costa Mesa, CA....714-979-8712
Barkentin, Pamela/1218 N LaCienga, Los Angeles, CA 213-854-1941
Barnes, John/PO Box 77003, San Francisco, CA 415-431-5264
Barnhurst, Noel/34 Mountain Spring Ave, San Francisco, CA....415-731-9979
Barros, Robert/1813 E Sprague Ave, Spokane, WA 509-535-6455
Barta, Patrick/1274 Folsom, San Francisco, CA 415-626-6085
Bartay Studio/66 Retiro Way, San Francisco, CA 415-563-0551
Bartholick, Robin/89 Yesler Way 4th Fl, Seattle, WA 206-467-1001
Barton, Hugh G/33464 Bloomberg Rd, Eugene, OR 503-747-8184
Bartone, Laurence/335 Fifth St, San Francisco, CA....415-974-6010
Bartruff, Dave/PO Box 800, San Anselmo, CA 415-457-1482
Basse, Cary Photographers/6927 Forbes Ave, Van Nuys, CA 818-781-4856
Bates, Frank/5158 Highland View Ave, Los Angeles, CA....213-258-5272
Batista-Moon Studio/1620 Montgomery #300, San Francisco, CA 415-777-5566
Bayer, Dennis/130 Ninth St, San Francisco, CA....415-255-9467
Bear, Brent/8659 Hayden Pl, Culver City, CA 213-558-4471
Beebe, Morton/150 Lombard St #808, San Francisco, CA 415-362-3530
Behrman, C H/8036 Kentwood, Los Angeles, CA 213-216-6611
Belcher, Richard/2565 Third St #206, San Francisco, CA 415-641-8912
Bell, Robert/1360 Logan Ave #105, Costa Mesa, CA....714-957-0772
Benchmark Photo/1442 N Hundley, Anaheim, CA 714-630-7965
Bencze, Louis/2442 NW Market St #86, Seattle, WA....206-283-6314
Benet, Ben/333 Fifth St #A, San Francisco, CA 415-974-5433
Bennion, Chris/5234 36th Ave NE, Seattle, WA....206-526-9981
Benson, Gary L/11110 34th Pl SW, Seattle, WA (P 233)....206-242-3232
Benson, Hank/653 Bryant St, San Francisco, CA 415-543-8153
Benson, John/130 Ninth St #302, San Francisco, CA....415-621-5247
Benton, Richard/4810 Pescadero, San Diego, CA....619-224-0278
Berman, Steve/7955 W 3rd, Los Angeles, CA....213-933-9185
Bernstein, Andrew/1450 N Chester, Pasadena, CA....818-797-3430
Bernstein, Gary/8735 Washington Blvd, Culver City, CA 213-550-6891
Bertholomey, John/17962 Sky Park Cir #J, Irvine, CA 714-261-0575
Betz, Ted R/527 Howard Top Fl, San Francisco, CA 415-777-1260
Bez, Frank/71 Zaca Lane, San Luis Obispo, CA....805-541-2878
Bielenberg, Paul/2447 Lanterman Terr, Los Angeles, CA....213-669-1085
Big City Visual Prdctn/1039 Seventh Ave #12, San Diego, CA 619-232-3366
Biggs, Ken/1147 N Hudson Ave, Los Angeles, CA 213-462-7739
Bilecky, John/5047 W Pico Blvd, Los Angeles, CA 213-931-1610
Bilyell, Martin/643 SE 74th Ave, Portland, OR 503-238-0349
Bishop, Bruce/1830 17th St, San Francisco, CA....415-552-4254
Bjoin, Henry/146 N La Brea Ave, Los Angeles, CA....213-937-4097
Black, Laurie/22085 Salamo Rd, West Lynn, OR 503-665-5939
Blair, Richard/2207 Fourth St, Berkeley, CA 415-548-8350
Blakeley, Jim/1061 Folsom St, San Francisco, CA 415-558-9300
Blakeman, Bob/710 S Santa Fe, Los Angeles, CA....213-624-6662
Blattel, David/19730 Observation Dr, Topanga, CA 818-848-1166
Blaustein, Alan/885 Autumn Ln, Mill Valley, CA 415-383-1511
Blaustein, John/911 Euclid Ave, Berkeley, CA 415-525-8133
Bleyer, Pete/807 N Sierra Bonita Ave, Los Angeles, CA 213-653-6567
Bloch, Steven J/431 NW Flanders, Portland, OR (P 234)....503-224-8018
Bloch, Tom/30 S Salinas, Santa Barbara, CA 805-965-1512
Blumensaadt, Mike/306 Edna, San Francisco, CA 415-333-6178
Bobo/Alexander/206 First Ave S, Seattle, WA 206-343-9426
Bolanos, Edgar/PO Box 16328, San Francisco, CA....415-585-7805
Bonini,Steve/615 SE Alder, Portland, OR....503-239-5421
Boonisar, Peter/PO Box 2274, Atascadero, CA....805-466-5577
Borges, Phil/4222 48th Ave S, Seattle, WA....206-284-2805
Boudreau, Bernard/1015 N Cahuenga Blvd, Hollywood, CA 213-467-2602
Boulger & Kanuit/503 S Catalina, Redondo Beach, CA....213-540-6300
Bowen, John E/PO Box 1115, Hilo, HI 808-959-9460
Boyd, Bill/201 E Haley St, Santa Barbara, CA....805-962-9193
Boyd, Jack/2038 Calvert Ave, Costa Mesa, CA....714-556-8332
Boyer, Dale/PO Box 391535, Mountain View, CA....415-968-9656
Boyer, Neil/1416 Aviation Blvd, Redondo Beach, CA 213-374-0443
Boyer, Paul/225 Taylor St, Port Townsend, WA....206-385-4038
Braasch, Gary/PO Box 1465, Portland, OR....503-368-5091
Brabant, Patricia/245 S Van Ness 3rd Fl, San Francisco, CA....415-864-0591
Bracke, Vic/912 E 3rd St #106, Los Angeles, CA 213-625-1531
Bradley, Glenn/4618 W Jefferson, Los Angeles, CA 213-737-5156
Bradley, Leverett/Box 1793, Santa Monica, CA....213-394-0908
Brandon, Randy/PO Box 1010, Girdwood, AK....907-563-3351
Brazil, Larry/41841 Albrae St, Freemont, CA....415-657-1311
Brenneis, Jon/2576 Shattuck, Berkeley, CA 415-845-3377
Brewer, Art/27324 Camino Capistrano #161, Laguna Nigel, CA....714-582-9085
Brewer, Bill/620 Moulton Ave #213, Los Angeles, CA 213-227-6861
Brewer, James/4649 Beverly Blvd #103, Los Angeles, CA 213-461-6241
Brian, Rick/555 S Alexandria Ave, Los Angeles, CA....213-387-3017
Brinegar, Scott/1088 Irvine Blvd #518, Tustin, CA 714-731-5630
Britt, Jim/3221 Hutchinson Ave, Los Angeles, CA 213-836-6317
Broaddus, Steve/6442 Santa Monica Blvd, Los Angeles, CA 213-466-9866
Brod, Garry/6502 Santa Monica Blvd, Hollywood, CA....213-463-7887
Brookhause, Win/2316 Porter St #11, Los Angeles, CA 213-488-9143
Brown, Matt/PO Box 956, Anacortes, WA....206-293-3540
Browne, Rick/145 Shake Tree Ln, Scotts Valley, CA....408-438-3919
Browne, Turner/10546 Greenwood Ave N, Seattle, WA 206-367-3782
Brun, Kim/5555-L Santa Fe St, San Diego, CA....619-483-2124
Bubar, Julie/12559 Palero Rd, San Diego, CA 619-234-4020
Buchanan, Craig/1026 Folsom St #207, San Francisco, CA....415-861-5566
Buckley, Jim/1310 Kawaihao St, Honolulu, HI....808-538-6128
Burke, Kevin/1015 N Cahuenga Blvd, Los Angeles, CA 213-467-0266
Burke, Leslie/947 La Cienega, Los Angeles, CA 213-652-7011
Burke/Triolo /940 E 2nd St #2, Los Angeles, CA....213-687-4730
Burkhart, Howard Photo/1783 S Holt Ave, Los Angeles, CA 213-836-9654
Burkholder, Jeff/Life Images/3984 Park Circle Lane, Carmichael, CA (P 235) 916-944-2128
Burman & Steinheimer/2648 Fifth Ave, Sacramento, CA....916-457-1908
Burnside Photography/1201 1st Ave S #316, Seattle, WA 206-624-0070
Burr, Bruce/2867 1/2 W 7th St, Los Angeles, CA 213-388-3361

Burr, Lawrence/76 Manzanita Rd, Fairfax, CA............415-456-9158
Burroughs, Robert/6713 Bardonia St, San Diego, CA 619-469-6922
Burt, Pat/1412 SE Stark, Portland, OR..........503-284-9989
Burton, Irwin/4743 21st Ave NE, Seattle, WA 206-522-5263
Burton, Steve/PO Box 52092, Pacific Grove, CA 408-372-1610
Bush, Chan/PO Box 819, Montrose, CA..........818-957-6558
Bush, Charles/940 N Highland Ave, Los Angeles, CA 213-466-6630
Bush, Dave/2 St George Alley, San Francisco, CA 415-981-2874
Busher, Dick/7042 20th Place NE, Seattle, WA.........206-523-1426
Butler, Erik/655 Bryant St, San Francisco, CA 415-777-1656
Bydalek, Martin/PO Box 45848, Seattle, WA.........206-587-2372

C

C & I Photography/275 Santa Ana Ct, Sunnyvale, CA 408-733-5855
Cable, Ron/17835 Skypark Cir #N, Irvine, CA 714-261-8910
Caccavo, James/1000 S Crescent Hts Blvd, Los Angeles, CA.........213-939-9594
Cacitti, Stanley R/589 Howard, San Francisco, CA 415-974-5668
Cahoon, John/1419-C Elliott Ave West, Seattle, WA.........206-282-6111
Cameron, Martin/2952 Naples St, Sacramento, CA 916-387-0711
Campbell Comm Photo/8586 Miramar Pl, San Diego, CA.........619-587-0336
Campbell, Tom + Assoc/PO Box 1409, Topanga Canyon, CA.........213-473-6054
Campbell, Willis Preston/1015 Cedar St, Santa Cruz, CA..........408-425-5700
Campos, Michael/705 13th St, San Diego, CA..........619-233-9914
Cannon, Bill/516 Yale Ave North, Seattle, WA.........206-682-7031
Caplan, Stan/2224 Main St, Santa Monica, CA.........213-464-6636
Capps, Alan/137 S La Peer Dr, Los Angeles, CA.........213-276-3724
Capra, Robert/1256 Lindell Dr, Walnut Creek, CA 415-947-0323
Caputo, Tony/1040 N Las Palmas Ave, Los Angeles, CA.........213-464-6636
Carey, Ed/438 Treat Ave, San Francisco, CA 415-621-2349
Carlson, Craig/266 J Street, Chula Vista, CA.........619-422-4937
Carlson, Joe/901 El Centro, S Pasadena, CA.........213-682-1020
Carofano, Ray/1011 1/4 W 190th St, Gardena, CA.........213-515-0310
Carpenter, Brent Studio/19 Kala Moreya, Laguna Niguel, CA.........312-787-1774
Carpenter, Mert/202 Granada Way, Los Gatos, CA
(P 236) **408-370-1663**
Carroll, Bruce/517 Dexter Ave N, Seattle, WA.........206-623-2119
Carroll, Tom/26712 Calle Los Alamos, Capistrano Beach, CA.........714-493-2665
Carruth, Kerry/9428 Eton Ave #H, Chatsworth, CA.........818-718-4014
Cartwright, Casey/434 9th St, San Francisco, CA 415-621-7393
Casado, John/1858 Fanning St, Los Angeles, CA.........213-666-5123
Casilli, Mario/2366 N Lake Ave, Altadena, CA 213-681-4476
Casler, Christopher/1600 Viewmont Dr, Los Angeles, CA.........213-854-7733
Cato, Eric/7224 Hillside Ave #38, Los Angeles, CA.........213-851-5606
Caulfield, Andy/PO Box 41131, Los Angeles, CA.........213-258-3070
Chamberlain, Paul/319 1/2 S Robertson Blvd, Beverly Hills, CA.........213-659-4647
Chaney, Brad/1750 Army St #H, San Francisco, CA..........415-826-2030
Chapman, Peter/4437 Fox Hollow Rd #7, Eugene, OR.........617-662-5462
Charles, Cindy/631 Carolina St, San Francisco, CA 415-821-4457
Chase, Julie/400 Treat Ave #E, San Francisco, CA 415-863-4749
Chen, James/1917 Anacapa St, Santa Barbara, CA.........805-569-1849
Chen, Ken/11622 Idaho Ave #6, Los Angeles, CA.........213-826-8272
Chernus, Ken/9531 Washington Blvd, Culver City, CA.........213-838-3116
Chesser, Mike/5290 W Washington Blvd, Los Angeles, CA 213-934-5211
Chester, Mark/PO Box 99501, San Francisco, CA 415-922-7512
Chin, K P/PO Box 421737, San Francisco, CA 415-282-3041
Chmielewski, David/230-C Polaris, Mountain View, CA.........415-969-6639
Christmas, Michael/9863 Pacific Heights Blvd #A,
San Diego, CA (P 238) **619-554-0226**
Chubb, Ralph/340 Tesconi Cicle #B, Santa Rosa, CA.........707-579-9995
Chung, Ken-Lei/5200 Venice Blvd, Los Angeles, CA 213-938-9117
Ciskowski, Jim/2444 Wilshire Blvd #B100, Santa Monica, CA 213-829-7375
Clark, Richard/8305 Wilshire Blvd #672, Los Angeles, CA 213-933-7407
Clark, Tom/2042 1/2 N Highland, Hollywood, CA.........213-851-1650
Clarke, Chandra/860 2nd St, San Francisco, CA 415-957-9393
Clayton, John/160 South Park, San Francisco, CA 415-495-4562
Clement, Michele/221 11th St, San Francisco, CA 415-558-9540
Clifton, Carr/PO Box 71, Taylorsville, CA 916-284-6205
Cobb, Bruce/1537-A 4th St #102, San Rafael, CA 415-454-0619
Cobb, Rick/10 Liberty Ship Way, Sausalito, CA 415-332-8739
Coccia, Jim/PO Box 81313, Fairbanks, AK.........907-479-4707
Cogen, Melinda/1112 N Beachwood Dr, Hollywood, CA.........213-467-9414
Cohen, Hilda/637 N Harper Ave, Los Angeles, CA.........213-655-4004
Coit, Jim/1205 J St #A, San Diego, CA.........619-234-2874
Cole, Steve/16710 Orange Ave #A-4, Paramount, CA 213-408-1008
Coleman, Arthur Photography/303 N Indian Ave, Palm Springs, CA 619-325-7015
Colladay, Charles/705 13th Ave, San Diego, CA.........619-231-2920
Collison, James/6950 Havenurst, Van Nuys, CA.........818-995-3171

Coluzzi, Tony Photo/897 Independence Ave #2B, Mtn View, CA 415-969-2955
Connell, John/4120 Birch St #108, Newport Beach, CA 714-995-3212
Conrad, Chris/333 Second Ave W, Seattle, WA 206-284-5663
Cook, Kathleen Norris/PO Box 2159, Laguna Hills, CA 714-770-4619
Corell, Volker/3797 Lavell Dr, Los Angeles, CA..........213-255-3336
Corey, Carl/1503 Abbot Kinney Blvd, Venice, CA 213-399-3313
Cormier, Glenn/828 K St #305, San Diego, CA 619-237-5006
Cornfield, Jim/8609 Venice Blvd, Los Angeles, CA 213-204-5747
Cornwell, David/1311 Kalakaua Ave, Honolulu, HI 808-949-7000
Corwin, Jeff/CPC Assoc/1910 Weepah Way, Los Angeles, CA 213-656-7449
Courbet, Yves/6516 W 6th St, Los Angeles, CA 213-655-2181
Courtney, William/4524 Rutgers Way, Sacramento, CA 916-487-8501
Cowin, Morgin/5 Windsor Ave, San Rafael, CA 415-459-7722
Crane, Wally/PO Box 81, Los Altos, CA..........415-960-1990
Crepea, Nick/12137 Kristy Lane, Saratoga, CA 408-257-5704
Crosier, Dave/11435 37th Ave Sw, Seattle, WA 206-682-6445
Crowley, Eliot/3221 Benda Pl, Hollywood, CA 213-851-5110
Cummings, Ian/2400 Kettner Blvd, San Diego, CA 619-231-1270
Cummins, Jim/1527 13th Ave, Seattle, WA 206-322-4944
Curtis, Jeff/1109 N 35th St, Seattle, WA.........206-634-3707
Curtis, Mel Photography/2400 E Lynn St, Seattle, WA 206-323-1230

D

Dahlstrom Photography Inc/2312 NW Savier St, Portland, OR.............503-222-4910
Dajani, Haas/2501 14th Ave W #23, Seattle, WA 206-282-7643
Daniel, Jay/816 W Francisco BLvd, San Rafael, CA 415-459-1495
Daniels, Charles/905 N Cole Ave #2120, Hollywood, CA.........213-463-7513
Dannehl, Dennis/3303 Beverly Blvd, Los Angeles, CA.........213-388-3888
Davenport, Jim/PO Box 296, Chula Vista, CA.........619-549-8733
David/Gayle Photo/3223-B 1st Ave S , Seattle, WA
(P 239) **206-624-5207**
Davidson, Dave/25003 S Beeson Rd, Beavercreek, OR 503-228-1268
Davidson, Jerry/3923 W Jefferson Blvd, Los Angeles, CA 213-735-1552
Davis, Tim/PO Box 1278, Palo Alto, CA.........415-327-4192
Day, Bob/3360 21st St, San Francisco, CA 415-387-0191
Dayton, Ted/1112 N Beachwood, Los Angeles, CA.........213-462-0712
DBS Photo/1088 Irvine Blvd #518, Tustin, CA
(P 228) **714-731-5630**
De Gennaro Assoc/902 South Norton Ave, Los Angeles, CA.........213-935-5179
DeCastro, Mike/2415 De La Cruz, Santa Clara, CA 408-988-8696
DeCruyenaere, Howard/1825 E Albion Ave, Santa Ana, CA 714-997-4446
DeGabriele, Dale/900 1st Ave S #305, Seattle, WA
(P 240) **206-624-9928**
Degler, Curtis/1050 Carolan Ave #311, Burlingame, CA 415-342-7381
Del Re, Sal/211-E East Columbine Ave, Santa Ana, CA 714-432-1333
Delzell, Bill/2325 3rd St #409, San Francisco, CA 415-626-3467
Demerdjian, Jacob/3331 W Beverly Blvd, Montebello, CA.........213-724-9630
Denman, Frank B/1201 First Ave S, Seattle, WA 206-325-9260
Denny, Michael/2631 Ariane Dr, San Diego, CA 619-272-9104
Dent, Fritz/Seattle, WA (P 241) **206-385-9645**
DePaola, Mark/1560 Benedict Cnyn Dr, Beverly Hills, CA.........213-550-5910
Der Cruyenaere, Howard/1825 E Albion Ave, Santa Ana, CA 714-997-4446
Der, Rick Photography/50 Mandell St #10, San Francisco, CA.........415-824-8580
Deras, Frank/342 N Ferndale Ave, Mill Valley, CA 415-381-2324
Derhacopian, Ronald/3109 Beverly Blvd, Los Angeles, CA.........213-388-6724
DeSilva, Dennis/3449 San Pablo Dam Rd, El Sobrante, CA.........415-222-0385
Devol, Thomas/236 W First Ave, Chico, CA 916-894-8277
DeVries, Nancy/2915 Redhill Ave A-202, Costa Mesa, CA.........213-874-2200
DeWilde, Roc/953 Mt View Dr #119, Lafayette, CA 415-676-8190
DeYoung, Skip/1112 N Beachwood, Los Angeles, CA.........213-462-0712
Diaz, Armando/19 S Park, San Francisco, CA 415-495-3552
Digital Art/3000 S Robertson Blvd #260, Los Angeles, CA.........213-836-7631
Dockery, Alan/4679 Hollywood Blvd, Los Angeles, CA.........213-662-8153
Doll, Tom/4186 Serranto Valley Blvd #J, San Diego, CA.........619-452-1683
Dominick/833 N LaBrea Ave, Los Angeles, CA 213-934-3033
Donaldson, Peter/118 King St, San Francisco, CA 415-957-1102
Dow, Curtis/642 7th St, San Francisco, CA 415-431-3105
Dow, Larry/1537 W 8th St, Los Angeles, CA 213-483-7970
Drake, Brian/1209 NE 126th St, Vancouver, WA.........206-574-6199
Dreiwitz, Herb/3906 Franklin Ave, Los Angeles, CA 213-662-0622
Dresser, Rod/1620 Montgomery St, San Francisco, CA 415-824-8448
Dressler, Rick/1322 Bell Ave #M, Tustin, CA 714-730-9113
Driver, Wallace/2540 Clairemont Dr #305, San Diego, CA 619-275-3159
Drobek, Carol/1260 Broadway #106, San Francisco, CA.........415-776-6188
Duff, Rodney/4901 Morena Blvd #323, San Diego, CA.........619-270-4082
Duffey, Robert/9691 Campus Dr, Anaheim, CA..........714-956-4731
Duka, Lonnie/919 Oriole Dr, Laguna Beach, CA 714-494-7057

Dumentz, Barbara/39 E Walnut St, Pasadena, CA....213-467-6397
Dunbar, Clark/1260-B Pear Ave, Mountain View, CA....415-964-4225
Dunmire, Larry/PO Box 338, Balboa Island, CA....714-673-4058
Dunn, Roger/544 Weddell Dr #3, Sunnyvale, CA....408-730-1630
Durke, Vernon/842 Folsom St #128, San Francisco, CA....415-648-1262
Dyer, Larry/1659 Waller St, San Francisco, CA....415-668-8049

E

Ealy, Dwayne/2 McLaren #B, Irvine, Ca....714-951-5089
Earnest, Robert G/1625 Boyd St, Santa Ana, CA....714-259-9190
Eckert, Peter/2136 SE 7th Ave, Portland, OR....503-234-2344
Edelman, Howard/4739 Hillsdale Dr, Los Angeles, CA....213-221-0309
Edmunds, Dana/188 N King St, Honolulu, HI....808-521-7711
Edwards, Grant P/1470 Rancho Encinitas Dr, Olivenhain, CA....619-458-1999
Ehrlich, Seth/1046 N Orange Dr, Hollywood, CA....213-462-5256
Elgin, John-Paul/20812 Vose St, Canoga Park, CA....818-347-7719
Elias, Robert Studio/959 N Cole, Los Angeles, CA....213-460-2988
Elk, John III/3163 Wisconsin, Oakland, CA....415-531-7469
Emanuel, Manny/2257 Hollyridge Dr, Hollywood, CA....213-465-0259
Emberly, Gordon/1479 Folsom, San Francisco, CA....415-621-9714
English, Rick/1162 Bryant St, San Francisco, CA....415-255-0751
Enkelis, Liane/764 Sutter Ave, Palo Alto, CA....415-326-3253
Epstein, Rachel/PO Box 772, Ukiah, CA....707-468-0514
Ergenbright, Ric/PO Box 1067, Bend, OR....503-389-7662
Ersland, Bill/PO Box 556, Stillwater, MN....612-430-1878
Esgro, Dan/PO Box 38536, Los Angeles, CA....213-932-1919
Eskenazy, Marcel/1231 24th St #4, Santa Monica, CA....213-828-4464
Estel, Suzanne/2325 3rd St, San Francisco, CA....415-864-3661
Evans, Douglas/111 S Lander #304, Seattle, WA....206-621-8549
Evans, Marty/6850-K Vineland Ave, N Hollywood, CA....818-762-5400

F

Fabrick, Ken/1320 Venice Blvd #308, Venice, CA....213-822-1030
Fahey, Michael/608 3rd St, San Raphael, CA....415-459-8777
Falconer, Michael/610 22nd St, San Francisco, CA....415-626-7774
Falk, Randolph/123 16th Ave, San Francisco, CA....415-751-8800
Faries, Tom/8520 Ostrich Circle, Fountain Valley, CA....714-775-5767
Farmer, Roscoe/PO Box 1909, San Francisco, CA....415-474-8457
Faubel, Warren/627 S Highland Ave, Los Angeles, CA....213-939-8822
Feldman, Marc/6442 Santa Monica Blvd, Hollywood, CA....213-463-4829
Feller, Bob/Worldway Ctr #91435, Los Angeles, CA....213-670-1177
Felt, Jim/1316 SE 12th Ave, Portland, OR....503-238-1748
Felzman, Joe/4504 SW Corbett Ave #120, Portland, OR....503-224-7983
Finnegan, Kristin/3045 NW Thurman St, Portland, OR....503-241-2701
Firebaugh, Steve/6750 55th Ave S, Seattle, WA (P 224,225)....206-721-5151
Fischer, Curt/51 Stillman St, San Francisco, CA....415-974-5568
Fischer, Hanna/1118 Drake Dr, Davis, CA....916-756-0338
Fisher, Arthur Vining/271 Missouri St, San Francisco, CA....415-626-5483
Fitch, Wanelle/1142 Manhattan Ave #333, Manhattan Beach, CA....213-546-2490
Flavin, Frank/901 W 54th St, Anchorage, AK....907-561-1606
Flood, Alan/206 14th Ave, San Mateo, CA....415-572-0439
Fogg, Don/400 Treat St #E, San Francisco, CA....415-974-5244
Foothorap, Robert/426 Bryant St, San Francisco, CA....415-957-1447
Forsman, John/8696 Crescent Dr, Los Angeles, CA....213-933-9339
Forster, Bruce/431 NW Flanders, Portland, OR....503-222-5222
Fort, Daniel/PO Box 11324, Costa Mesa, CA....714-546-5709
Fowler, Bradford/1522 Sanborn Ave, Los Angeles, CA....213-464-5708
Fox, Charles/PO Box 60432, Palo Alto, CA....415-327-3556
Frankel, Tracy/641 Bay St, Santa Monica, CA....213-396-2766
Franklin, Charly/3352 20th St, San Francisco, CA....415-543-5400
Franz-Moore, Paul/421 Tehama, San Francisco, CA....415-495-6183
Franzen, David/746 Ilaniwai St #200, Honolulu, HI (P 242)....808-537-9921
Frazier, Jules/PO Box 84345, Seattle, WA....206-283-3633
Frazier, Kim Andrew/PO Box 998, Lake Oswego, OR....503-697-8798
Freed, Jack/749 N La Brea, Los Angeles, CA....213-931-1015
Freeman, Davis/7331 20th Ave NW, Seattle, WA....206-783-0582
Freeman, Hunter/1123 S Park, San Francisco, CA....415-495-1900
Freis, Jay/416 Richardson St, Sausalito, CA....415-332-6709
French, Nancy/7421 Laurel Canyon Blvd #14, North Hollywood, CA....818-982-5448
French, Peter/PO Box 100, Kamuela, HI....808-889-6488
Fridge, Stephen/PO box 410413, San Francisco, CA....415-550-6711
Fried, Robert/29 Aries Lane, Novato, CA....415-898-6153
Friedlander, Ernie/275 Sixth St, San Francisco, CA....415-777-3373
Friedman, Todd/PO Box 3737, Beverly Hills, CA....213-474-6715
Friend, David/3886 Ampudia St, San Diego, CA....619-260-1603
Frisch, Stephen/ICB - Gate 5 Rd, Sausalito, CA....415-332-4545
Frisella, Josef/340 S Clark Dr, Beverly Hills, CA....213-659-7676
Fritz, Michael/PO Box 4386, San Diego, CA....619-281-3297
Fritz, Steve/3201 San Gabriel Ave, Glendale, CA....213-629-8052
Fritze, Jack/2106 S Grand, Santa Ana, CA....714-545-6466
Fruchtman, Jerry/8735 Washington Blvd, Culver City, CA....213-839-7891
Fry, George B III/PO Box 2465, Menlo Park, CA....415-323-7663
Fujioka, Robert/715 Stierlin Rd, Mt View, CA....415-960-3010
Fukuda, Steve/454 Natoma, San Francisco, CA....415-543-9339
Fukuhara, Richard Yutaka/1032-2 Taft Ave, Orange, CA....714-998-8790
Fuller, George/4091 Lincoln Ave, Oakland, CA....415-530-3814
Furuta, Carl/7360 Melrose Ave, Los Angeles, CA....213-655-1911

G

Gage, Rob/789 Pearl St, Laguna Beach, CA....714-494-7265
Gallagher, John/PO Box 4070, Seattle, WA....206-937-2422
Galvan, Gary/4626 1/2 Hollywood Blvd, Los Angeles, CA....213-667-1457
Garcia, Elma/2565 Third St #308, San Francisco, CA....415-641-9992
Gardner, Robert/800 S Citrus Ave, Los Angeles, CA....213-931-1108
Gasperini, Robert/PO Box 954, Folsom, CA....916-985-6474
Gates, Valerie/1235 S Bedford St, Los Angeles, CA....213-271-0979
Gebhardt Productions/3400 13th Ave SW, Seattle, WA....206-624-8784
Gelert, Rex/2660 S Grand Ave, Snata Ana, CA....714-751-2727
Gelineau, Val/1265 S Cochran, Los Angeles, CA....213-465-6149
Gendreau, Raymond/2201 Broadway Ave E, Seattle, WA....206-527-1989
Gerretsen, Charles/1714 N Wilton Pl, Los Angeles, CA....213-462-6342
Gersten, Paul/1021 1/2 N La Brea, Los Angeles, CA....213-850-6045
Gervais, Lois/923 E 3rd St, Los Angeles, CA....213-617-3338
Gervase, Mark/PO Box 38573, Los Angeles, CA....213-877-0928
Ghelerter, Michael/1020 41st St, Emeryville, CA....415-547-8456
Giannetti Photography/730 Clementina St, San Francisco, CA....415-864-0270
Gick, Peter/659 W Dryden St #5, Glendale, CA....818-500-0880
Giefer, Sebastian/3132 Hollyridge Dr, Hollywood, CA....213-461-1122
Gilbert, Elliot/311 N Curson Ave, Los Angeles, CA....213-939-1846
Gillette, Richard/PO Box 1400, 6856 Lois Ln, Forestville, CA....707-887-1718
Gilmore, Ed/54 Palm Ave, San Francisco, CA....415-861-7882
Giraud, Steve/2960 Airway Ave #B-103, Costa Mesa, CA....714-751-8191
Gleis, Nick/4040 Del Rey #7, Marina Del Rey, CA....213-823-4229
Glendinning, Edward/1001 East 1st St, Los Angeles, CA....213-617-1630
Glenn, Joel/439 Bryant St, San Francisco, CA....415-957-1273
Gnass, Jeff/PO Box 91490, Portland, OR....503-629-2020
Goavec, Pierre/2335 3rd St #201, San Francisco, CA....415-552-7331
Goble, James/620 Moulton Ave #205, Los Angeles, CA....213-222-7661
Goble, Jeff/300 Second Ave W, Seattle, WA....206-285-8765
Godwin, Bob/1427 E 4th St #1, Los Angeles, CA....213-269-8001
Going, Michael/1117 N Wilcox Pl, Los Angeles, CA....213-465-6853
Goldman, Larry/23674 Stagg, West Hills, CA....818-347-6865
Goldner, David/833 Traction Ave, Los Angeles, CA....212-617-0761
Goodman, Todd/2412-B Bayview Dr, Manhattan Beach, CA....213-453-3621
Gordon, Jon/2052 Los Feliz Dr, Thousand Oaks, CA....805-496-1485
Gordon, Larry Dale/225 Crossroads #410, Carmel, CA....408-624-1313
Gorman, Greg/1351 Miller Dr, Los Angeles, CA....213-650-5540
Gottlieb, Mark/1915 University Ave, Palo Alto, CA....415-321-8761
Gowans, Edward/10316 NW Thompson Rd, Portland, OR....503-223-4573
Grady, Noel/277 Rodney Ave, Encinitas, CA....619-753-8630
Graham, Don/1545 Marlay Dr, Los Angeles, CA....213-656-7117
Graham, Ellen/614 N Hillcrest Rd, Beverly Hills, CA....213-275-6195
Graham, Jay/6 Bridge Ave #8, San Anselmo, CA....415-459-3839
Graves, Robert/30 NW 1st Ave #202, Portland, OR....503-226-0099
Gray, Dennis/8705 W Washington Blvd, Culver City, CA....213-559-1711
Gray, Todd/1962 N Wilcox, Los Angeles, CA....213-466-6088
Greene, Jim Photo/PO Box 2150, Del Mar, CA....619-270-8121
Greenleigh, John/756 Natoma, San Francisco, CA....415-864-4147
Gregg, Barry/84 University #210, Seattle, WA....206-285-8695
Grigg, Robert/1050 N Wilcox Ave, Hollywood, CA....213-469-6316
Grimm, Tom & Michelle/PO Box 83, Laguna Beach, CA....714-494-1336
Grison, Herve/4917 W Washington Blvd, Los Angeles, CA....213-464-5608
Griswold, Eric/1210 SE Gideon, Portland, OR....503-232-7010
Grodske, Kirk/19235-7 Hamlin St, Reseda, CA....818-344-5966
Groenekamp, Greg/3710 Dunn Dr #3, Los Angeles, CA....213-838-2466
Groutage, Monty/2214 S Fairview Rd, Santa Ana, CA....714-751-8734
Gunn, Lorenzo/POB 13352, San Diego, CA....619-280-6010

H

Hadel, Gregg E/15431 Red Hill, Tustin, CA (P 232)....714-259-9224

Hagopian, Jim/915 N Mansfield Ave, Hollywood, CA 213-856-0018
Hagyard, Dave/1205 E Pike, Seattle, WA 206-322-8419
Haislip, Kevin/PO Box 1862, Portland, OR 503-254-8859
Hale, Bruce H/421 Bryant St, San Francisco, CA 415-882-9695
Hall, Bill Photo/917 20th St, Sacramento, CA 916-443-3330
Hall, George/601 Minnesota St, San Francisco, CA 415-821-7373
Hall, Norman/55 New Montgomery St #807, San Francisco, CA 415-543-8070
Hall, Steven/645 N Eckhoff St #P, Orange, CA..............714-634-1132
Hall, William/19881 Bushard St, Huntington Bch, CA 714-968-2473
Halle, Kevin/8165 Commerce Ave, San Diego, CA..............619-549-8881
Hamilton, David W/455 S Eliseo Dr #10, Greenbrea, CA 415-461-5901
Hamman, Rich/3015 Shipway Ave, Long Beach, CA............213-421-5708
Hammid, Tino/6305 Yucca St #500, Los Angeles, CA 213-461-8017
Hammond, Paul/1200 Carlisle, San Mateo, CA..............415-574-9192
Hampton, Wally/4190 Rockaway Beach, Bainbridge Isl, WA 206-842-9900
Hanauer, Mark/2228 21st St, Santa Monica, CA 213-462-2421
Hands, Bruce/PO Box 16186, Seattle, WA..............206-938-8620
Hansen, Jim/2800 S Main St #1, Santa Ana, CA 714-545-1343
Hara/265 Prado Rd #4, San Luis Obispo, CA..............805-543-6907
Harding, C B/660 N Thompson St, Portland, OR..............503-281-9907
Harmel, Mark/714 N Westbourne, West Hollywood, CA 213-659-1633
Harrington, Kim/1420 45th St 326, Emeryville, CA..............415-653-6554
Harrington, Marshall/2775 Kurtz St #2, San Diego, CA 619-291-2775
Harris, Paul/4601 Larkwood Ave, Woodland Hills, CA 818-347-8294
Hart, G K/780 Bryant St, San Francisco, CA 415-495-4278
Hart, Jerome/4612 NE Alameda, Portland, OR
(P 243) **503-224-3003**
Hartman, Raiko/1060 N Lillian Way, Los Angeles, CA 213-278-4700
Harvey, Stephen/7801 W Beverly Blvd, Los Angeles, CA............213-934-5817
Hastings, Ryan/309 S Cloverdale, Seattle, WA 206-762-8691
Hathaway, Steve/400 Treat Ave #F, San Francisco, CA 415-255-2100
Hawkes, William/5757 Venice Blvd, Los Angeles, CA 213-931-7777
Hawley, Larry/6502 Santa Monica Blvd, Hollywood, CA 213-466-5864
Healy, Brian/333-A 7th St, San Francisco, CA..............415-861-1008
Heffernan, Terry/352 6th St, San Francisco, CA 415-626-1999
Hellerman, Robert/920 N Citrus Ave, Los Angeles, CA 213-466-6030
Henderson, Tom/11722 Sorrento Vly Rd #A, San Diego, CA 619-481-7743
Hendrick, Howard/839 Bridge Rd, San Leandro, CA 415-483-1483
Herrin, Kelly/1623 South Boyd, Santa Ana, ca 714-261-1102
Herrmann, Karl/3165 S Barrington Ave #F, Los Angeles, CA............213-397-5917
Herron, Matt/PO Box 1860, Sausalito, CA 415-479-6994
Hersch, Claudia/600 Moulton Ave #203, Los Angeles, CA 213-342-0226
Hershey, Bruce/4790 Irvine Blvd #105-220, Irvine, CA............714-248-5288
Hess, Geri/134 S Roxbury Dr, Beverly Hills, CA 213-276-3638
Hewett, Richard/5725 Buena Vista Terr, Los Angeles, CA 213-254-4577
Hicks, Alan/PO Box 4186, Portland, OR..............503-226-6741
Hicks, Jeff/41 E Main St, Los Gatos, CA..............408-395-2277
Higgins, Donald/201 San Vincente Blvd #14, Santa Monica, CA..........213-393-8858
Hildreth, Jim/2565 3rd St #220, San Francisco, CA
(P 244) **415-821-7398**
Hill, Dennis/20 N Raymond Ave #14, Pasadena, CA 818-795-2589
Hiller, Geoff/44 Jersey St, San Francisco, CA..............415-824-7020
Hines, Richard/734 E 3rd St, Los Angeles, CA 213-625-2333
Hirshew, Lloyd/750 Natoma, San Francisco, CA 415-861-3902
Hishi, James/612 S Victory Blvd, Burbank, CA 213-849-4871
Hixson, Richard/3330 Vincent Rd #1, Pleasant Hills, CA............415-621-0246
Hodes, Brian Black/812 S Robertson Blvd, Los Angeles, CA 213-282-0500
Hodges, Rose/2325 3rd St #401, San Francisco, CA 415-550-7612
Hodges, Walter/1605 Twelfth Ave #25, Seattle, WA............206-325-9550
Hoffman, Davy/1923 Colorado Ave, Santa Monica, CA............213-453-4661
Hoffman, Paul/4500 19th St, San Francisco, CA 415-863-3575
Hofmann, Mark/827 N Fairfax Ave, Los Angeles, CA............213-450-4236
Hogg, Peter/1221 S La Brea, Los Angeles, CA............213-937-0642
Holden, Andrew/17944-M Sky Park Circle, Irvine, CA 714-553-9455
Holder, Leland/23311 Via Linda #6, Mission Viejo, CA 714-583-9215
Hollenbeck, Cliff/Box 4247 Pioneer Sq, Seattle, WA 206-682-6300
Holmes, Mark/PO Box 556, Mill Valley, CA 415-383-6783
Holmes, Robert/PO Box 556, Mill Valley, CA 415-383-6783
Holmes, Tim/217 NE 8th St, Portland, OR..............503-230-0468
Holmgren, Robert/319 Central Ave., Menlow
Park, CA (P 245) **415-325-6837**
Holt, David/1624 Cotner Ave #B, Los Angeles, CA 213-478-1188
Honowitz, Ed/39 E Walnut St, Pasadena, CA 818-584-4050
Hopkins, Stew/414 Rose Ave, Venice, CA..............213-399-3527
Horikawa, Michael/508 Kamakee St, Honolulu, HI..............808-538-7378
Housel, James F/84 University St #409, Seattle, WA 206-682-6181
Howe, Christina/3652 Francis Ave N #201, Seattle, WA............206-869-9348
Hudetz, Larry/11135 SE Yamhill, Portland, OR..............503-245-6001

Huling, Rod/84 University #207, Seattle, WA 206-622-8486
Hunt, Phillip/3435 Army St #206, San Francisco, CA 415-821-9879
Hunter, Jeff/4626 1/2 Hollywood Blvd, Los Angeles, CA 213-669-0468
Huss, John/520 Murray Canyon Dr, Palm Springs, CA 619-325-3563
Huss, W John/520 Murray Canyon Dr, Palm Springs, CA............619-325-3563
Hussey, Ron/229 Argonne #2, Long Beach, CA............213-439-4438
Hylen, Bo/1640 S LaCienega, Los Angeles, CA............213-271-6543
Hyun, Douglass/13601 Ventura Blvd #174, Sherman Oaks, CA..........818-789-4729

I

Illusion Factory/4657 Abargo St, Woodland Hills, CA 818-883-4501
Imstepf, Charles/620 Moulton Ave #216, Los Angeles, CA............213-222-8773
Ingham, Stephen/2717 NW St Helens Rd, Portland, OR............503-274-9788
Iri, Carl/5745 Scrivener, Long Beach, CA..............213-658-5822
Irwin, Dennis/164 Park Ave, Palo Alto, CA..............415-321-7959
Isaacs, Robert/1646 Mary Ave, Sunnyvale, CA 408-245-1690
Isola, Vincent/185 Moffatt Blvd, Mountain View, CA 415-967-2301
Iverson, Michele/1527 Princeton #2, Santa Monica, CA............213-829-5717
Iwaya, Hiroshi/1314 NW Irving St #703, Portland, OR 503-223-2385

J

Jacobs, Larry/1527 13th Ave, Seattle, WA 206-325-2975
Jacobs, Michael/646 N Cahuenga Blvd, Los Angeles, CA 213-461-0240
Jaffee, Robert/140 Nursery St, Ashland, OR..............503-482-3808
James, Patrick/1412 Santa Cruz, San Pedro, CA............213-519-1357
Jang, Michael/587 9th Ave, San Francisco, CA..............415-751-3431
Jansen, Peter/122 Martina St, Pt Richmond, CA 415-235-2958
Jarrett, Michael/16812 Red Hill, Irvine, CA..............714-250-3377
Jenkin, Bruce/1305 E St/Gertrude Pl #D, Santa Ana, CA 714-546-2949
Jensen, John/449 Bryant St, San Francisco, CA..............415-957-9449
Johannesson Photography/1162 E Valencia Dr, Fullerton, CA 714-738-1152
Johnson, Charles/2124 3rd Ave W, Seattle, WA............206-284-6223
Johnson, Conrad/350 Sunset Ave, Venice, CA 213-392-0541
Johnson, Edward/11823 Blythe St, N Hollywood, CA............818-765-2890
Johnson, Geoffry/PO Box 6186, Albany, CA 415-528-9005
Johnson, Payne B/4650 Harvey Rd, San Diego, CA............619-299-4567
Johnson, Ron Photo/2104 Valley Glen, Orange, CA 714-637-1145
Johnson, Stuart/688 S Santa Fe Ave #301, Los Angeles, CA 213-744-1844
Jones, William B/2171 India St #B, San Diego, CA 619-235-8892

K

Kaake, Phillip/47 Lusk, San Francisco, CA..............415-546-4079
Kaehler, Wolfgang/13641 NE 42nd St, Bellevue, WA 206-881-6581
Kaestner, Reed/2120 J Durante Blvd #4, Del Mar, CA 619-755-1200
Kaldor, Curt W/1011 Grandview Dr, S San Francisco, CA............415-583-8704
Kallewaard, Susan/4450 Enterprise #112, Fremont, CA............415-651-7202
Kam, Henrick/2325 3rd St #408, San Francisco, CA............415-861-7093
Kamens, Les/333-A 7th St, San Francisco, CA 415-621-1888
Kamin, Bonnie/PO Box 745, Fairfax, CA 415-456-5913
Kaplan, Fred/5618 Berkshire Dr, Los Angeles, CA 213-227-8858
Kaplan, K B/901 E St #300, San Rafael, CA 415-456-5370
Karageorge, Jim/610 22nd St #309, San Francisco,
CA (P 248,249) **415-648-3444**
Karau, Timothy/4213 Collis Ave, Los Angeles, CA..............213-221-9749
Kasmier, Richard/441 E Columbine #I, Santa Ana, CA............714-545-4022
Kasparowitz, Josef/PO Box 14408, San Luis Obispo, CA............805-544-8209
Katano, Nicole/112 N Harper, Los Angeles, CA..............213-655-1717
Kato, Sig/940 East 2nd St #3, Los Angeles, CA............213-617-0708
Katzenberger, George/211-D E Columbine St, Santa Ana, CA 714-545-3055
Kauffman, Helen/9017 Rangeley Ave, Los Angeles, CA............213-275-3569
Kaufman, Mitch/2244 Walnut Grove Ave/POB 194, Rosemead, CA 818-302-7983
Kearney, Ken/8048 Soquel Dr, Aptos, CA............408-688-4546
Keenan, Elaine Faris/421 Bryan St, San Francisco, CA............415-546-9246
Keenan, Larry/421 Bryant St, San Francisco, CA 415-495-6474
Kehl, Robert/769 22nd St, Oakland, CA 415-452-0501
Keller, Greg/769 22nd St, Oakland, CA..............415-452-0501
Kelley, Tom/8525 Santa Monica Blvd, Los Angeles, CA............213-657-1780
Kermani, Shahn/109 Minna St #210, San Francisco, CA 415-567-6073
Kerns, Ben/1201 First Ave S, Seattle, WA 206-621-7636
Kilberg, James/3371 Cahuenga Blvd W, Los Angeles, CA 213-874-9514
Killian, Glen/1270 Rio Vista, Los Angeles, CA..............213-263-6567
Kim, James/5765 Thorwood Dr, Santa Barbara, CA............805-964-1400
Kimball, Ron/1960 Colony, Mt View, CA 415-948-2939
Kimball-Nanessence/PO Box 2408, Julian, CA 619-762-0765
Kimura, Margaret/940 N Highland Ave, Los Angeles, CA............213-467-1923

King, CR/2420 24th St, San Francisco, CA 415-652-5112
King, Kathleen/1932 1st Ave, Seattle, WA 206-443-2800
King, Nicholas/3102 Moore St, San Diego, CA 619-296-8200
King, Taylor/620 Moulton Ave #210, Los Angeles, CA 213-225-9722
Kious, Gary/9800 Sepulvada Blvd #304, Los Angeles, CA 213-536-4880
Kirkland, Douglas/9060 Wonderland Park Ave, Los Angeles, CA 213-656-8511
Kirkpatrick, Mike/1115 Forest Way, Brookdale, CA 408-395-1447
Klein, Karey/1513 NE 92nd St, Seattle, WA 206-528-0691
Kleinman, Kathryn/3020 Bridgeway #315, Sausalito, CA 415-331-5070
Kobayashi, Ken/1750-H Army St, San Francisco, CA 415-826-4382
Koch, Jim/1360 Logan Ave #106, Costa Mesa, CA 714-957-5719
Kodama & Moriarty Photo/4081 Glencoe Ave, Marina Del Rey, CA 213-306-7574
Koehler, Rick/1622 Edinger #A, Tustin, CA 714-259-8787
Kohler, Heinz/125 Electric Dr, Pasadena, CA 213-564-1130
Kolodny, Jeff/20335 Arminta, Canoga Park, CA 818-718-9010
Koosh, Dan/PO Box 6038, Westlake Village, CA 818-991-2105
Kopp, Pierre/PO Box 8337, Long Beach, CA 213-430-8534
Kopriva, Greg/16150 NE 85th St #222, Redmond, WA 206-292-1662
Korn, Steve/1818 Barry #208, Los Angeles, CA 213-478-8560
Kosta, Jeffrey/2565 Third St #306, San Francisco, CA 415-285-7001
Kramer, David/3109 1/2 Beverly Blvd, Los Angeles, CA 213-388-6747
Krasner, Carin/3239 Helms Ave, Los Angeles, CA 213-280-0082
Kredenser, Peter/2551 Angelo Dr, Los Angeles, CA 213-278-6356
Krisel, Ron/1925 Pontius Ave, Los Angeles, CA 213-477-5519
Krosnick, Alan/2800 20th St, San Francisco, CA 415-285-1819
Krueger, Gary/PO Box 543, Montrose, CA 818-249-1051
Krupp, Carl/PO Box 910, Merlin, OR 503-479-6699
Kubly, Jon/604 Moulton, Los Angeles, CA 213-224-8947
Kuhn, Chuck/206 Third Ave S, Seattle, WA 206-624-4706
Kuhn, Robert/3022 Valevista Tr, Los Angeles, CA 213-461-3656
Kunin, Claudia/2359 Loma Vista Pl, Los Angeles, CA 213-661-0351
Kunkel, Larry/729 Minna Alley, San Francisco, CA 415-621-0729
Kunstadt, Hilda/4450 La Barca Dr, Tarzana, CA 818-342-0051
Kurihara, Ted/601 22nd St, San Francisco, CA 415-285-3200
Kurisu, Kaz/819 1/2 N Fairfax, Los Angeles, CA 213-655-7287
Kurtz, Steve/PO Box 625, Soquel, CA 408-425-1090
Kurzweil, Gordon M/211 15th St, Santa Monica, CA 213-395-0624

L

Lamb & Hall/7318 Melrose, Los Angeles, CA 213-931-1775
Lammers, Bud/211-A East Columbine, Santa Ana, CA 714-546-4441
Lamont, Dan/2227 13th Ave E, Seattle, WA 206-324-7757
Lamotte, Michael/828 Mission St, San Francisco, CA 415-777-1443
Lan, Graham/PO Box 211, San Anselmo, CA 415-492-0308
Landau, Robert/7274 Sunset Blvd #3, Los Angeles, CA 213-851-2995
Landecker, Tom/288 7th St, San Francisco, CA 415-864-8888
Landreth, Doug/1940 124th Ave NE #A-108, Bellevue, WA 206-453-0466
Lane, Bobbi/7213 Santa Monica Blvd, Los Angeles, CA 213-874-0557
Langdon, Harry/8275 Beverly Blvd, Los Angeles, CA 213-651-3212
Langston, Karen/905 N Cole Ave #2100, Los Angeles, CA 213-463-7513
Lanker, Brian/1993 Kimberly Dr, Eugene, OR 503-485-4011
Lanzer, Jack/16952 Dulca Ynez Lane, Pacific Palisades, CA 213-459-1213
LaRocca, Jerry/3734 SE 21st Ave, Portland, OR 503-232-5005
Larson, Dean/7668 Hollywood Blvd, Los Angeles, CA 213-876-1033
Larson, Randy/5110 N Denver Ave, Portland, OR 503-283-0114
LaTona, Kevin/159 Western Ave W #454, Seattle, WA 206-285-5779
Lauderborn, Lawrence/301 8th St #213, San Francisco, CA 415-863-1132
Law, Graham/PO Box 211, San Anselmo, CA 415-898-5385
Lawder, John/2672 S Grand, Santa Ana, CA 714-557-3657
Lawlor, John/723 N Cahuenga Blvd, Los Angeles, CA 213-468-9050
Lawne, Judith/6863 Sunnycove, Hollywood, CA 213-874-3095
Lawson, Greg/PO Box 1680, Ramona, CA 619-789-8878
Lea, Thomas/181 Alpine, San Francisco, CA 415-864-5941
Leatart, Brian/520 N Western, Los Angeles, CA 213-856-0121
LeBon, David/1148 2nd St, Manhattan Beach, CA 213-375-4877
LeCoq, John Land/2527 Fillmore St, San Francisco, CA 415-563-4724
Lee, Larry/PO Box 4688, North Hollywood, CA 805-259-1226
Lee, Roger Allyn/601 Fourth St Loft 128, San Francisco, CA 415-543-6463
Lee, Sherwood/632 Alta Vista Circle, Pasadena, CA 213-255-1338
Leeson, Tom & Pat/PO Box 2498, Vancouver, WA (P273) 206-256-0436
Legname, Rudi/389 Clementina St, San Francisco, CA 415-777-9569
Lehman, Danny/6643 W 6th St, Los Angeles, CA 213-652-1930
Leiber, Gregory/PO Box 985, Ashland, OR 503-770-8006
Leighton, Ron/1360 Logan #105, Costa Mesa, CA 714-641-5122
Leng, Brian/1021 1/2 N La Brea, Los Angeles, CA 213-469-8624
LeNoue, Wayne/1441 Kearny St, San Francisco, CA 415-981-1776
Levasheff, Michael/12001 Foothill Blvd #73, Lakeview Terrace, CA 213-946-2511
Levenson, Alan/1402 N Sierra Bonita Ave, Los Angeles, CA 213-851-8837
Levy, Paul/2830 S Robertson Blvd, Los Angeles, CA 213-838-2252
Levy, Richard J/1015 N Kings Rd #115, Los Angeles, CA 213-654-0335
Levy, Ronald/PO Box 3416, Soldotna, AK 907-262-1383
Lewin, Elyse/820 N Fairfax, Los Angeles, CA 213-655-4214
Lewine, Rob/8929 Holly Pl, Los Angeles, CA 213-654-0830
Lewis, Cindy/2554 Lincoln Blvd #1090, Marina Del Rey, CA 213-301-1977
Lewis, Don/2350 Stanley Hills Dr, Los Angeles, CA 213-656-2138
Leyden, Michael/PO Box 29131, Honolulu, HI 808-924-2513
Lezo, Roman/14464-B Benefit St, Sherman Oaks, CA 818-789-2700
Li, Jeff/8954 Ellis Ave, Los Angeles, CA 213-837-5377
Lidz, Jane/33 Nordhoff St, San Francisco, CA 415-587-3377
Liles, Harry/1060 N Lillian Way, Hollywood, CA 213-466-1612
Lin, Martin/6502 Nagel Ave, Van Nuys, CA 818-994-4876
Lindsey, Gordon/2311 Kettner Blvd, San Diego, CA 619-234-4432
Lindstrom, Mel/2510 Old Middlefield Way #H, Mountain View, CA 415-962-1313
Linn, Alan/5121 Santa Fe St #B, San Diego, CA 619-483-2122
Linna, Jim/900 1st Ave S #206, Seattle, WA 206-624-7344
Livzey, John/1510 N Las Palmas, Hollywood, CA 213-469-2992
London, Matthew/15326 Calle Juanito, San Diego, CA 619-457-3251
Londoner, Hank/231 N Swall Dr, Beverly Hills, CA 213-354-0293
Longwood, Marc/3045 65th St #6, Sacramento, CA (P 251) 916-731-5373
Louie, Ming/14 Otis St, San Francisco, CA 415-558-8663
Lovell, Buck/2145 W La Palma, Anaheim, ca 714-635-9040
Lovell, Craig/80 Laurel Dr, Carmel Valley, CA 408-659-4445
Lund, John M/860 Second St, San Francisco, CA 415-957-1775
Lund, John William/741 Natoma St, San Francisco, CA 415-552-7764
Lyon, Fred/237 Clara St, San Francisco, CA 415-974-5645
Lyons, Marv/2865 W 7th St, Los Angeles, CA 213-384-0732

M

Madden, Daniel J/PO Box 965, Los Alamitos, CA 213-429-3621
Madison, David/2330 Old Middlefield Rd, Mountain View, CA 415-961-6297
Magnuson, Mitchell D/23206 Normandie Ave #4, Torrance, CA 213-539-6355
Maharat, Chester/15622 California St, Tustin, CA 714-832-6203
Maher, John/2406 NE 12th Ave, Portland, OR 503-282-3815
Maloney, Jeff/265 Sobrante Way #D, Sunnyvale, CA 408-739-4030
Malphettes, Benoit/816 S Grand St, Los Angeles, CA 213-629-9054
Mar, Tim/PO Box 3488, Seattle, WA 206-583-0093
Marcus, Ken/6916 Melrose Ave, Los Angeles, CA 213-937-7214
Marenda, Frank/721 Hill St #105, Santa Monica, CA 213-399-5206
Mareschal, Tom/5816 182nd Pl SW, Lynnwood, WA 206-771-6932
Margolies, Paul/22 Rosemont Pl, San Francisco, CA 415-621-3306
Markovich, Robert/7985 Maria Dr, Riverside, CA 714-681-0508
Marley, Stephen/1160 Industrial Way, San Carlos, CA 415-966-8301
Marra, Ben/310 First Ave S #333, Seattle, WA 206-624-7344
Marriott, John/1830 McAllister, San Francisco, CA 415-922-2920
Marsden, Dominic/3783 W Cahuenga Blvd, Studio City, CA 818-508-5222
Marshall, Jim Photo/3622 16th St, San Francisco, CA 415-864-3622
Marshall, John Lewis/2210 Wilshire Blvd #427, Santa Monica, CA 213-478-7464
Marshall, Kent/899 Pine St #1912, San Francisco, CA 415-641-0932
Marshutz, Roger/1649 S La Cienega Blvd, Los Angeles, CA 213-273-1610
Martin, Brent/37744 Thisbe Ct, Palmdale, CA 805-274-0967
Martin, Greg/700-D W 58th St, Anchorage, AK 907-563-6112
Martin, John F/118 King St, San Francisco, CA 415-957-1355
Mason, Don/80 S Jackson #306, Seattle, WA 206-624-1668
Mason, Pablo/3026 North Park Way, San Diego, CA 619-298-2200
Mastandrea, Michael/PO Box 68944, Seattle, WA 206-244-6756
Masterson, Ed/11211-S Sorrento Val Rd, San Diego, CA 619-457-3251
Matsuda, Paul/920 Natoma St, San Francisco, CA 415-626-6146
Mauskopf, Norman/615 W California Blvd, Pasadena, CA 818-578-1878
Maxwell, Craig/725 Clementina, San Francisco, CA 415-861-4131
May, P Warwick/PO Box 19308, Oakland, CA 415-530-7319
McAfee, Lynn/12745 Moorpark #10, Studio City, CA 818-761-1317
McClain, Stan/39 E Walnut St, Pasadena, CA 818-795-8828
McClaran, Robby/PO Box 14573, Portland, OR 503-234-6588
McCormack, Mark/2707 Garnet, San Diego, CA 619-581-5050
McCrary, Jim/211 S LaBrea Ave, Los Angeles, CA 213-936-5115
McCumsey, Robert/3535 E Coast Hwy, Corona Del Mar, CA 714-720-1624
McDonald, Fred/650 9th St, San Francisco, CA 415-751-3565
McEvilley, John/1428 Havenhurst, Los Angeles, CA 213-656-7476
McIntyre, Gerry/2100 Q Street, Sacramento, CA 916-321-1278
McGuire, Gary/1248 S Fairfax Ave, Los Angeles, CA 213-938-2481
McKinney, Andrew/1628 Folsom St, San Francisco, CA 415-621-8415
McLane, Mark/214 Via Sevilla, Santa Barbara, CA 805-966-5783

McMahon, Steve/1164 S LaBrea, Los Angeles, CA................213-937-3345
McNally, Brian/9937 Durant Dr, Beverly Hills, CA................213-462-6565
McNeil, Larry/7107 Witchinghour Ct, Citrus Hts, CA................916-722-0302
McRae, Colin/1063 Folsom, San Francisco, CA................415-863-0119
McVay, Matt/PO Box 1103, Mercer Island, WA................206-236-1343
Mears, Jim/1471 Elliot Ave W, Seattle, WA................206-284-0929
Mejia, Michael/244 9th St, San Francisco, CA................415-621-7670
Melgar Photographers Inc/2971 Corvin Dr, Santa Clara, CA................408-733-4500
Mendenhall, Jim/PO Box 4114, Fullerton, CA................714-447-8555
Menuez, Doug/PO Box 2284, Sausalito, CA................415-332-8154
Menzel, Peter J/180 Franklin St, Napa, CA................707-255-4720
Menzie, W Gordon/2311 Kettner Blvd, San Diego, CA................619-234-4431
Merfeld, Ken/3951 Higuera St, Culver City, CA................213-837-5300
Michels, Bob Photo/821 5th Ave N, Seattle, WA................206-282-6894
Migdale, Lawrence/6114 LaSalle Ave #433, Oakland, CA................415-482-4422
Miglaras, Yanis/525 1st St #104, Lkae Oswego, OR................503-635-5616
Mihulka, Chris/PO Box 1515, Springfield, OR................503-741-2289
Miles, Reid/1136 N Las Palmas, Hollywood, CA................213-462-6106
Milholland, Richard/911 N Kings Rd #113, Los Angeles, CA................213-650-5458
Milkie Studio Inc/127 Boylston Ave E, Seattle, WA................206-324-3000
Miller, Bill/12429 Ventura Court, Studio City, CA................818-506-5112
Miller, Dennis/1467 12th St #C, Manhattan Beach, CA................213-546-3205
Miller, Donald/447 S Hewitt, Los Angeles, CA................213-680-1896
Miller, Earl/3212 Bonnie Hill Dr, Los Angeles, CA................213-851-4947
Miller, Jeff/300 Second Ave West, Seattle, WA................206-285-5975
Miller, Jim/1122 N Citrus Ave, Los Angeles, CA................213-466-9515
Miller, Jordan/506 S San Vicente Blvd, Los Angeles, CA................213-655-0408
Miller, Martin/5039 September St, San Diego, CA................619-276-4208
Miller, Peter Read/3413 Pine Ave, Manhattan Beach, CA................213-545-7511
Miller, Ray/PO Box 450, Balboa, CA................714-646-5748
Miller, Robert/11684 Ventura Blvd #500, Studio City, CA................818-563-1227
Miller, Wynn/4083 Glencoe Ave, Marina Del Rey, CA................213-821-4948
Milliken, Brad/3341 Bryant St, Palo Alto, CA................415-424-8211
Milne, Robbie/400 E Pine St, Seattle, WA................206-329-3757
Milroy/McAleer/711 W 17th St #G-7, Costa Mesa,
CA (P 253)................**714-722-6402**
Mineau, Joe/8921 National Blvd, Los Angeles, CA................213-558-3878
Mishler, Clark/1238 G St, Anchorage, AK................907-279-0892
Mitchell, David Paul/564 Deodar lane, Bradbury, CA................415-540-6518
Mitchell, Josh/1984 N Main St #501, Los Angeles, CA................213-225-5674
Mitchell, Margaretta K/280 Hillcrest Rd, Berkeley, CA................415-655-4920
Mizono, Robert/650 Alabama St, San Francisco, CA................415-648-3993
Mock, Dennis/13715 Sparren Ave, San Diego, CA................619-693-3201
Molenhouse, Craig/PO Box 7678, VAn Nuys, CA................818-901-9306
Molina, Jimi/6961 Havenhurst Ave, Van Nuys, CA................818-786-1566
Montague, Chuck/18005 Skypark Cir #E, Irvine, CA................714-250-0254
Montes de Oca, Arthur/4302 Melrose Ave, Los Angeles, CA................213-665-5141
Moore, Gary/1125 E Orange Ave, Monrovia, CA................818-359-9414
Moran, Edward/5264 Mount Alifan Dr, San Diego, CA................619-693-1041
Morduchowicz, Daniel/600 Moulton Ave #203, Los Angeles, CA................213-223-1867
Morfit, Mason/897 Independence Ave #D, Mountain View, CA................415-969-2209
Morgan, Jay P/618 Moulton Ave #D, Los Angeles, CA................213-224-8288
Morgan, Mike/16252 E Construction, Irvine, CA................714-551-3391
Morgan, Scott/612-C Hampton Dr, Venice, CA................213-392-1863
Morrell, Paul/300 Brannan St #207, San Francisco, CA................415-543-5887
Morris, Steve/PO Box 40261, Santa Barbara, CA................805-965-4859
Mosgrove, Will/85 Liberty Ship Way #110, Sausalito, CA................415-331-1526
Moskowitz, Karen/1205 SE Pike, Seattle, WA................206-325-0142
Moss, Gary/1124 Oak Grove Dr, Los Angeles, CA
(P 226,227)................**213-255-2404**
Motil, Guy/253 W Canada, San Clemente, CA................714-492-1350
Muckley, Mike Photography/8057 Raytheon Rd #3, San Diego, CA................619-565-6033
Mudford, Grant/5619 W 4th St #2, Los Angeles, CA................213-936-9145
Muench, David Photo, Inc./PO Box 30500,
Santa Barbara, CA (P 254)................**805-967-4488**
Muench, Marc/PO Box 30500, Santa Barbara, CA................805-967-4488
Muna, R J/63 Encina Ave, Palo Alto, CA................415-328-1131
Murphy, Suzanne/2442 Third St, Santa Monica, CA................213-399-6652
Murray, Michael/15431 Redhill Ave #E, Tustin, CA................714-259-9222
Murray, William III/15454 NE 182nd Pl, Woodinville, WA................206-485-4011
Musilek, Stan/2141 3rd St, San Francisco, CA................415-621-5336
Myer, Eric/2441 N Topanga Canyon Blvd, Topanga, CA................213-455-1514
Myers, Jeffry W Photography/1218 3rd Ave #510, Seattle, WA................206-325-1767

N

Nacca, Nick/6316 Riverdale St, San Diego, CA................619-280-9900
Nadler, Jeff/520 N Western Ave, Los Angeles, CA................213-467-2135

Nakashima, Les/600 Moulton Ave #101A, Los Angeles, CA................213-226-0506
Namaguchi, Charlene/17718 NE 160th Pl, Woodinville, WA................206-487-3498
Nance, Ancil/600 SW 10th St #530, Portland, OR................503-223-9534
Nation, Bill/937 N Cole #7, Los Angeles, CA................213-937-4888
Nease, Robert/441 E Columbine #E, Santa Ana, CA................714-545-6557
Nebeux, Michael/13450 S Western Ave, Gardena, CA................213-532-0949
Neil, Thomas/PO Box 901682, Palmdale, CA................213-202-0051
Neill, William/PO Box 162, Yosemite Nat Park, CA................209-379-2841
Nels/311 Avery St, Los Angeles, CA................213-680-2414
Nese, Robert/1215 E Colorado St #204, Glendale, CA................818-247-2149
Newman, Greg/1356 Brampton Rd, Pasadena, CA................213-257-6247
Nishihira, Robert/6150 Yarrow Dr #G, Carlsbad, CA................619-438-0366
Nissing, Neil B/711 S Flower, Burbank, CA................213-849-1811
Noble, Richard/7618 Melrose Ave, Los Angeles, CA................213-655-4711
Nolton, Gary/107 NW Fifth Ave, Portland, OR................503-228-0844
Normark, Don/1622 Taylor Ave N, Seattle, WA................206-284-9393
Northlight Photo/123 Lake St S, Kirkland, WA................206-881-9306
Norwood, David/9023 Washington Blvd, Culver City, CA................213-204-3323
Nourok, Jonathan/2343 E 17th St #201, Long Beach, CA................213-433-5600
Noyle, Ric/733 Auahi St, Honolulu, HI................808-524-8269
NTA Photo/600 Moulton Ave #101-A, Los Angeles, CA................213-226-0506
Nuding, Peter/2423 Old Middlefield Way #K, Mountain View, CA................415-967-4854
Nyerges, Suzanne/413 S Fairfax, Los Angeles, CA................213-938-0151

O

O'Brien, Tom/450 S La Brea, Los Angeles, CA................213-938-2008
O'Connor, Kelly/PO Box 2151, Los Gatos, CA................408-378-5600
O'Hara, Yoshi/6341 Yucca St, Hollywood, CA................213-466-8031
O'Rear, Chuck/PO Box 361, St Helena, CA................707-963-2663
Ogilvie, Peter/20 Millard Rd, Larkspur, CA................415-924-5507
Ohno, Aki/940 E 2nd St #3, Los Angeles, CA................213-617-1685
Oldenkamp, John/3331 Adams Ave, San Diego, CA................619-283-0711
Olson, George/451 Vermont, San Francisco, CA................415-864-8686
Olson, Jon/4045 32nd Ave SW, Seattle, WA................206-932-7074
Olson, Rosanne W/5200 Latona Ave NE, Seattle, WA................206-633-3775
Orazem, Scott/1150 1/2 Elm Dr, Los Angeles, CA................213-277-7447
Osbornem Bill/3118 196th Ave, Sumner, WA................206-862-1977
Oshiro, Jeff/2534 W 7th St, Los Angeles, CA................213-383-2774
Otto, Glenn/10625 Magnolia Blvd, North Hollywood, CA................818-762-5724
Ounjian, Michael/612 N Myers St, Burbank, CA................818-842-0880
Ovregaard, Keith/765 Clementina St, San Francisco, CA................415-621-0687
Oyama, Rick/1265 S Cochran, Los Angeles, CA................213-465-6149

P

Pacheco, Robert/11152 3/4 Morrison, N Hollywood, CA................818-761-1320
Pacific Image/930 Alabama, San Francisco, CA................415-282-2525
Pack, Bill/90 Natoma, San Francisco, CA................415-882-4460
Pack, Ross/175 Cohasset Rd #6, Chico, CA................916-891-3442
Pacura, Tim/756 Natoma St, San Francisco, CA................415-552-3512
Pagos, Terry/3622 Albion Pl N, Seattle, WA................206-633-4616
Pan, Richard/722 N Hoover St, Los Angeles, CA................213-661-6638
Panography/1514 Fruitvale, Oakland, CA................415-261-3327
Papazian, David/618 NW Glisan, Portland, OR................503-227-2930
Pape, Ross/1369 Lansing Ave, San Jose, CA................415-595-4242
Parker, Douglas/3279 Lowry Rd, Los Angeles, CA................213-660-6145
Parker, Suzanne/601 Minnesota, San Francisco, CA................415-821-7373
Parks, Ayako/4572 Mariners Bay, Oceanside, CA................714-240-8347
Parks, Jeff/12936 133rd Pl NE, Kirkland, WA................206-821-5450
Parks, Peggy/21 Broadview Dr, San Rafael, CA................415-457-5300
Parrish, Al/3501 Buena Vista Ave, Glendale, CA................818-957-3726
Parry, Karl/8800 Venice Blvd, Los Angeles, CA................213-558-4446
Pasley, Paul/418 Grande Ave, Davis, CA................916-753-0501
Pasquali, Art/1061 Sunset Blvd, Los Angeles, CA................213-250-0134
Patterson, Robert/915 N Mansfield Ave, Hollywood, CA................213-462-4401
Paullus, Bill/PO Box 432, Pacific Grove, CA................408-679-1624
Pavloff, Nick/PO Box 2339, San Francisco, CA................415-452-2468
Peacock, Christian/930 Alabama St, San Francisco, CA................415-641-8088
Pearson, Lee/1746 North Ivar, Los Angeles, CA................212-691-0122
Pedrick, Frank/PO Box 5541, Berkeley, CA................415-849-2722
Peebles, Doug/445 Ilwahi Loop, Kailua, HI................808-254-1082
Penoyar, Barbara/911 E Pike St #211, Seattle, WA................206-324-5632
Percey, Roland/626 N Hoover, Los Angeles, CA................213-660-7305
Perla, Dario/18 LaJacque Ct, Sacramento, CA................916-555-1212
Perry, David/837 Traction Ave #104, Los Angeles, CA................213-625-3567
Perry, David E/PO Box 4165 Pioneer Sq Sta,
Seattle, WA (P 256)................**206-932-6614**

Peterson, Bryan/PO Box 892, Hillsboro, OR....503-985-3276
Peterson, Darrell/84 University #306, Seattle, WA....206-624-1762
Peterson, Richard/733 Auahi St, Honolulu, HI....808-536-8222
Peterson, Richard Studio/711 8th Ave #A, San Diego, CA....619-236-0284
Peterson, Scott/2565 3rd St #224, San Francisco, CA....415-285-5112
Petrucelli, Tony/17522 Von Karman Ave, Irvine, CA....714-458-6914
Pett, Laurence J/5907 Cahill Ave, Tarzana, CA....818-344-9453
Petzke, Karl/610 22 St #305, San Francisco, CA....415-626-5979
Pfleger, Mickey/PO Box 280727, San Francisco, CA....415-355-1772
Pharoah, Rick/2830 Shoreview Circle, Westlake Village, CA....805-496-7196
Phase Infinity/Ron Jones/6730 Lusk Blvd #F106, San Diego, CA....619-546-0551
Philby, Donal/3102 Moore St, San Diego, CA....619-692-0770
Phillips, Lee/4964 Norwich Place, Newark, CA....415-794-7447
Photography Northwest/1415 Elliot Ave W, Seattle, WA....206-285-5249
Pinckney, Jim/PO Box 1149, Carmel Valley, CA....408-659-3002
Piper, Jim/922 SE Ankeny, Portland, OR....503-231-9622
Pisano, Robert/911 E Pike St #301, Seattle, WA....206-324-6093
Piscitello/Svensson /11440 Chandler Blvd #1200, N Hollywood, CA....818-769-2659
Pizur, Joe/194 Ohukai Rd, Kihie, Maui, HI....808-879-6633
Place, Chuck/2940 Lomita Rd, Santa Barbara, CA....805-682-6089
Pleasant, Ralph B/8755 W Washington Blvd, Culver City, CA....213-202-8997
Ploch, Thomas/30 S Salinas, Santa Barbara, CA....805-965-1312
Plummer, Bill/963 Yorkshire Ct, Lafayette, CA....415-284-1535
Plummer, Doug/501 N 36th St #409, Seattle, WA (P 257)....206-789-8174
Poppleton, Eric/1755 Correa Way, Los Angeles, CA....213-471-2845
Porter, James/3955 Birch St #F, Newport Beach, CA....714-852-8756
Poulsen, Chriss/104-A Industrial Center, Sausalito, CA....415-331-3495
Powers, David/2699 18th St, San Francisco, CA....415-641-7766
Powers, Lisa/1112 Beachwood, Los Angeles, CA....213-465-5546
Powers, Michael/3045 65th St #7, Sacramento, CA....916-451-5606
Prater, Yvonne/Box 940 Rt 1, Ellensburg, WA....509-925-1774
Preuss, Karen/369 Eleventh Ave, San Francisco, CA....415-752-7545
Pribble, Paul/911 Victoria Dr, Arcadia, CA....213-262-8305
Price, Tony/PO Box 5216, Portland, OR....503-239-4228
Pritchett, Bill/1771 Yale St, Chula Vista, CA....619-421-6005
Pritzker, Burton/456 Denton Way, Santa Rosa, CA....707-578-5461
Proehl, Steve/916 Rodney Dr, San Leandro, CA....415-483-3683
Professional Photo Srvcs/1011 Buenos Ave #A-B, San Diego, CA....619-299-4410
Pronobus Photo/653 Commercial Rd, Palm Springs, CA....619-320-8944
Pruitt, Brett/720 Iwilei Rd #260, Honolulu, HI....808-521-1929

R

Rahn, Stephen/259 Clara St, San Francisco, CA....415-495-3556
Ramey, Michael/2905 W Thurman, Seattle, WA....206-329-6936
Rampy, Tom/PO Box 3980, Laguna Hills, CA....714-850-4048
Ramsey, Gary/1412 Ritchey #A, Santa Ana, CA....714-547-0782
Rand, Marvin/1310 W Washington Blvd, Venice, CA....213-306-9779
Randall, Bob/1118 Mission St, S Pasadena, CA....818-441-1003
Randlett, Mary/Box 10536, Bainbridge Island, WA....206-842-3935
Randolph, Tom/324 Sunset Ave, Venice, CA....213-399-7058
Rantzman, Karen/2474-A Virginia St , Berkeley, CA....415-841-6103
Rapoport, Aaron/3119 Beverly Blvd, Los Angeles, CA....213-738-7277
Rappaport, Rick/2725 NE 49th St, Portland, OR....503-249-0705
Rausin, Chuck/1020 Woodcrest Ave, La Habra, CA....213-697-0408
Rawcliffe, David/7609 Beverly Blvd, Los Angeles, CA....213-938-6287
Rayniak, J Bart/3510 N Arden Rd, Otis Orchards, WA....509-924-0004
Reed, Bob/1816 N Vermont Ave, Los Angeles, CA....213-662-9703
Reed, Joe/3401 W 5th St #120, Oxnard, CA (P 231)....800-888-5504
Reiff, Robert/1920 Main St #2, Santa Monica, CA....213-938-3064
Reitzel, Bill/1001 Bridgeway #537, Sausalito, CA....415-457-7385
Rhoney, Ann/2264 Green St, San Francisco, CA....415-922-4775
Rich, Bill/109 Minna #459, San Francisco, CA....415-775-8214
Rigelhof, John/527 Barrington Ave #16, Los Angeles, CA....213-471-6306
Riggs, Anthony/447 York Dr, Benencia, CA....707-747-6948
Riggs, Robin/3785 Cahuenga W, N Hollywood, CA....818-506-7753
Ripley, John/290 Green St #5, San Francisco, CA (P 258)....415-781-4940
Rish, Glenn/656 Orchid Ave, Montecito, CA....805-969-9186
Ritts, Herb/7927 Hillside Ave, Los Angeles, CA....213-876-6366
Robbins, Bill/7016 Santa Monica Blvd, Los Angeles, CA....213-930-1382
Roberts, Chris J/84 University St #410, Portland, OR....206-628-3643
Robin, David/818 Brannan St, San Francisco, CA....415-863-8900
Rodal, Arney A/395 Winslow Way E, Bainbridge Island, WA....206-842-4989
Rodney, Andrew/501 N Detroit St, LA, CA (P 229)....213-939-7427
Rogers, Art/PO Box 777, Point Reyes, CA....415-495-4515
Rogers, Ken/PO Box 3187, Beverly Hills, CA....213-553-5532
Rogers, Martin/1764 North Point, San Francisco, CA....415-929-0999
Rogers, Peter/15621 Obsidian Ct, Chino Hills, CA....714-597-4394
Rojas, Art/2465 N Batavia, Orange, CA....714-921-1710
Rokeach, Barrie/499 Vermont Ave, Berkeley, CA....415-527-5376
Rolston, Matthew/8259 Melrose Ave, Los Angeles, CA....213-658-1151
Rose, Peter/2056 NW Pettygrove, Portland, OR....503-228-1288
Rosenberg, Alan/3024 Scott Blvd, Santa Clara, CA....408-986-8484
Rosewood, Russell/PO Box 663, Truckee, CA....916-587-3377
Ross, Alan C/202 Culper Ct, Hermosa Beach, CA....213-379-2015
Ross, Dave/1619 Tustin Ave, Costa Mesa, CA....714-642-0315
Ross, James Studio/2565 3rd St #220, San Francisco, CA....408-725-1571
Rothman, Michael/1816 N Vermont Ave, Los Angeles, CA....213-662-9703
Roundtree, Deborah/1316 Third St #3, Santa Monica, CA....213-394-3088
Rowan, Bob/209 Los Banos Ave, Walnut Creek, CA....415-930-8687
Rowe, Wayne/56 7 North Beverly Glen, Los Angeles, CA....213-475-7810
Rowell, Galen/1483-A Solano Ave, Albany, CA....415-524-9343
Rubin, Ken/4140 Arch Dr #209, Studio City, CA....818-508-9028
Rubins, Richard/3268 Motor Ave, Los Angeles, CA....213-287-0350
Ruppert, Michael/5086 W Pico, Los Angeles, CA....213-938-3779
Ruscha, Paul/940-F N Highland Ave, Los Angeles, CA....213-465-3516
Russo, Michael/12100 Wilshire Blvd #1800, Los Angeles, CA....213-442-1800
Ruthsatz, Richard/8735 Washington Blvd, Culver City, CA....213-838-6312
Ryder Photo/136 14th St Apt B, Seal Beach, CA....315-622-3499

S

Sabatini, Ken/915 1/2 N Mansfield Ave, Hollywood, CA....213-462-7744
Sabransky, Cynthia/3331 Adams Ave, San Diego, CA....619-283-0711
Sacks, Ron/PO Box 5532, Portland, OR....503-641-4051
Sadlon, Jim/118 King St #530, San Francisco, CA....415-541-0977
Safron, Marshal Studios/1041 N McCadden Pl, Los Angeles, CA....213-461-5676
Sakai, Steve/724 S Stanley Ave #2, Los Angeles, CA....213-460-4811
Saks, Stephen/807 Laurelwood Dr, San Mateo, CA....415-574-4534
Salas, Michael/398 Flower St, Costa Mesa, CA....714-722-9908
Saloutos, Pete/6851 Blue Sky Lane, Bainbridge Island, WA (P 222,223)....206-842-0832
Samerjan, Peter/743 N Fairfax, Los Angeles, CA....213-653-2940
Sanchez, Kevin/1200 Indiana, San Francisco, CA....415-285-1770
Sanders, Paul/7378 Beverly Blvd, Los Angeles, CA....213-933-5791
Sanderson, Mark/2307 Laguna canyon Rd, Laguna Beach, CA....714-497-4615
Sandison, Teri/8705 W Washington Blvd, Culver City, CA....213-559-6446
Santos, Bill/5711 Florin Perkins Rd#1, Sacramento, CA....916-383-7969
Santullo, Nancy/7213 Santa Monica Blvd, Los Angeles, CA....213-874-1940
Sarpa, Jeff/11821 Mississippi Ave, Los Angeles, CA....213-479-4988
Sasso, Gene/1285 Laurel Ave, Pomona, CA....714-623-7424
Saunders, Paul/9272 Geronimo #111, Irvine, CA....714-768-4624
Scavo, Joe/1088 Irvine Blvd #518, Tustin, CA....714-731-5630
Scharf, David/2100 Loma Vista Pl, Los Angeles, CA....213-666-8657
Schelling, Susan/244 Ninth St, San Francisco, CA....415-621-2992
Schenck, Rocky/2210 N Beachwood Dr #10, Los Angeles, CA....213-465-1547
Schenker, Larry/2830 S Robertson Blvd, Los Angeles, CA....213-837-2020
Schermeister, Phil/472 22nd Ave, San Francisco, CA....415-386-0218
Schiff, Darryll/8153 W Blackburn Ave, Los Angeles, CA....213-658-6179
Schiffman, Bonnie/7515 Beverly Blvd, Los Angeles, CA....213-965-0899
Schubert, John/11478 Burbank Blvd, N Hollywood, CA....213-935-6044
Schultz, Jeff/PO Box 241452, Anchorage, AK....907-561-5636
Schwager, Ron/PO Box 6157, Chico, CA....916-891-6682
Schwartz, Stuart/301 8th St #204, San Francisco, CA....415-863-8393
Schwob, Bill/5675-B Landragan, Emeryville, CA....415-547-2232
Scoffone, Craig/1169 Husted Ave, San Jose, CA....408-723-7011
Scott, Mark/1208 S Genesee, Hollywood, CA....213-931-9319
Sebastian Studios/5161-A Santa Fe St, San Diego, CA....619-581-9111
Sedam, Mike/PO Box 1679, Bothell, WA....206-488-9375
Segal, Susan Photography/11738 Moor Pk #B, Studio City, CA....818-763-7612
Seidemann, Bob/1183 S Tremaine Ave, Los Angeles, CA....213-938-2786
Selig, Jonathan/29206 Heathercliff Rd, Malibu, CA....213-457-5856
Selland Photography/461 Bryant St, San Francisco, CA....415-495-3633
Semple, Rick/1115 E Pike, Seattle, WA....206-325-1400
Sessions, David/2210 Wilshire Blvd #205, Santa Monica, CA....213-394-8379
Sexton, Richard/128 Laidley St, San Francisco, CA....415-550-8345
Shaneff, Carl/1200 College Walk #105, Honolulu, HI....808-533-3010
Sharpe, Dick/2475 Park Oak Dr, Los Angeles, CA....213-462-4597
Shaul, Wendy/7556 Rio Mondego Dr, Sacramento, CA....916-429-0288
Shelton, Randy/10925 SW 108th St, Tigard, OR....503-684-6271
Shirley, Ron/8755 W Washington, Culver City, CA....213-204-2177
Sholik, Stan/1946 E Blair Ave, Santa Ana, CA....714-250-9275
Short, Glenn/14641 La Maida, Sherman Oaks, CA....818-990-5599
Shorten, Chris/60 Federal St, San Francisco, CA....415-543-4883

Shrum, Steve/PO Box 6360, Ketchikan, AK 907-225-5453
Shuman, Ronald/1 Menlo Pl, Berkeley, CA................................415-527-7241
Shvartzman, Ed/31210 La Vaya Dr #212, Westlake Village, CA...........818-707-3227
Sibley, Scott/764 Bay, San Francisco, CA 415-673-7468
Silk, Gary Photography/4164 Wanda Dr, Los Angeles, CA................213-664-9639
Silva, Keith/771 Clementina Alley, San Francisco, CA 415-863-5655
Silverek, Don/914 Ripley St, Santa Rosa, CA 707-525-1155
Silverman, Jay Inc/920 N Citrus Ave, Hollywood, CA 213-466-6030
Sim, Veronica/4961 W Sunset Blvd, Los Angeles, CA 213-656-4816
Simon, Wolfgang/PO Box 807, La Canada, CA..........................818-790-1605
Simpson, Stephen/701 Kettner Blvd #124, San Diego, CA 619-239-6638
Sinick, Gary/3246 Ettie St, Oakland, CA 415-655-4538
Sirota, Peggy/4391 Vanalden Ave, Tarzana, CA 818-344-2020
Sjef's Fotographie/2311 NW Johnson St, Portland, OR 503-223-1089
Sjoberg/742 N LaCienega, Los Angeles, CA 213-659-7158
Skirball, Aggie/9724 Lockford St, Los Angeles, CA 213-837-9267
Skott, Michael/Rt 1/ Box 66D, East Sound, WA 206-376-5284
Skrivan, Tom/1081 Beach Park Blvd #205, Foster City, CA 415-574-4847
Slabeck, Bernard/2565 Third St #316, San Francisco, CA 415-282-8202
Slatery, Chad/11869 Nebraska Ave, Los Angeles, CA 213-820-6603
Slaughter, Paul D/771 El Medio Ave, Pacific Palisades, CA 213-454-3694
Slenzak, Ron/7106 Waring Ave, Los Angeles, CA 213-934-9088
Sloben, Marvin/7834 Nightingale Way, San Diego, CA 619-239-2828
Slobodian, Scott/6519 Fountain Ave, Los Angeles, CA 213-464-2341
Smith, Charles J/7163 Construction Crt, San Diego, CA 619-271-6525
Smith, Don/1773 14th Ave S, Seattle, WA 206-324-5748
Smith, Elliott /PO Box 5268, Berkeley, CA..............................415-654-9235
Smith, Gary Photos/75 South Main #303, Seattle, WA 206-343-7105
Smith, Gil/2865 W 7th St, Los Angeles, CA 213-384-1016
Smith, Steve/228 Main St #E, Venice, CA 213-392-4982
Smith, Todd/7316 Pyramid Dr, Hollywood, CA 213-969-9832
Snook, Randy/3385-B Lanatt St , Sacramento, CA 916-455-1360
Snyder, Mark/2415 Third St #265, San Francisco, CA 415-861-7514
Sokol, Mark/6518 Wilkinson Ave, North Hollywood, CA................818-506-4910
Sollecito, Tony/1120-B W Evelyn Ave, Sunnyvale, CA 408-773-8118
Solomon, Marc/PO Box 480574, Los Angeles, CA 213-935-1771
Spahn, Brian/2565 3rd St #339, San Francisco, CA 415-282-6630
Speier, Brooks/6022 Haviland Ave, Whittier, CA........................213-695-3552
Spiker, Scott/824 S Logan, Moscow, ID 208-882-5102
Spradling, David/2515 Patricia Ave, Los Angeles, CA 213-559-9870
Spring, Bob & Ira/18819 Olympic View Dr, Edmonds, WA 206-776-4685
Springmann, Christopher/PO Box 745, Point Reyes, CA 415-663-8428
St Jivago Desanges/PO Box 24AA2, Los Angeles, CA 213-931-1984
Stahn, David/920 Natoma, San Francisco, CA..........................415-864-1453
Stampfli, Eric/50 Mendell #10, San Francisco, CA 415-824-2305
Stanley, Maria/2170 Chatsworth, San Diego, CA 619-224-2848
Stanley, Paul/3911 Pacific Hwy #100, San Diego, CA 619-293-3535
Starkman, Rick/1656 Freda Lane, Cardiff, CA 619-943-1468
Starr, Ron Photo/PO Box 339, Santa Cruz, CA 408-426-6634
Steele, Melissa/PO Box 280727, San Francisco, CA 415-355-1772
Stein, Robert/319 1/2 S Robertson Blvd, Beverly Hills, CA 213-652-2030
Steinberg, Bruce/2128 18th St, San Francisco, CA 415-864-0739
Steiner, Glenn Rakowsky/3102 Moore St, San Diego, CA 619-299-0197
Steinke, Paula/830 NE 10th St, North Bend, WA 206-746-7738
Stenjem, Scott/111 S Lander #103, Seattle, WA 206-682-4260
Sterling, Doug/1827 Steiner St, San Francisco, CA 415-441-2318
Stevens, Bob/608 Moulton Ave, Los Angeles, CA 213-224-8082
Stillman, Richard/10 Shady Oak Ct, Danville, CA 415-736-9600
Stinson, John/376 W 14th St, San Pedro, CA 213-831-8495
Stock, Richard Photography/1205 Raintree Circle, Culver City, CA 213-559-3344
Stockton, Michael/10660 Olive Grove Ave, Sunland, CA..............818-352-3607
Stone, Pete/1410 NW Johnson, Portland, OR 503-224-7125
Stormont, Bill/28279 Rainbow Valley Rd, Eugene, OR................503-485-1684
Strandoo, Paul/1318 10th Ave, San Francisco, CA 415-661-1650
Strathy, Donna R/PO Box 12575, Seattle, WA 206-325-1837
Strauss, Andrew/6442 Santa Monica Blvd, Los Angeles, CA................213-464-5394
Street-Porter, Tim/6938 Camrose Dr, Los Angeles, CA 213-874-4278
Strickland, Steve/Box 3486, San Bernardino, CA........................714-883-4792
Stryker, Ray/900 First Ave S, Seattle, WA 206-623-9653
Studio AV/1201 1st Ave S #310, Seattle, WA 206-292-9931
Studio B/5121-B Santa Fe St, San Diego, CA 619-483-2122
Su, Andrew/5733 Benner St, Los Angeles, CA 213-256-0598
Sugar, James/45 Midway Ave, Mill Valley, CA 415-388-3344
Sullivan, Jeremiah S/PO Box 7870, San Diego, CA 619-236-0711
Sund, Harald/PO Box 16466, Seattle, WA 206-938-1080
Sutton, John/333 Fifth St, San Francisco, CA 415-974-5452
Svendsen, Linda/3915 Bayview Circle, Concord, CA..................415-676-8299
Swank & Newell/1551 Third Ave, Walnut Creek, CA 415-930-9229

Swarthout, Walter & Assoc/370 Fourth St, San Francisco, CA 415-543-2525
Swartz, Fred/135 S LaBrea, Los Angeles, CA............................213-939-2789
Swenson, John/4353 W 5th St #D, Los Angeles, CA..................213-384-1782

T

Tachibana, Kenji/1067 26th Ave East, Seattle, WA 206-325-2121
Taggart, Fritz/1117 N Wilcox Pl, Los Angeles, CA 213-469-8227
Tarleton, Gary/2589 NW 29th, Corvalis, OR 503-752-3759
Taub, Doug/5800 Fox View Dr, Malibu, CA..............................213-457-8600
Tauber, Richard/4221 24th St, San Francisco, CA 415-824-6837
Teeter, Jeff/2205 Dixon St, Chico, CA 916-895-3255
Teke/4338 Shady Glade Ave, Studio City, CA 818-985-9066
Theis, Rocky/1457 Ridgeview Dr, San Diego, CA 619-527-0776
Thimmes, Timothy/8749 Washington Blvd, Culver City, CA 213-204-6851
Thomas, Neil/PO Box 901682, Palmdale, CA............................213-202-0051
Thompson, Michael/7811 Alabama Ave #14, Canoga Park, CA.......818-883-7870
Thompson, Philip/1109 Longwood Ave, Los Angeles, CA 213-939-6307
Thompson, William/PO Box 4460, Seattle, WA 206-621-9069
Thomson, Sydney (Ms)/PO Box 1032, Keaau, HI 808-966-8587
Thornton, Tyler/4706 Oakwood Ave, Los Angeles, CA 213-465-0425
Tilger, Stewart/71 Columbia #206, Seattle, WA 206-682-7818
Tise, David/975 Folsom St, San Francisco, CA 415-777-0669
Tomsett, Rafe/5380 Carol Way, Riverside, CA 714-686-6638
Tracy, Tom/1 Maritime Plaza #1300, San Francisco, CA 415-340-9811
Trafficanda, Gerald/1111 N Beachwood Dr, Los Angeles, CA 213-466-1111
Trailer, Martin/8615 Commerce Ave, San Diego, CA 619-549-8881
Trierweiler, Henry/6316 Riverdale St, San Diego, CA 619-280-0073
Trindl, Gene/10619 Camarillo St, Toluca Lake, CA 213-877-4848
Trousdale, Mark/2849-A Fillmore St, San Francisco, CA..............415-391-0564
Tschoegel, Chris/600 Moulton Ave #101-A, Los Angeles, CA..........213-226-0506
Tucker, Kim/2428 Canyon Dr, Los Angeles, CA 213-465-9233
Turk, Roger/PO Box 3133, Redland, WA 206-881-9306
Turner & DeVries/1200 College Walk #212, Honolulu, HI 808-537-3115
Turner, John Terence/173 37th Ave E, Seattle, WA 206-325-9073
Turner, Richard P/Box 64205 Rancho Pk Sta, Los Angeles, CA..........213-279-2121
Tuschman, Mark/300 Santa Monica, Menlo Park, CA 415-322-4157
Tussey, Ron/57 Sunshine Ave, Sausalito, CA 415-331-1427

UV

Ueda, Richard/618 Moulton Ave St E, Los Angeles, CA................213-224-8709
Undheim, Timothy/1039 Seventh Ave, San Diego, CA 619-232-3366
Unger, Trudy/PO Box 536, Mill Valley, CA................................415-381-5683
Uniack/8933 National Blvd, Los Angeles, CA 213-938-0287
**Upton, Tom/1879 Woodland Ave, Palo Alto, CA
(P 262)**..**415-325-8120**
Urie, Walter Photography/1810 E Carnegie, Santa Ana, CA 714-261-6302
Vallance, Doug/4314 Campus Dr, San Diego, CA 619-231-2855
Vallely, Dwight/2027 Charleen Circle, Carlsbad, CA 619-434-3828
VanderHeiden, Terry/563 E Lewelling Blvd, San Lorenzo, CA 415-278-2411
Vanderpoel, Fred/1118 Harrison, San Francisco, CA 415-621-4405
Vanderschuit, Carl & Joan/627 8th Ave, San Diego, CA 619-232-4332
VanSciver, Diane/3500 SE 22nd Ave, Portland, OR....................503-239-7817
Vega, Raul/3511 W 6th Tower Suite, Los Angeles, CA................213-387-2058
Veitch, Julie/5757 Venice Blvd, Los Angeles, CA 213-936-4231
Venera, Michael/527 Howard St, San Francisco, CA 415-543-3562
Venezia, Jay/1373 Edgecliffe Dr, Los Angeles, CA 213-665-7382
Vereen, Jackson/570 Bryant St, San Francisco, CA 415-777-5272
Viarnes, Alex/Studio 33/Clementina, San Francisco, CA 415-543-1195
**Viewfinders/3401 W 5th St #120, Oxnard, CA
(P 231)**..**805-984-3117**
Vignes, Michelle/654 28th St, San Francisco, CA 415-550-8039
Villaflor, Francisco/PO Box 883274, San Francisco, CA 415-921-4238
Visually Speaking/3609 E Olympic Blvd, Los Angeles, CA 213-269-9141
Vogt, Laurie/17522 Von Karman, Invine, CA 714-497-1549
Vollenweider, Thom/3430 El Cajon Blvd, San Diego, CA 619-280-3070
Vollick, Tom/5245 Melrose, Los Angeles, CA 213-464-4415
Von Tragen, Fritz/2407 SE 10th Ave, Portland, OR....................503-236-2139

W

Wade, William/5608 E 2nd St, Long Beach, CA..........................213-439-6826
Wahlstrom, Richard/650 Alabama St 3rd Fl, San Francsico, CA 415-550-1400
Wallace, Marlene/1624 S Cotner, Los Angeles, CA 213-826-1027
Walters, Don/4886 Woodthrush Rd, Pleasanton, CA 415-462-1305
Warden, John/9201 Shorecrest Dr, Anchorage, AK 907-243-1667
Warren Aerial Photography/1585 E Locust, Pasadena, CA 818-899-5978

Wasserman, David/252 Caselli, San Francisco, CA ... 415-552-4428
Watanabe, David/14355 132nd Ave NE, Kirkland, WA ... 206-823-0692
Waterfall, William/1160-A Nuuanu, Honolulu, HI ... 808-521-6863
Watson, Alan/710 13th St #300, San Diego, CA ... 619-239-5555
Watson, Stuart/620 Moulton Ave, Los Angeles, CA ... 213-221-3886
Waz, Anthony/1115 S Trotwood Ave, San Pedro, CA ... 213-548-3758
Weaver, James/PO Box 2091, Manteca, CA ... 209-823-6368
Weibel, Joyce/10050 N Foothill Blvd, Cupertino, CA ... 408-973-1564
Weinkle, Mark/1213 Channing Way, Berkeley, CA ... 415-540-6277
Weintraub, David L/1452 Broadway, San Francisco, CA ... 415-931-7776
Werner, Jeffery R/4910 1/4 McConnell, Los Angeles, CA ... 213-821-2384
Werts, Bill/732 N Highland, Los Angeles, CA ... 213-464-2775
Wetzel, Kerry/330 SE Union, Portland, OR ... 503-233-3947
Wexler, Glen/736 N Highland, Los Angeles, CA ... 213-465-0268
Wheeler, Richard/1116 4th St, San Rafael, CA (P 263) ... 415-457-6914
White, Barbara/712 Emerald Bay, Laguna Beach, CA ... 714-494-2479
White, Lee/1172 S LaBrea Ave, Los Angeles, CA ... 213-934-5993
White, Randall/1514 Fruitvale, Oakland, CA ... 415-261-3327
Whitfield, Brent/816 S Grand Ave #202, Los Angeles, CA ... 213-624-7511
Whitmore, Ken/1038 N Kenter, Los Angeles, CA ... 213-472-4337
Whittaker, Steve Photo/1155-C Chess Dr Unit F, Foster City, CA ... 415-574-5424
Wiener, Leigh/2600 Carman Crest Dr, Los Angeles, CA ... 213-876-0990
Wietstock, Wilfried/877 Valencia St, San Francisco, CA ... 415-285-4221
Wildschut, Sjef/2311 NW Johnson, Portland, OR ... 503-223-1089
Wilhelm, Dave/2565 Third St #303, San Francisco, CA ... 415-826-9399
Wilkings, Steve/Box 22810, Honolulu, HI ... 808-732-6288
Williams, Bill Photo/9601 Owensmouth #13, Chatsworth, CA ... 818-341-9833
Williams, David Jordan/6122 W Colgate, Los Angeles, CA ... 213-936-3170
Williams, Harold/705 Bayswater Ave, Burlingame, CA ... 415-340-7017
Williams, Keith/PO Box 17891, Irvine, CA ... 714-259-9165
Williams, Sandra/PO Box 16130, San Diego, CA ... 619-283-3100
Williams, Steven Burr/8260 Grandview, Los Angeles, CA ... 213-650-7906
Williams, Waldon/2069 E 3rd St #11, Long Beach, CA ... 213-434-1782
Williamson, Scott/1901 E Carnegie #1G, Santa Ana, CA ... 714-261-2550
Wilson, Bruce/1022 1st Ave S, Seattle, WA ... 206-621-9182
Wilson, Don/10754 2nd Ave NW, Seattle, WA ... 206-367-4075
Wilson, Douglas M/10133 NE 113th Pl, Kirkland, WA ... 206-822-8604
Wimberg, Mercier/8751 W Washington Blvd, Culver City, CA ... 213-839-7521
Wimpey, Christopher/627 Eighth Ave, San Diego, CA ... 619-232-3222
Windus, Scott/928 N Formosa Ave, Los Angeles, CA ... 213-874-3160
Wing, Frank/2325 Third, San Francisco, CA ... 415-626-8066
Winholt, Bryan/PO Box 331, Sacramento, CA ... 916-969-1112
Winter, Nita Photography/176 Caselli Ave, San Francisco, CA ... 415-626-6588
Witbeck, Sandra/581 Seaver Dr, Mill Valley, CA ... 415-383-6834
Witmer, Keith/16203 George St, Los Gatos, CA ... 408-395-9618
Wittner, Dale/507 Third Ave #209, Seattle, WA ... 206-623-4545
Wolf, Bernard/3111 4th St #306, Santa Monica, CA ... 213-399-6803
Wolfe, Dan E/45 E Walnut, Pasadena, CA ... 213-681-3130
Wolman, Baron/PO Box 1959, Sebastopol, CA ... 707-823-8123
Wong, Darrell/PO Box 10307, Honolulu, HI ... 808-737-5269
Wong, Ken/3431 Wesley St, Culver City, CA ... 213-836-3118
Wood, Darrell/517 Aloha St, Seattle, WA ... 206-283-7900
Woodward, Jonathan/5121 Santa Fe St #A, San Diego, CA ... 619-270-5501
Woolslair, James/17229 Newhope St #H, Fountain Valley, CA ... 714-957-0349
Wortham, Robert/521 State St, Glendale, CA ... 818-243-6400
Wright, Armand/4026 Blairmore Ct, San Jose, CA ... 408-629-0559
Wyatt, Tom Photography/585 Mission St, San Francisco, CA ... 415-543-2813

YZ

Yellin, Jan/PO Box 81, N Hollywood, CA ... 818-508-5669
Young, Bill/PO Box 27344, Honolulu, HI ... 808-595-7324
Young, Edward/PO Box 3802, Carmel, CA ... 408-520-7035
Young, Irene/888 44th St, Oakland, CA ... 415-654-3846
Yudelman, Dale/1833 9th St, Santa Monica, CA ... 213-452-5482
Zaboroskie, K Gypsy/5584 Mission, San Francisco, CA ... 415-239-4230
Zachary, Neil/4111 Lincoln Blvd #100, Marina Del Rey, CA ... 213-399-5775
Zajack, Greg/1517 W Alton Ave, Santa Ana, CA ... 714-432-8400
Zak, Ed/80 Tehama St, San Francisco, CA ... 415-781-1611
Zanzinger, David/2411 Main St, Santa Monica, CA ... 213-399-8802
Zaruba, Jeff/911 E Pike #233, Seattle, WA ... 206-328-9035
Zens, Michael/84 University St, Seattle, WA ... 206-623-5249
Zimberoff, Tom/31 Wolfback Ridge Rd, Sausalito, CA ... 415-331-3100
Zimmerman, Dick/8743 W Washington Blvd, Los Angeles, CA ... 213-204-2911
Zimmerman, John/9135 Hazen Dr, Beverly Hills, CA ... 213-273-2642
Zippel, Arthur/2110 E McFadden #D, Santa Ana, CA ... 714-835-8400
Zurek, Nikolay/276 Shipley St, San Francisco, CA ... 415-777-9210
Zwart, Jeffrey R/1900-E East Warner, Santa Ana, CA ... 714-261-5844
Zyber, Tom/1305 E St/Gertrude Pl #D, Santa Ana, CA ... 714-546-2949

INTERNATIONAL

Arce, Francisco M/Rio San Lorenzo 511B, Garza Garcia, NL, MX ... 83-567-696
Austen, David Robert/GPO Box 2480, Sydney, Australia, (P 266) ... 61-02-957-2511
Bako, Andrew/3047 4th St SW, Calgary, AB ... 403-243-9789
Bochsler, Tom/3514 Mainway, Burlington, ON ... 416-529-9011
Bruemmer, Fred/5170 Cumberland Ave, Montreal, QU ... 514-482-5098
Burgess, Ralph/PO Box 36, Chrstnsted/St Croix, VI ... 809-773-6541
Carruthers, Alan/3605 Jeanne-Mamce, Montreal, QU ... 514-288-4333
Carter, Garry/179 Waverly, Ottawa, ON ... 613-233-3306
Chalifour, Benoit/1030 St Alexandre #812, Montreal, QU ... 514-879-1869
Chin, Albert/1150 Homer St, Vancouver, BC ... 604-685-2000
Clark, Harold/9 Lloyd Manor, Islington, ON ... 416-236-2958
Cochrane, Jim/25 1/2 York St #1, Ottawa, ON ... 613-234-3099
Cohen, Nancy/95 Atchison St, Crows Nest, NSW,Australia, (P 267) ... 61-02-929-7748
Cordero, Felix L/1259 Ponce DeKeon #6-5, Santurce, PR ... 809-725-3465
Cralle, Gary/83 Elm Ave #205, Toronto, ON ... 416-923-2920
Cruz, Edgard O/Parque de la Fuente #C17, Bairoa Pk Caguas, PR ... 809-746-0458
Dancs, Andras/518 Beatty St #603, Vancouver, BC ... 604-684-6760
Day, Michael/264 Seaton St, Toronto, ON ... 416-920-9135
Dee, Stuart/4725 W 6th Ave, Vancouver, BC ... 604-224-3122
Dickson, Nigel/507 King St E #100, Toronto, ON ... 416-366-4477
Dojc, Yuri/74 Bathurst St, Toronto, ON ... 416-366-8081
First Light Assoc/78 Rusholme Rd, Toronto, ON ... 416-532-6108
French, Graham/387 Richmond St E, Toronto, ON ... 416-860-0300
Gagnon, Francine/1981, Ave McGill Coll,bur 725, Montreal, QU ... 514-762-4654
Galvin, Kevin/Oblatterwallstr 44, 8900 Augsburg/GR, ... 49821 156393
Gelabert, Bill/PO Box 3231, Old San Juan, PR ... 809-725-4696
Goldstein, Larry/21 E 5th St, Vancouver, BC ... 604-877-1117
Harquail, John/67 Mowat Ave #40, Toronto, ON ... 416-535-1620
Hayes, Eric/836 LeHave St, Bridgewtr, NS ... 902-543-0256
Henderson, Gordon/182 Gariepy Crescent, Edmonton, AB ... 403-483-8049
Hirsch, Alan/1259 Ponce de Leon #6C, San Juan, PR ... 809-723-2224
Jarp, Leam/186 Brunswick Ave, Toronto, ON ... 416-696-7002
Joseph, Nabil/445 St Pierre St #402, Montreal, QU ... 514-842-2444
Labelle, Lise/4282 A Rue Delorimier, Montreal, QU ... 514-596-0010
LaCourciere, Mario/1 Rue Hamel, Quebec, QU ... 418-694-1744
Lacroix, Pat/25 Brant St, Toronto, ON ... 416-864-1858
Loynd, Mel/208 Queen St S, Streetsville, ON ... 416-821-0477
Malka, Daniel/1030 St Alexandre #203, Montreal, QU ... 514-397-9704
McCall, Stuart/518 Beatty St #603, Vancouver, BC ... 604-684-6760
Merrithew, Jim/PO Box 1510, Almonte, ON ... 613-729-3862
Milne, Brian/78 Rusholme Rd, Toronto, ON ... 416-532-6108
Monk, Russell/443 King St W, Toronto, ON ... 416-599-8231
Moore, Marvin/5240 Blowers St, Halifax, NS ... 902-420-1559
Mullen, Kevin/71 Sunhurst Crescent SE, Calgary, AB ... 403-256-5749
Murray, Derik/1128 Homer St, Vancouver, BC ... 604-669-7468
Nexus Productions/10-A Ashdale Ave, Toronto, ON ... 416-463-5078
Olthuis, Stan/524 Queen St E, Toronto, ON ... 416-860-0300
Outerbridge, Graeme/PO Box 182, Southampton 8,Bermuda, ... 809-298-0888
Ramirez, George/303 Canals St, Santurce, PR ... 809-724-5727
Ranson Photographers Ltd/26 Airport Rd, Edmonton, AB ... 403-454-9674
Reus-Breuer, Sandra/Cal Josefa Cabrera Final #3, Rio Piedras, PR ... 809-767-1568
Rondel, Benjamin/2012-155 Marlee Ave, Toronto, ON ... 416-785-8680
Rostron, Philip/489 Wellington St W, Toronto, ON ... 416-596-6587
Semeniuk, Robert/78 Rusholme Rd, Toronto, ON ... 416-532-6108
Share, Jed/Tokyo/Casa Ino 302/5-9-24 Inokashira, Tokyo, JP ... 212-562-8931
Staley, Bill/1160 21st St, W Vancouver, BC ... 604-922-6695
Stegel, Mark/9 Davis Ave #300, Toronto, ON ... 416-462-3244
Taback, Sidney/415 Eastern Ave, Toronto, ON ... 416-463-5718
Teschl, Josef/31 Brock Ave #203, Toronto, ON ... 416-743-5146
Vogt, Jurgen/936 E 28th Ave, Vancouver, BC ... 604-876-5817
Von Baich, Paul/78 Rusholme Rd, Toronto, ON ... 416-532-6108
Watts, Ron/78 Rusholme Rd, Toronto, ON ... 416-532-6108
Whetstone, Wayne/149 W Seventh Ave, Vancouver, BC ... 604-873-8471
Williamson, John/224 Palmerston Ave, Toronto, ON ... 416-530-4511
Zenuk, Alan/PO Box 3531, Vancouver,, BC ... 604-733-8271
Zimbel, George/1538 Sherbrooke W #813, Montreal, QU ... 514-931-6387
Zoom Photo/427 Queen St West, Toronto, ON ... 416-593-0690

STOCK

NYC

American Heritage Picture Library/60 Fifth Ave....212-206-5500
American Library Color Slide Co/121 W 27th St 8th Fl....212-255-5356
Animals Animals/65 Bleecker St 9th Fl....212-982-4442
Animals Unlimited/10 W 20th St....212-633-0200
Archive Films/530 W 25th St....212-620-3955
Arnold, Peter Stock/1181 Broadway 4th Fl....212-481-1190
Art Resource Inc/65 Bleecker St 9th Fl....212-505-8700
Beck's Studio/37-44 82nd St, Jackson Heights....718-424-8751
Bettmann Archive/902 Broadway....212-777-6200
Black Star/Stock/116 E 27th St 5th Fl....212-679-3288
Camera Five Inc/6 W 20th St....212-989-2004
Camp, Woodfin Assoc/116 E 27th St....212-481-6900
Coleman, Bruce Inc/381 Fifth Ave 2nd Fl....212-683-5227
Comstock/30 Irving Pl....212-889-9700
Contact Press Images/116 E 27th St 8th Fl....212-481-6910
Cooke, Jerry/161 E 82nd St....212-288-2045
Culver Pictures Inc/150 W 22nd St 3rd Fl....212-645-1672
Design Conceptions/Elaine Abrams/112 Fourth Ave....212-254-1688
DeWys, Leo Inc/1170 Broadway....212-689-5580
DMI Inc/341 First Ave....212-777-8135
DPI Inc/19 W 21st St #901....212-627-4060
Ellis Wildlife Collection/69 Cranberry St, Brooklyn Hts....718-935-9600
Ewing Galloway/, New York,....212-719-4720
Fashions In Stock/21-45 78th St, E Elmhurst....718-721-1373
Flying Camera Inc/114 Fulton St....212-619-0808
Focus on Sports/222 E 46th St....212-661-6860
FPG International/251 Park Ave S....212-777-4210
Fundamental Photographs/210 Forsythe St....212-473-5770
Gamma-Liaison Photo Agency/11 E 26th St 17th fl....212-447-2515
The Granger Collection/1841 Broadway....212-586-0971
Gross, Lee Assoc/366 Madison Ave....212-682-5240
Heyl, Fran Assoc/230 Park Ave #2525....212-581-6470
Heyman, Ken/37 Bank St....212-627-2028
The Image Bank/111 Fifth Ave (Back Cover)....212-529-6700
Image Resources/224 W 29th St....212-736-2523
Images Press Service/22 E 17th St #226....212-675-3707
Index Stock International Inc/126 Fifth Ave....212-929-4644
International Stock Photos/113 E 31st St #1A....212-696-4666
Keystone Press Agency Inc/202 E 42nd St....212-924-8123
Lewis, Frederick Inc/134 W 29th St #1003....212-594-8816
Life Picture Service/Rm 28-58 Time-Life Bldg....212-522-4800
London Features Int'l USA Ltd/215 W 84th St #406....212-724-8780
Magnum Photos Inc/72 Spring St 12th Fl....212-966-9200
Maisel, Jay/190 Bowery....212-431-5013
MediChrome/232 Madison Ave....212-679-8480
Memory Shop Inc/109 E 12th St....212-473-2404
Monkmeyer Press Photo Agency/118 E 28th St #615....212-689-2242
Nance Lee/215 W 84th St #406....212-724-8780
NBA Entertainment/38 E 32nd St....212-532-6223
Omni Photo Communication/5 E 22nd St #6N....212-995-0805
Onyx Enterprises/110 Greene St #804....212-925-5440
Outline/596 Broadway....212-226-8790
Photo Files/1235 E 40th St, Brooklyn....718-338-2245
Photo Researchers Inc/60 E 56th St....212-758-3420
Photofest/47 W 13th St 2nd Fl....212-633-6330
Photography Bureau/400 Lafayette St #4G....212-255-3333
Photography for Industry/1697 Broadway....212-757-9255
Photonica/141 Fifth Ave #8S....212-505-9000
Photoreporters/875 Ave of Americas #1003....212-736-7602
Phototake/4523 Broadway #7G....212-942-8185
Pictorial Parade/530 W 25th St....212-840-2026
Rangefinder Corp/275 Seventh Ave....212-689-1340
RDR Productions/351 W 54th St....212-586-4432
Reese, Kay/225 Central Park West....212-799-1133
Reference Pictures/900 Broadway #802....212-254-0008
Retna Ltd/36 W 56th St #3A....212-489-1230
Roberts, H Armstrong/1181 Broadway....212-685-3870
Science Photo Library Int'l/118 E 28th St #715....212-683-4028
Shashinka Photo/501 Fifth Ave #2108....212-490-2180
Sochurek, Howard Inc/680 Fifth Ave....212-582-1860
Sovfoto-Eastphoto Agency/225 W 34th St #1505....212-564-5485
Spano/Roccanova/16 W 46th St....212-840-7450
Sports Illustrated Pictures/Time-Life Bldg 20th Fl....212-522-2803
Steinhauser, Art Ent/305 E 40th St....212-953-1722
The Stock Market/360 Park Ave S....800-999-0800
Stockphotos Inc/373 Park Ave S 6th Fl....212-686-1196
The Stock Shop/232 Madison Ave....212-679-8480
The Strobe Studio Inc/214 E 24th St #3D....212-532-1977
Superstock/11 W 19th St 6th Fl....212-633-0200
Sygma Photo News/225 W 57th St 7th Fl....212-765-1820
Tamin Productions/440 West End Ave #4E....212-807-6691
Taurus Photos/118 E 28th St....212-683-4025
Telephoto/8 Thomas St....212-406-2440
Time Picture Synd/Time & Life Bldg....212-522-3866
Uncommon Stock/1181 Broadway 4th Fl....212-481-1190
UPI/Bettmann Newsphotos/902 Broadway 5th Fl....212-777-6200
Wheeler Pictures/Comstock/30 Irving Place....212-564-5430
Wide World Photos Inc/50 Rockefeller Plaza....212-621-1930
Winiker, Barry M/173 W 78th St....212-580-0841

NORTHEAST

Allen, John Inc/116 North Ave, Park Ridge, NJ....201-391-3299
Anthro-Photo/33 Hurlbut St, Cambridge, MA....617-497-7227
Arms, Jonathan/1517 Maurice Dr, Woodbridge, VA....703-490-3810
Authenticated News Int'l/29 Katonah Ave, Katonah, NY....914-232-7726
Bergman, LV & Assoc/East Mountain Rd S, Cold Spring, NY....914-265-3656
Blizzard, William C/PO Box 1696, Beckley, WV....304-755-0094
Camerique Stock Photography/45 Newbury St, Boston, MA....617-267-6450
Camerique Stock Photography/1701 Skippack Pike, Blue Bell, PA....215-272-4000
Camp, Woodfin Inc/2025 Penn Ave NW #1011, Washington, DC....202-223-8442
Cape Scapes/542 Higgins Crowell Rd, West Yarmouth, MA....508-362-8222
Chandoha, Walter/RD 1 PO Box 287, Annandale, NJ....908-782-3666
Chimera Productions/PO Box 1742, Clarksburg, WV....304-623-5368
Consolidated News Pictures/209 Penn Ave SE, Washington, DC....202-543-3203
Cyr Color Photo/PO Box 2148, Norwalk, CT....203-838-8230
DCS Enterprises/12806 Gaffney Rd, Silver Spring, MD....301-622-2323
DeRenzis, Philip/421 N 23rd St, Allentown, PA (P 270)....215-776-6465
Devaney Stock Photos/755 New York Ave #306, Huntington, NY....516-673-4477
Earth Scenes/Animals Animals/17 Railroad Ave, Chatham, NY....518-392-5500
Ewing Galloway/100 Merrick Rd, Rockville Centre, NY....516-764-8620
F/Stop Pictures Inc/PO Box 359, Springfield, VT....802-885-5261
Folio/3417 1/2 M St NW, Washington, DC....202-965-2410
Galloway, Ewing/100 Merrick Road, Rockville Center, NY....516-764-8620
Garber, Bette S/3160 Walnut St, Thorndale, PA (P 271)....215-380-0342
Headhunters/2619 Lovegrove St, Baltimore, MD....301-338-1820
Heilman, Grant/506 W Lincoln Ave, Lititz, PA....717-626-0296
The Image Bank/Boston, MA(Back Cover)....617-267-8866
Image Photos/Main St, Stockbridge, MA....413-298-5500
Image Specialists/12 Sharon St, Medford, MA....617-483-1422
The Image Works Inc/PO Box 443, Woodstock, NY....914-679-5603
Jones, G P - Stock/45 Newbury St, Boston, MA....617-267-6450
Lambert, Harold M/2801 W Cheltenham Ave, Philadelphia, PA....215-224-1400
Light, Paul/1430 Massachusetts Ave, Cambridge, MA....617-628-1052
Lumiere/512 Adams St, Centerport, NY....516-271-6133
Myers Studios/5575 Big Tree Rd, Orchard Park, NY....716-662-6002
Natural Selection/177 St Paul St, Rochester, NY....716-232-1502
New England Stock Photo/PO Box 815, Old Saybrook, CT....203-388-1741
North Wind Picture Archives/RR 1 Box 172/Federal St, Alfred, ME....207-490-1940
Philiba, Allan A/3408 Bertha Dr, Baldwin, NY....516-623-7841
Photo/Nats/33 Aspen Ave, Auburndale, MA....617-969-9531
The Picture Cube/89 Broad St, Boston, MA....617-367-1532
DPicture Group/830 Eddy St, Providence, RI....401-461-9333
Positive Images/317 N Main St, Natick, MA....508-653-7610
Rainbow/PO Box 573, Housatonic, MA....413-274-6211
Reis,Jon/Photolink/141 The Commons, Ithica, NY....607-272-0642
Roberts, H Armstrong/4203 Locust St, Philadelphia, PA....215-386-6300
Rotman, Jeff/14 Cottage Ave, Somerville, MA....617-666-0874
Sandak/GK Hall/180 Harvard Ave, Stamford, CT....203-348-3722
Seitz & Seitz/1006 N Second Ave #1A, Harrisburg, PA....717-232-7944
Sequis Stock Photo/9 W 29th St, Baltimore, MD....301-467-7300
Sickles Photo Reporting/PO Box 98, Maplewood, NJ....201-763-6355
Sportschrome/10 Brynkerhoff Ave 2nd Fl, Palisades Park, NJ....201-568-1412
Starwood/PO Box 40503, Washington, DC....202-362-7404
Stock Advantage/213 N 12th St, Allentown, PA....215-776-7381
Stock Boston Inc/36 Gloucester St, Boston, MA....617-266-2300

Sutton, Bug/6 Carpenter St, Salem, MA 508-741-0806
Undersea Systems/PO Box 29M, Bay Shore, NY...........................516-666-3127
Uniphoto Picture Agency/3205 Grace St NW, Washington, DC 202-333-0500
View Finder Stock Photo/2310 Penn Ave, Pittsburgh, PA 412-391-8720
Weidman, H Mark/2112 Goodwin Lane, North Wales, PA 215-646-1745
Woppel, Carl/PO Box 199, Islip, NY..516-581-7762

S O U T H E A S T

Bryant, Doug/PO Box 80155, Baton Rouge, LA..............................504-387-1620
Camera MD Studios/8290 NW 26 Pl, Ft Lauderdale, FL......................305-741-5560
Florida Image File/222 2nd St N, St Petersburg, FL..........................813-894-8433
Fotoconcept/408 SE 11th Ct, Ft Lauderdale, FL...............................305-463-1912
The Image Bank/, Naples, FL, (Back Cover).................**813-566-3444**
The Image Bank/3490 Piedmont Rd NE #1106,
Atlanta, GA, (Back Cover)   **404-233-9920**
Image File/526 11th Ave, St Petersburg, FL...................................813-894-8433
Instock Inc/516 NE 13th St, Ft Lauderdale, FL................................305-527-4111
Kutnyak, Catherine/644 S Third St #202, Louisville, KY.....................502-589-5799
National Stock Network/8960 SW 114th St, Miami, FL........................305-233-1703
Phelps, Catherine Stock Photo/2403 Dellwood Dr NW, Atlanta, GA......404-264-0264
Photo Options/1432 Linda Vista Dr, Birmingham, AL........................205-979-8412
Photri(Photo Research Int'l)/3701 S George Mason Dr/C-2 No,
Falls Church, VA...703-836-4439
Picturesque/1520 Brookside Dr #3, Raleigh, NC............................919-828-0023
Pinckney, Jim Photo/PO Box 22887, Lake Buena Vista, FL 407-239-8855
Sandved-Coleman Photo/12539 N Lake Court, Fairfax, VA.................703-968-6769
Sharp Shooters/4950 SW 72nd Ave #114, Miami, FL.......................305-666-1266
Silver Image Photo/5128 NW 58th Ct, Gainesville, FL 904-373-5771
Southern Stock/3601 W Commercial Blvd #33, Ft Lauderdale, FL 305-486-7117
Sports File/1674 Meridan Ave #407, Miami, FL.............................305-672-1674
Stills Inc/3288 Marjon Dr, Atlanta, GA......................................404-451-6749
Stock Options/851 French St, New Orleans, LA.............................504-486-7700
Stockfile/2107 Park Ave, Richmond, VA.....................................804-358-6364
The Waterhouse/PO Box 2487, Key Largo, FL...............................305-451-3737

M I D W E S T

A-Stock Photo Finde/230 N Michigan #1100, Chicago, IL 312-645-0611
Artstreet/111 E Chestnut #12B, Chicago, IL................................312-664-3049
Brooks & VanKirk/855 W Blackhawk St, Chicago, IL 312-642-7766
Bundt, Nancy/1908 Kenwood Pkw, Minneapolis, MN.....................612-377-7773
Camerique Stock Photo/233 E Wacker Dr #4305, Chicago, IL 312-938-4466
Campbell Stock/28000 Middlebelt Rd #260, Farmington Hills, MI......313-626-5233
Click/ Chicago Ltd/213 W Institute Pl #503, Chicago, IL..................312-787-7880
Custom Medical Stock Photo/3819 N Southport Ave, Chicago, IL.......312-248-3200
Fay, Mark/7301 Ohms Ln #375, Edina, MN................................612-835-5447
Frozen Images/400 First Ave N #626, Minneapolis, MN...................612-339-3191
Gartman, Marilyn/510 N Dearborn, Chicago, IL............................312-661-1656
Gibler, Mike/Rt 5 Zion Rd, Jefferson City, MO.............................314-635-2450
Hedrich-Blessing/11 W Illinois St, Chicago, IL............................312-321-1151
Historical Picture Service/921 W Van Buren #201, Chicago, IL..........312-346-0599
Ibid Inc/935 West Chestnut, Chicago, IL...................................312-733-8000
The Image Bank/822 Marquette Ave, Minneapolis,
MN, (Back Cover)   **612-332-8935**
The Image Bank/510 N Dearborn #930, Chicago, IL
(Back Cover) **312-329-1817**
Images of Nature/PO Box 241185/8206 J St, Omaha, NE..................800-228-9686
Journalism Services Stock/118 E 2nd St, Lockport, IL.....................312-951-0269
Nawrocki Stock Photo/332 S Michigan Ave #1630, Chicago, IL...........312-427-8625
Panoramic Stock Images/230 N Michigan Ave, Chicago, IL..............312-236-8545
Photographic Resources/6633 Delmar St #200, St Louis, MO.............314-721-5838
The Photoletter/Pine Lake Farm, Osceola, WI..............................715-248-3800
Pix International/300 N State #3926, Chicago, IL...........................312-321-9071
Schroeder, Loranelle/400 First Ave N #626, Minneapolis, MN............612-339-3191
Stone, Tony Worldwd/233 East Ontario, Chicago, IL.....................312-787-7880
Studio B Stock/107 W Van Buren #211, Chicago, IL......................312-939-4677
Thill, Nancy/537 South Dearborn, Chicago, IL.............................312-939-7770
Third Coast Stock/PO Box 92397, Milwaukee, WI.........................414-765-9442
Zehrt, Jack/PO Box 122A Rt5, Pacific, MO.................................314-458-3600

S O U T H W E S T

Adstock Photos/6219 North 9th Place, Phoenix, AZ 602-437-8772
Condroy, Scott/4810 S 40th St #3A; Phoenix, AZ 602-437-8772

Golfoto Inc/224 North Independence, Enid, OK 405-234-8284
The Image Bank/, Houston, TX, (Back Cover) **713-668-0066**
The Image Bank/3500 Maple Ave #1150, Dallas,
TX, (Back Cover)   **214-631-3808**
Image Venders/1222 N Winnetka, Dallas, TX................................214-943-5411
Ives, Tom/2250 El Moraga, Tucson, AZ......................................602-743-0750
Lee, E Doris/5810 Star Lane, Houston, TX 713-977-1768
McLaughlin, Herb & Dorothy/2344 W Holly, Phoenix, AZ...................602-258-6551
Photo Assoc of Texas/PO Box 887, Tomball, TX............................713-351-5740
Photobank/313 E Thomas Rd #102, Phoenix, AZ...........................602-265-5591
Raphaele/Digital Transparencies Inc/616 Hawthorne, Houston, TX......713-524-2211
Running Productions/PO Box 1237, Flagstaff, AZ...........................602-774-2923
The Stock House Inc/9261 Kirby, Houston, TX..............................713-796-8400
Visual Images West Inc/600 E Baseline Rd #B-6, Tempe, AZ..............602-820-5403

R O C K Y M T N

Ambrose, Paul Studios/34341 Hwy 550 North, Durango, CO 303-259-5925
Aspen Stock Photo/PO Box 4063, Aspen, CO.............................303-925-8280
Bair, Royce & Assoc/6640 South 2200 West, Salt Lake City, UT 801-569-1155
Dannen, Kent/Donna/851 Peak View/Moraine Rte, Estes Park, CO 303-586-5794
F Stock/PO Box 3956, Ketchum, ID..208-726-1378
Miles, Kent/465 Ninth Ave, Salt Lake City, UT.............................801-364-5755
Profiles West/PO Box 1199, Buena Vista, CO..............................719-395-8671
Stack, Tom & Assoc/3645 Jeannine Dr, Colorado Springs, CO............719-570-1000
The Stock Broker/450 Lincoln St #110, Denver, CO.......................303-698-1734
Stock Imagery/711 Kalamath St, Denver, CO..............................303-592-1091
The Stock Solution/6640 South, 2200 West, Salt Lake City, UT 801-569-1155
Williams, Hal/PO Box 10436, Aspen, CO...................................303-920-2802

W E S T C O A S T

Adventure Photo/56 E Main St, Ventura, CA................................805-643-7751
After Image Inc/6100 Wilshire Blvd #240, Los Angeles, CA................213-938-1700
Alaska Pictorial Service/Drawer 6144, Anchorage, AK.....................907-344-1370
All Sports Photo USA/320 Wilshire Blvd #200, Santa Monica, CA 213-395-2955
Allstock/1530 Westlake Ave N, Seattle, WA................................206-282-8116
Beebe, Morton & Assoc/150 Lombard St #808, San Francisco, CA.....415-362-3530
Big City Visual Prdctns/1039 Seventh Ave #12, San Diego, CA............619-232-3366
Burr, Lawrence/76 Manzanita Rd, Fairfax, CA...............................415-456-9158
Camerique Stock Photo/6640 Sunset Blvd #100, Hollywood, CA........213-469-3900
Catalyst/PO Box 689, Haines, AK...907-766-2670
Dae Flights/PO Box 1086, Newport Beach, CA.............................714-676-3902
Dritsas, George/207 Miller Ave, Mill Valley, CA............................415-381-5485
Earth Images/PO Box 10352, Bainbridge Isl, WA..........................206-842-7793
Ergenbright, Ric Photo/PO Box 1067, Bend, OR 503-389-7662
Focus West/4112 Adams Ave, San Diego, CA.............................619-280-3595
Four by Five Inc/99 Osgood Place, San Francisco, CA.....................415-781-4433
French, Peter/PO Box 100, Kamuela, HI....................................808-889-6488
Gibson, Mark/PO Box 14542, San Francisco, CA..........................415-524-8118
Great American Stock/7566 Trade St, San Diego, CA......................619-297-2205
Grubb, T D/5806 Deerhead Rd, Malibu, CA................................213-457-5539
Havens, Carol/POB 662, Laguna Beach, CA...............................714-497-1908
The Image Bank/, San Francisco, CA, (Back Cover) **415-788-2208**
The Image Bank/4526 Wilshire Blvd, Los Angeles,
CA, (Back Cover)   **213-656-9003**
The New Image Inc/38 Quail Ct 200, Walnut Creek, CA....................415-934-2405
Jeton/513 Harrington Ave NE, Renton, WA 206-226-1408
Kimball, Ron Stock/1960 Colony, Mt View, CA.............................415-948-2939
Leeson, Tom & Pat/PO Box 2498, Vancouver, WA
(P 273)   **206-256-0436**
Live Stock Photo/190 Parnassus Ave #5, San Francisco, CA 415-753-6261
Long Photo Inc/57865 Rickenbacher Rd, Los Angeles, CA.................213-888-9944
Madison, David/2330 Old Middlefield Rd, Mt View, CA....................415-961-6297
Motion Picture & TV Photo Archive/11821 Mississippi Ave, LA, CA......213-478-2379
MPTV PhotoArchive/11821 Mississippi Ave, Los Angeles, CA............213-478-2379
Muench, David Photo Inc/PO Box 30500, Santa Barbara, CA..............805-967-4488
NFL Photos/6701 Center Dr W #1111, Los Angeles, CA...................213-215-3813
Northern Light Studio/2407 SE 10th Ave, Portland, OR....................503-236-2139
O'Hara, Pat/PO Box 955, Port Angeles, WA................................206-457-4212
Pacific Stock/PO Box 90517, Honolulu, HI 800-321-3239
Peebles, Douglas Photography/445 Iliwahi Loop, Kailua, HI.............808-254-1082
Photo 20/20/PO Box 674, Berkeley, CA.....................................415-526-0921
Photo File/110 Pacific Ave #102, San Francisco, CA.......................415-397-3040
Photo Network/1541 Parkway Loop #J, Tustin, CA.........................714-259-1244
Photo Vault/1045 17th St, San Francisco, CA..............................415-552-9682

I N T E R N A T I O N A L

GRAPHIC
DESIGNERS
NYC

A

Abramson, Michael R Studio/401 Lafayette St 7th Fl 212-683-1271
Adams, Gaylord Design/236 E 36th St 212-684-4625
Adlemann, Morton/30 W 32nd St 212-564-8258
Adler, Stan Assoc/1140 Ave of Americas 212-719-1944
Adlerblum, Marleen/1133 Broadway #1225 212-807-8429
Adzema, Diane/17 Bleecker St 212-982-5657
AKM Associates/41 E 42nd St 212-687-7636
Alastair Brown Benjamin Assoc/419 Park Ave S 212-213-8719
Aliman, Elie/134 Spring St 212-925-9621
Allied Graphic Arts/1515 Broadway 212-730-1414
ALZ Design/11 Waverly Pl #1J 212-473-7620
American Express Publishing Co/1120 Ave of Americas 212-382-5600
Anagram Design Grp/10-40 Jackson Ave, Long Island City 718-786-2020
Anagraphics Inc/104 W 29th St 2nd Fl 212-279-2370
Ancona Design Atelier/524 W 43rd St 212-947-8287
Andersen, Bill/27 Minkel Rd, Ossining 914-762-4867
Anspach Grossman Portugal/711 Third Ave, 12th flr 212-692-9000
Antler & Baldwin Graphics/7 E 47th St 212-751-2031
Antupit and Others Inc/16 E 40th St 212-686-2552
Appelbaum Company/176 Madison Ave 4th Fl 212-213-1130
Ariel Peeri Design/135 E 27th St 212-686-0131
Arkadia Group/41 W 25th St 212-645-6226
Arnell-Bickford Assoc/100 Grand St 212-219-8400
Aron, Michael & Co/20 W 20th St 212-627-4054
Art Department/2 W 46th St 212-391-1826
Athey, Diane/425 W 23rd St 212-787-7415
Avanti Graphics/568 Broadway 212-966-6661

B

Balasas, Cora/651 Vanderbilt St 718-633-7753
Balch, Barbara/One Union Sq #903 212-242-0026
Bantam Books Inc/666 Fifth Ave 212-765-6500
Barnes, Miriam/2 Tudor City Pl #7D South 212-697-0441
Barnett Design Group/270 Lafayette St #801 212-431-7130
Barry David Berger Assoc/9 E 19th St 212-477-4100
Barry, Jim/69 W 68th St 212-873-6787
Becker Hockfield Design Assoc/35 E 21st St 212-505-7050
Beckerman, Ann Design/50 W 29th St 212-684-0496
Bel Air Assoc/745 Fifth Ave 17th Fl 212-838-1060
Benvenutti, Chris/12 W 27th St 12t Fl 212-696-0880
Bergman, Eliot, Inc./362 W. 20th St #201 (P 22,23) 212-645-0414
Bernhardt/Fudyma/133 E 36th St 212-889-9337
Bernstein, Harvey/160 Fifth Ave #804 212-243-4149
Besalel, Ely/235 E 49th St 212-759-7820
Bessen Tully & Lee/220 E 23rd St 12th Fl 212-213-1911
Binns & Lubin/80 Fifth Ave 212-989-0090
Biondo, Charles Design Assoc/389 W 12th St 212-645-5300
Black, Roger/PO Box 860/Radio City Sta 212-459-7553
Blackburn, Bruce/331 Park Ave South 10th Fl 212-777-5335
Bloch, Graulich & Whelan, Inc/333 Park Ave S 212-473-7033
Boker Group/37 W 26th St 212-686-1132
Bonnell Design Associates Inc/409 W 44th St 212-757-4420
Bordnick, Jack & Assoc/224 W 35th St 212-563-1544
Borejko, Barbara/124 W 24th St 4th Fl 212-463-9292
Botero, Samuel Assoc/150 E 58th St 212-935-5155
Bradford, Peter/11 E 22nd St 212-982-2090
Brainchild Designs/108 E 16th St 212-420-1222
Braswell, Lynn/320 Riverside Dr 212-222-8761
Bree/Taub Design/648 Broadway #703 212-254-8383
Brochure People/14 E 38th St #1466 212-696-9185
Brodsky Graphics/270 Madison Ave #605 212-684-2600
Brown, Kirk Q/1092 Blake Ave, Brooklyn 718-346-8281
Bryant & Co/2 Astor Pl 212-254-5122
Buckley Designs Inc/310 E 75th St 212-861-0626

Burns, Tom Assoc Inc/330 E 42nd St 212-594-9883
By Design/14 E 38th St 212-684-0388
Byrde Richard & Pound/251 Park Ave S 14th Fl 212-777-7000
Byrne, Susan/133 W 19th St 10th Fl 212-807-6671

C

Cain, David/200 W 20th St #607 212-633-0258
Calfo Assoc/20 W 20th St 9th Fl 212-627-3800
Cannan, Bill & Co Inc/529 W 42nd St #2Q 212-563-1004
Cantor, Andrew/4 W 37th St 6th Fl 212-629-0130
Canzani Graphics/11 W 30th St 212-643-1050
Caravello Studios/165 W 18th St 212-620-0620
Carlo & Associates/900 Boadway - 5th Floor 212-420-1110
Carnase, Inc/30 E 21st St 212-679-9880
Carpenter Graphic Design/72 Spring St 212-431-6666
Carson, Carol/138 W 88th St 212-580-0514
Cetta, Al/111 Bank St 212-989-9696
Chajet Design Group Inc/148 E 40th St 212-684-3669
Chang, Ivan/30 E 10th St 212-777-6102
Chapman, Sandra S/122 Ashland Pl #7E, Brooklyn 718-855-7396
Charles, Irene Assoc/104 E 40th St #206 212-765-8000
Chermayeff & Geismar/15 E 26th St 12th Fl 212-532-4499
Chin, E T Assoc/1160 Third Ave 212-645-6800
Chu, H L & Co Ltd/39 W 29th St 212-889-4818
Cliffer, Jill/9 E 16th St 212-691-7013
Cohen, Hayes Design/36-35 193rd St #3, Flushing
(P 20) 718-321-7307
Cohen, Norman Design/201 E 28th St #8K 212-679-3906
Collins, Thomas/156 Fifth Ave #1035 212-627-1656
Comart Assoc/360 W 31st St 212-714-2550
Condon, J & M/126 Fifth Ave 212-242-7811
Corchia Woliner Assoc/130 W 56th St 212-977-9778
Corey & Company/155 Sixth Ave 15th Fl 212-924-4311
Corpographics, Inc./47 West St 212-483-9065
Corporate Annual Reports Inc./112 E 31st St 212-889-2450
Corporate Graphics Inc/655 Third Ave 212-599-1820
Cosgrove Assoc Inc/223 E 31st St 212-889-7202
Cotler, Sheldon Inc/80 W 40th St 212-719-9590
Cousins, Morison S & Assoc/599 Broadway 8th Fl 212-751-3390
Cranner, Brian Inc/454 W 46th St #2D South 212-582-2030
Craven Design/234 Fifth Ave 212-696-4680
Creamer Dickson Basford/1633 Broadway 212-887-8670
Crow, John/34 W 37th St 212-594-2636
Csoka/Benato/Fleurant Inc/134 W 26th St 212-242-6777
Curtis Design Inc./928 Broadway #1104 212-475-3680

D

D'Astolfo, Frank Design/80 Warren St #32 212-732-3052
Daniels Design/150 E 35th St 212-889-0071
Danne, Richard & Assoc/126 Fifth Ave 212-645-7400
Davis, Jed/303 Lexington Ave 212-481-8481
Davis-Delaney-Arrow Inc/141 E 25th St 212-686-2500
Deharek & Poulin Assoc/320 W 13th St 212-929-5445
Delgado, Lisa/22 W 21st St 212-645-0097
Delphan Company/515 Madison Ave #3300 212-371-6700
DeMartin-Marona-Cranstoun-Downes/630 Third Ave 14th Fl 212-682-9044
DeMartino Design/584 Broadway 212-941-9200
Design Five/2637 Broadway 212-222-8133
Design Loiminchay/503 Broadway 5th Fl 212-941-7488
The Design Office/38 E 23rd St 212-420-1722
Design Plus/156 Fifth Ave #1232 212-645-2686
Designed to Print/130 W 25th St 212-924-2090
Designers Three/25 W 43rd St 212-221-5900
Designframe/1 Union Square 212-924-2426
Deutsch Design/530 Broadway 212-966-7710
Diamond Art Studio/11 E 36th St 212-685-6622
Dickens, Holly/60 E 42nd St #505 212-682-1490
DiComo, Charles & Assoc/120 E #4th St #12K 212-689-8670
DiFranza Williamson Inc/16 W 22nd St 212-463-8302
Displaycraft/41-21 28th St, Long Island City 718-784-8186
Donovan & Green Inc/1 Madison Ave 212-725-2233
Doret, Michael/12 E 14th St #4D 212-929-1688
Douglas, Barry Design/300 E 71st St #4H 212-734-4137
Downey Weeks + Toomey/519 Eighth Ave 22nd Fl 212-564-8260
Drate, Spencer/160 Fifth Ave #613 212-620-4672
Dreyfuss, Henry Assoc/423 W 55th St 212-957-8600

Dubins, Milt Designer Inc/353 W 22nd St....212-691-0232
Dubourcq, Hilaire/110 Christopher St....212-924-1564
Dubrow, Oscar Assoc/18 E 48th St....212-688-0698
Duffy, William R/201 E 36th St....212-682-6755
Dvorak Goodspeed & Assoc/165 Lexington Ave....212-475-4580
Dwyer, Tom/420 Lexington Ave....212-986-7108

EF

Eckstein, Linda/534 Laguardia Pl #5S....212-522-2552
Edgar, Lauren/26 E 20th St 8th Fl....212-673-6060
Edge, Dennis Design/36 E 38th St....212-679-0927
Eichinger, Inc/595 Madison Ave....212-421-0544
Emerson/Wajdowicz/1123 Broadway....212-807-8144
Environetics Inc/145 E 32nd St 8th Fl....212-481-9700
Environment Planning Inc/342 Madison Ave....212-661-3744
Erikson Assoc./345 Park Ave....212-688-0048
Etheridge, Palombo, Sedewitz/1500 Broadway....212-944-2530
Eucalyptus Tree Studio/73 Leonard St....212-226-0331
Falkins, Richard Design/15 W 44th St....212-840-3045
FDC Planning & Design Corp/434 E 57th St....212-355-7200
Fineberg Associates/333 E 68th St....212-734-1220
Flaherty, David/449 W 47th St #3....212-262-6536
Florville, Patrick Design Research/94-50 39 Ave, Rego Park....718-475-2278
Flying Eye Graphics/208 Fifth Ave/Unit 2....212-725-0658
Forman, Yale Designs Inc/11 Riverside Dr....212-799-1665
Fredy, Sherry/111 W 24th St....212-627-1867
Freyss, Christina/267 Broadway 2nd Fl....212-571-1130
Friday Saturday Sunday Inc/210 E 15th St....212-353-2060
Friedlander, Ira/502 E 84th St....212-580-9800
Friedman, Adam/820 Second Ave 6th Fl....212-682-6300
Froom, Georgia/62 W 39th St #803....212-944-0330
Fulgoni, Louis/233 W 21st St #4D....212-243-2959
Fulton & Partners/330 W 42nd St, 11th Fl....212-695-1625
Fultz, Patrick/166 Lexington Ave....212-545-7483

G

Gale, Robert A Inc/970 Park Ave....212-535-4791
Gamarello, Paul/21 E 22nd St #4G....212-485-4774
Gardner, Beau Assoc Inc/541 Lexington Ave 18th Fl....212-832-2426
Gaster, Joanne/201 E 30th St #43....212-686-0860
Gentile Studio/333 E 46th St....212-986-7743
George, Hershell/30 W 15th St....212-929-4321
Gerstman & Meyers Inc./60 W 55th St....212-586-2535
Gianninoto Assoc, Inc./133 E 54th St #2D....212-759-5757
Giber, Lauren/152 E 22nd St....212-473-2062
Giovanni Design Assoc./230 E 44th St #2L....212-972-2145
Gips & Balkind & Assoc/244 E 58th St....212-421-5940
Girth, Marcy/213 E 34th St #3A....212-685-0734
Glaser, Milton/207 E 32nd St....212-889-3161
Glazer & Kalayjian/301 E 45th St (P 14,15)....212-687-3099
Glusker Group/154 W 57th St....212-757-4438
Goetz Graphics/60 Madison Ave....212-679-4250
Gold, Susan/136 W 22nd St....212-645-6977
Goldman, Neal Assoc/230 Park Ave #1507....212-687-5058
Goodman/Orlick Design, Inc/461 West 47th St. 4th Fl....212-974-0297
Gorbaty, Norman Design/14 E 38th St....212-684-1665
Gordon, Sam & Assoc/226 W 4th St....212-741-9294
Gorman, Chris Assoc/305 Madison Ave....212-983-3375
Grant, Bill/119 Amherst St, Brooklyn....718-891-4936
Graphic Art Resource Assoc/257 W 10th St....212-929-0017
Graphic Chart & Map Co/236 W 26th St #8SE....212-463-0190
Graphic Expression/330 E 59th St....212-759-7788
Graphic Media/12 W 27th St 12th Fl....212-696-0880
Graphics by Nostradamus/250 W 57th St #1128A....212-581-1362
Graphics for Industry/8 W 30th St....212-889-6202
Graphics Institute/1633 Broadway....212-887-8670
Graphics to Go/133 E 36th St....212-889-9337
Gray, George/385 West End Ave....212-873-3607
Green, Douglas/251 E 51st St....212-752-6284
Grid, Steve C/118 E 28th St #908....212-889-1888
Griffler Designs/17 E 67th St....212-794-2625
Grunfeld Graphics Ltd/80 Varick St....212-431-8700
Gucciardo & Shapokas/244 Madison Ave....212-683-9378
Guth, Marcy/213 E 34th St #3A....212-685-0734

H

Halle, Doris/355 South End Ave #4C....212-321-2671
Halversen, Everett/874 58th St, Brooklyn....718-438-4200
Handler Group Inc/55 W 45th St....212-391-0951
Haynes, Leslie/134 E 22nd St....212-777-7390
HBO Studio Productions Inc/120 E 23rd St....212-477-8600
Head Productions/267 Wycoff St, Brooklyn....718-624-1906
Hecker, Mark Studio/321 W 11th St....212-620-9050
Heimall, Bob Inc/250 W 57th St #1206....212-245-4525
Hernandez, Raymond/994 Ocean Ave, Brooklyn....718-462-9072
Holzsager, Mel Assoc Inc/275 Seventh Ave....212-741-7373
Hopkins/Baumaun Group/236 W 26th St....212-727-2929
Horvath & Assoc Studios Ltd/93-95 Charles St....212-741-0300
Hub Graphics/18 E 16th St 4th Fl....212-675-8500
Human Factors/Industrial Design Inc/575 8th Ave....212-730-8010
Hunter, Rona Fischer/25 Fifth Ave #12F....212-598-4390
Huttner & Hillman/19 W 21st St 10th Fl....212-463-0776

IJ

Image Communications Inc/85 Fifth Ave....212-807-9677
Incredible Interactivity/26 W 23rd St 5th Fl....212-627-3321
Inkwell Inc/5 W 30th St....212-279-2066
Inner Thoughts/118 E 25th St....212-674-1277
Intersight Design Inc/419 Park Ave S....212-696-0700
Jaben, Seth Design/47 E 3rd St #3....212-673-5631
Jaffe Communications, Inc/122 E 42nd St....212-697-4310
Jensen Assoc/145 6th Ave #PH....212-645-3115
Jensen, Bill/145 Sixth Ave PH....212-645-3115
Johnston, Shaun & Susan/890 West End Ave #11E....212-663-4686
Jonson Pedersen Hinrichs & Shakery/141 Lexington Ave....212-889-9611

K

Kaeser & Wilson Design/330 Seventh Ave....212-563-2455
Kahn, Al Group/221 W 82nd St....212-580-3517
Kahn, Donald/39 W 29th St 12th Fl....212-889-8898
Kallir Phillips Ross Inc./605 Third Ave....212-878-3700
Kaplan, Barbara/875 Ave of Americas #1606....212-564-7706
Karlin, Bernie/41 E 42nd St #PH....212-687-7636
Kass Communications/505 Eighth Ave 19th Fl....212-868-3133
Kass, Milton Assoc Inc/1966 Broadway #35....212-874-0418
Kaufthial, Henry/220 W 19th St #1200....212-633-0222
Kaye Graphics/151 Lexington Ave....212-924-7800
Keithley & Assoc/32 W 22nd St 6th Fl....212-807-8388
Kleb Associates/25 W 45th St....212-246-2847
KLN Publishing Services Inc/36 E 30th St....212-686-8200
Kneapler, John/99 Lexington Ave 2nd Fl....212-696-1150
Ko Noda and Assoc International/950 Third Ave....212-759-4044
Kollberg-Johnson Assoc Inc/254 Fifth Ave....212-686-3648
Koppel & Scher Inc/156 Fifth Ave 13th Fl East....212-627-9330
Kosarin, Linda/400 W 58th St #5F....212-889-3050

L

Lake, John/38 E 57th St 7th Fl....212-644-3850
Lamlee, Stuart/55 W 86th St....212-772-2200
The Lamplight Group/342 Madison Ave....212-682-6270
Leach, Richard/62 W 39th St #803....212-869-0972
Lee & Young Communications/One Park Ave....212-689-4000
Lesley-Hille Inc/32 E 21st St....212-677-7570
Lester & Butler/437 Fifth Ave....212-889-0578
Levine, William V & Assoc/31 E 28th St....212-683-7177
Levirne, Joel/151 W 46th St....212-869-8370
Lieber/Brewster Corp Design/324 W 87th St....212-874-2874
Lieberman, Ron/109 W 28th St....212-947-0653
Liebert Studios Inc/6 E 39th St #1200....212-686-4520
Lika Association/160 E 38th St....212-490-3660
Lind Brothers Inc/111 Eighth Ave 7th Fl....212-924-9280
Lippincott & Margulies Inc/499 Park Ave....212-832-3000
Little Apple Art/409 Sixth Ave, Brooklyn....718-499-7045
Lombardo, Joe/98 Riverside Dr #15-G....212-580-7611
Lukasiewicz Design Inc/119 W 57th St....212-581-3344
Lundgren, Ray Graphics/122 E 42nd St #216....212-370-1686
Luth & Katz Inc/40 E 49th St 9th Fl....212-644-5777

M

M & Co Design Group/50 W 17th St 12th Fl	212-243-0082
Madridejos, Fernando/130 W 67th St #1B	212-724-7339
Maggio, Ben Assoc Inc/420 Lexington Ave #1650	212-697-8600
Maggio, J P Design Assoc Inc/561 Broadway	212-725-9660
Maleter, Mari/25-34 Crescent St, Astoria	718-726-7124
Marchese, Frank/444 E 82nd St	212-988-6267
Marcus, Eric/386 Waverly Ave, Brooklyn	718-789-1799
Masuda, Coco/1 Union Sq #803	212-255-8141
Mauro, Frank Assoc Inc/18 W 45th St	212-719-5570
Mayo-Infurna Design/10 E 21st St 13th Fl	212-888-7883
McDonald, B & Assoc/1140 Ave of the Americas	212-869-9717
McGovern & Pivoda/39 W 38th St	212-840-2912
McNicholas, Florence/1419 8th Ave, Brooklyn	718-965-0203
Mendola Design/420 Lexington Ave	212-986-5680
Mentkin, Robert/51 E 97th St	212-534-5101
Merrill, Abby Studio Inc/153 E 57th St	212-753-7565
Metzdorf, Lyle/821 Broadway 3rd Fl	212-353-0101
Meyers, Ann/118 E 37th St	212-689-3680
Miller, Irving D Inc/33 Great Neck Rd, Great Neck	516-466-6585
Mirenburg, Barry/413 City Island Ave, City Island	718-885-0835
Mitchell, E M Inc/820 Second Ave	212-986-5595
Mizerek Design/48 E 43rd St 2nd Fl	212-986-5702
Modular Marketing Inc/1841 Broadway	212-581-4690
Monczyk, Allen/210 fifth Ave	212-385-6633
Mont, Howard Assoc Inc/132 E 35th St	212-683-4360
Morris, Dean/307 E 6th St #4B	212-420-0673
Moshier, Harry & Assoc/18 E 53rd St	212-873-6130
Moskof & Assoc/154 W 57th St #133	212-333-2015
Mossberg, Stuart Design Assoc/11 W 73rd St	212-873-6130
Muir, Cornelius, Moore/79 5th Ave	212-463-7715
Mulligan, Don/418 Central PK W #81	212-666-6079
Murtha Desola Finsilver Fiore/800 Third Ave	212-832-4770

NO

N B Assoc Inc/435 Fifth Ave	212-684-8074
Nelson, George & Assoc Inc/PO Box 243 Madison Sq Sta	212-777-4300
Nichols, Mary Ann/80 Eighth Ave #900	212-727-9818
Nicholson Design/148 W 24th St 12th Fl	212-206-1530
Noneman & Noneman Design/230 E 18th St	212-473-4090
Notovitz & Perrault Design Inc/47 E 19th St 4th Fl	212-677-9700
Novus Visual Communications Inc/18 W 27th St	212-689-2424
O & J Design/9 W 29th St 5th Fl	212-779-9654
O'Neil, Brian/95 Fifth Ave 8th Fl	212-691-1510
Oak Tree Graphics Inc/570 Seventh Ave	212-398-9355
Offenhartz, Harvey Inc/1414 Ave of Americas	212-751-3241
Ong & Assoc/11 W 19th St 6th Fl	212-633-6702
Orlov, Christian/42 W 69th St	212-873-2381
Ortiz, Jose Luis/66 W 77th St	212-877-3081
Oz Communications Inc/36 E 30th St	212-686-8200

P

Page Arbitrio Resen Ltd/305 E 46th St	212-421-8190
Pahmer, Hal/8 W 30th St 7th Fl	212-889-6202
Palladino, Tony/400 E 56th St	212-751-0068
Paragraphics/427 3rd St, Brooklyn	718-965-2231
Parsons School of Design/66 Fifth Ave	212-741-8900
Patel, Harish Design Assoc/218 Madison Ave	212-686-7425
Peckolick & Prtnrs/112 E 31st St	212-532-6166
Pellegrini & Assoc/16 E 40th St	212-686-4481
Pencils Portfolio Inc/333 E 49th St	212-355-2468
Penpoint Studio Inc/444 Park Ave S	212-243-5435
Penraat Jaap Assoc/315 Central Park West	212-873-4541
Pentagram/212 Fifth Ave 17th Fl	212-683-7000
Performing Dogs/45 E 19th St	212-260-1880
Perlman-Withers/305 E 46th St 15th Fl	212-935-2552
Perlow, Paul/123 E 54th St #6E	212-758-4358
Peterson Blythe & Cato/216 E 45th St	212-557-5566
Pettis, Valerie/88 Lexington Ave #7G	212-683-7382
Pirman, John/57 W 28th St	212-679-2866
Platinum Design Inc/14 W 23rd St 2nd Fl	212-366-4000
Plumb Design Group Inc/57 E 11th St 7th Fl	212-673-3490
Pouget, Evelyn/23 E 7th St	212-228-7935
Prendergast, J W & Assoc Inc/605 Third Ave	212-687-8805

Pushpin Group/215 Park Ave S #1300	212-674-8080

QR

Quon, Mike Design Office/568 Broadway #703	212-226-6024
RC Graphics/157 E 57th St	212-755-1383
RD Graphics/151 Lexington Ave #5F	212-889-5612
Regn-Califano Inc/330 W 42nd St #1300	212-239-0380
Riss, Micha/25 W 45th St 2nd Fl	212-704-4000
Robinson, Mark/904 President St, Brooklyn	718-638-9067
Rogers, Ana/20 W 20th St 7th Fl	212-741-4687
Rogers, Richard Inc/300 E 33rd St	212-685-3666
Romero, Javier/9 W 19th St 5th Fl	212-727-9445
Rosebush Visions/154 W 57th St #826	212-398-6600
Rosenthal, Herb & Assoc Inc/207 E 32nd St	212-685-1814
Ross Culbert Lavery Russman/15 W 20th St 9th Fl	212-206-0044
Ross/Pento Inc/301 W 53rd St	212-757-5604
Rothschild, Joyce/305 E 46th St 15th Fl	212-888-8680
Rudoy, Peter/1619 Broadway 10th Fl	212-265-7600
Russell, Anthony Inc/170 Fifth Ave 11th Fl	212-255-0650
Russo, Rocco Anthony/31 W 21st St 6th Fl	212-213-4710

S

Sabanosh, Michael/433 W 34th St #18B	212-947-8161
Saiki & Assoc/154 W 18th St #2D	212-255-0466
Sakin, Sy/17 E 48th St	212-688-3141
Saks, Arnold/350 E 81st St 4th Fl	212-861-4300
Saksa Art & Design/41 Union Sq W #1001	212-255-5539
Salavetz, Judith/160 Fifth Ave #613	212-620-4672
Salisbury & Salisbury Inc/15 W 44th St	212-575-0770
Salpeter, Paganucci, Inc/142 E 37th St	212-683-3310
Sandgren Associates Inc/60 E 42nd St	212-679-4650
Sarda, Thomas/875 Third Ave 4th Fl	212-303-8326
Sawyer, Arnie Studio/15 W 28th St 4th Fl	212-685-4927
Say It In Neon/434 Hudson St	212-691-7977
Schaefer-Cassety Inc/42 W 39th St	212-840-0175
Schaeffer/Boehm Ltd/315 W 35th St	212-947-4345
Schecht, Leslie/505 Henry St, Brooklyn	718-834-1843
Schechter Group Inc/212 E 49th St	212-752-4400
Schecterson, Jack Assoc Inc/274 Madison Ave	212-889-3950
Scheinzeit, Teri/27 W 24th St	212-627-5355
Schumach, Michael P/159-10 Sanford Ave, Flushing	718-539-5328
SCR Design Organization/1114 First Ave	212-752-8496
Seidman, Gene/20 W 20th St #703	212-741-4687
Shapiro, Ellen Assoc/141 Fifth Ave 12th Fl	212-460-8544
Shareholders Reports/600 Third Ave 14th Fl	212-686-9099
Shaw, Paul/785 West End Ave	212-666-3738
Sherin & Matejka Inc/404 Park Ave S	212-686-8410
Sherowitz, Phyllis/310 E 46th St	212-532-8933
Shreeve, Draper Design/28 Perry St	212-675-7534
Siegel & Gale Inc/1185 Ave of Americas 8th Fl	212-730-0101
Siegel, Marion/87 E 2nd St #4A	212-460-9817
Silberlicht, Ira/210 W 70th St	212-595-6252
Silverman, Bob Design/216 E 49th St 2nd Fl	212-371-6472
Singer, Paul Design/494 14th St, Brooklyn	718-449-8172
Sloan, William/236 W 26th St #805	212-463-7025
Smith, Edward Design/1133 Broadway #1211	212-255-1717
Smith, Laura/12 E 14th St #4D	212-206-9162
Sochynsky, Ilona/200 E 36th St	212-686-1275
Solay/Hunt/28 W 44th St 21st Fl	212-840-3313
Solazzo Design/928 Broadway #700	212-529-3320
Sorvino Ligasan Design Assoc/1616 York Ave. #5	212-879-8197
St Vincent Milone & McConnells/1156 Sixth Ave	212-921-1414
Stern & Levine/12 W 27th St	212-545-0450
Stevenson, Bob/48 W 21st St 9th Fl	212-206-1724
Stewart Design Group/1 Union Sq W #814	212-979-2248
Stillman, Linda/1556 Third Ave	212-410-3225
Stuart, Gunn & Furuta/95 Madison Ave	212-689-0077
Studio 42/1472 Broadway #506	212-354-7298
Swatek and Romanoff Design Inc/156 Fifth Ave #1100	212-807-0236
Systems Collaborative Inc/52 Duane St	212-608-0584

TU

Taurins Design Assoc/280 Madison Ave	212-679-5955
Tauss, Jack George/484 W 43rd St #40H	212-279-1658
Taylor & Ives/989 Sixth Ave	212-244-0750

Taylor, Stan Inc/6 E 39th St...212-685-4741
Tercovich, Douglas Assoc Inc/575 Madison Ave.............212-838-4800
Three/444 East 82nd St #12C.......................................212-988-6267
Tobias, William/6 W 18th St...212-741-1712
Toomey, Michael/345 W 88th St.....................................212-877-5817
Toriello, Steven/846 Carroll St, Brooklyn.......................718-230-4867
Tribich/Glasman Design/150 E 35th St............................212-679-6016
Tscherny, George Design/238 E 72nd St.........................212-734-3277
Tunstull Studio/201 Clinton Ave #14G, Brooklyn.............718-834-8529
Ultra Arts Inc/150 E 35th St..212-679-7493
Un, David/130 W 25th St...212-924-2090

VW

Valk, John/245 E 24th St...212-889-4490
Viewpoint Graphics/10 Park Ave.....................................212-685-0560
Visible Studio Inc/99 Lexington Ave................................212-683-8530
Visual Accents Corp/30 Irving Pl....................................212-777-7766
Wallace/Church Assoc/330 E 48th St..............................212-755-2903
Waters, John Assoc Inc/3 W 18th St 8th Fl.....................212-807-0717
Waters, Pamela Studio Inc/320 W 13th St.......................212-620-8100
Webster, Robert Inc/331 Park Ave S................................212-677-2966
Weissman, Walter/463 West St #B332.............................212-989-9694
Whelan Design Office/144 W 27th St...............................212-691-4404
Wijtvliet, Ine/440 E 56th St...212-319-4444
Wilson, Rex Co/330 Seventh Ave.....................................212-594-3646
Winterson, Finn/401 Eighth Ave #43, Brooklyn...............212-219-2711
Wizard Graphics Inc/36 E 30th St...................................212-686-8200
Wolf, Henry Production Inc/167 E 73rd St.......................212-472-2500
Wolff, Rudi Inc/135 Central Park West.............................212-873-5800
Word-Wise/325 W 45th St..212-246-0430
Works/45 W 27th St...212-696-1666

YZ

Yoshimura-Fisher Graphic Design/284 Lafayette St.........212-431-4776
Young Goldman Young Inc/320 E 46th St.........................212-697-7820
Yurick, Michael/250 W 103rd St #7F................................212-850-1612
Zahor & Bender/200 E 33rd St...212-686-1121
Zazula, Hy Inc/2 W 46th St 2nd Fl...................................212-581-2747
Zeitsoff, Elaine/241 Central Park West............................212-580-1282
Zimmerman & Foyster/22 E 21st St.................................212-674-0259
Zimmerman, Amy/19 Salem Lane, Port Washington.........212-598-0133
Zuzzolo Graphics/99-31 64th Ave #F2, Rego Pk.............718-830-7116

NORTHEAST

AB

Action Incentive/2 Townlake Cir, Rochester, NY.............716-427-2410
Adam Filippo & Moran/1206 Fifth Ave, Pittsburgh, PA....412-261-3720
Adler-Schwartz Graphics/6 N Park Dr #107 Park Ctr, Hunt Valley, MD.410-628-0600
Advertising Design Assoc Inc/1220 Ridgley St, Baltimore, MD............301-752-2181
Altschul, Charles/356 Riverbank Rd, Stamford, CT...........203-329-7251
American Tech Systems/5 Suburban Park Dr, Billerica, MA.....617-272-8890
Aries Graphics/Massabesic, Manchester, NH..................603-668-0811
The Artery/12 W Biddle St, Baltimore, MD.......................301-752-2979
Arts and Words/1025 Conn Ave NW #300, Washington, DC.....202-463-4880
Ashton, David & Co/611 Cathedral St, Baltimore, MD......301-727-1151
The Avit Corp/1355 15th St #100, Fort Lee, NJ................201-886-1100
Baese, Gary/2229 N Charles St, Baltimore, MD................301-235-2226
Bain, S Milo/3 Shaw Lane, Hartsdale, NY.......................914-946-0144
BAIRDesign/38 Sunset Ave, W Bridgewater, MA...............508-580-9903
Baker, Arthur/PO Box 29, Germantown, NY......................518-537-4438
Baldassini, Paul/234 Clarendon St, Boston, MA...............617-236-0190
Baldwin, James/1467 Jordan Ave, Crofton, MD................301-721-1896
Bally Design Inc/420 N Craig St, Pittsburgh, PA..............412-621-9009
Barton-Gillet/10 S Gay St, Baltimore, MD.......................301-685-6800
Belser, Burkey/1818 N St NW #110, Washington, DC........202-775-0333
Bennardo, Churik Design Inc/1311 Old Freeport Rd, Pittsburgh, PA....412-963-0133
Blake + Barancik Design/135 S 18th St #403A, Philadelphia, PA.........215-977-9540
Bodzioch, Leon/59 Smith St, Chelmsford, MA..................617-250-0265
Bogus, Sidney A & Assoc/22 Corey St, Melrose, MA........617-662-6660
Bomzer Design Inc/66 Canal St, Boston, MA....................617-227-5151
Bowers, John D/PO Box 101, Radnor, PA..........................215-688-5541
Bradbury, Robert & Assoc/26 Halsey Ln, Closter, NJ.......201-768-6395

Brady, John Design/130 7th St, Century Bldg, Pittsburgh, PA.............412-288-9300
Breckenridge Designs/2025 I St NW #300, Washington, DC.............202-833-5700
Breiner, Joanne/11 Webster St, Medford, MA...................617-354-8378
Bressler, Peter Design Assoc/301 Cherry St, Philadelphia, PA.............215-925-7100
Bridy, Dan/625 Stanwix St #2402, Pittsburgh, PA............412-288-9362
Brier, David/38 Park Ave, Rutherford, NJ.........................201-896-8476
Brown and Craig Inc/407 N Charles St, Baltimore, MD.....301-837-2727
Brownstone Group/8 Raymond St, S Norwalk, CT.............203-866-9970
Buckett, Bill Assoc/137 Gibbs St, Rochester, NY.............716-546-6580
Byrne, Ford/100 N 20th St, Philadelphia, PA....................215-564-0500

C

Cable, Jerry Design/133 Kuhl Rd, Flemington, NJ.............201-788-6750
Calingo, Diane/3711 Lawrence Ave, Kensington, MD.........301-949-3557
Cameron Inc/9 Appleton St, Boston, MA..........................617-338-4408
Campbell Harrington & Brear/352 W Market St, York, PA.717-846-2947
Carmel, Abraham/7 Peter Beet Dr, Peekskill, NY.............914-737-1439
Cascio, Chris/456 Glenbrook Rd, Stamford, CT................203-358-0519
Case/11 Dupont Circle NW #400, Washington, DC............202-328-5900
Chaparos Productions Limited/1112 6th St NW, Washington, DC.......202-289-4838
Charysyn & Charysyn/Route 42, Westkill, NY...................518-989-6720
Chase, David O Design Inc/E Genesee St, Skaneateles, NY....315-685-5715
Chronicle Design/1333 New Hampshire Ave NW, Washington, DC......202-828-3519
Cleary Design/118-A N Division St, Salisbury, MD............301-546-1040
Cliggett, Jack/703 Redwood Ave, Yeadon, PA..................215-623-1606
Colangelo, Ted Assoc/340 Pemberwick Rd, Greenwich, CT....203-531-3600
Colopy Dale Inc/850 Ridge Ave, Pittsburgh, PA................412-332-6706
Concept Packaging Inc/5 Horizon Rd, Ft Lee, NJ..............201-224-5762
Consolidated Visual Center Inc/2529 Kenilworth Ave, Tuxedo, MD.....301-772-7300
Cook & Shanosky Assoc/103 Carnegie Ctr #203, Princeton, NJ.........609-452-1666
Cooper, Steven/39 Bancroft Ave, Reading, MA.................617-944-8080
Corey & Company/, Boston, MA.......................................617-266-1850
The Creative Dept/130 S 17th, Philadelphia, PA...............215-988-0390
Cundy, David/82 Main St, New Caanan, CT......................203-972-3350
Curran & Connors Inc/333 Marcus Blvd, Hauppauge, NY....516-433-6600

D

D'Art Studio Inc/PO Box 299, N Scituate, MA..................617-545-7313
Dakota Design/900 W Valley Rd #601, Wayne, PA.............215-293-0900
Dale, Terry/2824 Hurst Terrace NW, Washington, DC........202-244-3866
Dawson Designers Associates/21 Dean St, Assonet, MA...617-644-2940
Dean, Jane/13 N Duke St, Lancaster, PA..........................717-295-4638
DeCesare, John/1091 Post Rd, Darien, CT.......................203-655-6057
DMCD/911 Washington St, Wilmington, DE.......................302-654-5277
Design Associates/1601 Kent St #1010, Arlington, VA.......703-243-7717
Design Comp Inc/5 Colony St #303, Meriden, CT.............203-235-6696
Design for Medicine Inc/301 Cherry St, Philadelphia, PA...215-925-7100
Design Group of Boston/437 Boylston St, Boston, MA.......617-437-1084
Design Resource/700 S Henderson Rd, King of Prussia, PA.215-265-8585
Design Trends/4 Broadway PO Box 119, Valhalla, NY.......914-948-0902
Designed Images/25 Chicopee St, Chicopee, MA.............413-594-2681
Dever, Jeffrey L/7619 S Arbory Lane, Laurel, MD.............301-776-2812
DiFiore Associates/625 Stanwix St #2507, Pittsburgh, PA..412-471-0608
Dimensional Illustrators/362 2nd St Pike, Southhampton, PA.215-953-1415
Dimmick, Gary/47 Riverview Ave, Pittsburgh, PA..............412-321-7225
Dohanos, Steven/271 Sturges Highway, Westport, CT.......203-227-3541
Downing, Allan/50 Francis St, Needham, MA....................617-449-4784

EF

Educ'l Media/Div/GU Med Ctr 3900 Reservoir Rd, Washington, DC......202-625-2211
Egress Concepts/20 Woods Bridge Rd, Katonah, NY.........914-232-8433
Erickson, Peter/46 Pleasant St, Marlboro, MA..................508-481-2288
Eucalyptus Tree Studio/2221 Morton St, Baltimore, MD....301-243-0211
Evans Garber & Paige/2631 Genesee St, Utica, NY...........315-733-2313
Fader Jones & Zarkades/797 Boylston St, Boston, MA......617-267-7779
Falcone & Assoc/13 Watchung Ave Box 637, Chatham, NJ.201-635-2900
Fannell Studio/298-A Columbus Ave, Boston, MA.............617-267-0895
Finnin, Teresa/655 Washington Blvd #602, Stamford, CT...203-348-4104
Forum Inc/1226 Post Rd, Fairfield, CT..............................203-259-5686
Fossella, Gregory Assoc/479 Commonwealth Ave, Boston, MA.617-267-4940
Foster, Stephen Design/17 51st St #5, Weehawken , NJ....201-866-9040
Fraser, Robert & Assoc Inc/1101 N Calvert St, Baltimore, MD.............301-685-3700
Freelance Studio/271 Rte 46 W #F109, Fairfield, NJ..........201-227-3904
Fresh Produce/328-B S Broadway, Baltimore, MD.............301-821-1815
Froelich Advertising Service/8 Wanamaker Ave, Mahwah, NJ.............201-529-1737

Frohman, Al/2277 4th St, East Meadow, NY 516-735-2771
Full Circle Design/726 Pacific St, Baltimore, MD 301-523-5903

G

Garrett, JB Studios/2050 W Stanton St, York, PA 717-846-7056
Gasser, Gene/300 Main St, Chatham, NJ 201-635-6020
Gateway Studios/225 Ross St, Pittsburgh, PA............................412-471-7224
Gatter Inc/68 Purchase St, Rye, NY 914-967-5600
GK+D Communications/2311 Calvert St NW, Washington, DC............202-328-0414
Glass, Al/3312 M St NW, Washington, DC 202-333-3993
Glenn, Raymond/39 Edgerton Rd, Wallinford, CT.......................203-269-5643
Glickman, Frank Inc/180 Mosshill Rd, Boston, MA 617-524-2200
Goldner, Linda/709 Rittenhouse Savoy, Philadelphia, PA 215-735-8370
Gonzalez, Andres/1435 Bedford St #8C, Stamford, CT 212-909-9358
Good, Peter Graphic Design/Pequot Press Bldg, Chester, CT............203-526-9597
Gorelick, Alan Design/High St Court, Morristown, NJ 201-898-1991
Graham Associates Inc/1899 L St NW, Washington, DC.............202-833-9657
Grant Marketing Assoc./1100 E Hector St, Conshohocken, PA............215-834-0550
The Graphic Suite/235 Shady Ave, Pittsburgh, PA......................412-661-6699
Graphicenter/1101 2nd St NE, Washington, DC 202-544-0333
Graphics By Gallo/1800-B Swann St NW, Washington, DC..........202-234-7700
Graphicus Corp/2025 Maryland Ave, Baltimore, MD....................301-727-5553
Graves Fowler & Assoc/14532 Carona Dr, Silver Spring, MD............301-236-9808
Grear, Malcolm Designers Inc/391 Eddy St, Providence, RI........401-331-5656
Green, Mel/31 Thorpe Rd, Needham Hts, MA..............................617-449-6777
Greenebaum Design/86 Walnut St, Natick, MA 617-655-8146
Greenfield, Peggy/2 Lewis Rd, Foxboro, MA 617-543-6644
Gregory & Clyburne/59 Grove St, New Canaan, CT.....................203-966-8343
Groff, Jay Michael/515 Silver Spring Ave, Silver Spring, MD......301-565-0431
Groth, Donna/13 Seventh ave E, East Northport, NY..................516-757-1182
Group Four Design/PO Box 717, Avon, CT....................................203-678-1570
Guancione, Karen/262 DeWitt Ave, Belleville, NJ.......................201-450-9490
Guerrette, Muriel/97-A Perry St, Unionville, CT............................203-675-9866
Gunn Associates/275 Newbury St, Boston, MA............................617-267-0618

H

Hain, Robert Assoc/346 Park Ave, Scotch Plains, NJ 201-322-1717
Hammond Design Assoc/35 Amherst St, Milford, NH...................603-673-5253
Harvey, Ed/PO Box 23755, Washington, DC.................................703-671-0880
Hegemann Associates/One S Franklin St, Nyack, NY 914-358-7348
Helms, Nina/25 Forest Ln, Westbury, NY......................................516-997-6567
Herbick & Held/1117 Wolfendale St, Pittsburgh, PA....................412-321-7400
Herman, Sid & Assoc/930 Massachusetts Ave, Cambridge, MA............617-876-6464
Heyck, Edith/36 Liberty St, Newburyport, MA..............................508-462-9027
Hill, Michael/2433 Maryland Ave, Baltimore, MD.........................301-366-8338
Hillmuth, James/3613 Norton Pl, Washington, DC 202-244-0465
Holl, RJ/ Art Directions/McBride Rd/Box 44, Wales, MA..............413-267-5024
Holloway, Martin/56 Mt Horeb Rd, Plainfield, NJ.........................201-563-0169
Hough, Jack Inc/25 Seirhill Rd, Norwalk, CT................................203-846-2666
Hrivnak, James/10822 Childs Ct, Silver Spring, MD....................301-681-9090
Huerta, Gerard/45 Corbin Dr, Darien, CT (P 21)............203-656-0505
Huyssen, Roger/45 Corbin Dr, Darien, CT (P 21)...........203-656-0200

IJ

Image Consultants/3 Overlook Dr, Amherst, NH 603-673-5512
Image Factory/2229 N Charles St, Baltimore, MD 301-235-2226
Impress/PO Box 761, Williamsburg, MA..413-268-3040
Independent Design/451 D St #811, Boston, MA..........................617-439-4944
Inkstone Design/32 Laurel St, Fairfield, CT 203-336-9599
Innovations & Development Inc/115 River Rd, Edgewater, NJ............201-941-5500
Irish, Gary Graphics/45 Newbury St, Boston, MA.........................617-247-4168
Itin, Helen/Visual Concepts/100 Cutler Rd, Greenwich, CT 203-637-7609
Jarrin Design Inc/PO Box 421, Pound Ridge, NY 914-764-4625
Jensen, R S/819 N Charles St, Baltimore, MD..............................301-727-3411
Jezierny, John Michael/20 Kenter Pl, Westville, CT......................203-689-8170
Johnson & Simpson Graphic Design/49 Bleeker St, Newark, NJ............201-624-7788
Johnson Design Assoc/403 Massachusetts Ave, Acton, MA........617-263-5345
Jones, Jerry/36 S Paca St #108, Baltimore, MD...........................301-727-4222
Jones, Tom & Jane Kearns/2803 18th St NW, Washington, DC............202-232-1921

K

Kahana Associates/419 Benjamin #A Fox Pavilion, Jenkintown, PA.....215-887-0422
Karp, Rudi/28 Dudley Ave, Landsowne, PA..................................215-284-5949
Katz-Wheeler Design/37 S 20th St, Philadelphia, PA 215-567-5668

Kaufman, Henry J & Assoc/2233 Wisconsin Ave NW, Washington, DC ..202-333-0700
KBH Graphics/1023 St Paul Street, Baltimore, MD 301-539-7916
Ketchum International/4 Gateway Ctr, Pittsburgh, PA 412-456-3693
King-Casey Inc/199 Elm St, New Canaan, CT 203-966-3581
Klim, Matt & Assoc/PO Box Y, Avon Park N, Avon, CT................203-678-1222
Klotz, Don/296 Millstone Rd, Wilton, CT.......................................203-762-9111
Knabel, Lonnie/34 Station St, Brookline, MA................................617-566-4464
Knox, Harry & Assoc/9914 Locust St, Glenndale, MD.................304-464-1665
Kostanecki, Andrew Inc/47 Elm St, New Canaan, CT..................203-966-1681
Kovanen, Erik/102 Twin Oak Lane, Wilton, CT.............................203-762-8961
Kramer/Miller/Lomden/Glossman/1528 Waverly, Philadelphia, PA........215-545-7077
Krohne, David/2727 29th St NW, Washington, DC.......................202-265-2371
Krone Graphic Design/426 S 3rd St, Lemoyne, PA 717-774-7431
Kulhanek, Paul/Letter Perfect/167 Cherry St #177, Milford, CT.............203-876-0697

L

LAM Design Inc/661 N Broadway, White Plains, NY 914-948-4777
Langdon, John/4529 Pine St, Philadelphia, PA.............................215-476-4312
Lapham/Miller Assoc/34 Essex St, Andora, MA............................617-367-0110
Latham Brefka Associates/833 Boylston St, Boston, MA.............617-536-8787
Laufer, Joseph Mark/2308 Lombard St #1B, Philadelphia, PA............215-545-2191
Lausch, David Graphics/2613 Maryland Ave, Baltimore, MD 301-235-7453
Lebbad, James A/24 Independence Way, Titusville, NJ................212-645-5260
Lebowitz, Mo/2599 Phyllis Dr, N Bellemore, NY...........................516-826-3397
Leeds, Judith K Studio/14 Rosemont Ct, N Caldwell, NJ.............201-226-3552
Lees, John & Assoc/930 Massachusetts Ave, Cambridge, MA 617-876-6465
Lenney, Ann/2737 Devonshire Pl NW, Washington, DC...............202-667-1786
Leotta Designers Inc/303 Harry St, Conshohocken, PA...............215-828-8820
Lester Associates Inc/100 Snake Hill Rd Box D, West Nyack, NY 914-358-6100
Levinson Zaprauskis Assoc/15 W Highland Ave, Philadelphia, PA.......215-248-5242
Lewis, Hal Design/104 S 20th St, Philadelphia, PA......................215-563-4461
Lion Hill Studio/1233 W Mt Royal Ave, Baltimore, MD.................301-837-6218
Livingston Studio/29 Robbins Ave, Elmsford, NY.........................914-592-4220
Lizak, Matt/Blackplain Rd RD #1, N Smithfield, RI........................401-766-8885
Logan, Denise/203 Rugby Ave, Rochester, NY.............................716-235-0893
Löse, Hal/533 W Hortter St, Philadelphia, PA (P 32)....215-849-7635
Loukin, Serge Inc/PO Box 425, Solomons, MD.............................212-645-2788
Luebbers Inc/2300 Walnut St #732, Philadelphia, PA..................215-567-2360
Luma/702 N Eutaw St, Baltimore, MD...301-523-5903
Lussier, Mark/38 Cove Ave, E Norwalk, CT..................................203-852-0363
Lyons, Lisa/9 Deanne St, Gardiner, ME...207-582-1602

M

MacIntosh, Rob Communication/93 Massachusetts, Boston, MA.........617-267-4912
Magalos, Christopher/3308 Church Rd, Cherry Hill, NJ................609-667-7433
Maglio, Mark/PO Box 872, Plainville, CT.......................................203-793-0771
Major Assoc/1101 N Calvert #1703, Baltimore, MD 301-752-6174
Mandala/520 S Third St, Philadelphia, PA.....................................215-923-6020
Mandle, James/300 Forest Ave, Paramus, NJ..............................201-967-7900
Mansfield, Malcolm/20 Aberdeen St, Boston, MA.........................617-437-1922
Marcus, Sarna/4720 Montgomery Ln #903, Bethesda, MD..........301-951-7044
Mariuzza, Pete/146 Hardscrabble Rd, Briarcliff Manor, NY 914-769-3310
Martucci Studio/116 Newbury St, Boston, MA 617-266-6960
MDB Communications Inc/932 Hungerford Dr #23, Rockville, MD.......301-279-9093
Media Concepts/25 N Main St, Assonet, MA.................................617-437-1382
Melanson, Donya Assoc/437 Main St, Charlestown, MA..............617-241-7300
Melone, Michael/RD 3 Box 123, Canonsburg, PA.........................412-746-5165
Mendez, Nancy/4800 Chevy Chase Dr #508, Chevy Chase, MD.........301-656-2676
Merry, Ann (Merry Men)/246 Western Ave, Sherborn, MA.............508-655-4955
Meyer, Bonnie/259 Collignon Way #2A, River Vale, NJ................201-666-5763
Micolucci, Nicholas Assoc/515 Schumaker Rd, King of Prussia, PA 215-265-3320
Miho, J Inc/46 Chalburn Rd, Redding, CT......................................203-938-3214
Mitchell & Company/1029 33rd St NW, Washington, DC...............202-342-6025
Monti, Ron/106 W University, Baltimore, MD 301-366-8952
Morlock Graphics/722 Camberly Cir #C7, Towson, MD................301-825-5080
Moss, John C/4805 Bayard Blvd, Chevy Chase, MD.....................301-320-3912
Mueller & Wister/1211 Chestnut St #607, Philadelphia, PA..........215-568-7260
Muller-Munk, Peter Assoc/2100 Smallman St, Pittsburgh, PA......412-261-5161
Myers, Gene Assoc/5575 Hampton, Pittsburgh, PA......................412-661-6314

NO

Nason Design Assoc/329 Newbury, Boston, MA 617-266-7286
Navratil Art Studio/905 Century Bldg, Pittsburgh, PA...................412-471-4322
New York Design/1984 Monroe Ave, Rochester, NY.....................716-473-5100
Nimeck, Fran/RD 4/ 358-A Riva Ave , North Brunswick, NJ 201-821-8741

Noi Viva Design/220 Ferris Ave, White Plains, NY..........................914-946-1951
Nolan & Assoc/4100 Cathedral Ave NW, Washington, DC..................202-363-6553
North Charles St Design/222 W Saratoga St, Baltimore, MD...............301-539-4040
Odyssey Design Group/918 F St NW #200, Washington, DC..............202-783-6240
Ollio Studio/Fulton Bldg, Pittsburgh, PA..412-281-4483
On Target/1185 E Putnam Ave, Riverside, CT.................................203-637-8300

P

Paganucci, Bob/17 Terry Ct, Montvale, NJ......................................201-391-1752
Paine/ Bluett/ Paine Inc/4617 Edgefield Rd, Bethesda, MD 301-493-8445
Panke, Nick/116 Wintonbury Ave, Bloomfield, CT 203-242-6576
Parry, Ivor/, Eastchester, NY..914-961-7338
Parshall, C A Inc/200 Henry St, Stamford, CT..................................212-947-5971
Pasinski, Irene Assoc/6026 Penn Circle S, Pittsburgh, PA...................412-661-9000
Patterson, Margaret/234 Clarendon St, Boston, MA 617-424-1236
Peck, Gail M/1637 Harvard St NW, Washington, DC 202-667-7448
The Peregrine Group/375 Sylvan Ave, Englewood Cliffs, NJ................201-567-8585
Perspectives In Comm/1637 Harvard St NW, Washington, DC.............202-667-7448
Pesanelli, David Assoc/14508 Barkwood Dr, Rockville, MD 301-871-7355
Petty, Daphne/1460 Belmont St NW, Washington, DC.......................202-667-8222
Phase One Graphics/315 Market St, Sudbury, PA 717-286-1111
Phillips Design Assoc/25 Dry Dock Ave, Boston, MA.........................617-423-7676
Picture That Inc/880 Briarwood Rd, Newtown Square, PA...................215-353-8833
Pilz, Misty/324 Elm St, Monroe, CT..203-261-7665
Pinkston, Steve /212 W Miner St, West Chester, PA.........................215-692-2939
Planert, Paul Design Assoc/4650 Baum Blvd, Pittsburgh, PA 412-621-1275
Plataz, George/516 Martin Bldg, Pittsburgh, PA 412-322-3177
Porter, Eric/37 S 20th St, Philadelphia, PA 215-563-1904
Presentation Assocs/1346 Connecticut Ave NW, Washington, DC 202-333-0080
Production Studio/382 Channel Dr, Port Washington, NY....................516-944-6688
Profile Press Inc/40 Greenwood Ave, E Islip, NY 516-277-6319
Prokell, Jim/307 4th Ave #1100, Pittsburgh, PA 412-232-3636
Publication Services Inc/990 Hope St, PO Box 4625, Stamford, CT 203-348-7351

R

Rajcula, Vincent/176 Long MEadow Hill, Brookfield, CT......................203-775-2420
Ralcon Inc/431 W Market St, West Chester, PA.................................215-692-2840
Rand, Paul Inc/87 Goodhill Rd, Weston, CT......................................203-227-5375
Redtree Associates/1740 N St NW, Washington, DC...........................202-628-2900
Renaissance Communications/7835 Eastern Ave, Silver Spring, MD...301-587-1505
Research Planning Assoc/1831 Chestnut St, Philadelphia, PA 215-561-9700
Richardson/Smith/139 Lewis Wharf, Boston, MA................................617-367-1491
Richman, Mel/15 N Presidential Blvd, Bala Cynwyd, PA 215-667-8900
Rieb, Robert/10 Reichert Circle, Westport, CT...................................203-227-0061
Ringel, Leonard Design/18 Wheeler Rd, Kendall Park, NJ...................201-297-9084
Ritter, Richard Design Inc/31 Waterloo Ave, Berwyn, PA....................215-296-0400
Ritzau van Dijk Design/7 Hart Ave, Hopewell, NJ 609-466-2797
RKM Inc/5307 29th St NW, Washington, DC 202-364-0148
Rogalski Assoc/186 Lincoln St, Boston, MA......................................617-451-2111
Romax Studio/32 Club Circle, Stamford, CT.....................................203-324-4260
Rosborg Inc/15 Commerce Rd, Newton, CT......................................203-426-3171
Roth, J H Inc/13 Inwood Ln E, Peekskill, NY.....................................914-737-6784
Roth, Judee/103 Cornelia St, Boonton, NJ 201-316-5411
Rubin, Marc Design Assoc/PO Box 440, Breesport, NY......................607-739-0871
RZA Inc/122 Mill Pond Rd, Park Ridge, NJ 201-391-8500

S

Samerjan/Edigraph /45 Cantitoe St, RFD 1, Katonah, NY...................914-232-3725
Sanchez/138 S 20th St, Philadelphia, PA 215-564-2223
Schneider Design/2633 N Charles St, Baltimore, MD..........................301-467-2611
Schoenfeld, Cal/6 Colony Ct #B, Parsippany, NJ 201-263-1635
Schrecongost, Paul/284 Liberty St, Salem, WV.................................304-782-3499
Selame Design Assocs/2330 Washington St, Newton Lwr Falls, MA 617-969-6690
Shapiro, Deborah/150 Bentley Ave, Jersey City, NJ 201-432-5198
Silvia, Ken/15 Story St, Cambridge, MA...617-451-1995
Simpson Booth Designers/14 Arrow St, Cambridge, MA 617-661-2630
Smarilli Graphics Inc/602 N front St, Warmleysburg, PA.....................717-737-8141
Smith, Agnew Moyer/850 Ridge Ave, Pittsburgh, PA..........................412-322-6333
Smith, Doug/17 Althea Lane, Larchmont, NY.....................................914-834-3997
Smith, Gail Hunter/PO Box 217, Barnegat Light, NJ 609-494-9136
Smith, Tyler Art Direction/127 Dorrance St, Providence, RI 401-751-1220
Smizer Design/59 Wareham St, Boston, MA......................................617-423-3350
Snowden Associates Inc/5217 Wisconsin Ave NW, Washington, DC ...202-362-8944
Soree, Sal/97 Forest Hill Rd, W Orange, NJ......................................201-325-3591
Sparkman & Bartholomew/1120 Conn. Ave #270, Washington, DC 202-785-2414

Spectrum Boston/79-A Chestnut St, Boston, MA 617-367-1008
Stamler Design/220 Marlborough St #1, Boston, MA.........................617-262-6250
Stansbury Ronsaville Wood Inc/17 Pinewood St, Annapolis, MD.........301-261-8662
Star Design Inc/PO Box 30, Moorestown, NJ....................................609-235-8150
Steel Art Co Inc/75 Brainerd Rd, Allston, MA....................................617-566-4079
Stettler, Wayne Design/2311 Fairmount Ave, Philadelphia, PA............215-235-1230
Stockman & Andrews Inc/684 Warren Ave, E Providence, RI 401-438-0694
Stolt, Jill Design/1239 University Ave, Rochester, NY.........................716-461-2594
Stuart, Neil/RD 1 Box 64, Mahopac, NY..914-618-1662
The Studio Group/1713 Lanier Pl NW, Washington, DC......................202-332-3003
Studio Six Design/6 Lynn Dr, Springfield, NJ....................................201-379-5820
Studio Three/118 South St, Philadelphia, PA....................................215-925-4700

TV

Takajian, Asdur/17 Merlin Ave, N Tarrytown, NY 914-631-5553
Tapa Graphics/20 Bluff Rd, Thorndale, PA.......................................215-384-7081
Taylor, Pat/3540 'S' St NW, Washington, DC....................................202-338-0962
Telesis/107 E 25th, Baltimore, MD..301-235-2000
Tetrad Design/21 Southgate, Annapolis, MD 301-269-1326
Third Millenium Comm/979 Summer St, Stamford, CT........................203-325-9104
Thompson, Bradbury/Jones Park, Riverside, CT................................203-637-3614
Thomson/Corcetto & Co/4 Park Plaza #205, Wyomissing, PA............215-376-5170
Toelke, Cathleen/PO Box 487, Rhinebeck, NY..................................914-876-8776
Torode, Barbara/2311 Lombard St, Philadelphia, PA..........................215-732-6792
Total Collateral Grp/992 Old Eagles School Rd, Wayne, PA................215-687-8016
Town Studios Inc/212 9th St Victory Bldg, Pittsburgh, PA...................412-471-5353
Troller, Fred Assoc Inc/12 Harbor Ln, Rye, NY..................................914-698-1405
Van Der Sluys Graphics Inc/3303 18th St NW, Washington, DC 202-265-3443
Vance Wright Adams & Assoc/930 N Lincoln Ave, Pittsburgh, PA........412-322-1800
VanDine, Horton,et al, Inc/100 Ross St, Pittsburgh, PA.......................412-261-4280
Vann, Bob/5306 Knox St, Philadelphia, PA.......................................215-843-4841
Vinick, Bernard Assoc Inc/211 Wethersfield Ave, Hartford, CT.............203-525-4293
Viscom Inc/PO Box 10498, Baltimore, MD.......................................301-764-0005
Visual Research Corp/360 Commonwealth Ave, Boston, MA...............617-536-2111
The Visualizers/1100 E Carson St, Pittsburgh, PA..............................412-488-0944

WYZ

Warkulwiz Design/1704 Locust St, Philadelphia, PA...........................215-546-0880
Wasserman's, Myron Design Gp/113 Arch St, Philadelphia, PA...........215-922-4545
Weadock, Rutka/1627 E Baltimore St, Baltimore, MD 301-563-2100
Webb & Co/839 Beacon St, Boston, MA...617-262-6980
Weems, Samuel/One Arcadia Pl, Boston, MA....................................617-288-8888
Weymouth Design/234 Congress St, Boston, MA...............................617-542-2647
Whibley, Edward/4733 Bethesda Ave #345, Bethesda, MD.................301-951-5200
Wickham & Assoc Inc/1215 Connecticut Ave NW, Washington, DC.....202-296-4860
Wiggin, Gail/23 Old Kings Hwy S, Darien, CT...................................203-655-1920
Willard, Janet Design Assoc/4284 Route 8, Allison Park, PA...............412-486-8100
Williams Associates/200 Broadway #205, Lynnfield, MA.....................617-599-1818
Wilsonwork Graphic Design/1811 18th St NW, Washington, DC..........202-332-9016
Winick, Sherwin/115 Willow Ave #2R, Hoboken, NJ...........................201-659-9116
Wolf, Anita/49 Melcher St, Boston, MA..617-426-3929
Wood, William/68 Windsor Pl, Glen Ridge, NJ...................................201-743-5543
Wright, Kent M Assoc Inc/22 Union Ave, Sudbury, MA 617-443-9909
WW2 Design/250 Post Rd E, Westport, CT..203-454-2550
Yavorsky, Fredrick/2300 Walnut St #617, Philadelphia, PA.................215-564-6690
Yeo, Robert/746 Park Ave, Hoboken, NJ..201-659-3277
Yurdin, Carl Indust Design/2 Harborview Rd, Port Washington, NY......516-944-7811
Zeb Graphics/1312 18th St NW, Washington, DC...............................202-293-1687
Zingone, Robin/32 GodmanRd, Madison, CT.....................................212-288-8045
Zmiejko & Assoc Design Agcy/PO Box 126, Freeland, PA...................717-636-2304

SOUTHEAST

AB

Ace Art/171 Walnut St, New Orleans, LA..504-861-2222
Alphabet Group/1441 Peachtree NE, Atlanta, GA 404-892-6500
Alphacom Inc/14955 NE Sixth Ave, N Miami, FL................................305-949-5588
Art Services/1135 Spring St, Atlanta, GA..404-892-2105
Arts & Graphics/4010 Justine Dr, Annandale, VA 703-941-2560
Arunski, Joe & Assoc/8600 SW 86th Ave, Miami, FL..........................305-473-4114
The Associates Inc/5319 Lee Hwy, Arlington, VA...............................703-534-3940
Aurelio & Friends Inc/11110 SW 128th Ave, Miami, FL.......................305-385-0723
Austin, Jeremiah/1483 Chain Bridge Rd #300, McLean, VA.................703-893-7004

Baskin & Assoc/1021 Prince St, Alexandria, VA....................703-836-3316
Bender, Diane/2729 S Cleveland St, Arlington, VA.................703-521-1006
Beveridge and Associates, Inc/2020 N 14th St #444, Arlington, VA.....202-243-2888
Blair Incorporated/5819 Seminary Rd, Bailey's Crossroads, VA............703-820-9011
Bodenhamer, William S Inc/7380 SW 121st St, Miami, FL............305-253-9284
Bonner Advertising Art/1315 Washington Ave, New Orleans, LA 504-895-7938
Bowles, Aaron/1686 Sierra Woods Ct, Reston, VA.................703-437-4102
Brimm, Edward & Assoc/140 S Ocean Blvd, Palm Beach, FL 305-655-1059
Brothers Bogusky/11950 W Dixie Hwy, Miami, FL..................305-891-3642
Bugdal Group/7130 SW 48th St, Miami, FL.......................305-665-6686
Burch, Dan Associates/2338 Frankfort, Louisville, KY 502-895-4881

C

Carlson Design/1218 NW 6th St, Gainesville, FL 904-373-3153
Chartmasters Inc/3525 Piedmont,7 Pdmt Ctr, Atlanta, GA 404-262-7610
Clavena, Barbara/6000 Stone Lake, Birgmingham, AL 205-991-8909
Coastline Studios/489 Semoran Blvd #109, Casselberry, FL 407-339-1166
Communications Gphcs Gp/3717 Columbia Pk #211, Arlington, VA....703-979-8500
Cooper-Copeland Inc/1151 W Peachtree St NW, Atlanta, GA 404-892-3472
Corporate Design/Plaza Level-Colony Sq, Atlanta, GA 404-876-6062
Creative Design Assoc/9330 Silver Thorn Rd, Lake Park, FL 305-627-2467
Creative Services Inc/2317 Esplanade St, New Orleans, LA..........504-943-0842
Creative Services Unlimited/3080 N Tamiami Tr #3, Naples, FL...........813-262-0201
Critt Graham & Assoc/1190 W Orvid Hills Dr #T45, Atlanta, GA 404-320-1737

DF

DeRose, Andrea Legg/13 East Mason Ave, Alexandria, VA.................703-836-3204
Design Inc/9304 St Marks Pl, Fairfax, VA 703-273-5053
Design Workshop Inc/7430 SW 122nd St, Miami, FL.................305-378-1039
Designcomp/202 Dominion Rd NE, Vienna, VA 703-938-1822
Dodane, Eric/8525 Richland Colony Rd, Knoxville, TN...............615-693-6857
First Impressions/4411 W Tampa Bay Blvd, Tampa, FL...............813-875-0555
Foster, Kim A/1801 SW 11th St, Miami, FL 305-642-1801

GHI

Gerbino Advertising/2000 W Commercial Blvd, Ft Lauderdale, FL.......305-776-5050
Gestalt Associates, Inc/1509 King St, Alexandria, VA.................703-683-1126
Get Graphic Inc/160 Maple Ave E #201, Vienna, VA...............202-938-1822
Grafik Communication/300 Montgomery St, Alexandria, VA............703-683-4686
Graphic Arts Inc/1433 Powhatan St, Alexandria, VA................703-683-4303
Graphic Consultants Inc/5133 Lee Hwy, Arlington, VA 703-536-8377
Graphics Group/6111 PchtreeDunwdy Rd#G101, Atlanta, GA............404-391-9929
Graphicstudio/12305 NE 12th Ct, N Miami, FL 305-893-1015
Great Incorporated/601 Madison St, Alexandria, VA 703-836-6020
Gregg, Bill Adv Design/2465 SW 18th Ave A-3309, Miami, FL...........305-854-7657
Group 2 Atlanta/3500 Piedmont Rd, Atlanta, GA 404-262-3239
Hall Graphics/2600 Douglas Rd #608, Coral Gables, FL...............305-443-8346
Hall, Steve Graphics/14200 SW 136th St, Miami, FL 305-255-2900
Hauser, Sydney/9 Fillmore Dr, Sarasota, FL 813-388-3021
Hendrix, Jean/PO Box 5754, High Point, NC 919-840-4970
Herchak, Stephen/1735 St Julian Pl, Columbia, SC 803-799-1800
Identitia Incorporated/1000 N Ashley Dr #515, Tampa, Fl...............813-221-3326

JK

Jensen, Rupert & Assoc Inc/1800 Peachtree Rd #525, Atlanta, GA.....404-352-1010
Johnson Design Gp/3426 N Washington Blvd #102, Arlington, VA 703-525-0808
Jordan Barrett & Assoc/6701 Sunset Dr, Miami, FL 305-667-7051
Kelly & Co Graphic Design Inc/7490 30th Ave N, St Petersburg, FL 813-341-1009
Kjeldsen, Howard Assoc Inc/PO Box 420508, Atlanta, GA 404-266-1897
Klickovich Graphics/1638 Eastern Parkway, Louisville, KY 502-459-0295

LM

Landers Design/4607 NW 6th St #3F, Gainesville, FL 904-375-2353
Lowell, Shelley Design/1449 Bates Ct NE, Atlanta, GA 404-636-9149
Marks, David/726 Hillpine Dr NE, Atlanta, GA..................404-872-1824
Mason, Marlise/7534 Woodberry Ln, Falls Church, VA...............703-573-4365
Maxine, J & Martin Adv/1497 Chain Bridge Rd #204, McLean, VA 703-356-5222
McGurren Weber Ink/705 King St 3rd Fl, Alexandria, VA.............703-548-0003
MediaFour Inc/7638 Trail Run Rd, Falls Church, VA.................703-573-6117
Moore, William "Casey"/4242 Inverness Rd, Duluth, GA.............404-449-9553
Morgan-Burchette Assoc/6935 Arlington Rd, Bethesda, MD............703-549-2393
Morris, Robert Assoc Inc/6015 B NW 31 Ave, Ft Lauderdale, FL..........305-973-4380
Muhlhausen, John Design Inc/1146 Green St, Roswell, GA.................404-642-1146

P

Parallel Group Inc/3091 Maple Dr, Atlanta, GA 404-261-0988
Parks, Dick Comm/500 Montgomery St #701, Alexandria, VA 202-255-5500
Pertuit, Jim & Assoc Inc/302 Magazine St #400, New Orleans, LA 504-568-0808
Pierre, Keith Design/8000 Colony Circle S #305, Tamarac, FL...........305-726-0401
PL&P Advertising Studio/1280 SW 36th Ave, Pompano Beach, FL 307-977-9327
Platt, Don Advertising Art/1399 SE 9th Ave, Hialeah, FL 305-888-3296
Point 6/770 40th Court NE, Ft Lauderdale, FL....................305-563-6939
Polizos, Arthur Assoc/220 W Freemason St, Norfolk, VA 804-622-7033
Positively Main St Graphics/290 Coconut Ave, Sarasota, FL..............813-366-4959
PRB Design Studio/1900 Howell Brnch Rd #3, Winter Park, FL...........305-671-7992
Pre-Press Studio Design/1105N Royal St, Alexandria, VA 703-548-9194
Prep Inc/2615-B Shirlington Rd, Arlington, VA 703-979-6575
Price Weber Market Comm Inc/2101 Production Dr, Louisville, KY.......502-499-9220

QR

Quantum Communications/1730 N Lynn St #400, Arlington, VA...........703-841-1400
Rasor & Rasor/1145-D Executive Cir, Cary, NC 919-467-3353
Reed, Veronica/503 Lake Drive, Virginia Beach, VA 804-422-0371
Reinsch, Michael/32 Palmetto Bay Rd, Hilton Head Island, SC 803-842-3298
Richards Design Group/4722 Old Kingston Pike, Knoxville, TN............615-584-3319
Richardson, Hank/2675 Paces Ferry Rd #225, Atlanta, GA 404-433-0973
Rodriguez, Emilio Jr/8270 SW 116 Terrace, Miami, FL 305-235-4700

S

Sager Assoc Inc/739 S Orange Ave, Sarasota, FL 813-366-4192
Salmon, Paul/5826 Jackson's Oak Ct, Burke, VA 703-250-4943
Santa & Assoc/3960 N Andrews Ave, Ft Lauderdale, FL.............305-561-0551
Schulwolf, Frank/524 Hardee Rd, Coral Gables, FL 305-665-2129
Sirrine, J E/PO Box 5456, Greenville, SC.......................803-298-6000
Stewart Lopez Assoc/550 W Kentucky St, Louisville, KY...............502-583-5502
Studio + Co/13353 Sorento Valley Dr, Largo, FL 813-595-2275

TVW

Tash, Ken/6320 Castle Pl, Falls Church, VA 703-237-1712
Thayer Dana Industrial Design/Route 1, Monroe, VA 804-929-6359
Thomas, Steve Design/409 East Blvd, Charlotte, NC 704-332-4624
Turpin Design Assoc/1762 Century Blvd #B, Atlanta, GA 404-320-6963
Varisco, Tom Graphic Design/1925 Esplanade, New Orleans, LA........504-949-2888
Visualgraphics Design/1211 NW Shore Blvd, Tampa, FL.............813-877-3804
Whitford, Kim/242 Mead Rd, Decatur, GA.......................404-371-0860
Whitver, Harry K Graphic Design/208 Reidhurst Ave, Nashville, TN 615-320-1795
Winner, Stewart Inc/550 W Kentucky St, Louisville, KY...............502-583-5502
Wood, Tom/3925 Peachtree Rd NE, Atlanta, GA....................404-262-7424

MIDWEST

AB

Aarons, Allan Design/666 Dundee Rd #1701, Northbrook, IL...............312-291-9800
Abrams, Kym Design/711 S Dearborn #205, Chicago, IL.....................312-341-0709
Ades, Leonards Graphic Design/1200 Shermer Rd, Northbrook, IL.....312-564-8863
AKA Design/7380 Marietta St, St Louis, MO.......................314-781-3389
Album Graphics/1950 N Ruby St, Melrose Park, IL 312-344-9100
Allied Design Group/1701 W Chase, Chicago, IL..................312-743-3330
Ampersand Assoc/2454 W 38th St, Chicago, IL..................312-523-2282
Anderson Studios/209 W Jackson Blvd, Chicago, IL................312-922-3039
Art Forms Inc/5150 Prospect Ave, Cleveland, OH 216-361-3855
Arvind Khatkate Design/4837 W Jerome St, Skokie, IL.............312-679-4129
Babcock & Schmid Assoc/3689 Ira Rd, Bath, OH 216-666-8826
Bagby Design/225 N Michigan #2025, Chicago, IL 312-861-1288
Banka Mango Design Inc/274 Merchandise Mart, Chicago, IL.........312-467-0059
Barfuss Creative/1331 Lake Dr SE, Grand Rapids, MI 616-459-8888
Barnes, Jeff/666 N Lake Shore Dr #1408, Chicago, IL.............312-951-0996
Bartels & Cartsens/3284 Ivanhoe, St Louis, MO 314-781-4350
Benjamin, Burton E Assoc/3391 Summit, Highland Park, IL...............312-432-8089
Berg, Don/207 E Michigan, Milwaukee, WI 414-276-7828
Bieger, Walter Assoc/1689 W County Rd F, Arden Hills, MN 612-636-8500
Billman, Jennifer/760 Burr Oak Dr, Westmont, IL.................312-323-3616
Blake, Hayward & Co/834 Custer Ave, Evanston, IL................312-864-9800
Bobel, Jane/7543 Juler Ave, Cincinnati, OH 513-791-5337

Boller-Coates-Spadero/445 W Erie, Chicago, IL 312-787-2783
Bowlby, Joseph A/53 W Jackson #711, Chicago, IL 312-922-0890
Bradford-Cout Graphic Design/9933 Lawler, Skokie, IL 312-539-5557
Brooks Stevens Assoc Inc/1415 W Donges Bay Rd, Mequon, WI 414-241-3800

C

Campbell Art Studio/2145 Luray Ave, Cincinnati, OH...........................513-221-3600
Campbell Creative Group/8705 N Port Washington, Milwaukee, WI.....414-351-4150
Carter, Don W/ Industrial Design/8809 E 59th St, Kansas City, MO.......816-356-1874
Centaur Studios Inc/310 Mansion House Ctr, St Louis, MO...................314-421-6485
Chartmasters Inc/150 E Huron St, Chicago, IL 312-787-9040
Chen, Shih-chien/2839 35th St, Edmonton , AB....................................403-462-8617
Clifford, Keesler/6642 West H Ave, Kalamazoo, MI..............................616-375-0688
Combined Services Inc/501 Lynnhurst Ave, St Paul, MN 612-646-3339
Contours Consulting Design Group/864 Stearns Rd, Bartlett, IL...........312-837-4100
Coons/Beirise Design Assoc/2344 Ashland Ave, Cincinnati, OH.........513-751-7459
Cox, Stephen/424 S Clay, St Louis, MO 314-965-2150
Crosby, Bart/676 St Clair St, Chicago, IL...312-951-2800

D

Day, David Design & Assoc/700 Walnut St, Cincinnati, OH..................513-621-4060
DeBrey Design/6014 Blue Circle #D, Minneapolis, MN.........................612-935-2292
Dektas Eger Inc/1077 Celestial St, Cincinnati, OH...............................513-621-7070
Design Alliance Inc/114 E 8th St, Cincinnati, OH.................................513-621-9373
Design Axis/12 Westerville Sq #330, Westerville, OH...........................614-448-7995
Design Consultants/505 N Lakeshore Dr #4907, Chicago, IL...............312-642-4670
Design Factory/7543 Floyd, Overland Park, KS....................................913-383-3085
The Design Group/2976 Triverton Pike, Madison, WI............................608-274-5393
Design Group Three/1114 W Armitage Ave, Chicago, IL 312-337-1775
Design Marketing/900 N Franklin #610, Chicago, IL.............................312-787-9409
Design Marks Corp/1462 W Irving Park, Chicago, IL............................312-327-3669
Design North Inc/8007 Douglas Ave, Racine, WI 414-639-2080
The Design Partnership/124 N 1st St, Minneapolis, MN........................612-338-8889
Design One/437 Marshman St, Highland Park, IL 312-433-4140
Design Planning Group/223 W Erie, Chicago, IL..................................312-943-8400
Design Train/434 Hidden Valley Ln, Cincinnati, OH..............................513-761-7099
Design Two Ltd/600 N McClurg Ct #330, Chicago, IL...........................312-642-9888
Deur, Paul/109 Ottawa NW, Grand Rapids, MI.....................................616-458-5661
Di Cristo & Slagle Design/741 N Milwaukee, Milwaukee, WI 414-273-0980
Dickens Design Group/13 W Grand, Chicago, IL..................................312-222-1850
Dimensional Designs Inc/1101 Southeastern Ave, Indianapolis, IN......317-637-1353
Doty, David Design/661 W Roscoe, Chicago, IL...................................312-348-1200
Douglas Design/2165 Lakeside Ave, Cleveland, OH 216-621-2558
Dresser, John Design/180 Crescent Knoll E, Libertyville, IL.................312-362-4222
Dynamic Graphics Inc/6000 N Forrest Park Dr, Peoria, IL....................309-688-9800

EF

Egger/Assoc Inc/812 Busse Hwy, Park Ridge, IL.................................312-296-9100
Ellies, Dave Indstrl Design/2015 W 5th Ave, Columbus, OH 614-488-7995
Elyria Graphics/147 Winckles St, Elyria, OH..216-365-9384
Emphasis 7 Communications/43 E Ohio #1000, Chicago, IL.................312-951-8887
Engelhardt Design/1738 Irving Ave S, Minneapolis, MN 612-377-3389
Environmental Graphics/1101 Southeastern Ave, Indianapolis, IN 317-634-1458
Epstein & Assoc/11427 Bellflower, Cleveland, OH 216-421-1600
Falk, Robert Design Group/4425 W Pine, St Louis, MO........................314-531-1410
Feldkamp-Malloy/180 N Wabash, Chicago, IL......................................312-263-0633
Ficho & Corley Inc/875 N Michigan Ave, Chicago, IL...........................312-787-1011
Fleishman-Hillard, Inc/1 Memorial Dr, St Louis, MO.............................314-982-1700
Flexo Design/57 W Grand, Chicago, IL..312-321-1368
Ford & Earl Assoc Inc/28820 Mound Rd, Warren, MI...........................313-536-1999
Frederiksen Design/609 S Riverside Dr, Villa Park, IL..........................312-343-5882
Frink, Chin, Casey Inc/505 E Grant, Minneapolis, MN..........................612-333-6539

G

Gellman, Stan Graphic Design Studio/4509 Laclede, St Louis, MO 314-361-7676
Gerhardt & Clemons/848 Eastman St, Chicago, IL..............................312-337-3443
Glenbard Graphics Inc/333 Kimberly Dr, Carol Stream, IL...................312-653-4550
Goldsholl Assoc/420 Frontage Rd, Northfield, IL..................................312-446-8300
Goldsmith Yamasaki Specht Inc/840 N Michigan Ave, Chicago, IL......312-266-8404
Golon, Mary/4401 Estes St, Lincolnwood, IL.......................................312-679-0062
Gournoe, M Inc/60 E Elm, Chicago, IL...312-787-5157
Graphic Corp/727 E 2nd St PO Box 4806, Des Moines, IA 515-247-8500
Graphic House Inc/672 Woodbridge, Detroit, MI..................................313-259-7790
Graphic Specialties Inc/2426 East 26th St, Minneapolis, MN................612-722-6601

Graphica Corp/3184 Alpine, Troy, MI...313-649-5050
Graphics Group/8 S Michigan Ave, Chicago, IL...................................312-782-7421
Graphics-Cor Associates/549 W Randolph St, Chicago, IL...................312-332-3379
Greenberg, Jon Assoc Inc/2338 Coolidge, Berkley, MI........................313-548-8080
Greenlee-Hess Ind Design/750 Beta Dr, Mayfield Village, OH..............216-461-2112
Greiner, John & Assoc/311 N Ravenwood, Chicago, IL 312-644-2973
Griffin Media Design/802 Wabash Ave, Chesterton, IN 219-929-8602
Grusin, Gerald Design/232 E Ohio St, Chicago, IL...............................312-944-4945

HI

Hans Design/663 Greenwood Rd, Northbrook, IL.................................312-272-7980
Hanson Graphic/301 N Water St, Milwaukee, WI..................................414-347-1266
Harley, Don E Associates/1740 Livingston Ave, West St Paul, MN.......612-455-1631
Harris, Judy/550 Willow Creek Ct, Clarendon Hill, IL............................312-789-3821
Hawthorne/Wolfe/1818 Chouteau, St Louis, MO..................................314-231-1844
Herbst Lazar Rogers & Bell Inc/345 N Canal, Chicago, IL 312-454-1116
Hirsch, David Design Group Inc/205 W Wacker Dr, Chicago, IL...........312-329-1500
Hirsh Co/8051 N Central Park Ave, Skokie, IL.....................................312-267-6777
Hoekstra, Grant Graphics/333 N Michigan Ave, Chicago, IL................312-641-6940
Hoffar, Barron & Co/11 E Hubbard 7th Fl, Chicago, IL.........................312-922-0890
Horvath, Steve Design/301 N Water St, Milwaukee, WI 414-271-3992
Identity Center/1340-Q Remington Rd, Schaumburg, IL.......................312-843-2378
IGS Design/455 W Fort St,Detroit, MI...313-964-3000
Indiana Design Cons/102 N 3rd St 300 Rvr Cty Bldg, Lafayette, IN......317-423-5469
Industrial Technological Assoc/30675 Solon Rd, Cleveland, OH 216-349-2900
Ing, Victor Design/5810 Lincoln, Morton Grove, IL...............................312-965-3459
Intelplex/12215 Dorsett Rd, Maryland Hts, MO....................................314-739-9996

JK

J M H Corp/1200 Waterway Blvd, Indianapolis, IN 317-639-2535
Johnson, Stan Design Inc/21185 W Gumina Rd, Brookfield, WI 414-783-6510
Johnson, Stewart Design Studio/218 W Walnut, Milwaukee, WI...........414-265-3377
Jones, Richmond/2530 W Eastwood St, Chicago, IL............................312-588-4900
Joss Design Group/232 E Ohio, Chicago, IL 312-828-0055
Kaulfuss Design/200 E Ontario St, Chicago, IL....................................312-943-2161
KDA Industrial Des Consultants/1785-B Cortland Ct, Addison, IL 312-495-9466
Keller Lane & Waln/8 S Michigan #814, Chicago, IL.............................312-782-7421
Kerr, Joe/405 N Wabash #2013, Chicago, IL.......................................312-661-0097
Kornick & Lindsay/161 E Erie #107, Chicago, IL..................................312-280-8664
Kovach, Ronald Design/719 S Dearborn, Chicago, IL..........................312-461-9888
Krueger Wright Design/3744 Bryant Ave S, Minneapolis, MN..............612-827-7570

L

Laney, Ron/15 Fern St/Box 423, St Jacob, IL.......................................618-644-5883
Larsen Design/7101 York Ave S, Minneapolis, MN...............................612-835-2271
Larson Design/7101 York Ave South, Minneapolis, MN........................612-835-2271
Lehrfeld, Gerald/43 E Ohio, Chicago, IL...312-944-0651
Lenard, Catherine/700 N Green St #301N, Chicago, IL 312-248-6937
Lerdon, Wes Assoc/3070 Riverside Dr, Columbus, OH........................614-486-8188
Lesniewicz/Navarre/222 N Erie St, Toledo, OH....................................419-243-7131
Lighthaus Design Grp/4050 Pennsylvania #360, Kansas City, MO 816-931-9554
Lipson Associates Inc/2349 Victory Pkwy, Cincinnati, OH....................513-961-6225
Lipson Associates Inc/666 Dundee Rd #103, Northbrook, IL 312-291-0500
Liska & Assoc/213 W Institute Pl #605, Chicago, IL.............................312-943-5910
Lubell, Robert/2946 E Lincolnshire, Toledo, OH...................................419-531-2267

MNO

Maddox, Eva Assoc Inc/440 North Wells, Chicago, IL 312-670-0092
Madsan/Kuester/1 Main @ River Pl #500, Minneapolis, MN.................612-378-1895
Manning Studios Inc/613 Main St, Cincinnati, OH................................513-621-6959
Marsh, Richard Assoc Inc/203 N Wabash #1400, Chicago, IL.............312-236-1331
McConnell, Brian/3508 S 12th Ave, Minneapolis, MN...........................612-724-4069
McDermott, Bill Grphc Des/1410 Hanley Indust Ct, St Louis, MO.........314-962-6286
McGuire, Robert L Design/7943 Campbell, Kansas City, MO................816-523-9164
McMurray Design Inc/405 N Wabash Ave, Chicago, IL 312-527-1555
Media Corporation/3070 Riverside Dr, Columbus, OH..........................614-488-7767
Media Loft/333 Washington Ave N 3210, Minneapolis, MN...................612-375-1086
Minnick, James Design/535 N Michigan Ave, Chicago, IL.....................312-527-1864
Miska, John/192 E Wallings Rd, Cleveland, OH....................................216-526-0464
Moonink Inc/233 N Michigan Ave, Chicago, IL 312-565-0040
Murrie White Drummond Leinhart/58 W Huron, Chicago, IL..................312-943-5995
Naughton, Carol & Assoc/213 W Institute Pl #708, Chicago, IL............312-951-5353
Nemetz, Jeff/900 N Franklin #600, Chicago, IL 312-664-8112
Nottingham-Spirk Design Inc/11310 Juniper Rd, Cleveland, OH...........216-231-7830

Oak Brook Graphics, Inc/287 W Butterfield Rd, Elmhurst, IL 312-832-3200
Obata Design/1610 Menard, St Louis, MO 314-241-1710
Oberg, Richard/327 15th Ave, Moline, IL..319-359-3831
Osborne-Tuttle/233 E Wacker Dr #2409, Chicago, IL.............................312-565-1910
Oskar Designs/616 Sheridan Rd, Evanston, IL.......................................312-328-1734
Overlock Howe Conultng Gp/447 Conway Meadows, St Louis, MO.....314-533-4484

PQ

Painter/Cesaroni Design, Inc/1865 Grove St, Glenview, IL...................312-724-8840
Palmer Design Assoc/3330 Old Glenview Rd, Wilmette, IL....................312-256-7448
Paragraphs Design/414 N Orleans #310, Chicago, IL............................312-828-0200
Paramount Technical Service Inc/31811 Vine St, Cleveland, OH..........216-585-2550
Perlstein, Warren/560 Zenith Dr, Glenview, IL.......................................312-827-7884
Peterson, Ted/23 N Lincoln St, Hinsdale, IL 312-920-1091
Phares Associates Inc/Hills Tech Dr, Farmington Hills, MI...................313-553-2232
Picard Didier Inc/13160 W Burleigh St, Brookfield, WI..........................414-783-7400
Pinzke, Herbert/1935 N Kenmore, Chicago, IL......................................312-528-2277
Pitlock Design/300 N Michigan #200, South Bend, IN 219-233-8606
Pitt Studios/1370 Ontario St #1430, Cleveland, OH..............................216-241-6720
Porter/Matjasich Assoc/154 W Hubbard St #504, Chicago, IL..............312-670-4355
Pride and Performance/970 Raymond Ave, St Paul, MN........................612-646-4800
Prodesign Inc/2500 Niagara Ln, Plymouth, MI.......................................612-476-1200
Purviance, George Marketing Comm/7404 Bland Dr, Clayton, MO 314-721-2765
Pycha and Associates/16 E Pearson, Chicago, IL.................................312-944-3679
Qually & Co Inc/30 E Huron #2502, Chicago, IL....................................312-944-0237

RS

Ramba Graphics/1575 Merwin Ave, Cleveland, OH................................216-621-1776
Red Wing Enterprises/666 N Lake Shore Dr #211, Chicago, IL............312-951-0441
Redgrafix/19750 W Observatory Rd, New Berlin, WI..............................414-542-5547
Redmond, Patrick/757 Raymond Ave #300E/Securty, St Paul, MN 612-224-7155
RHI Inc/213 W Institute Pl, Chicago, IL..312-943-2585
Richardson/Smith Inc/10350 Olentangy River Rd, Worthington, OH.....614-885-3453
Roberts Webb & Co/111 E Wacker Dr, Chicago, IL................................312-861-0060
Roth, Randall/535 N Michigan #2312, Chicago, IL.................................312-467-0140
Rotheiser, Jordan I/1725 McGovern St, Highland Park, IL.....................312-433-4288
Samata Assoc/213 W Main Street, West Dundee, IL.............................312-428-8600
Sargent, Ann Design/432 Ridgewood Ave, Minneapolis, MN.................612-870-9995
Savlin/Petertil/1335 Dodge Ave, Evanston, IL.......................................312-328-3366
Schlatter Group Inc/40 E Michigan Mall, Battle Creek, MI....................616-964-0898
Schmidt, Wm M Assoc/20296 Harper Ave, Harper Woods, MI 313-881-8075
Selfridge, Mary/817 Desplaines St, Plainfield, IL...................................815-436-7197
Seltzer, Meyer Design & Illust/744 W Buckingham Pl, Chicago, IL 312-348-2885
Sherman, Roger Assoc Inc/13530 Michigan Ave, Dearborn, MI...........313-582-8844
Shilt, Jennifer/1010 Jorie Blvd, Oak Brook, IL.......................................312-325-8657
Sigalos, Alex/520 N Michigan Ave #606, Chicago, IL............................312-321-0349
Simanis, Vito/4 N 013 Randall Rd, St Charles, IL...................................312-584-1683
Simons, I W Industrial Design/975 Amberly Pl, Columbus, OH 614-451-3796
Skidmore Sahratian/2100 W Big Beaver Rd, Troy, MI...........................313-643-6000
Skolnick, Jerome/200 E Ontario, Chicago, IL..312-944-4568
Slavin Assoc Inc/229 W Illinois, Chicago, IL..312-822-0559
Smith, Glen Co/119 N 4th St #411, Minneapolis, MN............................612-338-8235
Sosin, Bill/415 W Superior St, Chicago, IL...312-751-0974
Source & Co/116 S Michigan Ave 16th Fl, Chicago, IL..........................312-236-7620
Spatial Graphics Inc/7131 W Lakefield Dr, Milwaukee, WI....................414-545-4444
Speare, Ray/730 N Franklin #501, Chicago, IL......................................312-943-5808
Staake, Bob Design/1009 S Berry Rd #3D, Saint Louis, MO.................314-961-2303
Stepan Design/52 Carlisle Rd, Hawthorne Woods, IL............................312-364-4121
Strizek, Jan/213 W Institute Pl, Chicago, IL...312-664-4772
Stromberg, Gordon H Visual Design/5423 Artesian, Chicago, IL...........312-275-9449
Studio 7/2770 State St NE, Middlebranch, OH.......................................216-454-1622
Studio One Graphics/16329 Middlebelt, Livonia, MI..............................313-522-7505
Studio One Inc/4640 W 77th St, Minneapolis, MN.................................612-831-6313
Svolos, Maria/1936 W Estes, Chicago, IL..312-338-4675
Swoger Grafik/12 E Scott St, Chicago, IL...312-943-2491
Synthesis Concepts/360 N Michigan Ave #1111, Chicago, IL..............312-787-1201

TUV

T & Company/3553 W Peterson Ave, Chicago, IL 312-463-1336
Tassian, George Org/702 Gwynne Bldg, Cincinnati, OH.......................513-721-5566
Taylor & Assoc/8601 Urbandale Rd, Des Moines, IA.............................515-276-0992
Tepe Hensler & Westerkamp/632 Vine St #1100, Cincinnati, OH.........513-241-0100
Teubner, Peter & Assoc/2341 N Cambridge St, Chicago, IL 312-248-6797
Thorbeck & Lambert Inc/1409 Willow, Minneapolis, MN 612-871-7979
Three & Assoc/2245 Gilbert Ave, Cincinnati, OH...................................513-281-1600

Toth, Joe/20000 Eldra Rd, Rocky River, OH..216-356-0745
Unicom/4100 W River Ln, Milwaukee, WI...414-354-5440
UVG & N/4415 W Harrison St, Hillside, IL...312-449-1500
Vallarta, Frederick Assoc Inc/40 E Delaware, Chicago, IL....................312-944-7300
Vanides-Mlodock/323 S Franklin St, Chicago, IL...................................312-663-0595
Vann, Bill Studio/1706 S 8th St, St Louis, MO.......................................314-231-2322
Vista Three Design/4820 Excelsior Blvd, Minneapolis, MN 612-920-5311
Visual Image Studio/1599 Selby Ave #22, St Paul, MN 612-644-7314

WXZ

Wallner Harbauer Bruce & Assoc/500 N Michigan Ave, Chicago, IL....312-787-6787
Weber Conn & Riley/444 N Michigan #2440, Chicago, IL......................312-527-4260
Weiss, Jack Assoc/409 Custer Ave #3, Evanston, IL.............................312-866-7480
Widmer, Stanley Assoc/Staples Airport Ind Park, RR2, Staples, MN....218-894-3466
Willson, William/100 E Ohio St #314, Chicago, IL..................................312-642-5328
Wooster + Assoc/314 Walnut, Winnetka, IL...312-726-7944
Wright Design/3744 Bryant Ave S, Minneapolis, MN.............................617-666-4880
Xeno/PO Box 10030, Chicago, IL..312-327-1989
Ziegler, Nancy/420 Lake Cook Rd #110, Deerfield, IL 312-945-2225

SOUTHWEST

AB

A&M Associates Inc/2727 N Central Ave, Box 21503, Phoenix, AZ......602-263-6504
Ad-Art Studios/813 6th Ave, Ft Worth, TX..817-335-9603
The Ad Department/1412 Texas St, Ft Worth, TX 817-335-4012
Advertising Inc/2202 E 49th St, Tulsa, OK...918-747-8871
Alexander, Martha/1419 Kirby Drive, Houston, TX.................................713-529-0133
Anderson Pearlstone & Assoc/PO Box 6528, San Antonio, TX 512-826-1897
Ark, Chuck/3825 Bowser Ave, Dallas, TX..214-522-5356
Arnold Harwell McClain/4131 N Central Expwy #510, Dallas, TX.........214-521-6400
Art Source Design/PO Box 2193, Grapevine, TX...................................817-481-2212
The Art Works/4409 Maple St, Dallas, TX..214-521-2121
Basham, Clay/3003 W Alabama #101, Houston, TX...............................713-529-8742
Baugh, Larry/1417 N Irving Hts, Irving, TX...214-438-5696
Beals Advertising Agency/5005 N Penn, Oklahoma City, OK 405-848-8513
The Belcher Group Inc/8300 Bissonnet #240, Houston, TX..................713-271-2727
Benhase, Meg/9541 E Myra Dr, Tucson, AZ...602-721-0330
Bleu Design Assoc/345 E Windsor, Phoenix, AZ....................................602-279-1131
Boughton, Cindy/1617 Fannin #2801, Houston, TX...............................713-951-9113
Brooks & Pollard Co/1650 Union Nat'L Plaza, Little Rock, AR..............501-375-5561

CD

Central Advertising Agency/1 Tandy Circle #300, Fort Worth, TX.........817-390-3011
Chandler, Jeff/PO Box 224427, Dallas, TX 214-946-1348
Chesterfield Interiors Inc/2213 Cedar Springs, Dallas, TX....................214-747-2211
Coffee Design Inc/5810 Star Ln, Houston, TX..713-780-0571
Connatser & Co/30 Highland Park Vill #201, Dallas, TX........................214-522-7373
Copeland, Kyle/11744 Wilcrest Dt #201, Houston, TX...........................713-499-6181
Crane, Susan Inc/8197 Chancellor Row, Dallas, TX..............................214-631-6490
Cranford/ Johnson & Assoc/1st Comm Bldg #2200, Little Rock, AR 501-376-6251
Design Bank/PO Box 33459, Austin, TX..512-445-7584
Design Enterprises, Inc/9434 Viscount Blvd #180, El Paso, TX 915-594-7100
Designmark/1800 W Loop South #1390, Houston, TX...........................713-626-0953
Drebelbis, Marsha/8150 Brookriver Dr #208S, Dallas, TX....................214-951-0266

EFG

Eisenberg Inc/4924 Cole, Dallas, TX..214-528-5990
Executive Image/8557 Wrld Trd Ctr/Box 581342, Dallas, TX................214-733-0496
Ford, Deborah/202 Senter Valley, Irving, TX...214-579-9472
Friesenhahn, Michelle/717 W Ashby, San Antonio, TX..........................512-342-1997
Funk, Barbara/3174 Catamore Ln, Dallas, TX..214-350-8534
Galen, D/5335 Bent Tree Forest #192, Dallas, TX.................................214-385-7855
Gluth & Weaver/3911 Stony Brook, Houston, TX...................................713-784-4141
The Goodwin Co/7598 N Mesa #200, El Paso, TX.................................915-584-1176
Gregory Dsgn Group/3636 Lemmon #302, Dallas, TX..........................214-522-9360
Grimes, Don/3514 Oak Grove, Dallas, TX..214-526-0040

HIJ

Hanagriff King Design/4151 SW Freeway, Houston, TX.........................714-622-4260
Harman, Gary/1025 S Jennings #403, Ft Worth, TX 817-332-7687

Herman, Ben/701 Pennsylvania, Fort Worth, TX 817-731-9941
Hermsen Design Assoc/5626 Preston Oaks #34-D, Dallas, TX 214-233-5090
Herring, Jerry/1216 Hawthorne, Houston, TX.....713-526-1250
High, Richard/4500 Montrose #D, Houston, TX 713-521-2772
Hill, Chris/3512 Lake, Houston, TX.....713-523-7363
Hixo/2905 San Gabriel #302, Austin, TX.....512-477-0050
Hood Hope & Assoc/8023 E 63rd Box 35408, Tulsa, OK 918-250-9511
Hubler-Rosenburg Assoc/1405-A Turtle Creek, Dallas, TX.....214-742-2491
Image Excellence/3312 Shore Crest, Dallas, TX.....214-352-9958
Image Group Studio/2808 Cole St, Dallas, TX.....214-745-1411
Jacob, Jim/3524 Villanova, Dallas, TX.....214-696-3953
Jettun, Carol/4212 Cumberland Rd, Ft Worth, TX.....817-737-4708
Johnson, Carla/9010 Windy Crest, Dallas, TX.....214-522-1449
Jones, Donald/10529 Sinclair, Dallas, TX.....214-327-0819

KLM

Kilmer/Geer/5650 Kirby Dr #205, Houston, TX 713-668-1708
Konig Design Group/4001 Broadway, San Antonio, TX.....512-824-7387
Ledbetter, James/10818 Ridge Spring, Dallas, TX 214-341-4858
Lindgren Design/5350 Interfirst Two, Dallas, TX.....214-742-3573
Loucks Atelier/2900 Weslyan #685, Houston, TX 713-877-8551
Lowe Runkle Co/6801 Broadway Extension, Oklahoma City, OK.....405-848-6800
Lyons, Dan/5510 Abrams #109A, Dallas, TX.....214-368-4890
Martin, Hardy/2540 Walnut Hill Dr #1525, Dallas, TX.....214-351-1275
Martin, Randy/701 E Plano Pkwy, Dallas, TX.....214-881-1647
Mays, Stan/5004 Mimosa, Bellaire, TX 713-668-6575
McCulley, Mike/412 Knollwood Ct, Euless, TX.....214-528-4889
McEuen, Roby/600 Eighth Ave, Ft Worth, TX.....817-335-5153
McFarlin, Steven/208 W Keaney #103, Mesquite, TX.....214-289-1893
McGrath, Michael Design/1201 Richardson Dr, Richardson, TX.....214-644-4358
Moore Co/5427 Redfield, Dallas, TX.....214-631-9443
Morales, Frank Design/12770 Coit Rd #905, Dallas, TX.....214-233-0667
Morris, Carroll/4835 LBJ Frwy #479, Dallas, TX.....214-233-6616
Morrison & Assoc/3900 Lemmon #2, Dallas, TX.....214-528-7410

NOP

Neumann, Steve & Friends/3000 Richmond #103, Houston, TX.....713-629-7501
Overton, Janet/2927 Bay Oaks Dr, Dallas, TX.....214-357-1272
Owens & Assoc Adv/2600 N Central Ave #1700, Phoenix, AZ 602-264-5691
Pencil Point/14330 Midway #210, Dallas, TX.....214-233-0776
Pirtle Design/4528 McKinney Ave #104, Dallas, TX 214-522-7520

RS

Richards Brock Miller Mitchel/7007 Twin Hill #200, Dallas, TX.....214-987-4800
Sawyer, Sandra/1319 Ballinger, Ft Worth, TX.....817-332-1611
Slaton, Richard/3514 Oak Grove #9, Dallas, TX.....214-231-3000
Squires, James/2913 N Canton, Dallas, TX.....214-939-9194
Strickland, Michael & Co/3000 Post Oak Blvd #140, Houston, TX.....713-961-1323
Struthers, Yvonne/2110 Mossy Oak, Arlington, TX.....214-469-1377
Sullivan, Jack Design Group/1320 N 7th Ave, Phoenix, AZ.....602-271-0117
Suntar Designs/PO Box 1901, Prescott, AZ 602-778-2714
Sweeney, Jim/250 Decker, Irving, TX.....214-258-1705

TUVW

Texas Art & Media/500 W 13th St #220, Ft Worth, TX 817-334-0443
Turnipseed, Allan/2719-C Laclede, Dallas, TX.....214-871-2828
Unigraphics/2700 Oak Lawn, Dallas, TX.....214-526-0930
Vanmar Assoc/1440 Empire Central #458, Dallas, TX.....214-630-7603
Warden, Bill/438 Wellington Dr, Mesquite, TX.....214-634-8434
WW3 Papagalos/313 E Thomas #208, Phoenix, AZ.....602-279-2933

ROCKY MTN

ABC

Allison & Schiedt/219 E 7th Ave, Denver, CO.....303-830-1110
Ampersand Studios/315 St Paul, Denver, CO.....303-388-1211
Arnold Design Inc/1635 Ogden, Denver, CO.....303-832-7156
Barnstorm Design/2527 W Colo Ave #201, Colorado Springs, CO 303-630-7200
Brogren/Kelly & Assoc/3113 E Third Ave #220, Denver, CO.....303-399-3851
CommuniCreations/2130 S Bellaire, Denver, CO.....303-759-1155
Cuerden Advertising Design/1730 Gaylord St, Denver, CO 303-321-4163

DEFG

Danford, Chuck/1556 Williams St, Denver, CO 303-320-1116
Design Center/734 W 800 S, Salt Lake City, UT.....801-532-6122
Duo Graphics/3907 Manhattan Ave, Ft Collins, CO.....303-463-2788
Engen, Scott/9058 Greenhills Dr, Sandy, UT.....801-942-3125
Entercom/425 S Cherry St #200, Denver, CO.....303-393-0405
Fleming, Ron/901 14th St N, Great Falls, MT.....406-761-7887
Genesis Design/604 W 6th Ave, Denver, CO.....617-881-2471
Gibby, John Design/1140 E 1250 N, Layton, UT.....801-544-0736
Graphic Concepts Inc/145 Pierpont Ave, Salt Lake City, UT 801-359-2191
Graphien Design/6950 E Belleview #250, Englewood, CO.....303-779-5858
Gritz Visual Graphics/5595 Arapahoe Rd, Boulder, CO.....303-449-3840

MOR

Martin, Janet/1112 Pearl, Boulder, CO 303-442-8202
Matrix Design/100 Filmore 3240, Denver, CO.....303-388-9353
Matrix International Inc/3773 Cherry Creek Dr N #690, Denver, CO.....303-388-9353
Monigle, Glenn/150 Adams, Denver, CO.....303-388-9358
Montano, Daniel/1616 W 17th St #371, Denver, CO.....303-628-5440
Multimedia/450 Lincoln #100, Denver, CO.....303-777-5480
Okland Design Assoc/1970 SW Temple, Salt Lake City, UT.....801-484-7861
Radetsky Design Associates/2342 Broadway, Denver, CO.....303-629-7375

TVW

Tandem Design Group Inc/217 E 7th Ave, Denver, CO.....303-831-9251
Taylor, Robert W Design Inc/2260 Baseline Rd #205, Boulder, CO 303-443-1975
Visual Communications/4475 E Hinsdale Pl, Littleton, CO.....303-773-0128
Visual Images Inc/1626 Franklin, Denver, CO.....303-388-5366
Weller Institute for Design/2240 Monarch Dr, Park City, UT 801-649-9859
Worthington, Carl A Partnership/1309 Spruce St, Boulder, CO 303-449-8900

WEST COAST

A

A & H Design/11844 Rncho Brndo #120-72, Rancho Bernardo, CA.....619-486-0777
Ace Design/310 Industrial Ctr Bldg, Sausalito, CA 415-332-9390
Adv Design & Prod Sevc/1929 Emerald St #3, San Diego, CA.....619-483-1393
Advertising Designers/818 North La Brea Ave, Los Angeles, CA.....213-463-8143
Advertising/Design Assoc/1906 Second Ave, Walnut Creek, CA.....415-421-7000
AGI/424 N Larchmont Blvd, Los Angeles, CA.....213-462-0821
Alatorre, Sean/1341 Ocean Ave #259, Santa Monica, CA 213-209-3765
Alvarez Group/3171 Cadet Court, Los Angeles, CA.....213-876-3491
Anderson, Lance/22 Margrave Pl #5, San Francisco, CA.....415-788-5893
Andrysiak, Michele/13534 Cordary Ave #14, Hawthorne, CA.....213-973-8480
Antisdel Image Group/3252 De La Cruz, Santa Clara, CA.....408-988-1010
Art Works Design/3325 W Desert Inn Rd #1, Las Vegas, NV 702-365-1970
Art Zone/404 Piikoi St PH, Honolulu, HI.....808-537-6647
Artists In Print/Bldg 314, Fort Mason Center, San Francisco, CA.....415-673-6941
Artmaster Studios/547 Library St, San Fernando, CA.....818-365-7188
Artworks Design/115 N Sycamore St, Los Angeles, CA 213-933-5763
Asbury & Assoc/3450 E Spring St, Long Beach, CA 213-595-6481

B

Bailey, Robert Design Group/0121 SW Bancroft St, Portland, OR.....503-228-1381
Banuelos Design/111 S Orange St, Orange, CA 714-771-4335
Baptiste, Bob/20360 Orchard Rd, Saratoga, CA 408-867-6569
Barnes, Herb Graphics/1844 Monterey Rd, S Pasadena, CA 213-682-2420
Basic Designs Inc/Box 479 Star Rt, Sausalito, CA.....415-388-5141
Bass, Yager and Assoc/7039 Sunset Blvd, Hollywood, CA.....213-466-9701
Bay Graphics/2550 9th St #101, Berkeley, CA 415-843-0701
Beggs Langley Design/619 Maybell Ave, Palo Alto, CA.....415-857-9539
Bennett, Douglas Design/1966 Harvard Ave E, Seattle, WA 206-324-9966
Beuret, Janis/404 Piikoi St PH, Honolulu, HI.....808-537-6647
Bhang, Samuel Design Assoc/824 S Burnside, Los Angeles, CA 213-382-1126
The Blank Co/1048 Lincoln Ave, San Jose, CA.....408-289-9095
Blik, Tyler/715 'J' St #102, San Diego, CA.....619-232-5707
Bloch & Associates/2800 28th St #105, Santa Monica, CA.....213-450-8863
Boelter, Herbert A/1544 El Miradero, Glendale, CA.....818-242-4206
Bohn, Richard/595 W Wilson St, Costa Mesa, CA 714-548-6669
Boyd, Douglas Design/6624 Melrose Ave, Los Angeles, CA 213-933-8383

Bramson + Assoc/7400 Beverly Blvd, Los Angeles, CA 213-938-3595
Breitmeyer & Assoc/10011 N Foothill Blvd #110, Cupertino, CA 408-257-4600
Bright & Associates, Inc/3008 Main St, Santa Monica, CA 213-450-2488
Britton Design/1045 Sansome #311, San Francisco, CA 415-989-4119
Brown, Bill/1054 S Robertson Blvd #203, Los Angeles, CA 213-652-9380
Burns & Associates Inc/2700 Sutter St, San Francisco, CA 415-567-4404
Burridge, Robert/2508 Castillo St #2, Santa Barbara, CA 805-964-2087
Business Graphics/1717 N Highland, Los Angeles, CA.......................213-467-0292

C

Camozzi, Teresa/770 California St, San Francisco, CA 415-392-1202
Carlsòn, Keith Advertising Art/251 Kearny St, San Francisco, CA 415-397-5130
Catalog Design & Prod/1485 Bay Shore Blvd, San Francisco, CA........415-468-5500
Chan Design/1334 Lincoln Blvd #150, Santa Monica, CA 213-393-3735
Chase, Margo/2255 Bancroft Ave, Los Angeles, CA 213-668-1055
Church, Jann/110 Newport Ctr Dr #160, Newport Beach, CA 714-640-6224
Churchill, Steven/4757 Cardin St, San Diego, CA 619-560-1225
Clark, Tim/8800 Venice Blvd, Los Angeles, CA.................................213-202-1044
Clasen, Gene/1355 Redondo Ave #10, Long Beach, CA 213-985-0051
Coak, Steve/2870 N Haven Lane, Altadena, CA.................................818-797-5477
The Coakley Heagerty Co/122 Saratoga Ave # 28, Santa Clara, CA....408-249-6242
Coates Advertising/115 SW Ash St #323, Portland, OR......................503-241-1124
Cognata Associates Inc/2247 Webster, San Francisco, CA 415-931-3800
Colorplay Design Studio/323 W 13th Ave, Eugene, OR.......................503-687-8262
Conber Creations/3326 NE 60th, Portland, OR..................................503-288-2938
Corporate Comms Group/310 Washington St, Marina Del Rey, CA 213-821-9086
Corporate Graphics/LA/11849 W Olympic Blvd #204, L A, CA 213-478-8211
Cowart, Jerry/1144-C S Robertson Blvd, Los Angeles, CA.................213-278-5605
Crawshaw, Todd Design/345-D Folsom, San Francisco, CA................145-777-3939
Creative Source/6671 W Sunset Blvd #1519, Los Angeles, CA...........213-462-5731
Crisp, Alan/1430 Mercy St, Mountain View, CA.................................415-965-8966
Cronan, Michael Patrick/1 Zoe St, San Francisco, CA........................415-543-6745
Cross Assoc/455 Market St #1200, San Francisco, CA.......................415-777-2731
Cross, James/10513 W Pico Blvd, Los Angeles, CA 213-474-1484
Crouch + Fuller Inc/853 Camino Del Mar, Del Mar, CA.......................619-450-9200
Curtis, Todd/2032 14th St #7, Santa Monica, CA..............................213-452-0738

D

Dahm & Assoc Inc/26735 Shorewood Rd, Rncho Palos Verdes, CA....213-373-4408
Dancer Fitzgerald & Sample/1010 Battery St, San Francisco, CA 415-981-6250
Danziger, Louis/7001 Melrose Ave, Los Angeles, CA.........................213-935-1251
Dawson, Chris/7250 Beverly Blvd #101, Los Angeles, CA 213-937-5867
Dayne, Jeff The Studio/731 NE Everett, Portland, OR........................503-232-8777
Daystar Design/4641 Date Ave #1, La Mesa, CA................................619-463-5014
Dellaporta Adv & Graphic/2020 14th St, Santa Monica, CA................213-452-3832
DeMaio Graphics/7101 Baird St #3, Reseda, CA................................818-342-1800
Design & Direction/947 61st St #18, Oakland, CA.............................415-654-6282
Design Bank Graphic Design/9605 Sepulveda #5, Sepulveda, CA 818-894-9123
Design Corps/501 N Alfred St, Los Angeles, CA................................213-651-1422
Design Direction Group/595 S Pasadena Ave, Pasadena, CA..............818-792-4765
Design Element/8624 Wonderland Ave, Los Angeles, CA....................213-656-3293
Design Graphics/2647 S Magnolia, Los Angeles, CA..........................213-749-7347
Design Group West/853 Camino Del Mar, Del Mar, CA........................619-450-9200
Design Office/55 Stevenson, San Francisco, CA................................415-543-4760
Design Projects Inc/16133 Ventura Blvd #600, Encino, CA.................818-995-0303
Design Vectors/408 Columbus Ave #2, San Francisco, CA.................415-391-0399
The Design Works/2205 Stoner Ave, Los Angeles, CA........................213-477-3577
The Designory Inc/351 E 6th St, Long Beach, CA 213-432-5707
Detanna & Assoc/12400 Wilshire Blvd #1160, Los Angeles, CA.........213-207-1778
Diniz, Carlos/676 S Lafayette Park Pl, Los Angeles, CA.....................213-387-1171
Doane, Dave Studio/215 Riverside Dr, Orange, CA............................714-548-7285
Doerfler Design/8742 Villa La Jolla Dr #29, La Jolla, CA....................619-455-0506
Dupre Design/415 2nd St, Coronado, CA..619-435-8369
Dyer-Cahn/8360 Melrose Ave 3rd Fl, Los Angeles, CA......................213-937-4100
Dyna Pac/7926 Convoy St, San Diego, CA..619-560-0280

EF

Ehrig & Assoc/4th & Vine Bldg 8th Fl, Seattle, WA...........................206-623-6666
Engle, Ray & Assoc/626 S Kenmore, Los Angeles, CA.......................213-381-5001
Faia, Don/39 E Main St #6, Los Gatos, CA 408-354-1530
Farber, Melvyn Design Group/406 Bonhill Rd, Los Angeles, CA..........213-829-2668
Finger, Julie Design Inc/8467 Melrose Pl, Los Angeles, CA...............213-653-0541
Floyd Design & Assoc/3451 Golden Gate Way, Lafayette, CA.............415-283-1735
Follis, Dean/2124 Venice Blvd, Los Angeles, CA...............................213-735-1283
Fox, BD & Friends Advertising/6671 Sunset Blvd, L A, CA 213-464-0131

Frazier, Craig/173 7th St, San Francisco, CA 415-863-9613
Furniss, Stephanie Design/1327 Via Sessi, San Rafael, CA 415-459-4730
Fusfield, Robert/8306 Wilshire Blvd #2550, Beverly Hills, CA 213-933-2818

G

Garnett, Joe/12121 Wilshire Blvd #322, Los Angeles, CA 213-826-9378
Georgopoulos/Imada Design/5410 Wilshire Blvd #405, L A, CA 213-933-6425
Gerber Advertising Agency/1305 SW 12th Ave, Portland, OR 503-221-0100
Gillian/Craig Assoc/165 Eighth St #301, San Francisco, CA...............415-558-8988
Girvin, Tim Design/1601 Second Ave 5th Fl, Seattle, WA...................206-623-7808
Gladych, Marianne/10641 Missouri Ave, Los Angeles, CA..................213-474-1915
Global West Studio/201 N Occidental Blvd, Los Angeles, CA..............213-384-3331
The Gnu Group/2200 Bridgeway Blvd, Sausalito, CA..........................415-332-8010
Gold, Judi/8738 Rosewood Ave, West Hollywoood, CA......................213-659-4690
Gordon, Roger/10799 N Gate St, Culver City, CA..............................213-559-8287
Gould & Assoc/10549 Jefferson, Culver City, CA..............................213-879-1900
Graformation/5233 Bakman Ave, N Hollywood, CA............................818-985-1224
Graphic Data/804 Tourmaline POB 99991, San Diego, CA..................619-274-4511
Graphic Designers Inc/3325 Wilshire Blvd #610, Los Angeles, CA......213-381-3977
Graphic Studio/811 N Highland Ave, Los Angeles, CA........................213-466-2666
Graphicom Design/201 Castro St 2nd Fl, Mountain View, CA 415-969-5611

H

Harrington and Associates/11480 Burbank Blvd, N Hollywood, CA 818-508-7322
Harte-Yamashita & Forest/5735 Melrose Ave, Los Angeles, CA...........213-462-6486
Hauser, S G Assoc Inc/24009 Ventura Blvd #200, Calabasas, CA.......818-884-1727
Hausman, Joan/247 High St, Palo Alto, CA.......................................415-325-7957
Helgesson, Ulf Ind Dsgn/4285 Canoga Ave, Woodland Hills, CA.........818-883-3772
Holden, Cynthia/275 S Oakland Ave #308, Pasadena, CA..................818-584-6944
Hornall Anderson Dsgn Works/1008 Western Ave 6th Fl, Seattle, WA ...206-467-5800
Hosick, Frank Design/PO Box H, Vashon Island, WA 206-463-5454
Hubert, Laurent/850 Arbor Rd, Menlo Park, CA.................................415-321-5182
Hyde, Bill/751 Matsonia, Foster City, CA...415-345-6955

IJ

Ikkanda, Richard/2800 28th St #105, Santa Monica, CA....................213-450-4881
Imag'Inez/5 Oak Flat Rd, Orinda, CA..415-254-2444
Image Stream/5450 W Washington Blvd, Los Angeles, CA..................213-933-9196
Imagination Creative Services/80 Justin, San Francisco, CA...............408-988-8696
Imagination Graphics/2760 S Harbor Blvd #A, Santa Ana, CA.............714-662-3114
J J & A/405 S Flower, Burbank, CA...213-849-1444
Jaciow Design Inc/201 Castro St, Mountain View, CA........................415-962-8860
Jerde Partnership/2798 Sunset Blvd, Los Angeles, CA.......................213-413-0130
Johnson Rodger Design/704 Silver Spur Rd, Rolling Hills, CA.............213-377-8860
Johnson, Iskra/1605 12th St, Seattle, WA..206-323-8256
Johnson, Paige Graphic Design/535-B Ramona St, Palo Alto, CA........415-327-0488
Joly Major Prod Dsgn Gp/4773 Sonoma Hwy #82, Santa Rosa, CA.....415-641-1933
Jones, Brent Design/328 Hayes St, San Francisco, CA.......................415-626-8337
Jones, Jacqueline/Pier 9, San Francisco, CA.....................................415-982-8484
Jones, Steve/1081 Nowita Pl, Venice, CA...213-396-9111
Jonson Pedersen Hinrichs/620 Davis St, San Francisco, CA...............415-981-6612
Juett, Dennis & Assoc/672 S Lafayette Pk Pl #48, Los Angeles, CA ...213-385-4373

KL

K S Wilshire Inc/10494 Santa Monica Blvd, Los Angeles, CA 213-879-9595
Kageyama, David Designer/2119 Smith Tower, Seattle, WA 206-622-7281
Kessler, David & Assoc/1300 N Wilton Pl, Hollywood, CA..................213-462-6043
Klein/1111 S Robertson Blvd, Los Angeles, CA.................................213-278-5600
Kleiner, John A Graphic Design/2627 10th Ct #4, Santa Monica, CA...216-472-7442
Kuey, Patty/20341 Ivy Hill Ln, Yorba Linda, CA.................................714-970-5286
Lacy, N Lee Assoc Ltd/8446 Melrose Pl, Los Angeles, CA..................213-852-1414
Lancaster Design/1810 14th St, Santa Monica, CA............................213-450-2999
Landes & Assoc/20313 Mason Court, Torrance, CA 213-540-0907
Landor Associates/Ferryboat Klamath Pier 5, San Francisco, CA 415-955-1200
Larson, Ron/940 N Highland Ave, Los Angeles, CA............................213-465-8451
Leimer Cross Design/120 Lakeside Ave #210, Seattle, WA................206-325-9504
Leong, Russell Design/524-A Ramona St, Palo Alto, CA.....................415-321-2443
Leonhardt Group/411 First Ave S #400, Seattle, WA 206-624-0551
Lesser, Joan/Etcetera/3565 Greenwood Ave, Los Angeles, CA...........213-397-4575
Letter Perfect/6606 Soundview Dr, Gig Harbor, WA...........................206-851-5158
Levine, Steve & Co/228 Main St, #5, Venice, CA...............................213-399-9336
Logan Carey & Rehag/353 Folsom St, San Francisco, CA...................415-543-7080
Loveless, J R Design/3617 MacArthur Blvd #511, Santa Ana, CA 714-754-0886
Lumel-Whiteman Assoc/4721 Laurel Cnyn #203, N Hollywood, CA.....818-769-5332

M

Mabry, Michael/212 Sutter St, San Francisco, CA...................................415-982-7336
Maddu, Patrick & Co/1842 Third Ave, San Diego, CA 619-238-1340
Malone, Julie/5 Hutton Centre Dr #840, Santa Anna, CA 714-557-5011
Manwaring, Michael Office/1005 Sansome St, San Francisco, CA 415-421-3595
Marketing Comm Grp/124 S Arrowhead Ave, San Bernadino, CA........714-885-4976
Marketing Tools/384 Trailview Rd, Encinitas, CA...................................619-942-6042
Markofski, Don/525 S Myrtle #212, Monrovia, CA.................................818-446-1222
Marra & Assoc/2800 NW Thurman, Portland, OR.................................503-227-5207
Matthews, Robert/1101 Boise Dr, Campbell, CA 408-378-0878
Mayeda, Scott/3115 Felton St, San Diego, CA......................................619-284-9692
McCargar Design/2915 Redhill Ave #A-202, Costa Mesa, CA 415-363-2130
McKee, Dennis/350 Townsend St, San Francisco, CA 415-543-7107
Media Services Corp/10 Aladdin Ter, San Francisco, CA.....................415-928-3033
Meek, Kenneth/90 N Berkeley, Pasadena, CA......................................818-449-9722
Miller, Marcia/425 E Hyde Park, Ingelwood, CA...................................213-677-4171
Mize, Charles Advertising Art/300 Broadway #29, San Francisco, CA.415-421-1548
Mizrahi, Robert/6256 San Harco Circle, Buena Park, CA 714-527-6182
Mobius Design Assoc/7250 Beverly Blvd #101, Los Angeles, CA 213-937-0331
Molly Designs Inc/15 Chrysler, Irvine, CA 714-768-7155
Murphy, Harry & Friends/58 Hickory Rd, Fairfax, CA............................415-454-1672
Murray/Bradley Inc/1904 Third Ave #432, Seattle, WA.........................206-622-7082

N

N Graphic/480 2nd St #101, San Francisco, CA 415-896-5806
Naganuma, Tony K Dsgn/1100 Montgomery St, San Francisco, CA 415-433-4484
Nagel & Degastaldi Co/530 Lytton Ave #309, Palo Alto, CA 415-328-0251
Neill, Richard/9724 Olive St, Bloomington, CA.....................................714-877-5824
Nicholson Design/662 Ninth Ave, San Diego, CA.................................619-235-9000
Nicolini Associates/4046 Maybelle Ave, Oakland, CA...........................415-531-5569
Niehaus, Don/2380 Malcolm Ave, Los Angeles, CA.............................213-279-1559
Nine West/9 West State St, Pasadena, CA...818-799-2727
Nordenhook Design/901 Dove St #115, Newport Beach, CA 714-752-8631

OP

Olson Design Inc/853 Camino Del Mar, Del Mar, CA...........................619-450-9200
Orr, R & Associates Inc/22282 Pewter Ln, El Toro, CA.........................714-770-1277
Osborn, Michael Design/105 South Park, San Francisco, CA...............415-495-4292
Oshima, Carol/1659 E Sachs Place, Covina, CA 818-966-0796
Package Deal/18211 Beneta Way, Tustin, CA..714-541-2440
Pease, Robert & Co/11 Orchard St, Alamo, CA.....................................415-820-0404
Pentagram Design/620 Davis St, San Francisco, CA 415-981-6612
Persechini & Co/357 S Robertson Blvd, Beverly Hills, CA....................213-657-6175
Peterson, Scott Design/13965 SW Linda lane, Beaverton, OR.............503-641-8685
Petzold & Assoc/11830 SW Kerr Pkwy #350, Lake Oswego, OR 503-246-8320
Pittard, Billy/6335 Homewood Ave, Hollywood, CA 213-462-2300
Popovich, Mike/15428 E Valley Blvd, City of Industry, CA 818-336-6958
Powers Design International/822 Production Pl, Newport Beach, CA....714-645-2265
Primo Angeli Graphics/590 Folsom St, San Francisco, CA 415-974-6100
The Quorum/305 NE Mapleleaf Pl, Seattle, WA.....................................206-522-6872

R

Rankin, Bob Assoc/103rd St NE #4, Bellevue, WA 206-641-4020
Reid, Scott/432 State St, Santa Barbara, CA...805-963-8926
Reineck & Reineck/1425 Cole St, San Francisco, CA...........................415-566-3614
Reis, Gerald & Co/560 Sutter St #301, San Francisco, CA 415-421-1232
Rickabaugh Design/213 SW Ash #209, Portland, OR 503-223-2191
Ritola, Roy Inc/714 Sansome St, San Francisco, CA............................415-788-7010
RJL Design Graphics/44110 Old Warm Springs Blvd, Fremont, CA.....415-657-2038
Roberts, Eileen/PO Box 1261, Carlsbad, CA...619-439-7800
Robinson, David/3607 Fifth Ave #6, San Diego, CA..............................619-298-2021
Rogow & Bernstein Dsgn/5971 W 3rd St, Los Angeles, CA 213-936-9916
Runyan, Richard Design/12016 Wilshire Blvd, W Los Angeles, CA 213-477-8878
Runyan, Robert Miles/200 E Culver Blvd, Playa Del Rey, CA 213-823-0975
Rupert, Paul Design/708 Montgomery St, San Francisco, CA...............415-391-2966

S

Sackheim, Morton Ent/170 N Robertson Blvd, Beverly Hills, CA...........213-652-0220
San Diego Art Prdctns/2752 Imperial Ave, San Diego, CA....................619-239-6666
Sanchez/Kamps Assoc/60 W Green St, Pasadena, CA........................213-793-4017
Schaefer, Robert Television Art/738 N Cahuenga, Hollywood, CA........213-462-7877
Schockner, Jan/80 Wellington Ave/Box 307, Ross, CA..........................415-456-7711

Schorer, R Thomas/27580 Silver Spur Rd #201, Palos Verdes, CA 213-377-0207
Schwab, Michael Design/118 King St, San Francisco, CA....................415-546-7559
Schwartz, Bonnie/Clem/2941 4th Ave, San Diego, CA 619-291-8878
Seiniger & Assoc/8201 W 3rd, Los Angeles, CA...................................213-653-8665
Shenon, Mike/576 Cambridge Ave, Palo Alto, CA.................................415-493-6878
Shimokochi/Reeves Design/4465 Wilshire Blvd, Los Angeles, CA 213-937-3414
Sidjakov, Nicholas/3727 Buchanan, San Francisco, CA.......................415-931-7500
Signworks/7710 Aurora Ave N, Seattle, WA...206-525-2718
Slavin, David/400 S Beverly Dr #305, Beverly Hills, CA 213-277-7036
Smidt, Sam/666 High St, Palo Alto, CA..415-327-0707
The Smith Group/520 NW Davis St #325, Portland, OR........................503-224-1905
Sorensen, Hugh Industrial Design/841 Westridge Way, Brea, CA.........714-529-8493
Soyster & Ohrenschall Inc/575 Sutter St, San Francisco, CA 415-956-7575
Spear, Jeffrey A/1228 11th St #201, Santa Monica, CA........................213-395-3939
Sperling, Lauren/128 S Bowling Green Way, Los Angeles, CA 213-472-9957
The Stansbury Co/9304 Santa Monica Blvd, Beverly Hills, CA 213-273-1138
Starr Seigle McCombs Inc/1001 Bishop Sq #19, Honolulu, HI.............808-524-5080
Stephenz Group/300 Orchard City Dr #133, Campbell, CA...................408-379-4883
Strong, David Design Group/2030 First Ave #201, Seattle, WA 206-447-9160
The Studio/45 Houston, San Francisco, CA 415-928-4400
Studio A/5801-A S Eastern Ave, Los Angeles, CA................................213-721-1802
Sugi, Richard Design & Assoc/844 Colorado Blvd #202, L A, CA........213-385-4169
Superior Graphic Systems/1700 W Anaheim St, Long Beach, CA........213-433-7421
Sussman & Prejza/1651 18th St, Santa Monica, CA 213-829-3337

TV

Tackett/Barbaria/1990 3rd St #400, Sacramento, CA 916-442-3200
Teague, Walter Dorwin Assoc/14727 NE 87th St, Redmond, WA.........206-883-8684
Thomas & Assoc/532 Colorado Ave, Santa Monica, CA 213-451-8502
Thomas, Greg/2238 1/2 Purdue Ave, Los Angeles, CA.........................213-479-8477
Thomas, Keith M Inc/3211 Shannon, Santa Ana, CA.............................714-261-1161
Torme, Dave/1868 Buchanan St, San Francisco, CA.............................415-931-3322
Trade Marx/1100 Pike St, Seattle, WA..206-623-7676
Tribotti Designs/15234 Morrison St, Sherman Oaks, CA.......................818-784-6101
Tycer Fultz Bellack/1731 Embarcadero Rd, Palo Alto, CA 415-856-1600
VanNoy & Co Inc/19750 S Vermont, Torrance, CA................................213-329-0800
Vantage Adv & Mktng/433 Callan Ave POB 3095, San Leandro, CA....415-352-3640
Visual Resources Inc/1556 N Fairfax, Los Angeles, CA 213-851-6688
Voltec Associates/560 N Larchmont, Los Angeles, CA 213-467-2106

W

Walton, Brenda/910 2nd St 2nd Fl, Sacramento, CA 916-448-4998
Weideman and Assocs/4747 Vineland Ave, North Hollywood, CA 818-769-8488
Wells, John/407 Jackson St, San Francisco, CA....................................415-956-3952
Wertman, Chuck/559 Pacific Ave, San Francisco, CA...........................415-433-4452
West, Suzanne Design/124 University Ave #201, Palo Alto, CA 415-324-8068
White + Assoc/137 N Virgil Ave #204, Los Angeles, CA 213-380-6319
Whitely, Mitchell Assoc/716 Montgomery St, San Francisco, CA 415-398-2920
Wiley, Jean/1700 I St #200, Sacramento, CA...916-447-4633
Wilkins & Peterson Grphc Des/206 Third Ave S #300, Seattle, WA.....206-624-1695
Willardson + Assoc/103 W California, Glendale, CA 818-242-5688
Williams & Ziller Design/330 Fell St, San Francisco, CA 415-621-0330
Williams, John/330 Fell St, San Francisco, CA.......................................415-621-0330
Williamson & Assoc Inc/8800 Venice Blvd, Los Angeles, CA................213-836-0143
Winters, Clyde Design/2200 Mason St, San Francisco, CA....................415-391-5643
Wong, Rick/379-A Clementina, San Francisco, CA 415-243-0588
Woo, Calvin Assoc/4015 Ibis St, San Diego, CA....................................619-299-0431
Workshop West/9720 Wilshire Blvd #700, Beverly Hills, CA 213-278-1370

YZ

Yanez, Maurice & Assoc/901 S Sixth Ave #448, Hacienda Hts, CA......818-792-0778
Yee, Ray/424 Larchmont Blvd, Los Angeles, CA 213-465-2514
Young & Roehr Adv/6415 SW Canyon Ct, Portland, OR........................503-297-4501
Yuguchi Krogstad/3378 W 1st St, Los Angeles, CA...............................213-383-6915
Zamparelli & Assoc/1450 Lomita Dr, Pasadena, CA..............................818-799-4370

INTERNATIONAL

Levine, Ron/1619 Williams St #202, Montreal, QU.................................212-727-1967
Design Innovations Inc/75 Berkeley St, Toronto , ON............................416-362-8470
Pacific Rim Design/720 E 27th Ave, Vancouver , BC 604-879-6689

LABS & RETOUCHERS

NYC

ACL Photolab/239 W 39th St.................................212-354-5280
ACS Studios/2 West 46th St..................................212-944-2622
Alchemy Color Ltd/239 W 39th St...........................212-354-5280
American Blue Print Co Inc/7 E 47th St....................212-751-2240
American Photo Print Co/285 Madison Ave...............212-532-2424
American Photo Print Co/350 Fifth Ave....................212-736-2885
Apco-Apeda Photo Co/525 W 52nd St....................212-586-5755
Appel, Albert/114 E 32nd St..................................212-779-3765
Arkin-Medo/30 E 33rd St......................................212-685-1969
Arno Spectrum/230 E 44th St................................212-687-3359
AT & S Retouching/230 E 44th St...........................212-986-0977
Atlantic Blue Print Co/575 Madison Ave...................212-755-3388
Aurora Retouching/10 W 19th St............................212-255-0620
Authenticolor Labs Inc/227 E 45th St......................212-867-7905
Avekta Productions Inc/164 Madison Ave.................212-686-4550
Benjamin, Bernard/1763 Second Ave.......................212-722-7773
Berger, Jack/41 W 53rd St....................................212-245-5705
Berkey K & L/222 E 44th St...................................212-661-5600
Bishop Studio Inc/236 E 36th St.............................212-889-3525
Blae, Ken Studios/1501 Broadway..........................212-869-3488
Broderson, Charles Backdrops/873 Broadway #612....212-925-9392
C & C Productions/445 E 80th St............................212-472-3700
Carlson & Forino Studios/230 E 44th St...................212-697-7044
Chroma Copy/423 West 55th St.............................212-399-2420
Color Masters Inc/143 E 27th St............................212-889-7464
Color Perfect Inc/200 Park Ave S...........................212-777-1210
Color Vision Photo Finishers/642 9th Avenue............212-757-2787
Color Wheel Inc/227 E 45th St...............................212-697-2434
Colorama Labs/165 W 46th St...............................212-382-0233
Colorite Film Processing/115 E 31st St.....................212-532-2116
Colotone Litho Seperator/24 E 38th St #1B..............212-545-7155
Columbia Blue & Photoprint Co/14 E 39th St............212-532-9424
Commerce Photo Print Co/106 Fulton......................212-964-2256
Compo Photocolor/1290 Ave of Americas................212-758-1690
Copy-Line Corp/40 W 37th St................................212-563-3535
Copycolor/8 W 30th St..212-725-8252
Copytone Inc/115 W 46th St 8th fl..........................212-575-0235
Cordero, Felix/159 E 104th St................................212-289-2861
Corona Color Studios Inc/10 W 33rd St...................212-239-4990
Cortese, Phyllis/306 E 52nd St..............................212-421-4664
Crowell, Joyce/333 E 30th St................................212-683-3055
Crown Photo/165 W 46th St.................................212-382-0233
Dai Nippon Printing/2 Park Ave.............................212-397-1880
Diamond Art Studio/11 E 36th St...........................212-685-6622
Diamond, Richard/155 E 42nd St...........................212-697-4720
DiPierro-Turiel/210 E 47th St.................................212-752-2260
Duggal Color Projects Inc/9 W 20th St....................212-924-6363
EAD Color/29 W 38th St......................................212-869-9870
Egelston Retouching Services/333 Fifth Ave 3rd Fl.....212-213-9095
Exact Photo/247 W 30th St...................................212-564-2568
Farmakis, Andreas/835 Third Ave..........................212-758-5280
Filmstat/520 Fifth Ave...212-840-1676
Finley Photographics Inc/509 Madison Ave...............212-751-3932
Flax, Sam Inc/39 W 19th St 9th fl...........................212-620-3000
Foto-Style Lab/5 W 20th St...................................212-242-0706
Fotos In Color/1 W 20th St....................................212-691-8360
Four Colors Photo Lab Inc/10 E 39th St...................212-889-3399
Frenchys Color Lab/10 E 38th St............................212-889-7787
Frey, Louis Co Inc/902 Broadway...........................212-477-0300
Gilbert Studio/127 W 24th St.................................212-255-7805
Giraldi, Bob Prodctns/581 Sixth Ave.......................212-691-9200
Graphic Images Ltd/119 W 23rd St.........................212-727-9277
Grubb, Louis D/155 Riverside Dr............................212-873-2561
GW Color Lab/36 E 23rd St..................................212-677-3800
H-Y Photo Service/16 E 52nd St............................212-371-3018
Hadar, Eric/10 E 39th St.....................................212-889-2092
Horvath Productions/335 W 12th St........................212-924-8492
Hudson Reproductions Inc/601 W 26th St................212-989-3400

Jaeger, Elliot/49 W 45th St...................................212-840-6278
Jellybean Photographics Inc/99 Madison Ave 14th Fl...212-679-4888
Katz, David Studio/6 E 39th St...............................212-889-5038
KG Studios Inc/56 W 45th St.................................212-840-7930
King Camera/1165 Broadway.................................212-685-4784
Kurahara, Joan/225 Lafayette St............................212-226-3628
LaFerla, Sandro/92 Vandam St..............................212-620-0693
Larson Color Lab/123 Fifth Ave..............................212-674-0610
Lawrence Color Systems/250 W 40th St...................212-944-7039
Lieberman, Ken Laboratories/118 W 22nd St 4th Fl....212-633-0500
Loy-Taubman Inc/34 E 30th St...............................212-685-6871
Lucas, Bob/10 E 38th St......................................212-725-2090
Lukon Art Service Ltd/22 W 45th St #401.................212-575-0474
Mann & Greene Color Inc/320 E 39th St..................212-949-7575
Mann & Greene Quality Color/305 E 46th St.............212-753-2200
Marshall, Henry/2 W 45th St.................................212-944-7771
Martin, Tulio G Studio/234 W 56th St 4th fl...............212-245-6489
Martin/Arnold Color Systems/150 Fifth Ave #429.......212-675-7270
McCurdy & Cardinale Color Lab/65 W 36th St...........212-695-5140
McWilliams, Clyde/151 West 46th St.......................212-221-3644
Miller, Norm & Steve/17 E 48th St..........................212-752-4830
Modernage Photo Services/1150 Ave of Americas......212-752-3993
Moser, Klaus T Ltd/127 E 15th St...........................212-475-0038
Motal Custom Darkrooms/25 W 45th St 3rd Fl...........212-719-5454
Murray Hill Photo Print Inc/32 W 39th St..................212-921-4175
My Lab Inc/42 W 24th St......................................212-255-3771
National Reprographics Co/44 W 18th St..................212-366-7000
New York Flash Rental/704 Broadway 10th fl.............212-353-0600
Olden Camera/1265 Broadway..............................212-725-1234
Ornaal Color Photos/24 W 25th St..........................212-675-3850
Paccione, E S Inc/150 E 56th St.............................212-755-0965
Palevitz, Bob/333 E 30th St..................................212-684-6026
Photographic Color Specialists/10-36 47th Rd, Long Island City....718-786-4770
Photographics Unlimited/17 W 17th St.....................212-255-9678
Precision Chromes Inc/32 W 38th St.......................212-575-0120
Prussack, Phil/155 E 55th St.................................212-755-2470
Rainbow Graphics & Chrome Services/49 W 45th St...212-869-3232
Rasulo Graphics Service/36 E 31st St......................212-686-2861
Regal Velox/575 Eighth Ave..................................212-714-1500
Reiter Dulberg/250 W 54th St................................212-582-6871
Rivera and Schiff Assoc Inc/39 W 32nd St................212-695-8546
Rogers Color Lab Corp/165 Madison Ave.................212-683-6400
San Photo-Art Service/165 W 29th St......................212-594-0850
Scala Fine Arts Publishers Inc/65 Bleecker St............212-420-9160
Scope Assoc/56 W 22nd St...................................212-243-0032
Slide by Slide/445 E 80th St..................................212-879-5091
Slide Shop Inc/220 E 23rd St.................................212-725-5200
Spector, Hy Studios/47 W 34th St..........................212-594-5766
Steinhauser, Art Retouching/305 E 40th St...............212-953-1722
Studio Chrome Lab Inc/36 W 25th St......................212-989-6767
Studio Macbeth Inc/130 W 42nd St........................212-921-8922
Studio X/20 W 20th St...212-989-9233
T R P Slavin Colour Services/37 W 26th St................212-683-6100
Tanksley, John Studios Inc/210 E 47th St.................212-752-1150
The Darkroom Inc/222 E 46th St............................212-687-8920
Todd Photoprint Inc/1600 Broadway.......................212-245-2440
Trio Studio/65 W 55th St......................................212-247-6349
Twenty/Twenty Photographers Place/20 W 20th St....212-675-2020
Ultimate Image/443 Park Ave S 7th Fl......................212-683-4838
Verilen Reproductions/350 W 51st St......................212-971-4000
Vogue Wright Studios/423 West 55th St...................212-977-3400
Wagner Photoprint Co/121 W 50th St......................212-245-4796
Ward, Jack Color Service/220 E 23rd St....................212-725-5200
Way Color Inc/420 Lexington Ave...........................212-687-5610
Welbeck Studios Inc/39 W 38th St..........................212-869-1660
Wolsk, Bernard/20 E 46th St.................................212-818-9024
Zazula, Hy Assoc/2 W 46th St...............................212-819-0444

NORTHEAST

Able Art Service/8 Winter St, Boston, MA.................617-482-4558
Alfie Custom Color/155 N Dean St, Englewood, NJ.....201-569-2028
Alves Photo Service/14 Storrs Ave, Braintree, MA.......617-843-5555
Artography Labs/2419 St Paul St, Baltimore, MD........301-467-5575
Asman Custom Photo Service/926 Penn Ave SE, Washington, DC....202-547-7713
Blakeslee Lane Studio/916 N Charles St, Baltimore, MD....301-727-8800
Blow-Up/2441 Maryland Ave, Baltimore, MD.............301-467-3636

Bonaventure Color Labs/425 Guy St, Montreal, QU............514-989-9551
Boris Color Lab/451 D St, Boston, MA...........617-439-3200
Boston Photo Service/112 State St, Boston, MA 617-523-0508
Calverts Inc/938 Highland Ave, Needham Hts, MA..........617-444-8000
Campbell Photo & Printing/2601 Everts St NE, Washington, DC..........202-526-0385
Central Color/1 Prospect Ave, White Plains, NY 914-681-0218
Chester Photo/398 Centrl Pk Ave/Grnvl Plz, Scarsdale, NY 914-472-8088
Cinema Services/116 North Ave, Parkridge, NJ...........201-391-3463
Collett, Al Retouching/8 Covenger Dr, Medford, NJ...........609-953-9470
Color Film Corp/100 Maple St, Stoneham, MA............617-279-0080
Color Services/120 Hampton Ave, Needham, MA...........617-444-5101
Colorlab/5708 Arundel Ave, Rockville, MD...........301-770-2128
Colortek/109 Beach St, Boston, MA 617-451-0894
Colotone Litho Separator/260 Branford/PO Box 97, N Branford, CT.....203-481-6190
Complete Photo Service/703 Mt Auburn St, Cambridge, MA...........617-864-5954
Dunigan, John V/62 Minnehaha Blvd, PO Box 70, Oakland, NJ 201-337-6656
Durkin, Joseph/5 Harwood Rd, Natick, MA...........508-653-7182
Eastman Kodak/343 State St, Rochester, NY 716-724-4688
EPD Photo Service/67 Fulton Ave, Hempstead, NY 516-486-5300
Five-Thousand K/281 Summer St, Boston, MA 617-542-5995
Foto Fidelity Inc/35 Leon St, Boston, MA...........617-267-6487
G F I Printing & Photo Co/2 Highland St, Port Chester, NY 914-937-2823
Gourdon, Claude Photo Lab/60 Sir Louis VI, St Lambert, QU........514-671-4604
Graphic Accent/446 Main St PO Box 243, Wilmington, MA..........508-658-7602
Iderstine, Van/148 State Hwy 10, E Hanover, NJ............201-887-7879
Image Inc/1919 Pennsylvania Ave, Washington, DC 202-833-1550
K E W Color Labs/112 Main St, Norwalk, CT............203-853-7888
Light-Works Inc/120 Pine St, Burlington, VT 802-658-6815
Lighthaus/109 Broad St, Boston, MA...........617-426-5643
Medina Studios Inc/26 Milburn Ave, Springfield, NJ 201-467-2141
Meyers, Tony/W 70 Century Rd, Paramus, NJ............201-265-6000
Modern Mass Media/Box 950, Chatham, NJ 201-635-6000
MotoPhoto/81 Closter Plaza, Closter, NJ 201-784-0655
Musy, Mark/PO Box 755, Buckingham, PA...........215-794-8851
National Color Labs Inc/306 W 1st Ave, Roselle, NJ............201-241-1010
National Photo Service/1475 Bergen Blvd, Fort Lee, NJ 212-860-2324
Northeast Color Research/40 Cameron Ave, Somerville, MA...........617-666-1161
Ogunquit Photo School/Po Box 2234, Ogunquit, ME...........207-646-7055
Photo Dynamics/PO Box 731, 70 Jackson Dr, Cranford, NJ.............201-272-8880
Photo-Colortura/67 Brookside Ave, Boston, MA...........617-522-5132
Regester Photo Service/50 Kane St, Baltimore, MD...........301-633-7600
Retouching Graphics/205 Roosevelt Ave, Massapequa Pk, NY 516-541-2960
Riter, Warren/2291 Enfield, Pittsford, NY...........716-381-4368
Snyder, Jeffrey/915 E Street NW, Washington, DC............202-347-5777
Starlab Photo/4727 Miller Ave, Washington, DC...........301-986-5300
STI Group/606 W Houstatonic St, Pittsfield, MA 413-443-7900
STI Group Inc/326 Springside Ave, Pittsfield, MA...........413-443-7900
Stone Reprographics/44 Brattle St, Cambridge, MA...........617-495-0200
Subtractive Technology/338-B Newbury St, Boston, MA 617-437-1887
Superior Photo Retouching Svc/1955 Mass Ave, Cambridge, MA.......617-661-9094
Technical Photography Inc/1275 Bloomfield Ave, Fairfield, NJ 201-227-4646
Visual Horizons/180 Metropark, Rochester, NY 716-424-5300
Wilson, Paul/25 Huntington Ave, Boston, MA...........617-437-1236

SOUTHEAST

A Printers Film Service/904-D Norwalk, Greensboro, NC 919-852-1275
AAA Blue Print Co/3649 Piedmont Rd, Atlanta, GA 404-261-1580
Alderman Co/325 Model Farm Rd, High Point, NC............919-889-6121
Allen Photo/2800 Shirlington Rd, Arlington, VA 703-524-7121
Associated Photographers/19 SW 6th St, Miami, FL...........305-373-4774
Atlanta Blue Print/1052 W Peachtree St N E, Atlanta, GA............404-873-5911
Atlanta Blue-Print & Graphics Co/1052 W Peachtree St, Atlanta, GA ...404-873-5976
Barral, Yolanda/100 Florida Blvd, Miami, FL............305-261-4767
Bristow Photo Service/2018 Wilson St, Hollywood, FL 305-920-1377
Chromatics/625 Fogg St, Nashville, TN............615-254-0063
Color Copy Inc/520 Whaley, Columbia, SC............803-256-0225
Color Image-Atlanta/478 Armour Circle, Atlanta, GA............404-876-0209
The Color Lab/111 NE 21st St, Miami, FL............305-576-3207
E-Six Lab/678 Tenth St NW, Atlanta, GA............404-885-1293
Eagle Photographics/3612 Swann Ave, Tampa, FL............813-870-2495
Florida Photo Inc/781 NE 125th St, N Miami, FL............305-891-6616
Florida Precision Graphics/5745 Columbia Cir, W Palm Beach, FL 407-842-9500
Fordyce Photography/4873 NW 36th St, Miami, FL............305-885-3406
Gables Blueprint Co/4075 Ponce De Leone Blvd, Coral Gables, FL 305-443-7146
General Color Corporation/604 Brevard Ave, Cocoa, FL............407-631-1602
Infinite Color/2 East Glebe Rd, Alexandria, VA............703-549-2242

Janousek & Assoc Inc/3041 NE Exprsswy #2, Atlanta, GA............404-458-8989
Laser Color Labs/Fairfield Dr, W Palm Beach, FL 407-848-2000
Mid-South Color Laboratories/496 Emmet, Jackson, TN...........901-422-6691
Northside Blueprint Co/5141 New Peachtree Rd, Atlanta, GA 404-458-8411
Par Excellence/2900 Youree Dr, Shreveport, LA...........318-869-2533
Photo-Pros/635 A Pressley Rd, Charlotte, NC...........704-525-0551
Qualex Illustrated/1200 N Dixie Hwy, Hollywood, FL...........305-927-8411
Reynolds, Charles/1715 Kirby Pkwy, Memphis, TN...........901-754-2411
Rich, Bob Video/12495 NE 6th Ave, Miami, FL...........305-893-6137
Rothor Color Labs/1251 King St, Jacksonville, FL...........904-388-7717
S & S Pro Color Inc/2719 S MacDill Ave, Tampa, FL...........813-831-1811
Sheffield & Board/18 E Main St, Richmond, VA...........804-649-8870
Taffae, Syd/3550 N Bayhomes Dr, Miami, FL...........305-667-5252
Thomson Photo Lab Inc/4210 Ponce De Leon Blvd, Coral Gables, FL.305-443-0669
Uniphoto Color/1120 Ashford Ave , Condado, PR...........809-722-3653
World Color Inc/1281 US #1 North, Ormond Beach, FL...........904-677-1332

MIDWEST

A-1 Photo Service/105 W Madison St #907, Chicago, IL 312-346-2248
AC Color Lab Inc/2310 Superior, Cleveland, OH...........216-621-4575
Ad Photo/2056 E 4th St, Cleveland, OH...........216-621-9360
Advantage Printers/1307 S Wabash, Chicago, IL...........312-663-0933
Amato Photo Color/818 S 75th St, Omaha, NE...........402-393-8380
Anderson Graphics/521 N 8th St, Milwaukee, WI...........414-276-4445
Andre's Foto Lab/160 E Illinois St, Chicago, IL...........312-321-0900
Arrow Photo Copy/523 S Plymouth Ct, Chicago, IL...........312-427-9515
Artstreet/111 E Chestnut #12B, Chicago, IL...........312-664-3049
Astra Photo Service/6 E Lake, Chicago, IL...........312-372-4366
Astro Color Labs/61 W Erie St, Chicago, IL...........312-280-5500
BGM Color Labs/497 King St E, Toronto, ON...........416-947-1325
Boulevard Photo/333 N Michigan Ave, Chicago, IL...........312-263-3508
Buffalo Photo Co/430 W Erie, Chicago, IL...........312-787-6476
Carriage Barn Studio/2360 Riverside Dr, Beloit, WI...........608-365-2405
Chroma Studios/2300 Maryland Ln, Columbus, OH...........614-471-1191
Color Central/612 N Michigan Ave, Chicago, IL...........312-321-1696
Color Concept/566 W Adams, Chicago, IL...........312-939-3397
Color Darkroom Corp/3320 W Vliet St, Milwaukee, WI...........414-344-3377
Color Detroit Inc/310 Livernois, Ferndale, MI...........313-546-1800
Color International Labs/593 N York St, Elmhurst, IL...........708-279-6632
Color Perfect Inc/7450 Woodward, Detroit, MI...........313-872-5115
Color Systems/5719 N Milwaukee Ave, Chicago, IL...........312-763-6664
Commercial Colorlab Service/41 So Stolp, Aurora, IL...........708-892-9330
Copy-Matics/6324 W Fond du Lac Ave, Milwaukee, WI 414-462-2250
Cutler-Graves/10 E Ontario, Chicago, IL...........312-988-9393
Diamond Graphics/6324 W Fond du Lac Ave, Milwaukee, WI...........414-462-2250
Drake, Brady Copy Center/1113 Orive St, St Louis, MO...........314-421-1311
Dzuroff Studios/1020 Huron Rd E, Cleveland, OH...........216-696-0120
Emulsion Stripping Ltd/4 N Eighth Ave, Maywood, IL...........708-344-8100
Fotis Photo/270B Merchandise Mart, Chicago, IL...........312-337-7300
Fromex/188 W Washington, Chicago, IL...........312-853-0067
Gamma Photo Lab Inc/314 W Superior St, Chicago, IL...........312-337-0022
Graphic Lab Inc/124 E Third St, Dayton, OH...........513-461-3774
Graphic Spectrum/523 S Plymouth Ct, Chicago, IL...........312-427-9515
Grossman Knowling Co/7350 John C Lodge, Detroit, MI...........813-871-0690
Hill, Vince Studio/119 W Hubbard, Chicago, IL...........312-644-6690
J D H Inc/2206 Superior Viaduct, Cleveland, OH...........216-771-0346
Jahn & Ollier Engraving/817 W Washington Blvd, Chicago, IL 312-666-7080
Janusz, Robert E Studios/1020 Huron Rd, Cleveland, OH...........216-621-9845
John, Harvey Studio/823 N 2nd St, Milwaukee, WI...........414-271-7170
K & S Photographics/1155 Handley Industrial Ct, St Louis, MO...........314-962-7050
K & S Photographics/222 N Canal, Chicago, IL...........312-207-1212
Kai-Hsi Studio/160 E Illinois St, Chicago, IL 312-642-9853
Kier Photo Service/1627 E 40th St, Cleveland, OH...........216-431-4670
Kolorstat Studios/415 N Dearborn St, Chicago, IL...........312-644-3729
LaDriere Studios/1565 W Woodward Ave, Bloomfield Hills, MI 313-644-3932
Lim, Luis Retouching/405 N Wabash, Chicago, IL...........312-645-0746
Lubeck, Larry & Assoc/405 N Wabash Ave, Chicago, IL 312-726-5580
Merrill-David Inc/3420 Prospect Ave, Cleveland, OH...........216-391-0988
Meteor Photo Company/1099 Chicago Rd, Troy, MI...........313-583-3090
Multiprint Co Inc/5555 W Howard, Skokie, IL...........708-677-7770
Munder Color/2771 Galilee Ave, Zion, IL...........312-764-4435
National Photo Service/114 W Illinois St, Chicago, IL 312-644-5211
NCL Graphics/1970 Estes Ave, Elk Grove Village, IL...........708-593-2610
Noral Color Corp/5560 N Northwest Hwy, Chicago, IL...........312-775-0991
Norman Sigele Studios/270 Merchandise Mart, Chicago, IL...........312-642-1757
O'Brien's Agency Inc/924 Terminal Rd, Lansing, MI 517-321-0188

Pallas Photo Labs/207 E Buffalo, Milwaukee, WI.............................414-272-2525
Pallas Photo Labs/319 W Erie St, Chicago, IL..............................312-787-4600
Parkway Photo Lab/57 W Grand Ave, Chicago, IL..........................312-467-1711
Photocopy Inc/104 E Mason St, Milwaukee, WI 414-272-1255
Photographic Specialties/1718 Washington Ave N, Minneapolis, MN.....612-332-6303
Photomatic Corp/59 E Illinois St, Chicago, IL.................................312-527-2929
Precision Photo Lab/5758 N Webster St, Dayton, OH 513-898-7450
Procolor/909 Hennepin Ave, Minneapolis, MN...............................612-332-7721
Professional Photo Colour Service/126 W Kinzie, Chicago, IL...........312-644-0888
Quantity Photo Co/119 W Hubbard St, Chicago, IL.........................312-644-8288
Race Frog Stats/62 N Water, Milwaukee, WI..................................414-276-7828
Reichart, Jim Studio/2301 W Mill Rd, Milwaukee, WI......................414-228-9089
Reliable Photo Service/415 N Dearborn, Chicago, IL.......................312-644-3723
Repro Inc/912 W Washington Blvd, Chicago, IL..............................312-666-3800
Rhoden Photo & Press Service/7833 S Cottage Grove, Chicago, IL.....312-488-4815
Robin Color Lab/2106 Central Parkway, Cincinnati, OH 513-381-5116
Ross-Ehlert/225 W Illinois, Chicago, IL...312-644-0244
Schellhorn Photo Techniques/3916 N Elston Ave, Chicago, IL...........312-267-5141
Scott Studios Inc/500 N Mannheim/Unit 1, Hillsdale, IL..................708-449-3800
SE Graphics Ltd/795 E Kings St, Hamilton, ON.............................416-545-8484
Standard Studios Inc/3270 Merchandise Mart, Chicago, IL..............312-944-5300
The Stat Center/668 Euclid Ave #817, Cleveland, OH 216-861-5467
Trans Fx/362 W Erie, Chicago, IL..312-943-2664
Transparency Duplicating Service/113 N May St, Chicago, IL............312-733-4464
UC Color Lab/3936 N Pulaski Rd, Chicago, IL................................312-545-9641

SOUTHWEST

A-1 Blue Print Co Inc/2220 W Alabama, Houston, TX......................713-526-3111
Alamo Photolabs/3814 Broadway, San Antonio, TX.........................512-828-9079
Allied & WBS/6305 N O'Connor #111, Irving, TX.............................214-869-0100
Burns, Floyd & Lloyd Ind/4223 Richmond Ave #2D, Houston, TX 713-622-8255
BWC/4930 Maple Ave, Dallas, TX 214-528-4200
Casey Color Inc/2115 S Harvard Ave, Tulsa, OK............................918-744-5004
Century Copi-Technics Inc/2008 Jackson St, Dallas, TX...................214-521-1991
Color Mark Laboratories/2202 E McDowell Rd, Phoenix, AZ...............602-273-1253
Custom Photographic Labs/601 W ML King Blvd, Austin, TX..............512-474-1177
Dallas Photolab/3942 Irving Blvd, Dallas, TX 214-630-4351
Five-P Photo Processing/2122 E Governor's Circle, Houston, TX..........713-688-4488
H & H Blueprint & Supply Co/5042 N 8th St, Phoenix, AZ.................602-279-5701
Hot Flash Photographics/5933 Bellaire Blvd #114, Houston, TX..........713-666-9510
Kolor Print Inc/PO Box 747, Little Rock, AR...................................501-375-5581
Magna Professional Color Lab/2601 N 32nd St, Phoenix, AZ.............602-955-0700
Master Printing Co Inc/220 Creath St, Jonesboro, AR 501-932-4491
Meisel Photographic Corp/9645 Wedge Chapel, Dallas, TX...............214-350-6666
NPL/1926 W Gray, Houston, TX...713-527-9300
Photographic Works Lab/3550 E Grant Rd, Tucson, AZ.....................602-327-7291
PhotoGraphics/1700 S Lamar #104, Austin, TX................................512-447-0963
Pounds Photo Lab Inc/2507 Manor Way, Dallas, TX.........................214-350-5671
Pro Photo Lab Inc/2700 N Portland, Oklahoma City, OK 405-942-3743
Raphaele/Digital Transparencies Inc/616 Hawthorne, Houston, TX......713-524-2211
River City Silver/906 Basse Rd, San Antonio, TX............................512-734-2020
Spectro Photo Labs Inc/3111 Canton St, Dallas, TX........................214-748-3151
Steffan Studio/1905 Skillman, Dallas, TX......................................214-827-6128
Texas World Entrtnmnt/8133 Chadbourne Rd, Dallas, TX..................214-351-6103
The Color Place/2927 Morton St, Fort Worth, TX.............................817-335-3515
The Color Place/1330 Conant St, Dallas, TX..................................214-631-7174
Total Color Inc/2242 Monitor St, Dallas, TX...................................214-634-1484
True Color Photo/710 W Sheridan Ave, Oklahoma City, OK................405-232-6441

ROCKY MTN

Cies/Sexton Photo Lab/275 S Hazel Ct, Denver, CO 303-935-3535
Pallas Photo Labs/700 Kalamath, Denver, CO 303-893-0101

WEST COAST

A & I Color Lab/933 N Highland, Los Angeles, CA..........................213-464-8361
Alan's Custom Lab/1545 Wilcox, Hollywood, CA.............................213-461-1975
ASA Prodctns/Rental Darkrooms/905 N Cole Ave #2100,
Hollywood, CA...213-463-7513
Atkinson-Stedco Color Film Svc/7610 Melrose Ave, L A, CA.............213-655-1255
Baker, Bill Photography/265 29th St, Oakland, CA 415-832-7685
Chromeworks Color Processing/425 Bryant St, San Francisco, CA......415-957-9481
Color Etcetera/740 Cahuenga Blvd, Los Angeles, CA 213-461-4591

Color Lab Inc/742 Cahuenga Blvd, Los Angeles, CA........................213-461-2916
Custom Photo Lab/123 Powell St, San Francisco, CA 415-956-2374
The Darkroom/9227 Reseda Blvd, Northridge, CA...........................818-885-1153
The Darkroom Custom B&W Lab/897-2B Independence Ave,
Mountain View, CA 415-969-2955
Faulkner Color Lab/1200 Folsom St, San Francisco, CA...................415-861-2800
Focus Foto Finishers/138 S La Brea Ave, Los Angeles, CA...............213-934-0013
Frosh, R L & Sons Scenic Studio/4114 Sunset Blvd, L A, CA............213-662-1134
G P Color Lab/201 S Oxford Ave, Los Angeles, CA..........................213-386-7901
Gamma Photographic Labs/351 9th St, San Francisco, CA................415-864-8155
Gibbons Color Lab/606 N Almont Dr, Los Angeles, CA.....................213-275-6806
Gornick Film Production/4200 Camino Real, Los Angeles, CA............213-223-8914
Graphic Process Co/979 N LaBrea, Los Angeles, CA.......................213-850-6222
Hecht Custom Photo/Graphics/1711 N Orange Dr, Hollywood, CA 213-466-7106
Hollywood Fotolab/6413 Willoughby Ave, Hollywood, CA...................213-469-5421
Imperial Color Lab/965 Howard St, San Francisco, CA.....................415-777-4020
Ivey-Seright/424 8th Ave North, Seattle, WA..................................206-623-8113
Jacobs, Ed/937 S Spaulding, Los Angeles, CA...............................213-935-1064
Jacobs, Robert Retouching/6010 Wilshire #505, Los Angeles, CA 213-931-3751
Kinney, Paul Productions/1990 Third St, Sacramento, CA..................916-447-8868
Landry, Carol/7926 Convoy Ct, San Diego, CA...............................619-560-1778
Lee Film Processing/8584 Venice Blvd, Los Angeles, CA..................213-559-0296
M P S Photo Services/17406 Mt Cliffwood Cir, Fountain Valley, CA.......714-540-9515
Maddocks, J H/4766 Melrose Ave, Los Angeles, CA 213-660-1321
Marin Color Lab/41 Belvedere St, San Rafael, CA...........................415-456-8093
Modern Photo Studio/5625 N Figueroa, Los Angeles, CA..................213-255-1527
Modernage/470 E Third St, Los Angeles, CA..................................213-628-8194
Newell Color Lab/630 Third St, San Francisco, CA...........................415-974-6870
Pacific Production & Location/424 Nahua St, Honolulu, HI................808-924-2513
Paragon Photo/731 1/2 N LaBrea, Los Angeles, CA.........................213-933-5865
Petron Corp/5443 Fountain Ave, Los Angeles, CA 213-461-4626
Pevehouse, Jerry Studio/3409 Tweedy Blvd, South Gate, CA............213-564-1336
Photoking Lab/6612 W Sunset Blvd, Los Angeles, CA......................213-466-2977
Prisma Color Inc/5623 Washington Blvd, Los Angeles, CA................213-728-7151
Professional Color Labs/96 Jessie, San Francisco, CA 415-397-5057
Quantity Photos Inc/5432 Hollywood Blvd, Los Angeles, CA..............213-467-6178
Rapid Color Inc/1236 S Central Ave, Glendale, CA..........................213-245-9211
Retouching Chemicals/5478 Wilshire Blvd, Los Angeles, CA..............213-935-9452
Revilo Color/4650 W Washington Blvd, Los Angeles, CA..................213-936-8681
RGB Lab Inc/816 N Highland, Los Angeles, CA...............................213-469-1959
Snyder, Len/238 Hall Dr, Orinda, CA..415-254-8687
Stat House/8126 Beverly Blvd, Los Angeles, CA.............................213-653-8200
Still Photo Lab/1210 N LaBrea, Los Angeles, CA.............................213-465-6106
Studio Photo Service/6920 Melrose Ave, Hollywood, CA...................213-935-1223
Timars/918 N Formosa, Los Angeles, CA 213-876-0175
Tom's Chroma Lab/514 No LaBrea, Los Angeles, CA 213-933-5637
Vloeberghs, Jerome/333 Kearny St, San Francisco, CA....................415-982-1287
Waters Art Studio/1820 E Garry St #207, Santa Ana, CA..................714-250-4466
Wild Studio/1311 N Wilcox Ave, Hollywood, CA 213-463-8369
Williams, Alan & Assoc Inc/4370 Tujunga Ave, Los Angeles, CA.........213-653-2243
Wolf Color Lab/1616 Cahuenga Blvd, Los Angeles, CA.....................213-463-0766
Zammit, Paul/5478 Wilshire Blvd #300, Los Angeles, CA..................213-933-8563
Ziba Photographics/591 Howard St, San Francisco, CA....................415-543-6221

INTERNATIONAL

Absolute Color Slides/197 Dundas E, Toronto , ON 416-868-0413
Assoc Photo Labs/1820 Gilford, Montreal, QU................................514-523-1139
Benjamin Film Labs/287 Richmond St, Toronto, ON 416-863-1166
Color Studio Labs/1553 Dupont, Toronto, ON.................................416-531-1177
Corley D & S Ltd/3610 Nashua Dr #7, Mississaugua, ON..................416-675-3511
Gallery Color Lab/620 W Richmond St, Toronto, ON 416-367-9770
Jones & Morris Ltd/24 Carlaw Ave, Toronto, ON 416-465-5466
Transparency Processing Service/324 W Richmond St, Toronto, ON ...416-593-0434

LIGHTING

NYC

Altman Stage Lighting Co Inc/57 Alexander, Yonkers, NY..................212-569-7777
Artistic Neon by Gasper/75-49 61st St, Glendale, NY 718-821-1550
Balcar Lighting Systems/38 Greene St 3rd fl...................................212-219-3501
Barbizon Electric Co Inc/426 W 55th St...212-586-1620
Bernhard Link Theatrical Inc/320 W 37th St....................................212-629-3522

Big Apple Lights Corp/533 Canal St...212-226-0925
Camera Mart/456 W 55th St...212-757-6977
Electra Displays/133 W 25th St...212-255-0438
Feature Systems Inc/512 W 36th St...212-736-0447
Ferco/601 W 50th St...212-245-4800
Filmtrucks, Inc/311 Washington St, Jersey City, NJ..........................201-432-9140
Fiorentino, Imero Assoc Inc/33 W 60th St..212-246-0600
Litelab Theatrical & Disco Equip/76 Ninth Ave.................................212-675-4357
Lowel Light Mfg Inc/140 58th St, Brooklyn.......................................718-921-0600
Movie Lights Ltd/207 E 15th St..212-673-5522
Paris Film Productions Ltd/31-00 47th Ave, Long Island City 718-482-7633
Production Arts Lighting/636 Eleventh Ave.......................................212-489-0312
Stage Lighting Discount Corp/318 W 47th St....................................212-489-1370
Stroblite Co Inc/430 W 14th St #507..212-929-3778

N O R T H E A S T

Barbizon Light of New England/3 Draper St, Woburn, MA..................617-935-3920
Capron Lighting & Sound/278 West St, Needham, MA.......................617-444-8850
Cestare, Thomas Inc/188 Herricks Rd, Mineola, NY..........................516-742-5550
Heller, Brian/200 Olney St, Providence, RI.......................................401-751-1381
Kliegl Bros Universal/5 Aerial Way, Syosset, NY..............................516-937-3900
Lighting Products, GTE Sylvania/Lighting Center, Danvers, MA.........508-777-1900
Limelight Productions/Route 102, Lee, MA.......................................413-298-3771
Lycian Stage Lighting/PO Box D, Sugar Loaf, NY.............................914-469-2285
Martarano, Sal Jr/9B West 1st St, Freeport, NY................................516-378-5815
McManus Enterprises/111 Union Ave, Bala Cynwyd, PA...................215-664-8600
Packaged Lighting Systems/29-41 Grant, PO Box 285, Walden, NY....914-778-3515
R & R Lighting Co/813 Silver Spring Ave, Silver Spring, MD..............301-589-4997
Ren Rose Locations/4 Sandalwood Dr, Livingston, NJ.......................201-992-4264

S O U T H E A S T

Aztec Stage Lighting/1370 4th St, Sarasota, FL................................813-366-8848
Kupersmith, Tony/320 Highland Ave NE, Atlanta, GA........................404-577-5319

M I D W E S T

Duncan, Victor Inc/23801 Ind Park Dr #100, Farmington Hls, MI..........313-471-1600
Grand Stage Lighting Co/630 W Lake, Chicago, IL............................312-332-5611
S & A Studio Lighting/1345 W Argyle St, Chicago, IL.........................312-989-8808

S O U T H W E S T

ABC Theatrical Rental & Sales/825 N 7th St, Phoenix, AZ.................602-258-5265
Astro Audio-Visual/1336 W Clay, Houston, TX..................................713-528-7119
Duncan, Victor Inc/6305 N O'Connor/Bldg 4, Irving, TX.....................214-869-0200
FPS Inc/6309 N O'Connor Rd #200, Irving, TX.................................214-869-9535

W E S T   C O A S T

Adaboy Rental Service/806 Rancho Rd, Thousand Oaks, CA.............805-495-8606
American Mobile Power Co/3218 W Burbank Blvd, Burbank, CA.........818-845-5474
Astro Generator Rentals/2835 Bedford St, Los Angeles, CA..............213-838-3958
Castex Rentals/1044 N Cole Ave, Los Angeles, CA...........................213-462-1468
Cine Turkey/2624 Reppert Ct, Los Angeles, CA...............................213-654-6495
Cineworks Superstage/1119 N Hudson Ave, Hollywood, CA...............213-464-0296
Cool Light Co Inc/5723 Auckland Ave, North Hollywood, CA..............818-761-6116
Fiorentino, Imero/7060 Hollywood Blvd #1000, Hollywood, CA...........213-467-4020
Hollywood Mobile Systems/7021 Hayvenhurst St, Van Nuys, CA........818-782-6558
Leoinetti Co/5609 Sunset Blvd, Hollywood, CA..................................213-469-2987
Mole Richardson/937 N Sycamore Ave, Hollywood, CA......................213-851-0111
Raleigh Studios/5300 Melrose Ave, Hollywood, CA............................213-466-3111

S T U D I O   R E N T A L S

N Y C

All Mobile Video/221 W 26th St...212-675-2211
American Museum of the Moving Image/30 Fifth Ave @ 36th St,

Astoria...718-784-4520
Antonio/Stephen Ad Photo/5 W 30th St 4th Fl..................................212-629-9542
Boken Inc/513 W 54th St..212-581-5507
C & C Visual/1500 Broadway 4th fl..212-869-4900
Camera Mart Inc/456 W 55th St..212-757-6977
Cine Studio/241 W 54th St..212-581-1916
Codalight Rental Studios/151 W 19th St...212-206-9333
Contact Studios/165 W 47th St..212-354-6400
DeFilippo/215 E 37th St...212-986-5444
Devlin Videoservice/1501 Broadway #408..212-391-1313
Duggal Color Projects/9 W 20th St...212-242-7000
Farkas Films Inc/385 Third Ave...212-679-8212
Horvath & Assoc Studios/95 Charles St..212-741-0300
Mothers Sound Stages/210 E 5th St..212-260-2050
National Video Industries/15 W 17th St...212-691-1300
New York Flash Rental/704 Broadway 10th fl....................................212-353-0600
North Light Studios/122 W 26th St...212-989-5498
Osonitsch, Robert/112 Fourth Ave...212-533-1920
Phoenix State Ltd/537 W 59th St...212-581-7721
Professional Photo Supply/141 W 20th St...212-924-1200
Reeves Entertainment/708 Third Ave...212-573-8888
Rotem Studio/259 W 30th St...212-947-9455
Schnoodle Studios/54 Bleecker St...212-431-7788
Silva-Cone Studios/260 W 36th St...212-279-0900
Studio 2B/1200 Broadway...212-679-5537
Yellow Dot/47 E 34th St...212-532-4010

N O R T H E A S T

Bay State Film Productions Inc/35 Springfield St, Agawam, MA...........413-786-4454
Color Leasing Studio/330 Rt 46 East, Fairfield, NJ............................201-575-1118
Editel/651 Beacon St, Boston, MA...617-267-6400
Impact Studios/1084 N Delaware Ave, Philadelphia, PA....................215-426-3988
Ren Rose Locations/4 Sandalwood Dr, Livingston, NJ.......................201-992-4264
September Productions Inc/1 Appleton St, Boston, MA.......................617-482-9900
Ultra Photo Works/468 Commercial Ave, Palisades Pk, NJ................201-592-7730
Videocom Inc/502 Sprague St, Dedham, MA....................................617-329-4080
WGGB-TV/PO Box 40, Springfield, MA...413-733-4040
WLNE-TV/430 County St, New Bedford, MA......................................508-992-6666

S O U T H E A S T

The Great Southern Stage/15221 NE 21st Ave, N Miami Bch, FL.........305-947-0430
Wien/Murray Studio/2480 West 82nd St #8, Hialeah, FL....................305-828-7400

M I D W E S T

Lewis, Tom/2511 Brumley Dr, Flossmoor, IL.....................................708-799-1156
Mike Jones Film Corp/5250 W 74, Minneapolis, MN...........................612-835-4490
Rainey, Pat/4031 N Hamlin Ave, Chicago, IL....................................312-463-0281
Sosin, Bill/415 W Superior St, Chicago, IL..312-751-0974

S O U T H W E S T

AIE Studios/3905 Braxton, Houston, TX...713-781-2110
Arizona Cine Equipment/2125 E 20th St, Tucson, AZ........................602-623-8268
Hayes, Bill Film & Video/11500 Braesview #2405, San Antonio, TX......512-493-3551
Pearlman Productions Inc/2401 W Belfort, Houston, TX.....................713-668-3601
Stokes, Bill Assoc/5642 Dyer, Dallas, TX...214-363-0161

W E S T   C O A S T

ASA Productions/Studio/905 Cole Ave #2100, Hollywood, CA.............213-463-7513
Blakeman, Bob Studios/710 S Santa Fe, Los Angeles, CA.................213-624-6662
Carthay Studio/5907 W Pico Blvd, Los Angeles, CA..........................213-938-2101
Cine-Rent West Inc/991 Tennessee St, San Francisco, CA................415-864-4644
Cine-Video/948 N Cahuenga Blvd, Los Angeles, CA..........................213-464-6200
Columbia Pictures/Columbia Plaza, Burbank, CA..............................818-954-6000
Disney, Walt Productions/500 S Buena Vista St, Burbank, CA.............818-560-1000
Dominick/833 N LaBrea Ave, Los Angeles, CA.................................213-934-3033
Eliot, Josh Studio/706 W Pico Blvd, Los Angeles, CA.......................213-742-0367
Hollywood National Studios/6605 Eleanor Ave, Hollywood, CA...........213-467-6272
Hollywood Stage/6650 Santa Monica Blvd, Los Angeles, CA..............213-466-4393

KCLP TV/915 N LaBrea, Los Angeles, CA 213-850-2236
Kelley, Tom Studios/8525 Santa Monica Blvd, Los Angeles, CA 213-657-1780
Kings Point Corporation/8599 Venice Blvd, Los Angeles, CA 213-559-4925
Liles, Harry Productions Inc/1060 N Lillian Way, Los Angeles, CA........213-466-1612
MGM Studios/10000 W Washington, Culver City, CA 213-280-6000
Norwood, David/9023 Washington Blvd, Culver City, CA 213-204-3323
Omega Studio Rentals/5755 Santa Monica Blvd, Hollywood, CA 213-466-8201
Paramount/5555 Melrose, Los Angeles, CA................................213-468-5000
Raleigh Studios/5300 Melrose Ave, Hollywood, CA 213-466-3111
Studio Center CBS/4024 Radford Ave, Studio City, CA....................818-760-5000
Studio Resources/1915 University Ave, Palo Alto, CA......................415-321-8763
Sunset/Gower Studio/1438 N Gower, Los Angeles, CA....................213-467-1001
Superstage/1119 N Hudson, Hollywood, CA..............................213-464-0296
Trans-American Video/1541 Vine St, Los Angeles, CA....................213-466-2141
Twentieth Century Fox/10201 W Pico Blvd, Los Angeles, CA 213-277-2211
Universal City Studios/Universal Studios, Universal City, CA...............818-777-1000
Warner Brothers/4000 Warner Blvd, Burbank, CA 818-954-6000

ANIMATORS

NYC

A P A/230 W 10th St 212-929-9436
ALZ Productions/11 Waverly Pl #1J 212-473-7620
Animated Productions Inc/1600 Broadway 212-265-2942
Animation Services Inc/221 W 57th St 11th Fl...........................212-333-5656
Animus Films/2 W 47th St..212-391-8716
Avekta Productions Inc/164 Madison Ave 212-686-4550
Beckerman, Howard/35-38 169th St, Flushing, NY 212-869-0595
Blechman, R O/2 W 47th St 212-869-1630
Broadcast Arts Inc/632 Broadway 212-254-5400
Charisma Communications/32 E 57th St 212-832-3020
Charlex Inc/2 W 45th St..212-719-4600
Cinema Concepts/321 W 44th St.......................................212-541-9220
Clark, Ian/229 E 96th St..212-289-0998
Computer Graphics Lab/100 Glen Cove Ave, Glen Cove, NY 516-484-1944
Dale Cameragraphics Inc/12 W 27th St 212-696-9440
Darino Films/222 Park Ave S...212-228-4024
Devlin Productions Inc/1501 Broadway #408 212-391-1313
Doros Animation Inc/156 Fifth Ave.....................................212-627-7220
Feigenbaum Productions Inc/5 W 37th St 3rd fl 212-704-9670
Film Opticals/144 E 44th St 212-697-4744
Gati, John/154 W 57th St #832 212-582-9060
Grossman, Robert/19 Crosby St 212-925-1965
ICON Communications/717 Lexington Ave...............................212-688-5155
International Production Center/514 W 57th St 212-582-6530
Kimmelman, Phil & Assoc Inc/9 E 37th St 10th fl 212-679-8400
Lieberman, Jerry/76 Laight St...212-431-3452
Locomo Productions/875 West End Ave 212-222-4833
Marz Productions Inc/118 E 25th St 212-477-3900
Metropolis Graphics/28 E 4th St 212-677-0630
Motion Picker Studio/416 Ocean Ave, Brooklyn 718-856-2763
Musicvision, Inc/185 E 85th St 212-860-4420
Omnibus Computer Gaphics/508 W 57th St 212-975-9050
Ovation Films/81 Irving Pl..212-529-4111
Rembrandt Films/59 E 54th St 212-758-1024
Shadow Light Prod, Inc/163 W 23rd St 5th fl...........................212-689-7511
Stark, Philip/245 W 29th St 15th Fl 212-868-5555
The Fantastic Animation Machine/12 E 46th St 212-697-2525
Today Video, Inc/45 W 45th St 212-391-1020
Videart Inc/39 W 38th St..212-840-2163
Video Works/24 W 40th St..212-869-2500

NORTHEAST

Aviation Simulations International Inc/Box 358, Huntington, NY 516-271-6476
Consolidated Visual Center/2529 Kenilworth Ave, Tuxedo, MD 301-772-7300
Hughes, Gary Inc/PO Box 426, Glen Echo, MD..........................301-229-1100
Pansophic/1825 Q St NW, Washington, DC 202-232-7733
Penpoint Prod Svc/331 Newbury St, Boston, MA........................617-266-1331
Pilgrim Film Service/2504 50th Ave, Hyattsville, MD 301-773-7072

SOUTHEAST

Cinetron Computer Systems Inc/6700 IH 85 North, Norcross, GA........404-448-9463

MIDWEST

AGS & R Studios/314 W Superior, Chicago, IL 312-649-4500
Ball, John & Assoc/203 N Wabash, Chicago, IL 312-332-6041
Boyer Studio/1324 Greenleaf, Evanston, IL..............................708-491-6363
Filmack Studios Inc/1327 S Wabash, Chicago, IL.........................312-427-3395
Freese & Friends Inc/1429 N Wells, Chicago, IL..........................312-642-4475
Goldsholl Assoc/420 Frontage Rd, Northfield, IL.........................708-446-8300
Kinetics/444 N Wabash, Chicago, IL....................................312-644-2767
Mike Jones Film Corp/5250 W 74, Minneapolis, MN.....................612-835-4490
Pilot Prod/2821 Central St, Evanston, IL.................................708-328-3100
Quicksilver Assoc Inc/16 W Ontario, Chicago, IL 312-943-7622
Simott & Associates/676 N La Salle, Chicago, IL.........................312-440-1875

WEST COAST

Bass/Yeager Associates/7039 Sunset Blvd, Hollywood, CA 213-466-9701
Bosustow Entertainment/3000 Olympic Blvd, Santa Monica, CA..........213-315-4888
Cinema Research Corp/6860 Lexington Ave, Hollywood, CA..............213-460-4111
Clampett, Bob Prod/729 Seward St, Hollywood, CA......................213-466-0264
Duck Soup Productions Inc/1026 Montana Ave, Santa Monica, CA....213-451-0771
Energy Productions/2690 Beechwood Dr, Los Angeles, CA 213-462-3310
Filmcore/849 N Seward, Hollywood, CA.................................213-464-7303
Filmfair/10900 Ventura Blvd, Studio City, CA............................213-877-3191
Kurtz & Friends/2312 W Olive Ave, Burbank, CA.........................213-461-8188
Littlejohn, William Prod Inc/23425 Malibu Colony Dr, Malibu, CA..........213-456-8620
Lumeni Productions/1727 N Ivar, Hollywood, CA.........................213-462-2110
Melendez, Bill Prod Inc/439 N Larchmont Blvd, Los Angeles, CA 213-463-4101
Murakami Wolf Swenson Films/4222 W Burbank Blvd, Burbank, CA....818-846-0611
New Hollywood Inc/1302 N Cahuenga Blvd, Hollywood, CA 213-466-3686
R & B EFX/1806 Victory Blvd, Glendale, CA 818-956-8406
Raintree Productions Ltd/666 N Robertson Blvd, Hollywood, CA 213-652-8330
Spungbuggy Works Inc/948 N Fairfax, Hollywood, CA 213-657-8070
Title House/738 Cahuenga Blvd, Los Angeles, CA.......................213-469-8171
U P A Pictures Inc/14101 Valley Heart Dr #200, Sherman Oaks, CA....818-990-3800

MODELS & TALENT

NYC

Abrams Artists/420 Madison Ave 212-935-8980
Adams, Bret/448 W 44th St..212-765-5630
Agency for Performing Arts/888 Seventh Ave............................212-582-1500
Agents for the Arts/1650 Broadway 212-247-3220
Amato, Michael Theatrical Entrps/1650 Broadway 212-247-4456
American Intl Talent/303 W 42nd St 212-245-8888
Anderson, Beverly/1501 Broadway......................................212-944-7773
Associated Booking/1995 Broadway.....................................212-874-2400
Astor, Richard/1697 Broadway 212-581-1970
Avenue Models/295 Madison Ave 46th Fl 212-972-5495
Barbizon Agency of Rego Park/95-20 63rd Rd 718-275-2100
Barry Agency/165 W 46th St..212-869-9310
Bauman & Hiller/250 W 57th St...212-757-0098
Beilin, Peter/230 Park Ave..212-949-9119
Bloom, J Michael/233 Park Ave S..212-529-5800
Buchwald, Don & Assoc Inc/10 E 44th St 212-867-1070
Carson-Adler/250 W 57th St 212-307-1882
Cataldi, Richard Agency/180 Seventh Ave 212-741-7450
Celebrity Look-Alikes/2067 Broadway..................................212-532-7676
Click Model Management/881 Seventh Ave #1013........................212-315-2200
Coleman-Rosenberg/210 E 58th St 212-838-0734
Columbia Artists/165 W 57th St 212-397-6900
DeVore, Ophelia/350 Fifth Ave #1816 212-629-6400
Eisen, Dulcina Assoc/154 E 61st St 212-355-6617
Fields, Marje/165 W 46th St 212-764-5740

Focus Model Management/611 Broadway #523............................212-677-1200
Ford Models Inc/344 E 59th St..212-753-6500
Funny Face/440 E 62nd St..212-752-6090
Gage Group Inc/315 W 57th St #4H......................................212-541-5250
Greco, Maria & Assoc/1261 Broadway 212-213-5500
Hadley, Peggy Ent/250 W 57th St...212-246-2166
Harter-Manning & Assoc/111 E 22nd St 4th Fl....................212-529-4555
Harth, Ellen Inc/149 Madison Ave...212-686-5600
Hartig, Michael Agency Ltd/114 E 28th St............................212-684-0010
Henderson-Hogan/405 W 44th St...212-765-5190
HV Models/18 E 53rd St..212-751-3005
International Creative Management/40 W 57th St..................212-556-5600
Jacobsen Wilder Kesten/419 Park Ave So.............................212-686-6100
Jan J Agency/213 E 38th St 3rd fl...212-682-0202
Jordan, Joe Talent Agency/156 Fifth Ave 212-463-8455
Kahn, Jerry Inc/853 Seventh Ave 212-245-7317
KMA Associates/211 W 56th St #17D...................................212-581-4610
Kolmar-Luth Entertainment Inc/165 W 46th St #1202.........212-921-8989
Kroll, Lucy/390 West End Ave...212-877-0556
L B H Assoc/1 Lincoln Plaza...212-787-2609
Larner, Lionel Ltd/130 W 57th St..212-246-3105
Leigh, Sanford Entrprs Ltd/440 E 62nd St...........................212-752-4450
Leighton, Jan/205 W 57th St...212-757-5242
Lewis, Lester Assoc/400 E 52nd St......................................212-758-2480
Mannequin Fashion Models Inc/150 E 58th St 35th Fl.........212-755-1456
Martinelli Attractions/888 Eighth Ave...................................212-586-0963
McDermott Enterprises/216 E 39th St...................................212-889-1583
McDonald/ Richards/156 Fifth Ave 212-627-3100
Models Service Agency/1457 Broadway 212-944-8896
Models Talent Int'l/1457 Broadway 212-302-8450
Morris, William Agency/1350 Sixth Ave 212-586-5100
Mystique Models/928 Broadway #704...................................212-228-7807
Oppenheim-Christie/13 E 37th St...212-213-4330
Oscard, Fifi/19 W 44th St #1500...212-764-1100
Our Agency/112 E 23rd St PH...212-982-5626
Packwood, Harry Talent Ltd/250 W 57th St..........................212-586-8900
Palmer, Dorothy/235 W 56th St...212-765-4280
Petite Model Management/123 E 54th St #9A.......................212-759-9304
Phoenix Artists/311 W 43rd St..212-586-9110
Plus Models/49 W 37th St...212-997-1785
Prelly People & Co/296 Fifth Ave 212-714-2060
Premier Talent Assoc/3 E 54th St 212-758-4900
Rogers-Lerman/37 E 28th St #506.......................................212-889-8233
Roos, Gilla Ltd/16 W 22nd St 212-727-7820
Ryan, Charles Agency/1841 Broadway 212-245-2225
Schuller, William Agency/1276 Fifth Ave 212-532-6005
Select Artists Reps/337 W 43rd St #1B.................................212-586-4300
Silver Kass Massetti/East Ltd/145 W 45th St 212-391-4545
Smith, Susan Ltd/192 Lexington Ave.....................................212-545-0500
Stars/303 E 60th St...212-758-3545
STE Representation/888 Seventh Ave 212-246-1030
Stroud Management/119 W 57th St..212-688-0226
Talent Reps Inc/20 E 53rd St..212-752-1835
The Starkman Agency/1501 Broadway 212-921-9191
Theater Now Inc/1515 Broadway 212-840-4400
Thomas, Michael Agency/305 Madison 212-867-0303
Total Look/10 Bay St Landing #A4L, St George SI 718-816-1532
Tranum Robertson Hughes Inc/2 Dag Hammarskjold Plaza 212-371-7500
Triad Artists/888 Seventh Ave 212-489-8100
Universal Attractions/225 W 57th St......................................212-582-7575
Van Der Veer People Inc/401 E 57th St 212-688-2880
Wilhelmina Models/9 E 37th St..212-532-6800
Wright, Ann Assoc/136 E 57th St 212-832-0110
Zoli/3 W 18th St 212-758-7336

NORTHEAST

Cameo Models/437 Boylston St, Boston, MA........................617-536-6004
Conover, Joyce Agency/33 Gallowae, Westfield, NJ 201-232-0908
Copley 7 Models & Talent/142 Berkeley St, Boston, MA......617-267-4444
Leach, Dennis/585 Dartmouth St, Westbury, NY..................516-334-3084
Models Unlimited/4475 S Clinton Ave #7, South Plainfield, NJ 201-769-8959
National Talent Assoc/40 Railroad Ave, Valley Stream, NY 516-825-8707
Somers, Jo/142 Berkeley St, Boston, MA 617-267-4444
The Ford Model Mgmt/297 Newbury St, Boston, MA............617-266-6939

SOUTHEAST

A del Corral Model & Talen/5830 Argonne Blvd, New Orleans, LA.......504-288-8963
Act 1 Casting Agency/1220 Collins Ave #200, Miami Beach, FL..........305-672-0200
Amaro Agency/661 Blanding Blvd, Orange Park, FL.............904-276-3408
Atlanta Models & Talent Inc/3030 Peachtree Rd NW, Atlanta, GA.......404-261-9627
Brown, Bob Puppet Prod/1415 S Queen St, Arlington, VA...703-920-1040
Burns, Dot Model & Talent Agcy/478 Severn Ave, Tampa, FL..............813-251-5882
Carolina Talent/220 East Blvd #C, Charlotte, NC 704-332-3218
Cassandra Models Agency/513 W Colonial Dr #6, Orlando, FL 407-423-7872
The Casting Directors Inc/1524 NE 147th St, North Miami, FL...........305-944-8559
Central Casting of FL/PO Box 7154, Ft Lauderdale, FL.......305-379-7526
Directions Talent Agency/338 N Elm St, Greensboro, NC....919-373-0955
Falcon, Travis Modeling Agency/17070 Collins Ave, Miami, FL 305-947-7957
Flair Models/PO Box 17372, Nashville, TN...........................615-361-3737
Irene Marie Models/728 Ocean Dr, Miami Beach, FL...........305-672-2929
JTA Talent/820 East Blvd, Charlotte, NC...............................704-377-5987
Lewis, Millie Modeling School/1228 S Pleasantburg Dr, Greenville, SC....803-299-1101
Lewis, Millie Modeling School/10 Calendar Ct #A, Forest Acres, SC....803-782-7338
Mar Bea Talent Agency/6100 Hollywood Blvd, Hollywood, FL 305-964-7401
Marilyn's Modeling Agency/601 Norwalk St, Greensboro, NC..............919-292-5950
Polan, Marian Talent Agency/PO Box 7154, Ft Lauderdale, FL...........305-525-8351
Pommier, Michele/1200 Anastasia/Biltmore, Coral Gables, FL...........305-667-8710
Powers, John Robert School/828 SE 4th St, Fort Lauderdale, FL........305-467-2838
Professional Models Guild & Wkshp/1819 Charlotte Dr, Charlotte, NC....704-377-9299
Serendipity/2989 Piedmont Rd NE, Atlanta, GA....................404-237-4040
Steinhart-Norton Talent/2940 N Lynnhaven Rd, Virginia Bch, VA.........804-486-5550
Talent & Model Land, Inc/1501 12th Ave S, Nashville, TN....615-385-2723
Ted Schmidt/2149 NE 63rd St, Ft Lauderdale, FL.................212-751-7070
Theatrics Etcetera/PO Box 11862, Memphis, TN..................901-278-7454
Top Billing Inc/PO Box 121089, Nashville, TN.......................615-327-1133
Wellington Models & Talent/823 E Las Olas Blvd, Ft Lauderdale, FL....305-728-8003

MIDWEST

A-Plus Talent Agency Corp/680 N Lakeshore Dr, Chicago, IL..............312-642-8151
Actors Etc Ltd/5102 Leavenworth, Omaha, NB 402-558-9750
Affiliated Talent & Casting Svc/Affiliate Bldg/1680 Crook, Troy, MI 313-244-8770
Creative Casting Inc/860 Lumber Exch/10 S 5th, Minneapolis, MN......612-375-0525
David & Lee Model Management/70 W Hubbard, Chicago, IL.............312-661-0500
IDC Services Inc/303 E Ohio St, Chicago, IL.........................312-943-7500
Limelight Assoc Inc/3460 Davis Lane, Cincinnati, OH...........513-651-2121
Moore, Eleanor Agency/1610 W Lake St, Minneapolis, MN ..612-827-3823
National Talent Assoc/6326 N Lincoln Ave, Chicago, IL.........312-539-8575
New Faces Models & Talent Inc/5217 Wayzata Blvd #210,
Minneapolis, MN..612-544-8668
Pastiche Models Inc/1514 Wealthy #280, Grand Rapids, MI..616-451-2181
Powers, John Robert/5900 Roche Dr, Columbus, OH 614-846-1047
Schucart, Norman Ent/1417 Green Bay Rd, Highland Park, IL.............708-433-1113
Sharkey Career Schools Inc/1299-H Lyons Rd Governours Sq,
Centerville, OH..513-434-4461
SR Talent Pool/206 S 44th St, Omaha, NE............................402-553-1164
Station 12-Producers Exp/1759 Woodgrove Ln, Bloomfield Hills, MI ...313-855-1188
Verblen, Carol Casting Svc/2408 N Burling, Chicago, IL.......312-348-0047

SOUTHWEST

Actors Clearinghouse/501 N IH 35, Austin, TX.....................512-476-3412
ARCA/ Freelance Talent/PO Box 5686, Little Rock, AR.........501-224-1111
Ball, Bobby Agency/808 E Osborn, Phoenix, AZ....................602-468-1292
Barbizon School & Agency/1619 W Bethany Home Rd, Phoenix, AZ...602-249-2950
Blair, Tanya Agency/4528 McKinney #107, Dallas, TX 214-522-9750
Creme de la Creme/5804 N Grand, Oklahoma City, OK........405-840-4419
Dawson, Kim Agency/PO Box 585060, Dallas, TX.................214-638-2414
Ferguson Modeling Agency/1100 W 34th St, Little Rock, AR................501-375-3519
Flair-Career Fashion & Modeling/8900 Menaul Rd, Albuquerque, NM 505-296-5571
Fosi's Talent Agency/2777 N Campbell Ave #209, Tucson, AZ............602-795-3534
Fullerton, Jo Ann/923 W Britton Rd, Oklahoma City, OK.......405-848-4839
Hall, K Agency/503 W 15th St, Austin, TX 512-476-7523
Harrison-Gers Agency/1707 Wilshire Blvd NW, Oklahoma City, OK 405-840-4515
Layman, Linda Agency/3546 E 51st St, Tulsa, OK.................918-744-0888
Mannequin Modeling Agency/204 E Oakview, San Antonio, TX 512-231-4540
Models of HoustonAgency/7887 San Felipe, Houston, TX 713-789-4973
Norton Agency/3900 Lemon Ave, Dallas, TX 214-528-9960
Parks, Page Model Reps/3131 McKinney #430, Dallas, TX.................214-871-9003

Southern Arizona Casting/2777 N Campbell Ave #209, Tucson, AZ 602-795-3534
Taylor, Peggy Talent Inc/4300 N Central Exprswy #110, Dallas, TX 214-826-7884
The Mad Hatter/10101 Harwin Rd, Houston, TX 713-988-3900
Wyse, Joy Agency/2600 Stemmons, Dallas, TX...........................214-638-8999

ROCKY MTN

Morris, Bobby Agency/1629 E Sahara Ave, Las Vegas, NV 702-733-7575

WEST COAST

Adrian, William Agency/1021 E Walnut, Pasadena, CA.........................213-681-5750
American Talent Inc/10850 Wilshire Blvd #530, Los Angeles, CA 213-470-4550
Anthony's , Tom Precision Driving/3418 N Knoll Dr, Hollywood, CA 213-466-8889
Artists Management Agency/835 Fifth Ave #411, San Diego, CA 619-233-6655
Barbizon Modeling Agy/15477 Ventura Blvd, Sherman Oaks, CA.......818-995-8238
Barbizon School of Modeling/452 Fashion Valley E, San Diego, CA....619-296-6366
Blanchard, Nina/957 Cole Ave, Los Angeles, CA 213-462-7274
Celebrity Look-Alikes/7060 Hollywood Blvd #1215, Hollywood, CA 213-272-2006
Commercials Unlimited/7461 Beverly Blvd, Los Angeles, CA...............213-937-2220
Cunningham, William D/261 S Robertson, Beverly Hills, CA 213-855-0200
Frazer Agency/4300 Stevens Creek Blvd, San Jose, CA....................408-554-1055
Garrick, Dale Intern'l Agency/8831 Sunset Blvd #402, L A, CA............213-657-2661
Grimme Agency/207 Powell St 6th fl, San Francisco, CA.....................415-392-9175
Heldfond, Joseph & Rix/1717 N Highland #414, Los Angeles, CA.......213-466-9111
International Creative Mngment/8899 Beverly Blvd, L A, CA 213-550-4000
Leonetti, Ltd/6526 Sunset Blvd, Los Angeles, CA 213-462-2345
Media Talent Center/4440 SW Corbet, Portland, OR 503-226-7131
Model Management Inc/1400 Castro St, San Francisco, CA 415-282-8855
Pacific Artists, Ltd/515 N La Cienaga, Los Angeles, CA 213-657-5990
Playboy Model Agency/8560 Sunset Blvd, Los Angeles, CA...............213-659-4080
Schwartz, Don Agency/8749 Sunset Blvd, Los Angeles, CA................213-657-8910
Seattle Models Guild/1809 7th Ave #303, Seattle, WA 206-622-1406
Smith's, Ron Celebrity Look-Alikes/7060 Hollywood Blvd/PH 1215,
Hollywood, CA 213-272-2006
Sohbi's Talent Agency/1750 Kalakaua Ave #116, Honolulu, HI.............808-946-6614
Stern, Charles Agency/11755 Wilshire Blvd #2320, L A, CA................213-479-1788
Studio Seven/304 E San Bernardino, Covina, CA 818-331-6351
Stunts Unlimited/3518 Cahuenga Blvd W, Los Angeles, CA 213-874-0050
Talent Management/935 NW 19th Ave, Portland, OR 503-223-1931
Tannen, Herb & Assoc/1800 N Vine St #120, Los Angeles, CA 213-466-6191

CASTING

NYC

Brinker, Jane/51 W 16th St 212-924-3322
Brown, Deborah Casting/250 W 57th St..212-581-0404
Burton, Kate/39 W 19th St 12th fl 212-243-6114
C & C Productions/445 E 80th St 212-472-3700
Carter, Kit & Assoc/160 W 95th St 212-864-3147
Cast Away Casting Service/14 Sutton Pl S..212-755-0960
Central Casting Corp of NY/200 W 54th St..212-582-4933
Claire Casting/333 Park Ave S 212-673-7373
Complete Casting/350 W 50th St..212-265-7460
Contemporary Casting Ltd/41 E 57th St..212-838-1818
Davidson/Frank Photo-Stylists/209 W 86th St #701 212-799-2651
DeSeta, Donna Casting/424 W 33rd St 212-239-0988
Digiaimo, Lou/513 W 54th St...212-691-6073
Fay, Sylvia/71 Park Ave 212-889-2626
Greco, Maria Casting/1261 Broadway 212-213-5500
Herman & Lipson Casting, Inc/24 W 25th St 212-807-7706
Howard, Stewart Assoc/22 W 27th St 10th fl 212-725-7770
Hughes/Moss Assoc/311 W 43rd St 212-307-6690
Jacobs, Judith/336 E 81st St 212-744-3758
Johnson/Liff/1501 Broadway 212-391-2680
Kressel, Lynn Casting/445 Park Ave 7th fl 212-605-9122
Navarro-Bertoni Casting Ltd/101 W 31st St 212-736-9272
Reed/Sweeney/Reed Inc/1780 Broadway 212-265-8541
Schneider Studio/119 W 57th St 212-265-1223
Shapiro, Barbara Casting/111 W 57th St 212-582-8228
Todd, Joy/37 E 28th St #700...212-685-3537
Weber, Joy Casting/250 W 57th St #1925 212-245-5220

Wollin, Marji/233 E 69th St...212-472-2528

NORTHEAST

Belajac, Donna & Co/1 Bigelow Sq #1924, Pittsburgh, PA..................412-391-1005
Central Casting/623 Pennsylvania Ave SE, Washington, DC................202-547-6300
Lawrence, Joanna Agency/82 Patrick Rd, Westport, CT.......................203-226-7239
Producers Audition Hotline/18156 Darnell Dr, Olney, MD 301-924-4327

SOUTHEAST

Central Casting/PO Box 7154, Ft Lauderdale, FL 305-379-7526
DiPrima, Barbara Casting/3390 Mary St #PH J, Coconut Grove, FL.....305-445-7630
Lancaster Models/785 Crossover, Memphis, TN 901-761-1046
Taylor Royal Casting/2308 South Rd, Baltimore, MD 301-466-5959

MIDWEST

Station 12 Producers Exp/1759 Woodgrove Ln, Bloomfield Hills, MI 313-855-1188

SOUTHWEST

Austin Actors Clearinghouse/501 North 1H 35, Austin, TX 512-476-3412
Blair, Tanya Agency/Artists Mngrs/4528 McKinney #107, Dallas, TX....214-522-9750
KD Studio/2600 Stemons #117, Dallas, TX 214-638-0484
New Visions/Box 372, Prescott, AZ..602-445-3382

WEST COAST

Abrams-Rubaloff & Lawrence/8075 W 3rd #303, Los Angeles, CA......213-935-1700
Associated Talent International/9744 Wilshire Blvd, Los Angeles, CA ..213-271-4662
BCI Casting/6565 Sunset Blvd #412, Los Angeles, CA 213-466-3400
C H N International/7428 Santa Monica Blvd, Los Angeles, CA 213-874-8252
Celebrity Look-Alikes/7060 Hollywood Blvd #1215, Hollywood, CA 213-272-2006
Commercials Unlimited/7461 Beverly Blvd, Los Angeles, CA...............213-937-2220
Creative Artists Agency Inc/9830 Wilshire Blvd, Beverly Hills, CA 213-277-4545
Cunningham, William /261 S Robertson Blvd, Beverly Hills, CA 213-855-0200
Davis, Mary Webb/515 N LaCienega, Los Angeles, CA......................213-652-6850
Garrick, Dale Internat'l Agency/8831 Sunset Blvd #402, L A, CA.........213-657-2661
Hecht, Beverly Agency/8949 Sunset Blvd #203, Los Angeles, CA.......213-278-3544
Heldfond, Joseph & Rix/1717 N Highland #414, Los Angeles, CA.......213-466-9111
Lien, Michael Casting/7461 Beverly Blvd, Los Angeles, CA 213-937-0411
Loo, Bessi Agency/8235 Santa Monica, W Hollywood, CA 213-650-1300
Mangum, Joan Agcy/9250 Wilshire Blvd #206, Beverly Hills, CA 213-274-6622
Morris, William Agency/151 El Camino Dr, Beverly Hills, CA.................213-274-7451
Pacific Artists Limited/515 N LaCienega Blvd, Los Angeles, CA 213-657-5990
Payment Management/935 NW 19th Ave, Portland, OR......................503-223-1931
Rose, Jack/7080 Hollywood Blvd #201, Los Angeles, CA...................213-463-7300
Schaeffer, Peggy Agency/10850 Riverside Dr, North Hollywood, CA ...818-985-5547
Schwartz, Don & Assoc/8749 Sunset Blvd, Los Angeles, CA 213-657-8910
Stern, Charles H Agency/11755 Wilshire Blvd #2320, L A, CA.............213-479-1788
Tannen, Herb & Assoc/1800 N Vine St #120, Los Angeles, CA 213-466-6191
Wilhelmina/West/8383 Wilshire Blvd #954, Beverly Hills, CA 213-653-5700

ANIMALS

NYC

All Tame Animals/250 W 57th St 212-245-6740
Animals for Advertising/310 W 55th St 212-245-2590
Cap Haggertys Theatrical Dogs/222 Seaman Ave 212-220-7771
Captain Haggertys Theatrical Dogs/1748 First Ave 212-410-7400
Chateau Stables/608 W 48th St 212-246-0520
Claremont Riding Academy/175 W 89th St 212-724-5100
Dawn Animal Agency/750 Eighth Ave 212-575-9396

NORTHEAST

Animal Actors Inc/Box 221, RD 3, Washington, NJ..............................201-689-7539

Long Island Game Farm & Zoo/Chapman Blvd, Manorville, NY 516-878-6644

SOUTHEAST

Dog Training by Bob Maida/7605 Old Centerville Rd, Manassas, VA ...703-631-2125

SOUTHWEST

Dallas Zoo in Marsalis Park/621 E Clarendon, Dallas, TX.....................214-670-6825
Estes, Bob Rodeos/138 E 6th St, Baird, TX.......................................915-854-1037
Fort Worth Zoological Park/2727 Zoological Park Dr., Fort Worth, TX ...817-870-7065
International Wildlife Park/601 Wildlife Parkway, Grand Prairie, TX 214-263-2203
Scott, Kelly Buggy & Wagon Rentals/Box 442, Bandera, TX................512-796-4943
Y O Ranch/Dept AS, Mountain Home, TX 512-640-3222

WEST COAST

Animal Action/PO Box 824, Arleta, CA 818-767-3003
Animal Actors of Hollywood/864 Carlisle Rd, Thousand Oaks, CA 805-495-2122
Birds and Animals/25191 Rivendell Dr, El Toro, CA 714-830-7845
Casa De Pets/13323 Ventura Blvd, Sherman Oaks, CA 818-986-2660
Di Sesso's, Moe Trained Wildlife/24233 Old Road, Newhall, CA 805-255-7969
Frank Inn Inc/30227 Hasley Canyon Rd, Castaic, CA 805-295-1205
Griffin, Gus/11281 Sheldon St, Sun Valley, CA................................818-767-6647
Martin, Steve Working Wildlife/PO Box 65, Acton, CA 805-268-0788
Pyramid Bird/1407 W Magnolia, Burbank, CA 818-843-5505
Schumacher Animal Rentals/14453 Cavette Pl, Baldwin Park, CA 818-338-4614
The American Mongrel/PO Box 2406, Lancaster, CA..........................805-942-7550
The Stansbury Co/9304 Santa Monica Blvd, Beverly Hills, CA 213-273-1138

HAIR & MAKE-UP

NYC

Abrams, Ron/126 W 75th St...212-580-0705
Imre, Edith Beauty Salon/33 E 65th St 212-772-3351
Jenrette, Pamela/300 Mercer St...212-673-4748
Laber, Honey Jeanne/235 W 102nd St #10D...................................212-662-3199
Narvaez, Robin/360 E 55th St 212-371-6378
Weithorn, Rochelle/431 E 73rd St 212-472-8668

SOUTHEAST

Irene Marie Models/728 Ocean Dr, Miami Beach, FL 305-672-2929
Parker, Julie Hill/PO Box 5412, Miami Lakes, FL................................305-362-5397

MIDWEST

Camylle/112 E Oak, Chicago, IL..312-943-1120
Cheveux/908 W Armitage, Chicago, IL..312-935-5212
International Guild of Make-Up/6970 N Sheridan, Chicago, IL..............312-761-8500
Kalagian, Maureen/Media Hair/Makeup Grp, Chicago, IL...................312-472-6550
Okains Costume & Theater/2713 W Jefferson, Joliet, IL......................815-741-9303
Sguardo, Che/716 N Wells St, Chicago, IL......................................312-440-1616
Simmons, Sid Inc/2 E Oak, Chicago, IL...312-943-2333

SOUTHWEST

Dawson, Kim Agency/PO Box 585060, Dallas, TX...............................214-638-2414

WEST COAST

Gavilan/139 S Kings Rd, Los Angeles, CA..213-655-4452
Hamilton, Bryan J/197 Larrabee St, Los Angeles, CA 213-657-6066
Johns, Arthur Adjectives/901 Westbourne Dr, W Hollywood, CA 213-855-0225
Studio Seven/304 E San Bernardino, Covina, CA 818-331-6351
Total You Salon/1647 Los Angeles Ave, Simi, CA 805-526-4189

HAIR

NYC

Benjamin Salon/104 Washington Pl...212-255-3330
Daines, David Salon Hair Styling/833 Madison Ave.............................212-535-1563
George V Hair Stylist/501 Fifth Ave...212-687-9097
Monsieur Marc Inc/Carlyle/981 Madison 212-861-0700

NORTHEAST

Brocklebank, Tom/249 Emily Ave, Elmont, NY 516-775-5356

SOUTHEAST

Yellow Strawberry/107 E Las Olas Blvd, Ft Lauderdale, FL 305-463-4343

MIDWEST

Kalagian, Maureen/Media Hair/Makeup Grp, Chicago, IL....................312-472-6550

SOUTHWEST

Southern Hair Designs/3563 Far West Blvd, Austin, TX.......................512-346-1734

ROCKY MTN

Luezano Andrez Int Salon/2845 Wyandote, Denver, CO 303-458-0131

WEST COAST

Anatra Haircutters/530 N LaCienega, Los Angeles, CA 213-657-1495
Barronson Hair/11908 Ventura, Studio City, CA 818-763-4337
Edwards, Allen/345 N Camden, Beverly Hills, CA 213-274-8575
John, Michael Salon/414 N Camden Dr, Beverly Hills, CA 213-278-8333
Lorenz, Barbara/, , CA 213-657-0028
Menage a Trois/8822 Burton Way, Beverly Hills, CA 213-278-4431
Phillips, Marilyn/, , CA...213-923-6996
Trainoff, Linda/11830 B Moorpark, Studio City, CA 818-769-0373

MAKE-UP

NYC

Groves, Teri..818-562-1668
Lane, Judy/444 E 82nd St...212-861-7225
Make-Up Center Ltd/1013 Third Ave...212-751-2001
Make-Up Center Ltd/150 W 55th St..212-977-9494
Oakley, Sara/..212-749-5912
Ross, Rose Cosmetics/16 W 55th St...212-586-2590
Sartin, Janet of Park Ave Ltd/480 Park Ave 212-751-5858

NORTHEAST

Douglas, Rodney N/473 Avon Ave #3, Newark, NJ.............................201-375-2979
Gilmore, Robert Assoc Inc/990 Washington St, Dedham, MA..............617-329-6633
Something Special/1805 S Oakland St, Arlington, VA..........................703-892-0551

SOUTHEAST

Lajoan, Brenda/236 Sandalwood Trail, Winter Park, FL.......................407-645-2434
Star Styled of Miami/475 NW 42nd Ave, Miami, FL............................305-541-2424

MIDWEST

Kalagian, Maureen/Media Hair/Makeup Grp, Chicago, IL 312-472-6550

SOUTHWEST

ABC Theatrical Rental & Sales/825 N 7th St, Phoenix, AZ 602-258-5265
Corey, Irene/4147 Herschel Ave, Dallas, TX 214-821-9633
Dobes, Pat/1826 Nocturne, Houston, TX 713-465-8102
Schakosky, Laurie/17735 Windflower Way #10, Dallas, TX 214-250-1019
Stamm, Louis M/721 Edgehill Dr, Hurst, TX 817-268-5037

ROCKY MTN

Moon Sun Emporium/Pearl Street Mall, Boulder, CO 303-443-6851

WEST COAST

Anderson, Dorian Blackman/12751 Addison, N Hollywood, CA 818-761-2177
Blackman, Charles F/12751 Addison, N Hollywood, CA 818-761-2177
Blackman, Gloria/12751 Addison, N Hollywood, CA 818-761-2177
Copeland, Christine/, , ...213-938-8414
Cosmetic Connection/421 N Rodeo Dr, Beverly Hills, CA 213-550-6242
D'Ifray, T J/468 N Bedford Dr, Beverly Hills, CA 213-274-6776
Fradkin, Joanne c/o Pigments/8822 Burton Way, Beverly Hills, CA 213-858-7038
Henrriksen, Ole/8601 W Sunset Blvd, Los Angeles, CA 213-854-7700
Logan, KathrynCA 818-988-7038
Menage a Trois/8822 Burton Way, Beverly Hills, CA 213-278-4431
Nadia/CA 213-465-2009
Natasha/4221 1/2 Avocado St, Los Angeles, CA 213-663-1477
Romero, Bob/4085 Benedict Canyon Dr, Sherman Oaks, CA 818-981-3338
Tuttle, William/325 Aderno Way, Pacific Palisades, CA 213-454-2355
Westmore, Michae 818-763-3158
Westmore, Monty 818-762-2094
Wolf, BarbaraCA 213-466-4660

STYLISTS
NYC

Benner, Dyne (Food)/311 E 60th St 212-688-7571
Berman, Benicia/399 E 72nd St 212-737-9627
Cheverton, Linda/150 9th Avenue 212-475-6450
Chin, Fay/67 Vestry St 212-219-8770
Davidson/Frank Photo-Stylists/209 W 86th St #701 212-799-2651
George, Georgia A/404 E 55th St 212-759-4131
Goldberg, Hal/40 E 9th St 212-353-9622
Hammond, Claire/440 E 57th St 212-838-0712
Haynie, Cecille/105 W 13th St #7C 212-929-3690
Laber, Honey Jeanne/235 W 102nd St #10D 212-662-3199
Manetti, Palmer/336 E 53rd St 212-758-3859
McCabe, Christine/200 E 16th St #8B 212-995-8175
McCracken, Laura/73 Atlantic Ave, Brooklyn, NY 718-643-9206
Meshejian, Zabel/125 Washington Pl 212-242-2459
Sampson, Linda/431 W Broadway 212-925-6821
Scherman, Joan/450 W 24th St 212-620-0475
Schoenberg, Marv/878 West End Ave #10A 212-663-1418
Sheffy, Nina/838 West End Ave 212-662-0709
Sinclair, Joanna/Food Stylist 212-679-7575
Smith, Rose/400 E 56th St #19D 212-758-8711
Specht, Meredith/411 West End Ave 212-877-8333
Weithorn, Rochelle/431 E 73rd St 212-472-8668
West, Susan/59 E 7th St 212-982-8228

NORTHEAST

Maggio, Marlene - Aura Prdtns/55 Waterview Circle, Rochester, NY 716-381-8053
Rosemary's Cakes Inc/299 Rutland Ave, Teaneck, NJ 201-833-2417

SOUTHEAST

Foodworks/1541 Colonial Ter, Arlington, VA 703-524-2606
Kupersmith, Tony/320 Highland Ave NE, Atlanta, GA 404-577-5319
Reelistic Productions/6467 SW 48th St, Miami, FL 305-284-9989
Sampson, Linda/827 Ursulines, New Orleans, LA 503-523-3085

MIDWEST

Carlson, Susan/255 Linden Park Pl, Highland Park, IL 708-433-2466
Cheveux/908 W Armitage, Chicago, IL 312-935-5212
Erickson, Emily/3224 N Southport, Chicago, IL 312-281-4899
Marx, Wendy/4034 N Sawyer Ave, Chicago, IL 312-509-9292
Pace, Leslie/6342 N Sheridan, Chicago, IL 312-761-2480
Passman, Elizabeth/927 Noyes St, Evanston, IL 708-869-3484
The Set-up & Co/1049 E Michigan St, Indianapolis, IN 317-635-2323

SOUTHWEST

Riley, Kim Manske/10707 Sandpiper, Houston, TX 713-777-9416

WEST COAST

Alaimo, Doris/8800 Wonderland Ave, Los Angeles, CA 213-654-1544
Corwin, Aleka/2383 Silver Ridge Ave, Los Angeles, CA 213-665-7953
Davis, Rommie/4414 La Venta Dr, West Lake Village, CA 818-906-1455
Frank, Tobi/1269 N Hayworth, Los Angeles, CA 213-552-7921
Granas, Marilyn/220 S Palm Dr, Beverly Hills, CA 213-278-3773
Griswald, Sandra/963 North Point, San Francisco, CA 415-775-4272
Hamilton, Bryan J/197 Larrabee St, Los Angeles, CA 213-657-6066
Miller, Freyda/1412 Warner Ave, Los Angeles, CA 213-474-5034
Minot, Abby/61101 Thornhill Dr, Oakland, CA 415-339-9600
Olsen, Eileen/1619 N Beverly Dr, Beverly Hills, CA 213-273-4496
Russo, Leslie/327 10th, Santa Monica, CA 213-395-8461
Shatsy/9008 Harratt St, Hollywood, CA 213-652-2288
Skinner, Jeanette/15431 Redhill Ave #E, Tustin, CA 714-259-9224
Stillman, Denise/PO Box 7692, Laguna Niguel, CA 714-496-4841
Thomas, Lisa/9029 Rangely Ave, W Hollywood, CA 213-858-6903

COSTUMES
NYC

Academy Clothes Inc/1703 Broadway 212-765-1440
Austin Ltd/140 E 55th St 212-752-7903
Capezio Dance Theater Shop/1650 Broadway 212-245-2130
Chenko Studio/130 W 47th St 212-944-0215
David's Outfitters Inc/36 W 20th St 212-691-7388
Eaves-Brookes Costume/21-07 41st Ave, L I City, NY 718-729-1010
Grace Costumes Inc/244 W 54th St 212-586-0260
Ian's Boutique Inc/1151-A Second Ave 212-838-3969
Kulyk/72 E 7th St 212-674-0414
Martin, Alice Manougian/239 E 58th St 212-688-0117
Michael-Jon Costumes Inc/39 W 19th St 212-741-3440
New York City Ballet Costume Shop/16 W 61st St 212-247-3341
Purcell, Elizabeth/225 Lafayette St 212-925-1962
Rubie's Costume Co/1 Rubie Plaza, Richmond Hill, NY 718-846-1008
Stivanello Costume Co Inc/66-38 Clinton Ave, Maspeth, NY 718-651-7715
Tint, Francine/1 University Pl #PHB 212-475-3366
Universal Costume Co Inc/535 Eighth Ave 212-239-3222
Weiss & Mahoney Inc/142 Fifth Ave 212-675-1915
Winston, Mary Ellen/11 E 68th St 212-879-0766
Ynocencio, Jo/302 E 88th St 212-348-5332

NORTHEAST

At-A-Glance Rentals/712 Main, Boonton, NJ 201-335-1488
Costume Armour Inc/PO Box 85/2 Mill St, Cornwall, NY 914-534-9120
Douglas, Rodney N/473 Avon Ave #3, Newark, NJ 201-375-2979
Ren Rose Locations/4 Sandalwood Dr, Livingston, NJ 201-992-4264

Strutters/11 Paul Sullivan Way, Boston, MA 617-423-9299
Westchester Costume Rentals/540 Nepperhan Ave, Yonkers, NY 914-963-1333

S O U T H E A S T

ABC Costume/185 NE 59th St, Miami, FL 305-757-3492
Atlantic Costume Co/2089 Monroe Dr, Atlanta, GA...............................404-874-7511
Star Styled/475 NW 42nd Ave, Miami, FL...305-649-3030

M I D W E S T

Advance Theatrical Co/1900 N Narragansett, Chicago, IL 312-889-7700
Broadway Costumes Inc/954 W Washington, Chicago, IL 312-829-6400
Center Stage/Fox Valley Shopping Cntr, Aurora, IL...............................708-851-9191
Chicago Costume Co Inc/1120 W Fullerton, Chicago, IL.......................312-528-1264
Ennis, Susan/3045 N Southport, Chicago, IL..312-525-7483
Kaufman Costumes/5065 N Lincoln, Chicago, IL....................................312-561-7529
Magical Mystery Tour, Ltd/6010 Dempster, Morton Grove, IL................708-966-5090
Okains Costume & Theater/2713 W Jefferson, Joliet, IL.........................815-741-9303
The Set-up & Co/1049 E Michigan St, Indianapolis, IN...........................317-635-2323

S O U T H W E S T

ABC Theatrical Rental & Sales/825 N 7th St, Phoenix, AZ....................602-258-5265
Anykind-A Costumes/210 Hancock Shpng Ctr, Austin, TX 512-454-1610
Campioni, Frederick/1920 Broken Oak, San Antonio, TX.......................512-342-7780
Corey, Irene/4147 Herschel Ave, Dallas, TX..214-821-9633
Incredible Productions/3327 Wylie Dr, Dallas, TX..................................214-350-3633
Lucy Greer & Assoc. Casting/600 Shadywood Ln, Richardson, TX.....214-231-2086
Old Time Teenies Vintage Clothing/1126 W 6th St, Austin, TX 512-477-2022
Second Childhood/1116 W 6th St, Austin, TX 512-472-9696
Starline Costume Products/1286 Bandera Rd, San Antonio, TX............512-435-3535
Thomas, Joan S/6904 Spanky Branch Court, Dallas, TX 214-931-1900

R O C K Y   M T N

And Sew On-Jila/2035 Broadway, Boulder, CO 303-442-0130
Raggedy Ann Clothing & Costume/1213 E Evans Ave, Denver, CO.....303-733-7937

W E S T   C O A S T

Adele's of Hollywood/5034 Hollywood Blvd, Hollywood, CA..............213-663-2231
California Surplus Mart/6263 Santa Monica Blvd, Los Angeles, CA 213-465-5525
Capezio Dancewear/1777 Vine St, Hollywood, CA................................213-465-3744
CBS Wardrobe Dept/7800 Beverly Blvd, Los Angeles, CA 213-852-2345
Courtney, Elizabeth/8636 Melrose Ave, Los Angeles, CA 213-657-4361
E C 2 Costumes/431 S Fairfax, Los Angeles, CA...................................213-934-1131
Fantasy Costume/4649 1/2 San Fernando Rd, Glendale, CA 213-245-7367
International Costume Co/1423 Marcellina, Torrance, CA.....................213-320-6392
Kings Western Wear/6455 Van Nuys Blvd, Van Nuys, CA....................818-785-2586
LA Uniform Exchange/5239 Melrose Ave, Los Angeles, CA 213-469-3965
MGM/UA Studios Wardrobe Dept/10000 W Washington Blvd,
Culver City, CA 213-558-5600
Minot, Abby/61101 Thornhill Dr, Oakland, CA..415-339-9600
Nudies Rodeo Tailor/5015 Lanskershim Blvd, N Hollywood, CA..........818-762-3105
Palace Costume/835 N Fairfax, Los Angeles, CA..................................213-651-5458
Paramount Studios Wardrobe/5555 Melrose Ave, Hollywood, CA 213-468-5288
The Burbank Studios Wardrobe/4000 Warner Blvd, Burbank, CA 818-954-1218
Tuxedo Center/7360 Sunset Blvd, Los Angeles, CA..............................213-874-4200
United American Costume Co/12980 Raymer, N Hollywood, CA..........818-764-2239
Valu Shoe Mart/5637 Santa Monica Blvd, Los Angeles, CA.................213-469-8560
Western Costume Co/11041 Van Allen, N Hollywood, CA....................213-469-1451

P R O P S

N Y C

Abet Rent-A-Fur/231 W 29th St #304 212-268-6225
Abstracta Structures Inc/347 Fifth Ave 212-532-3710
Ace Galleries/67 E 11th St 212-991-4536

Adirondack Direct/300 E 44th St...212-687-8555
Alice's Antiques/505 Columbus Ave 212-874-3400
Alpha-Pavia Bookbinding Co Inc/601 W 26th St/2nd Mezz...................212-929-5430
Artistic Neon by Gasper/75-49 61st St, Glendale 718-821-1550
Baird, Bill Marionettes/139 W 17th St #3A...212-989-9840
Bill's Flower Mart/816 Ave of the Americas...212-889-8154
Brandon Memorabilia/PO Box 20165 212-691-9776
Breitrose Seltzer Stages/383 W 12th St 212-877-5085
Brooklyn Model Works/60 Washington Ave, Brooklyn...........................718-834-1944
Carroll Musical Instrument Svc/351 W 41st St...212-868-4120
Chateau Stables Inc/608 W 48th St 212-246-0520
Constructive Display/525 W 26th St 212-643-0086
Doherty Studios/2255 Broadway 212-877-5085
Eclectic Encore Props/620 W 26th St 4th fl 212-645-8880
Furs, Valerie/150 W 30th St..212-947-2020
Golden Equipment Co Inc/574 Fifth Ave 212-719-5121
Gordon Novelty Co/933 Broadway 212-254-8616
Harrison/Erickson Puppets/66 Pierrepont, Brooklyn 212-929-5700
Jeffers, Kathy-Modelmaking/151 W 19th St #3F......................................212-255-5196
Kaplan, Howard/820 Broadway 212-674-1000
Karpen, Ben/212 E 51st St..212-755-3450
Kempler, George J/160 Fifth Ave 212-989-1180
Kenmore Furniture Co Inc/352 Park Ave S 212-683-1888
Manhattan Model Shop/40 Great Jones St...212-473-6312
Maniatis, Michael Inc/48 W 22nd St 212-620-0398
Mason's Tennis Mart/911 Seventh Ave 212-757-5374
Matty's Studio Sales/2368 12th Ave 212-491-7070
Mendez, Raymond A/220 W 98th St #12B 212-864-4689
Messmore & Damon Inc/530 W 28th St..212-594-8070
Metro Scenic Studio Inc/129-02 Northern Blvd, Corona 718-844-2835
Modern Miltex Corp/130-25 180th St, Springfield Gardens 718-525-6000
Newell Art Galleries Inc/425 E 53rd St...212-758-1970
Paul De Pass Inc/220 W 71st St...212-362-2648
Plant Specialists Inc/42-25 Vernon Blvd, Long Island City 212-839-9414
Plastic Works!/2107 Broadway @ 73rd...212-362-1000
Plexability Ltd/200 Lexington Ave 212-679-7826
The Prop House Inc/653 11th Ave @ 47th 212-713-0760
The Prop Shop/26 College Pl, Brooklyn Heights, NY 718-522-4606
Props and Displays/132 W 18th St 212-620-3840
Props for Today/121 W 19th St..212-206-0330
Ray Beauty Supply Co Inc/721 Eighth Ave 212-757-0175
Ridge, John Russell/ 212-929-3410
Say It In Neon/319 Third Ave, Brooklyn, NY 718-625-1481
Smith & Watson/305 E 63rd St 212-355-5615
Solco Plumbing & Baths/209 W 18th St..212-243-2569
Starbuck Studio - Acrylic props/162 W 21st St 212-807-7299
The Place for Antiques/993 Second Ave 212-308-4066
Theater Technology Inc/37 W 20th St 212-929-5380
Times Square Theatrical & Studio/318 W 47th St.....................................212-245-4155
Uncle Sam's Umbrella/161 W 57th St 212-247-7163
Whole Art Inc/580 Eighth Ave 19th fl 212-719-0620

N O R T H E A S T

Atlas Scenic Studios Ltd/46 Brookfield Ave, Bridgeport, CT 203-334-2130
Bestek Theatrical Productions/218 W Hoffman, Lindenhurst, NY..........516-225-0707
Geiger, Ed/12 Church St, Middletown, NJ 201-671-1707
Hart Scenic Studio/35-41 Dempsey Ave, Edgewater, NJ 212-947-7264
Rindner, Jack N Assoc/112 Water St, Tinton Falls, NJ 201-542-3548
Stewart, Chas H Co/69 Norman St, Everett, MA......................................617-625-2407
Strutters/11 Paul Sullivan Way, Boston, MA..617-423-9299
Zeller International/Main St/POB Z, Downsville, NY 212-627-7676

S O U T H E A S T

Arawak Marine/PO Box 7362, St Thomas, VI 809-775-6500
Dunwright Productions/15281 NE 21st Ave, N Miami Beach, FL 305-944-2464
Kupersmith, Tony/320 Highland Ave NE, Atlanta, GA.............................404-577-5319
Reelistic Productions/6467 SW 48th St, Miami, FL..................................305-284-9989
Sunshine Scenic Studios/1370 4th St, Sarasota, FL 813-366-8848

M I D W E S T

Advance Theatrical/1900 N Narragansett, Chicago, IL 312-889-7700
Becker Studios Inc/2824 W Taylor, Chicago, IL.......................................312-722-4040

Bregstone Assoc/500 S Wabash, Chicago, IL 312-939-5130
Cadillac Plastic and Chemical Co/953 N Larch Ave, Elmhurst, IL.........312-342-9200
Center Stage/Fox Valley Shopping Cntr, Aurora, IL..................708-851-9191
Chanco Ltd/3131 West Grand Ave, Chicago, IL.....................312-638-0363
Chicago Scenic Studios Inc/1711 W Fullerton, Chicago, IL 312-348-0115
Gard, Ron/2600 N Racine, Chicago, IL.............................312-975-6523
Hartman Furniture & Carpet Co/220 W Kinzie, Chicago, IL........312-664-2800
Hollywood Stage Lighting/5850 N Broadway, Chicago, IL 708-869-3340
House of Drane/410 N Ashland Ave, Chicago, IL..................312-829-8686
Okains Costume & Theater/2713 W Jefferson, Joliet, IL............815-741-9303
Scroungers Inc/351 Lyndale Ave S, Minneapolis, MN..............612-823-2346
Starr, Steve Studios/2654 N Clark St, Chicago, IL................312-525-6530
Studio Specialties/606 N Houston, Chicago, IL....................312-337-5131
The Model Shop/345 Canal St, Chicago, IL 312-454-9618
The Set-up & Co/1049 E Michigan St, Indianapolis, IN............317-635-2323

SOUTHWEST

Creative Video Productions/5933 Bellaire Blvd #110, Houston, TX.......713-661-0478
Doerr, Dean/11321 Greystone, Oklahoma City, OK 405-751-0313
Eats/PO Box 52, Tempe, AZ......................................602-966-7459
Marty, Jack/2225 South First, Garland, TX........................214-840-8708
Riley, Kim Manske/10707 Sandpiper, Houston, TX................713-777-9416
Southern Importers/4825 San Jacinto, Houston, TX 713-524-8236

WEST COAST

Abbe Rents/1001 La Brea, Los Angeles, CA 213-466-9582
Aldik Artificial Flowers Co/7651 Sepulveda Blvd, Van Nuys, CA..........818-988-5970
Allen, Walter Plant Rentals/4996 Melrose Ave, Hollywood, CA.............213-469-3621
Antiquarian Traders/650 LaPerre, West Hollywood, CA............213-289-0345
Antiquarian Traders/4851 S Alameda, Los Angeles, CA...........213-627-2144
Antiquarian Traders/8483 Melrose Ave, Los Angeles, CA 213-658-6394
Arnelle Sales Co Prop House/7926 Beverly Blvd, Los Angeles, CA 213-930-2900
Asia Plant Rentals/1215 225th St, Torrance, CA...................213-775-1811
Astrovision, Inc/7240 Valjean Ave, Van Nuys, CA 818-989-5222
Backings, c/o 20th Century Fox/10201 W Pico Blvd, L A, CA 213-277-0522
Baronian Manufacturing Co/1865 Farm Bureau Rd, Concord, CA.......415-671-7199
Barris Kustom Inc/10811 Riverside Dr, N Hollywood, CA 213-877-2352
Barton Surrey Svc/518 Fairview Ave, Arcadia, CA.................818-447-6693
Bischoff's/449 S San Fernando Blvd, Burbank, CA.................818-843-7561
Brown, Mel Furniture/5840 S Figueroa St, Los Angeles, CA........213-778-4444
Buccaneer Cruises/Berth 76W-33 Ports O'Call, San Pedro, CA......213-548-1085
The Burbank Studios Prop Dept/4000 Warner Blvd, Burbank, CA........818-954-6000
Carpenter, Brent Studio/19 Kala Moreya, Laguna Niguel, CA.........714-363-0825
Custom Neon/2210 S LaBrea, Los Angeles, CA 213-937-6366
D'Andrea Glass Etchings/3671 Tacoma Ave, Los Angeles, CA 213-223-7940
Decorative Paper Products/2481 Lilyvale Ave, Los Angeles, CA.........213-223-2676
Deutsch/Rattan/8611 Hayden Pl, Culver City, CA..................213-559-4949
Ellis Mercantile Co/169 N LaBrea Ave, Los Angeles, CA...........213-933-7334
Featherock Inc/20219 Bohama St, Chatsworth, CA................818-882-3888
First Street Furniture Store/1123 N Bronson Ave, Hollywood, CA.........213-462-6306
Flower Fashions/9960 Santa Monica Blvd, Beverly Hills, CA 213-272-6063
Grand American Fare/3110 Main St 3rd fl, Santa Monica, CA........213-450-4900
The Hand Prop Room/5700 Venice Blvd, Los Angeles, CA............213-931-1534
Hollywood Toys/6562 Hollywood Blvd, Los Angeles, CA............213-465-3119
House of Props Inc/1117 N Gower St, Hollywood, CA...............213-463-3166
Hume, Alex R/1024 W Burbank Blvd, Burbank, CA................213-849-1614
Malibu Florists/23823 Malibu Rd #300, Malibu, CA................213-456-1858
Marvin, Lennie Entrprs Ltd/1105 N Hollywood Way, Burbank, CA 818-841-5882
MGM Studios Prop/10000 W Washington Blvd, Culver City, CA 213-280-6000
Mole-Richardson/937 N Sycamore Ave, Hollywood, CA............213-851-0111
Moskatels/733 S San Julian St, Los Angeles, CA..................213-689-4830
Motion Picture Marine/616 Venice Blvd, Marina del Rey, CA.............213-822-1100
Music Center/5616 Santa Monica Blvd, Hollywood, CA 213-469-8143
Omega Cinema Props/5857 Santa Monica Blvd, Los Angeles, CA 213-466-8201
Paramount Studios Prop Dept/5555 Melrose Ave, Los Angeles, CA......213-468-5000
Post, Don Studios/8211 Lankershim Blvd, N Hollywood, CA............818-768-0811
Prop Service West/915 N Citrus Ave, Los Angeles, CA.............213-461-3371
Roschu/7100 Bear Ave, N Hollywood, CA 818-503-9392
Scale Model Co/4613 W Rosecrans Ave, Hawthorne, CA............213-679-1436
School Days Equipment Co/2525 Medford St, Los Angeles, CA 213-223-3474
Silvestri Studios/1733 W Cordova St, Los Angeles, CA.............213-735-1481
Special Effects Unlimited/752 N Cahuenga Blvd, Hollywood, CA.........213-466-3361
Spellman Desk Co/6159 Santa Monica Blvd, Hollywood, CA 213-467-0628
Studio Specialties/3013 Gilroy St, Los Angeles, CA 213-662-3031

Stunts Unlimited/3518 Cahuenga Blvd W, Los Angeles, CA 213-874-0050
Surf, Val/3810 Whitsett, N Hollywood, CA..........................818-769-6977
Tropizon Plant Rentals/1401 Pebble Vale, Monterey Park, CA 213-269-2010
Western Costume Company/11041 Van Allen, N Hollywood, CA.........213-469-1451

LOCATIONS
NYC

A Perfect Space/PO Box 1669.....................................212-941-0262
C & C Productions/445 E 80th St 212-472-3700
Cinema Galleries/517 W 35th St 1st Fl 212-627-1222
Davidson/Frank Photo-Stylists/209 W 86th St #701...............212-799-2651
Florentine Films, Inc/136 E 56th St #4C...........................212-486-0580
Howell, T J Interiors/301 E 38th St 212-532-6267
Joy of Movement/400 Lafayette St................................212-260-0459
Leach, Ed Inc/585 Dartmouth, Westbury, NY......................516-334-3084
Location Locators/225 E 63rd St...................................212-685-6363
Loft Locations/50 White St..212-966-6408
Marks, Arthur/24 Fifth Ave #829 212-673-0477
Myriad Communications, Inc/208 W 30th St 212-564-4340
Wolfson, Paula/227 W 10th St 212-741-3048

NORTHEAST

Betty Rankin/Location Unlimited/24 Briarcliff, Tenafly, NJ 201-567-2809
Forma, Belle/32 Vine Rd, Larchmont, NY 914-834-5554
Gilmore, Robert Assoc Inc/990 Washington St, Dedham, MA..............617-329-6633
Maine State Development Office/193 State St, Augusta, ME 207-289-2656
Maryland Film Commission/217 Redwood/9th fl, Baltimore, MD........301-333-6631
Massachusetts Film Off/10 Park Plaza #2310, Boston, MA..........617-973-8800
New Hampshire Vacation Travel/PO Box 856, Concord, NH 603-271-2666
NJ State Motion Pic Dev/1 Gateway Ctr, Newark, NJ................201-648-6279
Pennsylvania Film Bureau/455 Forum Bldg, Harrisburg, PA..............717-787-5333
PhotoSonics/1116 N Hudson St, Arlington, VA.....................703-522-1116
Proteus Location Services/9217 Baltimore Blvd, College Park, MD 301-441-2928
Ren Rose Locations/4 Sandalwood Dr, Livingston, NJ 201-992-4264
Rhode Island State Tourism Div/7 Jackson Walkway, Providence, RI ...800-556-2484
Rhode Island State Tourist Div/7 Jackson Walkway, Providence, RI 401-277-2601
Telesis Production/277 Alexander St #600, Rochester, NY 716-546-5417
Terry, Karen/131 Boxwood Dr, Kings Park, NY 516-724-3964
Verange, Joe - Century III/545 Boylston St, Boston, MA 617-267-9800
Vermont State Travel Division/134 State, Montpelier, VT 802-828-3236
Video One/100 Massachusetts Ave, Boston, MA....................617-266-2200
WV Film Commission/1900 Washington St E, Charleston, WV 800-225-5982

SOUTHEAST

Alabama State Film Office/340 N Hull St, Montgomery, AL 800-633-5898
Bruns, Ken & Gayle/7810 SW 48th Court, Miami, FL 305-666-2928
Darracott, David/2299 Sandford Rd, Decatur, GA 404-872-0219
Florida Film Bureau/107 W Gaines St, Tallahassee, FL..............904-487-1100
Georgia State Film Office/PO Box 1776, Atlanta, GA..................404-656-3591
Harris, George/2875 Mabry Lane NE, Atlanta, GA 404-231-0116
Irene Marie/728 Ocean Dr, Miami Beach, FL 305-672-2929
Kentucky Film Office/Berry Hill Mansion/Louisville, Frankfort, KY 502-564-3456
Kupersmith, Tony/320 Highland Ave NE, Atlanta, GA..............404-577-5319
Locations Extraordinaire/6794 Giralda Cir, Boca Raton, FL..............407-487-5050
McDonald, Stew/6905 N Coolidge Ave, Tampa, FL 813-886-3773
Mississippi State Film Office/PO Box 849, Jackson, MS...............601-359-3449
Natchez Convention & Visitors Bureau/Liberty Pk Hwy, Hwy 16,
Natchez, MS..601-446-6345
North Carolina Film Office/430 N Salisbury St, Raleigh, NC 919-733-9900
TN Film Entrtnmnt/Music Comm/320 6th Ave N/7th fl, Nashville, TN.....615-741-3456
TN State Econ & Comm Dev/320 6th Ave N/8th fl, Nashville, TN 615-741-1888
Virginia Division of Tourism/1021 E Cary St, Richmond, VA.................804-786-2051

MIDWEST

A-Stock Photo Finder/230 N Michigan #1100, Chicago, IL 312-645-0611
Carlson, Susan/255 Linden Park Pl, Highland Park, IL 708-433-2466
Illinois State Film Office/100 W Randolph #3-400, Chicago, IL 312-793-3600

Indiana State Tourism Development/1 N Capital, Indianapolis, IN 317-232-8860
Iowa Film Office/200 E Grand Ave, Des Moines, IA 800-779-3456
Kansas State Film Office/503 Kansas Ave, Topeka, KS........................913-296-4927
Manya Nogg Co/9773 Lafayette Plaza, Omaha, NB................................402-397-8887
Michigan St Trvl & Film Bureau/PO Box 30226, Lansing, MI 517-373-0670
Minnesota State Tourism Div/375 Jackson St #250, St Paul, MN 612-296-5029
Missouri State Tourism Comm/301 W High St, Jefferson City, MO 314-751-3051
ND State Business & Industrial/604 E Blvd Ave, Bismarck, ND 701-224-2810
Ohio Film Bureau/77 S High St, Columbus, OH 614-466-2284

SOUTHWEST

Alamo Village/PO Box 528, Brackettville, TX.......................................512-563-2580
Arizona Land Co/PO Box 63441, Phoenix, AZ 602-265-0108
Arkansas State Film Office/#1 Capital Mall, Little Rock, AR 501-682-7676
Blair, Tanya Agency/4528 McKinney #107, Dallas, TX 214-522-9750
Dawson, Kim Agency/PO Box 585060, Dallas, TX................................214-638-2414
Epic Film Productions/7630 Wood Hollow #237, Austin, TX 512-345-2563
Greenblatt, Linda/5150 Willis, Dallas, TX...214-361-7320
Kessel, Mark/2429 Hibernia, Dallas, TX 214-520-8686
MacLean, John/10017 Woodgrove, Dallas, TX 214-343-0181
OK State Tourism-Rec Dept/500 Will Rogers Bldg, Oklahoma City, OK405-521-3981
Oklahoma Film Comm/PO Box 26980, Oklahoma City, OK 405-843-9770
Ranchland - Circle R/5901 Cross Timbers Rd, Flower Mound, TX 817-430-1561
Ray, Al/2304 Houston Street, San Angelo, TX 915-949-2716
Ray, Rudolph/2231 Freeland Avenue, San Angelo, TX........................915-949-6784
San Antonio Zoo & Aquar/3903 N St Marys, San Antonio, TX 512-734-7184
Senn, Loyd C/PO Box 6060, Lubbock, TX 806-792-2000
Summers, Judy/3914 Law, Houston, TX..713-661-1440
Taylor, Peggy Talent/4300 N Central Exprswy #110, Dallas, TX 214-826-7884
Texas World Entrtnmnt/8133 Chadbourne Road, Dallas, TX 214-351-6103
Tucson Film Office/Box 27210, Tucson, AZ..602-791-4000

ROCKY MTN

Wyoming Film Comm/IH 25 & College Dr, Cheyenne, WY 307-777-7851

WEST COAST

California Film Comm/6922 Hollywood Blvd, Hollywood, CA 213-736-2465
Daniels, Karil, Point of View Prd/2477 Folsom St, San Francisco, CA ...415-821-0435
Excor Travel/1750 Kalakaua Ave #116, Honolulu, HI............................808-946-6614
Film Permits Unlimited/8058 Allott Ave, Van Nuys, CA 818-997-6197
Juckes, Geoff/1568 Loma Vista St, Pasadena, CA 818-791-3484
Juckes, Geoff/3185 Durand Dr, Hollywood, CA 213-465-6604
The Location Co/8646 Wilshire Blvd, Beverly Hills, CA.........................213-820-7770
Location Enterprises Inc/6725 Sunset Blvd, Los Angeles, CA 213-469-3141
Mindseye/767 Northpoint, San Francisco, CA 415-441-4578
Minot, Abby/61101 Thornhill Dr, Oakland, CA......................................415-339-9600
Newhall Ranch/23823 Valencia, Valencia, CA 818-362-1515
San Francisco Conv/Visitors Bur/900 Market St, San Francisco, CA 415-974-6900

SETS

NYC

Abstracta Structures/347 Fifth Ave 212-532-3710
Alcamo Marble Works/541 W 22nd St 212-255-5224
Baker, Alex/30 W 69th St..212-799-2069
Golden Office Interiors/574 Fifth Ave...212-719-5150
LaFerla, Sandro/92 Vandam St 212-620-0693
Lincoln Scenic Studio/560 W 34th St...212-244-2700
Nelson, Jane/21 Howard St 212-431-4642
Oliphant, Sarah/20 W 20th St 6th fl 212-741-1233
Plexability Ltd/200 Lexington Ave...212-679-7826
Theater Technology Inc/37 W 20th St...212-929-5380
Unique Surfaces/244 Mulberry 212-941-1866
Variety Scenic Studio/25-19 Borden Ave, Long Island City 718-392-4747
Yurkiw, Mark/568 Broadway..212-226-6338

NORTHEAST

Davidson, Peter/9R Conant St, Acton, MA 508-635-9780
The Focarino Studio/718 Fireplace Rd, East Hampton, NY..................516-324-7637
Foothills Theater Company/074 Worcester Ctr, Worcester, MA 508-754-3314
Ren Rose Locations/4 Sandalwood Dr, Livingston, NJ 201-992-4264
Videocom, Inc/502 Sprague St, Dedham, MA 617-329-4080

SOUTHEAST

The Great Southern Stage/15221 NE 21 Ave, N Miami Beach, FL........305-947-0430
Kupersmith, Tony/320 Highland Ave NE, Atlanta, GA..........................404-577-5319

MIDWEST

Backdrop Solution/311 N Desplaines Ave #607, Chicago, IL 312-993-0494
Becker Studio/2824 W Taylor, Chicago, IL..312-722-4040
Centerwood Cabinets/3700 Main St NE, Blaine, MN............................612-786-2094
Chicago Canvas & Supply/3719 W Lawrence Ave, Chicago, IL 312-478-5700
Gard, Ron/2600 N Racine, Chicago, IL...312-975-6523
Grand Stage Lighting Co/630 W Lake, Chicago, IL 312-332-5611
The Set-up & Co/1049 E Michigan St, Indianapolis, IN.........................317-635-2323

SOUTHWEST

Dallas Stage Lighting & Equipment/1818 Chestnut, Dallas, TX............214-428-1818
Dallas Stage Scenery Co, Inc/3917 Willow St, Dallas, TX....................214-821-0002
Dunn, Glenn E/7412 Sherwood Rd, Austin, TX.....................................512-441-0377
Freeman Exhibit Co/8301 Ambassador Row, Dallas, TX 214-638-8800
Reed, Bill Decorations/333 First Ave, Dallas, TX...................................214-823-3154
Texas Scenic Co Inc/5423 Jackwood Dr, San Antonio, TX 512-684-0091
Texas Set Design/3103 Oak Lane, Dallas, TX.......................................214-426-5511

WEST COAST

American Scenery/18555 Eddy St, Northridge, CA 818-886-1585
Backings, J C/10201 W Pico Blvd, Los Angeles, CA.............................213-277-0522
Carthay Set Services/5300 Melrose, Hollywood, CA 213-871-4400
Carthay Studio/5907 W Pico Blvd, Los Angeles, CA.............................213-938-2101
CBS Special Effects/7800 Beverly Blvd, Los Angeles, CA 213-852-2345
Erecter Set Inc/1150 S LaBrea, Los Angeles, CA 213-938-4762
Grosh, RL & Sons/4114 Sunset Blvd, Los Angeles, CA........................213-662-1134
Hollywood Stage/6650 Santa Monica Blvd, Los Angeles, CA 213-466-4393
Pacific Studios/8315 Melrose Ave, Los Angeles, CA.............................213-653-3093
Shafton Inc/5500 Cleon Ave, N Hollywood, CA.....................................818-985-5025
Superstage/1119 N Hudson, Los Angeles, CA 213-464-0296
Triangle Scenery/1215 Bates Ave, Los Angeles, CA 213-662-8129

Index